The Montessori Reader

The Montessori Reader

by Maria Montessori

The Montessori Method
Dr. Montessori's Own Handbook
The Absorbent Mind

Wilder Publications, LLC.
PO Box 3005
Radford VA 24143-3005

ISBN 10: 1-60459-579-5
ISBN 13: 978-1-60459-579-6

The Montessori Method

Table of Contents

Preface to the American Edition

In February, 1911, Professor Henry W. Holmes, of the Division of Education at Harvard University, did me the honour to suggest that an English translation be made of my Italian volume, "*Il Metodo della Pedagogia Scientifica applicato all' educazione infantile nelle Case dei Bambini.*" This suggestion represented one of the greatest events in the history of my educational work. To-day, that to which I then looked forward as an unusual privilege has become an accomplished fact.

The Italian edition of "*Il Metodo della Pedagogia Scientifica*" had no preface, because the book itself I consider nothing more than the preface to a more comprehensive work, the aim and extent of which it only indicates. For the educational method for children from three to six years set forth here is but the earnest of a work that, developing the same principle and method, shall cover in a like manner the successive stages of education. Moreover, the method which obtains in the *Casa dei Bambini* offers, it seems to me, an experimental field for the study of man, and promises, perhaps, the development of a science that shall disclose other secrets of nature.

In the period that has elapsed between the publication of the Italian and American editions, I have had, with my pupils, the opportunity to simplify and render more exact certain practical details of the method, and to gather additional observations concerning discipline. The results attest the vitality of the method, and the necessity for an extended scientific collaboration in the near future, and are embodied in two new chapters written for the American edition. I know that my method has been widely spoken of in America, thanks to Mr. S. S. McClure, who has presented it through the pages of his well-known magazine. Indeed, many Americans have already come to Rome for the purpose of observing personally the practical application of the method in my little schools. If, encouraged by this movement, I may express a hope for the future, it is that my work in Rome shall become the centre of an efficient and helpful collaboration.

To the Harvard professors who have made my work known in America and to *McClure's Magazine*, a mere acknowledgement of what I owe them is a barren response; but it is my hope that the method itself, in its effect upon the children of America, may prove an adequate expression of my gratitude.

Maria Montessori

Introduction

An audience already thoroughly interested awaits this translation of a remarkable book. For years no educational document has been so eagerly expected by so large a public, and not many have better merited general anticipation. That this widespread interest exists is due to the enthusiastic and ingenious articles in *McClure's Magazine* for May and December, 1911, and January, 1912; but before the first of these articles appeared a number of English and American teachers had given careful study to Dr. Montessori's work, and had found it novel and important. The astonishing welcome accorded to the first popular expositions of the Montessori system may mean much or little for its future in England and America; it is rather the earlier approval of a few trained teachers and professional students that commends it to the educational workers who must ultimately decide upon its value, interpret its technicalities to the country at large, and adapt it to English and American conditions. To them as well as to the general public this brief critical Introduction is addressed.

It is wholly within the bounds of safe judgment to call Dr. Montessori's work remarkable, novel, and important. It is remarkable, if for no other reason, because it represents the constructive effort of a woman. We have no other example of an educational system–original at least in its systematic wholeness and in its practical application–worked out and inaugurated by the feminine mind and hand. It is remarkable, also, because it springs from a combination of womanly sympathy and intuition, broad social outlook, scientific training, intensive and long-continued study of educational problems, and, to crown all, varied and unusual experience as a teacher and educational leader. No other woman who has dealt with Dr. Montessori's problem–the education of young children–has brought to it personal resources so richly diverse as hers. These resources, furthermore, she has devoted to her work with an enthusiasm, an absolute abandon, like that of Pestalozzi and Froebel, and she presents her convictions with an apostolic ardour which commands attention. A system which embodies such a capital of human effort could not be unimportant. Then, too, certain aspects of the system are in themselves striking and significant: it adapts to the education of normal children methods and apparatus originally used for deficients; it is based on a radical conception of liberty for the pupil; it entails a highly formal training of separate sensory, motor, and mental capacities; and it leads to rapid, easy, and substantial mastery of the elements of reading, writing, and arithmetic. All this will be apparent to the most casual reader of this book.

None of these things, to be sure, is absolutely new in the educational world. All have been proposed in theory; some have been put more or less completely into practice. It is not unjust, for instance, to point out that much of the material used by Dr. Walter S. Fernald, Superintendent of the Massachusetts Institution for the Feeble-Minded at Waverly, is almost identical with the Montessori material, and that Dr. Fernald has long maintained that it could be used to good effect in the education of normal children. (It may interest American readers to know that Séguin, on whose work that of Dr. Montessori is based, was once head of the school at Waverly.) So, too, formal training in various psycho-physical processes has been much urged of late by a good many workers in experimental pedagogy, especially by Meumann. But before Montessori, no one had produced a system in which the elements named above were combined. She conceived it, elaborated it in practice, and established it in schools. It is indeed the final result, as Dr. Montessori proudly asserts, of years of experimental effort both on her own part and on the part of her great predecessors; but the crystallisation of these experiments in a programme of education for normal children is due to Dr. Montessori alone. The incidental features which she has frankly taken over from other modern educators she has chosen because they fit into the fundamental form of her own scheme, and she has unified them all in her general conception of method. The system is not original in the sense in which Froebel's system was original; but as a system it is the novel product of a single woman's creative genius.

As such, no student of elementary education ought to ignore it. The system doubtless fails to solve all the problems in the education of young children; possibly some of the solutions it proposes are partly or completely mistaken; some are probably unavailable in English and American schools; but a system of education does not have to attain perfection in order to merit study, investigation, and experimental use. Dr. Montessori is too large-minded to claim infallibility, and too thoroughly scientific in her attitude to object to careful scrutiny of her scheme and the thorough testing of its results. She expressly states that it is not yet complete. Practically, it is highly probable that the system ultimately adopted in our schools will combine elements of the Montessori programme with elements of the kindergarten programme, both "liberal" and "conservative." In its actual procedure school work must always be thus eclectic. An all-or-nothing policy for a single system inevitably courts defeat; for the public is not interested in systems as systems, and refuses in the end to believe that any one system contains every good thing. Nor can we doubt that this attitude is essentially sound. If we continue, despite the pragmatists, to believe in absolute principles, we may yet remain skeptical about the logic of their reduction to practice–at least in any fixed programme of education. We are not yet justified, at any rate, in adopting one programme to the exclusion of every other simply because it is based on the most intelligible or the most inspiring philosophy. The pragmatic test must also be applied, and rigorously. We must try out several combinations, watch and record the results, compare them, and proceed cautiously to new experiments. This procedure is desirable for every stage and grade of education, but especially for the earliest stage, because there it has been least attempted and is most difficult. Certainly a system so radical, so clearly defined, and so well developed as that of Dr. Montessori offers for the thoroughgoing comparative study of methods in early education new material of exceptional importance. Without accepting every detail of the system, without even accepting unqualifiedly its fundamental principles, one may welcome it, thus, as of great and immediate value. If early education is worth studying at all, the educator who devotes his attention to it will find it necessary to define the differences in principle between the Montessori programme and other programmes, and to carry out careful tests of the results obtainable from the various systems and their feasible combinations.

One such combination this Introduction will suggest, and it will discuss also the possible uses of the Montessori apparatus in the home; but it may be helpful first to present the outstanding characteristics of the Montessori system as compared with the modern kindergarten in its two main forms.

Certain similarities in principle are soon apparent. Dr. Montessori's views of childhood are in some respects identical with those of Froebel, although in general decidedly more radical. Both defend the child's right to be active, to explore his environment and develop his own inner resources through every form of investigation and creative effort. Education is to guide activity, not repress it. Environment cannot create human power, but only give it scope and material, direct it, or at most but call it forth; and the teacher's task is first to nourish and assist, to watch, encourage, guide, induce, rather than to interfere, prescribe, or restrict. To most American teachers and to all kindergartners this principle has long been familiar; they will but welcome now a new and eloquent statement of it from a modern viewpoint. In the practical interpretation of the principle, however, there is decided divergence between the Montessori school and the kindergarten. The Montessori "directress" does not teach children in groups, with the practical requirement, no matter how well "mediated," that each member of the group shall join in the exercise. The Montessori pupil does about as he pleases, so long as he does not do any harm.

Montessori and Froebel stand in agreement also on the need for training of the senses; but Montessori's scheme for this training is at once more elaborate and more direct than Froebel's. She has devised out of Séguin's apparatus a comprehensive and scientific scheme for formal gymnastic of the senses; Froebel originated a series of objects designed for a much broader and more creative use by the children, but by no means so closely adapted to the training of sensory discrimination. The Montessori material carries out the fundamental principle of Pestalozzi, which he tried in vain to embody in a successful system of his own: it "develops piece by piece the pupil's mental capacities" by training separately, through repeated exercises, his several senses and his ability to distinguish, compare, and handle typical objects. In the kindergarten system, and particularly in the "liberal" modifications of it, sense training is incidental to constructive and imaginative activity in which the children are pursuing larger ends than the mere arrangement of forms or colours. Even in the most formal work in kindergarten design the children are "making a picture," and are encouraged to tell what it looks like-"a star," "a kite," "a flower."

As to physical education, the two systems agree in much the same way: both affirm the need for free bodily activity, for rhythmic exercises, and for the development of muscular control; but whereas the kindergarten seeks much of all this through group games with an imaginative or social content, the Montessori scheme places the emphasis on special exercises designed to give formal training in separate physical functions.

In another general aspect, however, the agreement between the two systems, strong in principle, leaves the Montessori system less formal rather than more formal in practice. The principle in this case consists of the affirmation of the child's need for social training. In the conservative kindergarten this training is sought once more, largely in group games. These are usually imaginative, and sometimes decidedly symbolic: that is, the children play at being farmers, millers, shoemakers, mothers and fathers, birds, animals, knights, or soldiers; they sing songs, go through certain semi-dramatic activities–such as "opening the pigeon house," "mowing the grass," "showing the good child to the knights," and the like; and each takes his part in the representation of some typical social situation. The social training involved in these games is formal only in the sense that the children are not engaged, as the Montessori children often are, in a real social enterprise, such as that of serving dinner, cleaning the room, caring for animals, building a toy house, or making a garden. It cannot be too strongly emphasized that even the most conservative kindergarten does not, on principle, exclude "real" enterprises of this latter sort; but in a three-hour session it does rather little with them. Liberal kindergartners do more, particularly in Europe, where the session is often longer. Nor does the Montessori system wholly exclude imaginative group games. But Dr. Montessori, despite an evidently profound interest not only in social training, but also in aesthetic, idealistic, and even religious development, speaks of "games and foolish stories" in a casual and derogatory way, which shows that she is as yet unfamiliar with the American kindergartner's remarkable skill and power in the use of these resources. (Of course the American kindergartner does not use "foolish" stories; but stories she does use, and to good effect.) The Montessori programme involves much direct social experience, both in the general life of the school and in the manual work done by the pupils; the kindergarten extends the range of the child's social consciousness through the imagination. The groupings of the Montessori children are largely free and unregulated; the groupings of kindergarten children are more often formal and prescribed.

On one point the Montessori system agrees with the conservative kindergarten, but not with the liberal: it prepares directly for the mastery of the school arts. There can be no doubt that Dr. Montessori has devised a peculiarly successful scheme for teaching children to write, an effective method for the introduction of reading, and good material for early number work. Both types of kindergarten increase, to be sure, the child's general capacity for expression: kindergarten activity adds to his stock of ideas, awakens and guides his imagination, increases his vocabulary, and trains him in the effective use of it. Children in a good kindergarten hear stories and tell them, recount their own experiences, sing songs, and recite verses, all in a company of friendly but fairly critical listeners, which does even more to stimulate and guide expression than does the circle at home. But even the conservative kindergarten does not teach children to write and to read. It does teach them a good deal about number; and it may fairly be questioned whether it does not do more fundamental work in this field than the Montessori system itself. The Froebelian gifts offer exceptional opportunity for concrete illustration of the conceptions of *whole* and *part*, through the creation of wholes from parts, and the breaking up of wholes into parts. This aspect of number is at least as important as the series aspect, which children get in counting and for which the Montessori "Long Stair" provides such good material. The Froebelian material may be used very readily for counting, however, and the Montessori material gives some slight opportunity for uniting and dividing. So far as preparation for arithmetic is concerned, a combination of the two bodies of material is both feasible and desirable. The liberal kindergarten, meanwhile, abandoning the use of the gifts and occupations for mathematical purposes, makes no attempt to prepare its pupils directly for the school arts.

Compared with the kindergarten, then, the Montessori system presents these main points of interest: it carries out far more radically the principle of unrestricted liberty; its materials are intended for the direct and formal training of the senses; it includes apparatus designed to aid in the purely physical development of the children; its social training is carried out mainly by means of present and actual social activities; and it affords direct preparation for the school arts. The kindergarten, on the other hand, involves a certain amount of group-teaching, in which children are held–not necessarily by the enforcement of authority, yet by authority, confessedly, when other means fail–to definite activities; its materials are intended primarily for creative use by the children and offer opportunity for mathematical analysis and the teaching of design; and its procedure is rich in resources for the imagination. One thing should be made entirely clear and emphatic: in none of these characteristics are the two systems rigidly antagonistic. Much kindergarten activity is free, and the principle of prescription is not wholly given over by the "Houses of Childhood"–witness their *Rules and Regulations*; the kindergarten involves direct sense training, and the Montessori system admits some of the Froebel blocks for building and design; there are many purely muscular activities in the kindergarten, and some of the usual kindergarten games are used by Montessori; the kindergarten conducts some gardening, care of animals, construction-work, and domestic business, and the Montessori system admits a few imaginative social plays; both systems (but not the liberal form of the kindergarten) work directly toward the school arts. Since the difference between the two programmes is one of arrangement, emphasis, and degree, there is no fundamental reason why a combination especially adapted to English and American schools cannot be worked out.

The broad contrast between a Montessori school and a kindergarten appears on actual observation to be this: whereas the Montessori children spend almost all their time handling *things*, largely according to their individual inclination and under individual guidance, kindergarten children are generally engaged in group work and games with an imaginative background and appeal. A possible principle of adjustment between the two systems might be stated thus: work with objects designed for formal sensory, motor, and intellectual training should be done individually or in purely voluntary groups; imaginative and social activity should be carried on in regulated groups. This principle is suggested only as a possible basis for education during the kindergarten age; for as children grow older they must be taught in classes, and they naturally learn how to carry out imaginative and social enterprises in free groups, and the former often alone. Nor should it be supposed that the principle is suggested as a rule to which there can be no exception. It is suggested simply as a general working hypothesis, the value of which must be tested in experience. Although it has long been observed by kindergartners themselves that group-work with the Froebelian materials, especially such work as involves geometrical analysis and formal design, soon tires the children, it has been held that the kindergartner could safeguard her pupils from loss of interest or real fatigue by watching carefully for the first signs of weariness and stopping the work promptly on their appearance. For small groups of the older children, who can do work of this sort with ease and enjoyment, no doubt the inevitable restraint of group teaching is a negligible factor, the fatiguing effects of which any good kindergartner can forestall. But for younger children a régime of complete freedom would seem to promise better results–at least so far as work with objects is concerned. In games, on the other hand, group teaching means very little restraint and the whole process is less tiring any way. To differentiate in method between these two kinds of activity may be the best way to keep them both in an effective educational programme.

To speak of an effective educational programme leads at once, however, to an important aspect of the Montessori system, quite aside from its relation to the kindergarten, with which this Introduction must now deal. This is the social aspect, which finds its explanation in Dr. Montessori's own story of her first school. In any discussion of the availability of the Montessori system in English and American schools–particularly in American public schools and English "Board" schools–two general conditions under which Dr. Montessori did her early work in Rome should be borne in mind. She had her pupils almost all day long, practically controlling their lives in their waking hours; and her pupils came for the most part from families of the laboring class. We cannot expect to achieve the results Dr. Montessori has achieved if we have our pupils under our guidance only two or three hours in the morning, nor can we expect exactly similar results from children whose heredity and experience make them at once more sensitive, more active, and less amenable to suggestion than hers. If we are to make practical application of the Montessori scheme we must not neglect to consider the modifications of it which differing social conditions may render necessary.

The conditions under which Dr. Montessori started her original school in Rome do not, indeed, lack counterpart in large cities the world over. When one reads her eloquent "Inaugural Address" it is impossible not to wish that a "School within the Home" might stand as a centre of hopeful child life in the midst of every close-built city block. Better, of course, if there were no hive-like city tenements at all, and if every family could give to its own children on its own premises enough of "happy play in grassy places." Better if every mother and father were in certain ways an expert in child psychology and hygiene. But while so many unfortunate thousands still live in the hateful cliff-dwellings of our modern cities, we must welcome Dr. Montessori's large conception of the social function of her "Houses of Childhood" as a new gospel for the schools which serve the city poor. No matter what didactic apparatus such schools may use, they should learn of Dr. Montessori the need of longer hours, completer care of the children, closer co-operation with the home, and larger aims. In such schools, too, it is probable that the two fundamental features of Dr. Montessori's work–her principle of liberty and her scheme for sense training–will find their completest and most fruitful application.

It is just these fundamental features, however, which will be most bitterly attacked whenever the social status of the original *Casa dei Bambini* is forgotten. Anthropometric measurements, baths, training in personal self-care, the serving of meals, gardening, and the care of animals we may hear sweepingly recommended for all schools, even for those with a three-hour session and a socially favored class of pupils; but the need for individual liberty and for the training of the senses will be denied even in the work of schools where the conditions correspond closely to those at San Lorenzo. Of course no practical educator will actually propose bathtubs for all schools, and no doubt there will be plenty of wise conversation about transferring to a given school any function now well discharged by the homes that support it. The problems raised by the proposal to apply in all schools the Montessori conception of discipline and the Montessori sense-training are really more difficult to solve. Is individual liberty a universal educational principle, or a principle which must be modified in the case of a school with no such social status as that of the original "House of Childhood"? Do all children need sense training, or only those of unfavorable inheritance and home environment? No serious discussion of the Montessori system can avoid these questions. What is said in answer to them here is written in the hope that subsequent discussion may be somewhat influenced to keep in view the really deciding factor in each case–the actual situation in the school.

There is occasion enough in these questions, to be sure, for philosophical and scientific argument. The first question involves an ethical issue, the second a psychological issue, and both may be followed through to purely metaphysical issues. Dr. Montessori believes in liberty for the pupil because she thinks of life "as a superb goddess, ever advancing to new conquests." Submission, loyalty, self-sacrifice seem to her, apparently, only incidental necessities of life, not essential elements of its eternal form. There is obvious opportunity here for profound difference of philosophic theory and belief. She seems to hold, too, that sense perception forms the sole basis for the mental and hence for the moral life; that "sense training will prepare the ordered foundation upon which the child may build up a clear and strong mentality," including, apparently, his moral ideas; and that the cultivation of purpose and of the imaginative and creative capacities of children is far less important than the development of the power to learn from the environment by means of the senses. These views seem to agree rather closely with those of Herbart and to some extent with those of Locke. Certainly they offer material for both psychological and ethical debate. Possibly, however, Dr. Montessori would not accept the views here ascribed to her on the evidence of this book; and in any case these are matters for the philosopher and the psychologist. A pedagogical issue is never wholly an issue of high principle.

Can it reasonably be maintained, then, that an actual situation like that in the first "House of Childhood" at Rome is the only situation in which the Montessori principle of liberty can justifiably find full application? Evidently the Roman school is a true Republic of Childhood, in which nothing need take precedence of the child's claim to pursue an active purpose of his own. Social restraints are here reduced to a minimum; the children must, to be sure, subordinate individual caprice to the demands of the common good, they are not allowed to quarrel or to interfere with each other, and they have duties to perform at stated times; but each child is a citizen in a community governed wholly in the interests of the equally privileged members thereof, his liberty is rarely interfered with, he is free to carry out his own purposes, and he has as much influence in the affairs of the commonwealth as the average member of an adult democracy. This situation is never duplicated in the home, for a child is not only a member of the family, whose interests are to be considered with the rest, but literally a subordinate member, whose interests must often be frankly set aside for those of an adult member or for those of the household itself. Children must come to dinner at dinner time, even if continued digging in the sand would be more to their liking or better for their general development of muscle, mind, or will. It is possible, of course, to refine on the theory of the child's membership in the family community and of the right of elders to command, but practically it remains true that the common conditions of family life prohibit any such freedom as is exercised in a Montessori school. In the same way a school of large enrollment that elects to cover in a given time so much work that individual initiative cannot be trusted to compass it, is forced to teach certain things at nine o'clock and others at ten, and to teach in groups; and the individual whose life is thus cabined and confined must get what he can. For a given school the obvious question is, Considering the work to be done in the time allowed, can we give up the safeguards of a fixed programme and group teaching? The deeper question lies here: Is the work to be done in itself so important that it is worth while to have the children go through it under compulsion or on interest induced by the teacher? Or to put it another way: May not the work be so much less important than the child's freedom that we had better trust to native curiosity and cleverly devised materials anyway and run the risk of his losing part of the work, or even the whole of it?

For schools beyond the primary grade there will be no doubt as to the answer to this question. There are many ways in which school work may safely be kept from being the deadening and depressing process it so often is, but the giving up of all fixed and limited schedules and the prescriptions of class teaching is not one of them. Even if complete liberty of individual action were possible in schools of higher grade, it is not certain that it would be desirable: for we must learn to take up many of our purposes in life under social imperative. But with young children the question becomes more difficult. What work do we wish to make sure that each child does? If our schools can keep but half a day, is there time enough for every child to cover this work without group teaching at stated times? Is the prescription and restraint involved in such group teaching really enough to do the children any harm or to make our teaching less effective? Can we not give up prescription altogether for parts of the work and minimise it for others? The general question of individual liberty is thus reduced to a series of practical problems of adjustment. It is no longer a question of total liberty or no liberty at all, but a question of the practical mediation of these extremes. When we consider, furthermore, that the teacher's skill and the attractiveness of her personality, the alluring power of the didactic apparatus and the ease with which it enables children to learn, to say nothing of a cheerful and pleasant room and the absence of set desks and seat, may all work together to prevent scheduled teaching in groups from becoming in the least an occasion for restraint, it is plain that in any given school there may be ample justification for abating the rigour of Dr. Montessori's principle of freedom. Every school must work out its own solution of the problem in the face of its particular conditions.

The adoption of sense-training would seem to be much less a matter for variable decision. Some children may need less than others, but for all children between the ages of three and five the Montessori material will prove fascinating as well as profitable. A good deal of modern educational theory has been based on the belief that children are interested only in what has social value, social content, or "real use"; yet a day with any normal child will give ample evidence of the delight that children take in purely formal exercises. The sheer fascination of tucking cards under the edge of a rug will keep a baby happy until any ordinary supply of cards is exhausted; and the wholly sensory appeal of throwing stones into the water gives satisfaction enough to absorb for a long time the attention of older children–to say nothing of grown-ups. The Montessori apparatus satisfies sense hunger when it is keen for new material, and it has besides a puzzle-interest which children eagerly respond to. Dr. Montessori subordinates the value of the concrete mental content her material supplies to its value in rendering the senses more acute; yet it is by no means certain that this content–purely formal as it is–does not also give the material much of its importance. Indeed, the refinement of sensory discrimination may not in itself be particularly valuable. What Professor G.M. Whipple says on this point in his *Manual of Mental and Physical Tests* (p. 130) has much weight:

> The use of sensory tests in correlation work is particularly interesting. In general, some writers are convinced that keen discrimination is a prerequisite to keen intelligence, while others are equally convinced that intelligence is essentially conditioned by "higher" processes, and

only remotely by sensory capacity–barring, of course, such diminution of capacity as to interfere seriously with the experiencing of sensations, as in partial deafness or partial loss of vision. While it is scarcely the place here to discuss the evolutionary significance of discriminative sensitivity, it may be pointed out that the normal capacity is many times in excess of the actual demands of life, and that it is consequently difficult to understand why nature has been so prolific and generous; to understand, in other words, what is the sanction for the seemingly hypertrophied discriminative capacity of the human sense organs. The usual "theological explanations" of our sensory life fail to account for this discrepancy. Again, the very fact of the existence of this surplus capacity seems to negative at the outset the notion that sensory capacity can be a conditioning factor in intelligence–with the qualification already noted.

It is quite possible that the real pedagogical value of the Montessori apparatus is due to the fact that it keeps children happily engaged in the exercise of their senses and their fingers when they crave such exercise most and to the further fact that it teaches them without the least strain a good deal about forms and materials. These values are not likely to be much affected by differing school conditions.

In the use of the material for sense-training, English and American teachers may find profit in two general warnings. First, it should not be supposed that sense training alone will accomplish all that Dr. Montessori accomplishes through the whole range of her school activities. To fill up most of a morning with sense-training is to give it (except perhaps in the case of the youngest pupils) undue importance. It is not even certain that the general use of the senses will be much affected by it, to say nothing of the loss of opportunity for larger physical and social activity. Second, the isolation of the senses should be used with some care. To shut off sight is to take one step toward sleep, and the requirement that a child concentrate his attention, in this situation, on the sense perceptions he gets by other means than vision must not be maintained too long. No small strain is involved in mental action without the usual means of information and control.

The proposal, mentioned above, of a feasible combination of the Montessori system and the kindergarten may now be set forth. If it is put very briefly and without defense or prophecy, it is because it is made without dogmatism, simply in the hope that it will prove suggestive to some open-minded teacher who is willing to try out any scheme that promises well for her pupils. The conditions supposed are those of the ordinary American public-school kindergarten, with a two-year programme beginning with children three and a half or four years old, a kindergarten with not too many pupils, with a competent kindergartner and assistant kindergartner, and with some help from training-school students.

The first proposal is for the use of the Montessori material during the better part of the first year instead of the regular Froebelian material. To the use of the Montessori devices–including the gymnastic apparatus–some of the time now devoted to pictures and stories should also be applied. It is not suggested that no Froebelian material should be used, but that the two systems be woven into each other, with a gradual transition from the free, individual use of the Montessori objects to the same sort of use of the large sizes of the Froebelian gifts, especially the second, third and fourth. When the children seem to be ready for it, a certain amount of the more formal work with the gifts should be begun. In the second year the Froebelian gift work should predominate, without absolute exclusion of the Montessori exercises. In the latter part of the second year the Montessori exercises preparatory to writing should be introduced. Throughout the second year the full time for stories and picture work should be given to them, and in both years the morning circle and the games should be carried on as usual. The luncheon period should of course remain the same. One part of Dr. Montessori's programme the kindergartner and her assistant should use every effort to incorporate in their work–the valuable training in self-help and independent action afforded in the care of the materials and equipment by the children themselves. This need not be confined to the Montessori apparatus. Children who have been trained to take out, use, and put away the Montessori objects until they are ready for the far richer variety of material in the Froebelian system, should be able to care for it also. Of course if there are children who can return in the afternoon, it would be very interesting to attempt the gardening, which both Froebel and Montessori recommend, and the Montessori vase-work.

For the possible scorn of those to whom all compromise is distasteful, the author of this Introduction seeks but one compensation–that any kindergartner who may happen to adopt this suggestion will let him study the results.

As to the use of the Montessori system in the home, one or two remarks must suffice. In the first place, parents should not expect that the mere presence of the material in the nursery will be enough to work an educational miracle. A Montessori directress does no common "teaching", but she is called upon for very skillful and very tiring effort. She must watch, assist, inspire, suggest, guide, explain, correct, inhibit. She is supposed, in addition, to contribute by her work to the upbuilding of a new science of pedagogy; but her educational efforts-and education is not an investigative and experimental effort, but a practical and constructive one-are enough to exhaust all her time, strength and ingenuity. It will do no harm-except perhaps to the material itself-to have the Montessori material at hand in the home, but it must be used under proper guidance if it is to be educationally effective. And besides, it must not be forgotten that the material is by no means the most important feature of the Montessori programme. The best use of the Montessori system in the home will come through the reading of this book. If parents shall learn from Dr. Montessori something of the value of child life, of its need for activity, of its characteristic modes of expression, and of its possibilities, and shall apply this knowledge wisely, the work of the great Italian educator will be successful enough.

This Introduction cannot close without some discussion, however limited, of the important problems suggested by the Montessori method of teaching children to write and to read. We have in American schools admirable methods for the teaching of reading; by the Aldine method, for instance, children of fair ability read without difficulty ten or more readers in the first school year, and advance rapidly toward independent power. Our instruction in writing, however, has never been particularly noteworthy. We have been trying recently to teach children to write a flowing hand by the "arm movement", without much formation of separate letters by the fingers, and our results seem to prove that the effort with children before the age of ten is not worth while. Sensible school officers are content to let children in the first four grades write largely by drawing the letters, and there has been a fairly general conviction that writing is not in any case especially important before the age of eight or nine. In view of Dr. Montessori's success in teaching children of four and five to write with ease and skill, must we not revise our estimate of the value of writing and our procedure in teaching it? What changes may we profitably introduce in our teaching of reading?

Here again our theory and our practice have suffered from the headstrong advocacy of general principles. Because by clumsy methods children used to be kept at the task of learning the school arts to the undoubted detriment of their minds and bodies, certain writers have advocated the total exclusion of reading and writing from the early grades. Many parents refuse to send their children to school until they are eight, preferring to let them "run wild". This attitude is well justified by school conditions in some places; but where the schools are good, it ignores not only the obvious advantages of school life quite aside from instruction in written language, but also the almost complete absence from strain afforded by modern methods. Now that the Montessori system adds a new and promising method to our resources, it is the more unreasonable: for as a fact normal children are eager to read and write at six, and have plenty of use for these accomplishments.

This does not mean, however, that reading and writing are so important for young children that they should be unduly emphasised. If we can teach them without strain, let us do so, and the more effectively the better; but let us remember, as Dr. Montessori does, that reading and writing should form but a subordinate part of the experience of a child and should minister in general to his other needs. With the best of methods the value of reading and writing before six is questionable. Our conscious life is bookish enough as it is, and it would seem on general grounds a safer policy to defer written language until the age of normal interest in it, and even then not to devote to it more time than an easy and gradual mastery demands.

Of the technical advantages of the Montessori scheme for writing there can be little doubt. The child gains ready control over his pencil through exercises which have their own simple but absorbing interest; and if he does not learn to write with an "arm movement", we may be quite content with his ability to draw a legible and handsome script. Then he learns the letters–their forms, their names, and how to make them–through exercises which have the very important technical characteristic of involving a *thorough sensory analysis* of the material to be mastered. Meumann has taught us of late the great value in all memory work of complete impression through prolonged and intensive analytical study. In the teaching of spelling, for instance, it is comparatively useless to devise schemes for remembering unless the original impressions are made strong and elaborate; and it is only by careful, varied, and detailed sense impression that such material as the alphabet can be thus impressed. So effective is the Montessori scheme for impressing the letters–especially because of its novel use of the sense of touch–that the children learn how to make the whole alphabet before the abstract and formal character of the material leads to any diminution of interest or enthusiasm. Their initial curiosity over the characters they see their elders use is enough to carry them through.

In Italian the next step is easy. The letters once learned, it is a simple matter to combine them into words, for Italian spelling is so nearly phonetic that it presents very little difficulty to any one who knows how to pronounce. It is at just this point that the teaching of English reading by the Montessori method will find its greatest obstacle. Indeed, it is the unphonetic character of English spelling that has largely influenced us to give up the alphabet method of teaching children to read. Other reasons, to be sure, have also induced us to teach by the word and the sentence method; but this one has been and will continue to be the deciding factor. We have found it more effective to teach children whole words, sentences, or rhymes by sight, adding to sense impressions the interest aroused by a wide range of associations, and then analysing the words thus acquired into their phonetic elements to give the children independent power in the acquisition of new words. Our marked success with this method makes it by no means certain that it is "in the characteristic process of natural development" for children to build up written words from their elements-sounds and syllables. It would seem, on the contrary, as James concluded, that the mind works quite as naturally in the opposite direction-grasping wholes first, especially such as have a practical interest, and then working down to their formal elements. In the teaching of spelling, of course, the wholes (words) are already known at sight-that is, the pupil recognises them easily in reading-and the process aims at impressing upon the child's mind the exact order of their constituent elements. It is because reading and spelling are in English such completely separate processes that we can teach a child to read admirably without making him a "good speller" and are forced to bring him to the latter glorious state by new endeavours. We gain by this separation both in reading and in spelling, as experience and comparative tests-popular superstition to the contrary notwithstanding-have conclusively proved. The mastery of the alphabet by the Montessori method will be of great assistance in teaching our children to write, but of only incidental assistance in teaching them to read and to spell.

Once more, then, this Introduction attempts to suggest a compromise. In the school arts the programme used to such good effect in the Italian schools and the programme which has been so well worked out in English and American schools may be profitably combined. We can learn much about writing and reading from Dr. Montessori-especially from the freedom her children have in the process of learning to write and in the use of their newly acquired power, as well as from her device for teaching them to read connected prose. We can use her materials for sense training and lead as she does to easy mastery of the alphabetic symbols. Our own schemes for teaching reading we can retain, and doubtless the phonetic analysis they involve we shall find easier and more effective because of our adoption of the Montessori scheme for teaching the letters. The exact adjustment of the two methods is of course a task for teachers in practice and for educational leaders.

To all educators this book should prove most interesting. Not many of them will expect that the Montessori method will regenerate humanity. Not many will wish to see it–or any method–produce a generation of prodigies such as those who have been heralded recently in America. Not many will approve the very early acquisition by children of the arts of reading and writing. But all who are fair-minded will admit the genius that shines from the pages which follow, and the remarkable suggestiveness of Dr. Montessori's labors. It is the task of the professional student of education to-day to submit all systems to careful comparative study, and since Dr. Montessori's inventive power has sought its tests in practical experience rather than in comparative investigation, this duller task remains to be done. But however he may scrutinise the results of her work, the educator who reads of it here will honour in the Dottoressa Maria Montessori the enthusiasm, the patience, and the constructive insight of the scientist and the friend of humanity.

Henry W. Holmes

Harvard University,

February 22,1912.

A Critical Consideration of the New Pedagogy in its Relation to Modern Science

It is not my intention to present a treatise on Scientific Pedagogy. The modest design of these incomplete notes is to give the results of an experiment that apparently opens the way for putting into practice those new principles of science which in these last years are tending to revolutionise the work of education.

Much has been said in the past decade concerning the tendency of pedagogy, following the footsteps of medicine, to pass beyond the purely speculative stage and base its conclusions on the positive results of experimentation. Physiological and experimental psychology which, from Weber and Fechner to Wundt, has become organised into a new science, seems destined to furnish to the new pedagogy that fundamental preparation which the old-time metaphysical psychology furnished to philosophical pedagogy. Morphological anthropology applied to the physical study of children, is also a strong element in the growth of the new pedagogy.

But in spite of all these tendencies, Scientific Pedagogy has never yet been definitely constructed nor defined. It is something vague of which we speak, but which does not, in reality, exist. We might say that it has been, up to the present time, the mere intuition or suggestion of a science which, by the aid of the positive and experimental sciences that have renewed the thought of the nineteenth century, must emerge from the mist and clouds that have surrounded it. For man, who has formed a new world through scientific progress, must himself be prepared and developed through a new pedagogy. But I will not attempt to speak of this more fully here.

Several years ago, a well-known physician established in Italy a *School of Scientific Pedagogy*, the object which was to prepare teachers to follow the new movement which had begun to be felt in the pedagogical world. This school had, for two or three years, a great success, so great, indeed, that teachers from all over Italy flocked to it, and it was endowed by the City of Milan with a splendid equipment of scientific material. Indeed, its beginnings were most propitious, and liberal help was afforded in the hope that it might be possible to establish, through the experiments carried on there, "the science of forming man".

The enthusiasm which welcomed this school was, in a large measure, due to the warm support given it by the distinguished anthropologist, Giuseppe Sergi, who for more than thirty years had earnestly laboured to spread among the teachers of Italy the principles of a new civilisation based upon education. "To-day in the social world," said Sergi, "an imperative need makes itself felt–the reconstruction of educational methods; and he who fights for this cause, fights for human regeneration." In his pedagogical writings collected in a volume under the title of "*Educazione ed Istruzione*" (Pensieri), * he gives a résumé of the lectures in which he encouraged this new movement, and says that he believes the way to this desired regeneration lies in a methodical study of the one to be educated, carried on under the guidance of pedagogical anthropology and of experimental psychology.

"For several years I have done battle for an idea concerning the instruction and education of man, which appeared the more just and useful the more deeply I thought upon it. My idea was that in order to establish natural, rational methods, it was essential that we make numerous, exact, and rational observations of man as an individual, principally during infancy, which is the age at which the foundations of education and culture must be laid.

"To measure the head, the height, etc., does not indeed mean that we are establishing a system of pedagogy, but it indicates the road which we may follow to arrive at such a system, since if we are to educate an individual, we must have a definite and direct knowledge of him."

The authority of Sergi was enough to convince many that, given such a knowledge of the individual, the art of educating him would develop naturally. This, as often happens, led to a confusion of ideas among his followers, arising now from too literal interpretation, now from an exaggeration, of the master's ideas. The chief trouble lay in confusing the experimental study of the pupil, with his education. And since the one was the road leading to the other, which should have grown from it naturally and rationally, they straightway gave the name of Scientific Pedagogy to what was in truth pedagogical anthropology. These new converts carried as their banner, the "Biographical Chart", believing that once this ensign was firmly planted upon the battle-field of the school, the victory would be won.

The so-called School of Scientific Pedagogy, therefore, instructed the teachers in the taking of anthropometric measurements, in the use of esthesiometric instruments, in the gathering of Psychological Data–and the army of new scientific teachers was formed.

It should be said that in this movement Italy showed herself to be abreast of the times. In France, in England, and especially in America, experiments have been made in the elementary schools, based upon a study of anthropology and psychological pedagogy, in the hope of finding in anthropometry and psychometry, the regeneration of the school. In these attempts it has rarely been the *teachers* who have carried on the research; the experiments have been, in most cases, in the hands of physicians who have taken more interest in their special science than in education. They have usually sought to get from their experiments some contribution to psychology, or anthropology, rather than to attempt to organise their work and their results toward the formation of the long-sought Scientific Pedagogy. To sum up the situation briefly, anthropology and psychology have never devoted themselves to the question of educating children in the schools, nor have the scientifically trained teachers ever measured up to the standards of genuine scientists.

The truth is that the practical progress of the school demands a genuine *fusion* of these modern tendencies, in practice and thought; such a fusion as shall bring scientists directly into the important field of the school and at the same time raise teachers from the inferior intellectual level to which they are limited to-day. Toward this eminently practical ideal the University School of Pedagogy, founded in Italy by Credaro, is definitely working. It is the intention of this school to raise Pedagogy from the inferior position it has occupied as a secondary branch of philosophy, to the dignity of a definite science, which shall, as does Medicine, cover a broad and varied field of comparative study.

And among the branches affiliated with it will most certainly be found Pedagogical Hygiene, Pedagogical Anthropology, and Experimental Psychology.

Truly, Italy, the country of Lombroso, of De-Giovanni, and of Sergi, may claim the honour of being pre-eminent in the organisation of such a movement. In fact, these three scientists may be called the founders of the new tendency in Anthropology: the first leading the way in criminal anthropology, the second in medical anthropology, and the third in pedagogical anthropology. For the good fortune of science, all three of them have been the recognised leaders of their special lines of thought, and have been so prominent in the scientific world that they have not only made courageous and valuable disciples, but have also prepared the minds of the masses to receive the scientific regeneration which they have encouraged. (For reference, see my treatise "Pedagogical Anthropology.") *

Surely all this is something of which our country may be justly proud.

To-day, however, those things which occupy us in the field of education are the interests of humanity at large, and of civilisation, and before such great forces we can recognise only one country-the entire world. And in a cause of such great importance, all those who have given any contribution, even though it be only an attempt not crowned with success, are worthy of the respect of humanity throughout the civilised world. So, in Italy, the schools of Scientific Pedagogy and the Anthropological Laboratories, which have sprung up in the various cities through the efforts of elementary teachers and scholarly inspectors, and which have been abandoned almost before they became definitely organised, have nevertheless a great value by reason of the faith which inspired them, and because of the doors they have opened to thinking people.

It is needless to say that such attempts were premature and sprang from too slight a comprehension of new sciences still in the process of development. Every great cause is born from repeated failures and from imperfect achievements. When St. Francis of Assisi saw his Lord in a vision, and received from the Divine lips the command-"Francis, rebuild my Church!"-he believed that the Master spoke of the little church within which he knelt at that moment. And he immediately set about the task, carrying upon his shoulders the stones with which he meant to rebuild the fallen walls. It was not until later that he became aware of the fact that his mission was to renew the Catholic Church through the spirit of poverty. But the St. Francis who so ingenuously carried the stones, and the great reformer who so miraculously led the people to a triumph of the spirit, are one and the same person in different stages of development. So we, who work toward one great end, are members of one and the same body; and those who come after us will reach the goal only because there were those who believed and laboured before them. And, like St. Francis, we have believed that by carrying the hard and barren stones of the experimental laboratory to the old and crumbling walls of the school, we might rebuild it. We have looked upon the aids offered by the materialistic and mechanical sciences with the same hopefulness with which St. Francis looked upon the squares of granite, which he must carry upon his shoulders.

Thus we have been drawn into a false and narrow way, from which we must free ourselves, if we are to establish true and living methods for the training of future generations.

To prepare teachers in the method of the experimental sciences is not an easy matter. When we shall have instructed them in anthropometry and psychometry in the most minute manner possible, we shall have only created machines, whose usefulness will be most doubtful. Indeed, if it is after this fashion that we are to initiate our teachers into experiment, we shall remain forever in the field of theory. The teachers of the old school, prepared according to the principles of metaphysical philosophy, understood the ideas of certain men regarded as authorities, and moved the muscles of speech in talking of them, and the muscles of the eye in reading their theories. Our scientific teachers, instead, are familiar with certain instruments and know how to move the muscles of the hand and arm in order to use these instruments; besides this, they have an intellectual preparation which consists of a series of typical tests, which they have, in a barren and mechanical way, learned how to apply.

The difference is not substantial, for profound differences cannot exist in exterior technique alone, but lie rather within the inner man. Not with all our initiation into scientific experiment have we prepared *new masters*, for, after all, we have left them standing without the door of real experimental science; we have not admitted them to the noblest and most profound phase of such study,-to that experience which makes real scientists.

And, indeed, what is a scientist? Not, certainly, he who knows how to manipulate all the instruments in the physical laboratory, or who in the laboratory of the chemist handles the various reactives with deftness and security, or who in biology knows how to make ready the specimens for the microscope. Indeed, it is often the case that an assistant has a greater dexterity in experimental technique than the master scientist himself. We give the name scientist to the type of man who has felt experiment to be a means guiding him to search out the deep truth of life, to lift a veil from its fascinating secrets, and who, in this pursuit, has felt arising within him a love for the mysteries of nature, so passionate as to annihilate the thought of himself. The scientist is not the clever manipulator of instruments, he is the worshipper of nature and he bears the external symbols of his passion as does the follower of some religious order. To this body of real scientists belong those who, forgetting, like the Trappists of the Middle Ages, the world about them, live only in the laboratory, careless often in matters of food and dress because they no longer think of themselves; those who, through years of unwearied use of the microscope, become blind; those who in their scientific ardour inoculate themselves with tuberculosis germs; those who handle the excrement of cholera patients in their eagerness to learn the vehicle through which the diseases are transmitted; and those who, knowing that a certain chemical preparation may be an explosive, still persist in testing their theories at the risk of their lives. This is the spirit of the men of science, to whom nature freely reveals her secrets, crowning their labours with the glory of discovery.

There exists, then, the "spirit" of the scientist, a thing far above his mere "mechanical skill," and the scientist is at the height of his achievement when the spirit has triumphed over the mechanism. When he has reached this point, science will receive from him not only new revelations of nature, but philosophic syntheses of pure thought.

It is my belief that the thing which we should cultivate in our teachers is more the *spirit* than the mechanical skill of the scientist; that is, the *direction* of the *preparation* should be toward the spirit rather than toward the mechanism. For example, when we considered the scientific preparation of teachers to be simply the acquiring of the technique of science, we did not attempt to make these elementary teachers perfect anthropologists, expert experimental psychologists, or masters of infant hygiene; we wished only to *direct them* toward the field of experimental science, teaching them to manage the various instruments with a certain degree of skill. So now, we wish to *direct* the teacher, trying to awaken in him, in connection with his own particular field, the school, that scientific *spirit* which opens the door for him to broader and bigger possibilities. In other words, we wish to awaken in the mind and heart of the educator an *interest in natural phenomena* to such an extent that, loving nature, he shall understand the anxious and expectant attitude of one who has prepared an experiment and who awaits a revelation from it.*

The instruments are like the alphabet, and we must know how to manage them if we are to read nature; but as the book, which contains the revelation of the greatest thoughts of an author, uses in the alphabet the means of composing the external symbols or words, so nature, through the mechanism of the experiment, gives us an infinite series of revelations, unfolding for us her secrets.

Now one who has learned to spell mechanically all the words in his spelling-book, would be able to read in the same mechanical way the words in one of Shakespeare's plays, provided the print were sufficiently clear. He who is initiated solely into the making of the bare experiment, is like one who spells out the literal sense of the words in the spelling-book; it is on such a level that we leave the teachers if we limit their preparation to technique alone.

We must, instead, make of them worshippers and interpreters of the spirit of nature. They must be like him who, having learned to spell, finds himself, one day, able to read behind the written symbols the *thought* of Shakespeare, or Goethe, or Dante. As may be seen, the difference is great, and the road long. Our first error was, however, a natural one. The child who has mastered the spelling-book gives the impression of knowing how to read. Indeed, he does read the signs over the shop doors, the names of newspapers, and every word that comes under his eyes. It would be very natural if, entering a library, this child should be deluded into thinking that he knew how to read the sense of all the books he saw there. But attempting to do this, he would soon feel that "to know how to read mechanically" is nothing, and that he needs to go back to school. So it is with the teachers whom we have thought to prepare for scientific pedagogy by teaching them anthropometry and psychometry.

But let us put aside the difficulty of preparing scientific masters in the accepted sense of the word. We will not even attempt to outline a programme of such preparation, since this would lead us into a discussion which has no place here. Let us suppose, instead, that we have already prepared teachers through long and patient exercises for the *observation of nature*, and that we have led them, for example, to the point attained by those students of natural sciences who rise at night and go into the woods and fields that they may surprise the awakening and the early activities of some family of insects in which they are interested. Here we have the scientist who, though he may be sleepy and tired with walking, is full of watchfulness, who is not aware that he is muddy or dusty, that the mist wets him, or the sun burns him; but is intent only upon not revealing in the least degree his presence, in order that the insects may, hour after hour, carry on peacefully those natural functions which he wishes to observe. Let us suppose these teachers to have reached the standpoint of the scientist who, half blind, still watches through his microscope the spontaneous movements of some particular infusory animalcule. These creatures seem to this scientific watcher, in their manner of avoiding each other and in their way of selecting their food, to possess a dim intelligence. He then disturbs this sluggish life by an electric stimulus, observing how some group themselves about the positive pole, and others about the negative. Experimenting further, with a luminous stimulus, he notices how some run toward the light, while others fly from it. He investigates these and like phenomena; having always in mind this question: whether the fleeing from or running to the stimulus be of the same character as the avoidance of one another or the selection of food–that is, whether such differences are the result of choice and are due to that dim consciousness, rather than to physical attraction or repulsion similar to that of the magnet. And let us suppose that this scientist, finding it to be four o'clock in the afternoon, and that he has not yet lunched, is conscious, with a feeling of pleasure, of the fact that he has been at work in his laboratory instead of in his own home, where they would have called him hours ago, interrupting his interesting observation, in order that he might eat.

Let us imagine, I say, that the teacher has arrived, independently of his scientific training, at such an attitude of interest in the observation of natural phenomena. Very well, but such a preparation is not enough. The master, indeed, is destined in his particular mission not to the observation of insects or of bacteria, but of man. He is not to make a study of man in the manifestations of his daily physical habits as one studies some family of insects, following their movements from the hour of their morning awakening. The master is to study man in the awakening of his intellectual life.

The interest in humanity to which we wish to educate the teacher must be characterised by the intimate relationship between the observer and the individual to be observed; a relationship which does not exist between the student of zoology or botany and that form of nature which he studies. Man cannot love the insect or the chemical reaction which he studies, without sacrificing a part of himself. This self-sacrifice seems to one who looks at it from the standpoint of the world, a veritable renunciation of life itself, almost a martyrdom.

But the love of man for man is a far more tender thing, and so simple that it is universal. To love in this way is not the privilege of any especially prepared intellectual class, but lies within the reach of all men.

To give an idea of this second form of preparation, that of the spirit, let us try to enter into the minds and hearts of those first followers of Christ Jesus as they heard Him speak of a Kingdom not of this world, greater far than any earthly kingdom, no matter how royally conceived. In their simplicity they asked of Him, "Master, tell us who shall be greatest in the Kingdom of Heaven?" To which Christ, caressing the head of a little child who, with reverent, wondering eyes, looked into His face, replied, "Whosoever shall become as one of these little ones, he shall be greatest in the Kingdom of Heaven." Now let us picture among those to whom these words were spoken, an ardent, worshipping soul, who takes them into his heart. With a mixture of respect and love, of sacred curiosity and of a desire to achieve this spiritual greatness, he sets himself to observe every manifestation of this little child. Even such an observer placed in a classroom filled with little children will not be the new educator whom we wish to form. But let us seek to implant in the soul the self-sacrificing spirit of the scientist with the reverent love of the disciple of Christ, and we shall have prepared the *spirit* of the teacher. From the child itself he will learn how to perfect himself as an educator.

Let us consider the attitude of the teacher in the light of another example. Picture to yourself one of our botanists or zoologists experienced in the technique of observation and experimentation; one who has travelled in order to study "certain fungi" in their native environment. This scientist has made his observations in open country and, then, by the aid of his microscope and of all his laboratory appliances, has carried on the later research work in the most minute way possible. He is, in fact, a scientist who understands what it is to study nature, and who is conversant with all the means which modern experimental science offers for this study.

Now let us imagine such a man appointed, by reason of the original work he has done, to a chair of science in some university, with the task before him of doing further original research work with hymenoptera. Let us suppose that, arrived at his post, he is shown a glass-covered case containing a number of beautiful butterflies, mounted by means of pins, their outspread wings motionless. The student will say that this is some child's play, not material for scientific study, that these specimens in the box are more fitly a part of the game which the little boys play, chasing butterflies and catching them in a net. With such material as this the experimental scientist can do nothing.

The situation would be very much the same if we should place a teacher who, according to our conception of the term, is scientifically prepared, in one of the public schools where the children are repressed in the spontaneous expression of their personality till they are almost like dead beings. In such a school the children, like butterflies mounted on pins, are fastened each to his place, the desk, spreading the useless wings of barren and meaningless knowledge which they have acquired.

It is not enough, then, to prepare in our Masters the scientific spirit. We must also make ready the school for their observation. The school must permit the *free, natural manifestations* of the *child* if in the school scientific pedagogy is to be born. This is the essential reform.

No one may affirm that such a principle already exists in pedagogy and in the school. It is true that some pedagogues, led by Rousseau, have given voice to impracticable principles and vague aspirations for the liberty of the child, but the true concept of liberty is practically unknown to educators. They often have the same concept of liberty which animates a people in the hour of rebellion from slavery, or perhaps, the conception of *social liberty*, which although it is a more elevated idea is still invariably restricted. "Social liberty" signifies always one more round of Jacob's ladder. In other words it signifies a partial liberation, the liberation of a country, of a class, or of thought.

That concept of liberty which must inspire pedagogy is, instead, universal. The biological sciences of the nineteenth century have shown it to us when they have offered us the means for studying life. If, therefore, the old-time pedagogy foresaw or vaguely expressed the principle of studying the pupil before educating him, and of leaving him free in his spontaneous manifestations, such an intuition, indefinite and barely expressed, was made possible of practical attainment only after the contribution of the experimental sciences during the last century. This is not a case for sophistry or discussion, it is enough that we state our point. He who would say that the principle of liberty informs the pedagogy of to-day, would make us smile as at a child who, before the box of mounted butterflies, should insist that they were alive and could fly. The principle of slavery still pervades pedagogy, and, therefore, the same principle pervades the school. I need only give one proof–the stationary desks and chairs. Here we have, for example, a striking evidence of the errors of the early materialistic scientific pedagogy which, with mistaken zeal and energy, carried the barren stones of science to the rebuilding of the crumbling walls of the school. The schools were at first furnished with the long, narrow benches upon which the children were crowded together. Then came science and perfected the bench. In this work much attention was paid to the recent contributions of anthropology. The age of the child and the length of his limbs were considered in placing the seat at the right height. The distance between the seat and the desk was calculated with infinite care, in order that the child's back should not become deformed, and, finally, the seats were separated and the width so closely calculated that the child could barely seat himself upon it, while to stretch himself by making any lateral movements was impossible. This was done in order that he might be separated from his neighbour. These desks are constructed in such a way as to render the child visible in all his immobility. One of the ends sought through this separation is the prevention of immoral acts in the schoolroom. What shall we say of such prudence in a state of society where it would be considered scandalous to give voice to principles of sex morality in education, for fear we might thus contaminate innocence? And, yet, here we have science lending itself to this hypocrisy, fabricating machines! Not only this; obliging science goes farther still, perfecting the benches in such a way as to permit to the greatest possible extent the immobility of the child, or, if you wish, to repress every movement of the child.

It is all so arranged that, when the child is well-fitted into his place, the desk and chair themselves force him to assume the position considered to be hygienically comfortable. The seat, the foot-rest, the desks are arranged in such a way that the child can never stand at his work. He is allotted only sufficient space for sitting in an erect position. It is in such ways that schoolroom desks and benches have advanced toward perfection. Every cult of the so-called scientific pedagogy has designed a model scientific desk. Not a few nations have become proud of their "national desk,"–and in the struggle of competition these various machines have been patented.

Undoubtedly there is much that is scientific underlying the construction of these benches. Anthropology has been drawn upon in the measuring of the body and the diagnosis of the age; physiology, in the study of muscular movements; psychology, in regard to perversion of instincts; and, above all, hygiene, in the effort to prevent curvature of the spine. These desks were indeed scientific, following in their construction the anthropological study of the child. We have here, as I have said, an example of the literal application of science to the schools.

I believe that before very long we shall all be struck with great surprise by this attitude. It will seem incomprehensible that the fundamental error of the desk should not have been revealed earlier through the attention given to the study of infant hygiene, anthropology, and sociology, and through the general progress of thought. The marvel is greater when we consider that during the past years there has been stirring in almost every nation a movement toward the protection of the child.

I believe that it will not be many years before the public, scarcely believing the descriptions of these scientific benches, will come to touch with wondering hands the amazing seats that were constructed for the purpose of preventing among our school children curvature of the spine!

The development of these scientific benches means that the pupils were subjected to a régime, which, even though they were born strong and straight, made it possible for them to become humpbacked! The vertebral column, biologically the most primitive, fundamental, and oldest part of the skeleton, the most fixed portion of our body, since the skeleton is the most solid portion of the organism–the vertebral column, which resisted and was strong through the desperate struggles of primitive man when he fought against the desert-lion, when he conquered the mammoth, when he quarried the solid rock and shaped the iron to his uses, bends, and cannot resist, under the yoke of the school.

It is incomprehensible that so-called *science* should have worked to perfect an instrument of slavery in the school without being enlightened by one ray from the movement of social liberation, growing and developing throughout the world. For the age of scientific benches was also the age of the redemption of the working classes from the yoke of unjust labor.

The tendency toward social liberty is most evident, and manifests itself on every hand. The leaders of the people make it their slogan, the labouring masses repeat the cry, scientific and socialistic publications voice the same movement, our journals are full of it. The underfed workman does not ask for a tonic, but for better economic conditions which shall prevent malnutrition. The miner who, through the stooping position maintained during many hours of the day, is subject to inguinal rupture, does not ask for an abdominal support, but demands shorter hours and better working conditions, in order that he may be able to lead a healthy life like other men.

And when, during this same social epoch, we find that the children in our schoolrooms are working amid unhygienic conditions, so poorly adapted to normal development that even the skeleton becomes deformed, our response to this terrible revelation is an orthopedic bench. It is much as if we offered to the miner the abdominal brace, or arsenic to the underfed workman.

Some time ago a woman, believing me to be in sympathy with all scientific innovations concerning the school, showed me with evident satisfaction a *corset or brace for pupils*. She had invented this and felt that it would complete the work of the bench.

Surgery has still other means for the treatment of spinal curvature. I might mention orthopedic instruments, braces, and a method of periodically suspending the child, by the head or shoulders, in such a fashion that the weight of the body stretches and thus straightens the vertebral column. In the school, the orthopedic instrument in the shape of the desk is in great favour; to-day someone proposes the brace–one step farther and it will be suggested that we give the scholars a systematic course in the suspension method!

All this is the logical consequence of a material application of the methods of science to the decadent school. Evidently the rational method of combating spinal curvature in the pupils, is to change the form of their work–so that they shall no longer be obliged to remain for so many hours a day in a harmful position. It is a conquest of liberty which the school needs, not the mechanism of a bench.

Even were the stationary seat helpful to the child's body, it would still be a dangerous and unhygienic feature of the environment, through the difficulty of cleaning the room perfectly when the furniture cannot be moved. The footrests, which cannot be removed, accumulate the dirt carried in daily from the street by the many little feet. To-day there is a general transformation in the matter of house furnishings. They are made lighter and simpler so that they may be easily moved, dusted, and even washed. But the school seems blind to the transformation of the social environment.

It behooves us to think of what may happen to the *spirit* of the child who is condemned to grow in conditions so artificial that his very bones may become deformed. When we speak of the redemption of the workingman, it is always understood that beneath the most apparent form of suffering, such as poverty of the blood, or ruptures, there exists that other wound from which the soul of the man who is subjected to any form of slavery must suffer. It is at this deeper wrong that we aim when we say that the workman must be redeemed through liberty. We know only too well that when a man's very blood has been consumed or his intestines wasted away through his work, his soul must have lain oppressed in darkness, rendered insensible, or, it may be, killed within him. The *moral* degradation of the slave is, above all things, the weight that opposes the progress of humanity–humanity striving to rise and held back by this great burden. The cry of redemption speaks far more clearly for the souls of men than for their bodies.

What shall we say then, when the question before us is that of *educating children?*

We know only too well the sorry spectacle of the teacher who, in the ordinary schoolroom, must pour certain cut and dried facts into the heads of the scholars. In order to succeed in this barren task, she finds it necessary to discipline her pupils into immobility and to force their attention. Prizes and punishments are every-ready and efficient aids to the master who must force into a given attitude of mind and body those who are condemned to be his listeners.

It is true that to-day it is deemed expedient to abolish official whippings and habitual blows, just as the awarding of prizes has become less ceremonious. These partial reforms are another prop approved of by science, and offered to the support of the decadent school. Such prizes and punishments are, if I may be allowed the expression, the *bench* of the soul, the instrument of slavery for the spirit. Here, however, these are not applied to lessen deformities, but to provoke them. The prize and the punishment are incentives toward unnatural or forced effort, and, therefore we certainly cannot speak of the natural development of the child in connection with them. The jockey offers a piece of sugar to his horse before jumping into the saddle, the coachman beats his horse that he may respond to the signs given by the reins; and, yet, neither of these runs so superbly as the free horse of the plains.

And here, in the case of education, shall man place the yoke upon man?

True, we say that social man is natural man yoked to society. But if we give a comprehensive glance to the moral progress of society, we shall see that little by little, the yoke is being made easier, in other words, we shall see that nature, or life, moves gradually toward triumph. The yoke of the slave yields to that of the servant, and the yoke of the servant to that of the workman.

All forms of slavery tend little by little to weaken and disappear, even the sexual slavery of woman. The history of civilisation is a history of conquest and of liberation. We should ask in what stage of civilisation we find ourselves and if, in truth, the good of prizes and of punishments be necessary to our advancement. If we have indeed gone beyond this point, then to apply such a form of education would be to draw the new generation back to a lower level, not to lead them into their true heritage of progress.

Something very like this condition of the school exists in society, in the relation between the government and the great numbers of the men employed in its administrative departments. These clerks work day after day for the general national good, yet they do not feel or see the advantage of their work in any immediate reward. That is, they do not realise that the state carries on its great business through their daily tasks, and that the whole nation is benefited by their work. For them the immediate good is promotion, as passing to a higher class is for the child in school. The man who loses sight of the really big aim of his work is like a child who has been placed in a class below his real standing: like a slave, he is cheated of something which is his right. His dignity as a man is reduced to the limits of the dignity of a machine which must be oiled if it is to be kept going, because it does not have within itself the impulse of life. All those petty things such as the desire for decorations or medals, are but artificial stimuli, lightening for the moment the dark, barren path in which he treads.

In the same way we give prizes to school children. And the fear of not achieving promotion, withholds the clerk from running away, and binds him to his monotonous work, even as the fear of not passing into the next class drives the pupil to his book. The reproof of the superior is in every way similar to the scolding of the teacher. The correction of badly executed clerical work is equivalent to the bad mark placed by the teacher upon the scholar's poor composition. The parallel is almost perfect.

But if the administrative departments are not carried on in a way which would seem suitable to a nation's greatness; if corruption too easily finds a place; it is the result of having extinguished the true greatness of man in the mind of the employee, and of having restricted his vision to those petty, immediate facts, which he has come to look upon as prizes and punishments. The country stands, because the rectitude of the greater number of its employees is such that they resist the corruption of the prizes and punishments, and follow an irresistible current of honesty. Even as life in the social environment triumphs against every cause of poverty and death, and proceeds to new conquests, so the instinct of liberty conquers all obstacles, going from victory to victory.

It is this personal and yet universal force of life, a force often latent within the soul, that sends the world forward.

But he who accomplishes a truly human work, he who does something really great and victorious, is never spurred to his task by those trifling attractions called by the name of "prizes," nor by the fear of those petty ills which we call "punishments." If in a war a great army of giants should fight with no inspiration beyond the desire to win promotion, epaulets, or medals, or through fear of being shot, if these men were to oppose a handful of pygmies who were inflamed by love of country, the victory would go to the latter. When real heroism has died within an army, prizes and punishments cannot do more than finish the work of deterioration, bringing in corruption and cowardice.

All human victories, all human progress, stand upon the inner force.

Thus a young student may become a great doctor if he is spurred to his study by an interest which makes medicine his real vocation. But if he works in the hope of an inheritance, or of making a desirable marriage, or if indeed he is inspired by any material advantage, he will never become a true master or a great doctor, and the world will never make one step forward because of his work. He to whom such stimuli are necessary, had far better never become a physician. Everyone has a special tendency, a special vocation, modest, perhaps, but certainly useful. The system of prizes may turn an individual aside from this vocation, may make him choose a false road, for him a vain one, and forced to follow it, the natural activity of a human being may be warped, lessened, even annihilated.

We repeat always that the world *progresses* and that we must urge men forward to obtain progress. But progress comes from the *new things that are born*, and these, not being foreseen, are not rewarded with prizes: rather, they often carry the leader to martyrdom. God forbid that poems should ever be born of the desire to be crowned in the Capitol! Such a vision need only come into the heart of the poet and the muse will vanish. The poem must spring from the soul of the poet, when he thinks neither of himself nor of the prize. And if he does win the laurel, he will feel the vanity of such a prize. The true reward lies in the revelation through the poem of his own triumphant inner force.

There does exist, however, an external prize for man; when, for example, the orator sees the faces of his listeners change with the emotions he has awakened, he experiences something so great that it can only be likened to the intense joy with which one discovers that he is loved. Our joy is to touch, and conquer souls, and this is the one prize which can bring us a true compensation.

Sometimes there is given to us a moment when we fancy ourselves to be among the great ones of the world. These are moments of happiness given to man that he may continue his existence in peace. It may be through love attained or because of the gift of a son, through a glorious discovery or the publication of a book; in some such moment we feel that there exists no man who is above us. If, in such a moment, someone vested with authority comes forward to offer us a medal or a prize, he is the important destroyer of our real reward–"And who are you?" our vanished illusion shall cry, "Who are you that recalls me to the fact that I am not the first among men? Who stands so far above me that he may give me a prize?" The prize of such a man in such a moment can only be Divine.

As for punishments, the soul of the normal man grows perfect through expanding, and punishment as commonly understood is always a form of *repression*. It may bring results with those inferior natures who grow in evil, but these are very few, and social progress is not affected by them. The penal code threatens us with punishment if we are dishonest within the limits indicated by the laws. But we are not honest through fear of the laws; if we do not rob, if we do not kill, it is because we love peace, because the natural trend of our lives leads us forward, leading us ever farther and more definitely away from the peril of low and evil acts.

Without going into the ethical or metaphysical aspects of the question, we may safely affirm that the delinquent before he transgresses the law, has, *if he knows of the existence of a punishment,* felt the threatening weight of the criminal code upon him. He has defied it, or he has been lured into the crime, deluding himself with the idea that he would be able to avoid the punishment of the law. But there has occurred within his mind, a *struggle between the crime and the punishment.* Whether it be efficacious in hindering crime or not, this penal code is undoubtedly made for a very limited class of individuals; namely, criminals. The enormous majority of citizens are honest without any regard whatever to the threats of the law.

The real punishment of normal man is the loss of the consciousness of that individual power and greatness which are the sources of his inner life. Such a punishment often falls upon men in the fullness of success. A man whom we would consider crowned by happiness and fortune may be suffering from this form of punishment. Far too often man does not see the real punishment which threatens him.

And it is just here that education may help.

To-day we hold the pupils in school, restricted by those instruments so degrading to body and spirit, the desk–and material prizes and punishments. Our aim in all this is to reduce them to the discipline of immobility and silence,–to lead them,–where? Far too often toward no definite end.

Often the education of children consists in pouring into their intelligence the intellectual content of school programmes. And often these programmes have been compiled in the official department of education, and their use is imposed by law upon the teacher and the child.

Ah, before such dense and wilful disregard of the life which is growing within these children, we should hide our heads in shame and cover our guilty faces with our hands!

Sergi says truly: "To-day an urgent need imposes itself upon society: the reconstruction of methods in education and instruction, and he who fights for this cause, fights for human regeneration."

History of Methods

If we are to develop a system of scientific pedagogy, we must, then, proceed along lines very different from those which have been followed up to the present time. The transformation of the school must be contemporaneous with the preparation of the teacher. For if we make of the teacher an observer, familiar with the experimental methods, then we must make it possible for her to observe and to experiment in the school. The fundamental principle of scientific pedagogy must be, indeed, the *liberty of the pupil*;–such liberty as shall permit a development of individual, spontanous manifestations of the child's nature. If a new and scientific pedagogy is to arise from the *study of the individual,* such study must occupy itself with the observation of *free* children. In vain should we await a practical renewing of pedagogical methods from methodical examinations of pupils made under the guidance offered to-day by pedagogy, anthropology, and experimental psychology.

Every branch of experimental science has grown out of the application of a method peculiar to itself. Bacteriology owes its scientific content to the method of isolation and culture of microbes. Criminal, medical, and pedagogical anthropology owe their progress to the application of anthropological methods to individuals of various classes, such as criminals, the insane, the sick of the clinics, scholars. So experimental psychology needs as its starting point an exact definition of the technique to be used in making the experiment.

To put it broadly, it is important to define *the method, the technique,* and from its application to *await* the definite result, which must be gathered entirely from actual experience. One of the characteristics of experimental sciences is to proceed to the making of an experiment *without preconceptions of any sort* as to the final result of the experiment itself. For example, should we wish to make scientific observations concerning the development of the head as related to varying degrees of intelligence, one of the conditions of such an experiment would be to ignore, in the taking of the measurements, which were the most intelligent and which the most backward among the scholars examined. And this because the preconceived idea that the most intelligent should have the head more fully developed will inevitably alter the results of the research.

He who experiments must, while doing so, divest himself of every preconception. It is clear then that if we wish to make use of a method of experimental psychology, the first thing necessary is to renounce all former creeds and to proceed by means of the *method* in the search for truth.

We must not start, for example, from any dogmatic ideas which we may happen to have held upon the subject of child psychology. Instead, we must proceed by a method which shall tend to make possible to the child complete liberty. This we must do if we are to draw from the observation of his spontaneous manifestations conclusions which shall lead to the establishment of a truly scientific child psychology. It may be that such a method holds for us great surprises, unexpected possibilities.

Child psychology and pedagogy must establish their content by successive conquests arrived at through the method of experimentation.

Our problem then, is this: to establish the *method peculiar* to experimental pedagogy. It cannot be that used in other experimental sciences. It is true that scientific pedagogy is rounded out by hygiene, anthropology, and psychology, and adopts in part the technical method characteristic of all three, although limiting itself to a special study of the individual to be educated. But in pedagogy this study of the individual, though it must accompany the very different work of *education,* is a limited and secondary part of the science as a whole.

This present study deals in part with the *method* used in experimental pedagogy, and is the result of my experiences during two years in the "Children's Houses." I offer only a beginning of the method, which I have applied to children between the ages of three and six. But I believe that these tentative experiments, because of the surprising results which they have given, will be the means of inspiring a continuation of the work thus undertaken.

Indeed, although our educational system, which experience has demonstrated to be excellent, is not yet entirely completed, it nevertheless constitutes a system well enough established to be practical in all institutions where young children are cared for, and in the first elementary classes.

Perhaps I am not exact when I say that the present work springs from two years of experience. I do not believe that these later attempts of mine could alone have rendered possible all that I set forth in this book. The origin of the educational system in use in the "Children's Houses" is much more remote, and if this experience with normal children seems indeed rather brief, it should be remembered that it sprang from preceding pedagogical experiences with abnormal children, and that considered in this way, it represents a long and thoughtful endeavour.

About fifteen years ago, being assistant doctor at the Psychiatric Clinic of the University of Rome, I had occasion to frequent the insane asylums to study the sick and to select subjects for the clinics. In this way I became interested in the idiot children who were at that time housed in the general insane asylums. In those days thyroid organotherapy was in full development, and this drew the attention of physicians to deficient children. I myself, having completed my regular hospital services, had already turned my attention to the study of children's diseases.

It was thus that, being interested in the idiot children, I became conversant with the special method of education devised for these unhappy little ones by Edward Séguin, and was led to study thoroughly the idea, then beginning to be prevalent among the physicians, of the efficacy of "pedagogical treatment" for various morbid forms of disease such as deafness, paralysis, idiocy, rickets, etc. The fact that pedagogy must join with medicine in the treatment of disease was the practical outcome of the thought of the time. And because of this tendency the method of treating disease by gymnastics became widely popular. I, however, differed from my colleagues in that I felt that mental deficiency presented chiefly a pedagogical, rather than mainly a medical, problem. Much was said in the medical congresses of the medico-pedagogic method for the treatment and education of the feeble minded, and I expressed my differing opinion in an address on *Moral Education* at the Pedagogical Congress of Turin in 1898. I believe that I touched a chord already vibrant, because the idea, making its way among the physicians and elementary teachers, spread in a flash as presenting a question of lively interest to the school.

In fact I was called upon by my master, Guido Baccelli, the great Minister of Education, to deliver to the teachers of Rome a course of lectures on the education of feeble-minded children. This course soon developed into the State Orthophrenic School, which I directed for more than two years.

In this school we had an all-day class of children composed of those who in the elementary schools were considered hopelessly deficient. Later on, through the help of a philanthropic organisation, there was founded a Medical Pedagogic Institute where, besides the children from the public schools, we brought together all of the idiot children from the insane asylums in Rome.

I spent these two years with the help of my colleagues in preparing the teachers of Rome for a special method of observation and education of feeble-minded children. Not only did I train teachers, but what was much more important, after I had been in London and Paris for the purpose of studying in a practical way the education of deficients, I gave myself over completely to the actual teaching of the children, directing at the same time the work of the other teachers in our institute.

I was more than an elementary teacher, for I was present, or directly taught the children, from eight in the morning to seven in the evening without interruption. These two years of practice are my first and indeed my true degree in pedagogy. From the very beginning of my work with deficient children (1898 to 1900) I felt that the methods which I used had in them nothing peculiarly limited to the instruction of idiots. I believed that they contained educational principles *more rational* than those in use, so much more so, indeed, that through their means an inferior mentality would be able to grow and develop. This feeling, so deep as to be in the nature of an intuition, became my controlling idea after I had left the school for deficients, and, little by little, I became convinced that similar methods applied to normal children would develop or set free their personality in a marvellous and surprising way.

It was then that I began a genuine and thorough study of what is known as remedial pedagogy, and, then, wishing to undertake the study of normal pedagogy and of the principles upon which it is based, I registered as a student of philosophy at the University. A great faith animated me, and although I did not know that I should ever be able to test the truth of my idea, I gave up every other occupation to deepen and broaden its conception. It was almost as if I prepared myself for an unknown mission.

The methods for the education of deficients had their origin at the time of the French Revolution in the work of a physician whose achievements occupy a prominent place in the history of medicine, as he was the founder of that branch of medical science which to-day is known as Otiatria (diseases of the ear).

He was the first to attempt a methodical education of the sense of hearing. He made these experiments in the institute for deaf mutes founded in Paris by Pereire, and actually succeeded in making the semi-deaf hear clearly. Later on, having in charge for eight years the idiot boy known as "the wild boy of Aveyron," he extended to the treatment of all the senses those educational methods which had already given such excellent results in the treatment of the sense of hearing. A student of Pinel, Itard was the first educator to practise *the observation* of the pupil in the way in which the sick are observed in the hospitals, especially those suffering from diseases of the nervous system.

The pedagogic writings of Itard are most interesting and minute descriptions of educational efforts and experiences, and anyone reading them to-day must admit that they were practically the first attempts at experimental psychology. But the merit of having completed a genuine educational system for deficient children was due to Edward Séguin, first a teacher and then a physician. He took the experiences of Itard as his starting point, applying these methods, modifying and completing them during a period of ten years' experience with children taken from the insane asylums and placed in a little school in Rue Pigalle in Paris. This method was described for the first time in a volume of more than six hundred pages, published in Paris in 1846, with the title: "Traitement Moral, Hygiène et Education des Idiots." Later Séguin emigrated to the United States of America where he founded many institutions for deficients, and where, after another twenty years of experience, he published the second edition of his method, under a very different title: "Idiocy and its Treatment by the Physiological Method." This volume was published in New York in 1866, and in it Séguin had carefully defined his method of education, calling it the *physiological method*. He no longer referred in the title to a method for the "education of idiots" as if the method were special to them, but spoke now of idiocy treated by a physiological method. If we consider that pedagogy always had psychology as its base, and that Wundt defines a "physiological psychology," the coincidence of these ideas must strike us, and lead us to suspect in the physiological method some connection with physiological psychology.

While I was assistant at the Psychiatric Clinic, I had read Edward Séguin's French book, with great interest. But the English book which was published in New York twenty years later, although it was quoted in the works about special education by Bourneville, was not to be found in any library. I made a vain quest for it, going from house to house of nearly all the English physicians, who were known to be specially interested in deficient children, or who were superintendents of special schools. The fact that this book was unknown in England, although it had been published in the English language, made me think that the Séguin system had never been understood. In fact, although Séguin was constantly quoted in all the publications dealing with institutions for deficients, the educational *applications* described, were quite different from the applications of Séguin's system.

Almost everywhere the methods applied to deficients are more or less the same as those in use for normal children. In Germany, especially, a friend who had gone there in order to help me in my researches, noticed that although special materials existed here and there in the pedagogical museums of the schools for deficients, these materials were rarely used. Indeed, the German educators hold the principle that it is well to adapt to the teaching of backward children, the same method used for normal ones; but these methods are much more objective in Germany than with us.

At the Bicêtre, where I spent some time, I saw that it was the didactic apparatus of Séguin far more than his *method* which was being used, although the French text was in the hands of the educators. The teaching there was purely mechanical, each teacher following the rules according to the letter. I found, however, wherever I went, in London as well as in Paris, a desire for fresh counsel and for new experiences, since far too often Séguin's claim that with his methods the education of idiots was actually possible, had proved only a delusion.

After this study of the methods in use throughout Europe I concluded my experiments upon the deficients of Rome, and taught them throughout two years. I followed Séguin's book, and also derived much help from the remarkable experiments of Itard.

Guided by the work of these two men, I had manufactured a great variety of didactic material. These materials, which I have never seen complete in any institution, became in the hands of those who knew how to apply them, a most remarkable and efficient means, but unless rightly presented, they failed to attract the attention of the deficients.

I felt that I understood the discouragement of those working with feeble-minded children, and could see why they had, in so many cases, abandoned the method. The prejudice that the educator must place himself on a level with the one to be educated, sinks the teacher of deficients into a species of apathy. He accepts the fact that he is educating an inferior personality, and for that very reason he does not succeed. Even so those who teach little children too often have the idea that they are educating babies and seek to place themselves on the child's level by approaching him with games, and often with foolish stories. Instead of all this, we must know how to call to the *man* which lies dormant within the soul of the child. I felt this, intuitively, and believed that not the didactic material, but my voice which called to them, *awakened* the children, and encouraged them to use the didactic material, and through it, to educate themselves. I was guided in my work by the deep respect which I felt for their misfortune, and by the love which these unhappy children know how to awaken in those who are near them.

Séguin, too, expressed himself in the same way on this subject. Reading his patient attempts, I understand clearly that the first didactic material used by him was *spiritual*. Indeed, at the close of the French volume, the author, giving a résumé of his work, concludes by saying rather sadly, that all he has established will be lost or useless, if the *teachers* are not prepared for their work. He holds rather original views concerning the preparation of teachers of deficients. He would have them good to look upon, pleasant-voiced, careful in every detail of their personal appearance, doing everything possible to make themselves attractive. They must, he says, render themselves attractive in voice and manner, since it is their task to awaken souls which are frail and weary, and to lead them forth to lay hold upon the beauty and strength of life.

This belief that we must act upon the spirit, served as a sort of *secret key*, opening to me the long series of didactic experiments so wonderfully analysed by Edward Séguin,-experiments which, properly understood, are really most efficacious in the education of idiots. I myself obtained most surprising results through their application, but I must confess that, while my efforts showed themselves in the intellectual progress of my pupils, a peculiar form of exhaustion prostrated me. It was as if I gave to them some vital force from within me. Those things which we call encouragement, comfort, love, respect, are drawn from the soul of man, and the more freely we give of them, the more do we renew and reinvigorate the life about us.

Without such inspiration the most perfect *external stimulus* may pass unobserved. Thus the blind Saul, before the glory of the sun, exclaimed, "This?-It is the dense fog!"

Thus prepared, I was able to proceed to new experiments on my own account. This is not the place for a report of these experiments, and I will only note that at this time I attempted an original method for the teaching of reading and writing, a part of the education of the child which was most imperfectly treated in the works of both Itard and Séguin.

I succeeded in teaching a number of the idiots from the asylums both to read and to write so well that I was able to present them at a public school for an examination together with normal children. And they passed the examination successfully.

These results seemed almost miraculous to those who saw them. To me, however, the boys from the asylums had been able to compete with the normal children only because they had been taught in a different way. They had been helped in their psychic development, and the normal children had, instead, been suffocated, held back. I found myself thinking that if, some day, the special education which had developed these idiot children in such a marvellous fashion, could be applied to the development of normal children, the "miracle" of which my friends talked would no longer be possible. The abyss between the inferior mentality of the idiot and that of the normal brain can never be bridged if the normal child has reached his full development.

While everyone was admiring the progress of my idiots, I was searching for the reasons which could keep the happy healthy children of the common schools on so low a plane that they could be equalled in tests of intelligence by my unfortunate pupils!

One day, a directress in the Institute for Deficients, asked me to read one of the prophecies of Ezekiel which had made a profound impression upon her, as it seemed to prophesy the education of deficients.

"The hand of the Lord was upon me, and carried me out in the spirit of the Lord, and set me down in the midst of the valley which was full of bones.

"And caused me to pass by them round about: and, behold, there were very many in the open valley; and, lo, they were very dry.

"And he said unto me, Son of man, can these bones live ? And I answered, O Lord God, thou knowest.

"Again he said unto me, Prophesy upon these bones, and say unto them, O ye dry bones, hear the word of the Lord.

"Thus saith the Lord God unto these bones; Behold, I will cause breath to enter into you, and ye shall live:

"And I will lay sinews upon you, and will bring up flesh upon you, and cover you with skin, and put breath in you, and ye shall live; and ye shall know that I am the Lord.

"So I prophesied as I was commanded: and as I prophesied, there was a noise, and behold a shaking, and the bones came together, bone to his bone.

"And when I beheld, lo, the sinews and the flesh came up upon them, and the skin covered them above: but there was no breath in them.

"Then said he unto me, Prophesy unto the wind, prophesy, son of man, and say to the wind, Thus saith the Lord God; Come from the four winds, O breath, and breathe upon these slain, that they may live.

"So I prophesied as He commanded me, and the breath came into them, and they lived, and stood up upon their feet, an exceeding great army.

"Then he said unto me, Son of man, these bones are the whole house of Israel: behold, they say, Our bones are dried, and our hope is lost: we are cut off for our parts."

In fact, the words-"I will cause breath to enter into you, and ye shall live," seem to me to refer to the direct individual work of the master who encourages, calls to, and helps his pupil, preparing him for education. And the remainder-"I will lay sinews upon you, and will bring up flesh upon you," recalled the fundamental phrase which sums up Séguin's whole method,-"to lead the child, as it were, by the hand, from the education of the muscular system, to that of the nervous system, and of the senses." It was thus that Séguin taught the idiots how to walk, how to maintain their equilibrium in the most difficult movements of the body-such as going up stairs, jumping, etc., and finally, to feel, beginning the education of the muscular sensations by touching, and reading the difference of temperature, and ending with the education of the particular senses.

But if the training goes no further than this, we have only led these children to adapt themselves to a low order of life (almost a vegetable existence). "Call to the Spirit," says the prophecy, and the spirit shall enter into them, and they shall have life. Séguin, indeed, led the idiot from the vegetative to the intellectual life, "from the education of the senses to general notions, from general notions to abstract thought, from abstract thought to morality." But when this wonderful work is accomplished, and by means of a minute physiological analysis and of a gradual progression in method, the idiot has become a man, he is still an inferior in the midst of his fellow men, an individual who will never be able fully to adapt himself to the social environment: "Our bones are dried, and our hope is lost; we are cut off for our parts."

This gives us another reason why the tedious method of Séguin was so often abandoned; the tremendous difficulty of the means, did not justify the end. Everyone felt this, and many said, "There is still so much to be done for normal children!"

Having through actual experience justified my faith in Séguin's method, I withdrew from active work among deficients, and began a more thorough study of the works of Itard and Séguin. I felt the need of meditation. I did a thing which I had not done before, and which perhaps few students have been willing to do,-I translated into Italian and copied out with my own hand, the writings of these men, from beginning to end, making for myself books as the old Benedictines used to do before the diffusion of printing.

I chose to do this by hand, in order that I might have time to weigh the sense of each word, and to read, in truth, the *spirit* of the author. I had just finished copying the 600 pages of Séguin's French volume when I received from New York a *copy* of the English book published in 1866. This old volume had been found among the books discarded from the private library of a New York physician. I translated it with the help of an English friend. This volume did not add much in the way of new pedagogical experiments, but dealt with the philosophy of the experiences described in the first volume. The man who had studied abnormal children for thirty years expressed the idea that the physiological method, which has as its base the individual study of the pupil and which forms its educative methods upon the analysis of physiological and psychological phenomena, must come also to be applied to normal children. This step, he believed, would show the way to a complete human regeneration.

The voice of Séguin seemed to be like the voice of the forerunner crying in the wilderness, and my thoughts were filled with the immensity and importance of a work which should be able to reform the school and education.

At this time I was registered at the University as a student of philosophy, and followed the courses in experimental psychology, which had only recently been established in Italian universities, namely, at Turin, Rome and Naples. At the same time I made researches in Pedagogic Anthropology in the elementary schools, studying in this way the methods in organisation used for the education of normal children. This work led to the teaching of Pedagogic Anthropology in the University of Rome.

I had long wished to experiment with the methods for deficients in a first elementary class of normal children, but I had never thought of making use of the homes or institutions where very young children were cared for. It was pure chance that brought this new idea to my mind.

It was near the end of the year 1906, and I had just returned from Milan, where I had been one of a committee at the International Exhibition for the assignment of prizes in the subjects of Scientific Pedagogy and Experimental Psychology. A great opportunity came to me, for I was invited by Edoardo Talamo, the Director General of the Roman Association for Good Building, to undertake the organisation of infant schools in its model tenements. It was Signor Talamo's happy idea to gather together in a large room all the little ones between the ages of three and seven belonging to the families living in the tenement. The play and work of these children was to be carried on under the guidance of a teacher who should have her own apartment in the tenement house. It was intended that every house should have its school, and as the Association for Good Building already owned more than 400 tenements in Rome the work seemed to offer tremendous possibilities of development. The first school was to be established in January, 1907, in a large tenement house in the Quarter of San Lorenzo. In the same Quarter the Association already owned fifty-eight buildings, and according to Signor Talamo's plans we should soon be able to open sixteen of these "schools within the house."

This new kind of school was christened by Signora Olga Lodi, a mutual friend of Signor Talamo and myself, under the fortunate title of *Casa dei Bambini* or *"The Children's House."* Under this name the first of our schools was opened on the sixth of January, 1907, at 58 Via dei Marsi. It was confided to the care of Candida Nuccitelli and was under my guidance and direction.

From the very first I perceived, in all its immensity, the social and pedagogical importance of such institutions, and while at that time my visions of a triumphant future seemed exaggerated, to-day many are beginning to understand that what I saw before was indeed the truth.

On the seventh of April of the same year, 1907, a second "Children's House" was opened in the Quarter of San Lorenzo; and on the eighteenth of October, 1908, another was inaugurated by the Humanitarian Society in Milan in the Quarter inhabited by workingmen. The workshops of this same society undertook the manufacture of the materials which we used.

On the fourth of November following, a third "Children's House" was opened in Rome, this time not in the people's Quarter, but in a modern building for the middle classes, situated in Via Famagosta, in that part of the city known as the Prati di Castello; and in January, 1909, Italian Switzerland began to transform its orphan asylums and children's homes in which the Froebel system had been used, into "Children's Houses" adopting our methods and materials.

The "Children's House" has a twofold importance: the social importance which it assumes through its peculiarity of being a school within the house, and its purely pedagogic importance gained through its methods for the education of very young children, of which I now made a trial.

As I have said, Signor Talamo's invitation gave me a wonderful opportunity for applying the methods used with deficients to normal children, not of the elementary school age, but of the age usual in infant asylums.

If a parallel between the deficient and the normal child is possible, this will be during the period of early infancy *when the child who has not the force to develop and he who is not yet developed* are in some ways alike.

The very young child has not yet acquired a secure coordination of muscular movements, and, therefore, walks imperfectly, and is not able to perform the ordinary acts of life: such as fastening and unfastening its garments. The sense organs, such as the power of accommodation of the eye, are not yet completely developed; the language is primordial and shows those defects common to the speech of the very young child. The difficulty of fixing the attention, the general instability, etc., are characteristics which the normal infant and the deficient child have in common. Preyer, also, in his psychological study of children has turned aside to illustrate the parallel between pathological linguistic defects, and those of normal children in the process of developing.

Methods which made growth possible to the mental personality of the idiot ought, therefore, to *aid the development of young children*, and should be so adapted as to constitute a hygienic education of the entire personality of a normal human being. Many defects which become permanent, such as speech defects, the child acquires through being neglected during the most important period of his age, the period between three and six, at which time he forms and establishes his principal functions.

Here lies the significance of my pedagogical experiment in the "Children's Houses." It represents the results of a series of trials made by me, in the education of young children, with methods already used with deficients. My work has not been in any way an application, pure and simple, of the methods of Séguin to young children, as anyone who will consult the works of the author will readily see. But it is none the less true that, underlying these two years of trial, there is a basis of experiment which goes back to the days of the French Revolution, and which represents the earnest work of the lives of Itard and Séguin.

As for me, thirty years after the publication of Séguin's second book, I took up again the ideas and, I may even say, the work of this great man, with the same freshness of spirit with which he received the inheritance of the work and ideas of his master Itard. For *ten years* I not only made practical experiments according to their methods, but through reverent meditation absorbed the works of these noble and consecrated men, who have left to humanity most vital proof of their obscure heroism.

Thus my ten years of work may in a sense be considered as a summing up of the forty years of work done by Itard and Séguin. Viewed in this light, fifty years of active work preceded and prepared for this apparently brief trial of only two years, and I feel that I am not wrong in saying that these experiments represent the successive work of three physicians, who from Itard to me show in a greater or less degree the first steps along the path of psychiatry.

As definite factors in the civilisation of the people, the "Children's Houses" deserve a separate volume. They have, in fact, solved so many of the social and pedagogic problems in ways which have seemed to be Utopian, that they are a part of that modem transformation of the home which must most surely be realised before many years have passed. In this way they touch directly the most important side of the social question–that which deals with the intimate or home life of the people.

It is enough here to reproduce the inaugural discourse delivered by me on the occasion of the opening of the second "Children's House" in Rome, and to present the rules and regulations * which I arranged in accordance with the wishes of Signor Talamo.

It will be noticed that the club to which I refer, and the dispensary which is also an out-patients' institution for medical and surgical treatment (all such institutions be- ing free to the inhabitants) have already been established. In the modern tenement–Casa Moderna in the Prati di Castello, opened November 4, 1908, through the philanthropy of Signor Talamo–they are also planning to annex a "communal kitchen."

Inaugural Address Delivered on the Occasion of the Opening of One of the "Children's Houses"

It may be that the life lived by the very poor is a thing which some of you here to-day have never actually looked upon in all its degradation. You may have only felt the misery of deep human poverty through the medium of some great book, or some gifted actor may have made your soul vibrate with its horror.

Let us suppose that in some such moment a voice should cry to you, "Go look upon these homes of misery and blackest poverty. For there have sprung up amid the terror and the suffering, oases of happiness, of cleanliness, of peace. The poor are to have an ideal house which shall be their own. In Quarters where poverty and vice ruled, a work of moral redemption is going on. The soul of the people is being set free from the torpor of vice, from the shadows of ignorance. The little children too have a 'House' of their own. The new generation goes forward to meet the new era, the time when misery shall no longer be deplored but destroyed. They go to meet the time when the dark dens of vice and wretchedness shall have become things of the past, and when no trace of them shall be found among the living." What a change of emotions we should experience! And how we should hasten here, as the wise men guided by a dream and a star hastened to Bethlehem!

I have spoken thus in order that you may understand the great significance, the real beauty, of this humble room, which seems like a bit of the house itself set apart by a mother's hand for the use and happiness of the children of the Quarter. This is the second "Children's House" * which has been established within the ill-favoured Quarter of San Lorenzo.

The Quarter of San Lorenzo is celebrated, for every newspaper in the city is filled with almost daily accounts of its wretched happenings. Yet there are many who are not familiar with the origin of this portion of our city.

It was never intended to build up here a tenement district for the people. And indeed San Lorenzo is not the *People's* Quarter, it is the Quarter of the *poor*. It is the Quarter where lives the underpaid, often unemployed workingman, a common type in a city which has no factory industries. It is the home of him who undergoes the period of surveillance to which he is condemned after his prison sentence is ended. They are all here, mingled, huddled together.

The district of San Lorenzo sprang into being between 1884 and 1888 at the time of the great building fever. No standards either social or hygienic guided these new constructions. The aim in building was simply to cover with walls square foot after square foot of ground. The more space covered, the greater the gain of the interested Banks and Companies. All this with a complete disregard of the disastrous future which they were preparing. It was natural that no one should concern himself with the stability of the building he was creating, since in no case would the property remain in the possession of him who built it.

When the storm burst, in the shape of the inevitable building panic of 1888 to 1890, these unfortunate houses remained for a long time untenanted. Then, little by little, the need of dwelling-places began to make itself felt, and these great houses began to fill. Now, those speculators who had been so unfortunate as to remain possessors of these buildings could not, and did not wish to add fresh capital to that already lost, so the houses constructed in the first place in utter disregard of all laws of hygiene, and rendered still worse by having been used as temporary habitations, came to be occupied by the poorest class in the city.

The apartments not being prepared for the working class, were too large, consisting of five, six, or seven rooms. These were rented at a price which, while exceedingly low in relation to the size, was yet too high for any one family of very poor people. This led to the evil of subletting. The tenant who has taken a six room apartment at eight dollars a month sublets rooms at one dollar and a half or two dollars a month to those who can pay so much, and a corner of a room, or a corridor, to a poorer tenant, thus making an income of fifteen dollars or more, over and above the cost of his own rent.

This means that the problem of existence is in great part solved for him, and that in every case he adds to his income through usury. The one who holds the lease traffics in the misery of his fellow tenants, lending small sums at a rate which generally corresponds to twenty cents a week for the loan of two dollars, equivalent to an annual rate of 500 per cent.

Thus we have in the evil of subletting the most cruel form of usury: that which only the poor know how to practise upon the poor.

To this we must add the evils of crowded living, promiscuousness, immorality, crime. Every little while the newspapers uncover for us one of these *intérieurs*: a large family, growing boys and girls, sleep in one room; while one corner of the room is occupied by an outsider, a woman who receives the nightly visits of men. This is seen by the girls and the boys; evil passions are kindled that lead to the crime and bloodshed which unveil for a brief instant before our eyes, in some lurid paragraph, this little detail of the mass of misery.

Whoever enters, for the first time, one of these apartments is astonished and horrified. For this spectacle of genuine misery is not at all like the garish scene he has imagined. We enter here a world of shadows, and that which strikes us first is the darkness which, even though it be midday, makes it impossible to distinguish any of the details of the room.

When the eye has grown accustomed to the gloom, we perceive, within, the outlines of a bed upon which lies huddled a figure–someone ill and suffering. If we have come to bring money from some society for mutual aid, a candle must be lighted before the sum can be counted and the receipt signed. Oh, when we talk of social problems, how often we speak vaguely, drawing upon our fancy for details instead of preparing ourselves to judge intelligently through a personal investigation of facts and conditions.

We discuss earnestly the question of home study for school children, when for many of them home means a straw pallet thrown down in the corner of some dark hovel. We wish to establish circulating libraries that the poor may read at home. We plan to send among these people books which shall form their domestic literature–books through whose influence they shall come to higher standards of living. We hope through the printed page to educate these poor people in matters of hygiene, of morality, of culture, and in this we show ourselves profoundly ignorant of their most crying needs. For many of them have no light by which to read!

There lies before the social crusader of the present day a problem more profound than that of the intellectual elevation of the poor; the problem, indeed, of *life*.

In speaking of the children born in these places, even the conventional expressions must be changed, for they do not "first see the light of day"; they come into a world of gloom. They grow among the poisonous shadows which envelope over-crowded humanity. These children cannot be other than filthy in body, since the water supply in an apartment originally intended to be occupied by three or four persons, when distributed among twenty or thirty is scarcely enough for drinking purposes!

We Italians have elevated our word "casa" to the almost sacred significance of the English word "home," the enclosed temple of domestic affection, accessible only to dear ones.

Far removed from this conception is the condition of the many who have no "casa," but only ghastly walls within which the most intimate acts of life are exposed upon the pillory. Here, there can be no privacy, no modesty, no gentleness; here, there is often not even light, nor air, nor water! It seems a cruel mockery to introduce here our idea of the home as essential to the education of the masses, and as furnishing, along with the family, the only solid basis for the social structure. In doing this we would be not practical reformers but visionary poets.

Conditions such as I have described make it more decorous, more hygienic, for these people to take refuge in the street and to let their children live there. But how often these streets are the scene of bloodshed, of quarrel, of sights so vile as to be almost inconceivable. The papers tell us of women pursued and killed by drunken husbands! Of young girls with the fear of worse than death, stoned by low men. Again, we see untellable things–a wretched woman thrown, by the drunken men who have preyed upon her, forth into the gutter. There, when day has come, the children of the neighbourhood crowd about her like scavengers about their dead prey, shouting and laughing at the sight of this wreck of womanhood, kicking her bruised and filthy body as it lies in the mud of the gutter!

Such spectacles of extreme brutality are possible here at the very gate of a cosmopolitan city, the mother of civilisation and queen of the fine arts, because of a new fact which was unknown to past centuries, namely, *the isolation of the masses of the poor.*

In the Middle Ages, leprosy was isolated: the Catholics isolated the Hebrews in the Ghetto; but poverty was never considered a peril and an infamy so great that it must be isolated. The homes of the poor were scattered among those of the rich and the contrast between these was a commonplace in literature up to our own times. Indeed, when I was a child in school, teachers, for the purpose of moral education, frequently resorted to the illustration of the kind princess who sends help to the poor cottage next door, or of the good children from the great house who carry food to the sick woman in the neighbouring attic.

To-day all this would be as unreal and artificial as a fairy tale. The poor may no longer learn from their more fortunate neighbours lessons in courtesy and good breeding, they no longer have the hope of help from them in cases of extreme need. We have herded them together far from us, without the walls, leaving them to learn of each other, in the abandon of desperation, the cruel lessons of brutality and vice. Anyone in whom the social conscience is awake must see that we have thus created infected regions that threaten with deadly peril the city which, wishing to make all beautiful and shining according to an aesthetic and aristocratic ideal, has thrust without its walls whatever is ugly or diseased.

When I passed for the first time through these streets, it was as if I found myself in a city upon which some great disaster had fallen. It seemed to me that the shadow of some recent struggle still oppressed the unhappy people who, with something very like terror in their pale faces, passed me in these silent streets. The very silence seemed to signify the life of a community interrupted, broken. Not a carriage, not even the cheerful voice of the ever-present street vender, nor the sound of the hand-organ playing in the hope of a few pennies, not even these things, so characteristic of poor quarters, enter here to lighten this sad and heavy silence.

Observing these streets with their deep holes, the doorsteps broken and tumbling, we might almost suppose that this disaster had been in the nature of a great inundation which had carried the very earth away; but looking about us at the houses stripped of all decorations, the walls broken and scarred, we are inclined to think that it was perhaps an earthquake which has afflicted this quarter. Then, looking still more closely, we see that in all this thickly settled neighbourhood there is not a shop to be found. So poor is the community that it has not been possible to establish even one of those popular bazars where necessary articles are sold at so low a price as to put them within the reach of anyone. The only shops of any sort are the low wine shops which open their evil-smelling doors to the passer-by. As we look upon all this, it is borne upon us that the disaster which has placed its weight of suffering upon these people is not a convulsion of nature, but poverty–poverty with its inseparable companion, vice.

This unhappy and dangerous state of things, to which our attention is called at intervals by newspaper accounts of violent and immoral crime, stirs the hearts and consciences of many who come to undertake among these people some work of generous benevolence. One might almost say that every form of misery inspires a special remedy and that all have been tried here, from the attempt to introduce hygienic principles into each house, to the establishment of crèches, "Children's Houses", and dispensaries.

But what indeed is benevolence? Little more than an expression of sorrow; it is pity translated into action. The benefits of such a form of charity cannot be great, and through the absence of any continued income and the lack of organisation it is restricted to a small number of persons. The great and widespread peril of evil demands, on the other hand, a broad and comprehensive work directed toward the redemption of the entire community. Only such an organisation, as, working for the good of others, shall itself grow and prosper through the general prosperity which it has made possible, can make a place for itself in this quarter and accomplish a permanent good work.

It is to meet this dire necessity that the great and kindly work of the Roman Association of Good Building has been undertaken. The advanced and highly modern way in which this work is being carried on is due to Edoardo Talamo, Director General of the Association. His plans, so original, so comprehensive, yet so practical, are without counterpart in Italy or elsewhere.

This Association was incorporated three years ago in Rome, its plan being to acquire city tenements, remodel them, put them into a productive condition, and administer them as a good father of a family would.

The first property acquired comprised a large portion of the Quarter of San Lorenzo, where to-day the Association possesses fifty-eight houses, occupying a ground space of about 30,000 square metres, and containing, independent of the ground floor, 1,600 small apartments. Thousands of people will in this way receive the beneficent influence of the protective reforms of the Good Building Association. Following its beneficent programme, the Association set about transforming these old houses, according to the most modern standards, paying as much attention to questions related to hygiene and morals as to those relating to buildings. The constructional changes would make the property of real and lasting value, while the hygienic and moral transformation would, through the improved condition of the inmates, make the rent from these apartments a more definite asset.

The Association of Good Building therefore decided upon a programme which would permit of a gradual attainment of their ideal. It is necessary to proceed slowly because it is not easy to empty a tenement house at a time when houses are scarce, and the humanitarian principles which govern the entire movement make it impossible to proceed more rapidly in this work of regeneration. So it is, that the Association has up to the present time transformed only three houses in the Quarter of San Lorenzo. The plan followed in this transformation is as follows:

A: To demolish in every building all portions of the structure not originally constructed with the idea of making homes, but, from a purely commercial standpoint, of making the rental roll larger. In other words, the new management tore down those parts of the building which encumbered the central court, thus doing away with dark, ill-ventilated apartments, and giving air and light to the remaining portion of the tenement. Broad airy courts take the place of the inadequate air and light shafts, rendering the remaining apartments more valuable and infinitely more desirable.

B: To increase the number of stairways, and to divide the room space in a more practical way. The large six or seven room suites are reduced to small apartments of one, two, or three rooms, and a kitchen.

The importance of such changes may be recognised from the economic point of view of the proprietor as well as from the standpoint of the moral and the material welfare of the tenant. Increasing a number of stairways diminishes that abuse of walls and stairs inevitable where so many persons must pass up and down. The tenants more readily learn to respect the building and acquire habits of cleanliness and order. Not only this, but in reducing the chances of contact among the inhabitants of the house, especially late at night, a great advance has been made in the matter of moral hygiene.

The division of the house into small apartments has done much toward this moral regeneration. Each family is thus set apart, *homes* are made possible, while the menacing evil of subletting together with all its disastrous consequences of overcrowding and immorality is checked in the most radical way.

On one side this arrangement lessens the burden of the individual lease holders, and on the other increases the income of the proprietor, who now receives those earnings which were the unlawful gain of the system of subletting. When the proprietor who originally rented an apartment of six rooms for a monthly rental of eight dollars, makes such an apartment over into three small, sunny, and airy suites consisting of one room and a kitchen, it is evident that he increases his income.

The moral importance of this reform as it stands to-day is tremendous, for it has done away with those evil influences and low opportunities which arise from crowding and from promiscuous contact, and has brought to life among these people, for the first time, the gentle sentiment of feeling themselves free within their own homes, in the intimacy of the family.

But the project of the Association goes beyond even this. The house which it offers to its tenants is not only sunny and airy, but in perfect order and repair, almost shining, and as if perfumed with purity and freshness. These good things, however, carry with them a responsibility which the tenant must assume if he wishes to enjoy them. He must pay an actual tax of *care* and *good will*. The tenant who receives a clean house must keep it so, must respect the walls from the big general entrance to the interior of his own little apartment. He who keeps his house in good condition receives the recognition and consideration due such a tenant. Thus all the tenants unite in an ennobling warfare for practical hygiene, an end made possible by the simple task of *conserving* the already perfect conditions.

Here indeed is something new! So far only our great national buildings have had a continued *maintenance fund*. Here, in these houses offered to the people, the maintenance is confided to a hundred or so workingmen, that is, to all the occupants of the building. This care is almost perfect. The people keep the house in perfect condition, without a single spot. The building in which we find ourselves to-day has been for two years under the sole protection of the tenants, and the work of maintenance has been left entirely to them. Yet few of our houses can compare in cleanliness and freshness with this home of the poor.

The experiment has been tried and the result is remarkable. The people acquire together with the love of homemaking, that of cleanliness. They come, moreover, to wish to beautify their homes. The Association helps this by placing growing plants and trees in the courts and about the halls.

Out of this honest rivalry in matters so productive of good, grows a species of pride new to this quarter; this is the pride which the entire body of tenants takes in having the best-cared-for building and in having risen to a higher and more civilised plane for living. They not only live in a house, but they *know how to live*, they *know how to respect* the house in which they live.

This first impulse has led to other reforms. From the clean home will come personal cleanliness. Dirty furniture cannot be tolerated in a clean house, and those persons living in a permanently clean house will come to desire personal cleanliness.

One of the most important hygienic reforms of the Association is that of *the baths*. Each remodeled tenement has a place set apart for bathrooms, furnished with tubs or shower, and having hot and cold water. All the tenants in regular turn may use these baths, as, for example, in various tenements the occupants go according to turn, to wash their clothes in the fountain of the court. This is a great convenience which invites the people to be clean. These hot and cold baths *within the house* are a great improvement upon the general public baths. In this way we make possible to these people, at one and the same time, health and refinement, opening not only to the sun, but to progress, those dark habitations once the *vile caves* of misery.

But in striving to realise its ideal of a semi-gratuitous maintenance of its buildings, the Association met with a difficulty in regard to those children under school age, who must often be left alone during the entire day while their parents went out to work. These little ones, not being able to understand the educative motives which taught their parents to respect the house, became ignorant little vandals, defacing the walls and stairs. And here we have another reform the expense of which may be considered as indirectly assumed by the tenants as was the care of the building. This reform may be considered as the most brilliant transformation of a tax which progress and civilisation have as yet devised. The "Children's House" is earned by the parents through the care of the building. Its expenses are met by the sum that the Association would have otherwise been forced to spend upon repairs. A wonderful climax, this, of moral benefits received! Within the "Children's House", which belongs exclusively to those children under school age, working mothers may safely leave their little ones, and may proceed with a feeling of great relief and freedom to their own work. But this benefit, like that of the care of the house, is not conferred without a tax of care and of good will. *The Regulations posted on the walls announce it thus:

"The mothers are obliged to send their children to the 'Children's House' clean, and to co-operate with the Directress in the educational work."

Two obligations: namely, the physical and moral care of their own children. If the child shows through its conversation that the educational work of the school is being undermined by the attitude taken in his home, he will be sent back to his parents, to teach them thus how to take advantage of their good opportunities. Those who give themselves over to low-living, to fighting, and to brutality, shall feel upon them the weight of those little lives, so needing care. They shall feel that they themselves have once more cast into the darkness of neglect those little creatures who are the dearest part of the family. In other words, the parents must learn to *deserve* the benefit of having within the house the great advantage of a school for their little ones.

"Good will", a willingness to meet the demands of the Association is enough, for the directress is ready and willing to teach them how. The regulations say that the mother must go at least once a week, to confer with the directress, giving an account of her child, and accepting any helpful advice which the directress may be able to give. The advice thus given will undoubtedly prove most illuminating in regard to the child's health and education, since to each of the "Children's Houses" is assigned a physician as well as a directress.

The directress is always at the disposition of the mothers, and her life, as a cultured and educated person, is a constant example to the inhabitants of the house, for she is obliged to live in the tenement and to be therefore a co-habitant with the families of all her little pupils. This is a fact of immense importance. Among these almost savage people, into these houses where at night no one dared to go about unarmed, there has come not only to teach, *but to live the very life they live*, a gentlewoman of culture, an educator by profession, who dedicates her time and her life to helping those about her! A true missionary, a moral queen among the people, she may, if she be possessed of sufficient tact and heart, reap an unheard-of harvest of good from her social work.

This house is verily *new*; it would seem a dream impossible of realisation, but it has been tried. It is true that there have been before this attempts made by generous persons to go and live among the poor to civilise them. But such work is not practical, unless the house of the poor is hygienic, making it possible for people of better standards to live there. Nor can such work succeed in its purpose unless some common advantage or interest unites all of the tenants in an effort toward better things.

This tenement is new also because of the pedagogical organisation of the "Children's House". This is not simply a place where the children are kept, not just an *asylum*, but a true school for their education, and its methods are inspired by the rational principles of scientific pedagogy.

The physical development of the children is followed, each child being studied from the anthropological standpoint. Linguistic exercises, a systematic sense-training, and exercises which directly fit the child for the duties of practical life, form the basis of the work done. The teaching is decidedly objective, and presents an unusual richness of didactic material.

It is not possible to speak of all this in detail. I must, however, mention that there already exists in connection with the school a bathroom, where the children may be given hot or cold baths and where they may learn to take a partial bath, hands, face, neck, ears. Wherever possible the Association has provided a piece of ground in which the children may learn to cultivate the vegetables in common use.

It is important that I speak here of the pedagogical progress attained by the "Children's House" as an institution. Those who are conversant with the chief problems of the school know that to-day much attention is given to a great principle, one that is ideal and almost beyond realisation,-the union of the family and the school in the matter of educational aims. But the family is always something far away from the school, and is almost always regarded as rebelling against its ideals. It is a species of phantom upon which the school can never lay its hands. The home is closed not only to the pedagogical progress, but often to social progress. We see here for the first time the possibility of realising the long-talked-of pedagogical ideal. We have put *the school within the house*; and this is not all. We have placed it within the house as the *property of the collectivity*, leaving under the eyes of the parents the whole life of the teacher in the accomplishment of her high mission.

This idea of collective ownership of the school is new and very beautiful and profoundly educational.

The parents know that the "Children's House" is their property, and is maintained by a portion of the rent they pay. The mothers may go at any hour of the day to watch, to admire, or to meditate upon the life there. It is in every way a continual stimulus to reflection, and a fount of evident blessing and help to their own children. We may say that the mothers *adore* the "Children's House", and the directress. How many delicate and thoughtful attentions these good mothers show the teacher of their little ones! They often leave sweets or flowers upon the sill of the schoolroom window, as a silent token, reverently, almost religiously, given.

And when after three years of such a novitiate, the mothers send their children to the common schools, they will be excellently prepared to co-operate in the work of education, and will have acquired a sentiment, rarely found even among the best classes; namely, the idea that they must *merit* through their own conduct and with their own virtue, the possession of an educated son.

Another advance made by the "Children's Houses" as an institution is related to scientific pedagogy. This branch of pedagogy, heretofore, being based upon the anthropological study of the pupil whom it is to educate, has touched only a few of the positive questions which tend to transform education. For a man is not only a biological but a social product, and the social environment of individuals in the process of education, is the home. Scientific pedagogy will seek in vain to better the new generation if it does not succeed in influencing also the environment within which this new generation grows! I believe, therefore, that in opening the house to the light of new truths, and to the progress of civilisation we have solved the problem of being able to modify directly, the *environment* of the new generation, and have thus made it possible to apply, in a practical way, the fundamental principles of scientific pedagogy.

The "Children's House" marks still another triumph; it is the first step toward the *socialisation of the house*. The inmates find under their own roof the convenience of being able to leave their little ones in a place, not only safe, but where they have every advantage.

And let it be remembered that *all* the mothers in the tenement may enjoy this privilege, going away to their works with easy minds. Until the present time only one class in society might have this advantage. Rich women were able to go about their various occupations and amusements, leaving their children in the hands of a nurse or a governess. To-day the women of the people who live in these remodeled houses, may say, like the great lady, "I have left my son with the governess or the nurse". More than this, they may add, like the princess of the blood, "And the house physician watches over them and directs their sane and sturdy growth". These women, like the most advanced class of English and American mothers, possess a "Biographical Chart", which, filled for the mother by the directress or the doctor, gives her the most practical knowledge of her child's growth and condition.

We are all familiar with the ordinary advantages of the communistic transformation of the general environment. For example, the collective use of railway carriages, of street lights, of the telephone, all these are great advantages. The enormous production of useful articles, brought about by industrial progress, makes possible to all, clean clothes, carpets, curtains, table-delicacies, better tableware, etc. The making of such benefits generally tends to level social caste. All this we have seen in its reality. But the communising of *persons* is new. That the collectivity shall benefit from the services of the servant, the nurse, the teacher–this is a modern ideal.

We have in the "Children's Houses" a demonstration of this ideal which is unique in Italy or elsewhere. Its significance is most profound, for it corresponds to a need of the times. We can no longer say that the convenience of leaving their children takes away from the mother a natural social duty of first importance; namely, that of caring for and educating her tender offspring. No, for to-day the social and economic evolution calls the working-woman to take her place among wage-earners, and takes away from her by force those duties which would be most dear to her! The mother must, in any event, leave her child, and often with the pain of knowing him to be abandoned. The advantages furnished by such institutions are not limited to the labouring classes, but extend also to the general middle-class, many of whom work with the brain. Teachers, professors, often obliged to give private lessons after school hours, frequently leave their children to the care of some rough and ignorant maid-of-all-work. Indeed, the first announcement of the "Children's House" was followed by a deluge of letters from persons of the better class demanding that these helpful reforms be extended to their dwellings.

We are, then, communising a "maternal function", a feminine duty, within the house. We may see here in this practical act the solving of many of woman's problems which have seemed to many impossible of solution. What then will become of the home, one asks, if the woman goes away from it? The home will be transformed and will assume the functions of the woman.

I believe that in the future of society other forms of communistic life will come.

Take, for example, the infirmary; woman is the natural nurse for the dear ones of her household. But who does not know how often in these days she is obliged to tear herself unwillingly from the bedside of her sick to go to her work? Competition is great, and her absence from her post threatens the tenure of the position from which she draws the means of support. To be able to leave the sick one in a "house-infirmary", to which she may have access any free moments she may have, and where she is at liberty to watch during the night, would be an evident advantage to such a woman.

And how great would be the progress made in the matter of family hygiene, in all that relates to isolation and disinfection! Who does not know the difficulties of a poor family when one child is ill of some contagious disease, and should be isolated from the others? Often such a family may have no kindred or friends in the city to whom the other children may be sent.

Much more distant, but not impossible, is the communal kitchen, where the dinner ordered in the morning is sent at the proper time, by means of a dumb-waiter, to the family dining-room. Indeed, this has been successfully tried in America. Such a reform would be of the greatest advantage to those families of the middle-class who must confide their health and the pleasures of the table to the hands of an ignorant servant who ruins the food. At present, the only alternative in such cases is to go outside the home to some café where a cheap table d'hôte may be had.

Indeed, the transformation of the house must compensate for the loss in the family of the presence of the woman who has become a social wage-earner.

In this way the house will become a centre, drawing unto itself all those good things which have hitherto been lacking: schools, public baths, hospitals, etc.

Thus the tendency will be to change the tenement houses, which have been places of vice and peril, into centres of education, of refinement, of comfort. This will be helped if, besides the schools for the children, there may grow up also *clubs* and reading-rooms for the inhabitants, especially for the men, who will find there a way to pass the evening pleasantly and decently. The tenement-club, as possible and as useful in all social classes as is the "Children's House", will do much toward closing the gambling-houses and saloons to the great moral advantage of the people. And I believe that the Association of Good Building will before long establish such clubs in its reformed tenements here in the Quarter of San Lorenzo; clubs where the tenants may find newspapers and books, and where they may hear simple and helpful lectures.

We are, then, very far from the dreaded dissolution of the home and of the family, through the fact that woman has been forced by changed social and economic conditions to give her time and strength to remunerative work. The home itself assumes the gentle feminine attributes of the domestic housewife. The day may come when the tenant, having given the proprietor of the house a certain sum, shall receive in exchange whatever is necessary to the *comfort* of life; in other words, the administration shall become the *steward* of the family.

The house, thus considered, tends to assume in its evolution a significance more exalted than even the English word "home" expresses. It does not consist of walls alone, though these walls be the pure and shining guardians of that intimacy which is the sacred symbol of the family. The home shall become more than this. It lives! It has a soul. It may be said to embrace its inmates with the tender, consoling arms of woman. It is the giver of moral life, of blessings; it cares for, it educates and feeds the little ones. Within it, the tired workman shall find rest and newness of life. He shall find there the intimate life of the family, and its happiness.

The new woman, like the butterfly come forth from the chrysalis, shall be liberated from all those attributes which once made her desirable to man only as the source of the material blessings of existence. She shall be, like man, an individual, she shall seek blessing and repose within the house, the house which has been reformed and communised.

She shall wish to be loved for herself and not as a giver of comfort and repose. She shall wish a love free from every form of servile labour. The goal of human love is not the egotistical end of assuring its own satisfaction–it is the sublime goal of multiplying the forces of the free spirit, making it almost Divine, and, within such beauty and light, perpetuating the species.

This ideal love is made incarnate by Frederick Nietzsche, in the woman of Zarathustra, who conscientiously wished her son to be better than she. "Why do you desire me?", she asks the man. "Perhaps because of the perils of a solitary life?

"In that case go far from me. I wish the man who has conquered himself, who has made his soul great. I wish the man who has conserved a clean and robust body. I wish the man who desires to unite with me, body and soul, to create a son! A son better, more perfect, stronger, than any created heretofore!"

To better the species consciously, cultivating his own health, his own virtue, this should be the goal of man's married life. It is a sublime concept of which, as yet, few think. And the socialised home of the future, living, provident, kindly; educator and comforter; is the true and worthy home of those human mates who wish to better the species, and to send the race forward triumphant into the eternity of life!

Rules and Regulations of the "Children's Houses"

The Roman Association of Good Building hereby establishes within its tenement house number , a "Children's House", in which may be gathered together all children under common school age, belonging to the families of the tenants.

The chief aim of the "Children's House" is to offer, free of charge, to the children of those parents who are obliged to absent themselves for their work, the personal care which the parents are not able to give.

In the "Children's House" attention is given to the education, the health, the physical and moral development of the children. This work is carried on in a way suited to the age of the children.

There shall be connected with the "Children's House" a Directress, a Physician, and a Caretaker.

The programme and hours of the "Children's House" shall be fixed by the Directress.

There may be admitted to the "Children's House" all the children in the tenement between the ages of three and seven.

The parents who wish to avail themselves of the advantages of the "Children's House" pay nothing. They must, however, assume these binding obligations:

(a) To send their children to the "Children's House" at the appointed time, clean in body and clothing, and provided with a suitable apron.

(b) To show the greatest respect and deference toward the Directress and toward all persons connected with the "Children's House", and to co-operate with the Directress herself in the education of the children. Once a week, at least, the mothers may talk with the Directress, giving her information concerning the home life of the child, and receiving helpful advice from her.

There shall be expelled from the "Children's House":

(a) Those children who present themselves unwashed, or in soiled clothing.

(b) Those who show themselves to be incorrigible.

(c) Those whose parents fail in respect to the persons connected with the "Children's House", or who destroy through bad conduct the educational work of the institution.

Pedagogical Methods Used in the "Children's Houses"

As soon as I knew that I had at my disposal a class of little children, it was my wish to make of this school a field for scientific experimental pedagogy and child psychology. I started with a view in which Wundt concurs; namely, that child psychology does not exist. Indeed, experimental researches in regard to childhood, as, for example, those of Preyer and Baldwin, have been made upon not more than two or three subjects, children of the investigators. Moreover, the instruments of psychometry must be greatly modified and simplified before they can be used with children, who do not lend themselves passively as subjects for experimentation. Child psychology can be established only through the method of external observation. We must renounce all idea of making any record of internal states, which can be revealed only by the introspection of the subject himself. The instruments of psychometric research, as applied to pedagogy, have up to the present time been limited to the esthesiometric phase of the study.

My intention was to keep in touch with the researches of others, but to make myself independent of them, proceeding to my work without preconceptions of any kind. I retained as the only essential, the affirmation, or, rather, the definition of Wundt, that "all methods of experimental psychology may be reduced to one, namely, carefully recorded observation of the subject".

Treating of children, another factor must necessarily intervene: the study of development. Here too, I retained the same general criterion, but without clinging to any dogma about the activity of the child according to age.

Anthropological Consideration

In regard to physical development, my first thought was given to the regulating of anthropometric observations, and to the selection of the most important observations to be made.

I designed an anthropometer provided with the metric scale, varying between .50 metre and 1.50 metres. A small stool, 30 centimetres high, could be placed upon the floor of the anthropometer for measurements taken in a sitting position. I now advise making the anthropometer with a platform on either side of the pole bearing the scale, so that on one side the total stature can be measured, and on the other the height of the body when seated. In the second case, the zero is indicated at 30 centimetres; that is, it corresponds to the seat of the stool, which is fixed. The indicators on the vertical post are independent one of the other and this makes it possible to measure two children at the same time. In this way the inconvenience and waste of time caused by having to move the seat about, is obviated, and also the trouble of having to calculate the difference in the metric scale.

Having thus facilitated the technique of the researches, I decided to take the measurements of the children's stature, seated and standing, every month, and in order to have these regulated as exactly as possible in their relation to development, and also to give greater regularity to the research work of the teacher, I made a rule that the measurements should be taken on the day on which the child completed each month of his age.

The spaces opposite each number are used to register the name of the child born on that day of the month. Thus the teacher knows which scholars she must measure on the days which are marked on the calendar, and she fills in his measurements to correspond with the month in which he was born. In this way a most exact registration can be arrived at without having the teacher feel that she is overburdened, or fatigued.

With regard to the weight of the child, I have arranged that it shall be taken every week on a pair of scales which I have placed in the dressing-room where the children are given their bath. According to the day on which the child is born, Monday, Tuesday, Wednesday, etc., we have him weighed when he is ready to take a bath. Thus the children's baths (no small matter when we consider a class of fifty) are sub-divided into seven days, and from three to five children go to the bath every day. Certainly, theoretically, a daily bath would be desirable, but in order to manage this a large bath or a number of small ones would be necessary, so that a good many children could be bathed at once. Even a weekly bath entails many difficulties, and sometimes has to be given up. In any case, I have distributed the taking of the weight in the order stated with the intention of thus arranging for and making sure of periodical baths.

It seems to me that anthropological measurements, the taking and recording of which I have just described, should be the only ones with which the schoolmistress need occupy herself; and, therefore, the only ones which should be taken actually within the school. It is my plan that other measurements should be taken by a physician, who either is, or is preparing to be, a specialist in infant anthropology.

The anthropometrical records should be arranged in an orderly way, while the simplicity of the mechanism, and the clearness of the charts, guarantee the making of such observations as I have considered fundamental. I advise that once a year the following measurements be taken: Circumference of the head; the two greater diameters of the head; the circumference of the chest; and the cephalic, ponderal, and stature indices. Further information concerning the selection of these measurements may be found in my treatise, "Antropologia Pedagogica". The physician is asked to take these measurements during the week, or at least within the month, in which the child completes a year of his age, and, if it is possible, on the birthday itself. In this way the task of the physician will also be made easier, because of its regularity. We have, at the most, fifty children in each of our schools, and the birthdays of these scattered over the 365 days of the year make it possible for the physician to take his measurements from time to time, so that the burden of his work is not heavy. It is the duty of the teacher to inform the doctor of the birthdays of the children.

The taking of these anthropological measurements has also an educational side to it, for the pupils, when they leave the "Children's House", know how to answer with clearness and certainty the following questions:–

On what day of the week were you born?

On what day of the month?

When does your birthday come?

And with all this they will have acquired habits of order, and, above all, they will have formed the habit of observing themselves. Indeed, I may say here, that the children take a great pleasure in being measured; at the first glance of the teacher and at the word stature, the child begins instantly to take off his shoes, laughing and running to place himself upon the platform of the anthropometer; placing himself of his own accord in the normal position so perfectly that the teacher needs only to arrange the indicator and read the result.

Aside from the measurements which the physician takes with the ordinary instruments (calipers and metal yard measure), he makes observations upon the children's colouring, condition of their muscles, state of their lymphatic glands, the condition of the blood, etc. He notices any malformations; describes any pathological conditions with care (any tendency of rickets, infant paralysis, defective sight, etc.). This objective study of the child will guide the doctor when he finds it advisable to talk with the parents concerning its condition. Following this, when the doctor has found it desirable, he makes a thorough, sanitary inspection of the home of the child, prescribing necessary treatment and eventually doing away with such troubles as eczema, inflammation of the ear, feverish conditions, intestinal disturbances, etc. This careful following of the case in hand is greatly assisted by the existence of the *dispensary within the house*, which makes feasible direct treatment and continual observation.

I have found that the usual questions asked patients who present themselves at the clinics, are not adapted for use in our schools, as the members of the families living in these tenements are for the greater part perfectly normal.

I therefore encourage the directress of the school to gather from her conversation with the mothers information of a more practical sort. She informs herself as to the education of the parents, their habits, the wages earned, the money spent for household purposes, etc., and from all this she outlines a history of each family, much on the order of those used by Le-Play. This method is, of course, practical only where the directress lives among the families of her scholars.

In every case, however, the physician's advice to the mothers concerning the hygienic care of each particular child, as well as his directions concerning hygiene in general, will prove most helpful. The directress should act as the go-between in these matters, since she is in the confidence of the mothers, and since from her, such advice comes naturally.

Environment: Schoolroom Furnishings

The method of *observation* must undoubtedly include the *methodical observation* of the morphological growth of the pupils. But let me repeat that, while this element necessarily enters, it is not upon this particular kind of observation that the method is established.

The method of observation is established upon one fundamental base–*the liberty of the pupils in their spontaneous manifestations.*

With this in view, I first turned my attention to the question of environment, and this, of course, included the furnishing of the schoolroom.

In considering an ample playground with space for a garden as an important part of this school environment, I am not suggesting anything new.

The novelty lies, perhaps, in my idea for the use of this open-air space, which is to be in direct communication with the schoolroom, so that the children may be free to go and come as they like, throughout the entire day. I shall speak of this more fully later on.

The principal modification in the matter of school furnishings is the abolition of desks, and benches or stationary chairs. I have had tables made with wide, solid, octagonal legs, spreading in such a way that the tables are at the same time solidly firm and very light, so light, indeed, that two four-year-old children can easily carry them about. These tables are rectangular and sufficiently large to accommodate two children along the long side, there being room for three if they sit rather close together. There are smaller tables at which one child can work alone.

I also designed and had manufactured little chairs. My first plan for these was to have them cane seated, but experience has shown the wear on these to be so great, that I now have chairs made entirely of wood. These are very light and of an attractive shape. In addition to these, I have in each schoolroom a number of comfortable little armchairs, some of wood and some of wicker.

Another piece of our school furniture consists of a little washstand, so low that it can be used by even a three-year-old child. This is painted with a waterproof enamel and, besides the broad, upper and lower shelves which hold the little white enameled basins and pitchers, there are small side shelves for the soap-dishes, nail-brushes, towels, etc. There is also a receptacle into which the basins may be emptied. Wherever possible, a small cupboard provides each child with a space where he may keep his own soap, nail-brush, tooth-brush, etc.

In each of our schoolrooms we have provided a series of long low cupboards, especially designed for the reception of the didactic materials. The doors of these cupboards open easily, and the care of the materials is confided to the children. The tops of these cases furnish room for potted plants, small aquariums, or for the various toys with which the children are allowed to play freely. We have ample blackboard space, and these boards are so hung as to be easily used by the smallest child. Each blackboard is provided with a small case in which are kept the chalk, and the white cloths which we use instead of the ordinary erasers.

Above the blackboards are hung attractive pictures, chosen carefully, representing simple scenes in which children would naturally be interested.

Among the pictures in our "Children's House" in Rome we have hung a copy of Raphael's "Madonna della Seggiola", and this picture we have chosen as the emblem of the "Children's Houses". For indeed, these "Children's Houses" represent not only social progress, but universal human progress, and are closely related to the elevation of the idea of motherhood, to the progress of woman and to the protection of her offspring. In this beautiful conception, Raphael has not only shown us the Madonna as a Divine Mother holding in her arms the babe who is greater than she, but by the side of this symbol of all motherhood, he has placed the figure of St. John, who represents humanity. So in Raphael's picture we see humanity rendering homage to maternity,–maternity, the sublime fact in the definite triumph of humanity. In addition to this beautiful symbolism, the picture has a great value as being one of the greatest works of art of Italy's greatest artist. And if the day shall come when the "Children's Houses" shall be established throughout the world, it is our wish that this picture of Raphael's shall have its place in each of the schools, speaking eloquently of the country in which they originated.

The children, of course, cannot comprehend the symbolic significance of the "Madonna of the Chair", but they will see something more beautiful than that which they feel in more ordinary pictures, in which they see mother, father, and children. And the constant companionship with this picture will awaken in their heart a religious impression.

This, then, is the environment which I have selected for the children we wish to educate.

I know the first objection which will present itself to the minds of persons accustomed to the old-time methods of discipline;–the children in these schools, moving about, will overturn the little tables and chairs, producing noise and disorder; but this is a prejudice which has long existed in the minds of those dealing with little children, and for which there is no real foundation.

Swaddling clothes have for many centuries been considered necessary to the new-born babe, walking-chairs to the child who is learning to walk. So in the school, we still believe it necessary to have heavy desks and chairs fastened to the floor. All these things are based upon the idea that the child should grow in immobility, and upon the strange prejudice that, in order to execute any educational movement, we must maintain a special position of the body;–as we believe that we must assume a special position when we are about to pray.

Our little tables and our various types of chairs are all light and easily transported, and we permit the child to *select* the position which he finds most comfortable. He can *make himself comfortable* as well as seat himself in his own place. And this freedom is not only an external sign of liberty, but a means of education. If by an awkward movement a child upsets a chair, which falls noisily to the floor, he will have an evident proof of his own incapacity; the same movement had it taken place amid stationary benches would have passed unnoticed by him. Thus the child has some means by which he can correct himself, and having done so he will have before him the actual proof of the power he has gained: the little tables and chairs remain firm and silent each in its own place. It is plainly seen that the *child has learned to command his movements.*

In the old method, the proof of discipline attained lay in a fact entirely contrary to this; that is, in the immobility and silence of the child himself. Immobility and silence which *hindered* the child from learning to move with grace and with discernment, and left him so untrained, that, when he found himself in an environment where the benches and chairs where not nailed to the floor, he was not able to move about without overturning the lighter pieces of furniture. In the "Children's Houses" the child will not only learn to move gracefully and properly, but will come to understand the reason for such deportment. The ability to move which he acquires here will be of use to him all his life. While he is still a child, he becomes capable of conducting himself correctly, and yet, with perfect freedom.

The Directress of the Casa dei Bambini at Milan constructed under one of the windows a long, narrow shelf upon which she placed the little tables containing the metal geometric forms used in the first lessons in design. But the shelf was too narrow, and it often happened that the children in selecting the pieces which they wished to use would allow one of the little tables to fall to the floor, thus upsetting with great noise all the metal pieces which it held. The directress intended to have the shelf changed, but the carpenter was slow in coming, and while waiting for him she discovered that the children had learned to handle these materials so carefully that in spite of the narrow and sloping shelf, the little tables no longer fell to the floor.

The children, by carefully directing their movements, had overcome the defect in this piece of furniture. The simplicity or imperfection of external objects often serves to develop the *activity* and the dexterity of the pupils. This has been one of the surprises of our method as applied in the "Children's Houses".

It all seems very logical, and now that it has been actually tried and put into words, it will no doubt seem to everyone as simple as the egg of Christopher Columbus.

Discipline

The pedagogical method of *observation* has for its base the *liberty* of the child; and *liberty is activity.*

Discipline must come through liberty. Here is a great principle which is difficult for the followers of common-school methods to understand. How shall one obtain *discipline* in a class of free children? Certainly in our system, we have a concept of discipline very different from that commonly accepted. If discipline is founded upon liberty, the discipline itself must necessarily be *active.* We do not consider an individual disciplined only when he has been rendered as artificially silent as a mute and as immovable as a paralytic. He is an individual *annihilated*, not *disciplined.*

We call an individual disciplined when he is master of himself, and can, therefore, regulate his own conduct when it shall be necessary to follow some rule of life. Such a concept of *active discipline* is not easy to comprehend or to apply. But certainly it contains a great *educational* principle, very different from the old-time absolute and undiscussed coercion to immobility.

A special technique is necessary to the teacher who is to lead the child along such a path of discipline, if she is to make it possible for him to continue in this way all his life, advancing indefinitely toward perfect self-mastery. Since the child now learns to *move* rather than to *sit still*, he prepares himself not for the school, but for life; for he becomes able, through habit and through practice, to perform easily and correctly the simple acts of social or community life. The discipline to which the child habituates himself here is, in its character, not limited to the school environment but extends to society.

The liberty of the child should have as its *limit* the collective interest; as its *form*, what we universally consider good breeding. We must, therefore, check in the child whatever offends or annoys others, or whatever tends toward rough or ill-bred acts. But all the rest,–every manifestation having a useful scope,–whatever it be, and under whatever form it expresses itself, must not only be permitted, but must be *observed* by the teacher. Here lies the essential point; from her scientific preparation, the teacher must bring not only the capacity, but the desire, to observe natural phenomena. In our system, she must become a passive, much more than an active, influence, and her passivity shall be composed of anxious scientific curiosity, and of absolute *respect* for the phenomenon which she wishes to observe. The teacher must understand and *feel* her position of *observer*: the *activity* must lie in the *phenomenon*.

Such principles assuredly have a place in schools for little children who are exhibiting the first psychic manifestations of their lives. We cannot know the consequences of suffocating a *spontaneous action* at the time when the child is just beginning to be active: perhaps we suffocate *life itself.* Humanity shows itself in all its intellectual splendour during this tender age as the sun shows itself at the dawn, and the flower in the first unfolding of the petals; and we must *respect* religiously, reverently, these first indications of individuality. If any educational act is to be efficacious, it will be only that which tends to *help* toward the complete unfolding of this life. To be thus helpful it is necessary rigorously to avoid the *arrest of spontaneous movements and the imposition of arbitrary tasks.* It is of course understood, that here we do not speak of useless or dangerous acts, for these must be *suppressed, destroyed.*

Actual training and practice are necessary to fit for this method teachers who have not been prepared for scientific observation, and such training is especially necessary to those who have been accustomed to the old domineering methods of the common school. My experiences in training teachers for the work in my schools did much to convince me of the great distance between these methods and those. Even an intelligent teacher, who understands the principle, find much difficulty in putting it into practice. She can not understand that her new task is apparently *passive*, like that of the astronomer who sits immovable before the telescope while the worlds whirl through space. This idea, that *life acts of itself*, and that in order to study it, to divine its secrets or to direct its activity, it is necessary to observe it and to understand it without intervening–this idea, I say, is very difficult for anyone to *assimilate* and to *put into practice.*

The teacher has too thoroughly learned to be the one free activity of the school; it has for too long been virtually her duty to suffocate the activity of her pupils. When in the first days in one of the "Children's Houses" she does not obtain order and silence, she looks about her embarrassed as if asking the public to excuse her, and calling upon those present to testify her innocence. In vain do we repeat to her that the disorder of the first moment is necessary. And finally, when we oblige her to do nothing but *watch*, she asks if she had not better resign, since she is no longer a teacher.

But when she begins to find it her duty to discern which are the acts to hinder and which are those to observe, the teacher of the old school feels a great void within herself and begins to ask if she will not be inferior to her new task. In fact, she who is not prepared finds herself for a long time abashed and impotent; whereas the broader the teacher's scientific culture and practice in experimental psychology, the sooner will come for her the marvel of unfolding life, and her interest in it.

Notari, in his novel, "My Millionaire Uncle," which is a criticism of modern customs, gives with that quality of vividness which is peculiar to him, a most eloquent example of the old-time methods of discipline. The "uncle" when a child was guilty of such a number of disorderly acts that he practically upset the whole town, and in desperation he was confined in a school. Here "Fufu," as he was called, experiences his first wish to be kind, and feels the first moving of his soul when he is near to the pretty little Fufetta, and learns that she is hungry and has no luncheon.

"He glanced around, looked at Fufetta, rose, took his little lunch basket, and without saying a word placed it in her lap.

"Then he ran away from her, and, without knowing why he did so, hung his head and burst into tears.

"My uncle did not know how to explain to himself the reason for this sudden outburst.

"He had seen for the first time two kind eyes full of sad tears, and he had felt moved within himself, and at the same time a great shame had rushed over him; the shame of eating near to one who had nothing to eat.

"Not knowing how to express the impulse of his heart, nor what to say in asking her to accept the offer of his little basket, nor how to invent an excuse to justify his offering it to her, he remained the victim of this first deep movement of his little soul.

"Fufetta, all confused, ran to him quickly. With great gentleness she drew away the arm in which he had hidden his face.

"'Do not cry, Fufu,' she said to him softly, almost as if pleading with him. She might have been speaking to her beloved rag doll, so motherly and intent was her little face, and so full of gentle authority, her manner.

"Then the little girl kissed him, and my uncle yielding to the influence which had filled his heart, put his arms around her neck, and, still silent and sobbing, kissed her in return. At last, sighing deeply, he wiped from his face and eyes the damp traces of his emotion, and smiled again.

"A strident voice called out from the other end of the courtyard:

"'Here, here, you two down there–be quick with you; inside, both of you!'

"It was the teacher, the guardian. She crushed that first gentle stirring in the soul of a rebel with the same blind brutality that she would have used toward two children engaged in a fight.

"It was the time for all to go back into the school–and everybody had to obey the rule."

Thus I saw my teachers act in the first days of my practice school in the "Children's Houses." They almost involuntarily recalled the children to immobility without *observing* and *distinguishing* the nature of the movements they repressed. There was, for example, a little girl who gathered her companions about her and then, in the midst of them, began to talk and gesticulate. The teacher at once ran to her, took hold of her arms, and told her to be still; but I, observing the child, saw that she was playing at being teacher or mother to the others, and teaching them the morning prayer, the invocation to the saints, and the sign of the cross: she already showed herself as a *director*. Another child, who continually made disorganised and misdirected movements, and who was considered abnormal, one day, with an expression of intense attention, set about moving the tables. Instantly they were upon him to make him stand still because he made too much noise. Yet this was one of the *first manifestations*, in this child, of movements that were *co-ordinated* and *directed toward a useful end*, and it was therefore an action that should have been respected. In fact, after this the child began to be quiet and happy like the others whenever he had any small objects to move about and to arrange upon his desk.

It often happened that while the directress replaced in the boxes various materials that had been used, a child would draw near, picking up the objects, with the evident desire of imitating the teacher. The first impulse was to send the child back to her place with the remark, "Let it alone; go to your seat." Yet the child expressed by this act a desire to be useful; the time, with her, was ripe for a lesson in order.

One day, the children had gathered themselves, laughing and talking, into a circle about a basin of water containing some floating toys. We had in the school a little boy barely two and a half years old. He had been left outside the circle, alone, and it was easy to see that he was filled with intense curiosity. I watched him from a distance with great interest; he first drew near to the other children and tried to force his way among them, but he was not strong enough to do this, and he then stood looking about him. The expression of thought on his little face was intensely interesting. I wish that I had had a camera so that I might have photographed him. His eye lighted upon a little chair, and evidently he made up his mind to place it behind the group of children and then to climb up on it. He began to move toward the chair, his face illuminated with hope, but at that moment the teacher seized him brutally (or, perhaps, she would have said, gently) in her arms, and lifting him up above the heads of the other children showed him the basin of water, saying, "Come, poor little one, you shall see too!"

Undoubtedly the child, seeing the floating toys, did not experience the joy that he was about to feel through conquering the obstacle with his own force. The sight of those objects could be of no advantage to him, while his intelligent efforts would have developed his inner powers. The teacher *hindered* the child, in this case, from educating himself, without giving him any compensating good in return. The little fellow had been about to feel himself a conqueror, and he found himself held within two imprisoning arms, impotent. The expression of joy, anxiety, and hope, which had interested me so much faded from his face and left on it the stupid expression of the child who knows that others will act for him.

When the teachers were weary of my observations, they began to allow the children to do whatever they pleased. I saw children with their feet on the tables, or with their fingers in their noses, and no intervention was made to correct them. I saw others push their companions, and I saw dawn in the faces of these an expression of violence; and not the slightest attention on the part of the teacher. Then I had to intervene to show with what absolute rigour it is necessary to hinder, and little by little suppress, all those things which we must not do, so that the child may come to discern clearly between good and evil.

If discipline is to be lasting, its foundations must be laid in this way and these first days are the most difficult for the directress. The first idea that the child must acquire, in order to be actively disciplined, is that of the difference between *good* and *evil*; and the task of the educator lies in seeing that the child does not confound *good* with *immobility* and *evil* with *activity*, as often happens in the case of the old-time discipline. And all this because our aim is to discipline *for activity, for work, for good;* not for *immobility*, not for *passivity*, not for *obedience.*

A room in which all the children move about usefully, intelligently, and voluntarily, without committing any rough or rude act, would seem to me a classroom very well disciplined indeed.

To seat the children in rows, as in the common schools, to assign to each little one a place, and to propose that they shall sit thus quietly observant of the order of the whole class as an assemblage–this can be attained later, as *the starting place of collective education.* For also, in life, it sometimes happens that we must all remain seated and quiet; when, for example, we attend a concert or a lecture. And we know that even to us, as grown people, this costs no little sacrifice.

If we can, when we have established individual discipline, arrange the children, sending each one to *his own place, in order*, trying to make them understand the idea that thus placed they look well, and that it is a *good thing* to be thus placed in order, that it is a *good and pleasing arrangement in the room*, this ordered and tranquil adjustment of theirs–then their remaining in their places, *quiet* and *silent*, is the result of a species of *lesson*, not an *imposition*. To make them understand the idea, without calling their attention too forcibly to the practice, to have them *assimilate a principle of collective order* –that is the important thing.

If, after they have understood this idea, they rise, speak, change to another place, they no longer do this without knowing and without thinking, but they do it because they *wish* to rise, to speak, etc.; that is, from that *state of repose and order*, well understood, they depart in order to undertake *some voluntary action*; and knowing that there are actions which are prohibited, this will give them a new impulse to remember to discriminate between good and evil.

The movements of the children from the state of order become always more co-ordinated and perfect with the passing of the days; in fact, they learn to reflect upon their own acts. Now (with the idea of order understood by the children) the observation of the way in which the children pass from the first disordered movements to those which are spontaneous and ordered–this is the book of the teacher; this is the book which must inspire her actions; it is the only one in which she must read and study if she is to become a real educator.

For the child with such exercises makes, to a certain extent, a selection of his own *tendencies*, which were at first confused in the unconscious disorder of his movements. It is remarkable how clearly *individual differences* show themselves, if we proceed in this way; the child, conscious and free, *reveals himself*.

There are those who remain quietly in their seats, apathetic, or drowsy; others who leave their places to quarrel, to fight, or to overturn the various blocks and toys, and then there are those others who set out to fulfil a definite and determined act–moving a chair to some particular spot and sitting down in it, moving one of the unused tables and arranging upon it the game they wish to play.

Our idea of liberty for the child cannot be the simple concept of liberty we use in the observation of plants, insects, etc.

The child, because of the peculiar characteristics of helplessness with which he is born, and because of his qualities as a social individual is circumscribed by *bonds* which *limit* his activity.

An educational method that shall have *liberty* as its basis must intervene to help the child to a conquest of these various obstacles. In other words, his training must be such as shall help him to diminish, in a rational manner, the *social bonds*, which limit his activity.

Little by little, as the child grows in such an atmosphere, his spontaneous manifestations will become more *clear, with the clearness of truth*, revealing his nature. For all these reasons, the first form of educational intervention must tend to lead the child toward independence.

Independence

No one can be free unless he is independent: therefore, the first, active manifestations of the child's individual liberty must be so guided that through this activity he may arrive at independence. Little children, from the moment in which they are weaned, are making their way toward independence.

What is a weaned child? In reality it is a child that has become independent of the mother's breast. Instead of this one source of nourishment he will find various kinds of food; for him the means of existence are multiplied, and he can to some extent make a selection of his food, whereas he was at first limited absolutely to one form of nourishment.

Nevertheless, he is still dependent, since he is not yet able to walk, and cannot wash and dress himself, and since he is not yet able to *ask* for things in a language which is clear and easily understood. He is still in this period to a great extent the *slave* of everyone. By the age of three, however, the child should have been able to render himself to a great extent *independent* and free.

That we have not yet thoroughly assimilated the highest concept of the term *independence*, is due to the fact that the social form in which we live is still *servile*. In an age of civilisation where servants exist, the concept of that *form of life* which is *independence* cannot take root or develop freely. Even so in the time of slavery, the concept of liberty was distorted and darkened.

Our servants are not our dependents, rather it is we who are dependent upon them.

It is not possible to accept universally as a part of our social structure such a deep human error without feeling the general effects of it in the form of moral inferiority. We often believe ourselves to be independent simply because no one commands us, and because we command others; but the nobleman who needs to call a servant to his aid is really a dependent through his own inferiority. The paralytic who cannot take off his boots because of a pathological fact, and the prince who dare not take them off because of a social fact, are in reality reduced to the same condition.

Any nation that accepts the idea of servitude and believes that it is an advantage for man to be served by man, admits servility as an instinct, and indeed we all too easily lend ourselves to *obsequious service*, giving to it such complimentary names as *courtesy, politeness, charity.*

In reality, *he who is served is limited* in his independence. This concept will be the foundation of the dignity of the man of the future; "I do not wish to be served, *because* I am not an impotent." And this idea must be gained before men can feel themselves to be really free.

Any pedagogical action, if it is to be efficacious in the training of little children, must tend to *help* the children to advance upon this road of independence. We must help them to learn to walk without assistance, to run, to go up and down stairs, to lift up fallen objects, to dress and undress themselves, to bathe themselves, to speak distinctly, and to express their own needs clearly. We must give such help as shall make it possible for children to achieve the satisfaction of their own individual aims and desires. All this is a part of education for independence.

We habitually *serve* children; and this is not only an act of servility toward them, but it is dangerous, since it tends to suffocate their useful, spontaneous activity. We are inclined to believe that children are like puppets, and we wash them and feed them as if they were dolls. We do not stop to think that the child *who does not do, does not know how to do.* He must, nevertheless, do these things, and nature has furnished him with the physical means for carrying on these various activities, and with the intellectual means for learning how to do them. And our duty toward him is, in every case, that of *helping him* to make a conquest of such useful acts as nature intended he should perform for himself. The mother who feeds her child without making the least effort to teach him to hold the spoon for himself and to try to find his mouth with it, and who does not at least eat herself, inviting the child to look and see how she does it, is not a good mother. She offends the fundamental human dignity of her son,–she treats him as if he were a doll, when he is, instead, a man confided by nature to her care.

Who does not know that to *teach* a child to feed himself, to wash and dress himself, is a much more tedious and difficult work, calling for infinitely greater patience, than feeding, washing and dressing the child one's self ? But the former is the work of an educator, the latter is the easy and inferior work of a servant. Not only is it easier for the mother, but it is very dangerous for the child, since it closes the way and puts obstacles in the path of the life which is developing

The ultimate consequences of such an attitude on the part of the parent may be very serious indeed. The grand gentleman who has too many servants not only grows constantly more and more dependent upon them, until he is, finally, actually their slave, but his muscles grow weak through inactivity and finally lose their natural capacity for action. The mind of one who does not work for that which he needs, but commands it from others, grows heavy and sluggish. If such a man should some day awaken to the fact of his inferior position and should wish to regain once more his own independence, he would find that he had no longer the force to do so. These dangers should be presented to the parents of the privileged social classes, if their children are to use independently and for right the special power which is theirs. Needless help is an actual hindrance to the development of natural forces.

Oriental women wear trousers, it is true, and :European women, petticoats; but the former, even more than the latter, are taught as a part of their education the art of *not moving.* Such an attitude toward woman leads to the fact that man works not only for himself, but for woman. And the woman wastes her natural strength and activity and languishes in slavery. She is not only maintained and served, she is, besides, diminished, belittled, in that individuality which is hers by right of her existence as a human being. As an individual member of society, she is a cypher. She is rendered deficient in all those powers and resources which tend to the preservation of life. Let me illustrate this:

A carriage containing a father, mother, and child, is going along a country road. An armed brigand stops the carriage with the well-known phrase, "Your money or your life." Placed in this situation, the three persons in the carriage act in very different ways. The man, who is a trained marksman, and who is armed with a revolver, promptly draws, and confronts the assassin. The boy, armed only with the freedom and lightness of his own legs, cries out and betakes himself to flight. The woman, who is not armed in any way whatever, neither artificially nor naturally (since her limbs, not trained for activity, are hampered by her skirts), gives a frightened gasp, and sinks down unconscious.

These three diverse reactions are in close relation to the state of liberty and independence of each of the three individuals. The swooning woman is she whose cloak is carried for her by attentive cavaliers, who are quick to pick up any fallen object that she may be spared all exertion.

The peril of servilism and dependence lies not only in that "useless consuming of life," which leads to helplessness, but in the development of individual traits which indicate all too plainly a regrettable perversion and degeneration of the normal man. I refer to the domineering and tyrannical behaviour with examples of which we are all only too familiar. The domineering habit develops side by side with helplessness. It is the outward sign of the state of feeling of him who conquers through the work of others. Thus it often happens that the master is a tyrant toward his servant. It is the spirit of the task-master toward the slave.

Let us picture to ourselves a clever and proficient workman, capable, not only of producing much and perfect work, but of giving advice in his workshop, because of his ability to control and direct the general activity of the environment in which he works. The man who is thus master of his environment will be able to smile before the anger of others, showing that great mastery of himself which comes from consciousness of his ability to do things. We should not, however, be in the least surprised to know that in his home this capable workman scolded his wife if the soup was not to his taste, or not ready at the appointed time. In his home, he is no longer the capable workman; the skilled workman here is the wife, who serves him and prepares his food for him. He is a serene and pleasant man where he is powerful through being efficient, but is domineering where he is served. Perhaps if he should learn how to prepare his soup he might become a perfect man! The man who, through his own efforts, is able to perform all the actions necessary for his comfort and development in life, conquers himself, and in doing so multiplies his abilities and perfects himself as an individual.

We must make of the future generation, *powerful men*, and by that we mean men who are independent and free.

Abolition of Prizes and of External Forms of Punishment

Once we have accepted and established such principles, the abolition of prizes and external forms of punishment will follow naturally. Man, disciplined through liberty, begins to desire the true and only prize which will never belittle or disappoint him,–the birth of human power and liberty within that inner life of his from which his activities must spring.

In my own experience I have often marvelled to see how true this is. During our first months in the "Children's Houses," the teachers had not yet learned to put into practice the pedagogical principles of liberty and discipline. One of them, especially, busied herself, when I was absent, in *remedying* my ideas by introducing a few of those methods to which she had been accustomed. So, one day when I came in unexpectedly, I found one of the most intelligent of the children wearing a large Greek cross of silver, hung from his neck by a fine piece of white ribbon, while another child was seated in an armchair which had been conspicuously placed in the middle of the room.

The first child had been rewarded, the second was being punished. The teacher, at least while I was present, did not interfere in any way, and the situation remained as I had found it. I held my peace, and placed myself where I might observe quietly.

The child with the cross was moving back and forth, carrying the objects with which he had been working, from his table to that of the teacher, and bringing others in their place. He was busy and happy. As he went back and forth he passed by the armchair of the child who was being punished. The silver cross slipped from his neck and fell to the floor, and the child in the armchair picked it up, dangled it on its white ribbon, looking at it from all sides, and then said to his companion: "Do you see what you have dropped?" The child turned and looked at the trinket with an air of indifference; his expression seemed to say; "Don't interrupt me," his voice replied "I don't care." "Don't you care, really?" said the punished one calmly. "Then I will put it on myself." And the other replied, "Oh, yes, put it on," in a tone that seemed to add, "and leave me in peace!"

The boy in the armchair carefully arranged the ribbon so that the cross lay upon the front of his pink apron where he could admire its brightness and its pretty form, then he settled himself more comfortably in his little chair and rested his arms with evident pleasure upon the arms of the chair. The affair remained thus, and was quite just. The dangling cross could satisfy the child who was being punished, but not the active child, content and happy with his work.

One day I took with me on a visit to another of the "Children's Houses" a lady who praised the children highly and who, opening a box she had brought, showed them a number of shining medals, each tied with a bright red ribbon.

"The mistress," she said "will put these on the breasts of those children who are the cleverest and the best."

As I was under no obligation to instruct this visitor in my methods, I kept silence, and the teacher took the box. At that moment, a most intelligent little boy of four, who was seated quietly at one of the little tables, wrinkled his forehead in an act of protest and cried out over and over again;–"Not to the boys, though, not to the boys!"

What a revelation! This little fellow already knew that he stood among the best and strongest of his class, although no one had ever revealed this fact to him, and he did not wish to be offended by this prize. Not knowing how to defend his dignity, he invoked the superior quality of his masculinity!

As to punishments, we have many times come in contact with children who disturbed the others without paying any attention to our corrections. Such children were at once examined by the physician. When the case proved to be that of a normal child, we placed one of the little tables in a corner of the room, and in this way isolated the child; having him sit in a comfortable little armchair, so placed that he might see his companions at work, and giving him those games and toys to which he was most attracted. This isolation almost always succeeded in calming the child; from his position he could see the entire assembly of his companions, and the way in which they carried on their work was an *object lesson* much more efficacious than any words of the teacher could possibly have been. Little by little, he would come to see the advantages of being one of the company working so busily before his eyes, and he would really wish to go back and do as the others did. We have in this way led back again to discipline all the children who at first seemed to rebel against it. The isolated child was always made the object of special care, almost as if he were ill. I myself, when I entered the room, went first of all directly to him, caressing him, as if he were a very little child. Then I turned my attention to the others, interesting myself in their work, asking questions about it as if they had been little men. I do not know what happened in the soul of these children whom we found it necessary to discipline, but certainly the conversion was always very complete and lasting. They showed great pride in learning how to work and how to conduct themselves, and always showed a very tender affection for the teacher and for me.

The Biological Concept of Liberty in Pedagogy

From a biological point of view, the concept of *liberty* in the education of the child in his earliest years must be understood as demanding those conditions adapted to the most favourable *development* of his entire individuality. So, from the physiological side as well as from the mental side, this includes the free development of the brain. The educator must be as one inspired by a deep *worship of life*, and must, through this reverence, *respect*, while he observes with human interest, the *development* of the child life. Now, child life is not an abstraction; *it is the life of individual children*. There exists only one real biological manifestation: the *living individual*; and toward single individuals, one by one observed, education must direct itself. By education must be understood the active *help* given to the normal expansion of the life of the child. The child is a body which grows, and a soul which de- develops,–these two forms, physiological and psychic, have one eternal font, life itself. We must neither mar nor stifle the mysterious powers which lie within these two forms of growth, but we must *await from them* the manifestations which we know will succeed one another.

Environment is undoubtedly a *secondary* factor in the phenomena of life; it can modify in that it can help or hinder, but it can never *create*. The modern theories of evolution, from Naegeli to De Vries, consider throughout the development of the two biological branches, animal and vegetable, this interior factor as the essential force in the transformation of the species and in the transformation of the individual. The origins of the *development*, both in the species and in the individual, *lie within*. The child does not grow *because* he is nourished, *because* he breathes, *because* he is placed in conditions of temperature to which he is adapted; he grows because the potential life within him develops, making itself visible; because the fruitful germ from which his life has come develops itself according to the biological destiny which was fixed for it by heredity. Adolescence does not come *because* the child laughs, or dances, or does gymnastic exercises, or is well nourished; but because he has arrived at that particular physiological state. Life makes itself manifest,–life creates, life gives:–and is in its turn held within certain limits and bound by certain laws which are insuperable. The *fixed* characteristics of the species do not change,– they can only vary.

This concept, so brilliantly set forth by De Vries in his Mutation Theory, illustrates also the limits of education. We can act on the *variations* which are in relation to the environment, and whose limits vary slightly in the species and in the individual, but we cannot act upon the *mutations*. The mutations are bound by some mysterious tie to the very font of life itself, and their power rises superior to the modifying elements of the environment.

A species, for example, cannot *mutate* or change into another species through any phenomenon of *adaptation*, as, on the other hand, a great human genius cannot be suffocated by any limitation, nor by any false form of education.

The *environment* acts more strongly upon the individual life the less fixed and strong this individual life may be. But environment can act in two opposite senses, favouring life, and stifling it. Many species of palm, for example, are splendid in the tropical regions, because the climatic conditions are favourable to their development, but many species of both animals and plants have become extinct in regions to which they were not able to adapt themselves.

Life is a superb goddess, always advancing, overthrowing the obstacles which environment places in the way of her triumph. This is the basic or fundamental truth,–whether it be a question of species or of individuals, there persists always the forward march of those victorious ones in whom this mysterious life-force is strong and vital.

It is evident that in the case of humanity, and especially in the case of our civil humanity, which we call society, the important and imperative question is that of the *care*, or perhaps we might say, the *culture* of human life.

How Lessons Should Be Given

"Let all thy words be counted."*Dante, Inf., canto X.*

Given the fact that, through the régime of liberty the pupils can manifest their natural tendencies in the school, and that with this in view we have prepared the environment and the materials (the objects with which the child is to work), the teacher must not limit her action to *observation*, but must proceed to *experiment*.

In this method the lesson corresponds to an *experiment*. The more fully the teacher is acquainted with the methods of experimental psychology, the better will she understand how to give the lesson. Indeed, a special technique is necessary if the method is to be properly applied. The teacher must at least have attended the training classes in the "Children's Houses," in order to acquire a knowledge of the fundamental principles of the method and to understand their application. The most difficult portion of this training is that which refers to the method for discipline.

In the first days of the school the children do not learn the idea of collective order; this idea follows and comes as a result of those disciplinary exercises through which the child learns to discern between good and evil. This being the case, it is evident that, at the outset the teacher *cannot give* collective lessons. Such lessons, indeed, will always be *very rare*, since the children being free are not
obliged to remain in their places quiet and ready to listen to the teacher, or to watch what she is doing. The collective lessons, in fact, are of very secondary importance, and have been almost abolished by us.

Characteristics of the Individual
Lessons:–conciseness,Simplicity, Objectivity.

The lessons, then, are individual, and *brevity* must be one of their chief characteristics. Dante gives excellent advice to teachers when he says, "Let thy words be counted." The more carefully we cut away useless words, the more perfect will become the lesson. And in preparing the lessons which she is to give, the teacher must pay special attention to this point, counting and weighing the value of the words which she is to speak.

Another characteristic quality of the lesson in the "Children's Houses" is its *simplicity*. It must be stripped of all that is not absolute truth. That the teacher must not lose herself in vain words, is included in the first quality of conciseness; this second, then, is closely related to the first: that is, the carefully chosen words must be the most simple it is possible to find, and must refer to the truth.

The third quality of the lesson is its *objectivity*. The lesson must be presented in such a way that the personality of the teacher shall disappear. There shall remain in evidence only the *object* to which she wishes to call the attention of the child. This brief and simple lesson must be considered by the teacher as an explanation of the object and of the use which the child can make of it.

In the giving of such lessons the fundamental guide must be the *method of observation*, in which is included and understood the liberty of the child. So the teacher shall *observe* whether the child interests himself in the object, how he is interested in it, for how long, etc., even noticing the expression of his face. And she must take great care not to offend the principles of liberty. For, if she provokes the child to make an unnatural effort, she will no longer know what is the *spontaneous* activity of the child. If, therefore, the lesson rigorously prepared in this brevity, simplicity and truth is not understood by the child, is not accepted by him as an explanation of the object,–the teacher must be warned of two things:–first, not to *insist* by repeating the lesson; and second, *not to make the child feel that he has made a mistake*, or that he is not understood, because in doing so she will cause him to make an effort to understand, and will thus alter the natural state which must be used by her in making her psychological observation. A few examples may serve to illustrate this point.

Let us suppose, for example, that the teacher wishes to teach to a child the two colours, red and blue. She desires to attract the attention of the child to the object. She says, therefore, "Look at this." Then, in order to teach the colours, she says, showing him the red, "This is *red*," raising her voice a little and pronouncing the word "red" slowly and clearly; then showing him the other colour, "This is *blue*." In order to make sure that the child has understood, she says to him, "Give me the red,"–"Give me the blue." Let us suppose that the child in following this last direction makes a mistake. The teacher does not repeat and does not insist; she smiles, gives the child a friendly caress and takes away the colours.

Teachers ordinarily are greatly surprised at such simplicity. They often say, "But everybody knows how to do that!" Indeed, this again is a little like the egg of Christopher Columbus, but the truth is that not everyone knows how to do this simple thing (to give a lesson with such simplicity). To *measure* one's own activity, to make it conform to these standards of clearness, brevity and truth, is practically a very difficult matter. Especially is this true of teachers prepared by the old-time methods, who have learned to labour to deluge the child with useless, and often, false words. For example, a teacher who had taught in the public schools often reverted to collectivity. Now in giving a collective lesson much importance is necessarily given to the simple thing which is to be taught, and it is necessary to oblige all the children to follow the teacher's explanation, when perhaps not all of them are disposed to give their attention to the particular lesson in hand. The teacher has perhaps commenced her lesson in this way:- "Children, see if you can guess what I have in my hand!" She knows that the children cannot guess, and she therefore attracts their attention by means of a falsehood. Then she probably says,-"Children, look out at the sky. Have you ever looked at it before? Have you never noticed it at night when it is all shining with stars? No! Look at my apron. Do you know what colour it is? Doesn't it seem to you the same colour as the sky? Very well then, look at this colour I have in my hand. It is the same colour as the sky and my apron. It is *blue*. Now look around you a little and see if you can find some thing in the room which is blue. And do you know what colour cherries are, and the colour of the burning coals in the fireplace, etc., etc."

Now in the mind of the child after he has made the useless effort of trying to guess there revolves a confused mass of ideas,-the sky, the apron, the cherries, etc. It will be difficult for him to extract from all this confusion the idea which it was the scope of the lesson to make clear to him; namely, the recognition of the two colours, blue and red. Such a work of selection is almost impossible for the mind of a child who is not yet able to follow a long discourse.

I remember being present at an arithmetic lesson where the children were being taught that two and three make five. To this end, the teacher made use of a counting board having coloured beads strung on its thin wires. She arranged, for example, two beads on the top line, then on a lower line three, and at the bottom five beads. I do not remember very clearly the development of this lesson, but I do know that the teacher found it necessary to place beside the two beads on the upper wire a little cardboard dancer with a blue skirt, which she christened on the spot the name of one of the children in the class, saying, "This is Mariettina." And then beside the other three beads she placed a little dancer dressed in a different colour, which she called "Gigina." I do not know exactly how the teacher arrived at the demonstration of the sum, but certainly she talked for a long time with these little dancers, moving them about, etc. If *I* remember the dancers more clearly than I do the arithmetic process, how must it have been with the children? If by such a method they were able to learn that two and three make five, they must have made a tremendous mental effort, and the teacher must have found it necessary to talk with the little dancers for a long time.

In another lesson a teacher wished to demonstrate to the children the difference between noise and sound. She began by telling a long story to the children. Then suddenly someone in league with her knocked noisily at the door. The teacher stopped and cried out–"What is it! What's happened! What is the matter! Children, do you know what this person at the door has done? I can no longer go on with my story, I cannot remember it any more. I will have to leave it unfinished. Do you know what has happened? Did you hear? Have you understood? That was a noise, that is a noise. Oh! I would much rather play with this little baby (taking up a mandolin which she had dressed up in a table cover). Yes, dear baby, I had rather play with you. Do you see this baby that I am holding in my arms?" Several children replied, "It isn't a baby." Others said, "It's a mandolin." The teacher went on–"No, no, it is a baby, really a baby. I love this little baby. Do you want me to show you that it is a baby? Keep very, very quiet then. It seems to me that the baby is crying. Or, perhaps it is talking, or perhaps it is going to say papa or mamma." Putting her hand under the cover, she touched the strings of the mandolin. "There! did you hear the baby cry? Did you hear it call out?" The children cried out–"It's a mandolin, you touched the strings, you made it play." The teacher then replied, "Be quiet, be quiet, children. Listen to what I am going to do." Then she uncovered the mandolin and began to play on it, saying, "This is sound."

To suppose that the child from such a lesson as this shall come to understand the difference between noise and sound is ridiculous. The child will probably get the impression that the teacher wished to play a joke, and that she is rather foolish, because she lost the thread of her discourse when she was interrupted by noise, and because she mistook a mandolin for a baby. Most certainly, it is the figure of the teacher herself that is impressed upon the child's mind through such a lesson, and not the object for which the lesson was given.

To obtain a *simple lesson* from a teacher who has been prepared according to the ordinary methods, is a very difficult task. I remember that, after having explained the material fully and in detail, I called upon one of my teachers to teach, by means of the geometric insets, the difference between a square and a triangle. The task of the teacher was simply to fit a square and a triangle of wood into the empty spaces made to receive them. She should then have shown the child how to follow with his finger the contours of the wooden pieces and of the frames into which they fit, saying, meanwhile, "This is a square–this is a triangle." The teacher whom I had called upon began by having the child touch the square, saying, "This is a line,–another,–another,–and another. There are four lines: count them with your little finger and tell me how many there are. And the corners,–count the corners, feel them with your little finger. See, there are four corners too. Look at this piece well. It is a square." I corrected the teacher, telling her that in this way she was not teaching the child to recognise a form, but was giving him an idea of sides, of angles, of number, and that this was a very different thing from that which she was to teach in this lesson. "But," she said, trying to justify herself, "it is the same thing." It is not, however, the same thing. It is the geometric analysis and the mathematics of the thing. It would be possible to have an idea of the form of the quadrilateral without knowing how to count to four, and, therefore, without appreciating the number of sides and angles. The sides and the angles are abstractions which in themselves do not exist; that which does exist is this piece of wood of a determined form. The elaborate explanations of the teacher not only confused the child's mind, but bridged over the distance that lies between the concrete and the abstract, between the form of an object and the mathematics of the form.

Let us suppose, I said to the teacher, that an architect shows you a dome, the form of which interests you. He can follow one of two methods in showing you his work: he can call attention to the beauty of line, the harmony of the proportions, and may then take you inside the building and up into the cupola itself, in order that you may appreciate the relative proportion of the parts in such a way that your impression of the cupola as a whole shall be founded on general knowledge of its parts, or he can have you count the windows, the wide or narrow cornices, and can, in fact, make you a design showing the construction; he can illustrate for you the static laws and write out the algebraic formulæ necessary in the calculation of such laws. In the first place, you will be able to retain in your mind the form of the cupola; in the second, you will have understood nothing, and will come away with the impression that the architect fancied himself speaking to a fellow engineer, instead of to a traveller whose object was to become familiar with the beautiful things about him. Very much the same thing happens if we, instead of saying to the child, "This is a square," and by simply having him touch the contour establish materially the idea of the form, proceed rather to a geometrical analysis of the contour.

Indeed, we should feel that we are making the child precocious if we taught him the geometric forms in the plane, presenting at the same time the mathematical concept, but we do not believe that the child is too immature to appreciate the simple *form*; on the contrary, it is no effort for a child to look at a square window or table,–he sees all these forms about him in his daily life. To call his attention to a determined form is to clarify the impression he has already received of it, and to fix the idea of it. It is very much as if, while we are looking absent-mindedly at the shore of a lake, an artist should suddenly say to us–"How beautiful the curve is that the shore makes there under the shade of that cliff." At his words, the view which we have been observing almost unconsciously, is impressed upon our minds as if it had been illuminated by a sudden ray of sunshine, and we experience the joy of having crystallised an impression which we had before only imperfectly felt.

And such is our duty toward the child: to give a ray of light and to go on our way.

I may liken the effects of these first lessons to the impressions of one who walks quietly, happily, through a wood, alone, and thoughtful, letting his inner life unfold freely. Suddenly, the chime of a distant bell recalls him to himself, and in that awakening he feels more strongly than before the peace and beauty of which he has been but dimly conscious.

To stimulate life,–leaving it then free to develop, to unfold,–herein lies the first task of the educator. In such a delicate task, a great art must suggest the moment, and limit the intervention, in order that we shall arouse no perturbation, cause no deviation, but rather that we shall help the soul which is coming into the fulness of life, and which shall live from its *own forces*. This *art* must accompany the *scientific method*.

When the teacher shall have touched, in this way, soul for soul, each one of her pupils, awakening and inspiring the life within them as if she were an invisible spirit, she will then possess each soul, and a sign, a single word from her shall suffice; for each one will feel her in a living and vital way, will recognise her and will listen to her. There will come a day when the directress herself shall be filled with wonder to see that all the children obey her with gentleness and affection, not only ready, but intent, at a sign from her. They will look toward her who has made them live, and will hope and desire to receive from her, new life.

Experience has revealed all this, and it is something which forms the chief source of wonder for those who visit the "Children's Houses." Collective discipline is obtained as if by magic force. Fifty or sixty children from two and a half years to six years of age, all together, and at a single time know how to hold their peace so perfectly that the absolute silence seems that of a desert. And, if the teacher, speaking in a low voice, says to the children, "Rise, pass several times around the room on the tips of your toes and then come back to your place in silence" all together, as a single person, the children rise, and follow the order with the least possible noise. The teacher with that one voice has spoken to each one; and each child hopes from her intervention to receive some light and inner happiness. And feeling so, he goes forth intent and obedient like an anxious explorer, following the order in his own way.

In this matter of discipline we have again something of the egg of Christopher Columbus. A concert-master must prepare his scholars one by one in order to draw from their collective work great and beautiful harmony; and each artist must perfect himself as an individual before he can be ready to follow the voiceless commands of the master's baton.

How different is the method which we follow in the public schools! It is as if a concert-master taught the same monotonous and sometimes discordant rhythm contemporaneously to the most diverse instruments and voices.

Thus we find that the most disciplined members of society are the men who are best trained, who have most thoroughly perfected themselves, but this is the training or the perfection acquired through contact with other people. The perfection of the collectivity cannot be that material and brutal solidarity which comes from mechanical organisation alone.

In regard to infant psychology, we are more richly endowed with prejudices than with actual knowledge bearing upon the subject. We have, until the present day, wished to dominate the child through force, by the imposition of external laws, instead of making an interior conquest of the child, in order to direct him as a human soul. In this way, the children have lived beside us without being able to make us know them. But if we cut away the artificiality with which we have enwrapped them, and the violence through which we have foolishly thought to discipline them, they will reveal themselves to us in all the truth of child nature.

Their gentleness is so absolute, so sweet, that we recognise in it the infancy of that humanity which can remain oppresed by every form of yoke, by every injustice; and the child's love of *knowledge* is such that it surpasses every other love and makes us think that in very truth humanity must carry within it that passion which pushes the minds of men to the successive conquest of thought, making easier from century to century the yokes of every form of slavery.

Exercises of Practical Life

Proposed Winter Schedule of Hours in The "Children's Houses"

Opening at Nine O'clock–Closing at Four O'clock

9-10. Entrance. Greeting. Inspection as to personal cleanliness. Exercises of practical life; helping one another to take off and put on the aprons. Going over the room to see that everything is dusted and in order. Language: Conversation period: Children give an account of the events of the day before. Religious exercises.

10-11. Intellectual exercises. Objective lessons interrupted by short rest periods. Nomenclature, Sense exercises.

11-11:30. Simple gymnastics: Ordinary movements done gracefully, normal position of the body, walking, marching in line, salutations, movements for attention, placing of objects gracefully.

11:30-12. Luncheon: Short prayer.

12-1. Free games.

1-2. Directed games, if possible, in the open air. During this period the older children in turn go through with the exercises of practical life, cleaning the room, dusting, putting the material in order. General inspection for cleanliness: Conversation.

2-3. Manual work. Clay modelling, design, etc.

3-4. Collective gymnastics and songs, if possible in the open air. Exercises to develop forethought: Visiting, and caring for, the plants and animals.

As soon as a school is established, the question of schedule arises. This must be considered from two points of view; the length of the school-day and the distribution of study and of the activities of life.

I shall begin by affirming that in the "Children's Houses," as in the school for deficients, the hours may be very long, occupying the entire day. For poor children, and especially for the "Children's Houses" annexed to workingmen's tenements, I should advise that the school-day should be from nine in the morning to five in the evening in winter, and from eight to six in summer.

These long hours are necessary, if we are to follow a directed line of action which shall be helpful to the growth of the child. It goes without saying, that in the case of little children such a long school-day should be interrupted by at least an hour's rest in bed. And here lies the great practical difficulty. At present we must allow our little ones to sleep in their seats in a wretched position, but I foresee a time, not distant, when we shall be able to have a quiet, darkened room where the children may sleep in low-swung hammocks. I should like still better to have this nap taken in the open air.

In the "Children's Houses" in Rome we send the little ones to their own apartments for the nap, as this can be done without their having to go out into the streets.

It must be observed that these long hours include not only the nap, but the luncheon. This must be considered in such schools as the "Children's Houses," whose aim is to help and to direct the growth of children in such an important period of development as that from three to six years of age.

The "Children's House" is a garden of child culture, and we most certainly do not keep the children for so many hours in school with the idea of making students of them!

The first step which we must take in our method is to *call* to the pupil. We call now to his attention, now to his interior life, now to the life he leads with others. Making a comparison which must not be taken in a literal sense,–it is necessary to proceed as in experimental psychology or anthropology when one makes an experiment,–that is, after having prepared the instrument (to which in this case the environment may correspond) we prepare the subject. Considering the method as a whole, we must begin our work by preparing the child for the forms of social life, and we must attract his attention to these forms.

In the schedule which we outlined when we established the first "Children's House," but which we have never followed entirely, (a sign that a schedule in which the material is distributed in arbitrary fashion is not adapted to the régime of liberty) we begin the day with a series of exercises of practical life, and I must confess that these exercises were the only part of the programme which proved thoroughly stationary. These exercises were such a success that they formed the beginning of the day in all of the "Children's Houses." First:

Cleanliness.

Order.

Poise.

Conversation.

As soon as the children arrive at school we make an inspection for cleanliness. If possible, this should be carried on in the presence of the mothers, but their attention should not be called to it directly. We examine the hands, the nails, the neck, the ears, the face, the teeth; and care is given to the tidiness of the hair. If any of the garments are torn or soiled or ripped, if the buttons are lacking, or if the shoes are not clean, we call the attention of the child to this. In this way, the children become accustomed to observing themselves and take an interest in their own appearance.

The children in our "Children's Houses" are given a bath in turn, but this, of course, can not be done daily. In the class, however, the teacher, by using a little washstand with small pitchers and basins, teaches the children to take a partial bath: for example, they learn how to wash their hands and clean their nails. Indeed, sometimes we teach them how to take a foot-bath. They are shown especially how to wash their ears and eyes with great care. They are taught to brush their teeth and rinse their mouths carefully. In all of this, we call their attention to the different parts of the body which they are washing, and to the different means which we use in order to cleanse them: clear water for the eyes, soap and water for the hands, the brush for the teeth, etc. We teach the big ones to help the little ones, and, so, encourage the younger children to learn quickly to take care of themselves.

After this care of their persons, we put on the little aprons. The children are able to put these on themselves, or, with the help of each other. Then we begin our visit about the schoolroom. We notice if all of the various materials are in order and if they are clean. The teacher shows the children how to clean out the little corners where dust has accumulated, and shows them how to use the various objects necessary in cleaning a room,–dust-cloths, dust-brushes, little brooms, etc. All of this, when the children are allowed *to do it by themselves,* is very quickly accomplished. Then the children go each to his own place. The teacher explains to them that the normal position is for each child to be seated in his own place, in silence, with his feet together on the floor, his hands resting on the table, and his head erect. In this way she teaches them poise and equilibrium. Then she has them rise on their feet in order to sing the hymn, teaching them that in rising and sitting down it is not necessary to be noisy. In this way the children learn to move about the furniture with poise and with care. After this we have a series of exercises in which the children learn to move gracefully, to go and come, to salute each other, to lift objects carefully, to receive various objects from each other politely. The teacher calls attention with little exclamations to a child who is clean, a room which is well ordered, a class seated quietly, a graceful movement, etc.

From such a starting point we proceed to the free teaching. That is, the teacher will no longer make comments to the children, directing them how to move from their seats, etc., she will limit herself to correcting the disordered movements.

After the directress has talked in this way about the attitude of the children and the arrangement of the room, she invites the children to talk with her. She questions them concerning what they have done the day before, regulating her inquiries in such a way that the children need not report the intimate happenings of the family but their individual behaviour, their games, attitude to parents, etc. She will ask if they have been able to go up the stairs without getting them muddy, if they have spoken politely to their friends who passed, if they have helped their mothers, if they have shown in their family what they have learned at school, if they have played in the street, etc. The conversations are longer on Monday after the vacation, and on that day the children are invited to tell what they have done with the family; if they have gone away from home, whether they have eaten things not usual for children to eat, and if this is the case we urge them not to eat these things and try to teach them that they are bad for them. Such conversations as these encourage the *unfolding* or development of language and are of great educational value, since the directress can prevent the children from recounting happenings in the house or in the neighbourhood, and can select, instead, topics which are adapted to pleasant conversation, and in this way can teach the children those things which it is desirable to talk about; that is, things with which we occupy ourselves in life, public events, or things which have happened in the different houses, perhaps, to the children themselves–as baptism, birthday parties, any of which may serve for occasional conversation. Things of this sort will encourage children to describe, themselves. After this morning talk we pass to the various lessons.

Refection–the Child's Diet

In connection with the exercises of practical life, it may be fitting to consider the matter of refection.

In order to protect the child's development, especially in neighbourhoods where standards of child hygiene are not yet prevalent in the home, it would be well if a large part of the child's diet could be entrusted to the school. It is well known to-day that the diet must be adapted to the physical nature of the child; and as the medicine of children is not the medicine of adults in reduced doses, so the diet must not be that of the adult in lesser quantitative proportions. For this reason I should prefer that even in the "Children's Houses" which are situated in tenements and from which little ones, being at home, can go up to eat with the family, school refection should be instituted. Moreover, even in the case of rich children, school refection would always be advisable until a scientific course in cooking shall have introduced into the wealthier families the habit of specialising in children's food.

The diet of little children must be rich in fats and sugar: the first for reserve matter and the second for plastic tissue. In fact, sugar is a stimulant to tissues in the process of formation.

As for the *form* of preparation, it is well that the alimentary substances should always be minced, because the child has not yet the capacity for completely masticating the food, and his stomach is still incapable of fulfilling the function of mincing food matter.

Consequently, soups, purées, and meat balls should constitute the ordinary form of dish for the child's table.

The nitrogenous diet for a child from two or three years of age ought to be constituted chiefly of milk and eggs, but after the second year broths are also to be recommended. After three years and a half meat can be given; or, in the case of poor children, vegetables. Fruits are also to be recommended for children.

Perhaps a detailed summary on child diet may be useful, especially for mothers.

Method of Preparing Broth for Little Children. (Age three to six; after that the child may use the common broth of the family.) The quantity of meat should correspond to 1 gramme for every cubic centimetre of broth and should be put in cold water. No aromatic herbs should be used, the only wholesome condiment being salt. The meat should be left to boil for two hours. Instead of removing the grease from the broth, it is well to add butter to it, or, in the case of the poor, a spoonful of olive oil; but substitutes for butter, such as margerine, etc., should never be used. The broth must be prepared *fresh*; it would be well therefore, to put the meat on the fire two hours before the meal, because as soon as broth is cool there begins to take place a separation of chemical substances, which are injurious to the child and may easily cause diarrhea.

Soups. A very simple soup, and one to be highly recommended for children, is bread boiled in salt water or in broth and abundantly seasoned with oil. This is the classic soup of poor children and an excellent means of nutrition. Very like this, is the soup which consists of little cubes of bread toasted in butter and allowed to soak in the broth which is itself fat with butter. Soups of grated bread also belong in this class.

Pastine, * especially the glutinous pastine, which are of the same nature, are undoubtedly superior to the others for digestibility, but are accessible only to the privileged social classes.

The poor should know how much more wholesome is a broth made from remnants of stale bread, than soups of coarse spaghetti–often dry and seasoned with meat juice. Such soups are most indigestible for little children.

Excellent soups are those consisting of purées of vegetables (beans, peas, lentils). To-day one may find in the shops dried vegetables especially adapted for this sort of soups. Boiled in salt water, the vegetables are peeled, put to cool and passed through a sieve (or simply compressed, if they are already peeled). Butter is then added, and the paste is stirred slowly into the boiling water, care being taken that it dissolves and leaves no lumps.

Vegetable soups can also be seasoned with pork. Instead of broth, sugared milk may be the base of vegetable purées.

I strongly recommend for children a soup of rice boiled in broth or milk; also cornmeal broth, provided it be seasoned with abundant butter, but not with cheese. (The porridge form–polenta, really cornmeal mush, is to be highly recommended on account of the long cooking.)

The poorer classes who have no meat-broth can feed their children equally well with soups of boiled bread and porridge seasoned with oil.

Milk and Eggs. These are foods which not only contain nitrogenous substances in an eminently digestible form, but they have the so-called *enzymes* which facilitate assimilation into the tissues, and, hence, in a particular way, favour the growth of the child. And they answer so much the better this last most important condition if they are *fresh* and *intact*, keeping in themselves, one may say, the life of the animals which produced them.

Milk fresh from the cow, and the egg while it is still warm, are assimilable to the highest degree. Cooking, on the other hand, makes the milk and eggs lose their special conditions of assimilability and reduces the nutritive power in them to the simple power of any nitrogenous substance.

To-day, consequently, there are being founded *special dairies for children* where the milk produced is sterile; the rigorous cleanliness of the surroundings in which the milk-producing animals live, the sterilisation of the udder before milking, of the hands of the milker, and of the vessels which are to contain the milk, the hermetic sealing of these last, and the refrigerating bath immediately after the milking, if the milk is to be carried far,—otherwise it is well to drink it warm, procure a milk free from bacteria which, therefore, has no need of being sterilised by boiling, and which preserves intact its natural nutritive powers.

As much may be said of eggs; the best way of feeding them to a child is to take them still warm from the hen and have him eat them just as they are, and then digest them in the open air. But where this is not practicable, eggs must be chosen fresh, and barely heated in water, that is to say, prepared *à la coque.*

All other forms of preparation, milk-soup, omelettes, and so forth, do, to be sure, make of milk and eggs an excellent food, more to be recommended than others; but they take away the specific properties of assimilation which characterise them.

Meat. All meats are not adapted to children, and even their preparation must differ according to the age of the child. Thus, for example, children from three to five years of age ought to eat only more or less finely-ground meats, whereas at the age of five children are capable of grinding meat completely by mastication; at that time it is well to *teach the child accurately how to masticate* because he has a tendency to swallow food quickly, which may produce indigestion and diarrhea.

This is another reason why school-refection in the "Children's Houses" would be a very serviceable as well as convenient institution, as the whole diet of the child could then be rationally cared for in connection with the educative system of the Houses.

The meats most adapted to children are so-called white meats, that is, in the first place, chicken, then veal; also the light flesh of fish, (sole, pike, cod).

After the age of four, filet of beef may also be introduced into the diet, but never heavy and fat meats like that of the pig, the capon, the eel, the tunny, etc., which are to be *absolutely excluded* along with mollusks and crustaceans, (oysters, lobsters), from the child's diet.

Croquettes made of finely ground meat, grated bread, milk, and beaten eggs, and fried in butter, are the most wholesome preparation. Another excellent preparation is to mould into balls the grated meat, with sweet fruit-preserve, and eggs beaten up with sugar.

At the age of five, the child may be given breast of roast fowl, and occasionally veal cutlet or filet of beef.

Boiled meat must never be given to the child, because meat is deprived of many stimulating and even nutritive properties by boiling and rendered less digestible.

Nerve Feeding Substances. Besides meat a child who has reached the age of four may be given fried brains and sweetbreads, to be combined, for example, with chicken croquettes.

Milk Foods. All cheeses are to be excluded from the child's diet.

The only milk product suitable to children from three to six years of age is fresh butter.

Custard. Custard is also to be recommended provided it be *freshly prepared*, that is immediately before being eaten, and *with very fresh* milk and eggs: if such conditions cannot be rigorously fulfilled, it is preferable to do without custard, which is not a necessity.

Bread. From what we have said about soups, it may be inferred that bread is an *excellent food* for the child. It should be well selected; the crumb is not very digestible, but it can be utilised, when it is dry, to make a bread broth; but if one is to give the child simply a piece of bread to eat, it is well to offer him the crust, the end of the loaf. Bread sticks are excellent for those who can afford them.

Bread contains many nitrogenous substances and is very rich in starches, but is lacking in fats; and as the fundamental substances of diet are, as is well known, three in number, namely, proteids, (nitrogenous substances), starches, and fats, bread is not a complete food; it is necessary therefore to offer the child buttered bread, which constitutes a complete food and may be considered as a sufficient and complete breakfast.

Green Vegetables. Children must never eat raw vegetables, such as salads and greens, but only cooked ones; indeed they are not to be highly recommended either cooked or raw, with the exception of spinach which may enter with moderation into the diet of children.

Potatoes prepared in a purée with much butter form, however, an excellent complement of nutrition for children.

Fruits. Among fruits there are excellent foods for children. They too, like milk and eggs, if freshly gathered, retain a *living* quality which aids assimilation.

As this condition, however, is not easily attainable in cities, it is necessary to consider also the diet of fruits which are not perfectly fresh and which, therefore, should be prepared and cooked in various ways. All fruits are not to be advised for children; the chief properties to be considered are the degree of *ripeness,* the *tenderness* and *sweetness* of the pulp, and its *acidity.* Peaches, apricots, grapes, currants, oranges, and mandarins, in their natural state, can be given to little children with great advantage. Other fruits, such as pears, apples, plums, should be cooked or prepared in syrup.

Figs, pineapples, dates, melons, cherries, walnuts, almonds, hazelnuts, and chestnuts, are excluded for various reasons from the diet of early childhood.

The preparation of fruit must consist in removing from it all indigestible parts, such as the peel, and also such parts as the child inadvertently may absorb to his detriment, as, for example, the seed.

Children of four or five should be taught early how carefully the seeds must be thrown away and how the fruits are peeled. Afterwards, the child so educated may be promoted to the honour of receiving a fine fruit intact, and he will know how to eat it properly.

The culinary preparation of fruits consists essentially in two processes: cooking, and seasoning with sugar.

Besides simple cooking, fruits may be prepared as marmalades and jellies, which are excellent but are naturally within the reach of the wealthier classes only. While jellies and marmalades may be allowed, candied fruits,–on the other hand,–*marrons glacés,* and the like, are absolutely excluded from the child's diet.

Seasonings. An important phase of the hygiene of child diet concerns seasonings–with a view to their rigorous limitation. As I have already indicated, sugar and some fat substances along with kitchen salt (sodium chloride) should constitute the principal part of the seasonings.

To these may be added *organic acids* (acetic acid, citric acid) that is, vinegar and lemon juice; this latter can be advantageously used on fish, on croquettes, on spinach, etc.

Other condiments suitable to little children are some aromatic vegetables like garlic and rue which disinfect the intestines and the lungs, and also have a direct anthelminthic action.

Spices, on the other hand, such as pepper, nutmeg, cinnamon, clove, and especially mustard, are to be absolutely abolished.

Drinks. The growing organism of the child is very rich in water, and, hence, needs a constant supply of moisture. Among the beverages, the best, and indeed the only one, to be unreservedly advised is pure fresh spring water. To rich children might be allowed the so-called table waters which are slightly alkaline, such as those of San Gemini, Acqua Claudia, etc., mixed with syrups, as, for example, syrup of black cherry.

It is now a matter of general knowledge that all fermented beverages, and those exciting to the nervous system, are injurious to children; hence, all alcoholic and caffeic beverages are absolutely eliminated from child diet. Not only liquors, but wine and beer, ought to be unknown to the child's taste, and coffee and tea should be inaccessible to childhood.

The deleterious action of alcohol on the child organism needs no illustration, but in a matter of such vital importance insistent repetition is never superfluous. Alcohol is a poison especially fatal to organisms in the process of formation. Not only does it arrest their total development (whence infantilism, idiocy), but also pre-disposes the child to nervous maladies (epilepsy, meningitis), and to maladies of the digestive organs, and metabolism (cirrhosis of the liver, dyspepsia, anæmia).

If the "Children's Houses" were to succeed in enlightening the people on such truths, they would be accomplishing a very lofty hygienic work for the new generations.

Instead of coffee, children may be given roasted and boiled barley, malt, and especially chocolate which is an excellent child food, particularly when mixed with milk.

Distribution of the Meals

Another chapter of child diet concerns the distribution of the meals. Here, one principle must dominate, and must be diffused, among mothers, namely, that the children shall be kept to rigorous meal hours in order that they may enjoy good health and have excellent digestion. It is true that there prevails among the people (and it is one of the forms of maternal ignorance most fatal to children) the prejudice that children in order to grow well must be eating almost continuously, without regularity, nibbling almost habitually a crust of bread. On the contrary, the child, in view of the special delicacy of his digestive system, has more need of regular meals than the adult has. It seems to me that the "Children's Houses" with very prolonged programmes are, for this reason, suitable places for child culture, as they can direct the child's diet. *Outside of their regular meal hours, children should not eat.*

In a "Children's House" with a long programme there ought to be two meals, a hearty one about noon, and a light one about four in the afternoon.

At the hearty meal, there should be soup, a meat dish, and bread, and, in the case of rich children, also fruits or custard, and butter on the bread.

At the four o'clock meal there should be prepared a light lunch, which from a simple piece of bread can range to buttered bread, and to bread accompanied by a fruit marmalade, chocolate, honey, custard, etc. Crisp crackers, biscuits, and cooked fruits, etc., might also be usefully employed. Very suitably the lunch might consist of bread soaked in milk or an egg *à la coque* with bread sticks, or else of a simple cup of milk in which is dissolved a spoonful of Mellin's Food. I recommend Mellin's Food very highly, not only in infancy, but also much later on account of its properties of digestibility and nutrition, and on account of its flavour, which is so pleasing to children.

Mellin's Food is a powder prepared from barley and wheat, and containing in a concentrated and pure state the nutritive substances proper to those cereals; the powder is slowly dissolved in hot water in the bottom of the same cup which is to be used for drinking the mixture, and very fresh milk is then poured on top.

The child would take the other two meals in his own home, that is, the morning breakfast and the supper, which latter must be *very light* for children so that shortly after they may be ready to go to bed. On these meals it would be well to give advice to mothers, urging them to help complete the hygienic work of the "Children's Houses," to the profit of their children.

The morning breakfast for the rich might be milk and chocolate, or milk and extract of malt, with crackers, or, better, with toasted bread spread with butter or honey; for the poor, a cup of fresh milk, with bread.

For the evening meal, a soup is to be advised (children should eat soups twice a day), and an egg *à la coque* or a cup of milk; or rice soup with a base of milk, and buttered bread, with cooked fruits, etc.

As for the alimentary rations to be calculated, I refer the reader to the special treatises on hygiene: although practically such calculations are of no great utility.

In the "Children's Houses," especially in the case of the poor, I should make extensive use of the vegetable soups and I should have cultivated in the garden plots vegetables which can be used in the diet, in order to have them plucked in their freshness, cooked, and enjoyed. I should try, possibly, to do the same for the fruits, and, by the raising of animals, to have fresh eggs and pure milk. The milking of the goats could be done directly by the larger children, after they had scrupulously washed their hands. Another important educative application which school-refection in the "Children's Houses" has to offer, and which concerns "practical life," consists in the preparing of the table, arranging the table linen, learning its nomenclature, etc. Later, I shall show how this exercise can gradually increase in difficulty and constitute a most important didactic instrument.

It is sufficient to intimate here that it is very important to teach the children to eat with cleanliness, both with respect to themselves and with respect to their surroundings (not to soil the napkins, etc.), and to use the table implements (which, at least, for the little ones, are limited to the spoon, and for the larger children extended to the fork and knife).

Muscular Education–Gymnastics

The generally accepted idea of gymnastics is, I consider, very inadequate. In the common schools we are accustomed to describe as gymnastics a species of collective muscular discipline which has as its aim that children shall learn to follow definite ordered movements given in the form of commands. The guiding spirit in such gymnastics is coercion, and I feel that such exercises repress spontaneous movements and impose others in their place. I do not know what the psychological authority for the selection of these imposed movements is. Similar movements are used in medical gymnastics in order to restore a normal movement to a torpid muscle or to give back a normal movement to a paralysed muscle. A number of chest movements which are given in the school are advised, for example, in medicine for those who suffer from intestinal torpidity, but truly I do not well understand what office such exercises can fulfil when they are followed by squadrons of normal children. In addition to these formal gymnastics we have those which are carried on in a gymnasium, and which are very like the first steps in the training of an acrobat. However, this is not the place for criticism of the gymnastics used in our common schools. Certainly in our case we are not considering such gymnastics. Indeed, many who hear me speak of gymnastics for infant schools very plainly show disapprobation and they will disapprove more heartily when they hear me speak of a gymnasium for little children. Indeed, if the gymnastic exercises and the gymnasium were those of the common schools, no one would agree more heartily than I in the disapproval expressed by these critics.

We must understand by *gymnastics* and in general by muscular education a series of exercises tending to *aid* the normal development of physiological movements (such as walking, breathing, speech), to protect this development, when the child shows himself backward or abnormal in any way, and to encourage in the children those movements which are useful in the achievement of the most ordinary acts of life; such as dressing, undressing, buttoning their clothes and lacing their shoes, carrying such objects as balls, cubes, etc. If there exists an age in which it is necessary to protect a child by means of a series of gymnastic exercises, between three and six years is undoubtedly the age. The special gymnastics necessary, or, better still, hygienic, in this period of life, refer chiefly to walking. A child in the general morphological growth of his body is characterised by having a torso greatly developed in comparison with the lower limbs. In the new-born child the length of the torso, from the top of the head to the curve of the groin, is equal to 68 per cent of the total length of the body. The limbs then arc barely 32 per cent of the stature. During growth these relative proportions change in a most noticeable way; thus, for example, in the adult the torso is fully half of the entire stature and, according to the individual, corresponds to 51 or 52 per cent of it.

This morphological difference between the new-born child and the adult is bridged so slowly during growth that in the first years of the child's life the torso still remains tremendously developed as compared with the limbs. In one year the height of the torso corresponds to 65 per cent of the total stature, in two years to 63, in three years to 62.

At the age when a child enters the infant school his limbs are still very short as compared with his torso; that is, the length of his limbs barely corresponds to 38 per cent of the stature. Between the years of six and seven the proportion of the torso to the stature is from 57 to 56 per cent. In such a period therefore the child not only makes a noticeable growth in height, (he measures indeed at the age of three years about 0.85 metre and at six years 1.05 metres) but, changing so greatly the relative proportions between the torso and the limbs, the latter make a most decided growth. This growth is related to the layers of cartilage which still exist at the extremity of the long bones and is related in general to the still incomplete ossification of the entire skeleton. The tender bones of the limbs must therefore sustain the weight of the torso which is then disproportionately large. We cannot, if we consider all these things, judge the manner of walking in little children by the standard set for our own equilibrium. If a child is not strong, the erect posture and walking are really sources of fatigue for him, and the long bones of the lower limbs, yielding to the weight of the body, easily become deformed and usually bowed. This is particularly the case among the badly nourished children of the poor, or among those in whom the skeleton structure, while not actually showing the presence of rickets, still seems to be slow in attaining normal ossification.

We are wrong then if we consider little children from this physical point of view as *little men*. They have, instead, characteristics and proportions that are entirely special to their age. The tendency of the child to stretch out on his back and kick his legs in the air is an expression of physical needs related to the proportions of his body. The baby loves to walk on all fours just because, like the quadruped animals, his limbs are short in comparison with his body. Instead of this, we divert these natural manifestations by foolish habits which we impose on the child. We hinder him from throwing himself on the earth, from stretching, etc., and we oblige him to walk with grown people and to keep up with them; and excuse ourselves by saying that we don't want him to become capricious and think he can do as he pleases! It is indeed a fatal error and one which has made bow-legs common among little children. It is well to enlighten the mothers on these important particulars of infant hygiene. Now we, with the gymnastics, can, and, indeed, should, help the child in his development by making our exercises correspond to the movement which he *needs to make*, and in this way save his limbs from fatigue.

One very simple means for helping the child in his activity was suggested to me by my observation of the children themselves. The teacher was having the children march, leading them about the courtyard between the walls of the house and the central garden. This garden was protected by a little fence made of strong wires which were stretched in parallel lines, and were supported at intervals by wooden palings driven into the ground. Along the fence, ran a little ledge on which the children were in the habit of sitting down when they were tired of marching. In addition to this, I always brought out little chairs, which I placed against the wall. Every now and then, the little ones of two and one half and three years would drop out from the marching line, evidently being tired; but instead of sitting down on the ground or on the chairs, they would run to the little fence and catching hold of the upper line of wire they would walk along sideways, resting their feet on the wire which was nearest the ground. That this gave them a great deal of pleasure, was evident from the way in which they laughed as, with bright eyes, they watched their larger companions who were marching about. The truth was that these little ones had solved one of my problems in a very practical way. They moved themselves along on the wires, pulling their bodies sideways. In this way, they moved their limbs *without throwing upon them the weight of the body*. Such an apparatus placed in the gymnasium for little children, will enable them to fulfil the need which they feel of throwing themselves on the floor and kicking their legs in the air; for the movements they make on the little fence correspond even more correctly to the same physical needs. Therefore, I advise the manufacture of this little fence for use in children's playrooms. It can be constructed of parallel bars supported by upright poles firmly fixed on to the heavy base. The children, while playing upon this little fence, will be able to look out and see with great pleasure what the other children are doing in the room.

Other pieces of gymnasium apparatus can be constructed upon the same plan, that is, having as their aim the furnishing of the child with a proper outlet for his individual activities. One of the things invented by Séguin to develop the lower limbs, and especially to strengthen the articulation of the knee in weak children, is the trampolino.

This is a kind of swing, having a very wide seat, so wide, indeed, that the limbs of the child stretched out in front of him are entirely supported by this broad seat. This little chair is hung from strong cords and is left swinging. The wall in front of it is reinforced by a strong smooth board against which the children press their feet in pushing themselves back and forth in the swing. The child seated in this swing exercises his limbs, pressing his feet against the board each time that he swings toward the wall. The board against which he swings may be erected at some distance from the wall, and may be so low that the child can see over the top of it. As he swings in this chair, he strengthens his limbs through the species of gymnastics limited to the lower limbs, and this he does without resting the weight of his body upon his legs. Other pieces of gymnastic apparatus, less important from the hygienic standpoint, but very amusing to the children, may be described briefly. "The Pendulum," a game which may be played by one child or by several, consists of rubber balls hung on a cord. The children seated in their little armchairs strike the ball, sending it from one to another. It is an exercise for the arms and for the spinal column, and is at the same time an exercise in which the eye gauges the distance of bodies in motion. Another game, called "The Cord," consists of a line, drawn on the earth with chalk, along which the children walk. This helps to order and to direct their free movements in a given direction. A game like this is very pretty, indeed, after a snowfall, when the little path made by the children shows the regularity of the line they have traced, and encourages a pleasant war among them in which each one tries to make his line in the snow the most regular.

The little round stair is another game, in which a little wooden stairway, built on the plan of the spiral, is used. This little stair is enclosed on one side by a balustrade on which the children can rest their hands. The other side is open and circular. This serves to habituate the children to climbing and descending stairs without holding on to the balustrade, and teaches them to move up and down with movements that are poised and self-controlled. The steps must be very low and very shallow. Going up and down on this little stair, the very smallest children can learn movements which they cannot follow properly in climbing ordinary stairways in their homes, in which the proportions are arranged for adults.

Another piece of gymnasium apparatus, adapted for the broad-jump, consists of a low wooden platform painted with various lines, by means of which the distance jumped may be gauged. There is a small flight of stairs which may be used in connection with this plane, making it possible to practise and to measure the high-jump.

I also believe that rope-ladders may be so adapted as to be suitable for use in schools for little children. Used in pairs, these would, it seems to me, help to perfect a great variety of movements, such as kneeling, rising, bending forward and backward, etc.; movements which the child, without the help of the ladder, could not make without losing his equilibrium. All of these movements are useful in that they help the child to acquire, first, equilibrium, then that co-ordination of the muscular movements necessary to him. They are, moreover, helpful in that they increase the chest expansion. Besides all this, such movements as I have described, reinforce the *hand* in its most primitive and essential action, *prehension;* –the movement which necessarily precedes all the finer movements of the hand itself. Such apparatus was successfully used by Séguin to develop the general strength and the movement of prehension in his idiotic children.

The gymnasium, therefore, offers a field for the most varied exercises, tending to establish the co-ordination of the movements common in life, such as walking, throwing objects, going up and down stairs, kneeling, rising, jumping, etc.

Free Gymnastics

By free gymnastics I mean those which are given without any apparatus. Such gymnastics are divided into two classes: directed and required exercises, and free games. In the first class, I recommend the march, the object of which should be not rhythm, but poise only. When the march is introduced, it is well to accompany it with the singing of little songs, because this furnishes a breathing exercise very helpful in strengthening the lungs. Besides the march, many of the games of Froebel which are accompanied by songs, very similar to those which the children constantly play among themselves, may be used. In the free games, we furnish the children with balls, hoops, bean bags and kites. The trees readily offer themselves to the game of "Pussy wants a corner," and many simple games of tag.

Educational Gymnastics

Under the name of educational gymnastics, we include two series of exercises which really form a part of other school work, as, for instance, the cultivation of the earth, the care of plants and animals (watering and pruning the plants, carrying the grain to the chickens, etc.). These activities call for various co-ordinated movements, as, for example, in hoeing, in getting down to plant things, and in rising; the trips which children make in carrying objects to some definite place, and in making a definite practical use of these objects, offer a field for very valuable gymnastic exercises. The scattering of minute objects, such as corn and oats, is valuable, and also the exercise of opening and closing the gates to the garden and to the chicken yard. All of these exercises are the more valuable in that they are carried on in the open air. Among our educational gymnastics we have exercises to develop co-ordinated movements of the fingers, and these prepare the children for the exercises of practical life, such as dressing and undressing themselves. The didactic material which forms the basis of these last named gymnastics is very simple, consisting of wooden frames, each mounted with two pieces of cloth, or leather, to be fastened and unfastened by means of the buttons and buttonholes, books and eyes, eyelets and lacings, or automatic fastenings.

In our "Children's Houses" we use ten of these frames, so constructed that each one of them illustrates a different process in dressing or undressing.

One: mounted with heavy pieces of wool which are to be fastened by means of large bone buttons–corresponds to children's dresses.

Two: mounted with pieces of linen to be fastened with pearl buttons–corresponds to a child's underwear.

Three: leather pieces mounted with shoe buttons–in fastening these leather pieces the children make use of the button-hook–corresponds to a child's shoes.

Four: pieces of leather which are laced together by means of eyelets and shoe laces.

Five: two pieces of cloth to be laced together. (These pieces are boned and therefore correspond to the little bodices worn by the peasants in Italy.)

Six: two pieces of stuff to be fastened by means of large hooks and eyes.

Seven: two pieces of linen to be fastened by means of small hooks and worked eyelets.

Eight: two pieces of cloth to be fastened by means of broad coloured ribbon, which is to be tied into bows.

Nine: pieces of cloth laced together with round cord, on the same order as the fastenings on many of the children's underclothes.

Ten: two pieces to be fastened together by means of the modern automatic fasteners.

Through the use of such toys, the children can practically analyse the movements necessary in dressing and undressing themselves, and can prepare themselves separately for these movements by means of repeated exercises. We succeed in teaching the child to dress himself without his really being aware of it, that is, without any direct or arbitrary command we have led him to this mastery. As soon as he knows how to do it, he begins to wish to make a practical application of his ability, and very soon he will be proud of being sufficient unto himself, and will take delight in an ability which makes his body free from the hands of others, and which leads him the sooner to that modesty and activity which develops far too late in those children of today who are deprived of this most practical form of education. The fastening games are very pleasing to the little ones, and often when ten of them are using the frames at the same time, seated around the little tables, quiet and serious, they give the impression of a workroom filled with tiny workers.

Respiratory Gymnastics

The purpose of these gymnastics is to regulate the respiratory movements: in other words, to teach the *art of breathing*. They also help greatly the correct formation of the child's *speech habits*. The exercises which we use were introduced into school literature by Professor Sala. We have chosen the simple exercises described by him in his treatise, "Cura della Balbuzie." * These include a number of respiratory gymnastic exercises with which are co-ordinated muscular exercises. I give here an example:

Mouth wide open, tongue held flat, hands on hips.

Breathe deeply, lift the shoulders rapidly, lowering the diaphragm.

Expel breath slowly, lowering shoulders slowly, returning to normal position.

The directress should select or devise simple breathing exercises, to be accompanied with arm movements, etc.

Exercises for proper use of *lips, tongue,* and *teeth.* These exercises teach the movements of the lips and tongue in the pronunciation of certain fundamental consonant sounds, reinforcing the muscles, and making them ready for these movements. These gymnastics prepare the organs used in the formation of language.

In presenting such exercises we begin with the entire class, but finish by testing the children individually. We ask the child to pronounce, *aloud* and with *force*, the first syllable of a word. When all are intent upon putting the greatest possible force into this, we call each child separately, and have him repeat the word. If he pronounces it correctly, we send him to the right, if badly, to the left. Those who have difficulty with the word, are then encouraged to repeat it several times. The teacher takes note of the age of the child, and of the particular defects in the movements of the muscles used in articulating. She may then touch the muscles which should be used, tapping for example, the curve of the lips, or even taking hold of the child's tongue and placing it against the dental arch, or showing him clearly the movements which she herself makes when pronouncing the syllable. She must seek in every way to aid the normal development of the movements necessary to the exact articulation of the word.

As the basis for these gymnastics we have the children pronounce the words: *pane–fame–tana–zina–stella–rana–gatto.*

In the pronunciation of *pane*, the child should repeat with much force, *pa, pa, pa,* thus exercising the muscles producing orbicular contraction of the lips.

In *fame* repeating *fa, fa, fa,* the child exercises the movements of the lower lip against the upper dental arch.

In *tana*, having him repeat *ta, ta, ta,* we cause him to exercise the movement of the tongue against the upper dental arch.

In *zina*, we provoke the contact of the upper and lower dental arches.

With *stella* we have him repeat the whole word, bringing the teeth together, and holding the tongue (which has a tendency to protrude) close against the upper teeth.

In *rana* we have him repeat *r, r, r,* thus exercising the tongue in the vibratory movements. In *gatto* we hold the voice upon the guttural *g.*

Nature in Education–Agricultural Labour: Culture of Plants and Animals

Itard, in a remarkable pedagogical treatise: "*Des premiers développements du jeune sauvage de l'Aveyron,*" expounds in detail the drama of a curious, gigantic education which attempted to overcome the psychical darkness of an idiot and at the same time to snatch a man from primitive nature.

The savage of the Aveyron was a child who had grown up in the natural state: criminally abandoned in a forest where his assassins thought they had killed him, he was cured by natural means, and had survived for many years free and naked in the wilderness, until, captured by hunters, he entered into the civilised life of Paris, showing by the scars with which his miserable body was furrowed the story of the struggles with wild beasts, and of lacerations caused by falling from heights.

The child was, and always remained, mute; his mentality, diagnosed by Pinel as idiotic, remained forever almost inaccessible to intellectual education.

To this child are due the first steps of positive pedagogy. Itard, a physician of deaf-mutes and a student of philosophy, undertook his education with methods which he had already partially tried for treating defective hearing–believing at the beginning that the savage showed characteristics of inferiority, not because he was a degraded organism, but for want of education. He was a follower of the principles of Helvetius: "Man is nothing without the work of man"; that is, he believed in the omnipotence of education, and was opposed to the pedagogical principle which Rousseau had promulgated before the Revolution: "*Tout est bien sortant des mains de l'Auteur des choses, tout dégénère dans les mains de l'homme,*"–that is, the work of education is deleterious and spoils the man.

The savage, according to the erroneous first impression of Itard, demonstrated experimentally by his characteristics the truth of the former assertion. When, however, he perceived, with the help of Pinel, that he had to do with an idiot, his philosophical theories gave place to the most admirable, tentative, experimental pedagogy.

Itard divides the education of the savage into two parts. In the first, he endeavours to lead the child from natural life to social life; and in the second, he attempts the intellectual education of the idiot. The child in his life of frightful abandonment had found one happiness; he had, so to speak, immersed himself in, and unified himself with, nature, taking delight in it-rains, snow, tempests, boundless space, had been his sources of entertainment, his companions, his love. Civil life is a renunciation of all this: but it is an acquisition beneficent to human progress. In Itard's pages we find vividly described the moral work which led the savage to civilisation, multiplying the needs of the child and surrounding him with loving care. Here is a sample of the admirably patient work of Itard as *observer of the spontaneous expressions* of his pupil: it can most truly give teachers, who are to prepare for the experimental method, an idea of the patience and the self-abnegation necessary in dealing with a phenomenon which is to be observed:

"When, for example, he was observed within his room, he was seen to be lounging with oppressive monotony, continually directing his eyes toward the window, with his gaze wandering in the void. If on such occasions a sudden storm blew up, if the sun, hidden behind the clouds, peeped out of a sudden, lighting the atmosphere brilliantly, there were loud bursts of laughter and almost convulsive joy. Sometimes, instead of these expressions of joy, there was a sort of frenzied rage: he would twist his arms, put his clenched fists upon his eyes, gnashing his teeth and becoming dangerous to those about him.

"One morning, when the snow fell abundantly while he was still in bed, he uttered a cry of joy upon awaking, leaped from his bed, ran to the window and then to the door; went and came impatiently from one to the other; then ran out undressed as he was into the garden. There, giving vent to his joy with the shrillest of cries, he ran, rolled in the snow, gathered it up in handfuls, and swallowed it with incredible avidity.

"But his sensations at sight of the great spectacles of nature did not always manifest themselves in such a vivid and noisy manner. It is worthy of note that in certain cases they were expressed by a quiet regret and melancholy. Thus, it was when the rigour of the weather drove everybody from the garden that the savage of the Aveyron chose to go there. He would walk around it several times and finally sit down upon the edge of the fountain.

"I have often stopped for *whole hours*, and with indescribable pleasure, to watch him as he sat thus-to see how his face, inexpressive or contracted by grimaces, gradually assumed an expression of sadness, and of melancholy reminiscence, while his eyes were fixed upon the surface of the water into which from time to time he would throw a few dead leaves.

"If when there was a full moon, a sheaf of mild beams penetrated into his room, he rarely failed to wake and to take his place at the window. He would remain there *for a large part of the night*, erect, motionless, with his head thrust forward, his eyes fixed on the countryside lighted by the moon, plunged in a sort of contemplative ecstasy, the immobility and silence of which were only interrupted at long intervals by a breath as deep as a sigh, which died away in a plaintive sound of lamentation."

Elsewhere, Itard relates that the boy did not know the *walking gait* which we use in civilised life, but only the *running gait*, and tells how he, Itard, ran after him at the beginning, when he took him out into the streets of Paris, rather than violently check the boy's running.

The gradual and gentle leading of the savage through all the manifestations of social life, the early adaptation of the teacher to the pupil rather than of the pupil to the teacher, the successive attraction to a new life which was to win over the child by its charms, and not be imposed upon him violently so that the pupil should feel it as a burden and a torture, are as many precious educative expressions which may be generalised and applied to the education of children.

I believe that there exists no document which offers so poignant and so eloquent a contrast between the life of nature and the life of society, and which so graphically shows that society is made up solely of renunciations and restraints. Let it suffice to recall the run, checked to a walk, and the loud-voiced cry, checked to the modulations of the ordinary speaking voice.

And, yet, without any violence, leaving to social life the task of charming the child little by little, Itard's education triumphs. It is true that civilised life is made by renunciation of the life of nature; it is almost the snatching of a man from the lap of earth; it is like snatching the newborn child from its mother's breast; but it is also a new life.

In Itard's pages we see the final triumph of the love of man over the love of nature: the savage of the Aveyron ends by *feeling* and preferring the affection of Itard, the caresses, the tears shed over him, to the joy of immersing himself voluptuously in the snow, and of contemplating the infinite expanse of the sky on a starry night: one day after an attempted escape into the country, he returns of his own accord, humble and repentant, to find his good soup and his warm bed.

It is true that man has created enjoyments in social life and has brought about a vigorous human love in community life. But nevertheless he still belongs to nature, and, especially when he is a child, he must needs draw from it the forces necessary to the development of the body and of the spirit. We have intimate communications with nature which have an influence, even a material influence, on the growth of the body. (For example, a physiologist, isolating young guinea pigs from terrestrial magnetism by means of insulators, found that they grew up with rickets.)

In the education of little children Itard's educative drama is repeated: we must prepare man, who is one among the living creatures and therefore belongs to nature, for social life, because social life being his own peculiar work, must also correspond to the manifestation of his natural activity.

But the advantages which we prepare for him in this social life, in a great measure escape the little child, who at the beginning of his life is a predominantly vegetative creature.

To soften this transition in education, by giving a large part of the educative work to nature itself, is as necessary as it is not to snatch the little child suddenly and violently from its mother and to take him to school; and precisely this is done in the "Children's Houses," which are situated within the tenements where the parents live, where the cry of the child reaches the mother and the mother's voice answers it.

Nowadays, under the form of child hygiene, this part of education is much cultivated: children are allowed to grow up in the open air, in the public gardens, or are left for many hours half naked on the seashore, exposed to the rays of the sun. It has been understood, through the diffusion of marine and Apennine colonies, that the best means of invigorating the child is to immerse him in nature.

Short and comfortable clothing for children, sandals for the feet, nudity of the lower extremities, are so many liberations from the oppressive shackles of civilisation.

It is an obvious principle that we should sacrifice to natural liberties in education only as much as is *necessary* for the acquisition of the greater pleasures which are offered by civilisation without *useless sacrifices*.

But in all this progress of modern child education, we have not freed ourselves from the prejudice which denies children spiritual expression and spiritual needs, and makes us consider them only as amiable vegetating bodies to be cared for, kissed, and set in motion. The *education* which a good mother or a good modern teacher gives today to the child who, for example, is running about in a flower garden is the counsel *not to touch the flowers*, not to tread on the grass; as if it were sufficient for the child to satisfy the physiological needs of his body by moving his legs and breathing fresh air.

But if for the physical life it is necessary to have the child exposed to the vivifying forces of nature, it is also necessary for his psychical life to place the soul of the child in contact with creation, in order that he may lay up for himself treasure from the directly educating forces of living nature. The method for arriving at this end is to set the child at agricultural labour, guiding him to the cultivation of plants and animals, and so to the intelligent contemplation of nature.

Already, in England Mrs. Latter has devised the *basis* for a method of child education by means of *gardening* and *horticulture*. She sees in the contemplation of developing life the bases of religion, since the soul of the child may go from the creature to the Creator. She sees in it also the point of departure for intellectual education, which she limits to drawing from life as a step toward art, to the ideas about plants, insects, and seasons, which spring from agriculture, and to the first notions of household life, which spring from the cultivation and the culinary preparation of certain alimentary products that children later serve upon the table, providing afterwards also for the washing of the utensils and tableware.

Mrs. Latter's conception is too one-sided; but her institutions, which continue to spread in England, undoubtedly complete the natural *education* which, up to this time limited to the physical side, has already been so efficacious in invigorating the bodies of English children. Moreover, her experience offers a positive corroboration of the practicability of agricultural teaching in the case of little children.

As for deficients, I have seen agriculture applied on a large scale to their education at Paris by the means which the kindly spirit of Baccelli tried to introduce into the elementary schools when he attempted to institute the "little educative gardens." In every *little garden* are sown different agricultural products, demonstrating practically the proper method and the proper time for seeding and for crop gathering, and the period of development of the various products; the manner of preparing the soil, of enriching it with natural or chemical manures, etc. The same is done for ornamental plants and for gardening, which is the work yielding the best income for deficients, when they are of an age to practise a profession.

But this side of education, though it contains, in the first place, an objective method of intellectual culture, and, in addition, a professional preparation, is not, in my opinion, to be taken into serious consideration for child education. The educational conception of this age must be solely that of aiding the psycho-physical development of the individual; and, this being the case, agriculture and animal culture contain in themselves precious means of moral education which can be analysed far more than is done by Mrs. Latter, who sees in them essentially a method of conducting the child's soul to religious feeling. Indeed, in this method, which is a progressive ascent, several gradations can be distinguished: I mention here the principal ones:

First. The child is initiated into observation of the phenomena of life. He stands with respect to the plants and animals in relations analogous to those in which the *observing* teacher stands towards him. Little by little, as interest and observation grow, his zealous care for the living creatures grows also, and in this way, the child can logically be brought to appreciate the care which the mother and the teacher take of him.

Second. The child is initiated into *foresight* by way of *auto-education;* when he knows that the life of the plants that have been sown depends upon his care in watering them, and that of the animals, upon his diligence in feeding them, without which the little plant dries up and the animals suffer hunger, the child becomes vigilant, as one who is beginning to feel a mission in life. Moreover, a voice quite different from that of his mother and his teacher calling him to his duties, is speaking here, exhorting him never to forget the task he has undertaken. It is the plaintive voice of the needy life which lives by his care. Between the child and the living creatures which he cultivates there is born a mysterious correspondence which induces the child to fulfil certain determinate acts without the intervention of the teacher, that is, leads him to an *auto-education.*

The rewards which the child reaps also remain between him and nature: one fine day after long patient care in carrying food and straw to the brooding pigeons, behold the little ones! behold a number of chickens peeping about the setting hen which yesterday sat motionless in her brooding place! behold one day the tender little rabbits in the hutch where formerly dwelt in solitude the pair of big rabbits to which he had not a few times lovingly carried the green vegetables left over in his mother's kitchen!

I have not yet been able to institute in Rome the breeding of animals, but in the "Children's Houses" at Milan there are several animals, among them a pair of pretty little white American fowl that live in a diminutive and elegant *chalet,* similar in construction to a Chinese pagoda: in front of it, a little piece of ground inclosed by a rampart is reserved for the pair. The little door of the *chalet* is locked at evening, and the children take care of it in turn. With what delight they go in the morning to unlock the door, to fetch water and straw, and with what care they watch during the day, and at evening lock the door after having made sure that the fowl lack nothing! The teacher informs me that among all the educative exercises this is the most welcome, and seems also the most important of all. Many a time when the children are tranquilly occupied in tasks, each at the work he prefers, one, two, or three, get up silently, and go out to cast a glance at the animals to see if they need care. Often it happens that a child absents himself for a long time and the teacher surprises him watching enchantedly the fish gliding ruddy and resplendent in the sunlight in the waters of the fountain.

One day I received from the teacher in Milan a letter in which she spoke to me with great enthusiasm of a truly wonderful piece of news. The little pigeons were hatched. For the children it was a great festival. They felt themselves to some extent the parents of these little ones, and no artificial reward which had flattered their vanity would ever have provoked such a truly fine emotion. Not less great are the joys which vegetable nature provides. In one of the " Children's Houses" at Rome, where there was no soil that could be cultivated, there have been arranged, through the efforts of Signora Talamo, flower-pots all around the large terrace, and climbing plants near the walls. The children never forget to water the plants with their little watering-pots.

One day I found them seated on the ground, all in a circle, around a splendid red rose which had bloomed in the night; silent and calm, literally immersed in mute contemplation.

Third. The children are initiated into the virtue of *patience and into confident expectation*, which is a form of faith and of philosophy of life.

When the children put a seed into the ground, and wait until it fructifies, and see the first appearance of the shapeless plant, and wait for the growth and the transformations into flower and fruit, and see how some plants sprout sooner and some later, and how the deciduous plants have a rapid life, and the fruit trees a slower growth, they end by acquiring a peaceful equilibrium of conscience, and absorb the first germs of that wisdom which so characterised the tillers of the soil in the time when they still kept their primitive simplicity.

Fourth. The children are inspired with a feeling for nature, which is maintained by the marvels of creation–that creation which *rewards* with a generosity not measured by the labour of those who help it to evolve the life of its creatures.

Even while at the work, a sort of correspondence arises between the child's soul and the lives which are developed under his care. The child loves naturally the manifestations of life: Mrs. Latter tells us how easily little ones are interested even in earthworms and in the movement of the larvae of insects in manure, without feeling that horror which we, who have grown up isolated from nature, experience towards certain animals. It is well then, to develop this feeling of trust and confidence in living creatures, which is, moreover, a form of love, and of union with the universe.

But what most develops a feeling of nature is the *cultivation* of the *living* things, because they by their natural development give back far more than they receive, and show something like infinity in their beauty and variety. When the child has cultivated the iris or the pansy, the rose or the hyacinth, has placed in the soil a seed or a bulb and periodically watered it, or has planted a fruit-bearing shrub, and the blossomed flower and the ripened fruit offer themselves as a *generous gift* of nature, a rich reward for a small effort; it seems almost as if nature were answering with her gifts to the feeling of desire, to the vigilant love of the cultivator, rather than striking a balance with his material efforts.

It will be quite different when the child has to gather the *material* fruits of his labour: motionless, uniform objects, which are consumed and dispersed rather than increased and multiplied.

The difference between the products of nature and those of industry, between divine products and human products–it is this that must be born spontaneously in the child's conscience, like the determination of a fact.

But at the same time, as the plant must give its fruit, so man must give his labour.

Fifth. The child follows the natural way of development of the human race. In short, such education makes the evolution of the individual harmonise with that of humanity. Man passed from the natural to the artificial state through agriculture: when he discovered the secret of intensifying the production of the soil, he obtained the reward of civilisation.

The same path must be traversed by the child who is destined to become a civilised man.

The action of educative nature so understood is very practically accessible. Because, even if the vast stretch of ground and the large courtyard necessary for physical education are lacking, it will always be possible to find a few square yards of land that may be cultivated, or a little place where pigeons can make their nest, things sufficient for spiritual education. Even a pot of flowers at the window can, if necessary, fulfil the purpose.

In the first "Children's House" in Rome we have a vast courtyard, cultivated as a garden, where the children are free to run in the open air–and, besides, a long stretch of ground, which is planted on one side with trees, has a branching path in the middle, and on the opposite side, has broken ground for the cultivation of plants. This last, we have divided into so many portions, reserving one for each child.

While the smaller children run freely up and down the paths, or rest in the shade of the trees, the *possessors of the earth* (children from four years of age up), are sowing, or hoeing, watering or examining, the surface of the soil watching for the sprouting of plants. It is interesting to note the following fact: the little reservations of the children are placed along the wall of the tenement, in a spot formerly neglected because it leads to a blind road; the inhabitants of the house, therefore, had the habit of throwing from those windows every kind of offal, and at the beginning our garden was thus contaminated.

But, little by little, without any exhortation on our part, solely through the respect born in the people's mind for the children's labour, nothing more fell from the windows, except the loving glances and smiles of the mothers upon the soil which was the beloved possession of their little children.

Manual Labour–the Potter's Art and Building

Manual labour is distinguished from manual gymnastics by the fact that the object of the latter is to exercise the hand, and the former, *to accomplish a determinate work*, being, or simulating, a socially useful object. The one perfects the individual, the other enriches the world; the two things are, however, connected because, in general, only one who has perfected his own hand can produce a useful product.

I have thought wise, after a short trial, to exclude completely Froebel's exercises, because weaving and sewing on cardboard are ill adapted to the physiological state of the child's visual organs where the powers of the accommodation of the eye have not yet reached complete development; hence, these exercises cause an *effort* of the organ which may have a fatal influence on the development of the sight. The other little exercises of Froebel, such as the foldingof paper, are exercises of the hand, not work.

There is still left plastic work,–the most rational among all the exercises of Froebel,–which consists in making the child reproduce determinate objects in clay.

In consideration, however, of the system of liberty which I proposed, I did not like to make the children *copy* anything, and, in giving them clay to fashion in their own manner, I did not direct the children to *produce useful things*; nor was I accomplishing an educative result, inasmuch as plastic work, as I shall show later, serves for the study of the psychic individuality of the child in his spontaneous manifestations, but not for his education.

I decided therefore to try in the "Children's Houses" some very interesting exercises which I had seen accomplisbed by an artist, Professor Randone, in the "School of Educative Art" founded by him. This school had its origin along with the society for young people, called *Giovinezza Gentile*, both school and society having the object of educating youth in gentleness towards their surroundings–that is, in respect for objects, buildings, monuments: a really important part of civil education, and one which interested me particularly on account of the "Children's Houses," since that institution has, as its fundamental aim, to teach precisely this respect for the walls, for the house, for the surroundings.

Very suitably, Professor Randone had decided that the society of *Giovinezza Gentile* could not be based upon sterile theoretical preachings of the principles of citizenship, or upon moral pledges taken by the children; but that it must proceed from an artistic education which should lead the youth to appreciate and love, and consequently respect, objects and especially monuments and historic buildings. Thus the "School of Educative Art" was inspired by a broad artistic conception including the reproduction of objects which are commonly met in the surroundings; the history and pre-history of their production, and the illustration of the principal civic monuments which, in Rome, are in large measure composed of archæological monuments. In order the more directly to accomplish his object, Professor Randone founded his admirable school in an opening in one of the most artistic parts of the walls of Rome, namely, the wall of Belisarius, overlooking the Villa Umberto Primo–a wall which has been entirely neglected by the authorities and by no means respected by the citizens, and upon which Randone lavished care, decorating it with graceful hanging gardens on the outside, and locating within it the School of Art which was to shape the *Giovinezza Gentile*.

Here Randone has tried, very fittingly, to rebuild and revive a form of art which was once the glory of Italy and of Florence–the potter's art, that is, the art of constructing vases.

The archæological, historical, and artistic importance of the vase is very great, and may be compared with the numismatic art. In fact the first object of which humanity felt the need was the *vase*, which came into being with the utilisation of fire, and before the discovery of the *production* of fire. Indeed the first food of mankind was cooked in a vase.

One of the things most important, ethnically, in judging the civilisation of a primitive people is the grade of perfection attained in *pottery*; in fact, the *vase* for domestic life and the axe for social life are the first sacred symbols which we find in the prehistoric epoch, and are the religious symbols connected with the temples of the gods and with the cult of the dead. Even to-day, religious cults have sacred vases in their Sancta Sanctorum.

People who have progressed in civilisation show their feeling for art and their æsthetic feeling also in *vases* which are multiplied in almost infinite form, as we see in Egyptian, Etruscan, and Greek art.

The vase then comes into being, attains perfection, and is multiplied in its uses and its forms, in the course of human civilisation; and the history of the vase follows the history of humanity itself. Besides the civil and moral importance of the vase, we have another and practical one, its literal *adaptability* to every modification of form, and its susceptibility to the most diverse ornamentation; in this, it gives free scope to the individual genius of the artist.

Thus, when once the handicraft leading to the construction of vases has been learned (and this is the part of the progress in the work, learned from the direct and graduated instruction of the teacher), anyone can modify it according to the inspiration of his own æsthetic taste and this is the artistic, individual part of the work. Besides this, in Randone's school the use of the potter's wheel is taught, and also the composition of the mixture for the bath of majolica ware, and baking the pieces in the furnace, stages of manual labour which contain an industrial culture.

Another work in the School of Educative Art is the manufacture of diminutive bricks, and their baking in the furnace, and the construction of diminutive *walls* built by the same processes which the masons use in the construction of houses, the bricks being joined by means of mortar handled with a trowel. After the simple construction of the wall,–which is very amusing for the children who build it, placing brick on brick, superimposing row on row,–the children pass to the construction of real *houses*,– first, resting on the ground, and, then, really constructed with foundations, after a previous excavation of large holes in the ground by means of little hoes and shovels. These little houses have openings corresponding to windows and doors, and are variously ornamented in their facades by little tiles of bright and multi-coloured majolica: the tiles themselves being manufactured by the children.

Thus the children learn to *appreciate* the objects and constructions which surround them, while a real manual and artistic labour gives them profitable exercise.

Such is the manual training which I have adopted in the "Children's Houses"; after two or three lessons the little pupils are already enthusiastic about the construction of vases, and they preserve very carefully their own products, in which they take pride. With their plastic art they then model little objects, eggs or fruits, with which they themselves fill the vases. One of the first undertakings is the simple vase of red clay filled with eggs of white clay; then comes the modelling of the vase with one or more spouts, of the narrow-mouthed vase, of the vase with a handle, of that with two or three handles, of the tripod, of the amphora.

For children of the age of five or six, the work of the potter's wheel begins. But what most delights the children is the work of building a wall with little bricks, and seeing a little house, the fruit of their own hands, rise in the vicinity of the ground in which are growing plants, also cultivated by them. Thus the age of childhood epitomises the principal primitive labours of humanity, when the human race, changing from the nomadic to the stable condition, demanded of the earth its fruit, built itself shelter, and devised vases to cook the foods yielded by the fertile earth.

Education of the Senses

In a pedagogical method which is experimental the education of the senses must undoubtedly assume the greatest importance. Experimental psychology also takes note of movements by means of sense measurements.

Pedagogy, however, although it may profit by psychometry is not designed to *measure* the sensations, but *educate* the senses. This is a point easily understood, yet one which is often confused. While the proceedings of esthesiometry are not to any great extent applicable to little children, the *education* of the *senses* is entirely possible.

We do not start from the conclusions of experimental psychology. That is, it is not the knowledge of the average sense conditions according to the age of the child which leads us to determine the educational applications we shall make. We start essentially from a method, and it is probable that psychology will be able to draw its conclusions from pedagogy so understood, and not *vice versa*.

The method used by me is that of making a pedagogical experiment with a didactic object and awaiting the spontaneous reaction of the child. This is a method in every way analogous to that of experimental psychology.

I make use of a material which, at first glance, may be confused with psychometric material. Teachers from Milan who had followed the course in the Milan school of experimental psychology, seeing my material exposed, would recognise among it, measures of the perception of colour, hardness, and weight, and would conclude that, in truth, I brought no new contribution to pedagogy since these instruments were already known to them.

But the great difference between the two materials lies in this: The esthesiometer carries within itself the possibility of *measuring*; my objects on the contrary, often do not permit a measure, but are adapted to cause the child to *exercise* the senses.

In order that an instrument shall attain such a pedagogical end, it is necessary that it shall not *weary* but shall *divert* the child. Here lies the difficulty in the selection of didactic material. It is known that the psychometric instruments are great *consumers of energy* –for this reason, when Pizzoli wished to apply them to the education of the senses, he did not succeed because the child was annoyed by them, and became tired. Instead, *the aim of education is to develop the energies.*

Psychometric instruments, or better, the instruments of *esthesiometry,* are prepared in their differential gradations upon the laws of Weber, which were in truth drawn from experiments made upon adults.

With little children, we must proceed to the making of trials, and must select the didactic materials in which they show themselves to be interested.

This I did in the first year of the "Children's Houses" adopting a great variety of stimuli, with a number of which I had already experimented in the school for deficients.

Much of the material used for deficients is abandoned in the education of the normal child–and much that is used has been greatly modified. I believe, however, that I have arrived at a *selection of objects* (which I do not here wish to speak of in the technical language of psychology as stimuli) representing the minimum *necessary* to a practical sense education.

These objects constitute the *didactic system* (or set of didactic materials) used by me. They are manufactured by the House of Labour of the Humanitarian Society at Milan.

A description of the objects will be given as the educational scope of each is explained. Here I shall limit myself to the setting forth of a few general considerations.

First. The difference in the reaction between deficient and normal children, in the presentation of didactic material made up of graded stimuli. This difference is plainly seen from the fact that the same didactic material used with deficients *makes education possible,* while with normal children it *provokes auto-education.*

This fact is one of the most interesting I have met with in all my experience, and it inspired and rendered possible the method of *observation* and *liberty.*

Let us suppose that we use our first object,–a block in which solid geometric forms are set. Into corresponding holes in the block are set ten little wooden cylinders, the bases diminishing gradually about ten millimetres. The game consists in taking the cylinders out of their places, putting them on the table, mixing them, and then putting each one back in its own place. The aim is to educate the eye to the differential perception of dimensions.

With the deficient child, it would be necessary to begin with exercises in which the stimuli were much more strongly contrasted, and to arrive at this exercise only after many others had preceded it.

With normal children, this is, on the other hand, the first object which we may present, and out of all the didactic material this is the game preferred by the very little children of two and a half and three years. Once we arrived at this exercise with a deficient child, it was necessary continually and actively to recall his attention, inviting him to look at the block and showing him the various pieces. And if the child once succeeded in placing all the cylinders properly, he stopped, and the game was finished. Whenever the deficient child committed an error, it was necessary to correct it, or to urge him to correct it himself, and when he was able to correct an error he was usually quite indifferent.

Now the normal child, instead, takes spontaneously a lively interest in this game. He pushes away all who would interfere, or offer to help him, and wishes to be alone before his problem.

It had already been noted that little ones of two or three years take the greatest pleasure in arranging small objects, and this experiment in the "Children's Houses" demonstrates the truth of this assertion.

Now, and here is the important point, the normal child attentively observes the relation between the size of the opening and that of the object which he is to place in the mould, and is greatly interested in the game, as is clearly shown by the expression of attention on the little face.

If he mistakes, placing one of the objects in an opening that is small for it, he takes it away, and proceeds to make various trials, seeking the proper opening. If he makes a contrary error, letting the cylinder fall into an opening that is a little too large for it, and then collects all the successive cylinders in openings just a little too large, he will find himself at the last with the big cylinder in his hand while only the smallest opening is empty. The didactic material *controls every error*. The child proceeds to correct himself, doing this in various ways. Most often he feels the cylinders or shakes them, in order to recognise which are the largest. Sometimes, he sees at a glance where his error lies, pulls the cylinders from the places where they should not be, and puts those left out where they belong, then replaces all the others. The normal child always repeats the exercise with growing interest.

Indeed, it is precisely in these errors that the educational importance of the didactic material lies, and when the child with evident security places each piece in its proper place, he has outgrown the exercise, and this piece of material becomes useless to him.

This self-correction leads the child to concentrate his attention upon the differences of dimensions, and to compare the various pieces. It is in just this comparison that the *psycho-sensory exercise* lies.

There is, therefore, no question here of teaching the child the *knowledge* of the dimensions, through the medium of these pieces. Neither is it our aim that the child shall know how to use, *without an error*, the material presented to him thus performing the exercises well.

That would place our material on the same basis as many others, for example that of Froebel, and would require again the *active* work of the *teacher*, who busies herself furnishing knowledge, and making haste to correct every error in order that the child may *learn the use of the objects*.

Here instead it is the work of the child, the auto-correction, the auto-education which acts, *for the teacher must not interfere* in the *slightest* way. No teacher can furnish the child with the *agility which he acquires* through gymnastic *exercises*: it is necessary that the pupil perfect himself through his own efforts. It is very much the same with the *education of the senses*.

It might be said that the same thing is true of every form of education; a man is not what he is because of the teachers he has had, but because of what he has done.

One of the difficulties of putting this method into practice with teachers of the old school, lies in the difficulty of preventing them from intervening when the little child remains for some time puzzled before some error, and with his eyebrows drawn together and his lips puckered, makes repeated efforts to correct himself. When they see this, the old-time teachers are seized with pity, and long, with an almost irresistible force, to help the child. When we prevent this intervention, they burst into words of compassion for the little scholar, but he soon shows in his smiling face the joy of having surmounted an obstacle.

Normal children repeat such exercises many times. This repetition varies according to the individual. Some children after having completed the exercise five or six times are tired of it. Others will remove and replace the pieces at least *twenty times*, with an expression of evident interest. Once, after I had watched a little one of four years repeat this exercise sixteen times, I had the other children sing in order to distract her, but she continued unmoved to take out the cylinders, mix them up and put them back in their places.

An intelligent teacher ought to be able to make most interesting individual psychological observations, and, to a certain point, should be able to measure the length of time for which the various stimuli held the attention.

In fact, when the child educates himself, and when the control and correction of errors is yielded to the didactic material, there *remains for the teacher nothing but to observe*. She must then be more of a psychologist than a teacher, and this shows the importance of a scientific preparation on the part of the teacher.

Indeed, with my methods, the teacher teaches *little* and observes *much*, and, above all, it is her function to direct the psychic activity of the children and their physiological development. For this reason I have changed the name of teacher into that of directress.

At first this name provoked many smiles, for everyone asked whom there was for this teacher to direct, since she had no assistants, and since she must leave her little scholars *in liberty*. But her direction is much more profound and important than that which is commonly understood, for this teacher directs *the life and the soul*.

Second. The education of the senses has, as its aim, the refinement of the differential perception of stimuli by means of repeated exercises.

There exists a *sensory culture*, which is not generally taken into consideration, but which is a factor in esthesiometry.

For example, in the mental *tests* which are used in France, or in a series of tests which De Sanctis has established for the *diagnosis* of the intellectual status, I have often seen used *cubes of different sizes placed at varying distances*. The child was to select the *smallest* and the *largest*, while the chronometer measured the time of reaction between the command and the execution of the act. Account was also taken of the errors. I repeat that in such experiments the factor of *culture* is forgotten and by this I mean *sensory culture*.

Our children have, for example, among the didactic material for the education of the senses, a series of ten cubes. The first has a base of ten centimetres, and the others decrease, successively, one centimetre as to base, the smallest cube having a base of one centimetre. The exercise consists in throwing the blocks, which are pink in colour, down upon a green carpet, and then building them up into a little tower, placing the largest cube as the base, and then placing the others in order of size until the little cube of one centimetre is placed at the top.

The little one must each time select, from the blocks scattered upon the green carpet, "the largest" block. This game is most entertaining to the little ones of two years and a half, who, as soon as they have constructed the little tower, tumble it down with little blows of the hand, admiring the pink cubes as they lie scattered upon the green carpet. Then, they begin again the construction, building and destroying a definite number of times.

If we were to place before these tests one of my children from three to four years, and one of the children from the first elementary (six or seven years old), my pupil would undoubtedly manifest a shorter period of reaction, and would not commit errors. The same may be said for the tests of the chromatic sense, etc.

This educational method should therefore prove interesting to students of experimental psychology as well as to teachers.

In conclusion, let me summarize briefly: Our didactic material renders auto-education possible, permits a methodical education of the senses. Not upon the ability of the teacher does such education rest, but upon the didactic system. This presents objects which, first, attract the spontaneous attention of the child, and, second, contain a rational gradation of stimuli.

We must not confuse the *education* of the senses, with the concrete ideas which may be gathered from our environment by means of the senses. Nor must this education of the senses be identical in our minds with the language through which is given the nomenclature corresponding to the concrete idea, nor with the acquisition of the abstract idea of the exercises.

Let us consider what the music master does in giving instruction in piano playing. He teaches the pupil the correct position of the body, gives him the idea of the notes, shows him the correspondence between the written notes and the touch and the position of the fingers, and then he leaves the child to perform the exercise by himself. If a pianist is to be made of this child, there must, between the ideas given by the teacher and the musical exercises, intervene long and patient application to those exercises which serve to give agility to the articulation of the fingers and of the tendons, in order that the coordination of special muscular movements shall become automatic, and that the muscles of the hand shall become strong through their repeated use.

The pianist must, therefore, *act for himself,* and the more his natural tendencies lead him to persist in these exercises the greater will be his success. However, without the direction of the master the exercise will not suffice to develop the scholar into a true pianist.

The directress of the "Children's House" must have a clear idea of the two factors which enter into her work–the guidance of the child, and the individual exercise.

Only after she has this concept clearly fixed in her mind, may she proceed to the application of a *method* to *guide* the spontaneous education of the child and to impart necessary notions to him.

In the opportune quality and in the manner of this intervention lies the *personal art* of the *educator*.

For example, in the "Children's House" in the Prati di Castello, where the pupils belong to the middle-class, I found, a month after the opening of the school, a child of five years who already knew how to compose any word, as he knew the alphabet perfectly–he had learned it in two weeks. He knew how to write on the blackboard, and in the exercises in free design he showed himself not only to be an observer, but to have some intuitive idea of perspective, drawing a house and chair very cleverly. As for the exercises of the chromatic sense, he could mix together the eight gradations of the eight colours which we use, and from this mass of sixty-four tablets, each wound with silk of a different colour or shade, he could rapidly separate the eight groups. Having done this, he would proceed with ease to arrange each colour series in perfect gradation. In this game the child would almost cover one of the little tables with a carpet of finely-shaded colours. I made the experiment, taking him to the window and showing him in full daylight one of the coloured tablets, telling him to look at it well, so that he might be able to remember it. I then sent him to the table on which all the gradations were spread out, and asked him to find the tablet like the one at which he had looked. He committed only very slight errors, often choosing the exact shade but more often the one next it, rarely a tint two grades removed from the right one. This boy had then a power of discrimination and a colour memory which were almost prodigious. Like all the other children, he was exceedingly fond of the colour exercises. But when I asked the name of the white colour spool, he hesitated for a long time before replying uncertainly "white." Now a child of such intelligence should have been able, even without the special intervention of the teacher, to learn the name of each colour.

The directress told me that having noticed that the child had great difficulty in retaining the nomenclature of the colours, she had up until that time left him to exercise himself freely with the games for the colour sense. At the same time he had developed rapidly a power over written language, which in my method is presented through a series of problems to be solved. These problems are presented as sense exercises. This child was, therefore, most intelligent. In him the discriminative sensory perceptions kept pace with great intellectual activities–attention and judgment. But his *memory for names* was inferior.

The directress had thought best not to interfere, as yet, in the teaching of the child. Certainly, the education of the child was a little disordered, and the directress had left the spontaneous explanation of his mental activities excessively free. However desirable it may be to furnish a sense education as a basis for intellectual ideas, it is nevertheless advisable at the same time to associate the *language* with these *perceptions*.

In this connection I have found excellent for use with normal children *the three periods* of which the lesson according to Séguin consists:

First Period. The association of the sensory perception with the name.

For example, we present to the child, two colours, red and blue. Presenting the red, we say simply, " This is red," and presenting the blue, "This is blue." Then, we lay the spools upon the table under the eyes of the child.

Second Period. Recognition of the object corresponding to the name. We say to the child, "Give me the red," and then, "Give me the blue."

Third Period. The remembering of the name corresponding to the object. We ask the child, showing him the object, "What is this?" and he should respond, "Red."

Séguin insists strongly upon these three periods, and urges that the colours be left for several instants under the eyes of the child. He also advises us never to present the colour singly, but always two at a time, since the contrast helps the chromatic memory. Indeed, I have proved that there cannot be a better method for teaching colour to the deficients, who, with this method were able to learn the colours much more perfectly than normal children in the ordinary schools who have had a haphazard sense education. For normal children however there exists a *period preceding* the Three Periods of Séguin–a period which contains the real *sense education*. This is the acquisition of a fineness of differential perception, which can be obtained *only* through auto-education.

This, then, is an example of the great superiority of the normal child, and of the greater effect of education which such pedagogical methods may exercise upon the mental development of normal as compared with deficient children.

The association of the name with the stimulus is a source of great pleasure to the normal child. I remember, one day, I had taught a little girl, who was not yet three years old, and who was a little tardy in the development of language, the names of three colours. I had the children place one of their little tables near a window, and seating myself in one of the little chairs, I seated the little girl in a similar chair at my right.

I had, on the table, six of the colour spools in pairs, that is two reds, two blues, two yellows. In the First Period, I placed one of the spools before the child, asking her to find the one like it. This I repeated for all three of the colours, showing her how to arrange them carefully in pairs. After this I passed to the Three Periods of Séguin. The little girl learned to recognise the three colours and to pronounce the name of each.

She was so happy that she looked at me for a long time, and then began to jump up and down. I, seeing her pleasure, said to her, laughing, "Do you know the colours?" and she replied, still jumping up and down, "Yes! YES!" Her delight was inexhaustible; she danced about me, waiting joyously for me to ask her the same question, that she might reply with the same enthusiasm, "Yes! Yes!"

Another important particular in the technique of sense education lies in *isolating the sense*, whenever this is possible. So, for example, the exercises on the sense of hearing can be given more successfully in an environment not only of silence, but even of darkness.

For the education of the senses in general, such as in the tactile, thermic, baric, and stereognostic exercises, we blindfold the child. The reasons for this particular technique have been fully set forth by psychology. Here, it is enough to note that in the case of normal children the blindfold greatly increases their interest, without making the exercises degenerate into noisy fun, and without having the child's attention attracted more to the *bandage* than to the sense-stimuli upon which we wish to *focus* the attention.   For example, in order to test the acuteness of the child's sense of hearing (a most important thing for the teacher to know), I use an empiric test which is coming to be used almost universally by physicians in the making of medical examinations. This test is made by modulating the voice, reducing it to a whisper. The child is blindfolded, or the teacher may stand behind him, speaking his name, in a *whisper* and from varying distances. I establish a *solemn silence* in the schoolroom, darken the windows, have the children bow their heads upon their hands which they hold in front of their eyes. Then I call the children by name, one by one, in a whisper, lighter for those who are nearer me, and more clearly for those farther away. Each child awaits, in the darkness, the faint voice which calls him, listening intently, ready to run with keenest joy toward the mysterious and much desired call.

The normal child may be blindfolded in the games where, for example, he is to recognise various weights, for this does help him to intensify and concentrate his attention upon the baric stimuli which he is to test. The blindfold adds to his pleasure, since he is proud of having been able to guess.

The effect of these games upon deficient children is very different. When placed in darkness, they often go to sleep, or give themselves up to disordered acts. When the blindfold is used, they fix their attention upon the bandage itself, and change the exercise into a game, which does not fulfil the end we have in view with the exercise.

We speak, it is true, of *games* in education, but it must be made clear that we understand by this term a free activity, ordered to a definite end; not disorderly noise, which distracts the attention.

The following pages of Itard give an idea of the patient experiments made by this pioneer in pedagogy. Their lack of success was due largely to errors which successive experiments have made it possible to correct, and in part to the mentality of his subject.

"IV: In this last experiment it was not necessary, as in the one preceding, to demand that the pupil repeat the sounds which he perceived. This double work, distributing his attention, was outside the plane of my purpose, which was to educate each organ separately. I, therefore, limited myself to following the simple perception of sounds. To be certain of this result, I placed my pupil in front of me with his eyes blinded, his fists closed, and had him extend a finger every time that I made a sound. He understood this arrangement, and as soon as the sound reached his ear, the finger was raised, with a species of impetuosity, and often with demonstrations of joy which left no doubt as to the pleasure the pupil took in these bizarre lessons. Indeed, whether it be that he found a real pleasure in the sound of the human voice, or that he had at last conquered the annoyance he at first felt on being deprived of the light for so long a time, the fact remains that more than once, during the intervals of rest, he came to me with his blindfold in his hand, holding it over his eyes, and jumping with joy when he felt my hands tying it about his head.

"V: Having thoroughly assured myself, through such experiments as the one described above, that all sounds of the voice, whatever their intensity, were perceived by Vittorio, I proceeded to the attempt of making him compare these sounds. It was no longer a case of simply noting the sounds of the voice, but of perceiving the differences and of appreciating all these modifications and varieties of tone which go to make up the music of the word. Between this task and the preceding there stretched a prodigious difference, especially for a being whose development was dependent upon gradual effort, and who advanced toward civilisation only because I led thitherward so gently that he was unconscious of the progress. Facing the difficulty now presented, I had need to arm myself more strongly than ever with patience and gentleness, encouraged by the hope that once I had surmounted this obstacle all would have been done for the sense of hearing.

"We began with the comparison of the vowel sounds, and here, too, made use of the hand to assure ourselves as to the result of our experiments. Each one of the fingers was made the sign of one of the five vowels. Thus the thumb represented A and was to be raised whenever this vowel was pronounced; the index finger was the sign for E; the middle finger for I; and so on.

"VI: Not without fatigue, and not for a long time, was I able to give a distinct idea of the vowels. The first to be clearly distinguished was O, and then followed A. The three others presented much greater difficulty, and were for a long time confused. At last, however, the ear began to perceive distinctly, and, then, there returned in all their vivacity, those demonstrations of joy of which I have spoken. This continued until the pleasure taken in the lessons began to be boisterous, the sounds became confused, and the finger was raised indiscriminately. The outbursts of laughter became indeed so excessive that I lost patience! As soon as I placed the blindfold over his eyes the shouts of laughter began."

Itard, finding it impossible to continue his educational work, decided to do away with the blindfold, and, indeed, the shouts ceased, but now the child's attention was distracted by the slightest movement about him. The blindfold was necessary, but the boy had to be made to understand that he must not laugh so much and that he was having a lesson. The corrective means of Itard and their touching results are worth reporting here!

"I wished to intimidate him with my manner, not being able to do so with my glance. I armed myself with a tambourine and struck it lightly whenever he made a mistake. But he mistook this correction for a joke, and his joy became more noisy than ever. I then felt that I must make the correction a little more severe. It was understood, and I saw, with a mixture of pain and pleasure, revealed in the darkened face of this boy the fact that the feeling of injury surpassed the unhappiness of the blow. Tears came from beneath the blindfold, he urged me to take it off, but, whether from embarrassment or fear, or from some inner preoccupation, when freed from the bandage he still kept his eyes tightly closed. I could not laugh at the doleful expression of his face, the closed eyelids from between which trickled an occasional tear! Oh, in this moment, as in many others, ready to renounce my task, and feeling that the time I had consecrated to it was lost, how I regretted ever having known this boy, and how severely I condemned the barren and inhuman curiosity of the men who in order to make scientific advancement had torn him away from a life, at least innocent and happy!"

Here also is demonstrated the great educative superiority of scientific pedagogy for normal children.

Finally, one particular of the technique consists in the *distribution of the stimuli.* This will be treated more fully in the description of the didactic system (materials) and of the sense education. Here it is enough to say that one should proceed from *few stimuli strongly contrasting, to many stimuli in gradual differentiation always more fine and imperceptible.* So, for example, we first present, together, red and blue; the shortest rod beside the longest; the thinnest beside the thickest, etc., passing from these to the delicately differing tints, and to the discrimination of very slight differences in length and size.

Education of the Senses and Illustrations of the Didactic Material: General Sensibility; the Tactile, Thermic, Baric, and Stereognostic Senses

The education of the tactile and the thermic senses go together, since the warm bath, and heat in general, render the tactile sense more acute. Since to exercise the tactile sense it is necessary to *touch*, bathing the hands in warm water has the additional advantage of teaching the child a principle of cleanliness–that of not touching objects with hands that are not clean. I therefore apply the general notions of practical life, regarding the washing of the hands, care of the nails, to the exercises preparatory to the discrimination of tactile stimuli.

The limitation of the exercises of the tactile sense to the cushioned tips of the fingers, is rendered necessary by practical life. It must be made a necessary phase of *education* because it prepares for a life in which man exercises and uses the tactile sense through the medium of these finger tips. Hence, I have the child wash his hands carefully with soap, in a little basin; and in another basin I have him rinse them in a bath of tepid water. Then I show him how to dry and rub his hands gently, in this way preparing for the regular bath. I next teach the child how to *touch*, that is, the manner in which he should touch surfaces. For this it is necessary to take the finger of the child and to draw *it very, very lightly over the surface.*

Another particular of the technique is to teach the child to hold his eyes closed while he touches, encouraging him to do this by telling him that he will be able to feel the differences better, and so leading him to distinguish, without the help of sight, the change of contact. He will quickly learn, and will show that he enjoys the exercise. Often, after the introduction of such exercises, it is a common thing to have a child come to you, and, closing his eyes, touch with great delicacy the palm of your hand or the cloth of your dress, especially any silken or velvet trimmings. They do verily *exercise* the tactile sense. They enjoy keenly touching any soft pleasant surface, and become exceedingly keen in discriminating between the differences in the sandpaper cards.

The Didactic Material consists of: *a* -a rectangular wooden board divided into two equal rectangles, one covered with very smooth paper, or having the wood polished until a smooth surface is obtained; the other covered with sandpaper. *b* -a tablet like the preceding covered with alternating strips of smooth paper and sandpaper.

I also make use of a collection of paper slips, varying through many grades from smooth, fine cardboard to coarsest sandpaper. The stuffs described elsewhere are also used in these lessons.

As to the Thermic Sense, I use a set of little metal bowls, which are filled with water at different degrees of temperature. These I try to measure with a thermometer, so that there may be two containing water of the same temperature.

I have designed a set of utensils which are to be made of very light metal, and filled with water. These have covers, and to each is attached a thermometer. The bowl touched from the outside gives the desired impression of heat.

I also have the children put their hands into cold, tepid, and warm water, an exercise which they find most diverting. I should like to repeat this exercise with the feet, but I have not had an opportunity to make the trial.

For the education of the baric sense (sense of weight), I use with great success little wooden tablets, six by eight centimetres, having a thickness of 1/2 centimetre. These tablets are in three different qualities of wood, wistaria, walnut, and pine. They weigh respectively, 24, 18, and 12 grammes, making them differ in weight by 6 grammes. These tablets should be very smooth; if possible, varnished in such a way that every roughness shall be eliminated, but so that the natural colour of the wood shall remain. The child, *observing* the colour, *knows* that they are of differing weights, and this offers a means of controlling the exercise. He takes two of the tablets in his hands, letting them rest upon the palm at the base of his outstretched fingers. Then he moves his hands up and down in order to gauge the weight. This movement should come to be, little by little, almost insensible. We lead the child to make his distinction purely through the difference in weight, leaving out the guide of the different colours, and closing his eyes. He learns to do this of himself, and takes great interest in "guessing."

The game attracts the attention of those near, who gather in a circle about the one who has the tablets, and who take turns in *guessing*. Sometimes the children spontaneously make use of the blindfold, taking turns, and interspersing the work with peals of joyful laughter.

Education of the Stereognostic Sense

The education of this sense leads to the recognition of objects through feeling, that is, through the simultaneous help of the tactile and muscular senses.

Taking this union as a basis, we have made experiments which have given marvellously successful educational results. I feel that for the help of teachers these exercises should be described.

The first didactic material used by us is made up of the bricks and cubes of Froebel. We call the attention of the child to the form of the two solids, have him feel them carefully and accurately, with his eyes open, repeating some phrase serving to fix his attention upon the particulars of the forms presented. After this the child is told to place the cubes to the right, the bricks to the left, always feeling them, and without looking at them. Finally the exercise is repeated, by the child blindfolded. Almost all the children succeed in the exercise, and after two or three times, are able to eliminate every error. There are twenty-four of the bricks and cubes in all, so that the attention may be held for some time through this "game"–but undoubtedly the child's pleasure is greatly increased by the fact of his being watched by a group of his companions, all interested and eager.

One day a directress called my attention to a little girl of three years, one of our very youngest pupils, who had repeated this exercise perfectly. We seated the little girl comfortably in an armchair, close to the table. Then, placing the twenty-four objects before her upon the table, we mixed them, and calling the child's attention to the difference in form, told her to place the cubes to the right and the bricks to the left. When she was blindfolded she began the exercise as taught by us, taking an object in each hand, feeling each and putting it in its right place. Sometimes she took two cubes, or two bricks, sometimes she found a brick in the right hand, a cube in the left. The child had to recognise the form, and to remember throughout the exercise the proper placing of the different objects. This seemed to me very difficult for a child of three years.

But observing her I saw that she not only performed the exercise easily, but that the movements with which we had taught her to feel the form were superfluous. Indeed the instant she had taken the two objects in her hands, if it so happened that she had taken a cube with the left hand and a brick in the right, she *exchanged* them *immediately*, and *then* began the laborious feeling the form which we had taught and which she perhaps, believed to be obligatory. But the objects had been recognised by her through *the first light touch*, that is, the *recognition was contemporaneous to the taking.*

Continuing my study of the subject, I found that this little girl was possessed of a remarkable *functional ambidexterity*—I should be very glad to make a wider study of this phenomenon having in view the desirability of a simultaneous education of both hands.

I repeated the exercise with other children and found that they *recognise* the objects before feeling their contours. This was particularly true of the *little ones*. Our educational methods in this respect furnished a remarkable exercise in associative gymnastics, leading to a rapidity of judgment which was truly surprising and had the advantage of being perfectly adapted to very young children.

These exercises of the stereognostic sense may be multiplied in many ways—they amuse the children who find delight in the recognition of a stimulus, as in the thermic exercises; for example—they may raise any small objects, toy soldiers, little balls, and, above all, the various *coins* in common use. They come to discriminate between small forms varying very slightly, such as corn, wheat, and rice.

They are very proud of *seeing without eyes,* holding out their hands and crying, "Here are my eyes!" "I can see with my hands!" Indeed, our little ones walking in the ways we have planned, make us marvel over their unforeseen progress, surprising us daily. Often, while they are wild with delight over some new conquest,-we watch, in deepest wonder and meditation.

Education of the Senses of Taste and Smell

This phase of sense education is most difficult, and I have not as yet had any satisfactory results to record. I can only say that the exercises ordinarily used in the tests of psychometry do not seem to me to be practical for use with young children.

The olfactory sense in children is not developed to any great extent, and this makes it difficult to attract their attention by means of this sense. We have made use of one test which has not been repeated often enough to form the basis of a method. We have the child smell fresh violets, and jessamine flowers. We then blindfold him, saying; "Now we are going to present you with flowers." A little friend then holds a bunch of violets under the child's nose, that he may guess the name of the flower. For greater or less intensity we present fewer flowers, or even one single blossom.

But this part of education, like that of the sense of taste, can be obtained by the child during the luncheon hour;–when he can learn to recognise various odours.

As to taste, the method of touching the tongue with various solutions, bitter or acid, sweet, salty, is perfectly applicable. Children of four years readily lend themselves to such games, which serve as a reason for showing them how to rinse their mouths perfectly. The children enjoy recognising various flavours, and learn, after each test, to fill a glass with tepid water, and carefully rinse their mouths. In this way the exercise for the sense of taste is also an exercise in hygiene.

Education of the Sense of Vision

I. Differential Visual Perception of Dimensions

First. Solid Insets: This material consists of three solid blocks of wood each 55 centimetres long, 6 centimetres high and 8 centimetres wide. Each block contains ten wooden pieces, set into corresponding holes. These pieces are cylindrical in shape and are to be handled by means of a little wooden or brass button which is fixed in the centre of the top. The cases of cylinders are in appearance much like the cases of weights used by chemists. In the first set of the series, the cylinders are all of equal height (55 millimetres) but differ in diameter. The smallest cylinder has a diameter of 1 centimetre, and the others increase in diameter at the rate of 1/2 centimetre. In the second set, the cylinders are all of equal diameter, corresponding to half the diameter of the largest cylinder in the preceding series–(27 millimetres). The cylinders in this set differ in height, the first being merely a little disk only a centimetre high, the others increase 5 millimetres each, the tenth one being 55 millimetres high. In the third set, the cylinders differ both in height and diameter, the first being 1 centimetre high and 1 centimetre in diameter and each succeeding one increasing 1/2 centimetre in height and diameter. With these insets, the child, working by himself, learns to differentiate objects according to *thickness*, according to *height*, and according to *size*.

In the schoolroom, these three sets may be played with by three children gathered about a table, an exchange of games adding variety. The child takes the cylinders out of the moulds, mixes them upon the table, and then puts each back into its corresponding opening. These objects are made of hard pine, polished and varnished.

Second. Large pieces in graded dimensions:–There are three sets of blocks which come under this head, and it is desirable to have two of each of these sets in every school.

(*a*) Thickness: this set consists of objects which vary from *thick* to *thin*. There are ten quadrilateral prisms, the largest of which has a base of 10 centimetres, the others decreasing by 1 centimetre. The pieces are of equal length, 20 centimetres. These prisms are stained a dark brown. The child mixes them, scattering them over the little carpet, and then puts them in order, placing one against the other according to the graduations of thickness, observing that the length shall correspond exactly. These blocks, taken from the first to the last, form a species of *stair*, the steps of which grow broader toward the top. The child may begin with the thinnest piece or with the thickest, as suits his pleasure. The control of the exercise is not certain, as it was in the solid cylindrical insets. There, the large cylinders could not enter the small opening, the taller ones would project beyond the top of the block, etc. In this game of the Big Stair, the *eye* of the child can easily recognise an error, since if he mistakes, the *stair* is irregular, that is, there will be a high step, behind which the step which should have ascended, decreases.

(*b*) Length: Long and Short Objects:–This set consists of *ten rods*. These are four-sided, each face being 3 centimetres. The first rod is a metre long, and the last a decimetre. The intervening rods decrease, from first to last, 1 decimetre each. Each space of 1 decimetre is painted alternately *red* or *blue*. The rods, when placed close to each other, must be so arranged that the colours correspond, forming so many transverse stripes–the whole set when arranged has the appearance of a rectangular triangle made up of organ pipes, which decrease on the side of the hypothenuse.

The child arranges the rods which have first been scattered and mixed. He puts them together according to the graduation of length, and observes the correspondence of colours. This exercise also offers a very evident control of error, for the regularity of the decreasing length of the stairs along the hypothenuse will be altered if the rods are not properly placed.

This most important set of blocks will have its principal application in arithmetic, as we shall see. With it, one may count from one to ten and may construct the addition and other tables, and it may constitute the first steps in the study of the decimal and metric system.

(c) Size: Objects, Larger and Smaller:–This set is made up of ten wooden cubes painted in rose-coloured enamel. The largest cube has a base of 10 centimetres, the smallest, of 1 centimetre, the intervening ones decrease 1 centimetre each. A little green cloth carpet goes with these blocks. This may be of oilcloth or cardboard. The game consists of building the cubes up, one upon another, in the order of their dimensions, constructing a little tower of which the largest cube forms the base and the smallest the apex. The carpet is placed on the floor, and the cubes are scattered upon it. As the tower is built upon the carpet, the child goes through the exercise of kneeling, rising, etc. The control is given by the irregularity of the tower as it decreases toward the apex. A cube misplaced reveals itself, because it breaks the line. The most common error made by the children in playing with these blocks at first, is that of placing the second cube as the base and placing the first cube upon it, thus confusing the two largest blocks. I have noted that the same error was made by deficient children in the repeated trials I made with the tests of De Sanctis. At the question, "Which is the largest?" the child would take, not the largest, but that nearest it in size.

Any of these three sets of blocks may be used by the children in a slightly different game. The pieces may be mixed upon a carpet or table, and then put in order upon another table at some distance. As he carries each piece, the child must walk without letting his attention wander, since he must remember the dimensions of the piece for which he is to look among the mixed blocks.

The games played in this way are excellent for children of four or five years; while the simple work of arranging the pieces in order upon the same carpet where they have been mixed is more adapted to the little ones between three and four years of age. The construction of the tower with the pink cubes is very attractive to little ones of less than three years, who knock it down and build it up time after time.

II. Differential Visual Perception of Form and Visual-tactile-muscular Perception

Didactic Material. Plane geometric *insets of wood:* The idea of these insets goes back to Itard and was also applied by Séguin.

In the school for deficients I had made and applied these insets in the same form used by my illustrious predecessors. In these there were two large tablets of wood placed one above the other and fastened together. The lower board was left solid, while the upper one was perforated by various geometric figures. The game consisted in placing in these openings the corresponding wooden figures which, in order that they might be easily handled, were furnished with a little brass knob.

In my school for deficients, I had multiplied the games calling for these insets, and distinguished between those used to teach colour and those used to teach form. The insets for teaching colour were all circles, those used for teaching form were all painted blue. I had great numbers of these insets made in graduations of colour, and in an infinite variety of form. This material was most expensive and exceedingly cumbersome.

In many later experiments with normal children, I have, after many trials, completely excluded the plane geometric insets as an aid to the teaching of colour, since this material offers no control of errors, the child's task being that of *covering* the forms before him.

I have kept the geometric insets, but have given them a new and original aspect. The form in which they are now made was suggested to me by a visit to the splendid manual training school in the Reformatory of St. Michael in Rome. I saw there wooden models of geometric figures, which could be set into corresponding frames or placed above corresponding forms. The scope of these materials was to lead to exactness in the making of the geometric pieces in regard to control of dimension and form; the *frame* furnishing the *control* necessary for the exactness of the work.

This led me to think of making modifications in my geometric insets, making use of the frame as well as of the inset. I therefore made a rectangular tray, which measured 30x20 centimetres. This tray was painted a dark blue and was surrounded by a dark frame. It was furnished with a cover so arranged that it would contain six of the square frames with their insets. The advantage of this tray is that the forms may be changed, thus allowing us to present any combination we choose. I have a number of blank wooden squares which make it possible to present as few as two or three geometric forms at a time, the other spaces being filled in by the blanks. To this material I have added a set of white cards, 10 centimetres square. These cards form a series presenting the geometric forms in other aspects. In the *first* of the series, the form is cut from blue paper and mounted upon the card. In the *second* box of cards, the *contour* of the same figures is mounted in the same blue paper, forming an outline one centimetre in width. On the *third* set of cards the contour of the geometric form is *outlined by a black line.* We have then the tray, the collection of small frames with their corresponding insets, and the set of the cards in three series.

I also designed a case containing six trays. The front of this box may be lowered when the top is raised and the trays may be drawn out as one opens the drawers of a desk. Each drawer contains six of the small frames with their respective insets. In the first drawer I keep the four plain wooden squares and two frames, one containing a rhomboid, and the other a trapezoid. In the second, I have a series consisting of a square, and five rectangles of the same length, but varying in width. The third drawer contains six circles which diminish in diameter. In the fourth are six triangles, in the fifth, five polygons from a pentagon to a decagon. The sixth drawer contains six curved figures (an ellipse, an oval, etc., and a flower-like figure formed by four crossed arcs).

Exercise with the Insets. This exercise consists in presenting to the child the large frame or tray in which we may arrange the figures as we wish to present them. We proceed to take out the insets, mix them upon the table, and then invite the child to put them back in place. This game may be played by even the younger children and holds the attention for a long period, though not for so long a time as the exercise with the cylinders. Indeed, I have never seen a child repeat this exercise more than five or six times. The child, in fact, expends much energy upon this exercise. He must *recognise* the form and must look at it carefully.

At first many of the children only succeed in placing the insets after many attempts, trying for example to place a triangle in a trapezoid, then in a rectangle, etc. Or when they have taken a rectangle, and recognise where it should go, they will still place it with the long side of the inset across the short side of the opening, and will only after many attempts, succeed in placing it. After three or four successive lessons, the child recognises the geometric figures with *extreme* facility and places the insets with a security which has a tinge of nonchalance, or of *slight contempt for an exercise that is too easy.* This is the moment in which the child may be led to a methodical observation of the forms. We change the forms in the frame and pass from contrasted frames to analogous ones. The exercise is easy for the child, who habituates himself to placing the pieces in their frames without errors or false attempts.

The first period of these exercises is at the time when the child is obliged to make repeated *trials* with figures that are strongly contrasted in form. The *recognition* is greatly helped by associating with the visual sense the muscular-tactile perception of the forms. I have the child touch the contour of the piece with the *index finger of his right hand,* and then have him repeat this with the contour of the frame into which the pieces must fit. We succeed in making this a *habit* with the child. This is very easily attained, since all children love to touch things. I have already learned, through my work with deficient children, that among the various forms of sense memory that of the muscular sense is the most precocious. Indeed, many children who have not arrived at the point of recognising a *figure by looking at it,* could recognise it by *touching it,* that is, by computing the movements necessary to the following of its contour. The same is true of the greater number of normal children;–confused as to where to place a figure, they turn it about trying in vain to fit it in, yet as soon as they have touched the two contours of the piece and its frame, they succeed in placing it perfectly. Undoubtedly, the association of the muscular-tactile sense with that of vision, aids in a most remarkable way the perception of forms and fixes them in memory.

In such exercises, the control is absolute, as it was in the solid insets. The figure can only enter the corresponding frame. This makes it possible for the child to work by himself, and to accomplish a genuine sensory auto-education, in the visual perception of form.

Exercise with the three series of cards. First series. We give the child the wooden forms and the cards upon which the white figure is mounted. Then we mix the cards upon the table; the child must arrange them in a line upon his table (which he loves to do), and then place the corresponding wooden pieces upon the cards. Here the control lies in the eyes. The child must *recognise* this figure, and place the wooden piece upon it so perfectly that it will cover and hide the paper figure. The eye of the child here corresponds to the frame, which *materially* led him at first to bring the two pieces together. In addition to covering the figure, the child is to accustom himself to *touching* the contour of the mounted figures as a part of the exercise (the child always voluntarily follows those movements); and after he has placed the wooden inset he again touches the contour, adjusting with his finger the superimposed piece until it exactly covers the form beneath.

Second Series. We give a number of cards to the child together with the corresponding wooden insets. In this second series, the figures are repeated by an outline of blue paper. The child through these exercises is passing gradually from the *concrete* to the *abstract.* At first, he handled only *solid objects.* He then passed to a *plane figure,* that is, to the plane which in itself does not exist. He is now passing to the *line,* but this line does not represent for him the abstract contour of a plane figure. It is to him the *path, which he has so often followed with his index finger;* this line is the *trace of a movement.* Following again the contour of the figure with his finger, the child receives the impression of actually leaving a trace, for the figure is covered by his finger and appears as he moves it. It is the eye now which guides the movement, but it must be remembered that this movement was *already prepared* for when the child touched the contours of the solid pieces of wood.

Third Series. We now present to the child the cards upon which the figures are drawn in black, giving him, as before, the corresponding wooden pieces. Here, he has actually passed to the *line;* that is, to an abstraction, yet here, too, there is the idea of the result of a movement.

This cannot be, it is true, the trace left by the finger, but, for example, that of a pencil which is guided by the hand in the same movements made before. These geometric figures in simple outline *have grown out* of a gradual series of representations which were concrete to vision and touch. These representations return to the mind of the child when he performs the exercise of superimposing the corresponding wooden figures.

III. Differential Visual Perception of Contours:–Education of the Chromatic Sense

In many of our *lessons on the colours,* we make use of pieces of brightly-coloured stuffs, and of balls covered with wool of different colours. The didactic material for the *education of the chromatic* sense is the following, which I have established after a long series of tests made upon normal children, (in the institute for deficients, I used as I have said above, the geometric inserts). The present material consists of small flat tablets, which are wound with coloured wool or silk. These tablets have a little wooden border at each end which prevents the silk-covered card from touching the table. The child is also taught to take hold of the piece by these wooden extremities, so that he need not soil the delicate colours. In this way, we are able to use this material for a long time without having to renew it.

I have chosen eight tints and each one has with it eight gradations of different intensity of colour. There are, therefore, sixty-four colour-tablets in all. The eight tints selected are *black (from grey to white), red, orange, yellow, green, blue, violet,* and *brown.* We have duplicate boxes of these sixty-four colours, giving us two of each exercise. The entire set, therefore, consists of one hundred twenty-eight tablets. They are contained in two boxes, each divided into eight equal compartments so that one box may contain sixty-four tablets.

Exercises with the Colour-tablets. For the earliest of these exercises, we select three strong colours: for example, *red, blue,* and *yellow,* in pairs. These six tablets we place upon the table before the child. Showing him one of the colours, we ask him to find its duplicate among the mixed tablets upon the table. In this way, we have him arrange the colour-tablets in a column, two by two, pairing them according to colour.

The number of tablets in this game may be increased until the eight colours, or sixteen tablets, are given at once. When the strongest tones have been presented, we may proceed to the presentation of the lighter tones, in the same way. Finally, we present two or three tablets of the same colour, but of different tone, showing the child how to arrange these in order of gradation. In this way, the eight gradations are finally presented.

Following this, we place before the child the eight gradations of two different colours (red and blue); he is shown how to separate the groups and then arrange each group in gradation. As we proceed, we offer groups of more nearly related colours; for example, blue and violet, yellow and orange, etc.

In one of the "Children's Houses," I have seen the following game played with the greatest success and interest, and with surprising *rapidity*. The directress places upon a table, about which the children are seated, as many colour groups as there are children, for example, three. She then calls each child's attention to the colour each is to select, or which she assigns to him. Then, she mixes the three groups of colours upon the table. Each child takes rapidly from the mixed heap of tablets all the gradations of his colour, and proceeds to arrange the tablets, which, when thus placed in a line, give the appearance of a strip of shaded ribbon.

In another "House," I have seen the children take the entire box, empty the sixty-four colour-tablets upon the table and after carefully mixing them, rapidly collect them into groups and arrange them in gradation, constructing a species of little carpet of delicately coloured and intermingling tints. The children very quickly acquire an ability before which we stand amazed. Children of three years are able to put all of the tints into gradation.

Experiments in Colour-memory. Experiments in colour-memory may be made by showing the child a tint, allowing him to look at it as long as he will, and then asking him to go to a distant table upon which all of the colours are arranged and to select from among them the tint similar to the one at which he has looked. The children succeed in this game remarkably, committing only slight errors. Children of five years enjoy this immensely, taking great pleasure in comparing the two spools and judging as to whether they have chosen correctly.

At the beginning of my work, I made use of an instrument invented by Pizzoli. This consisted of a small brown disk having a half-moon shape opening at the top. Various colours were made to pass behind this opening, by means of a rotary disk which was composed of strips of various colours. The teacher called the attention of the child to a certain colour, then turned the disk, asking him to indicate the same disk when it again showed itself in the opening. This exercise rendered the child inactive, preventing him from controlling the material. It is not, therefore, an instrument which can promote the *education* of the senses.

Exercise for the Discrimination of Sounds

It would be desirable to have in this connection the didactic material used for the "auricular education" in the principal institutions for deaf mutes in Germany and America. These exercises are an introduction to the acquisition of language, and serve in a very special way to centre the children's discriminative attention upon the "modulations of the sound of the human voice."

With very young children linguistic education must occupy a most important place. Another aim of such exercises is to educate the ear of the child to noises so that he shall accustom himself to distinguish every slight noise and compare it with *sounds*, coming to resent harsh or disordered noises. Such sense education has a value in that it exercises aesthetic taste, and may be applied in a most noteworthy way to practical discipline. We all know how the younger children disturb the order of the room by shouts, and by the noise of over-turned objects.

The rigorous scientific education of the sense of hearing is not practically applicable to the didactic method. This is true because the child cannot *exercise himself through his own activity* as he does for the other senses. Only one child at a time can work with any instrument producing the gradation of sounds. In other words, *absolute silence* is necessary for the discrimination of sounds.

Signorina Maccheroni, Directress, first of the "Children's House" in Milan and later in the one in Franciscan Convent at Rome, has invented and has had manufactured a series of thirteen bells hung upon a wooden frame. These bells are to all appearances, identical, but the vibrations brought about by a blow of a hammer produce the following thirteen notes:

The set consists of a double series of thirteen bells and there are four hammers. Having struck one of the bells in the first series, the child must find the corresponding sound in the second. This exercise presents grave difficulty, as the child does not know how to strike each time with the same force, and therefore produces sounds which vary in intensity. Even when the teacher strikes the bells, the children have difficulty distinguishing between sounds. So we do not feel that this instrument in its present form is entirely practical.

For the discrimination of sounds, we use Pizzoli's series of little whistles. For the gradation of noises, we use small boxes filled with different substances, more or less fine (sand or pebbles). The noises are produced by shaking the boxes.

In the lessons for the sense of hearing I proceed as follows: I have the teachers establish silence in the usual way and then I *continue* the work, making the silence more profound. I say, "St! St!" in a series of modulations, now sharp and short, now prolonged and light as a whisper. The children, little by little, become fascinated by this. Occasionally I say, "More silent still–more silent."

I then begin the sibilant St! St! again, making it always lighter and repeating "More silent still," in a barely audible whisper, "Now, I hear the clock, now I can hear the buzzing of a fly's wings, now I can hear the whisper of the trees in the garden."

The children, ecstatic with joy, sit in such absolute and complete silence that the room seems deserted; then I whisper, "Let us close our eyes." This exercise repeated, so habituates the children to immobility and absolute silence that, when one of them interrupts, it needs only a syllable, a gesture to call him back immediately to perfect order.

In the silence, we proceeded to the production of sounds and noises, making these at first strongly contrasted, then, more nearly alike. Sometimes we present the comparisons between noise and sound. I believe that the best results can be obtained with the primitive means employed by Itard in 1805. He used the drum and the bell. His plan was a graduated series of drums for the noises,-or, better, for the heavy harmonic sounds, since these belong to a musical instrument,-and a series of bells. The diapason, the whistles, the boxes, are not attractive to the child, and do not educate the sense of hearing as do these other instruments. There is an interesting suggestion in the fact that the two great human institutions, that of hate (war), and that of love (religion), have adopted these two opposite instruments, the drum and the bell.

I believe that after establishing silence it would be educational to ring well-toned bells, now calm and sweet, now clear and ringing, sending their vibrations through the child's whole body. And when, besides the education of the ear, we have produced a *vibratory* education of the ear, we have produced a *vibratory* education of the whole body, through these wisely selected sounds of the bells, giving a peace that pervades the very fibres of his being, then I believe these young bodies would be sensitive to crude noises, and the children would come to dislike, and to cease from making, disordered and ugly noises.

In this way one whose ear has been trained by a musical education suffers from strident or discordant notes. I need give no illustration to make clear the importance of such education for the masses in childhood. The new generation would be more calm, turning away from the confusion and the discordant sounds, which strike the ear to-day in one of the vile tenements where the poor live, crowded together, left by us to abandon themselves to the lower, more brutal human instincts.

Musical Education

This must be carefully guided by method. In general, we see little children pass by the playing of some great musicians as an animal would pass. They do not perceive the delicate complexity of sounds. The street children gather about the organ grinder, crying out as if to hail with joy the *noises* which will come instead of sounds.

For the musical education we must *create instruments* as well as music. The scope of such an instrument in addition to the discrimination of sounds, is to awaken a sense of rhythm, and, so to speak, to give the *impulse* toward calm and co-ordinate movements to those muscles already vibrating in the peace and tranquillity of immobility.

I believe that stringed instruments (perhaps some very much simplified harp) would be the most convenient. The stringed instruments together with the drum and the bells form the trio of the classic instruments of humanity. The harp is the instrument of "the intimate life of the individual." Legend places it in the hands of Orpheus, folk-lore puts it into fairy hands, and romance gives it to the princess who conquers the heart of a wicked prince.

The teacher who turns her back upon her scholars to play, (far too often badly), will never be the *educator* of their musical sense.

The child needs to be charmed in every way, by the glance as well as by the pose. The teacher who, bending toward them, gathering them about her, and leaving them free to stay or go, touches the chords, in a simple rhythm, puts herself in communication with them, *in relation with their very souls.* So much the better if this touch can be accompanied by her voice, and the children left free to follow her, no one being obliged to sing. In this way she can select as "adapted to education," those songs which were followed by all the children. So she may regulate the complexity of rhythm to various ages, for she will see now only the older children following the rhythm, now, also the little ones. At any rate, I believe that simple and primitive instruments are the ones best adapted to the awakening of music in the soul of the little child.

I have tried to have the Directress of the "Children's House" in Milan, who is a gifted musician, make a number of trials and experiments, with a view to finding out more about the muscular capacity of young children. She has made many trials with the pianoforte, observing how the children *are not sensitive* to the musical *tone,* but only to the *rhythm.* On a basis of rhythm she arranged simple little dances, with the intention of studying the influence of the rhythm itself upon the co-ordination of muscular movements. She was greatly surprised to discover the *educational disciplinary* effect of such music. Her children, who had been led with great wisdom and art through liberty to a *spontaneous* ordering of their acts and movements, had nevertheless lived in the streets and courts, and had an almost universal habit of jumping.

Being a faithful follower of the method of liberty, and not considering that *jumping* was a wrong act, she had never corrected them.

She now noticed that as she multiplied and repeated the rhythm exercises, the children little by little left off their ugly jumping, until finally it was a thing of the past. The directress one day asked for an explanation of this change of conduct. Several little ones looked at her without saying anything. The older children gave various replies, whose meaning was the same.

"It isn't nice to jump."

"Jumping is ugly."

"It's rude to jump."

This was certainly a beautiful triumph for our method!

This experience shows that it is possible to educate the child's *muscular sense,* and it shows how exquisite the refinement of this sense may be as it develops in relation to the *muscular memory,* and side by side with the other forms of sensory memory.

Tests for Acuteness of Hearing

The only entirely successful experiments which we have made so far in the "Children's Houses" are those of the *clock*, and of the *lowered* or whispered *voice*. The trial is purely empirical, and does not lend itself to the measuring of the sensation, but it is, however, most useful in that it helps us to an approximate knowledge of the child's auditory acuteness.

The exercise consists in calling attention, when perfect silence has been established, to the ticking of the clock, and to all the little noises not commonly audible to the ear. Finally we call the little ones, one by one from an adjoining room, pronouncing each name in a low voice. In preparing for such an exercise it is necessary to *teach* the children the real meaning of *silence*.

Toward this end I have several *games of silence*, which help in a surprising way to strengthen the remarkable discipline of our children.

I call the children's attention to myself, telling them to see how silent I can be. I assume different positions; standing, sitting, and maintain each pose *silently, without movement*. A finger moving can produce a noise, even though it be imperceptible. We may breathe so that we may be heard. But I maintain *absolute* silence, which is not an easy thing to do. I call a child, and ask him to do as I am doing. He adjusts his feet to a better position, and this makes a noise! He moves an arm, stretching it out upon the arm of his chair; it is a noise. His breathing is not altogether silent, it is not tranquil, absolutely unheard as mine is.

During these manoeuvres on the part of the child, and while my brief comments are followed by intervals of immobility and silence, the other children are watching and listening. Many of them are interested in the fact, which they have never noticed before; namely, that we make so many noises of which we are not conscious, and that there are *degrees* of *silence*. There is an absolute silence where nothing, *absolutely nothing* moves. They watch me in amazement when I stand in the middle of the room, so quietly that it is really as if "I were not." Then they strive to imitate me, and to do even better. I call attention here and there to a foot that moves, almost inadvertently. The attention of the child is called to every part of his body in an anxious eagerness to attain to immobility.

When the children are trying in this way, there is established a silence very different from that which we carelessly call by that name.

It seems as if life gradually vanishes, and that the room becomes, little by little, empty, as if there were no longer anyone in it. Then we begin to hear the tick-tock of the clock, and this sound seems to grow in intensity as the silence becomes absolute. From without, from the court which before seemed silent, there come varied noises, a bird chirps, a child passes. The children sit fascinated by that silence as if by some conquest of their own. "Here," says the directress, "here there is no longer anyone; the children have all gone away."

Having arrived at that point, we darken the windows, and tell the children to close their eyes, resting their heads upon their hands. They assume this position, and in the darkness the absolute silence returns.

"Now listen," we say. "A soft voice is going to call your name." Then going to a room behind the children, and standing within the open door, I call in a low voice, lingering over the syllables as if I were calling from across the mountains. This voice, almost occult, seems to reach the heart and to call to the soul of the child. Each one as he is called, lifts his head, opens his eyes as if altogether happy, then rises, silently seeking not to move the chair, and walks on the tips of his toes, so quietly that he is scarcely heard. Nevertheless his step resounds in the silence, amid the immobility which persists.

Having reached the door, with a joyous face, he leaps into the room, choking back soft outbursts of laughter. Another child may come to hide his face against my dress, another, turning, will watch his companions sitting like statutes, silent and waiting. The one who is called feels that he is privileged, that he has received a gift, a prize. And yet they know that all will be called, "beginning with the most silent one in the room." So each one tries to merit by his perfect silence the certain call. I once saw a little one of three years try to suffocate a sneeze, and succeed! She held her breath in her little breast, and resisted, coming out victorious. A most surprising effort!

This game delights the little ones beyond measure. Their intent faces, their patient immobility, reveal the enjoyment of a great pleasure. In the beginning, when the soul of the child was unknown to me, I had thought of showing them sweetmeats and little toys, promising to give them to the ones who were *called*, supposing that the gifts would be necessary to persuade the child to make the necessary effort. But I soon found that this was unnecessary.

The children, after they had made the effort necessary to maintain silence, enjoyed the sensation, took pleasure in the *silence* itself. They were like ships safe in a tranquil harbour, happy in having experienced something new, and to have won a victory over themselves. This, indeed, was their recompense. They *forgot* the promise of sweets, and no longer cared to take the toys, which I had supposed would attract them. I therefore abandoned that useless means, and saw, with surprise, that the game became constantly more perfect, until even children of three years of age remained immovable in the silence throughout the time required to call the entire forty children out of the room!

It was then that I learned that the soul of the child has its own reward, and its peculiar spiritual pleasures. After such exercises it seemed to me that the children became closer to me, certainly they became more obedient, more gentle and sweet. We had, indeed, been isolated from the world, and had passed several minutes during which the communion between us was very close, I wishing for them and calling to them, and they receiving in the perfect silence the voice which was directed personally toward each one of them, crowning each in turn with happiness.

A Lesson in Silence

I am about to describe a lesson which *proved* most successful in teaching the perfect silence to which it is possible to attain. One day as I was about to enter one of the "Children's Houses," I met in the court a mother who held in her arms her little baby of four months. The little one was swaddled, as is still the custom among the people of Rome–an infant thus in the swaddling bands is called by us a *pupa*. This tranquil little one seemed the incarnation of peace. I took her in my arms, where she lay quiet and good. Still holding her I went toward the schoolroom, from which the children now ran to meet me. They always welcomed me thus, throwing their arms about me, clinging to my skirts, and almost tumbling me over in their eagerness. I smiled at them, showing them the "*pupa*." They understood and skipped about me looking at me with eyes brilliant with pleasure, but did not touch me through respect for the little one that I held in my arms.

I went into the schoolroom with the children clustered about me. We sat down, I seating myself in a large chair instead of, as usual, in one of their little chairs. In other words, I seated myself solemnly. They looked at my little one with a mixture of tenderness and joy. None of us had yet spoken a word. Finally I said to them, "I have brought you a little teacher." Surprised glances and laughter. "A little teacher, yes, because none of you know how to be quiet as she does." At this all the children changed their positions and became quiet. "Yet no one holds his limbs and feet as quietly as she." Everyone gave closer attention to the position of limbs and feet. I looked at them smiling, "Yes, but they can never be as quiet as hers. You move a little bit, but she, not at all; none of you can be as quiet as she." The children looked serious. The idea of the superiority of the little teacher seemed to have reached them. Some of them smiled, and seemed to say with their eyes that the swaddling bands deserved all the merit. "Not one of you can be silent, voiceless as she." General silence. "It is not possible to be as silent as she, because,–listen to her breathing–how delicate it is; come near to her on your tiptoes."

Several children rose, and came slowly forward on tiptoe, bending toward the baby. Great silence. "None of you can breathe so silently as she." The children looked about amazed, they had never thought that even when sitting quietly they were making noises, and that the silence of a little babe is more profound than the silence of grown people. They almost ceased to breathe. I rose. "Go out quietly, quietly," I said, "walk on the tips of your toes and make no noise." Following them, I said, "And yet I still hear some sounds, but she, the baby, walks with me and makes no sound. She goes out silently." The children smiled. They understood the truth and the jest of my words. I went to the open window, and placed the baby in the arms of the mother who stood watching us.

The little one seemed to have left behind her a subtle charm which enveloped the souls of the children. Indeed, there is in nature nothing more sweet than the silent breathing of a new-born babe. There is an indescribable majesty about this human life which in repose and silence gathers strength and newness of life. Compared to this, Wordsworth's description of the silent peace of nature seems to lose its force. "What calm, what quiet! The one sound the drip of the suspended oar." The children, too, felt the poetry and beauty in the peaceful silence of a new-born human life.

General Notes on the Education of the Senses

I do not claim to have brought to perfection the method of sense training as applied to young children. I do believe, however, that it opens a new field for psychological research, promising rich and valuable results.

Experimental psychology has so far devoted its attention to *perfecting the instruments by which the sensations are measured*. No one has attempted the *methodical* preparation *of the individual for the sensations*. It is my belief that the development of psychometry will owe more to the attention given to the preparation of the *individual* than to the perfecting of the *instrument*.

But putting aside this purely scientific side of the question, the *education of the senses* must be of the greatest *pedagogical* interest.

Our aim in education in general is two-fold, biological and social. From the biological side we wish to help the natural development of the individual, from the social standpoint it is our aim to prepare the individual for the environment. Under this last head technical education may be considered as having a place, since it teaches the individual to make use of his surroundings. The education of the senses is most important from both these points of view. The development of the senses indeed precedes that of superior intellectual activity and the child between three and seven years is in the period of formation.

We can, then, help the development of the senses while they are in this period. We may graduate and adapt the stimuli just as, for example, it is necessary to help the formation of language before it shall be completely developed.

All education of little children must be governed by this principle–to help the natural *psychic* and *physical development* of the child.

The other aim of education (that of adapting the individual to the environment) should be given more attention later on when the period of intense development is past.

These two phases of education are always interlaced, but one or the other has prevalence according to the age of the child. Now, the period of life between the ages of three and seven years covers a period of rapid physical development. It is the time for the formation of the sense activities as related to the intellect. The child in this age develops his senses. His attention is further attracted to the environment under the form of passive curiosity.

The stimuli, and not yet the reasons for things, attract his attention. This is, therefore, the time when we should methodically direct the sense stimuli, in such a way that the sensations which he receives shall develop in a rational way. This sense training will prepare the ordered foundation upon which he may build up a clear and strong mentality.

It is, besides all this, possible with the education of the senses to discover and eventually to correct defects which to-day pass unobserved in the school. Now the time comes when the defect manifests itself in an evident and irreparable inability to make use of the forces of life about him. (Such defects as deafness and near-sightedness.) This education, therefore, is physiological and prepares directly for intellectual education, perfecting the organs of sense, and the nerve-paths of projection and association.

But the other part of education, the adaptation of the individual to his environment, is indirectly touched. We prepare with our method the infancy of the *humanity of our time*. The men of the present civilisation are pre-eminently observers of their environment because they must utilise to the greatest possible extent all the riches of this environment.

The art of to-day bases itself, as in the days of the Greeks, upon observation of the truth.

The progress of positive science is based upon its observations and all its discoveries and their applications, which in the last century have so transformed our civic environment, were made by following the same line–that is, they have come through observation. We must therefore prepare the new generation for this attitude, which has become necessary in our modern civilised life. It is an indispensable means–man must be so armed if he is to continue efficaciously the work of our progress.

We have seen the discovery of the Roentgen Rays born of observation. To the same methods are due the discovery of Hertzian waves, and vibrations of radium, and we await wonderful things from the Marconi telegraph. While there has been no period in which thought has gained so much from positive study as the present century, and this same century promises new light in the field of speculative philosophy and upon spiritual questions, the theories upon the matter have themselves led to most interesting metaphysical concepts. We may say that in preparing the method of observation, we have also prepared the way leading to spiritual discovery.

The education of the senses makes men observers, and not only accomplishes the general work of adaptation to the present epoch of civilisation, but also prepares them directly for practical life. We have had up to the present time, I believe, a most imperfect idea of what is necessary in the practical living of life. We have always started from ideas, and have *proceeded thence to motor activities*; thus, for example, the method of education has always been to teach intellectually, and then to have the child follow the principles he has been taught. In general, when we are teaching, we talk about the object which interests us, and then we try to lead the scholar, when he has understood, to perform some kind of work with the object itself; but often the scholar who has understood the idea finds great difficulty in the execution of the work which we give him, because we have left out of his education a factor of the utmost importance, namely, the perfecting of the senses. I may, perhaps, illustrate this statement with a few examples. We ask the cook to buy only 'fresh fish.' She understands the idea, and tries to follow it in her marketing, but, if the cook has not been trained to recognise through sight and smell the signs which indicate freshness in the fish, she will not know how to follow the order we have given her.

Such a lack will show itself much more plainly in culinary operations. A cook may be trained in book matters, and may know exactly the recipes and the length of time advised in her cook book; she may be able to perform all the manipulations necessary to give the desired appearance to the dishes, but when it is a question of deciding from the odor of the dish the exact moment of its being properly cooked, or with the eye, or the taste, the time at which she must put in some given condiment, then she will make a mistake if her senses have not been sufficiently prepared.

She can only gain such ability through long practice, and such practice on the part of the cook is nothing else than a *belated education* of the senses–an education which often can never be properly attained by the adult. This is one reason why it is so difficult to find good cooks.

Something of the same kind is true of the physician, the student of medicine who studies theoretically the character of the pulse, and sits down by the bed of the patient with the best will in the world to read the pulse, but, if his fingers do not know how to read the sensations his studies will have been in vain. Before he can become a doctor, he must gain a *capacity for discriminating between sense stimuli.*

The same may be said for the *pulsations* of the *heart,* which the student studies in theory, but which the ear can learn to distinguish only through practice.

We may say the same for all the delicate vibrations and movements, in the reading of which the hand of the physician is too often deficient. The thermometer is the more indispensable to the physician the more his sense of touch is unadapted and untrained in the gathering of the thermic stimuli. It is well understood that the physician may be learned, and most intelligent, without being a good practitioner, and that to make a good practitioner long practice is necessary. In reality, this *long practice* is nothing else than a tardy, and often inefficient, *exercise* of the senses. After he has assimilated the brilliant theories, the physician sees himself forced to the unpleasant labor of the semiography, that is to making a record of the symptoms revealed by his observation of and experiments with the patients. He must do this if he is to receive from these theories any practical results.

Here, then, we have the beginner proceeding in a stereotyped way to tests of *palpation,* percussion, and auscultation, for the purpose of identifying the throbs, the resonance, the tones, the breathings, and the various sounds which *alone* can enable him to formulate a diagnosis. Hence the deep and unhappy discouragement of so many young physicians, and, above all, the loss of time; for it is often a question of lost years. Then, there is the immorality of allowing a man to follow a profession of so great responsibility, when, as is often the case, he is so unskilled and inaccurate in the taking of symptoms. The whole art of medicine is based upon an education of the senses; the schools, instead, *prepare* physicians through a study of the classics. All very well and good, but the splendid intellectual development of the physician falls, impotent, before the insufficiency of his senses.

One day, I heard a surgeon giving, to a number of poor mothers, a lesson on the recognition of the first deformities noticeable in little children from the disease of rickets. It was his hope to lead these mothers to bring to him their children who were suffering from this disease, while the disease was yet in the earliest stages, and when medical help might still be efficacious. The mothers understood the idea, but they did not know how to recognise these first signs of deformity, because they were lacking in the sensory education through which they might discriminate between signs deviating only slightly from the normal.

Therefore those lessons were useless. If we think of it for a minute, we will see that almost all the forms of adulteration in food stuffs are rendered possible by the torpor of the senses, which exists in the greater number of people. Fraudulent industry feeds upon the lack of sense education in the masses, as any kind of fraud is based upon the ignorance of the victim. We often see the purchaser throwing himself upon the honesty of the merchant, or putting his faith in the company, or the label upon the box. This is because purchasers are lacking in the capacity of judging directly for themselves. They do not know how to distinguish with their senses the different qualities of various substances. In fact, we may say that in many cases intelligence is rendered useless by lack of practice, and this practice is almost always sense education. Everyone knows in practical life the fundamental necessity of judging with exactness between various stimuli.

But very often sense education is most difficult for the adult, just as it is difficult for him to educate his hand when he wishes to become a pianist. It is necessary to begin the education of the senses in the formative period, if we wish to perfect this sense development with the education which is to follow. The education of the senses should be begun methodically in infancy, and should continue during the entire period of instruction which is to prepare the individual for life in society.

Æsthetic and moral education are closely related to this sensory education. Multiply the sensations, and develop the capacity of appreciating fine differences in stimuli and we *refine* the sensibility and multiply man's pleasures.

Beauty lies in harmony, not in contrast; and harmony is refinement; therefore, there must be a fineness of the senses if we are to appreciate harmony. The æsthetic harmony of nature is lost upon him who has coarse senses. The world to him is narrow and barren. In life about us, there exist inexhaustible fonts of æsthetic enjoyment, before which men pass as insensible as the brutes seeking their enjoyment in those sensations which are crude and showy, since they are the only ones accessible to them.

Now, from the enjoyment of gross pleasures, vicious habits very often spring. Strong stimuli, indeed, do not render acute, but blunt the senses, so that they require stimuli more and more accentuated and more and more gross.

Onanism, so often found among normal children of the lower classes, alcoholism, fondness for watching sensual acts of adults–these things represent the enjoyment of those unfortunate ones whose intellectual pleasures are few, and whose senses are blunted and dulled. Such pleasures kill the man within the individual, and call to life the beast.

Indeed from the physiological point of view, the importance of the education of the senses is evident from an observation of the scheme of the diagrammatic arc which represents the functions of the nervous system. The external stimulus acts upon the organ of sense, and the impression is transmitted along the centripetal way to the nerve centre–the corresponding motor impulse is elaborated, and is transmitted along the centrifugal path to the organ of motion, provoking a movement. Although the arc represents diagrammatically the mechanism of reflex spinal actions, it may still be considered as a fundamental key explaining the phenomena of the more complex nervous mechanisms. Man, with the peripheral sensory system, gathers various stimuli from his environment. He puts himself thus in direct communication with his surroundings. The psychic life develops, therefore, in relation to the system of nerve centres; and human activity which is eminently social activity, manifests itself through acts of the individual–manual work, writing, spoken language, etc.–by means of the psychomotor organs.

Education should guide and perfect the development of the three periods, the two peripheral and the central; or, better still, since the process fundamentally reduces itself to the nerve centres, education should give to psychosensory exercises the same importance which it gives to psychomotor exercises.

Otherwise, we *isolate* man from his *environment*. Indeed, when with *intellectual culture* we believe ourselves to have completed education, we have but made thinkers, whose tendency will be to live without the world. We have not made practical men. If, on the other hand, wishing through education to prepare for practical life, we limit ourselves to exercising the psychomotor phase, we lose sight of the chief end of education, which is to put man in direct communication with the external world.

Since *professional work* almost always requires man to *make use of his surroundings*, the technical schools are not forced to return to the very beginnings of education, sense exercises, in order to supply the great and universal lack.

Intellectual Education

"...To lead the child from the education of the senses to ideas." Edward Séguin.

The sense exercises constitute a species of auto-education, which, if these exercises be many times repeated, leads to a perfecting of the child's psychosensory processes. The directress must intervene to lead the child from sensations to ideas–from the concrete to the abstract, and to the association of ideas. For this, she should use a method tending to isolate the inner attention of the child and to fix it upon the perceptions–as in the first lessons his objective attention was fixed, through isolation, upon single stimuli.

The teacher, in other words, when she gives a lesson must seek to limit the field of the child's consciousness to the object of the lesson, as, for example, during the sense education she isolated the sense which she wished the child to exercise.

For this, knowledge of a special technique is necessary. The educator must, *"to the greatest possible extent, limit his intervention; yet he must not allow the child to weary himself in an undue effort of auto-education. "*

It is here, that the factor of individual limitation and differing degrees of perception are most keenly felt in the teacher. In other words, in the quality of this intervention lies the art which makes up the individuality of the teacher.

A definite and undoubted part of the teacher's work is that of teaching an exact nomenclature.

She should, in most cases, pronounce the necessary names and adjectives without adding anything further. These words she should pronounce distinctly, and in a clear strong voice, so that the various sounds composing the word may be distinctly and plainly perceived by the child.

So, for example, touching the smooth and rough cards in the first tactile exercise, she should say, "This is smooth. This is rough," repeating the words with varying modulations of the voice, always letting the tones be clear and the enunciation very distinct. "Smooth, smooth, smooth. Rough, rough, rough."

In the same way, when treating of the sensations of heat and cold, she must say, "This is cold." "This is hot." "This is ice-cold." "This is tepid." She may then begin to use the generic terms, "heat," "more heat," "less heat," etc.

First. "The lessons in nomenclature must consist simply in provoking the association of the name with the object, or with the abstract idea which the name represents." Thus the *object* and the *name* must be united when they are received by the child's mind, and this makes it most necessary that no other word besides the name be spoken.

Second. The teacher must always *test* whether or not her lesson has attained the end she had in view, and her tests must be made to come within the restricted field of consciousness, provoked by the lesson on nomenclature.

The first test will be to find whether the name is still associated in the child's mind with the object. She must allow the necessary time to elapse, letting a short period of silence intervene between the lesson and the test. Then she may ask the child, pronouncing slowly and very clearly the name or the adjective she has taught: "Which is *smooth?* Which is *rough?* "

The child will point to the object with his finger, and the teacher will know that he has made the desired association. But if he has not done this, that is, if he makes a mistake, *she must not correct him,* but must suspend her lesson, to take it up again another day. Indeed, why correct him? If the child has not succeeded in associating the name with the object, the only way in which to succeed would be to *repeat* both the action of the sense stimuli and the *name;* in other words, to repeat the lesson. But when the child has failed we should know that he was not at that instant ready for the psychic association which we wished to provoke in him, and we must therefore choose another moment.

If we should say, in correcting the child "No, you have made a mistake," all these words, which, being in the form of a reproof, would strike him more forcibly than others (such as smooth or rough), would remain in the mind of the child, retarding the learning of the names. On the contrary, the *silence* which follows the error leaves the field of consciousness clear, and the next lesson may successfully follow the first. In fact, by revealing the error we may lead the child to make an undue *effort* to remember, or we may discourage him, and it is our duty to avoid as much as possible all unnatural effort and all depression.

Third. If the child has not committed any error, the teacher may provoke the motor activity corresponding to he idea of the object: that is, to the *pronunciation of the name.* She may ask him, "What is this?" and the child should respond, "Smooth." The teacher may then interrupt, teaching him how to pronounce the word correctly and distinctly, first, drawing a deep breath and, then, saying in a rather loud voice, "Smooth." When he does this the teacher may note his particular speech defect, or the special form of baby talk to which he may be addicted.

In regard to the *generalisation* of the ideas received, and by that I mean the application of these ideas to his environment, I do not advise any lessons of this sort for a certain length of time, even for a number of months. There will be children who, after having touched a few times the stuffs, or merely the smooth and rough cards, *will quite spontaneously touch the various surfaces about them*, repeating "Smooth! Rough! It is velvet! etc." In dealing with normal children, we must *await* this spontaneous investigation of the surroundings, or, as I like to call it, this *voluntary explosion* of the exploring spirit. In such cases, the children experience a joy at each *fresh discovery*. They are conscious of a sense of dignity and satisfaction which encourages them to seek for new sensations from their environment and to make themselves spontaneous *observers*.

The teacher should *watch* with the most solicitous care to see when and how the child arrives at this generalisation of ideas. For example, one of our little four-year olds while running about in the court one day suddenly stood still and cried out, "Oh! the sky is blue!" and stood for some time looking up into the blue expanse of the sky.

One day, when I entered one of the "Children's Houses," five or six little ones gathered quietly about me and began caressing, lightly, my hands, and my clothing, saying, "It is smooth." "It is velvet." "This is rough." A number of others came near and began with serious and intent faces to repeat the same words, touching me as they did so. The directress wished to interfere to release me, but I signed to her to be quiet, and I myself did not move, but remained silent, admiring this spontaneous intellectual activity of my little ones. The greatest triumph of our educational method should always be this: *to bring about the spontaneous progress of the child.*

One day, a little boy, following one of our exercises in design, had chosen to fill in with coloured pencils the outline of a tree. To colour the trunk he laid hold upon a red crayon. The teacher wished to interfere, saying, "Do you think trees have red trunks?" I held her back and allowed the child to colour the tree red. This design was precious to us; it showed that the child was not yet an observer of his surroundings. *My way of treating this was to encourage the child to make use of the games for the chromatic sense.* He went daily into the garden with the other children, and could at any time see the tree trunks.

When the sense exercises should have succeeded in attracting the child's spontaneous attention to colours about him, then, in some *happy moment* he would become aware that the tree trunks were not red, just as the other child during his play had become conscious of the fact that the sky was blue. In fact, the teacher continued to give the child outlines of trees to fill in. He one day chose a brown pencil with which to colour the trunk, and made the branches and leaves green. Later, he made the branches brown, also, using green only for the leaves.

Thus we have *the test* of the child's intellectual progress. We can not create observers by saying, "*observe*," but by giving them the power and the means for this observation, and these means are procured through education of the senses. Once we have *aroused* such activity, auto-education is assured, for refined well-trained senses lead us to a closer observation of the environment, and this, with its infinite variety, attracts the attention and continues the psychosensory education.

If, on the other hand, in this matter of sense education we single out definite concepts of the quality of certain objects, these very objects become associated with, or a part of, the training, which is in this way limited to those concepts taken and recorded. So the sense training remains unfruitful. When, for example, a teacher has given in the old way a lesson on the names of the colours, she has imparted an idea concerning that particular *quality*, but she has not educated the chromatic sense. The child will know these colours in a superficial way, forgetting them from time to time; and at best his appreciation of them will lie within the limits prescribed by the teacher. When, therefore, the teacher of the old methods shall have provoked the generalisation of the idea, saying, for example, "What is the colour of this flower?" "of this ribbon?" the attention of the child will in all probability remain torpidly fixed upon the examples suggested by her.

We may liken the child to a clock, and may say that with the old-time way it is very much as if we were to hold the wheels of the clock quiet and move the hands about the clock face with our fingers. The hands will continue to circle the dial just so long as we apply, through our fingers, the necessary motor force. Even so is it with that sort of culture which is limited to the work which the teacher does with the child. The new method, instead, may be compared to the process of winding, which sets the entire mechanism in motion.

This motion is in direct relation with the machine, and not with the work of winding. So the spontaneous psychic development of the child continues indefinitely and is in direct relation to the psychic potentiality of the child himself, and not with the work of the teacher. The movement, or the *spontaneous psychic activity* starts in our case from the education of the senses and is maintained by the observing intelligence. Thus, for example, the hunting dog receives his ability, not from the education given by his master, but from the *special acuteness* of his senses; and as soon as this physiological quality is applied to the right environment, the *exercise of hunting*, the increasing refinement of the sense perceptions, gives the dog the pleasure and then the passion for the chase. The same is true of the pianist who, refining at the same time his musical sense and the agility of his hand, comes to love more and more to draw new harmonies from the instrument. This double perfection proceeds until at last the pianist is launched upon a course which will be limited only by the personality which lies within him. Now a student of physics may know all the laws, of harmony which form a part of his scientific culture, and yet he may not know how to follow a most simple musical composition. His culture, however vast, will be bound by the definite limits of his science. Our educational aim with very young children must be to *aid the spontaneous development of the mental, spiritual, and physical personality,* and not to make of the child a cultured individual in the commonly accepted sense of the term. So, after we have offered to the child such didactic material as is adapted to provoke the development of his senses, we must wait until the activity known as observation develops. And herein lies the *art of the educator;* in knowing how to measure the action by which we help the young child's personality to develop. To one whose attitude is right, little children soon reveal *profound individual differences* which call for very different kinds of help from the teacher. Some of them require almost no intervention on her part, while others demand actual *teaching*. It is necessary, therefore, that the teaching shall be rigorously guided by the principle of limiting to the greatest possible point the active intervention of the educator. Here are a number of games and problems which we have used effectively in trying to follow this principle.

Games of the Blind

The Games of the Blind are used for the most part as exercises in general sensibility as follows:

The Stuffs. We have in our didactic material a pretty little chest composed of drawers within which are arranged rectangular pieces of stuff in great variety. There are velvet, satin, silk, cotton, linen, etc. We have the child touch each of these pieces, teaching the appropriate nomenclature and adding something regarding the quality, as coarse, fine, soft. Then, we call the child and seat him at one of the tables where he can be seen by his companions, blindfold him, and offer him the stuffs one by one. He touches them, smooths them, crushes them between his fingers and decides, "It is velvet,–It is fine linen,–It is rough cloth," etc. This exercise provokes general interest. When we offer the child some unexpected foreign object, as, for example, a sheet of paper, a veil, the little assembly trembles as it awaits his response.

Weight. We place the child in the same position, call his attention to the tablets used for the education of the sense of weight, have him notice again the already well-known differences of weight, and then tell him to put all the dark tablets, which are the heavier ones, at the right, and all the light ones, which are the lighter, to the left. We then blindfold him and he proceeds to the game, taking each time two tablets. Sometimes he takes two of the same colour, sometimes two of different colours, but in a position opposite to that in which he must arrange them on his desk. These exercises are most exciting; when, for example, the child has in his hands two of the dark tablets and changes them from one hand to the other uncertain, and finally places them together on the right, the children watch in a state of intense eagerness, and a great sigh often expresses their final relief. The shouts of the audience when the entire game is followed without an error, gives the impression that their little friend sees *with his hands* the colours of the tablets.

Dimension and Form. We use games similar to the preceding one, having the child distinguish between different coins, the cubes and bricks of Froebel, and dry seeds, such as beans and peas. But such games never awaken the intense interest aroused by the preceding ones. They are, however, useful and serve to associate with the various objects those qualities peculiar to them, and also to fix the nomenclature.

Application of the Education of the Visual Sense to the Observation of the Environment

Nomenclature. This is one of the most important phases of education. Indeed, nomenclature prepares for an *exactness* in the use of language which is not always met with in our schools. Many children, for example, use interchangeably the words thick and big, long and high. With the methods already described, the teacher may easily establish, by means of the didactic material, ideas which are very exact and clear, and may associate the proper word with these ideas.

Method of Using the Didactic Material

Dimensions. The directress, after the child has played for a long time with the three sets of solid insets and has acquired a security in the performance of the exercise, takes out all the cylinders of equal height and places them in a horizontal position on the table, one beside the other. Then she selects the two extremes, saying, "This is the *thickest* -This is the *thinnest.*" She places them side by side so that the comparison may be more marked, and then taking them by the little button, she compares the bases, calling attention to the great difference. She then places them again beside each other in a vertical positionin order to show that they are equal in height, and repeats several times, "thick-thin." Having done this, she should follow it with the test, asking, "Give me the thickest-Give me the thinnest," and finally she should proceed to the test of nomenclature, asking, "What is this?" In the lessons which follow this, the directress may take away the two extreme pieces and may repeat the lesson with the two pieces remaining at the extremities, and so on until she has used all the pieces. She may then take these up at random, saying, "Give me one a little thicker that this one," or "Give me one a little thinner than this one." With the second set of solid insets she proceeds in the same way. Here she stands the pieces upright, as each one has a base sufficiently broad to maintain it in this position, saying, "This is the highest" and "This is the lowest." Then placing the two extreme pieces side by side she may take them out of the line and compare the bases, showing that they are equal. From the extremes she may proceed as before, selecting each time the two remaining pieces most strongly contrasted.

With the third solid inset, the directress, when she has arranged the pieces in gradation, calls the child's attention to the first one, saying, "This is the largest," and to the last one, saying, "This is the smallest." Then she places them side by side and observes how they differ both in height and in base. She then proceeds in the same way as in the other two exercises.

Similar lessons may be given with the series of graduated prisms, of rods, and of cubes. The prisms are *thick* and *thin* and of equal *length*. The rods are *long* and *short* and of equal *thickness*. The cubes are *big* and *little* and differ in size and in height.

The application of these ideas to environment will come most easily when we measure the children with the anthropometer. They will begin among themselves to make comparisons, saying, "I am taller,-you are thicker." These comparisons are also made when the children hold out their little hands to show that they are clean, and the directress stretches hers out also, to show that she, too, has clean hands. Often the contrast between the dimensions of the hands calls forth laughter. The children make a perfect game of measuring themselves. They stand side by side; they look at each other; they decide. Often they place themselves beside grown persons, and observe with curiosity and interest the greatest difference in height.

Form. When the child shows that he can with security distinguish the forms of the plane geometric insets, the directress may begin the lessons in nomenclature. She should begin with two strongly-contrasted forms, as the square and the circle, and should follow the usual method, using the three periods of Séguin. We do not teach all the names relative to the geometric figures, giving only those of the most familiar forms, such as square,circle, rectangle, triangle, oval. We now call attention to the fact that there are *rectangles which are narrow and long,* and others which are *broad and short,* while the *squares* are equal on all sides and can be only big and little. These things are most easily shown with the insets, for, though we turn the square about, it still enters its frame, while the rectangle, if placed across the opening, will not enter. The child is much interested in this exercise, for which we arrange in the frame a square and a series of rectangles, having the longest side equal to the side of the square, the other side gradually decreasing in the five pieces.

In the same way we proceed to show the difference between the oval, the ellipse, and the circle. The circle enters no matter how it is placed, or turned about; the ellipse does not enter when placed transversely, but if placed lengthwise will enter even if turned upside down. The oval, however, not only cannot enter the frame if place transversely, but not even when turned upside down; it must be placed with the *large* curve toward the large part of the opening, and with the *narrow* curve toward the *narrow* portion of the opening.

The circles, *big* and *little,* enter their frames no matter how they are turned about. I do not reveal the difference between the oval and the ellipse until a very late stage of the child's education, and then not to all children, but only to those who show a special interest in the forms by choosing the game often, or by asking about the differences. I prefer that such differences should be recognised later by the child, spontaneously, perhaps in the elementary school.

It seems to many persons that in teaching these forms we are teaching *geometry,* and that this is premature in schools for such young children. Others feel that, if we wish to present geometric forms, we should use the *solids,* as being more concrete.

I feel that I should say a word here to combat such prejudices. To *observe* a geometric form is not to *analyse* it, and in the analysis geometry begins. When, for example, we speak to the child of sides and angles and explain these to him, even though with objective methods,as Froebel advocates (for example, the square has four sides and can be constructed with four sticks of equal length), then indeed we do enter the field of geometry, and I believe that little children are too immature for these steps. But the *observation of the form* cannot be too advanced for a child at this age. The plane of the table at which the child sits while eating his supper is probably a rectangle; the plate which contains his food is a circle, and we certainly do not consider that the child is too *immature* to be allowed to look at the table and the plate.

The insets which we present simply call the attention to a given *form*. As to the name, it is analogous to other names by which the child learns to call things. Why should we consider it premature to teach the child the words *circle, square, oval*, when in his home he repeatedly hears the word *round* used in connection with plates, etc.? He will hear his parents speak of the *square* table, the *oval* table, etc., and these words in common use will remain for a long time *confused* in his mind and in his speech, if we do not interpose such help as that we give in the teaching of forms.

We should reflect upon the fact that many times a child, left to himself, makes an undue effort to comprehend the language of the adults and the meaning of the things about him. Opportune and rational instruction *prevents* such an effort, and therefore does not *weary*, but *relieves*, the child and satisfies his desire for knowledge. Indeed, he shows his contentment by various expressions of pleasure. At the same time, his attention is called to the word which, if he is allowed to pronounce badly, develops in him an imperfect use of language.

This often arises from an effort on his part to imitate the careless speech of persons about him, while the teacher, by pronouncing clearly the word referring to the object which arouses the child's curiosity, prevents such effort and such imperfections.

Here, also, we face a widespread prejudice; namely, the belief that the child left to himself gives absolute repose to his mind. If this were so he would remain a stranger to the world, and, instead, we see him, little by little, spontaneously conquer various ideas and words. He is a traveller through life, who observes the new things among which he journeys, and who tries to understand the unknown tongue spoken by those about him. Indeed, he makes a great and *voluntary effort* to understand and to imitate. The instruction given to little children should be so directed as to *lessen this expenditure* of poorly directed effort, converting it instead into the enjoyment of conquest made easy and infinitely broadened. We are *the guides* of these travellers just entering the great world of human thought. We should see to it that we are intelligent and cultured guides, not losing ourselves in vain discourse, but illustrating briefly and concisely the work of art in which the traveller shows himself interested, and we should then respectfully allow him to observe it as long as he wishes to. It is our privilege to lead him to observe the most important and the most beautiful things of life in such a way that he does not lose energy and time in useless things, but shall find pleasure and satisfaction throughout his pilgrimage.

I have already referred to the prejudice that it is more suitable to present the geometric forms to the child in the *solid* rather than in the *plane*, giving him, for example, the *cube*, the *sphere*, the *prism*. Let us put aside the physiological side of the question showing that the visual recognition of the solid figure is more complex than that of the plane, and let us view the question only from the more purely pedagogical standpoint of *practical life*.

The greater number of objects which we look upon every day present more nearly the aspect of our plane geometric insets. In fact, doors, window-frames, framed pictures, the wooden or marble top of a table, are indeed *solid* objects, but with one of the dimensions greatly reduced, and with the two dimensions determining the form of the plane surface made most evident.

When the plane form prevails, we say that the window is rectangular, the picture frame oval, this table square, etc. *Solids having a determined form prevailing in the plane surface* are almost the only ones which come to our notice. And such solids are clearly represented by our *plane geometric insets*.

The child will *very often* recognise in his environment forms which he has learned in this way, but he will rarely recognise the *solid geometric forms*.

That the table leg is a prism, or a truncated cone, or an elongated cylinder, will come to his knowledge long after he has observed that the top of the table upon which he places things is rectangular. We do not, therefore, speak of the fact of recognising that a house is a prism or a cube. Indeed, the pure solid geometric forms never exist in the ordinary objects about us; these present, instead, a *combination of forms*. So, putting aside the difficulty of taking in at a glance the complex form of a house, the child recognises in it, not an *identity* of form, but an *analogy*.

He will, however, see the plane geometric forms perfectly represented in windows and doors, and in the faces of many solid objects in use at home.

Thus the knowledge of the forms given him in the plane geometric insets will be for him a species of magic *key*. opening the external world, and making him feel that he knows its secrets.

I was walking one day upon the Pincian Hill with a boy from the elementary school. He had studied geometric design and understood the analysis of plane geometric figures. As we reached the highest terrace from which we could see the Piazza del Popolo with the city stretching away behind it, I stretched out my hand saying, "Look, all the works of man are a great mass of geometric figures;" and, indeed, rectangles, ovals, triangles, and semicircles, perforated, or ornamented, in a hundred different ways the grey rectangular façades of the various buildings. Such uniformity in such an expanse of buildings seemed to prove the *limitation* of human intelligence, while in an adjoining garden plot the shrubs and flowers spoke eloquently of the infinite variety of forms in nature.

The boy had never made these observations; he had studied the angles, the sides and the construction of outlined geometric figures, but without thinking beyond this, and feeling only annoyance at this arid work. At first he laughed at the idea of man's massing geometric figures together, then he became interested, looked long at the buildings before him, and an expression of lively and thoughtful interest came into his face. To the right of the Ponte Margherita was a factory building in the process of construction, and its steel framework delineated a series of rectangles. "What tedious work!" said the boy, alluding to the workmen. And, then, as we drew near the garden, and stood for a moment in silence admiring the grass and the flowers which sprang so freely from the earth, "It is beautiful!" he said. But that word "beautiful" referred to the inner awakening of his own soul.

This experience made me think that in the observation of the plane geometric forms, and in that of the plants which they saw growing in their own little gardens, there existed for the children precious sources of spiritual as well as intellectual education. For this reason, I have wished to make my work broad, leading the child, not only to observe the forms about him, but to distinguish the work of man from that of nature, and to appreciate the fruits of human labour.

(a) *Free Design.* I give the child a sheet of white paper and a pencil, telling him that he may draw whatever he wishes to. Such drawings have long been of interest to experimental psychologists. Their importance lies in the fact that they reveal the *capacity* of the child for observing, and also show his individual tendencies. Generally, the first drawings are unformed and confused, and the teacher should ask the child *what he wished to draw*, and should write it underneath the design that it may be a record. Little by little, the drawings become more intelligible, and verily reveal the progress which the child makes in the observation of the forms about him. Often the most minute details of an object have been observed and recorded in the crude sketch. And, since the child draws what he wishes, he reveals to us which are the objects that most strongly attract his attention.

(b) *Design Consisting of the Filling in of Outlined Figures*. These designs are most important as they constitute "the preparation for writing." They do for the colour sense what *free design* does for the sense of *form*. In other words, they reveal the capacity of the child in *the matter of observation of colours*, as the free design showed us the extent to which he was an observer of form in the objects surrounding him. I shall speak more fully of this work in the chapter on *writing*. The exercises consist in filling in with coloured pencil, certain outlines drawn in black. These outlines present the simple geometric figures and various objects with which the child is familiar in the schoolroom, the home, and the garden. The child must *select* his colour, and in doing so he shows us whether he has observed the colours of the things surrounding him.

Free Plastic Work

These exercises are analogous to those in free design and in the filling in of figures with coloured pencils. Here the child makes whatever he wishes with *clay*; that is, he models those objects which he remembers most distinctly and which have impressed him most deeply. We give the child a wooden tray containing a piece of clay, and then we await his work. We possess some very remarkable pieces of clay work done by our little ones. Some of them reproduce, with surprising minuteness of detail, objects which they have seen. And what is most surprising, these models often record not only the form, but even the *dimensions* of the objects which the child handled in school.

Many little ones model the objects which they have seen at home, especially kitchen furniture, water-jugs, pots, and pans. Sometimes, we are shown a simple cradle containing a baby brother or sister. At first it is necessary to place written descriptions upon these objects, as it is necessary to do with the free design. Later on, however, the models are easily recognisable, and the children learn to reproduce the geometric solids. These clay models are undoubtedly very valuable material for the teacher, and make clear many individual differences, thus helping her to understand her children more fully. In our method they are also valuable as psychological manifestations of development according to age. Such designs are precious guides also for the teacher in the matter of her intervention in the child's education. The children who, in this work reveal themselves as observers, will probably become spontaneous observers of all the world about them, and may be led toward such a goal by the indirect help of exercises tending to fix and to make more exact the various sensations and ideas.

These children will also be those who arrive most quickly at the act of *spontaneous writing*. Those whose clay work remains unformed and indefinite will probably need the direct revelation of the directress, who will need to call their attention in some material manner to the objects around them.

Geometric Analysis of Figures; Sides, Angles, Centre, Base

The geometric analysis of figures is not adapted to very young children. I have tried a means for the *introduction* of such analysis, limiting this work to the *rectangle* and making use of a game which includes the analysis without fixing the attention of the child upon it. This game presents the concept most clearly.

The *rectangle* of which I make use is the plane of one of the children's tables, and the game consists in laying the table for a meal. I have in each of the "Children's Houses" a collection of toy table-furnishings, such as may be found in any toy-store. Among these are dinner-plates, soup-plates, soup-tureen, saltcellars, glasses, decanters, little knives, forks, spoons, etc. I have them lay the table for six, putting *two places* on each of the longer sides, and one place on each of the shorter sides. One of the children takes the objects and places them as I indicate. I tell him to place the soup-tureen in the *centre* of the table; this napkin in a *corner*. "Place this plate in the centre of the short *side*."

Then I have the child look at the table, and I say, "Something is lacking in this *corner*. We want another glass on this *side*. Now let us see if we have everything properly placed on the two longer sides. Is everything ready on the two shorter sides? Is there anything lacking in the four corners?"

I do not believe that we may proceed to any more complex analysis than this before the age of six years, for I believe that the child should one day take up one of the plane insets and *spontaneously* begin to count the sides and the angles. Certainly, if we taught them such ideas they would be able to learn, but it would be a mere learning of formulæ, and not applied experience.

Exercises in the Chromatic Sense

I have already indicated what colour exercises we follow. Here I wish to indicate more definitely the succession of these exercises and to describe them more fully.

Designs and Pictures. We have prepared a number of outline drawings which the children are to fill in with coloured pencil, and, later on, with a brush, preparing for themselves the water-colour tints which they will use. The first designs are of flowers, butterflies, trees and animals, and we then pass to simple landscapes containing grass, sky, houses, and human figures.

These designs help us in our study of the natural development of the child as an observer of his surroundings; that is, in regard to colour. The children *select the colours* and are left entirely free in their work. If, for example, they colour a chicken red, or a cow green, this shows that they have not yet become observers. But I have already spoken of this in the general discussion of the method. These designs also reveal the effect of the education of the chromatic sense. As the child selects delicate and harmonious tints, or strong and contrasting ones, we can judge of the progress he has made in the refinement of his colour sense.

The fact that the child must *remember* the colour of the objects represented in the design encourages him to observe those things which are about him. And then, too, he wishes to be able to fill in more difficult designs. Only those children who know how to keep the colour *within* the outline and to reproduce the *right colours* may proceed to the more ambitious work. These designs are very easy, and often very effective, sometimes displaying real artistic work. The directress of the school in Mexico, who studied for a long time with me, sent me two designs; one representing a cliff in which the stones were coloured most harmoniously in light violet and shades of brown, trees in two shades of green, and the sky a soft blue. The other represented a horse with a chestnut coat and black mane and tail.

Methods for the Teaching of Reading and Writing

Spontaneous Development of Graphic Language. While I was directress of the Orthophrenic School at Rome, I had already begun to experiment with various didactic means for the teaching of reading and writing. These experiments were practically original with me.

Itard and Séquin do not present any rational method through which writing may be learned. In the pages above quoted, it may be seen how Itard proceeded in the teaching of the alphabet and I give here what Séguin says concerning the teaching of writing.

"To have a child pass from design, to writing, which is its most immediate application, the teacher need only call D, a portion of a circle, resting its extremities upon a vertical; A, two obliques reunited at the summit and cut by a horizontal, etc., etc.

"We no longer need worry ourselves as to how the child shall learn to write: he designs, *then* writes. It need not be said that we should have the child draw the letters according to the laws of contrast and analogy. For instance, O beside I; B with P; T opposite L, etc."

According to Séguin, then, we do not need to *teach* writing. The child who draws, will write. But writing, for this author, means printed capitals! Nor does he, in any other place, explain whether his pupil shall write in any other way. He instead, gives much space to the description of *the design which prepares for,* and which *includes* writing. This method of design is full of difficulties and was only established by the combined attempts of Itard and Séguin.

"DESIGN. In design the first idea to be acquired is that of the plane destined to receive the design. The second is that of the trace or delineation. Within these two concepts lies all design, all linear creation.

"These two concepts are correlative, their relation generates the idea, or the capacity to produce the lines in this sense; that lines may only be called such when they follow a methodical and determined direction: the trace without direction is not a line; produced by chance, it has no name.

"The rational sign, on the contrary, has a name because it has a direction and since all writing or design is nothing other than a composite of the diverse directions followed by a line, we must, before approaching what is commonly called writing, *insist* upon these notions of plane and line. The ordinary child acquires these by instinct, but an insistence upon them is necessary in order to render the idiot careful and sensitive in their application. Through methodical design he will come into rational contact with all parts of the plane and will, guided by imitation, produce lines at first simple, but growing more complicated.

"The pupil may be taught: First, to trace the diverse species of lines. Second, to trace them in various directions and in different positions relative to the plane. Third, to reunite these lines to form figures varying from simple to complex. We must therefore, teach the pupil to distinguish straight lines from curves, vertical from horizontal, and from the various oblique lines; and must finally make clear the principal points of conjunction of two or more lines in forming a figure.

"This rational analysis of design, *from which writing will spring*, is so essential in all its parts, that a child who, before being confided to my care, already wrote many of the letters, has taken six days to learn to draw a perpendicular or a horizontal line; he spent fifteen days before imitating a curve and an oblique. Indeed the greater number of my pupils, are for a long time incapable of even imitating the movements of my hand upon the paper, before attempting to draw a line in a determined direction. The most imitative, or the least stupid ones, produce a sign diametrically opposite to that which I show them and all of them confound the points of conjunction of two lines no matter how evident this is. It is true that the thorough knowledge I have given them of lines and of configuration helps them to make the connection which must be established between the plane and the various marks with which they must cover the surface, but in the study rendered necessary by the deficiency of my pupils, the progression in the matter of the vertical, the horizontal, the oblique, and the curve must be determined by the consideration of the difficulty of comprehension and of execution which each offers to a torpid intelligence and to a weak unsteady hand.

"I do not speak here of merely having them perform a difficult thing, since I have them surmount a *series* of difficulties and for this reason I ask myself if some of these difficulties are not greater and some less, and if they do not grow one from the other, like theorems. Here are the ideas which have guided me in this respect.

"The vertical is a line which the eye and the hand follow directly, going up and down. The horizontal line is not natural to the eye, nor to the hand, which lowers itself and follows a curve (like the horizon from which it has taken its name), starting from the centre and going to the lateral extremity of the plane.

"The oblique line presupposes more complex comparative ideas,and the curve demands such firmness and so many differences in its relation to the plane that we would only lose time in taking up the study of these lines. The most simple line then, is the vertical, and this is how I have given my pupils an idea of it.

"The first geometric formula is this: only straight lines may be drawn from one given point to another.

"Starting from this axiom, which the hand alone can demonstrate, I have fixed two points upon the blackboard and have connected them by means of a vertical. My pupils try to do the same between the dots they have upon their paper, but with some the vertical descends to the right of the point and with others, to the left, to say nothing of those whose hand diverges in all directions. To arrest these various deviations which are often far more defects of the intelligence and of the vision, than of the hand, I have thought it wise to restrict the field of the plane, drawing two vertical lines to left and right of the points which the child is to join by means of a parallel line half way between the two enclosing lines. If these two lines are not enough, I place two rulers vertically upon the paper, which arrest the deviations of the hand absolutely. These material barriers are not, however, useful for very long. We first suppress the rulers and return to the two parallel lines, between which the idiot learns to draw the third line. We then take away one of the guiding lines, and leave, sometimes that on the right, sometimes that on the left, finally taking away this last line and at last, the dots, beginning by erasing the one at the top which indicates the starting point of the line and of the hand. The child thus learns to draw a vertical without material control, without points of comparison.

"The same method, the same difficulty, the same means of direction are used for the straight horizontal lines. If, by chance, these lines begin well, we must await until the child curves them, departing from the centre and proceeding to the extremity *as nature commands him*, and because of the reason which I have explained. If the two dots do not suffice to sustain the hand, we keep it from deviating by means of the parallel lines or of the rulers.

"Finally, have him trace a horizontal line, and by uniting with it a vertical ruler we form a right angle. The child will begin to understand, in this way, what the vertical and horizontal lines really are, and will see the relation of these two ideas as he traces a figure.

"In the sequence of the development of lines, it would seem that the study of the oblique should immediately follow that of the vertical and the horizontal, but this is not so! The oblique which partakes of the vertical in its inclination, and of the horizontal in its direction, and which partakes of both in its nature (since it is a straight line), presents perhaps, because of its relation to other lines, an idea too complex to be appreciated without preparation."

Thus Séguin goes on through many pages, to speak of the oblique in all directions, which he has his pupils trace between two parallels. He then tells of the four curves which he has them draw to right and left of a vertical and above and below a horizontal, and concludes: "So we find the solution of the problems for which we sought–the vertical line, the horizontal, the oblique, and four curves, whose union forms the circle, contain all possible lines, *all writing.*"

"Arrived at this point, Itard and I were for a long time at a standstill. The lines being known, the next step was to have the child trace regular figures, beginning of course, with the simplest. According to the general opinion, Itard had advised me to begin with the square and I had followed this advice *for three months*, without being able to make the child understand me."

After a long series of experiments, guided by his ideas of the genesis of geometric figures, Séguin became aware that the triangle is the figure most easily drawn.

"When three lines meet thus, they always form a triangle, while four lines may meet in a hundred different directions without remaining parallel and therefore without presenting a perfect square.

"From these experiments and many others, I have deduced the first principles of writing and of design for the idiot; principles whose application is *too simple* for me to discuss further."

Such was the proceeding used by my predecessors in the teaching of writing to deficients. As for reading, Itard proceeded thus: he drove nails into the wall and hung upon them, geometric figures of wood, such as triangles, squares, circles. He then drew the exact imprint of these upon the wall, after which he took the figures away and had the "boy of Aveyron" replace them upon the proper nails, guided by the design. From this design Itard conceived the idea of the plane geometric insets. He finally had large print letters made of wood and proceeded in the same way as with the geometric figures, that is, using the design upon the wall and arranging the nails in such a way that the child might place the letters upon them and then take them off again. Later, Séguin used the horizontal plane instead of the wall, drawing the letters on the bottom of a box and having the child superimpose solid letters. After twenty years, Séguin had not changed his method of procedure.

A criticism of the method used by Itard and Séguin for reading and writing seems to me superfluous. The method has two fundamental errors which make it inferior to the methods in use for normal children, namely: writing in printed capitals, and the preparation for writing through a study of rational geometry, which we now expect only from students in the secondary schools.

Séguin here confuses ideas in a most extraordinary way. He has suddenly jumped from the psychological observation of the child and from his relation to his environment, to the study of the origin of lines and their relation to the plane.

He says that the child *will readily design a vertical line,* but that the horizontal will soon become a curve, because "*nature commands it* " and this *command of nature* is represented by the fact that man sees the horizon as a curved line!

The example of Séguin serves to illustrate the necessity of a *special education* which shall fit man for *observation,* and shall direct *logical thought.*

The observation must be absolutely objective, in other words, stripped of preconceptions. Séguin has in this case the preconception that geometric design must prepare for writing, and that hinders him from discovering the truly natural proceeding necessary to such preparation. He has, besides, the preconception that the deviation of a line, as well as the inexactness with which the child traces it, are due to "*the mind and the eye, not to the hand,*" and so he wearies himself *for weeks and months in explaining* the direction of lines and in guiding *the vision* of the idiot.

It seems as if Séguin felt that a good method must start from a superior point, geometry; the intelligence of the child is only considered worthy of attention in its relation to abstract things. And is not this a common defect?

Let us observe mediocre men; they pompously assume erudition and disdain simple things. Let us study the clear thought of those whom we consider men of genius. Newton is seated tranquilly in the open air; an apple falls from the tree, he observes it and asks, "Why?" Phenomena are never insignificant; the fruit which falls and universal gravitation may rest side by side in the mind of a genius.

If Newton had been a teacher of children he would have led the child to look upon the worlds on a starry night, but an erudite person might have felt it necessary first to prepare the child to understand the sublime calculus which is the key to astronomy–Galileo Galilei observed the oscillation of a lamp swung on high, and discovered the laws of the pendulum.

In the intellectual life *simplicity* consists in divesting one's mind of every preconception, and this leads to the discovery of new things, as, in the moral life, humility and material poverty guide us toward high spiritual conquests.

If we study the history of discoveries, we will find that they have come from *real objective observation* and from *logical thought.* These are simple things, but rarely found in one man.

Does it not seem strange, for instance, that after the discovery by Laveran of the malarial parasite which invades the red blood-corpuscles, we did not, in spite of the fact that we know the blood system to be a system of closed vessels, even so much as *suspect the possibility* that a stinging insect might inoculate us with the parasite? Instead, the theory that the evil emanated from low ground, that it was carried by the African winds, or that it was due to dampness, was given credence. Yet these were vague ideas, while the parasite was a definite biological specimen.

When the discovery of the malarial mosquito came to complete logically the discovery of Laveran, this seemed marvellous, stupefying. Yet we know in biology that the reproduction of molecular vegetable bodies is by scission with alternate sporation, and that of molecular animals is by scission with alternate conjunction. That is, after a certain period in which the primitive cell has divided and sub-divided into fresh cells, equal among themselves, there comes the formation of two diverse cells, one male and one female, which must unite to form a single cell capable of recommencing the cycle of reproduction by division. All this being known at the time of Laveran, and the malarial parasite being known to be a protozoon, it would have seemed logical to consider its segmentation in the stroma of the red corpuscle as the phase of scission and to await until the parasite gave place to the sexual forms, which must necessarily come in the phase succeeding scission. Instead, the division was looked upon as spore-formation, and neither Laveran, nor the numerous scientists who followed the research, knew how to give an explanation of the appearance of the sexual forms. Laveran expressed an idea, which was immediately received, that these two forms were degenerate forms of the malarial parasite, and therefore incapable of producing the changes determining the disease. Indeed, the malaria was apparently cured at the appearance of the two sexual forms of the parasite, the conjunction of the two cells being impossible in the human blood. The theory-then recent-of Morel upon human degeneration accompanied by deformity and weakness, inspired Laveran in his interpretation, and everybody found the idea of the illustrious pathologist a fortunate one, because it was inspired by the great concepts of the Morellian theory.

Had anyone, instead, limited himself to reasoning thus: the original form of the malarial insect is a protozoon; it reproduces itself by scission, under our eyes; when the scission is finished, we see two diverse cells; one a half-moon, the other threadlike. These are the feminine and masculine cells which must, by conjunction, alternate the scission,-such a reasoner would have opened the way to the discovery. But *so simple* a process of reasoning did not come. We might almost ask ourselves how great would be the world's progress if a special form of education prepared men for pure observation and logical thought.

A great deal of time and intellectual force are lost in the world, because the false seems great and the truth so small and insignificant.

I say all this to defend the necessity, which I feel we face, of preparing the coming generations by means of more rational methods. It is from these generations that the world awaits its progress. We have already learned to make use of our surroundings, but I believe that we have arrived at a time when the necessity presents itself for *utilising* human force, through a scientific education.

To return to Séguin's method of writing, it illustrates another truth, and that is the tortuous path we follow in our teaching. This, too, is allied to an instinct for complicating things, analogous to that which makes us so prone to appreciate complicated things. We have Séguin teaching *geometry* in order to teach a child to write; and making the child's mind exert itself to follow geometrical abstractions only to come down to the simple effort of drawing a printed D. After all, must the child not have to make another effort in order to *forget* the print, and *learn* the script?

And even we in these days still believe that in order to learn to write the child must first make vertical strokes. This conviction is very general. Yet it does not seem natural that to write the letters of the alphabet, which are all rounded, it should be necessary to begin with straight lines and acute angles.

In all good faith, we wonder that it should be difficult to do away with the angularity and stiffness with which the beginner traces the beautiful curve of the O. * Yet, through what effort on our part, and on his, was he forced to fill pages and pages with rigid lines and acute angles! To whom is due this time honoured idea that the first sign to be traced must be a straight line? And why do we so avoid preparing for curves as well as angles?

Let us, for a moment, divest ourselves of such preconceptions and proceed in a more simple way. We may be able to relieve future generations of *all effort* in the matter of learning to write.

Is it necessary to begin writing with the making of vertical strokes? A moment of clear and logical thinking is enough to enable us to answer, no. The child makes too painful an effort in following such an exercise. The first steps should be the easiest, and the up and down stroke, is, on the contrary, one of the most difficult of all the pen movements. Only a professional penman could fill a whole page and preserve the regularity of such strokes, but a person who writes only moderately well would be able to complete a page of presentable writing. Indeed, the straight line is unique, expressing the shortest distance between two points, while *any deviation* from that direction signifies a line which is not straight. These infinite deviations are therefore easier than that *one* trace which is perfection.

If we should give to a number of adults the order to draw a straight line upon the blackboard, each person would draw a long line proceeding in a different direction, some beginning from one side, some from another,and almost all would succeed in making the line straight. Should we then ask that the line be drawn in a *particular direction*, starting from a determined point, the ability shown at first would greatly diminish, and we would see many more irregularities, or errors. Almost all the lines would be long-for the individual *must needs gather impetus* in order to succeed in making his line straight.

Should we ask that the lines be made short, and included within precise limits, the errors would increase, for we would thus impede the impetus which helps to conserve the definite direction. In the methods ordinarily used in teaching writing, we add, to such limitations, the further restriction that the instrument of writing must be held in a certain way, not as instinct prompts each individual.

Thus we approach in the most conscious and restricted way the first act of writing, which should be voluntary. In this first writing we still demand that the single strokes be kept parallel, making the child's task a difficult and barren one, since it has no purpose for the child, who does not understand the meaning of all this detail.

I had noticed in the note-books of the deficient children in France (and Voisin also mentions this phenomenon) that the pages of vertical strokes, although they began as such, ended in lines of C's. This goes to show that the deficient child, whose mind is less resistant than that of the normal child, exhausts, little by little, the initial effort of imitation, and the natural movement gradually comes to take the place of that which was forced or stimulated. So the straight lines are transformed into curves, more and more like the letter C. Such a phenomenon does not appear in the copy-books of normal children, for they resist, through effort, until the end of the page is reached, and, thus, as often happens, conceal the didactic error.

But let us observe the spontaneous drawings of normal children. When, for example, picking up a fallen twig, they trace figures in the sandy garden path, we never see short straight lines, but long and variously interlaced curves.

Séguin saw the same phenomenon when the horizontal lines he made his pupils draw became curves so quickly instead. And he attributed the phenomenon to the imitation of the horizon line!

That vertical strokes should prepare for alphabetical writing, seems incredibly illogical. The alphabet is made up of curves, therefore we must prepare for it by learning to make straight lines.

"But," says someone, "in many letters of the alphabet, the straight line does exist." True, but there is no reason why as a beginning of writing, we should select one of the details of a complete form. We may analyse the alphabetical signs in this way, discovering straight lines and curves, as by analysing discourse, we find grammatical rules. But we all *speak* independently of such rules, why then should we not write independently of such analysis, and without the separate execution of the parts constituting the letter?

It would be sad indeed if we could *speak* only *after* we had studied grammar! It would be much the same as demanding that before we *looked* at the stars in the firmament, we must study infinitesimal calculus; it is much the same thing to feel that before teaching an idiot to write, we must make him understand the abstract derivation of lines and the problems of geometry!

No less are we to be pitied if, in order to write, we must follow analytically the parts constituting the alphabetical signs. In fact the *effort* which we believe to be a necessary accompaniment to learning to write is purely artificial effort, allied, not to writing, but to the *methods* by which it is taught.

Let us for a moment cast aside every dogma in this connection. Let us take no note of culture, or custom. We are not, here, interested in knowing how humanity began to write, nor what may have been the origin of writing itself.

Let us put away the conviction, that long usage has given us, of the necessity of beginning writing by making vertical strokes; and let us try to be as clear and unprejudiced in spirit as the truth which we are seeking.

"*Let us observe an individual who is writing, and let us seek to analyse the acts he performs in writing,*" that is, the mechanical operations which enter into the execution of writing. This would be undertaking the *philosophical study of writing,* and it goes without saying that we should examine the individual who writes, not the *writing;* the *subject,* not the *object.* Many have begun with the object, examining the writing, and in this way many methods have been constructed.

But a method starting from the individual would be decidedly original–very different from other methods which preceded it. It would indeed signify a new era in writing, *based upon anthropology.*

In fact, when I undertook my experiments with normal children, if I had thought of giving a name to this new method of writing, I should have called it without knowing what the results would be, the *anthropological method.* Certainly, my studies in anthropology inspired the method, but experience has given me, as a surprise, another title which seems to me the natural one, "the method of *spontaneous* writing."

While teaching deficient children I happened to observe the following fact: An idiot girl of eleven years, who was possessed of normal strength and motor power in her hands, could not learn to sew, or even to take the first step, darning, which consists in passing the needle first over, then under the woof, now taking up, now leaving, a number of threads.

I set the child to weaving with the Froebel mats, in which a strip of paper is threaded transversely in and out among vertical strips of paper held fixed at top and bottom. I thus came to think of the analogy between the two exercises, and became much interested in my observation of the girl. When she had become skilled in the Froebel weaving, I led her back again to the sewing, and saw with pleasure that she was now able to follow the darning. From that time on, our sewing classes began with a regular course in the Froebel weaving.

I saw that the necessary movements of the hand in sewing *had been prepared without having the child sew,* and that we should really find the way to *teach* the child *how,* before *making him execute* a task. I saw especially that preparatory movements could be carried on, and reduced to a mechanism, by means of repeated exercises not in the work itself but in that which prepares for it. Pupils could then come to the real work, able to perform it without ever having directly set their hands to it before.

I thought that I might in this way prepare for writing, and the idea interested me tremendously. I marvelled at its simplicity, and was annoyed that *I had not thought before* of the method which was suggested to me by my observation of the girl who could not sew.

In fact, seeing that I had already taught the children to touch the contours of the plane geometric insets, I had now only to teach them to touch with their fingers the *forms of the letters of the alphabet.*

I had a beautiful alphabet manufactured, the letters being in flowing script, the low letters 8 centimetres high, and the taller ones in proportion. These letters were in wood, 1/2 centimetre in thickness, and were painted, the consonants in blue enamel, the vowels in red. The under side of these letter forms, instead of being painted, were covered with bronze that they might be more durable. We had only one copy of this wooden alphabet, but there were a number of cards upon which the letters were painted in the same colours and dimensions as the wooden ones. These painted letters were arranged upon the cards in groups, according to contrast, or analogy of form.

Corresponding to each letter of the alphabet, we had a picture representing some object the name of which began with the letter. Above this, the letter was painted in large script, and near it, the same letter, much smaller and in its printed form. These pictures served to fix the memory of the sound of the letter, and the small printed letter united to the one in script, was to form the passage to the reading of books. These pictures do not, indeed, represent a new idea, but they completed an arrangement which did not exist before. Such an alphabet was undoubtedly most expensive and when made by hand the cost was fifty dollars.

The interesting part of my experiment was, that after I had shown the children how to place the movable wooden letters upon those painted in groups upon the cards, I had them *touch them repeatedly in the fashion of flowing writing.*

I multiplied these exercises in various ways, and the children thus learned to make *the movements necessary to reproduce the form of the graphic signs without writing.*

I was struck by an idea which had never before entered my mind–that in writing we make *two diverse* forms of movement, for, besides the movement by which the form is reproduced, there is also that of *manipulating the instrument of writing.* And, indeed, when the deficient children had become expert in touching all the letters according to form, *they did not yet know how to hold a pencil.* To hold and to manipulate a little stick securely, corresponds to the *acquisition of a special muscular mechanism which is independent of the writing movement;* it must in fact go along with the motions necessary to produce all of the various letter forms. It is, then, *a distinct mechanism,* which must exist together with the motor memory of the single graphic signs. When I provoked in the deficients the movements characteristic of writing by having them touch the letters with their fingers, I exercised mechanically the psycho-motor paths, and fixed the muscular memory of each letter. There remained the preparation of the muscular mechanism necessary in holding and managing the instrument of writing, and this I provoked by adding two periods to the one already described. In the second period, the child touched the letter, not only with the index finger of his right hand, but with two, the index and the middle finger. In the third period, he touched the letters with a little wooden stick, held as a pen in writing. In substance I was making him repeat the same movements, now with, and now without, holding the instrument.

I have said that the child was to follow the visual image of the outlined letter. It is true that his finger had already been trained through touching the contours of the geometric figures, but this was not always a sufficient preparation. Indeed, even we grown people, when we trace a design through glass or tissue paper, cannot follow perfectly the line which we see and along which we should draw our pencil. The design should furnish some sort of control, some mechanical guide, for the pencil, in order to follow with *exactness* the trace, *sensible in reality only to the eye.*

The deficients, therefore, did not always follow the design exactly with either the finger or the stick. The didactic material did not offer *any control* in the work, or rather it offered only the uncertain control of the child's glance, which could, to be sure, see if the finger continued upon the sign, or not. I now thought that in order to have the pupil follow the movements more exactly, and to guide the execution more directly, I should need to prepare letter forms so indented, as to represent a *furrow* within which the wooden stick might run. I made the designs for this material, but the work being too expensive I was not able to carry out my plan.

After having experimented largely with this method, I spoke of it very fully to the teachers in my classes in didactic methods at the State Orthophrenic School. These lectures were printed, and I give below the words which, though they were placed in the hands of more than 200 elementary teachers, did not draw from them a single helpful idea. Professor Ferreri * in an article speaks with amazement of this fact.

"At this point we present the cards bearing the vowels painted in red. The child sees irregular figures painted in red. We give him the vowels in wood, painted red, and have him superimpose these upon the letters painted on the card. We have him touch the wooden vowels in the fashion of writing, and give him the name of each letter. The vowels are arranged on the cards according to analogy of form:

o e a

i   u

"We then say to the child, for example, 'Find o. Put it in its place.' Then, 'What letter is this?' We here discover that many children make mistakes in the letters if they only look at the letter.

"They could however tell the letter by touching it. Most interesting observations may be made, revealing various individual types: visual, motor.

"We have the child touch the letters drawn upon the cards,–using first the index finger only, then the index with the middle finger,–then with a small wooden stick held as a pen. The letter must be traced in the fashion of writing.

"The consonants are painted in blue, and are arranged upon the cards according to analogy of form. To these cards are annexed a movable alphabet in blue wood, the letters of which are to be placed upon the consonants as they were upon the vowels. In addition to these materials there is another series of cards, where, besides the consonant, are painted one or two figures the names of which begin with that particular letter. Near the script letter, is a smaller printed letter painted in the same colour.

"The teacher, naming the consonant according to the phonetic method, indicates the letter, and then the card, pronouncing the names of the objects painted there, and emphasizing the first letter, as, for example, '*p-pear*: give me the consonant *p* –put it in its place, touch it,' etc. *In all this we study the linguistic defects of the child.*

"Tracing the letter, in the fashion of writing, begins the muscular education which prepares for writing. One of our little girls taught by this method has reproduced all the letters with the pen, though she does not as yet recognise them all. She has made them about eight centimetres high, and with surprising regularity. This child also does well in hand work. The child who looks, recognises, and touches the letters in the manner of writing, prepares himself simultaneously for reading and writing.

"Touching the letters and looking at them at the same time, fixes the image more quickly through the co-operation of the senses. Later, the two facts separate; looking becomes reading; touching becomes writing. According to the type of the individual, some learn to read first, others to write."

I had thus, about the year 1899, initiated my method for reading and writing upon the fundamental lines it still follows. It was with great surprise that I noted the *facility* with which a deficient child, to whom I one day gave a piece of chalk, traced upon the blackboard, in a firm hand, the letters of the entire alphabet, writing for the first time.

This had arrived much more quickly than I had supposed. As I have said, some of the children wrote the letters *with a pen and yet could not recognise one of them.* I have noticed, also, in normal children, that the muscular sense is most easily developed in infancy, and this makes writing exceedingly easy for children. It is not so with reading, which requires a much longer course of instruction, and which calls for a superior intellectual development, since it treats of the *interpretation of signs*, and of the *modulation of accents of the voice*, in order that the word may be understood. And all this is a purely mental task, while in writing, the child, under dictation, *materially translates* sounds into signs, and moves, a thing which is always easy and pleasant for him. Writing develops in the little child with *facility* and *spontaneity*, analogous to the development of spoken language–which is a motor translation of audible sounds. Reading, on the contrary, makes part of an abstract intellectual culture, which is the interpretation of ideas from graphic symbols, and is only acquired later on.

My first experiments with normal children were begun in the first half of the month of November, 1907.

In the two "Children's Houses" in San Lorenzo, I had, from the date of their respective inaugurations (January 6 in one and March 7 in the other), used only the games of practical life, and of the education of the senses. I had not presented exercises for writing, because, like everybody else, I held the prejudice that it was necessary to begin as late as possible the teaching of reading and writing, and certainly to avoid it before the age of six.

But the children seemed to demand some *conclusion* of the exercises, which had already developed them intellectually in a most surprising way. They knew how to dress and undress, and to bathe, themselves; they knew how to sweep the floors, dust the furniture, put the room in order, to open and close boxes, to manage the keys in the various locks; they could replace the objects in the cupboards in perfect order, could care for the plants; they knew how to observe things, and how to see objects with their hands. A number of them came to us and frankly demanded to be taught to read and write. Even in the face of our refusal several children came to school and proudly showed us that they knew how to make an O on the blackboard.

Finally, many of the mothers came to beg us as a favour to teach the children to write, saying, "Here in the 'Children's Houses' the children are awakened, and learn so many things easily that if you only teach reading and writing they will soon learn, and will then be spared the great fatigue this always means in the elementary school." This faith of the mothers, that their little ones would, from us, be *able to learn to read and write without fatigue*, made a great impression upon me. Thinking upon the results I had obtained in the school for deficients, I decided during the August vacation to make a trial upon the reopening of the school in September. Upon second thought I decided that it would be better to take up the interrupted work in September, and not to approach reading and writing until October, when the elementary schools opened. This presented the added advantage of permitting us to compare the progress of the children of the first elementary with that made by ours, who would have begun the same branch of instruction at the same time.

In September, therefore, I began a search for someone who could manufacture didactic materials, but found no one willing to undertake it. I wished to have a splendid alphabet made, like the one used with the deficients. Giving this up, I was willing to content myself with the ordinary enamelled letters used upon shop windows, but I could find them in script form nowhere. My disappointments were many.

So passed the whole month of October. The children in the first elementary had already filled pages of vertical strokes, and mine were still waiting. I then decided to cut out large paper letters, and to have one of my teachers colour these roughly on one side with a blue tint. As for the touching of the letters, I thought of cutting the letters of the alphabet out of sandpaper, and of gluing them upon smooth cards, thus making objects much like those used in the primitive exercises for the tactile sense.

Only after I had made these simple things, did I become aware of the superiority of this alphabet to that magnificent one I had used for my deficients, and in the pursuit of which I had wasted two months! If I had been rich, I would have had that beautiful but barren alphabet of the past! We wish the old things because we cannot understand the new, and we are always seeking after that gorgeousness which belongs to things already on the decline, without recognising in the humble simplicity of new ideas the germ which shall develop in the future.

I finally understood that a paper alphabet could easily be multiplied, and could be used by many children at one time, not only for the recognition of letters, but for the composition of words. I saw that in the sandpaper alphabet I had found the looked-for guide for the fingers which touched the letter. This was furnished in such a way that no longer the sight alone, but the touch, lent itself directly to teaching the movement of writing with exactness of control.

In the afternoon after school, the two teachers and I, with great enthusiasm, set about cutting out letters from writing-paper, and others from sandpaper. The first, we painted blue, the second, we mounted on cards, and, while we worked, there unfolded before my mind a clear vision of the method in all its completeness, so simple that it made me smile to think I had not seen it before.

The story of our first attempts is very interesting. One day one of the teachers was ill, and I sent as a substitute a pupil of mine, Signorina Anna Fedeli, a professor of pedagogy in a Normal school. When I went to see her at the close of the day, she showed me two modifications of the alphabet which she had made. One consisted in placing behind each letter, a transverse strip of white paper, so that the child might recognise the direction of the letter, which he often turned about and upside down. The other consisted in the making of a cardboard case where each letter might be put away in its own compartment, instead of being kept in a confused mass as at first. I still keep this rude case made from an old pasteboard box, which Signorina Fedeli had found in the court and roughly sewed with white thread.

She showed it to me laughing, and excusing herself for the miserable work, but I was most enthusiastic about it. I saw at once that the letters in the case were a precious aid to the teaching. Indeed, it offered to the eye of the child the possibility of comparing all of the letters, and of selecting those he needed. In this way the didactic material described below had its origin.

I need only add that at Christmas time, less than a month and a half later, while the children in the first elementary were laboriously working to forget their wearisome pothooks and to prepare for making the curves of O and the other vowels, two of my little ones of four years old, wrote, each one in the name of his companions, a letter of good wishes and thanks to Signor Edoardo Talamo. These were written upon note paper without blot or erasure and the writing was adjudged equal to that which is obtained in the third elementary grade.

Description of the Method and Didactic Material Used

First Period: Exercise Tending to Develop the Muscular Mechanism Necessary in Holding and Using the Instrument in Writing

Design Preparatory to Writing.–Didactic Material. Small wooden tables; metal insets, outline drawings, coloured pencils. I have among my materials two little wooden tables, the tops of which form an inclined plane sloping toward a narrow cornice, which prevents objects placed upon the table from slipping off. The top of each table is just large enough to hold four of the square frames, into which the metal plane geometric insets are fitted, and is so painted as to represent three of these brown frames, each containing a square centre of the same dark blue as the centres of the metal insets.

The metal insets are in dimension and form a reproduction of the series of plane geometric insets in wood already described.

Exercises. Placed side by side upon the teacher's desk, or upon one of the little tables belonging to the children, these two little tables may have the appearance of being one long table containing eight figures. The child may select one or more figures, taking at the same time the frame of the inset. The analogy between these metal insets and the plane geometric insets of wood is complete. But in this case, the child can freely use the pieces, where before, he arranged them in the wooden frame. He first takes the metal frame, places it upon a sheet of white paper, and with a coloured pencil *draws around the contour of the empty centre.* Then, he takes away the frame, and upon the paper there remains a geometric figure.

This is the first time that the child has reproduced through design, a geometric figure. Until now, he has only placed the geometric insets above the figures delineated on the three series of cards. He now places upon the figure, which he himself has drawn, the metal inset, just as he placed the wooden inset upon the cards. His next act is to follow the contour of this inset with a pencil of a different colour. Lifting the metal piece, he sees the figure reproduced upon the paper, in two colours.

Here, for the first time is born the abstract concept of the geometric figure, for, from two metal pieces so different in form as the frame and the inset, there has resulted the same design, which is a *line* expressing a determined figure. This fact strikes the attention of the child. He often marvels to find the same figure reproduced by means of two pieces so different, and looks for a long time with evident pleasure at the duplicate design–almost as if it were *actually produced by* the objects which serve to guide his hand.

Besides all this, the child learns *to trace lines* determining figures. There will come a day in which, with still greater surprise and pleasure, he will trace graphic signs determining words.

After this, he begins the work which directly prepares for the formation of the muscular mechanism relative to the holding and manipulation of the instrument of writing. With a coloured pencil of his own selection, held as the pen is held in writing, he *fills* in the figure which he has outlined. We teach him not to pass outside the contour, and in doing so we attract his attention to this contour, and thus *fix* the idea that a line may determine a figure.

The exercise of filling in one figure alone, causes the child to perform repeatedly the movement of manipulation which would be necessary to fill ten copy-book pages with vertical strokes. And yet, the child feels no weariness, because, although he makes exactly the muscular co-ordination which is necessary to the work, he does so freely and in any way that he wishes, while his eyes are fixed upon a large and brightly coloured figure. At first, the children fill pages and pages of paper with these big squares, triangles, ovals, trapezoids; colouring them red, orange, green, blue, light blue, and pink.

Gradually they limit themselves to the use of the dark blue and brown, both in drawing the figure and in filling it in, thus reproducing the appearance of the metal piece itself. Many of the children, quite of their own accord, make a little orange-coloured circle in the centre of the figure, in this way representing the little brass button by which the metal piece is to be held. They take great pleasure in feeling that they have reproduced exactly, like true artists, the objects which they see before them on the little shelf.

Observing the successive drawings of a child, there is revealed to us a duplicate form of progression:

First. Little by little, the lines tend less and less to go outside the enclosing line until, at last, they are perfectly contained within it, and both the centre and the frame are filled in with close and uniform strokes.

Second. The strokes with which the child fills in the figures, from being at first short and confused, become gradually *longer, and more nearly parallel*, until in many cases the figures are filled in by means of perfectly regular up and down strokes, extending from one side of the figure to the other. In such a case, it is evident that the child is *master of the pencil.* The muscular mechanism, necessary to the management of the instrument of writing, *is established.* We may, therefore, by examining such designs, arrive at a clear idea of the maturity of the child in the matter of *holding the pencil or pen in hand.* To vary these exercises, we use the *outline drawings* already described. Through these designs, the manipulation of the pencil is perfected, for they oblige the child to make lines of various lengths, and make him more and more secure in his use of the pencil.

If we could count the lines made by a child in the filling in of these figures, and could transform them into the signs used in writing, they would fill many, many copy-books! Indeed, the security which our children attain is likened to that of children in our ordinary third elementary grade. When for the first time they take a pen or a pencil in hand, they know how to manage it almost as well as a person who has written for a long time.

I do not believe that any means can be found which will so successfully and, in so short a space of time, establish this mastery. And with it all, the child is happy and diverted. My old method for the deficients, that of following with a small stick the contours of raised letters, was, when compared with this, barren and miserable!

Even when the children *know how to write* they continue these exercises, which furnish an unlimited progression, since the designs may be varied and complicated. The children follow in each design essentially the same movements, and acquire a varied collection of pictures which grow more and more perfect, and of which they are very proud. For I not only *provoke*, but perfect, the writing through the exercises which we call preparatory. The control of the pen is rendered more and more secure, not by repeated exercises in the writing, but by means of these filled-in designs. In this way, my children *perfect themselves in writing, without actually writing.*

Second Period: Exercises Tending to Establish the Visual-muscular Image of the Alphabetical Signs: and to Establish the Muscular Memory of the Movements Necessary to Writing

Didactic Material. Cards upon which the single letters of the alphabet are mounted in sandpaper; larger cards containing groups of the same letters.

The cards upon which the sandpaper letters are mounted are adapted in size and shape to each letter. The vowels are in light-coloured sandpaper and are mounted upon dark cards, the consonants and the groups of letters are in black sandpaper mounted upon white cards. The grouping is so arranged as to call attention to contrasted, or analogous forms.

The letters are cut in clear script form, the shaded parts being made broader. We have chosen to reproduce the vertical script in use in the elementary schools.

Exercises. In teaching the letters of the alphabet, we begin with the *vowels* and proceed to the consonants, pronouncing the *sound*, not the name. In the case of the consonants, we immediately unite the sound with one of the vowel sounds, repeating the syllable according to the usual phonetic method. The teaching proceeds according to the three periods already illustrated.

First. Association of the visual and muscular-tactile sensation with the letter sound.

The directress presents to the child two of the cards upon which vowels are mounted (or two of the consonants, as the case may be). Let us suppose that we present the letters i and o, saying, "This is i! This is o!" As soon as we have given the sound of a letter, we have the child trace it, taking care to show him *how* to trace it, and if necessary guiding the index finger of his right hand over the sandpaper letter *in the sense of writing.*

"*Knowing how to trace* " will consist in *knowing the direction* in which a given graphic sign must be followed.

The child learns quickly, and his finger, already expert in the tactile exercise, *is led*, by the slight roughness of the fine sandpaper, over the exact track of the letter. *He may then repeat indefinitely* the movements necessary to produce the letters of the alphabet, without the fear of the mistakes of which a child writing with a pencil for the first time is so conscious. If he deviates, the smoothness of the card immediately warns him of his error.

The children, as soon as they have become at all expert in this tracing of the letters, take great pleasure in repeating it *with closed eyes*, letting the sandpaper lead them in following the form which they do not see. Thus the perception will be established by the direct muscular-tactile sensation of the letter. In other words, it is no longer the visual image of the letter, but the *tactile sensation*, which guides the hand of the child in these movements, which thus become fixed in the muscular memory.

There develop, contemporaneously, three sensations when the directress *shows the letter* to the child and has him trace it; the visual sensation, the tactile sensation, and the muscular sensation. In this way the *image of the graphic sign is fixed in a much shorter space of time* than when it was, according to ordinary methods, acquired only through the visual image. It will be found that the *muscular memory* is in the young child the most tenacious and, at the same time, the most ready. Indeed, he sometimes recognises the letters by touching them, when he cannot do so by looking at them. These images are, besides all this, contemporaneously associated with the alphabetical sound.

Second. Perception. *The child should know how to compare and to recognise the figures, when he hears the sounds corresponding to them.*

The directress asks the child, for example, "Give me o!–Give me i!" If the child does not recognise the letters by looking at them, she invites him to trace them, but if he still does not recognise them, the lesson is ended, and may be resumed another day. I have already spoken of the necessity of *not revealing* the error, and of not insisting in the teaching when the child does not respond readily.

Third. Language. *Allowing the letters to lie for some instants upon the table, the directress asks the child, "What is this?" and he should respond, o, i.*

In teaching the consonants, the directress pronounces only the *sound*, and as soon as she has done so unites with it a vowel, pronouncing the syllable thus formed and alternating this little exercise by the use of different vowels. She must always be careful to emphasize the sound of the consonant, repeating it by itself, as, for example, m, m, m, ma, me, mi, m, m. When the child *repeats* the sound he isolates it, and then accompanies it with the vowel.

It is not necessary to teach all the vowels before passing to the consonants, and as soon as the child knows one consonant he may begin to compose words. Questions of this sort, however, are left to the judgment of the educator.

I do not find it practical to *follow a special rule* in the teaching of the consonants. Often the curiosity of the child concerning a letter leads us to teach that desired consonant; a name pronounced may awaken in him a desire to know what consonants are necessary to compose it, and this *will*, or *willingness*, of the pupil is a much more *efficacious* means than any rule concerning the *progression* of the letters.

When the child pronounces *the sounds* of the consonants, he experiences an evident pleasure. It is a great novelty for him, this series of sounds, so varied and yet so distinct, *presenting* such enigmatic signs as the letters of the alphabet. There is mystery about all this, which provokes most decided interest. One day I was on the terrace while the children were having their free games; I had with me a little boy of two years and a half left with me, for a moment, by his mother. Scattered about upon a number of chairs, were the alphabets which we use in the school. These had become mixed, and I was putting the letters back into their respective compartments. Having finished my work, I placed the boxes upon two of the little chairs near me. The little boy watched me. Finally, he drew near to the box, and took one of the letters in his hand. It chanced to be an f. At that moment the children, who were running in single file, passed us, and, seeing the letter, called out in chorus the corresponding sound and passed on. The child paid no attention to them, but put back the f and took up an r. The children running by again, looked at him laughing, and then began to cry out "r, r, r ! r, r, r !" Little by little the baby understood that, when he took a letter in hand, the children, who were passing, cried out a sound. This amused him so much that I wished to observe how long he would persist in this game without becoming tired. He kept it up for *three-quarters of an hour!* The children had become interested in the child, and grouped themselves about him, pronouncing the sounds in chorus, and laughing at his pleased surprise. At last, after he had several times held up f, and had received from his public the same sound, he took the letter again, showing it to me, and saying, "f, f, f!" He had learned this from out the great confusion of sounds which he had heard: the long letter which had first arrested the attention of the running children, had made a great impression upon him.

It is not necessary to show how the separate pronunciation of the alphabetical sounds *reveals* the condition of the child's speech. Defects, which are almost all related to the *incomplete* development of the language itself, manifest themselves, and the directress may take note of them one by one. In this way she will be possessed of a record of the child's progress, which will help her in her individual teaching, and will reveal much concerning the development of the language in this particular child.

In the matter of *correcting linguistic defects*, we will find it helpful to follow the physiological rules relating to the child's development, and to modify the difficulties in the presentation of our lesson. When, however, the child's speech is sufficiently developed, and when he *pronounces all the sounds*, it does not matter which of the letters we select in our lessons.

Many of the defects which have become permanent in adults are due to *functional errors in the development* of the language during the period of infancy. If, for the attention which we pay to the correction of linguistic defects in children in the upper grades, we would substitute *a direction of the development of the language* while the child is still young, our results would be much more practical and valuable. In fact, many of the defects in pronunciation arise from the use of a *dialect*, and these it is almost impossible to correct after the period of childhood. They may, however, be most easily removed through the use of educational methods especially adapted to the perfecting of the language in little children.

We do not speak here of actual linguistic *defects* related to anatomical or physiological weaknesses, or to pathological facts which alter the function of the nervous system. I speak at present only of those irregularities which are due to a repetition of incorrect sounds, or to the imitation of imperfect pronunciation. Such defects may show themselves in the pronunciation of any one of the consonant sounds, and I can conceive of no more practical means for a methodical correction of speech defects than this exercise in pronunciation, which is a necessary part in learning the graphic language through my method. But such important questions deserve a chapter to themselves.

Turning directly to the method used in teaching writing, I may call attention to the fact that it is contained in the two periods already described. Such exercises have made it possible for the child to learn, and to fix, the muscular mechanism necessary to the proper holding of the pen, and to the making of the graphic signs. If he has exercised himself for a sufficiently long time in these exercises, he will be *potentially* ready to write all the letters of the alphabet and all of the simple syllables, without ever having taken chalk or pencil in his hand.

We have, in addition to this, begun the teaching of *reading* at the same time that we have been teaching *writing*. When we present a letter to the child and enunciate its sound, he fixes the image of this letter by means of the visual sense, and also by means of the muscular-tactile sense. He associates the sound with its related sign; that is, he relates the sound to the graphic sign. But *when he sees and recognises, he reads; and when he traces, he writes*. Thus his mind receives as one, two acts, which, later on, as he develops, will separate, coming to constitute the two diverse processes of *reading and writing*. By teaching these two acts contemporaneously, or, better, by their *fusion*, we place the child *before a new form of language* without determining which of the acts constituting it should be most prevalent.

We do not trouble ourselves as to whether the child in the development of this process, first learns to read or to write, or if the one or the other will be the easier. We must rid ourselves of all preconceptions, and must *await from experience* the answer to these questions. We may expect that individual differences will show themselves in the prevalence of one or the other act in the development of different children. This makes possible the most interesting psychological study of the individual, and should broaden the work of this method, which is based upon the free expansion of individuality.

Third Period: Exercises for the Composition of Words

Didactic Material. This consists chiefly of alphabets. The letters of the alphabet used here are identical in form and dimension with the sandpaper ones already described, but these are cut out of cardboard and are not mounted. In this way each letter represents an object which can be easily handled by the child and placed wherever he wishes it. There are several examples of each letter, and I have designed cases in which the alphabets may be kept. These cases or boxes are very shallow, and are divided and subdivided into many compartments, in each one of which I have placed a group of four copies of the same letter. The compartments are not equal in size, but are measured according to the dimensions of the letters themselves. At the bottom of each compartment is glued a letter which is not to be taken out. This letter is made of black cardboard and relieves the child of the fatigue of hunting about for the right compartment when he is replacing the letters in the case after he has used them. The vowels are cut from blue cardboard, and the consonants from red.

In addition to these alphabets we have a set of the capital letters mounted in sandpaper upon cardboard, and another, in which they are cut from cardboard. The numbers are treated in the same way.

Exercises. As soon as the child knows some of the vowels and the consonants we place before him the big box containing all the vowels and the consonants which he knows. The directress pronounces *very* clearly a word; for example, "mama," brings out the sound of the m very distinctly, repeating the sounds a number of times. Almost always the little one with an impulsive movement seizes an m and places it upon the table. The directress repeats "ma-ma." The child selects the a and places it near the m. He then composes the other syllable very easily. But the reading of the word which he has composed is not so easy. Indeed, he generally succeeds in reading it only after *a certain effort.* In this case I help the child, urging him to read, and reading the word with him once or twice, always pronouncing very distinctly, *mama, mama.* But once he has understood the mechanism of the game, the child goes forward by himself, and becomes intensely interested. We may pronounce any word, taking care only that the child understands separately the letters of which it is composed. He composes the new word, placing, one after the other, the signs corresponding to the sounds.

It is most interesting indeed to watch the child at this work. Intensely attentive, he sits watching the box, moving his lips almost imperceptibly, and taking one by one the necessary letters, rarely committing an error in spelling. The movement of the lips reveals the fact that he *repeats to himself an infinite number of times* the words whose sounds he is translating into signs. Although the child is able to compose any word which is clearly pronounced, we generally dictate to him only those words which are well-known, since we wish his composition to result in an idea. When these familiar words are used, he spontaneously rereads many times the word he has composed, repeating its sounds in a thoughtful, contemplative way.

The importance of these exercises is very complex. The child analyses, perfects, fixes his own spoken language,–placing an object in correspondence to every sound which he utters. The composition of the word furnishes him with substantial proof of the necessity for clear and forceful enunciation.

The exercise, thus followed, associates the sound which is heard with the graphic sign which represents it, and lays a most solid foundation for accurate and perfect spelling.

In addition to this, the composition of the words is in itself an exercise of intelligence. The word which is pronounced presents to the child a problem which he must solve, and he will do so by remembering the signs, selecting them from among others, and arranging them in the proper order. He will have the *proof* of the exact solution of his problem when he *rereads* the word–this word which he has composed, and which represents for all those who know how to read it, *an idea.*

When the child hears others read the word he has composed, he wears an expression of satisfaction and pride, and is possessed by a species of joyous wonder. He is impressed by this correspondence, carried on between himself and others by means of symbols. The written language represents for him the highest attainment reached by his own intelligence, and is at the same time, the reward of a great achievement.

When the pupil has finished the composition and the reading of the word we have him, according to the habits of order which we try to establish in connection with all our work, *"put away "* all the letters, each one in its own compartment. In composition, pure and simple, therefore, the child unites the two exercises of comparison and of selection of the graphic signs; the first, when from the entire box of letters before him he takes those necessary; the second, when he seeks the compartment in which each letter must be replaced. There are, then, three exercises united in this one effort, all three uniting to *fix the image of the graphic sign* corresponding to the sounds of the word. The work of learning is in this case facilitated in three ways, and the ideas are acquired in a third of the time which would have been necessary with the old methods. We shall soon see that the child, on hearing the word, or on thinking of a word which he already knows, *will see*, with his mind's eye, all the letters, necessary to compose the word, arrange themselves. He will reproduce this vision with a facility most surprising to us. One day a little boy four years old, running alone about the terrace, was heard to repeat many times, "To make Zaira, I must have z-a-i-r-a." Another time, Professor Di Donato, in a visit to the "Children's House," pronounced his own name for a four-year-old child. The child was composing the name, using small letters and making it all one word, and had begun thus–*diton*. The professor at once pronounced the word more distinctly; di *do* nato, whereupon the child, without scattering the letters, picked up the syllable *to* and placed it to one side, putting *do* in the empty space. He then placed an *a* after the *n*, and, taking up the *to* which he had put aside, completed the word with it. This made it evident that the child, when the word was pronounced more clearly, understood that the syllable *to* did not belong at that place in the word, realised that it belonged at the end of the word, and therefore placed it aside until he should need it. This was most surprising in a child of four years, and amazed all of those present. It can be explained by the clear and, at the same time, complex vision of the signs which the child must have, if he is to form a word which he hears spoken. This extraordinary act was largely due to the orderly mentality which the child had acquired through repeated spontaneous exercises tending to develop his intelligence.

These three periods contain the entire method for the acquisition of written language. The significance of such a method is clear. The psycho-physiological acts which unite to establish reading and writing are prepared separately and carefully. The muscular movements peculiar to the making of the signs or letters are prepared apart, and the same is true of the manipulation of the instrument of writing. The composition of the words, also, is reduced to a psychic mechanism of association between images heard and seen. There comes a moment in which the child, without thinking of it, fills in the geometric figures with an up and down stroke, which is free and regular; a moment in which he touches the letters with closed eyes, and in which he reproduces their form, moving his finger through the air; a moment in which the composition of words has become a psychic impulse, which makes the child, even when alone, repeat to himself "To make Zaira I must have z-a-i-r-a."

Now this child, it is true, *has never written*, but he has mastered all the acts necessary to writing. The child who, when taking dictation, not only knows how to compose the word, but instantly embraces in his thought its composition as a whole, will be able to write, since he knows how to make, with his eyes closed, the movements necessary to produce these letters, and since he manages almost unconsciously the instrument of writing.

More than this, the freedom with which the child has acquired this mechanical dexterity makes it possible for the impulse or spirit to act at any time through the medium of his mechanical ability. He should, sooner or later, come into his full power by way of a spontaneous explosion into writing. This is, indeed, the marvellous reaction which has come from my experiment with normal children. In one of the "Children's Houses," directed by Signorina Bettini, I had been especially careful in the way in which writing was taught, and we have had from this school most beautiful specimens of writing, and for this reason, perhaps I cannot do better than to describe the development of the work in this school.

One beautiful December day when the sun shone and the air was like spring, I went up on the roof with the children. They were playing freely about, and a number of them were gathered about me. I was sitting near a chimney, and said to a little five-year-old boy who sat beside me, "Draw me a picture of this chimney," giving him as I spoke a piece of chalk. He got down obediently and made a rough sketch of the chimney on the tiles which formed the floor of this roof terrace. As is my custom with little children, I encouraged him, praising his work. The child looked at me, smiled, remained for a moment as if on the point of bursting into some joyous act, and then cried out, "I can write! I can write!" and kneeling down again he wrote on the pavement the word "hand." Then, full of enthusiasm, he wrote also "chimney," "roof." As he wrote, he continued to cry out, "I can write! I know how to write!" His cries of joy brought the other children, who formed a circle about him, looking down at his work in stupefied amazement. Two or three of them said to me, trembling with excitement, "Give me the chalk. I can write too." And indeed they began to write various words: *mama, hand, John, chimney, Ada.*

Not one of them had ever taken chalk or any other instrument in hand for the purpose of writing. It was the *first time* that they had ever written, and they traced an entire word, as a child, when speaking for the first time, speaks the entire word.

The first word spoken by a baby causes the mother ineffable joy. The child has chosen perhaps the word "mother," seeming to render thus a tribute to maternity. The first word written by my little ones aroused within themselves an indescribable emotion of joy. Not being able to adjust in their minds the connection between the preparation and the act, they were possessed by the illusion that, having now grown to the proper size, they knew how to write. In other words, writing seemed to them only one among the many gifts of nature.

They believe that, as they grow bigger and stronger, there will come some beautiful day when they *shall know how to write.* And, indeed, this is what it is in reality. The child who speaks, first prepares himself unconsciously, perfecting the psycho-muscular mechanism which leads to the articulation of the word. In the case of writing, the child does almost the same thing, but the direct pedagogical help and the possibility of preparing the movements for writing in an almost material way, causes the ability to write to develop much more rapidly and more perfectly than the ability to speak correctly.

In spite of the ease with which this is accomplished, the preparation is not partial, but complete. The child possesses *all* the movements necessary for writing. And written language develops not gradually, but in an explosive way; that is, the child can write *any word.* Such was our first experience in the development of the written language in our children. Those first days we were a prey to deep emotions. It seemed as if we walked in a dream, and as if we assisted at some miraculous achievement.

The child who wrote a word for the first time was full of excited joy. He might be compared to the hen who has just laid an egg. Indeed, no one could escape from the noisy manifestations of the little one. He would call everyone to see, and if there were some who did not go, he ran to take hold of their clothes forcing them to come and see. We all had to go and stand about the written word to admire the marvel, and to unite our exclamations of surprise with the joyous cries of the fortunate author. Usually, this first word was written on the floor, and, then, the child knelt down before it in order to be nearer to his work and to contemplate it more closely.

After the first word, the children, with a species of frenzied joy, continued to write everywhere. I saw children crowding about one another at the blackboard, and behind the little ones who were standing on the floor another line would form consisting of children mounted upon chairs, so that they might write above the heads of the little ones. In a fury at being thwarted, other children, in order to find a little place where they might write, overturned the chairs upon which their companions were mounted. Others ran toward the window shutters or the door, covering them with writing. In these first days we walked upon a carpet of written signs. Daily accounts showed us that the same thing was going on at home, and some of the mothers, in order to save their pavements, and even the crust of their loaves upon which they found words written, made their children presents of *paper* and *pencil*. One of these children brought to me one day a little note-book entirely filled with writing, and the mother told me that the child had written all day long and all evening, and had gone to sleep in his bed with the paper and pencil in his hand.

This impulsive activity which we could not, in those first days control, made me think upon the wisdom of Nature, who develops the spoken language little by little, letting it go hand in hand with the gradual formation of ideas. Think of what the result would have been had Nature acted imprudently as I had done! Suppose Nature had first allowed the human being to gather, by means of the senses, a rich and varied material, and to acquire a store of ideas, and had then completely prepared in him the means for articulate language, saying finally to the child, mute until that hour, "Go-Speak!" The result would have been a species of sudden madness, under the influence of which the child, feeling no restraints, would have burst into an exhausting torrent of the most strange and difficult words.

I believe, however, that there exists between the two extremes a happy medium which is the true and practical way. We should lead the child more gradually to the conquest of written language, yet we should still have it come as a *spontaneous fact*, and his work should from the first be almost perfect.

Experience has shown us how to control this phenomenon, and how to lead the child more *calmly* to this new power. The fact that the children *see* their companions writing, leads them, through imitation, to write *as soon as* they can. In this way, when the child writes he does not have the entire alphabet at his disposal, and the number of words which he can write is limited. He is not even capable of making all of the words possible through a combination of the letters which he does know. He still has the great joy of the *first written word*, but this is no longer the source of *an overwhelming surprise*, since he sees just such wonderful things happening each day, and knows that sooner or later the same gift will come to all. This tends to create a calm and ordered environment, still full of beautiful and wonderful surprises.

Making a visit to the "Children's House," even during the opening weeks, one makes fresh discoveries. Here, for instance, are two little children, who, though they fairly radiate pride and joy, are writing tranquilly. Yet, these children, until yesterday, had never thought of writing!

The directress tells me that one of them began to write yesterday morning at eleven o'clock, the other, at three in the afternoon. We have come to accept the phenomenon with calmness, and tacitly recognise it as a *natural form of the child's development.*

The wisdom of the teacher shall decide when it is necessary to encourage a child to write. This can only be when he is already perfect in the three periods of the preparatory exercise, and yet does not write of his own accord. There is danger that in retarding the act of writing, the child may plunge finally into a tumultuous effort, due to the fact that he knows the entire alphabet and has no natural check.

The signs by which the teacher may almost precisely diagnose the child's maturity in this respect are: the *regularity* of the *parallel* lines which fill in the geometric figures; the recognition with closed eyes of the sandpaper letters; the security and readiness shown in the composition of words. Before intervening by means of a direct invitation to write, it is best to wait at least a week in the hope that the child may write spontaneously. When he has begun to write spontaneously the teacher may intervene to *guide* the progress of the writing. The first help which she may give is that of *ruling* the blackboard, so that the child may be led to maintain regularity and proper dimensions in his writing. The second, is that of inducing the child, whose writing is not firm, to *repeat the tracing* of the sandpaper letters. She should do this instead of *directly* correcting his actual writing, for the child does not perfect himself by repeating the act of writing, but by repeating the acts preparatory to writing. I remember a little beginner who, wishing to make his blackboard writing perfect, brought all of the sandpaper letters with him, and before writing touched two or three times *all of the letters needed in the words he wished to write.* If a letter did not seem to him to be perfect he erased it and *retouched* the letter upon the card before rewriting.

Our children, even after they have been writing for a year, continue to repeat the three preparatory exercises. They thus learn both to write, and to perfect their writing, without really going through the actual act. With our children, actual writing is a test, it springs from an inner impulse, and from the pleasure of explaining a superior activity; it is not an exercise. As the soul of the mystic perfects itself through prayer, even so in our little ones, that highest expression of civilisation, written language, is acquired and improved through exercises which are akin to, but which are not, writing.

There is educational value in this idea of preparing oneself before trying, and of perfecting oneself before going on. To go forward correcting his own mistakes, boldly attempting things which he does imperfectly, and of which he is as yet unworthy dulls the sensitiveness of the child's spirit toward his own errors. My method of writing contains an educative concept; teaching the child that prudence which makes him avoid errors, that dignity which makes him look ahead, and which guides him to perfection, and that humility which unites him closely to those sources of good through which alone he can make a spiritual conquest, putting far from him the illusion that the immediate success is ample justification for continuing in the way he has chosen.

The fact that all the children, those who are just beginning the three exercises and those who have been writing for months, daily repeat the same exercise, unites them and makes it easy for them to meet upon an apparently equal plane. Here there are no *distinctions* of beginners, and experts. All of the children fill in the figures with coloured pencils, touch the sandpaper letters and compose words with the movable alphabets; the little ones beside the big ones who help them. He who prepares himself, and he who perfects himself, both follow the same path. It is the same way in life, for, deeper than any social distinction, there lies an equality, a common meeting point, where all men are brothers, or, as in the spiritual life, aspirants and saints again and again pass through the same experiences.

Writing is very quickly learned, because we begin to teach it only to those children who show a desire for it by spontaneous attention to the lesson given by the directress to other children, or by watching the exercises in which the others are occupied. Some individuals *learn* without ever having received any lessons, solely through listening to the lessons given to others.

In general, all children of four are intensely interested in writing, and some of our children have begun to write at the age of three and a half. We find the children particularly enthusiastic about tracing the sandpaper letters.

During the first period of my experiments, when the children were shown the alphabet *for the first time*, I one day asked Signorina Bettini to bring out to the terrace where the children were at play, all of the various letters which she herself had made. As soon as the children saw them they gathered about us, their fingers outstretched in their eagerness to touch the letters. Those who secured cards were unable to touch them properly because of the other children, who crowded about trying to reach the cards in our laps. I remember with what an impulsive movement the possessors of the cards held them on high like banners, and began to march, followed by all the other children who clapped their hands and cried out joyously. The procession passed before us, and all, big and little, laughed merrily, while the mothers, attracted by the noise, leaned from the windows to watch the sight.

The average time that elapses between the first trial of the preparatory exercises and the first written word is, for children of four years, from a month to a month and a half. With children of five years, the period is much shorter, being about a month. But one of our pupils learned to use in writing all the letters of the alphabet in twenty days. Children of four years, after they have been in school for two months and a half, can write any word from dictation, and can pass to writing with ink in a note-book. Our little ones are generally experts after three months' time, and those who have written for six months may be compared to the children in the third elementary. Indeed, writing is one of the easiest and most delightful of all the conquests made by the child.

If adults learned as easily as children under six years of age, it would be an easy matter to do away with illiteracy. We would probably find two grave hinderances to the attainment of such a brilliant success: the torpor of the muscular sense, and those permanent defects of spoken language, which would be sure to translate themselves into the written language. I have not made experiments along this line, but I believe that one school year would be sufficient to lead an illiterate person, not only to write, but to express his thoughts in written language.

So much for the time necessary for learning. As to the execution, our children *write well* from the moment in which they begin. The *form* of the letters, beautifully rounded and flowing, is surprising in its similarity to the form of the sandpaper models. The beauty of our writing is rarely equalled by any scholars in the elementary schools, *who have not had special exercises in penmanship.* I have made a close study of penmanship, and I know how difficult it would be to teach pupils of twelve or thirteen years to write an entire word without lifting the pen, except for the few letters which require this. The up and down strokes with which they have filled their copy-book make flowing writing almost impossible to them.

Our little pupils, on the other hand, spontaneously, and with a marvellous security, write entire words without lifting the pen, maintaining perfectly the slant of the letters, and making the distance between each letter equal This has caused more than one visitor to exclaim, "If I had not seen it I should never have believed it." Indeed, penmanship is a superior form of teaching and is necessary to correct defects already acquired and fixed. It is a long work, for the child, *seeing* the model, must follow the *movements* necessary to reproduce it, while there is no direct correspondence between the visual sensation and the movements which he must make. Too often, penmanship is taught at an age when all the defects have become established, and when the physiological period in which the *muscular memory* is ready, has been passed.

We directly prepare the child, not only for writing, but also for *penmanship*, paying great attention to the *beauty of form* (having the children touch the letters in script form) and to the flowing quality of the letters. (The exercises in filling-in prepare for this.)

Reading

Didactic Material. The Didactic Material for the lessons in reading consists in slips of paper or cards upon which are written in clear, large script, words and phrases. In addition to these cards we have a great variety of toys.

Experience has taught me to distinguish clearly between *writing* and *reading*, and has shown me that the two acts *are not absolutely contemporaneous. Contrary to the usually accepted idea, writing precedes reading.* I do not consider as *reading* the test which the child makes *when he verifies* the word that he has written. He is translating signs into sounds, as he first translated sounds into signs. In this verification he already knows the word and has repeated it to himself while writing it. What I understand by reading is the *interpretation* of an idea from the written signs. The child who has not heard the word pronounced, and who recognises it when he sees it composed upon the table with the cardboard letters and who can tell what it means; this child *reads*. The word which he reads has the same relation to written language that the word which he hears bears to articulate language. Both serve to *receive the language* transmitted to us *by others*. So, until the child reads a transmission of ideas from the written word, *he does not read*.

We may say, if we like, that writing as described is a fact in which the psycho-motor mechanism prevails, while in reading, there enters a work which is purely intellectual. But it is evident how our method for writing prepares for reading, making the difficulties almost imperceptible. Indeed, writing prepares the child to interpret mechanically the union of the letter sounds of which the written word is composed. When a child in our school knows how to write, *he knows how to read the sounds* of which the word is composed. It should be noticed, however, that when the child composes the words with the movable alphabet, or when he writes, he has *time to think* about the signs which he must select to form the word. The writing of a word requires a great deal more time than that necessary for reading the same word.

The child who *knows how to write*, when placed before a word which he must interpret by reading, is silent for a long time, and generally reads the component sounds with the same slowness with which he would have written them. But *the sense of the word* becomes evident only when it is pronounced clearly and with the phonetic accent. Now, in order to place the phonetic accent the child must recognise the word; that is, he must recognise the idea which the word represents. The intervention of a superior work of the intellect is necessary if he is to read. Because of all this, I proceed in the following way with the exercises in reading, and, as will be evident, I do away entirely with the old-time primer.

I prepare a number of little cards made from ordinary writing-paper. On each of these I write in large clear script some well-known word, one which has already been pronounced many times by the children, and which represents an object actually present or well known to them. If the word refers to an object which is before them, I place this object under the eyes of the child, in order to facilitate his interpretation of the word. I will say, in this connection, the objects used in these writing games are for the most part toys of which we have a great many in the "Children's Houses." Among these toys, are the furnishings of a doll's house, balls, dolls, trees, flocks of sheep, or various animals, tin soldiers, railways, and an infinite variety of simple figures.

If writing serves to correct, or better, to direct and perfect the mechanism of the articulate language of the child, reading serves to help the development of ideas, and relates them to the development of the language. Indeed writing aids the physiological language and reading aids the social language.

We begin, then, as I have indicated, with the nomenclature, that is, with the reading of names of objects which are well known or present.

There is no question of beginning with words that are *easy or difficult*, for the child *already knows how to read any word*; that is, he knows how to read *the sounds which compose it*. I allow the little one to translate the written word slowly into sounds, and if the interpretation is exact, I limit myself to saying, "Faster." The child reads more quickly the second time, but still often without understanding. I then repeat, "Faster, faster." He reads faster each time, repeating the same accumulation of sounds, and finally the word bursts upon his consciousness. Then he looks upon it as if he recognised a friend and assumes that air of satisfaction which so often radiates our little ones. This completes the exercise for reading; It is a lesson which goes very rapidly, since it is only presented to a child who is already prepared through writing. Truly, we have buried the tedious and stupid A B C primer side by side with the useless copy-books!

When the child has read the word, he places the explanatory card under the object whose name it bears, and the exercise is finished.

One of our most interesting discoveries was made in the effort to devise a game through which the children might, without effort, learn to read words. We spread out upon one of the large tables a great variety of toys. Each one of them had a corresponding card upon which the name of the toy was written. We folded these little cards and mixed them up in a basket, and the children who knew how to read were allowed to take turns in drawing these cards from the basket. Each child had to carry his card back to his desk, unfold it quietly, and read it mentally, not showing it to those about him. He then had to fold it up again, so that the secret which it contained should remain unknown. Taking the folded card in his hand, he went to the table. He had then to pronounce clearly the name of a toy and present the card to the directress in order that she might verify the word he had spoken. The little card thus became current coin with which he might acquire the toy he had named. For, if he pronounced the word clearly and indicated the correct object, the directress allowed him to take the toy, and to play with it as long as he wished.

When each child had had a turn, the directress called the first child and let him draw a card from another basket. This card he read as soon as he had drawn it. It contained the name of one of his companions who did not yet know how to read, and for that reason could not have a toy. The child who had read the name then offered to his little friend the toy with which he had been playing. We taught the children to present these toys in a gracious and polite way, accompanying the act with a bow. In this way we did away with every idea of class distinction, and inspired the sentiment of kindness toward those who did not possess the same blessings as ourselves. This reading game proceeded in a marvellous way. The contentment of these poor children in possessing even for a little while such beautiful toys can be easily imagined.

But what was my amazement, when the children, having learned to understand the written cards, *refused* to take the toys! They explained that they did not wish to waste time in playing, and, with a species of insatiable desire, preferred to draw out and read the cards one after another!

I watched them, seeking to understand the secret of these souls, of whose greatness I had been so ignorant! As I stood in meditation among the eager children, the discovery that it was knowledge they loved, and not the silly *game*, filled me with wonder and made me think of the greatness of the human soul!

We therefore put away the toys, and set about making *hundreds* of written slips, containing names of children, cities, and objects; and also of colours and qualities known through the sense exercises. We placed these slips in open boxes, which we left where the children could make free use of them. I expected that childish inconstancy would at least show itself in a tendency to pass from one box to another; but no, each child finished emptying the box under his hand before passing to another, being verily *insatiable* in the desire to read.

Coming into the school one day, I found that the directress had allowed the children to take the tables and chairs out upon the terrace, and was having school in the open air. A number of little ones were playing in the sun, while others were seated in a circle about the tables containing the sandpaper letters and the movable alphabet.

A little apart sat the directress, holding upon her lap a long narrow box full of written slips, and all along the edge of her box were little hands, fishing for the beloved cards. "You may not believe me," said the directress, "but it is more than an hour since we began this, and they are not satisfied yet!" We tried the experiment of bringing balls, and dolls to the children, but without result; such futilities had no power beside the joys of *knowledge*.

Seeing these surprising results, I had already thought of testing the children with print, and had suggested that the directress *print* the word under the written word upon a number of slips. But the children forestalled us! There was in the hall a calendar upon which many of the words were printed in clear type, while others were done in Gothic characters. In their mania for reading the children began to look at this calendar, and, to my inexpressible amazement, read not only the print, but the Gothic script.

There therefore remained nothing but the presentation of a book, and I did not feel that any of those available were suited to our method.

The mothers soon had proofs of the progress of their children; finding in the pockets of some of them little slips of paper upon which were written rough notes of marketing done; bread, salt, etc. Our children were making lists of the marketing they did for their mothers! Other mothers told us that their children no longer ran through the streets, but stopped to read the signs over the shops.

A four-year-old boy, educated in a private house by the same method, surprised us in the following way. The child's father was a Deputy, and received many letters. He knew that his son had for two months been taught by means of exercises apt to facilitate the learning of reading and writing, but he had paid slight attention to it, and, indeed, put little faith in the method. One day as he sat reading, with the boy playing near, a servant entered, and placed upon the table a large number of letters that had just arrived. The little boy turned his attention to these, and holding up each letter read aloud the address. To his father this seemed a veritable miracle.

As to the average time required for learning to read and write, experience would seem to show that, starting from the moment in which the child writes, the passage from such an inferior stage of the graphic language to the superior state of reading averages a fortnight. *Security* in reading is, however, arrived at much more slowly than perfection in writing. In the greater majority of cases the child who writes beautifully, still reads rather poorly.

Not all children of the same age are at the same point in this matter of reading and writing. We not only do not force a child, but we do not even *invite* him, or in any way attempt to coax him to do that which he does not wish to do. So it sometimes happens that certain children, *not having spontaneously presented themselves* for these lessons, are left in peace, and do not know how to read or write.

If the old-time method, which tyrannized over the will of the child and destroyed his spontaneity, does not believe in making a knowledge of written language *obligatory* before the age of six, much less do we!

I am not ready to decide, without a wider experience, whether the period when the spoken language is fully developed is, in every case, the proper time for beginning to develop the written language.

In any case, almost all of the normal children treated with our method begin to write at four years, and at five know how to read and write, at least as well as children who have finished the first elementary. They could enter the second elementary a year in advance of the time when they are admitted to first.

Games for the Reading of Phrases. As soon as my friends saw that the children could read print, they made me gifts of beautifully illustrated books. Looking through these books of simple fairy lore, I felt sure that the children would not be able to understand them. The teachers, feeling entirely satisfied as to the ability of their pupils, tried to show me I was wrong, having different children read to me, and saying that they read much more perfectly than the children who had finished the second elementary.

I did not, however, allow myself to be deceived, and made two trials. I first had the teacher tell one of the stories to the children while I observed to what extent they were spontaneously interested in it. The attention of the children wandered after a few words. I had *forbidden* the teacher to recall to order those who did not listen, and thus, little by little, a hum arose in the schoolroom, due to the fact that each child, not caring to listen had returned to his usual occupation.

It was evident that the children, who seemed to read these books with such pleasure, *did not take pleasure in the sense*, but enjoyed the mechanical ability they had acquired, which consisted in translating the graphic signs into the sounds of a word they recognised. And, indeed, the children did not display the same *constancy* in the reading of books which they showed toward the written slips, since in the books they met with so many unfamiliar words.

My second test, was to have one of the children read the book to me. I did not interrupt with any of those explanatory remarks by means of which a teacher tries to help the child follow the thread of the story he is reading, saying for example: "Stop a minute. Do you understand? What have you read? You told me how the little boy went to drive in a big carriage, didn't you? Pay attention to what the book says, etc."

I gave the book to a little boy, sat down beside him in a friendly fashion, and when he had read I asked him simply and seriously as one would speak to a friend, "Did you understand what you were reading?" He replied: "No." But the expression of his face seemed to ask an explanation of my demand. In fact, the idea that *through the reading of a series of words the complex thoughts of others might be communicated to us*, was to be for my children one of the beautiful conquests of the future, a new source of surprise and joy

The *book* has recourse to *logical language*, not to the mechanism of the language. Before the child can understand and enjoy a book, the *logical language* must be established in him. Between knowing how to read the *words*, and how to read the *sense*, of a book there lies the same distance that exists between knowing how to pronounce a word and how to make a speech. I, therefore, stopped the reading from books and waited.

One day, during a free conversation period, *four* children arose at the same time and with expressions of joy on their faces ran to the blackboard and wrote phrases upon the order of the following:

"Oh, how glad we are that our garden has begun to bloom." It was a great surprise for me, and I was deeply moved. These children had arrived spontaneously at the art of *composition*, just as they had spontaneously written their first word.

The mechanical preparation was the same, and the phenomenon developed logically. Logical articulate language had, when the time was ripe, provoked the corresponding explosion in written language.

I understood that the time had come when we might proceed to the *reading of phrases*. I had recourse to the means used by the children; that is, I wrote upon the blackboard, "Do you love me?" The children read it slowly aloud, were silent for a moment as if thinking, then cried out, "Yes! Yes!" I continued to write; "Then make the silence, and watch me." They read this aloud, almost shouting, but had barely finished when a solemn silence began to establish itself, interrupted only by the sounds of the chairs as the children took positions in which they could sit quietly. Thus began between me and them a communication by means of written language, a thing which interested the children intensely. Little by little, they *discovered* the great quality of writing–that it transmits thought. Whenever I began to write, they fairly *trembled* in their eagerness to understand what was my meaning without hearing me speak a word.

Indeed, *graphic* language does not need spoken words. It can only be understood in all its greatness when it is completely isolated from spoken language.

This introduction to reading was followed by the following game, which is greatly enjoyed by the children. Upon a number of cards I wrote long sentences describing certain actions which the children were to carry out; for example, "Close the window blinds; open the front door; then wait a moment, and arrange things as they were at first." "Very politely ask eight of your companions to leave their chairs, and to form in double file in the centre of the room, then have them march forward and back on tiptoe, making no noise." "Ask three of your oldest companions who sing nicely, if they will please come into the centre of the room. Arrange them in a nice row, and sing with them a song that you have selected," etc., etc. As soon as I finished writing, the children seized the cards, and taking them to their seats read them spontaneously with great intensity of attention, and all *amid the most complete silence.*

I asked then, "Do you understand?" "Yes! Yes!" "Then do what the card tells you," said I, and was delighted to see the children rapidly and accurately follow the chosen action. A great activity, a movement of a new sort, was born in the room. There were those who closed the blinds, and then reopened them;

others who made their companions run on tiptoe, or sing; others wrote upon the blackboard, or took certain objects from the cupboards. Surprise and curiosity produced a general silence, and the lesson developed amid the most intense interest. It seemed as if some magic force had gone forth from me stimulating an activity hitherto unknown. This magic was graphic language, the greatest conquest of civilisation.

And how deeply the children understood the importance of it! When I went out, they gathered about me with expressions of gratitude and affection, saying, "Thank you! Thank you! Thank you for the lesson!"

This has become one of the favourite games: We first establish *profound silence*, then present a basket containing folded slips, upon each one of which is written a long phrase describing an action. All those children who know how to read may draw a slip, and read it *mentally* once or twice until they are certain they understand it. They then give the slip back to the directress and set about carrying out the action. Since many of these actions call for the help of the other children who do not know how to read, and since many of them call for the handling and use of the materials, a general activity develops amid marvellous order, while the silence is only interrupted by the sound of little feet running lightly, and by the voices of the children who sing. This is an unexpected revelation of the perfection of spontaneous discipline.

Experience has shown us that *composition* must *precede logical* reading, as writing preceded the reading of the word. It has also shown that reading, if it is to teach the child to *receive an idea*, should be *mental* and not *vocal*.

Reading aloud implies the exercise of two mechanical forms of the language–articulate and graphic–and is, therefore, a complex task. Who does not know that a grown person who is to read a paper in public prepares for this by making himself master of the content? Reading aloud is one of the most difficult intellectual actions. The child, therefore, who *begins* to read by interpreting thought *should read mentally*. The written language must isolate itself from the articulate, when it rises to the interpretation of logical thought. Indeed, it represents the language which *transmits thought at a distance*, while the senses and the muscular mechanism are silent. It is a spiritualised language, which puts into communication all men who know how to read.

Education having reached such a point in the "Children's Houses," the entire elementary school must, as a logical consequence, be changed. How to reform the lower grades in the elementary schools, eventually carrying them on according to our methods, is a great question which cannot be discussed here. I can only say that the *first elementary* would be completely done away with by our infant education, which includes it.

The elementary classes in the future should begin with children such as ours who know how to read and write; children who know how to take care of themselves; how to dress and undress, and to wash themselves; children who are familiar with the rules of good conduct and courtesy, and who are thoroughly disciplined in the highest sense of the term, having developed, and become masters of themselves, through liberty; children who possess, besides a perfect mastery of the articulate language, the ability to read written language in an elementary way, and who begin to enter upon the conquest of logical language.

These children pronounce clearly, write in a firm hand, and are full of grace in their movements. They are the earnest of a humanity grown in the cult of beauty-the infancy of an all-conquering humanity, since they are intelligent and patient observers of their environment, and possess in the form of intellectual liberty the power of spontaneous reasoning.

For such children, we should found an elementary school worthy to receive them and to guide them further along the path of life and of civilisation, a school loyal to the same educational principles of respect for the freedom of the child and for his spontaneous manifestations-principles which shall form the personality of these little men.

Language in Childhood

Graphic language, comprising dictation and reading, contains articulate language in its complete mechanism (auditory channels, central channels, motor channels), and, in the manner of development called forth by my method, is based essentially on articulate language.

Graphic language, therefore, may be considered from two points of view:

(a) That of the conquest of a new language of eminent social importance which adds itself to the articulate language of natural man; and this is the cultural significance which is commonly given to graphic language, which is therefore taught in the schools without any consideration of its relation to spoken language, but solely with the intention of offering to the social being a necessary instrument in his relations with his fellows.

(b) That of the relation between graphic and articulate language and, in this relation, of an eventual possibility of utilising the written language to perfect the spoken: a new consideration upon which I wish to insist and which gives to graphic language *a physiological importance.*

Moreover, as spoken language is at the same time a *natural function* of man and an instrument which he utilises for social ends, so written language may be considered in itself, in its *formation*, as an organic *ensemble* of new mechanisms which are established in the nervous system, and as an instrument which may be utilised for social ends.

In short, it is a question of giving to written language not only a physiological importance, but also a *period of development* independent of the high functions which it is destined to perform later.

It seems to me that graphic language bristles with difficulties in its beginning, not only because it has heretofore been taught by irrational methods, but because we have tried to make it perform, as soon as it has been acquired, the high function of teaching *the written language* which has been fixed by centuries of perfecting in a civilised people.

Think how irrational have been the methods we have used! We have analysed the graphic signs rather than the physiological acts necessary to produce the alphabetical signs; and this without considering that *any graphic sign* is difficult to achieve, because the visual representation of the signs have no hereditary connection with the motor representations necessary for producing them; as, for example, the auditory representations of the word have with the motor mechanism of the articulate language. It is, therefore, always a difficult thing to provoke a stimulative motor action unless we have already established the movement before the visual representation of the sign is made. It is a difficult thing to arouse an activity that shall produce a motion unless that motion shall have been previously established by practice and by the power of habit.

Thus, for example, the analysis of writing into *little straight lines and curves* has brought us to present to the child a sign without significance, which therefore does not interest him, and whose representation is incapable of determining a spontaneous motor impulse. The artificial act constituted, therefore, an *effort* of the will which resulted for the child in rapid exhaustion exhibited in the form of boredom and suffering. To this effort was added the effort of constituting *synchronously* the muscular associations co-ordinating the movements necessary to the holding and manipulating the instrument of writing.

All sorts of *depressing* feelings accompanied such efforts and conduced to the production of imperfect and erroneous signs which the teachers had to correct, discouraging the child still more with the constant criticism of the error and of the imperfection of the signs traced. Thus, while the child was urged to make an effort, the teacher depressed rather than revived his psychical forces.

Although such a mistaken course was followed, the graphic language, so painfully learned, was nevertheless to be *immediately* utilised for social ends; and, still imperfect and immature, was made to do service in the *syntactical construction of the language*, and in the ideal expression of the superior psychic centres. One must remember that in nature the spoken language is formed gradually; and it is already established in *words* when the superior psychic centres use these words in what Kussmaul calls *dictorium*, in the syntactical grammatical formation of language which is necessary to the expression of complex ideas; that is, in the language of the *logical mind*.

In short the mechanism of language is a necessary antecedent of the higher psychic activities which are to *utilise it*.

There are, therefore, two periods in the development of language: a lower one which prepares the nervous channel and the central mechanisms which are to put the sensory channels in relation with the motor channels; and a higher one determined by the higher psychic activities which are *exteriorized* by means of the preformed mechanisms of language.

Thus for example in the scheme which Kussmaul gives on the mechanism of articulate language we must first of all distinguish a sort of cerebral diastaltic arc (representing the pure mechanism of the word), which is established in the first formation of the spoken language. Let E be the ear, and T the motor organs of speech, taken as a whole and here represented by the tongue, A the auditory centre of speech, and M the motor centre. The channels EA and MT are peripheral channels, the former centripetal and the latter centrifugal, and the channel AM is the inter-central channel of association.

The centre A in which reside the auditive images of words may be again subdivided into three, as in the following scheme, viz.: Sound (So), syllables (Sy), and words (W).

That partial centres for sounds and syllables can really be formed, the pathology of language seems to establish, for in some forms of centro-sensory dysphasia, the patients can pronounce only sounds, or at most sounds and syllables.

Small children, too, are, at the beginning, particularly sensitive to simple sounds of language, with which indeed, and especially with *s*, their mothers caress them and attract their attention; while later the child is sensitive to syllables, with which also the mother caresses him, saying: *"ba, ba, punf, tuf!"*

Finally it is the simple word, dissyllabic in most cases, which attracts the child's attention.

But for the motor centres also the same thing may be repeated; the child utters at the beginning simple or double sounds, as for example *bl, gl, ch,* an expression which the mother greets with joy; then distinctly syllabic sounds begin to manifest themselves in the child: *ga, ba;* and, finally, the dissyllabic word, usually labial: *mama.*

We say that the spoken language begins with the child when the word pronounced by him signifies an idea; when for example, seeing his mother and recognising her he says *"mamma;* " and seeing a dog says, *"tettè;"* and wishing to eat says: *"pappa."*

Thus we consider *language begun* when it is established in relation to perception; while the language itself is still, in its psycho-motor mechanism, perfectly rudimentary.

That is, when above the diastaltic arc where the mechanical formation of the language is still unconscious, the recognition of the word takes place, that is, the word is perceived and associated with the object which it represents, language is considered to have begun.

On this level, *later*, language continues the process of perfecting in proportion as the hearing perceives better the component sounds of the words and the psycho-motor channels become more permeable to articulation.

This is the first stage of spoken language, which has its own beginning and its own development, leading, through the perceptions, to the *perfecting* of the primordial mechanism of the language itself; and at this stage precisely is established what we call *articulate language*, which will later be the means which the adult will have at his disposal to express his own thoughts, and which the adult will have great difficulty in perfecting or correcting when it has once been established: in fact a high stage of culture sometimes accompanies an imperfect articulate language which prevents the aesthetic expression of one's thought.

The development of articulate language takes place in the period between the age of two and the age of seven: the age of *perceptions* in which the attention of the child is spontaneously turned towards external objects, and the memory is particularly tenacious. It is the age also of *motility* in which all the psycho-motor channels are becoming permeable and the muscular mechanisms establish themselves. In this period of life by the mysterious bond between the auditory channel and the motor channel of the spoken language it would seem that the auditory perceptions have the direct power of *provoking* the complicated movements of articulate speech which develop instinctively after such stimuli as if awaking from the slumber of heredity. It is well known that it is only at this age that it is possible to acquire all the characteristic modulations of a language which it would be vain to attempt to establish later. The mother tongue alone is well pronounced because it was established in the period of childhood; and the adult who learns to speak a new language must bring to it the imperfections characteristic of the foreigner's speech: only children who under the age of seven years learn several languages at the same time can receive and reproduce all the characteristic mannerisms of accent and pronunciation. `

Thus also the *defects* acquired in childhood such as dialectic defects or those established by bad habits, become indelible in the adult.

What develops later, the *superior* language, the *dictorium*, no longer has its origin in the mechanism of language but in the intellectual development which makes use of the mechanical language. As the articulate language develops by the exercise of its mechanism and is enriched by perception, the *dictorium* develops with syntax and is enriched by *intellectual culture*.

Going back to the scheme of language we see that above the arc which defines the lower language, is established the *dictorium*, D,-from which now come the motor impulses of speech–which is established as *spoken language* fit to manifest the ideation of the intelligent man; this language will be enriched little by little by intellectual culture and perfected by the grammatical study of syntax.

Hitherto, as a result of a preconception, it has been believed that written language should enter only into the development of the *dictorium*, as the suitable means for the acquisition of culture and of permitting grammatical analysis and construction of the language. Since "spoken words have wings" it has been admitted that intellectual culture could only proceed by the aid of a language which was stable, objective, and capable of being analysed, such as the graphic language.

But why, when we acknowledge the graphic language as a precious, nay indispensable, instrument of intellectual education, for the reason that it *fixes the ideas* of men and permits of their analysis and of their assimilation in books, where they remain indelibly written as an ineffaceable memory of words which are therefore always present and by which we can analyse the syntactical structure of the language, why shall we not acknowledge that it is *useful* in the more humble task of *fixing* the *words* which represent perception and of analysing their component sounds?

Compelled by a pedagogical prejudice we are unable to separate the idea of a graphic language from that of a function which heretofore we have made it exclusively perform; and it seems to us that by teaching such a language to children still in the age of simple perceptions and of motility we are committing a serious psychological and pedagogical error.

But let us rid ourselves of this prejudice and consider the graphic language in itself, reconstructing its psycho-physiological mechanism. It is far more simple than the psycho-physiological mechanism of the articulate language, and is far more directly accessible to education.

Writing especially is surprisingly simple. For let us consider *dictated* writing: we have a perfect parallel with spoken language since a *motor* action must correspond with *heard* speech. Here there does not exist, to be sure, the mysterious hereditary relations between the heard speech and the articulate speech; but the movements of writing are far simpler than those necessary to the spoken word, and are performed by large muscles, all external, *upon which we can directly act*, rendering the motor channels permeable, and establishing psycho-muscular mechanisms.

This indeed is what is done by my method, which *prepares the movements directly*; so that the psycho-motor impulse of the heard speech *finds the motor channels already established*, and is manifested in the act of writing, like an explosion.

The real difficulty is in the *interpretation of the graphic signs*; but we must remember that we are in the age of *perceptions*, where the sensations and the memory as well as the primitive associations are involved precisely in the characteristic progress of natural development. Moreover our children are already prepared by various exercises of the senses, and by methodical construction of ideas and mental associations to perceive the graphic signs; something like a patrimony pf perceptive ideas offers material to the language in the process of development. The child who recognises a triangle and calls it a triangle can recognise a letter *s* and denominate it by the sound *s*. This is obvious.

Let us not talk of premature teaching; ridding ourselves of prejudices, let us appeal to experience which shows that in reality children proceed without effort, nay rather with evident manifestations of pleasure to the recognition of graphic signs presented as objects.

And with this premise let us consider the relations between the mechanisms of the two languages.

The child of three or four has already long begun his articulate language according to our scheme. But he finds himself in the period in which *the mechanism of articulate language is being perfected*; a period contemporary with that in which he is acquiring a content of language along with the patrimony of perception.

The child has perhaps not heard perfectly in all their component parts the words which he pronounces, and, if he has heard them perfectly, they may have been pronounced badly, and consequently have left an erroneous auditory perception. It would be well that the child, by exercising the motor channels of articulate language should establish exactly the movements necessary to a perfect articulation, *before* the age of easy motor adaptations is passed, and, by the fixation of erroneous mechanisms, the defects become incorrigible.

To this end the *analysis of speech* is necessary. As when we wish to perfect the language we first start children at composition and then pass to grammatical study; and when we wish to perfect the style we first teach to write grammatically and then come to the analysis of style–so when we wish to perfect the *speech* it is first necessary that the speech *exist*, and then it is proper to proceed to its analysis. When, therefore, the child *speaks*, but before the completion of the development of speech which renders it fixed in mechanisms already established, the speech should be analysed with a view to perfecting it.

Now, as grammar and rhetoric are not possible with the spoken language but demand recourse to the written language which keeps ever before the eye the discourse to be analysed, so it is with speech.

The analysis of the transient is impossible.

The language must be materialised and made stable. Hence the necessity of the written word or the word represented by graphic signs.

In the third stage of my method for writing, that is, composition of speech, is included the *analysis of the word* not only into signs, but into the component sounds; the signs representing its translation. The child, that is, *divides* the heard word which he perceives integrally as *a word*, knowing also its meanings, into sounds and syllables.

Let me call attention to the following diagram which represents the interrelation of the two mechanisms for writing and for articulate speech.

Whereas in the development of spoken language the sound composing the word might be imperfectly perceived, here in the teaching of the graphic sign corresponding to the sound (which teaching consists in presenting to the child a sandpaper letter, naming it *distinctly* and making the child *see* it and *touch* it), not only is the perception of the heard sound *clearly* fixed–separately and clearly–but this perception is associated with two others: the centro-motor perception and the centro-visual perception of the written sign.

The triangle VC, MC, So represents the association of three sensations in relation with the analysis of speech.

When the letter is presented to the child and he is made to touch and see it, while it is being named, the centripetal channels ESo; H, MC, So; V, VC, So are acting and when the child is made to name the letter, alone or accompanied by a vowel, the external stimulus acts in V and passes through the channels V, VC, So, M, T; *and* V, CV, So, Sy, M. T.

When these channels of association have been established by presenting visual stimuli in the graphic sign, the corresponding movements of articulate language can be provoked and studied one by one in their defects; while, by maintaining the visual stimulus of the graphic sign which provokes articulation and accompanying it by the auditory stimulus of the corresponding *sound* uttered by the teacher, their articulation can be perfected; this articulation is by innate conditions connected with the heard speech; that is, in the course of the pronunciation provoked by the visual stimulus, and during the repetition of the relative movements of the organs of language, the auditory stimulus which is introduced into the exercise contributes to the perfecting of the pronunciation of the isolated or syllabic sounds composing the spoken word.

When later the child writes under dictation, translating into signs the sounds of speech, he analyses the heard speech into its sounds, translating them into graphic movements through channels already rendered permeable by the corresponding muscular sensations.

Defects of Language Due to Lack of Education

Defects and imperfections of language are in part due to organic causes, consisting in malformations or in pathological alterations of the nervous system; but in part they are connected with functional defects acquired in the period of the formation of language and consist in an erratic pronunciation of the component sounds of the spoken word. Such errors are acquired by the child who hears words imperfectly pronounced, or *hears bad speech*. The dialectic accent enters into this category; but there are also vicious habits which make the natural defects of the articulate language of childhood persist in the child, or which provoke in him by imitation the defects of language peculiar to the persons who surrounded him in his childhood.

The normal defects of child language are due to the fact that the complicated muscular agencies of the organs of articulate language do not yet function well and are consequently incapable of reproducing the *sound* which was the sensory stimulus of a certain innate movement. The association of the movements necessary to the articulation of the spoken words is established little by little. The result is a language made of words with sounds which are imperfect and often lacking (whence incomplete words). Such defects are grouped under the name *bloesitas* and are especially due to the fact that the child is not yet capable of directing the movements of his tongue. They comprise chiefly: *sigmatism* or imperfect pronunciation of *s*; *rhotacism* or imperfect pronunciation of *r*; *lambdacism* or imperfect pronunciation of *l*; *gammacism* or imperfect pronunciation of *g*; *iotacism*, defective pronunciation of the gutturals; *mogilalia*, imperfect pronunciation of the labials, and according to some authors, as Preyer, mogilalia is made to include also the suppression of the first sound of a word.

Some defects of pronunciation which concern the utterance of the vowel sound as well as that of the consonant are due to the fact that the child *reproduces perfectly* sounds imperfectly heard.

In the first case, then, it is a matter of functional insufficiencies of the peripheral motor organ and hence of the nervous channels, and the cause lies in the individual; whereas in the second case the error is caused by the auditory stimulus and the cause lies outside.

These defects often persist, however attenuated, in the boy and the adult: and produce finally an erroneous language to which will later be added in writing orthographical errors, such for example as dialectic orthographical errors.

If one considers the charm of human speech one is bound to acknowledge the inferiority of one who does not possess a correct spoken language; and an aesthetic conception in education cannot be imagined unless special care be devoted to perfecting articulate language. Although the Greeks had transmitted to Rome the art of educating in language, this practice was not resumed by Humanism which cared more for the aesthetics of the environment and the revival of artistic works than for the perfecting of the man.

To-day we are just beginning to introduce the practice of correcting by pedagogical methods the serious defects of language, such as stammering; but the idea of *linguistic gymnastics* tending to its perfection has not yet penetrated into our schools as a *universal method*, and as a detail of the great work of the aesthetic perfecting of man.

Some teachers of deaf mutes and intelligent devotees of orthophony are trying nowadays with small practical success to introduce into the elementary schools the correction of the various forms of *bloesitas*, as a result of statistical studies which have demonstrated the wide diffusion of such defects among the pupils. The exercises consist essentially in *silence* cures which procure calm and repose for the organs of language, and in patient *repetition* of the *separate* vowel and consonant *sounds*; to these exercises is added also respiratory gymnastics. This is not the place to describe in detail the methods of these exercises which are long and patient and quite out of harmony with the teachings of the school. But in my methods are to be found all exercises for the corrections of language:

(a) *Exercises of Silence*, which prepare the nervous channels of language to receive new stimuli perfectly;

(b) *Lessons* which consist first of the distinct pronunciation by the teacher of *few words* (especially of nouns which must be associated with a concrete idea); by this means clear and perfect *auditory stimuli* of language are started, stimuli which are *repeated* by the teacher when the child has conceived the idea of the object represented by the word (recognition of the object); finally of the provocation of articulate language on the part of the child who must repeat *that word alone* aloud, pronouncing its separate sounds;

(c) *Exercises in Graphic Language*, which analyse the sounds of speech and cause them to be repeated separately in several ways: that is, when the child learns the separate letters of the alphabet and when he composes or writes words, repeating their sounds which he translates separately into composed or written speech;

(d) *Gymnastic Exercises*, which comprise, as we have seen, both *repiratory exercises* and those of *articulation*.

I believe that in the schools of the future the conception will disappear which is beginning to-day of "*correcting in the elementary schools* " the defects of language; and will be replaced by the more rational one of *avoiding them by caring for the development of language* in the "Children's Houses"; that is, in the very age in which language is being established in the child.

Teaching of Numeration; Introduction to Arithmetic

Children of three years already know how to count as far as two or three when they enter our schools. They therefore *very easily* learn numeration, which consists *in counting objects.* A dozen different ways may serve toward this end, and daily life presents many opportunities; when the mother says, for instance, "There are two buttons missing from your apron," or "We need three more plates at table."

One of the first means used by me, is that of counting with money. I obtain *new* money, and if it were possible I should have good reproductions made in cardboard. I have seen such money used in a school for deficients in London.

The *making of change* is a form of numeration so attractive as to hold the attention of the child. I present the one, two, and four centime pieces and the children, in this way learn to count to *ten.*

No form of instruction is more *practical* than that tending to make children familiar with the coins in common use, and no exercise is more useful than that of making change. It is so closely related to daily life that it interests all children intensely.

Having taught numeration in this empiric mode, I pass to more methodical exercises, having as didactic material one of the sets of blocks already used in the education of the senses; namely, the series of ten rods heretofore used for the teaching of length. The shortest of these rods corresponds to a decimetre, the longest to a metre, while the intervening rods are divided into sections a decimetre in length. The sections are painted alternately red and blue.

Some day, when a child has arranged the rods, placing them in order of length, we have him count the red and blue signs, beginning with the smallest piece; that is, one; one, two; one, two, three, etc., always going back to one in the counting of each rod, and starting from the side A. We then have him name the single rods from the shortest to the longest, according to the total number of the sections which each contains, touching the rods at the sides B, on which side the stair ascends. This results in the same numeration as when we counted the longest rod-1, 2, 3, 4, 5, 6, 7, 8, 9, 10. Wishing to know the number of rods, we count them from the side A and the same numeration results; 1, 2, 3, 4, 5, 6, 7, 8, 9, 10. This correspondence of the three sides of the triangle causes the child to verify his knowledge and as the exercise interests him he repeats it many times.

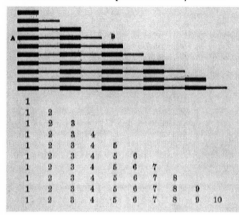

We now unite to the exercises in *numeration* the earlier, sensory exercises in which the child recognised the long and short rods. Having mixed the rods upon a carpet, the directress selects one, and showing it to the child, has him count the sections; for example, 5. She then asks him to give her the one next in length. He selects it *by his eye*, and the directress has him *verify* his choice by *placing the two pieces side by side and by counting their sections*. Such exercises may be repeated in great variety and through them the child learns to assign a *particular name to each one of the pieces in the long stair*. We may now call them piece number one; piece number two, etc., and finally, for brevity, may speak of them in the lessons as one, two, three, etc.

The Numbers as Represented by the Graphic Signs

At this point, if the child already knows how to write, we may present the figures cut in sandpaper and mounted upon cards. In presenting these, the method is the same used in teaching the letters. "This is one." "This is two." "Give me one." "Give me two." "What *number* is this?" The child traces the number with his finger as he did the letters.

Exercises with Numbers. Association of the graphic sign with the quantity.

I have designed two trays each divided into five little compartments. At the back of each compartment may be placed a card bearing a figure. The figures in the first tray should be 0, 1, 2, 3, 4, and in the second, 5, 6, 7, 8, 9.

The exercise is obvious; it consists in placing within the compartments a number of objects corresponding to the figure indicated upon the card at the back of the compartment. We give the children various objects in order to vary the lesson, but chiefly make use of large wooden pegs so shaped that they will not roll off the desk. We place a number of these before the child whose part is to arrange them in their places, one peg corresponding to the card marked one, etc. When he has finished he takes his tray to the directress that she may verify his work.

The Lesson on Zero. We wait until the child, pointing to the compartment containing the card marked zero, asks, "And what must I put in here?" We then reply, "Nothing; zero is nothing." But often this is not enough. It is necessary to make the child *feel* what we mean by *nothing.* To this end we make use of little games which vastly entertain the children. I stand among them, and turning to one of them who has already used this material, I say, "Come, dear, come to me *zero* times." The child almost always comes to me, and then runs back to his place. "But, my boy, you came *one* time, and I told you to come *zero* times." Then he begins to wonder. "But what must I do, then?" "Nothing; zero is nothing." "But how shall I do nothing?" "Don't do anything. You must sit still. You must not come at all, not any times. Zero times. No times at all." I repeat these exercises until the children understand, and they are then immensely amused at remaining quiet when I call to them to come to me zero times, or to throw me zero kisses. They themselves often cry out, "Zero is nothing! Zero is nothing!"

Exercises for the Memory of Numbers

When the children recognise the written figure, and when this figure signifies to them the numerical value, I give them the following exercise:

I cut the figures from old calendars and mount them upon slips of paper which are then folded and dropped into a box. The children draw out the slips, carry them still folded, to their seats, where they look at them and refold them, *conserving the secret.* Then, one by one, or in groups, these children (who are naturally the oldest ones in the class) go to the large table of the directress where groups of various small objects have been placed. Each one selects the *quantity* of objects corresponding to the number he has drawn. The number, meanwhile, has been left *at the child's place,* a slip of paper mysteriously folded. The child, therefore, must *remember* his number not only during the movements which he makes in coming and going, but while he collects his pieces, counting them one by one. The directress may here make interesting individual observations upon the number memory.

When the child has gathered up his objects he arranges them upon his own table, in columns of two, and if the number is uneven, he places the odd piece at the bottom and between the last two objects. The arrangement of the pieces is therefore as follows:-

```
o   o   o   o   o   o   o   o   o   o
X  XX  XX  XX  XX  XX  XX  XX  XX  XX
    X  XX  XX  XX  XX  XX  XX  XX
        X  XX  XX  XX  XX  XX
            X  XX  XX  XX
                X  XX
```

The crosses represent the objects, while the circle stands for the folded slip containing the figure. Having arranged his objects, the child awaits the verification. The directress comes, opens the slip, reads the number, and counts the pieces.

When we first played this game it often happened that the children took *more objects* than were called for upon the card, and this was not always because they did not remember the number, but arose from a mania for the having the greatest number of objects. A little of that instinctive greediness, which is common to primitive and uncultured man. The directress seeks to explain to the children that it is useless to have all those things upon the desk, and that the point of the game lies in taking the exact number of objects called for.

Little by little they enter into this idea, but not so easily as one might suppose. It is a real effort of self-denial which holds the child within the set limit, and makes him take, for example, only two of the objects placed at his disposal, while he sees others taking more. I therefore consider this game more an exercise of will power than of numeration. The child who has the *zero*, should not move from his place when he sees all his companions rising and taking freely of the objects which are inaccessible to him. Many times zero falls to the lot of a child who knows how to count perfectly, and who would experience great pleasure in accumulating and arranging a fine group of objects in the proper order upon his table, and in awaiting with security the teacher's verification.

It is most interesting to study the expressions upon the faces of those who possess zero. The individual differences which result are almost a revelation of the "character" of each one. Some remain impassive, assuming a bold front in order to hide the pain of the disappointment; others show this disappointment by involuntary gestures. Still others cannot hide the smile which is called forth by the singular situation in which they find themselves, and which will make their friends curious. There are little ones who follow every movement of their companions with a look of desire, almost of envy, while others show instant acceptance of the situation. No less interesting are the expressions with which they confess to the holding of the zero, when asked during the verification, "and you, you haven't taken anything?" "I have zero." "It is zero." These are the usual words, but the expressive face, the tone of the voice, show widely varying sentiments. Rare, indeed, are those who seem to give with pleasure the explanation of an extraordinary fact. The greater number either look unhappy or merely resigned.

We therefore give lessons upon the meaning of the game, saying, "It is hard to keep the zero secret. Fold the paper tightly and don't let it slip away. It is the most difficult of all." Indeed, after awhile, the very difficulty of remaining quiet appeals to the children and when they open the slip marked zero it can be seen that they are content to keep the secret.

Addition and Subtraction from One to Twenty: Multiplication and Division

The didactic material which we use for the teaching of the first arithmetical operations is the same already used for numeration; that is, the rods graduated as to length which, arranged on the scale of the metre, contain the first idea of the decimal system.

The rods, as I have said, have come to be called by the numbers which they represent; one, two, three, etc. They are arranged in order of length, which is also in order of numeration.

The first exercise consists in trying to put the shorter pieces together in such a way as to form tens. The most simple way of doing this is to take successively the shortest rods, from one up, and place them at the end of the corresponding long rods from nine down. This may be accompanied by the commands, "Take one and add it to nine; take two and add it to eight; take three and add it to seven; take four and add it to six." In this way we make four rods equal to ten. There remains the five, but, turning this upon its head (in the long sense), it passes from one end of the ten to the other, and thus makes clear the fact that two times five makes ten.

These exercises are repeated and little by little the child is taught the more technical language; nine plus one equals ten, eight plus two equals ten, seven plus three equals ten, six plus four equals ten, and for the five, which remains, two times five equals ten. At last, if he can write, we teach the signs *plus* and *equals* and *times*. Then this is what we see in the neat note-books of our little ones:

9 + 1 = 10

8 + 2 = 10   (5 X 2 = 10)

7 + 3 = 10

6 + 4 + 10

When all this is well learned and has been put upon the paper with great pleasure by the children, we call their attention to the work which is done when the pieces grouped together to form tens are taken apart, and put back in their original positions. From the ten last formed we take away four and six remains; from the next we take away three and seven remains; from the next, two and eight remains; from the last, we take away one and nine remains. Speaking of this properly we say, ten less four equals six; ten less three equals seven; ten less two equals eight; ten less one equals nine.

In regard to the remaining five, it is the half of ten, and by cutting the long rod in two, that is dividing ten by two, we would have five; ten divided by two equals five. The written record of all this reads:

10 – 4 = 6

10 – 3 = 7   (10 / 2 = 5)

10 – 2 = 8

10 – 1 = 9

Once the children have mastered this exercise they multiply it spontaneously. Can we make three in two ways? We place the one after the two and then write, in order that we may remember what we have done, 2+1=3. Can we make two rods equal to number four? 3+1=4, and 4-3=1; 4-1=3. Rod number two in its relation to rod number four is treated as was five in relation to ten; that is, we turn it over and show that it is contained in four exactly two times: 4 / 2=2; 2x2=4. Another problem: let us see with how many rods we can play this same game. We can do it with three and six; and with four and eight; that is,

2 x 2 = 4   3 x 2 = 6   4 x 2 = 8   5 x 2 = 10

10 / 2=5   8 / 2=4   6 / 2=3   4 / 2=2

At this point we find that the cubes with which we played the number memory games are of help:

From this arrangement, one sees at once which are the numbers which can be divided by two–all those which have not an odd cube at the bottom. These are the *even* numbers, because they can be arranged in pairs, two by two; and the division by two is easy, all that is necessary being to separate the two lines of twos that stand one under the other. Counting the cubes of each file we have the quotient. To recompose the primitive number we need only reassemble the two files thus 2x3=6. All this is not difficult for children of five years.

The repetition soon becomes monotonous, but the exercises may be most easily changed, taking again the set of long rods, and instead of placing rod number one after nine, place it after ten. In the same way, place two after nine, and three after eight. In this way we make rods of a greater length than ten; lengths which we must learn to name eleven, twelve, thirteen, etc., as far as twenty. The little cubes, too, may be used to fix these higher numbers

Having learned the operations through ten, we proceed with no difficulty to twenty. The one difficulty lies in the *decimal numbers* which require certain lessons.

Lessons on Decimals: Arithmetical Calculations Beyond Ten

The necessary didactic material consists of a number of square cards upon which the figure ten is printed in large type, and of other rectangular cards, half the size of the square, and containing the single numbers from one to nine. We place the numbers in a line; 1, 2, 3, 4, 5, 6, 7, 8 , 9, 10. Then, having no more numbers, we must begin over again and take the 1 again. This 1 is like that section in the set of rods which, in rod number 10, extends beyond nine. Counting along *the stair* as far as nine, there remains this one section which, as there are no more numbers, we again designate as 1; but this is a higher 1 than the first, and to distinguish it from the first we put near it a zero, a sign which means nothing. Here then is 10. Covering the zero with the separate rectangular number cards in the order of their succession we see formed: 11, 12, 13, 14, 15, 16, 17, 18, 19. These numbers are composed by adding to rod number 10, first rod number 1, then 2, then 3, etc., until we finally add rod number 9 to rod number 10, thus obtaining a very long rod, which, when its alternating red and blue sections are counted, gives us nineteen.

The directress may then show to the child the cards, giving the number 16, and he may place rod 6 after rod 10. She then takes away the card bearing 6, and places over the zero the card bearing the figure 8, whereupon the child takes away rod 6 and replaces it with rod 8, thus making 18. Each of these acts may be recorded thus: 10+6=16; 10+8=18, etc. We proceed in the same way to subtraction.

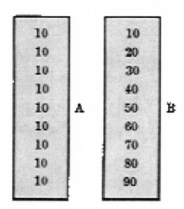

When the number itself begins to have a clear meaning to the child, the combinations are made upon one long card, arranging the rectangular cards bearing the nine figures upon the two columns of numbers shown in the figures A and B.

Upon the card A we superimpose upon the zero of the second 10, the rectangular card bearing the 1: and under this the one bearing two, etc. Thus while the one of the ten remains the same the numbers to the right proceed from zero to nine, thus:

In card B the applications are more complex. The cards are superimposed in numerical progression by tens.

Almost all our children count to 100, a number which was given to them in response to the curiosity they showed in regard to learning it.

I do not believe that this phase of the teaching needs further illustrations. Each teacher may multiply the practical exercises in the arithmetical operations, using simple objects which the children can readily handle and divide.

Sequence of Exercises

In the practical application of the method it is helpful to know the sequence, or the various series, of exercises which must be presented to the child successively.

In the first edition of my book there was clearly indicated a progression for each exercise; but in the "Children's Houses" we began contemporaneously with the most varied exercises; and it develops that there exist *grades* in the presentation of the material in its entirety. These grades have, since the first publication of the book, become clearly defined through experience in the "Children's Houses."

Sequence and Grades in the Presentation of Material and in the Exercises

First Grade

As soon as the child comes to the school he may be given the following exercises:

Moving the seats, in silence (practical life).

Lacing, buttoning, hooking, etc.

The cylinders (sense exercises).

Among these the most useful exercise is that of the cylinders (solid insets). The child here begins to *fix his attention.* He makes his first comparison, his first selection, in which he exercises judgment. Therefore he exercises his intelligence.

Among these exercises with the solid insets, there exists the following progression from easy to difficult:

(*a*) The cylinders in which the pieces are of the same height and of decreasing diameter.

(*b*) The cylinders decreasing in all dimensions.

(*c*) Those decreasing only in height.

Second Grade

Exercises of Practical Life. To rise and be seated in silence. To walk on the line.

Sense Exercises. Material dealing with dimensions. The Long Stair. The prisms, or Big Stair. The cubes. Here the child makes exercises in the recognition of dimensions as he did in the cylinders but under a very different aspect. The objects are much larger. The differences much more evident than they were in the preceding exercises, but here, *only the eye of the child* recognises the differences and controls the errors. In the preceding exercises, the errors were mechanically revealed to the child by the didactic material itself. The impossibility of placing the objects in order in the block in any other than their respective spaces gives this control. Finally, while in the preceding exercises the child makes much more simple movements (being seated he places little objects in order with his hands), in these new exercises he accomplishes movements which are decidedly more complex and difficult and makes small muscular efforts. He does this by moving from the table to the carpet, rises, kneels, carries heavy objects.

We notice that the child continues to be confused between the two last pieces in the growing scale, being for a long time unconscious of such an error after he has learned to put the other pieces in correct order. Indeed the difference between these pieces being throughout the varying dimensions the same for all, the relative difference diminishes with the increasing size of the pieces themselves. For example, the little cube which has a base of 2 centimetres is double the size, as to base, of the smallest cube which has a base of 1 centimetre, while the largest cube having a base of 10 centimetres, differs by barely 1/10 from the base of the cube next it in the series (the one of 9 centimetres base).

Thus it would seem that, theoretically, in such exercises we should begin with the smallest piece. We can, indeed, do this with the material through which size and length are taught. But we cannot do so with the cubes, which must be arranged as a little "tower." This column of blocks must always have as its base the largest cube.

The children attracted above all by the tower, begin very early to play with it. Thus we often see very little children playing with the tower, happy in believing that they have constructed it, when they have inadvertently used the next to the largest cube as the base. But when the child, repeating the exercise, *corrects himself of his own accord,* in a permanent fashion, we may be certain that *his eye* has become trained to perceive even the slightest differences between the pieces.

In the three systems of blocks through which dimensions are taught that of length has pieces differing from each other by 10 centimetres, while in the other two sets, the pieces differ only 1 centimetre. Theoretically it would seem that the long rods *should be the first to attract the attention* and to exclude errors. This, however, is not the case. The children are attracted by this set of blocks, but they commit the greatest number of errors in using it, and only after they have for a long time eliminated every error in constructing the other two sets, do they succeed in arranging the Long Stair perfectly. This may then be considered as the most difficult among the series through which dimensions are taught.

Arrived at this point in his education, the child is capable of fixing his attention, with interest, upon the thermic and tactile stimuli.

The progression in the sense development is not, therefore, in actual practice identical with the theoretical progression which psychometry indicates in the study of its subjects. Nor does it follow the progression which physiology and anatomy indicate in the description of the relations of the sense organs.

In fact, the tactile sense is the *primitive* sense; the organ of touch is the most *simple* and the most widely diffused. But it is easy to explain how the most simple sensations, the least complex organs, are not the first through which to attract the *attention* in a didactic presentation of sense stimuli.

Therefore, when the *education of the attention has been begun*, we may present to the child the rough and smooth surfaces (following certain thermic exercises described elsewhere in the book).

These exercises, if presented at the proper time, *interest* the children *immensely*. It is to be remembered that these games are of the *greatest importance* in the method, because upon them, in union with the exercises for the movement of the hand, which we introduce later, we base the acquisition of writing.

Together with the two series of sense exercises described above, we may begin what we call the "pairing of the colours," that is, the recognition of the identity of two colours. This is the first exercise of the chromatic sense.

Here, also, it is only the *eye* of the child that intervenes in the judgment, as it was with the exercises in dimension. This first colour exercise is easy, but the child must already have acquired a certain grade of education of the attention through preceding exercises, if he is to repeat this one with interest.

Meanwhile, the child has heard music; has walked on the line, while the directress played a rhythmic march. Little by little he has learned to accompany the music spontaneously with certain movements. This of course necessitates the repetition of the same music. (To acquire the sense of rhythm *the repetition of the same exercise is necessary*, as in all forms of education dealing with spontaneous activity.)

The exercises in silence are also repeated.

Third Grade

Exercises of Practical Life. The children wash themselves, dress and undress themselves, dust the tables, learn to handle various objects, etc.

Sense Exercises. We now introduce the child to the recognition of gradations of stimuli (tactile gradations, chromatic, etc.), allowing him to exercise himself freely.

We begin to present the stimuli for the sense of hearing (sounds, noises), and also the baric stimuli (the little tablets differing in weight).

Contemporaneously with the gradations we may present the *plane geometric insets.* Here begins the education of the movement of the hand in following the contours of the insets, an exercise which, together with the other and contemporaneous one of the recognition of tactile stimuli in gradation, *prepares for writing.*

The series of cards bearing the geometric forms, we give after the child recognises perfectly the same forms in the wooden insets. These cards serve to prepare for the *abstract signs* of which writing consists. The child learns to recognise a delineated form, and after all the preceding exercises have formed within him an ordered and intelligent personality, they may be considered the bridge by which he passes from the sense exercises to writing, from the *preparation*, to the actual *entrance into instruction.*

Fourth Grade

Exercises of Practical Life. The children set and clear the table for luncheon. They learn to put a room in order. They are now taught the most minute care of their persons in the making of the toilet. (How to brush their teeth, to clean their nails, etc.)

They have learned, through the rhythmic exercises on the line, to walk with perfect freedom and balance.

They know how to control and direct their own movements (how to make the silence,–how to move various objects without dropping or breaking them and without making a noise).

Sense Exercises. In this stage we repeat all the sense exercises. In addition we introduce the recognition of musical notes by the help of the series of duplicate bells.

Exercises Related to Writing. Design. The child passes to the *plane geometric insets in metal.* He has already co-ordinated the movements necessary to follow the contours. Here he no longer *follows them with his finger,* but with a pencil, leaving the double sign upon a sheet of paper. Then he fills in the figures with coloured pencils, holding the pencil as he will later hold the pen in writing.

Contemporaneously the child is taught to *recognise* and *touch* some of the letters of the alphabet made in sandpaper.

Exercises in Arithmetic. At this point, repeating the sense exercises, we present the Long Stair with a different aim from that with which it has been used up to the present time. We have the child *count* the different pieces, according to the blue and red sections, beginning with the rod consisting of one section and continuing through that composed of ten sections. We continue such exercises and give other more complicated ones.

In Design we pass from the outlines of the geometric insets to such outlined figures as the practice of four years has established and which will be published as models in design.

These have an educational importance, and represent in their content and in their gradations one of the most carefully studied details of the method.

They serve as a means for the continuation of the sense education and help the child to observe his surroundings. They thus add to his intellectual refinement, and, as regards writing, they prepare for the high and low strokes. After such practice it will be *easy for the child to make high or low letters,* and this will do away with the *ruled note-books* such as are used in Italy in the various elementary classes.

In the *acquiring* of the use of *written language* we go as far as the knowledge of the letters of the alphabet, and of composition with the movable alphabet.

In Arithmetic, as far as a knowledge of the figures. The child places the corresponding figures beside the number of blue and red sections on each rod of the Long Stair.

The children now take the exercise with the wooden pegs.

Also the games which consist in placing under the figures, on the table, a corresponding number of coloured counters. These are arranged in columns of twos, thus making the question of odd and even numbers clear. (This arrangement is taken from Séguin.)

Fifth Grade

We continue the preceding exercises. We begin more complicated rhythmic exercises.

In design we begin:

(*a*) The use of water colours.

(*b*) Free drawing from nature (flowers, etc.).

Composition of words and phrases with the movable alphabet.

(*a*) Spontaneous writing of words and phrases.

(*b*) Reading from slips prepared by the directress.

We continue the arithmetical operations which we began with the Long Stair.

The children at this stage present most interesting differences of development. They fairly *run* toward instruction, and order their *intellectual growth* in a way that is remarkable.

This joyous growth is what we so rejoice in, as we watch in these children, humanity, growing in the spirit according to its own deep laws. And only he who experiments can say how great may be the harvest from the sowing of such seed.

General Review of Discipline

The accumulated experience we have had since the publication of the Italian version has repeatedly proved to us that in our classes of little children, numbering forty and even fifty, the discipline is much better than in ordinary schools. For this reason I have thought that an analysis of the discipline obtained by our method–which is based upon liberty,–would interest my American readers.

Whoever visits a well kept school (such as, for instance, the one in Rome directed by my pupil Anna Maccheroni) is struck by the discipline of the children. There are forty little beings–from three to seven years old, each one intent on his own work; one is going through one of the exercises for the senses, one is doing an arithmetical exercise; one is handling the letters, one is drawing, one is fastening and unfastening the pieces of cloth on one of our little wooden frames, still another is dusting. Some are seated at the tables, some on rugs on the floor. There are muffled sounds of objects lightly moved about, of children tiptoeing. Once in a while comes a cry of joy only partly repressed, "Teacher! Teacher!" an eager call, "Look! see what I've done." But as a rule, there is entire absorption in the work in hand.

The teacher moves quietly about, goes to any child who calls her, supervising operations in such a way that any one who needs her finds her at his elbow, and whoever does not need her is not reminded of her existence. Sometimes, hours go by without a word. They seem "little men," as they were called by some visitors to the "Children's House"; or, as another suggested, "judges in deliberation."

In the midst of such intense interest in work it never happens that quarrels arise over the possession of an object. If one accomplishes something especially fine, his achievement is a source of admiration and joy to others: no heart suffers from another's wealth, but the triumph of one is a delight to all. Very often he finds ready imitators. They all seem happy and satisfied to do what they can, without feeling jealous of the deeds of others. The little fellow of three works peaceably beside the boy of seven, just as he is satisfied with his own height and does not envy the older boy's stature. Everything is growing in the most profound peace.

If the teacher wishes the whole assembly to do something, for instance, leave the work which interests them so much, all she needs to do is to speak a word in a low tone, or make a gesture, and they are all attention, they look toward her with eagerness, anxious to know how to obey. Many visitors have seen the teacher write orders on the blackboard, which were obeyed joyously by the children. Not only the teachers, but anyone who asks the pupils to do something is astonished to see them obey in the minutest detail and with obliging cheerfulness. Often a visitor wishes to hear how a child, now painting, can sing. The child leaves his painting to be obliging, but the instant his courteous action is completed, he returns to his interrupted work. Sometimes the smaller children finish their work before they obey.

A very surprising result of this discipline came to our notice during the examinations of the teachers who had followed my course of lectures. These examinations were practical, and, accordingly, groups of children were put at the disposition of the teachers being examined, who, according to the subject drawn by lot, took the children through a given exercise. While the children were waiting their turn, they were allowed to do just as they pleased. *They worked incessantly*, and returned to their undertakings as soon as the interruption caused by the examination was over. Every once in a while, one of them came to show us a drawing made during the interval. Miss George of Chicago was present many times when this happened, and Madame Pujols, who founded the first "Children's House" in Paris, was astonished at the patience, the perseverance, and the inexhaustible amiability of the children.

One might think that such children had been severely repressed were it not for their lack of timidity, for their bright eyes, for their happy, free aspect, for the cordiality of their invitations to look at their work, for the way in which they take visitors about and explain matters to them. These things make us feel that we are in the presence of the masters of the house; and the fervour with which they throw their arms around the teacher's knees, with which they pull her down to kiss her face, shows that their little hearts are free to expand as they will.

Anyone who has watched them setting the table must have passed from one surprise to another. Little four-year-old waiters take the knives and forks and spoons and distribute them to the different places; they carry trays holding as many as five water-glasses, and finally they go from table to table, carrying big tureens full of hot soup.

Not a mistake is made, not a glass is broken, not a drop of soup is spilled. All during the meal unobtrusive little waiters watch the table assiduously; not a child empties his soup-plate without being offered more; if he is ready for the next course a waiter briskly carries off his soup-plate. Not a child is forced to ask for more soup, or to announce that he has finished.

Remembering the usual condition of four-year-old children, who cry, who break whatever they touch, who need to be waited on, everyone is deeply moved by the sight I have just described, which evidently results from the development of energies latent in the depths of the human soul. I have often seen the spectators at this banquet of little ones, moved to tears.

But such discipline could never be obtained by commands, by sermonizings, in short, through any of the disciplinary devices universally known. Not only were the actions of those children set in an orderly condition, but their very lives were deepened and enlarged. In fact, such discipline is on the same plane with school-exercises extraordinary for the age of the children; and it certainly does not depend upon the teacher but upon a sort of miracle, occurring in the inner life of each child.

If we try to think of parallels in the life of adults, we are reminded of the phenomenon of conversion, of the superhuman heightening of the strength of martyrs and apostles, of the constancy of missionaries, of the obedience of monks. Nothing else in the world, except such things, is on a spiritual height equal to the discipline of the "Children's Houses."

To obtain such discipline it is quite useless to count on reprimands or spoken exhortations. Such means might perhaps at the beginning have an appearance of efficacy: but very soon, the instant that real discipline appears, all of this falls miserably to the earth, an illusion confronted with reality-"night gives way to day."

The first dawning of real discipline comes through work. At a given moment it happens that a child becomes keenly interested in a piece of work, showing it by the expression of his face, by his intense attention, by his perseverance in the same exercise. That child has set foot upon the road leading to discipline. Whatever be his undertaking-an exercise for the senses, an exercise in buttoning up or lacing together, or washing dishes-it is all one and the same.

On our side, we can have some influence upon the permanence of this phenomenon, by means of repeated "Lessons of Silence." The perfect immobility, the attention alert to catch the sound of the names whispered from a distance, then the carefully co-ordinated movements executed so as not to strike against chair or table, so as barely to touch the floor with the feet-all this is a most efficacious preparation for the task of setting in order the whole personality, the motor forces and the psychical.

Once the habit of work is formed, we must supervise it with scrupulous accuracy, graduating the exercises as experience has taught us. In our effort to establish discipline, we must rigorously apply the principles of the method. It is not to be obtained by words; no man learns self-discipline "through hearing another man speak." The phenomenon of discipline needs as preparation a series of complete actions, such as are presupposed in the genuine application of a really educative method. Discipline is reached always by indirect means. The end is obtained, not by attacking the mistake and fighting it, but by developing activity in spontaneous work.

This work cannot be arbitrarily offered, and it is precisely here that our method enters; it must be work which the human being instinctively desires to do, work towards which the latent tendencies of life naturally turn, or towards which the individual step by step ascends.

Such is the work which sets the personality in order and opens wide before it infinite possibilities of growth. Take, for instance, the lack of control shown by a baby; it is fundamentally a lack of muscular discipline. The child is in a constant state of disorderly movement: he throws himself down, he makes queer gestures, he cries. What underlies all this is a latent tendency to seek that coordination of movement which will be established later. The baby is a man not yet sure of the movements of the various muscles of the body; not yet master of the organs of speech. He will eventually establish these various movements, but for the present he is abandoned to a period of experimentation full of mistakes, and of fatiguing efforts towards a desirable end latent in his instinct, but not clear in his consciousness. To say to the baby, "Stand still as I do," brings no light into his darkness; commands cannot aid in the process of bringing order into the complex psycho-muscular system of an individual in process of evolution. We are confused at this point by the example of the adult who through a wicked impulse *prefers* disorder, and who may (granted that he can) obey a sharp admonishment which turns his will in another direction, towards that order which he recognises and which it is within his capacity to achieve. In the case of the little child it is a question of aiding the natural evolution of voluntary action. Hence it is necessary to teach all the co-ordinated movements, analysing them as much as possible and developing them bit by bit.

Thus, for instance, it is necessary to teach the child the various degrees of immobility leading to silence; the movements connected with rising from a chair and sitting down, with walking, with tiptoeing, with following a line drawn on the floor keeping an upright equilibrium. The child is taught to move objects about, to set them down more or less carefully, and finally the complex movements connected with dressing and undressing himself (analysed on the lacing and buttoning frames at school), and for even each of these exercises, the different parts of the movement must be analysed. Perfect immobility and the successive perfectioning of action, is what takes the place of the customary command, "Be quiet! Be still!" It is not astonishing but very natural that the child by means of such exercises should acquire self-discipline, so far as regards the lack of muscular discipline natural to his age. In short, he responds to nature because he is in action; but these actions being directed towards an end, have no longer the appearance of disorder but of work. This is discipline which represents an end to be attained by means of a number of conquests. The child disciplined in this way, is no longer the child he was at first, who knows how to *be* good passively; but he is an individual who has made himself better, who has overcome the usual limits of his age, who has made a great step forward, who has conquered his future in his present.

He has therefore enlarged his dominion. He will not need to have someone always at hand, to tell him vainly (confusing two opposing conceptions), "Be quiet! Be good!" The goodness he has conquered cannot be summed up by inertia: his goodness is now all made up of action. As a matter of fact, good people are those who advance towards the good–that good which is made up of their own self-development and of external acts of order and usefulness.

In our efforts with the child, external acts are the means which stimulate internal development, and they again appear as its manifestation, the two elements being inextricably intertwined. Work develops the child spiritually; but the child with a fuller spiritual development works better, and his improved work delights him,– hence he continues to develop spiritually. Discipline is, therefore, not a fact but a path, a path in following which the child grasps the abstract conception of goodness with an exactitude which is fairly scientific.

But beyond everything else he savours the supreme delights of that spiritual *order* which is attained indirectly through conquests directed towards determinate ends. In that long preparation, the child experiences joys, spiritual awakenings and pleasures which form his inner treasure-house–the treasure-house in which he is steadily storing up the sweetness and strength which will be the sources of righteousness.

In short, the child has not only learned to move about and to perform useful acts; he has acquired a special grace of action which makes his gestures more correct and attractive, and which beautifies his hands and indeed his entire body now so balanced and so sure of itself; a grace which refines the expression of his face and of his serenely brilliant eyes, and which shows us that the flame of spiritual life has been lighted in another human being.

It is obviously true that co-ordinated actions, developed spontaneously little by little (that is, chosen and carried out in the exercises by the child himself), must call for less effort than the disorderly actions performed by the child who is left to his own devices. True rest for muscles, intended by nature for action, is in orderly action; just as true rest for the lungs is the normal rhythm of respiration taken in pure air. To take action away from the muscles is to force them away from their natural motor impulse, and hence, besides tiring them, means forcing them into a state of degeneration; just as the lungs forced into immobility, would die instantly and the whole organism with them.

It is therefore necessary to keep clearly in mind the fact that rest for whatever naturally acts, lies in some specified form of action, corresponding to its nature.

To act in obedience to the hidden precepts of nature–that is rest; and in this special case, since man is meant to be an intelligent creature, the more intelligent his acts are the more he finds repose in them. When a child acts only in a disorderly, disconnected manner, his nervous force is under a great strain; while on the other hand his nervous energy is positively increased and multiplied by intelligent actions which give him real satisfaction, and a feeling of pride that he has overcome himself, that he finds himself in a world beyond the frontiers formerly set up as insurmountable, surrounded by the silent respect of the one who has guided him without making his presence felt.

This "multiplication of nervous energy" represents a process which can be physiologically analysed, and which comes from the development of the organs by rational exercise, from better circulation of the blood, from the quickened activity of all the tissues–all factors favourable to the development of the body and guaranteeing physical health. The spirit aids the body in its growth; the heart, the nerves and the muscles are helpful in their evolution by the activity of the spirit, since the upward path for soul and body is one and the same.

By analogy, it can be said of the intellectual development of the child, that the mind of infancy, although characteristically disorderly, is also "a means searching for its end," which goes through exhausting experiments, left, as it frequently is, to its own resources, and too often really persecuted. Once in our public park in Rome, the Pincian Gardens, I saw a baby of about a year and a half, a beautiful smiling child, who was working away trying to fill a little pail by shoveling gravel into it. Beside him was a smartly dressed nurse evidently very fond of him, the sort of nurse who would consider that she gave the child the most affectionate and intelligent care. It was time to go home and the nurse was patiently exhorting the baby to leave his work and let her put him into the baby-carriage. Seeing that her exhortations made no impression on the little fellow's firmness, she herself filled the pail with gravel and set pail and baby into the carriage with the fixed conviction that she had given him what he wanted.

I was struck by the loud cries of the child and by the expression of protest against violence and injustice which wrote itself on his little face. What an accumulation of wrongs weighed down that nascent intelligence ! The little boy did not wish to have the pail full of gravel; he wished to go through the motions necessary to fill it, thus satisfying a need of his vigorous organism. The child's unconscious aim was his own self-development; not the external fact of a pail full of little stones. The vivid attractions of the external world were only empty apparitions; the need of his life was a reality. As a matter of fact, if he had filled his pail he would probably have emptied it out again in order to keep on filling it up until his inner self was satisfied. It was the feeling of working towards this satisfaction which, a few moments before, had made his face so rosy and smiling; spiritual joy, exercise, and sunshine, were the three rays of light ministering to his splendid life.

This commonplace episode in the life of that child, is a detail of what happens to all children, even the best and most cherished. They are not understood, because the adult judges them by his own measure: he thinks that the child's wish is to obtain some tangible object, and lovingly helps him to do this: whereas the child as a rule has for his unconscious desire, his own self-development. Hence he despises everything already attained, and yearns for that which is still to be sought for. For instance, he prefers the action of dressing himself to the state of being dressed, even finely dressed. He prefers the act of washing himself to the satisfaction of being clean: he prefers to make a little house for himself, rather than merely to own it. His own self-development is his true and almost his only pleasure. The self-development of the little baby up to the end of his first year consists to a large degree in taking in nutrition; but afterwards it consists in aiding the orderly establishment of the psycho-physiological functions of his organism.

That beautiful baby in the Pincian Gardens is the symbol of this: he wished to co-ordinate his voluntary actions; to exercise his muscles by lifting; to train his eye to estimate distances; to exercise his intelligence in the reasoning connected with his undertaking; to stimulate his will-power by deciding his own actions; whilst she who loved him, believing that his aim was to possess some pebbles, made him wretched.

A similar error is that which we repeat so frequently when we fancy that the desire of the student is to possess a piece of information. We aid him to grasp intellectually this detached piece of knowledge, and, preventing by this means his self-development, we make him wretched. It is generally believed in schools that the way to attain satisfaction is "to learn something." But by leaving the children in our schools in liberty we have been able with great clearness to follow them in their natural method of spontaneous self-development.

To have learned something is for the child only a point of departure. When he has learned the meaning of an exercise, then he begins to enjoy repeating it, and he does repeat it an infinite number of times, with the most evident satisfaction. He enjoys executing that act because by means of it he is developing his psychic activities.

There results from the observation of this fact a criticism of what is done to-day in many schools. Often, for instance when the pupils are questioned, the teacher says to someone who is eager to answer, "No, not you, because you know it" and puts her question specially to the pupils who she thinks are uncertain of the answer. Those who do not know are made to speak, those who do know to be silent. This happens because of the general habit of considering the act of knowing something as final.

And yet how many times it happens to us in ordinary life to *repeat* the very thing we know best, the thing we care most for, the thing to which some living force in us responds. We love to sing musical phrases very familiar, hence enjoyed and become a part of the fabric of our lives. We love to repeat stories of things which please us, which we know very well, even though we are quite aware that we are saying nothing new. No matter how many times we repeat the Lord's Prayer, it is always new. No two persons could be more convinced of mutual love than sweethearts and yet they are the very ones who repeat endlessly that they love each other.

But in order to repeat in this manner, there must first exist the idea to be repeated. A mental grasp of the idea, is indispensable to the beginning of *repetition*. The exercise which develops life, consists *in the repetition, not in the mere grasp of the idea*. When a child has attained this stage, of repeating an exercise, he is on the way to self-development, and the external sign of this condition is his self-discipline.

This phenomenon does not always occur. The same exercises are not repeated by children of all ages. In fact, repetition corresponds to a *need*. Here steps in the experimental method of education. It is necessary to offer those exercises which correspond to the need of development felt by an organism, and if the child's age has carried him past a certain need, it is never possible to obtain, in its fulness, a development which missed its proper moment. Hence children grow up, often fatally and irrevocably, imperfectly developed.

Another very interesting observation is that which relates to the length of time needed for the execution of actions. Children, who are undertaking something for the first time are extremely slow. Their life is governed in this respect by laws especially different from ours. Little children accomplish slowly and perseveringly, various complicated operations agreeable to them, such as dressing, undressing, cleaning the room, washing themselves, setting the table, eating, etc. In all this they are extremely patient, overcoming all the difficulties presented by an organism still in process of formation. But we, on the other hand, noticing that they are "tiring themselves out" or "wasting time" in accomplishing something which we would do in a moment and without the least effort, put ourselves in the child's place and do it ourselves. Always with the same erroneous idea, that the end to be obtained is the completion of the action, we dress and wash the child, we snatch out of his hands objects which he loves to handle, we pour the soup into his bowl, we feed him, we set the table for him. And after such services, we consider him with that injustice always practiced by those who domineer over others even with benevolent intentions, to be incapable and inept. We often speak of him as "impatient" simply because we are not patient enough to allow his actions to follow laws of time differing from our own; we call him "tyrannical" exactly because we employ tyranny towards him. This stain, this false imputation, this calumny on childhood has become an integral part of the theories concerning childhood, in reality so patient and gentle.

The child, like every strong creature fighting for the right to live, rebels against whatever offends that occult impulse within him which is the voice of nature, and which he ought to obey; and he shows by violent actions, by screaming and weeping that he has been overborne and forced away from his mission in life. He shows himself to be a rebel, a revolutionist, an iconoclast, against those who do not understand him and who, fancying that they are helping him, are really pushing him backward in the highway of life. Thus even the adult who loves him, rivets about his neck another calumny, confusing his defence of his molested life with a form of innate naughtiness characteristic of little children.

What would become of us if we fell into the midst of a population of jugglers, or of lightning-change impersonators of the variety-hall? What should we do if, as we continued to act in our usual way, we saw ourselves assailed by these sleight-of-hand performers, hustled into our clothes, fed so rapidly that we could scarcely swallow, if everything we tried to do was snatched from our hands and completed in a twinkling and we ourselves reduced to impotence and to a humiliating inertia? Not knowing how else to express our confusion we would defend ourselves with blows and yells from these madmen, and they having only the best will in the world to serve us, would call us haughty, rebellious, and incapable of doing anything. We, who know our own *milieu*, would say to those people, "Come into our countries and you will see the splendid civilisation we have established, you will see our wonderful achievements." These jugglers would admire us infinitely, hardly able to believe their eyes, as they observed our world, so full of beauty and activity, so well regulated, so peaceful, so kindly, but all so much slower than theirs.

Something of this sort occurs between children and adults.

It is exactly in the repetition of the exercise that the education of the senses consists; their aim is not that the child shall *know* colours, forms and the different qualities of objects, but that he refine his senses through an exercise of attention, of comparison, of judgment. These exercises are true intellectual gymnastics. Such gymnastics, reasonably directed by means of various devices, aid in the formation of the intellect, just as physical exercises fortify the general health and quicken the growth of the body. The child who trains his various senses separately, by means of external stimuli, concentrates his attention and develops, piece by piece, his mental activities, just as with separately prepared movements he trains his muscular activities. These mental gymnastics are not merely psycho-sensory, but they prepare the way for spontaneous association of ideas, for ratiocination developing out of definite knowledge, for a harmoniously balanced intellect. They are the powder-trains that bring about those mental explosions which delight the child so intensely when he makes discoveries in the world about him, when he, at the same time, ponders over and glories in the new things which are revealed to him in the outside world, and in the exquisite emotions of his own growing consciousness; and finally when there spring up within him, almost by a process of spontaneous ripening, like the internal phenomena of growth, the external products of learning–writing and reading.

I happened once to see a two-year-old child, son of a medical colleague of mine, who, fairly fleeing away from his mother who had brought him to me, threw himself on the litter of things covering his father's desk, the rectangular writing-pad, the round cover of the ink-well. I was touched to see the intelligent little creature trying his best to go through the exercises which our children repeat with such endless pleasure till they have fully committed them to memory. The father and the mother pulled the child away, reproving him, and explaining that there was no use trying to keep that child from handling his father's desk-furniture, "The child is restless and naughty." How often we see all children reproved because, though they are told not to, they will "take hold of everything." Now, it is precisely by means of guiding and developing this natural instinct "to take hold of everything," and to recognise the relations of geometrical figures, that we prepare our little four-year-old men for the joy and triumph they experience later over the phenomenon of spontaneous writing.

The child who throws himself on the writing-pad, the cover to the ink-well, and such objects, always struggling in vain to attain his desire, always hindered and thwarted by people stronger than he, always excited and weeping over the failure of his desperate efforts, *is wasting* nervous force. His parents are mistaken if they think that such a child ever gets any real rest, just as they are mistaken when they call "naughty" the little man longing for the foundations of his intellectual edifice. The children in our schools are the ones who are really at rest, ardently and blessedly free to take out and put back in their right places or grooves, the geometric figures offered to their instinct for higher self-development; and they, rejoicing in the most entire spiritual calm, have no notion that their eyes and hands are initiating them into the mysteries of a new language.

The majority of our children become calm as they go through such exercises, because their nervous system is at rest. Then we say that such children are quiet and good; external discipline, so eagerly sought after in ordinary schools is more than achieved.

However, as a calm man and a self-disciplined man are not one and the same, so here the fact which manifests itself externally by the calm of the children is in reality a phenomenon merely physical and partial compared to the real *self-discipline* which is being developed in them.

Often (and this is another misconception) we think all we need to do, to obtain a voluntary action from a child, is to order him to do it. We pretend that this phenomenon of a forced voluntary action exists, and we call this pretext, "the obedience of the child." We find little children specially disobedient, or rather their resistance, by the time they are four or five years old, has become so great that we are in despair and are almost tempted to give up trying to make them obey. We force ourselves to praise to little children "the virtue of obedience" a virtue which, according to our accepted prejudices, should belong specially to infancy, should be the "infantile virtue" yet we fail to learn anything from the fact that we are led to emphasize it so strongly because we can only with the greatest difficulty make children practise it.

It is a very common mistake, this of trying to obtain by means of prayers, or orders, or violence, what is difficult, or impossible to get. Thus, for instance, we ask little children to be obedient, and little children in their turn ask for the moon.

We need only reflect that this "obedience" which we treat so lightly, occurs later, as a natural tendency in older children, and then as an instinct in the adult to realise that it springs spontaneously into being, and that it is one of the strongest instincts of humanity. We find that society rests on a foundation of marvellous obedience, and that civilisation goes forward on a road made by obedience. Human organisations are often founded on an abuse of obedience, associations of criminals have obedience as their key-stone.

How many times social problems centre about the necessity of rousing man from a state of "obedience" which has led him to be exploited and brutalised!

Obedience naturally is *sacrifice*. We are so accustomed to an infinity of obedience in the world, to a condition of self-sacrifice, to a readiness for renunciation, that we call matrimony the "blessed condition," although it is made up of obedience and self-sacrifice. The soldier, whose lot in life is to obey if it kills him is envied by the common people, while we consider anyone who tries to escape from obedience as a malefactor or a madman. Besides, how many people have had the deeply spiritual experience of an ardent desire to obey something or some person leading them along the path of life–more than this, a desire to sacrifice something for the sake of this obedience.

It is therefore entirely natural that, loving the child, we should point out to him that obedience is the law of life, and there is nothing surprising in the anxiety felt by nearly everyone who is confronted with the characteristic disobedience of little children. But obedience can only be reached through a complex formation of the psychic personality. To obey, it is necessary not only to wish to obey, but also to know how to. Since, when a command to do a certain thing is given, we presuppose a corresponding active or inhibitive power of the child, it is plain that obedience must follow the formation of the will and of the mind. To prepare, in detail, this formation by means of detached exercises is therefore indirectly, to urge the child towards obedience. The method which is the subject of this book contains in every part an exercise for the will-power, when the child completes co-ordinated actions directed towards a given end, when he achieves something he set out to do, when he repeats patiently his exercises, he is training his positive will-power. Similarly, in a very complicated series of exercises he is establishing through activity his powers of inhibition; for instance in the "lesson of silence," which calls for a long continued inhibition of many actions, while the child is waiting to be called and later for a rigorous self-control when he is called and would like to answer joyously and run to his teacher, but instead is perfectly silent, moves very carefully, taking the greatest pains not to knock against chair or table or to make a noise.

Other inhibitive exercises are the arithmetical ones, when the child having drawn a number by lot, must take from the great mass of objects before him, apparently entirely at his disposition, only the quantity corresponding to the number in his hand, whereas (as experience has proved) he would *like* to take the greatest number possible. Furthermore if he chances to draw the zero he sits patiently with empty hands. Still another training for the inhibitive will-power is in "the lesson of zero" when the child, called upon to come up zero times and give zero kisses, stands quiet, conquering with a visible effort the instinct which would lead him to "obey" the call. The child at our school dinners who carries the big tureen full of hot soup, isolates himself from every external stimulant which might disturb him, resists his childish impulse to run and jump, does not yield to the temptation to brush away the fly on his face, and is entirely concentrated on the great responsibility of not dropping or tipping the tureen. A little thing of four and a half, every time he set the tureen down on a table so that the little guests might help themselves, gave a hop and a skip, then took up the tureen again to carry it to another table, repressing himself to a sober walk. In spite of his desire to play he never left his task before he had passed soup to the twenty tables, and he never forgot the vigilance necessary to control his actions.

Will-power, like all other activities is invigorated and developed through methodical exercises, and all our exercises for will-power are also mental and practical. To the casual onlooker the child seems to be learning exactitude and grace of action, to be refining his senses, to be learning how to become his own master, how to be a man of prompt and resolute will.

We often hear it said that a child's will should be "broken" that the best education for the will of the child is to learn to give it up to the will of adults. Leaving out of the question the injustice which is at the root of every act of tyranny, this idea is irrational because the child cannot give up what he does not possess. We prevent him in this way from forming his own will-power, and we commit the greatest and most blameworthy mistake. He never has time or opportunity to test himself, to estimate his own force and his own limitations because he is always interrupted and subjected to our tyranny, and languishes in injustice because he is always being bitterly reproached for not having what adults are perpetually destroying.

There springs up as a consequence of this, childish timidity, which is a moral malady acquired by a will which could not develop, and which with the usual calumny with which the tyrant consciously or not, covers up his own mistakes, we consider as an inherent trait of childhood. The children in our schools are never timid. One of their most fascinating qualities is the frankness with which they treat people, with which they go on working in the presence of others, and showing their work frankly, calling for sympathy. That moral monstrosity, a repressed and timid child, who is at his ease nowhere except alone with his playmates, or with street urchins, because his will-power was allowed to grow only in the shade, disappears in our schools. He presents an example of thoughtless barbarism, which resembles the artificial compression of the bodies of those children intended for "court dwarfs," museum monstrosities or buffoons. Yet this is the treatment under which nearly all the children of our time are growing up spiritually.

As a matter of fact in all the pedagogical congresses one hears that the great peril of our time is the lack of individual character in the scholars; yet these alarmists do not point out that this condition is due to the way in which education is managed, to scholastic slavery, which has for its specialty the repression of will-power and of force of character. The remedy is simply to enfranchise human development.

Besides the exercises it offers for developing will-power, the other factor in obedience is the capacity to perform the act it becomes necessary to obey. One of the most interesting observations made by my pupil Anna Maccheroni (at first in the school in Milan and then in that in the Via Guisti in Rome), relates to the connection between obedience in a child and his "knowing how." Obedience appears in the child as a latent instinct as soon as his personality begins to take form. For instance, a child begins to try a certain exercise and suddenly some time he goes through it perfectly; he is delighted, stares at it, and wishes to do it over again, but for some time the exercise is not a success. Then comes a time when he can do it nearly every time he tries voluntarily but makes mistakes if someone else asks him to do it. The external command does not as yet produce the voluntary act. When, however, the exercise always succeeds, with absolute certainty, then an order from someone else brings about on the child's part, orderly adequate action; that is, the child *is able* each time to execute the command received. That these facts (with variations in individual cases) are laws of psychical development is apparent from everyone's experience with children in school or at home.

One often hears a child say, "I did do such and such a thing but now I can't!" and a teacher disappointed by the incompetence of a pupil will say, "Yet that child was doing it all right-and now he can't!"

Finally there is the period of complete development in which the capacity to perform some operation is permanently acquired. There are, therefore, three periods: a first, subconscious one, when in the confused mind of the child, order produces itself by a mysterious inner impulse from out the midst of disorder, producing as an external result a completed act, which, however, being outside the field of consciousness, cannot be reproduced at will; a second, conscious period, when there is some action on the part of the will which is present during the process of the development and establishing of the acts; and a third period when the will can direct and cause the acts, thus answering the command from someone else.

Now, obedience follows a similar sequence. When in the first period of spiritual disorder, the child does not obey it is exactly as if he were psychically deaf, and out of hearing of commands. In the second period he would like to obey, he looks as though he understood the command and would like to respond to it, but cannot,-or at least does not always succeed in doing it, is not "quick to mind" and shows no pleasure when he does. In the third period he obeys at once, with enthusiasm, and as he becomes more and more perfect in the exercises he is proud that he knows how to obey. This is the period in which he runs joyously to obey, and leaves at the most imperceptible request whatever is interesting him so that he may quit the solitude of his own life and enter, with the act of obedience into the spiritual existence of another.

To this order, established in a consciousness formerly chaotic, are due all the phenomena of discipline and of mental development, which open out like a new Creation. From minds thus set in order, when "night is separated from day" come sudden emotions and mental feats which recall the Biblical story of Creation. The child has in his mind not only what he has laboriously acquired, but the free gifts which flow from spiritual life, the first flowers of affection, of gentleness, of spontaneous love for righteousness which perfume the souls of such children and give promise of the "fruits of the spirit" of St. Paul–"The fruit of the Spirit is love, joy, peace, long-suffering gentleness, goodness, faith, meekness."

They are virtuous because they exercise patience in repeating their exercises, long-suffering in yielding to the commands and desires of others, good in rejoicing in the well-being of others without jealousy or rivalry; they live, doing good in joyousness of heart and in peace, and they are eminently, marvellously industrious. But they are not proud of such righteousness because they were not conscious of acquiring it as a moral superiority. They have set their feet in the path leading to righteousness, simply because it was the only way to attain true self-development and learning; and they enjoy with simple hearts the fruits of peace that are to be gathered along that path.

These are the first outlines of an experiment which shows a form of indirect discipline in which there is substituted for the critical and sermonizing teacher a rational organisation of work and of liberty for the child. It involves a conception of life more usual in religious fields than in those of academic pedagogy, inasmuch as it has recourse to the spiritual energies of mankind, but it is founded on work and on liberty which are the two paths to all civic progress.

Conclusions and Impressions

In the "Children's Houses," the old-time teacher, who wore herself out maintaining discipline of immobility, and who wasted her breath in loud and continual discourse, has disappeared.

For this teacher we have substituted the *didactic material*, which contains within itself the control of errors and which makes auto-education possible to each child. The teacher has thus become a *director* of the spontaneous work of the children. She is not a *passive* force, a *silent* presence.

The children are occupied each one in a different way, and the directress, watching them, can make psychological observations which, if collected in an orderly way and according to scientific standards, should do much toward the reconstruction of child psychology and the development of experimental psychology. I believe that I have by my method established the conditions necessary to the development of scientific pedagogy; and whoever adopts this method opens, in doing so, a laboratory of experimental pedagogy.

From such work, we must await the positive solution of all those pedagogical problems of which we talk to-day. For through such work there has already come the solution of some of these very questions: that of the liberty of the pupils; auto-education; the establishment of harmony between the work and activities of home life and school tasks, making both work together for the education of the child.

The problem of religious education, the importance of which we do not fully realise, should also be solved by positive pedagogy. If religion is born with civilisation, its roots must lie deep in human nature. We have had most beautiful proof of an instinctive love of knowledge in the child, who has too often been misjudged in that he has been considered addicted to meaningless play, and games void of thought. The child who left the game in his eagerness for knowledge, has revealed himself as a true son of that humanity which has been throughout centuries the creator of scientific and civil progress. We have belittled the son of man by giving him foolish and degrading toys, a world of idleness where he is suffocated by a badly conceived discipline. Now, in his liberty, the child should show us, as well, whether man is by nature a religious creature.

To deny, *a priori*, the religious sentiment in man, and to deprive humanity of the education of this sentiment, is to commit a pedagogical error similar to that of denying, *a priori*, to the child, the love of learning for learning's sake. This ignorant assumption led us to dominate the scholar, to subject him to a species of slavery, in order to render him apparently disciplined.

The fact that we assume that religious education is only adapted to the adult, may be akin to another profound error existing in education to-day, namely, that of over-looking the education of the senses at the very period when this education is possible. The life of the adult is practically an application of the senses to the gathering of sensations from the environment. A lack of preparation for this, often results in inadequacy in practical life, in that lack of poise which causes so many individuals to waste their energies in purposeless effort. Not to form a parallel between the education of the senses as a guide to practical life, and religious education as a guide to the moral life, but for the sake of illustration; let me call attention to how often we find inefficiency, instability, among irreligious persons, and how much precious individual power is miserably wasted.

How many men have had this · experience! And when that spiritual awakening comes late, as it sometimes does, through the softening power of sorrow, the mind is unable to establish an equilibrium, because it has grown too much accustomed to a life deprived of spirituality. We see equally piteous cases of religious fanaticism, or we look upon intimate dramatic struggles between the heart, ever seeking its own safe and quiet port, and the mind that constantly draws it back to the sea of conflicting ideas and emotions, where peace is unknown. These are all psychological phenomena of the highest importance; they present, perhaps, the gravest of all our human problems. We Europeans are still filled with prejudices and hedged about with preconceptions in regard to these matters. We are very slaves of thought. We believe that liberty of conscience and of thought consists in denying certain sentimental beliefs, while liberty never can exist where one struggles to stifle some other thing, but only where unlimited expansion is granted; where life is left free and untrammelled. He who really does not believe, does not fear that which he does not believe, and does not combat that which for him does not exist. If he believes and fights, he then becomes an enemy to liberty.

In America, the great positive scientist, William James, who expounds the physiological theory of emotions, is also the man who illustrates the psychological importance of religious "conscience." We cannot know the future of the progress of thought: here, for example, in the "Children's Houses" the triumph of *discipline* through the conquest of liberty and independence marks the foundation of the progress which the future will see in the matter of pedagogical methods. To me it offers the greatest hope for human redemption through education.

Perhaps, in the same way, through the conquest of liberty of thought and of conscience, we are making our way toward a great religious triumph. Experience will show, and the psychological observations made along this line in the "Children's Houses" will undoubtedly be of the greatest interest.

This book of methods compiled by one person alone, must be followed by many others. It is my hope that, starting from the *individual study of the child* educated with our method, other educators will set forth the results of their experiments. These are the pedagogical books which await us in the future.

From the practical side of the school, we have with our methods the advantage of being able to teach in one room, children of very different ages. In our "Children's Houses" we have little ones of two years and a half, who cannot as yet make use of the most simple of the sense exercises, and children of five and a half who because of their development might easily pass into the third elementary. Each one of them perfects himself through his own powers, and goes forward guided by that inner force which distinguishes him as an individual.

One great advantage of such a method is that it will make instruction in the rural schools easier, and will be of great advantage in the schools in the small provincial towns where there are few children, yet where all the various grades are represented. Such schools are not able to employ more than one teacher. Our experience shows that one directress may guide a group of children varying in development from little ones of three years old to the third elementary. Another great advantage lies in the extreme facility with which written language may be taught, making it possible to combat illiteracy and to cultivate the national tongue.

As to the teacher, she may remain for the whole day among children in the most varying stages of development, just as the mother remains in the house with children of all ages, without becoming tired.

The children work by themselves, and, in doing so, make a conquest of active discipline, and independence in all the acts of daily life, just as through daily conquests they progress in intellectual development. Directed by an intelligent teacher, who watches over their physical development as well as over their intellectual and moral progress, children are able with our methods to arrive at a splendid physical development, and, in addition to this, there unfolds within them, in all its perfection, the soul, which distinguishes the human being.

We have been mistaken in thinking that the natural education of children should be purely physical; the soul, too, has its nature, which it was intended to perfect in the spiritual life,-the dominating power of human existence throughout all time. Our methods take into consideration the spontaneous psychic development of the child, and help this in ways that observation and experience have shown us to be wise.

If physical care leads the child to take pleasure in bodily health, intellectual and moral care make possible for him the highest spiritual joy, and send him forward into a world where continual surprises and discoveries await him; not only in the external environment, but in the intimate recesses of his own soul.

It is through such pleasures as these that the ideal man grows, and only such pleasures are worthy of a place in the education of the infancy of humanity.

Our children are noticeably different from those others who have grown up within the grey walls of the common schools. Our little pupils have the serene and happy aspect and the frank and open friendliness of the person who feels himself to be master of his own actions. When they run to gather about our visitors, speaking to them with sweet frankness, extending their little hands with gentle gravity and well-bred cordiality, when they thank these visitors for the courtesy they have paid us in coming, the bright eyes and the happy voices make us feel that they are, indeed, unusual little men. When they display their work and their ability, in a confidential and simple way, it is almost as if they called for a maternal approbation from all those who watch them. Often, a little one will seat himself on the floor beside some visitor silently writing his name, and adding a gentle word of thanks. It is as if they wished to make the visitor feel the affectionate gratitude which is in their hearts.

When we see all these things and when, above all, we pass with these children from the busy activity of the schoolroom at work, into the absolute and profound silence which they have learned to enjoy so deeply, we are moved in spite of ourselves and feel that we have come in touch with the very souls of these little pupils.

The "Children's House" seems to exert a spiritual influence upon everyone. I have seen here, men of affairs, great politicians preoccupied with problems of trade and of state, cast off like an uncomfortable garment the burden of the world, and fall into a simple forgetfulness of self. They are affected by this vision of the human soul growing in its true nature, and I believe that this is what they mean when they call our little ones, wonderful children, happy children–the infancy of humanity in a higher stage of evolution than our own. I understand how the great English poet Wordsworth, enamoured as he was of nature, demanded the secret of all her peace and beauty. It was at last revealed to him–the secret of all nature lies in the soul of a little child. He holds there the true meaning of that life which exists throughout humanity. But this beauty which "lies about us in our infancy" becomes obscured; "shades of the prison house, begin to close about the growing boy . . . at last the man perceives it die away, and fade into the light of common day."

Truly our social life is too often only the darkening and the death of the natural life that is in us. These methods tend to guard that spiritual fire within man, to keep his real nature unspoiled and to set it free from the oppressive and degrading yoke of society. It is a pedagogical method informed by the high concept of Immanuel Kant: "Perfect art returns to nature."

Dr. Montessori's Own Handbook

Table of Contents

Preface

If a preface is a light which should serve to illumine the contents of a volume, I choose, not words, but human figures to illustrate this little book intended to enter families where children are growing up. I therefore recall here, as an eloquent symbol, Helen Keller and Mrs. Anne Sullivan Macy, who are, by their example, both teachers to myself – and, before the world, living documents of the miracle in education.

In fact, Helen Keller is a marvelous example of the phenomenon common to all human beings: the possibility of the liberation of the imprisoned spirit of man by the education of the senses. Here lies the basis of the method of education of which the book gives a succinct idea.

If one only of the senses sufficed to make of Helen Keller a woman of exceptional culture and a writer, who better than she proves the potency of that method of education which builds on the senses? If Helen Keller attained through exquisite natural gifts to an elevated conception of the world, who better than she proves that in the inmost self of man lies the spirit ready to reveal itself?

Helen, clasp to your heart these little children, since they, above all others, will understand you. They are your younger brothers: when, with bandaged eyes and in silence, they touch with their little hands, profound impressions rise in their consciousness, and they exclaim with a new form of happiness: "I see with my hands." They alone, then, can fully understand the drama of the mysterious privilege your soul has known. When, in darkness and in silence, their spirit left free to expand, their intellectual energy redoubled, they become able to read and write without having learnt, almost as it were by intuition, they, only they, can understand in part the ecstasy which God granted you on the luminous path of learning.

Maria Montessori

Introductory Remarks

Recent years have seen a remarkable improvement in the conditions of child life. In all civilized countries, but especially in England, statistics show a decrease in infant mortality.

Related to this decrease in mortality a corresponding improvement is to be seen in the physical development of children; they are physically finer and more vigorous. It has been the diffusion, the popularization of science, which has brought about such notable advantages. Mothers have learned to welcome the dictates of modern hygiene and to put them into practice in bringing up their children. Many new social institutions have sprung up and have been perfected with the object of assisting children and protecting them during the period of physical growth.

In this way what is practically a new race is coming into being, a race more highly developed, finer and more robust; a race which will be capable of offering resistance to insidious disease.

What has science done to effect this? Science has suggested for ns certain very simple rules by which the child has been restored as nearly as possible to conditions of a natural life, and an order and a guiding law have been given to the functions of the body. For example, it is science which suggested maternal feeding, the abolition of swaddling clothes, baths, life in the open air, exercise, simple short clothing, quiet and plenty of sleep. Rules were also laid down for the measurement of food adapting it rationally to the physiological needs of the child's life.

Yet with all this, science made no contribution that was entirely new. Mothers had always nursed their children, children had always been clothed, they had breathed and eaten before.

The point is, that the same physical acts which, performed blindly and without order, led to disease and death, when ordered rationally were the means of giving strength and life.

The great progress made may perhaps deceive us into thinking that everything possible has been done for children.

We have only to weigh the matter carefully, however, to reflect: Are our children only those healthy little bodies which to-day are growing and developing so vigorously under our eyes? Is their destiny fulfilled in the production of beautiful human bodies?

In that case there would be little difference between their lot and that of the animals which we raise that we may have good meat or beasts of burden.

Man's destiny is evidently other than this, and the care due to the child covers a field wider than that which is considered by physical hygiene. The mother who has given her child his bath and sent him in his perambulator to the park has not fulfilled the mission of the "mother of humanity" The hen which gathers her chickens together, and the cat which licks her kittens and lavishes on them such tender care, differ in no wise from the human mother in the services they render.

No, the human mother if reduced to such limits devotes herself in vain, feels that a higher aspiration has been stifled within her. She is yet the mother of man.

Children must grow not only in the body but in the spirit, and the mother longs to follow the mysterious spiritual journey of the beloved one who to-morrow will be the intelligent, divine creation, man.

Science evidently has not finished its progress. On the contrary, it has scarcely taken the first step in advance, for it has hitherto stopped at the welfare of the body. It must continue, however, to advance; on the same positive lines along which it has improved the health and saved the physical life of the children, it is bound in the future to benefit and to reenforce their inner life, which is the real human life. On the same positive lines science will proceed to direct the development of the intelligence, of character, and of those latent creative forces which lie hidden in the marvelous embryo of man's spirit.

As the child's body must draw nourishment and oxygen from its external environment, in order to accomplish a great physiological work, the work of growth, so also the spirit must take from its environment the nourishment which it needs to develop according to its own "laws of growth." It cannot be denied that the phenomena of development are a great work in themselves. The consolidation of the bones, the growth of the whole body, the completion of the minute construction of the brain, the formation of the teeth, all these are very real labors of the physiological organism, as is also the transformation which the organism undergoes during the period of puberty.

These exertions are very different from those put forth by mankind in so-called external work, that is to say, in "social production," whether in the schools where man is taught, or in the world where, by the activity of his intelligence, he produces wealth and transforms his environment.

It is none the less true, however, that they are both "work." In fact, the organism during these periods of greatest physiological work is least capable of performing external tasks, and sometimes the work of growth is of such extent and difficulty that the individual is overburdened, as with an excessive strain, and for this reason alone becomes exhausted or even dies.

Man will always be able to avoid "external work" by making use of the labor of others, but there is no possibility of shirking that inner work. Together with birth and death it has been imposed by nature itself, and each man must accomplish it for himself. This difficult, inevitable labor, this is the "work of the child."

When we say then that little children should rest, we are referring to one side only of the question of work. We mean that they should rest from that external visible work to which the little child through his weakness and incapacity cannot make any contribution useful either to himself or to others.

Our assertion, therefore, is not absolute; the child in reality is not resting, he is performing the mysterious inner work of his auto-formation. He is working to make a man, and to accomplish this it is not enough that the child's body should grow in actual size; the most intimate functions of the motor and nervous systems must also be established and the intelligence developed.

The functions to be established by the child fall into two groups: (1) the motor functions by which he is to secure his balance and learn to walk, and to coordinate his movements; (2) the sensory functions through which, receiving sensations from his environment, he lays the foundations of his intelligence by a continual exercise of observation, comparison and judgment. In this way he gradually comes to be acquainted with his environment and to develop his intelligence.

At the same time he is learning a language, and he is faced not only with the motor difficulties of articulation, sounds and words, but also with the difficulty of gaining an intelligent understanding of names and of the syntactical composition of the language.

If we think of an emigrant who goes to a new country ignorant of its products, ignorant of its natural appearance and social order, entirely ignorant of its language, we realize that there is an immense work of adaptation which he must perform before he can associate himself with the active life of the unknown people. No one will be able to do for him that work of adaptation. He himself must observe, understand, remember, form judgments, and learn the new language by laborious exercise and long experience.

What is to be said then of the child? What of this emigrant who comes into a new world, who, weak as he is and before his organism is completely developed, must in a short time adapt himself to a world so complex?

Up to the present day the little child has not received rational aid in the accomplishment of this laborious task. As regards the psychical development of the child we find ourselves in a period parallel to that in which the physical life was left to the mercy of chance and instinct — the period in which infant mortality was a scourge.

It is by scientific and rational means also that we must facilitate that inner work of psychical adaptation to be accomplished within the child, a work which is by no means the same thing as "any external work or production whatsoever."

This is the aim which underlies my method of infant education, and it is for this reason that certain principles which it enunciates, together with that part which deals with the technique of their practical application, are not of a general character, but have special reference to the particular case of the child from three to seven years of age, i.e., to the needs of a formative period of life.

My method is scientific, both in its substance and in its aim. It makes for the attainment of a more advanced stage of progress, in directions no longer only material and physiological. It is an endeavor to complete the course which hygiene has already taken, but in the treatment of the physical side alone.

If to-day we possessed statistics respecting the nervous debility, defects of speech, errors of perception and of reasoning, and lack of character in normal children, it would perhaps be interesting to compare them with statistics of the same nature, but compiled from the study of children who have had a number of years of rational education. In all probability we should find a striking resemblance between such statistics and those to-day available showing the decrease in mortality and the improvement in the physical development of children.

A "Children's House"

The "Children's House" is the environment which is offered to the child that he may be given the opportunity of developing his activities. This kind of school is not of a fixed type, but may vary according to the financial resources at disposal and to the opportunities afforded by the environment. It ought to be a real house; that is to say, a set of rooms with a garden of which the children are the masters. A garden which contains shelters is ideal, because the children can play or sleep under them, and can also bring their tables out to work or dine. In this way they may live almost entirely in the open air, and are protected at the same time from rain and sun.

The central and principal room of the building, often also the only room at the disposal of the children, is the room for "intellectual work." To this central room can be added other smaller rooms according to the means and opportunities of the place: for example, a bathroom, a diningroom, a little parlor or common-room, a room for manual work, a gymnasium and rest-room.

The special characteristic of the equipment of these houses is that it is adapted for children and not adults. They contain not only didactic material specially fitted for the intellectual development of the child, but also a complete equipment for the management of the miniature family. The furniture is light so that the children can move it about, and it is painted in some light color so that the children can wash it with soap and water. There are low tables of various sizes and shapes — square, rectangular and round, large and small. The rectangular shape is the most common as two or more children can work at it together. The seats are small wooden chairs, but there are also small wicker armchairs and sofas.

FIG. 1.—CUPBOARD WITH APPARATUS.

In the working-room there are two indispensable pieces of furniture. One of these is a very long cupboard with large doors. (Fig. 1.) It is very low so that a small child can set on the top of it small objects such as mats, flowers, etc. Inside this cupboard is kept the didactic material which is the common property of all the children.

The other is a chest of drawers containing two or three columns of little drawers, each of which has a bright handle (or a handle of some color to contrast with the background), and a small card with a name upon it. Every child has his own drawer, in which to put things belonging to him.

Round the walls of the room are fixed blackboards at a low level, so that the children can write or draw on them, and pleasing, artistic pictures, which are changed from time to time as circumstances direct. The pictures represent children, families, landscapes, flowers and fruit, and more often Biblical and historical incidents. Ornamental plants and flowering plants ought always to be placed in the room where the children are at work.

Another part of the working-room's equipment is seen in the pieces of carpet of various colors — red, blue, pink, green and brown. The children spread these rugs upon the floor, sit upon them and work there with the didactic material. A room of this kind is larger than the customary class-rooms, not only because the little tables and separate chairs take up more space, but also because a large part of the floor must be free for the children to spread their rugs and work upon them.

In the sitting-room, or "club-room," a kind of parlor in which the children amuse themselves by conversation, games, or music, etc., the furnishings should be especially tasteful. Little tables of different sizes, little armchairs and sofas should be placed here and there. Many brackets of all kinds and sizes, upon which may be put statuettes, artistic vases or framed photographs, should adorn the walls; and, above all, each child should have a little flower-pot, in which he may sow the seed of some indoor plant, to tend and cultivate it as it grows. On the tables of this sitting-room should be placed large albums of colored pictures, and also games of patience, or various geometric solids, with which the children can play at pleasure, constructing figures, etc. A piano, or, better, other musical instruments, possibly harps of small dimensions, made especially for children, completes the equipment. In this "club-room" the teacher may sometimes entertain the children with stories, which will attract a circle of interested listeners.

The furniture of the dining-room consists, in addition to the tables, of low cupboards accessible to all the children, who can themselves put in their place and take away the crockery, spoons, knives and forks, table-cloth and napkins. The plates are always of china, and the tumblers and water-bottles of glass. Knives are always included in the table equipment.

The Dressing-room. Here each child has his own little cupboard or shelf. In the middle of the room there are very simple wash stands, consisting of tables, on each of which stand a small basin, soap and nail-brush. Against the wall stand little sinks with water-taps. Here the children may draw and pour away their water. There is no limit to the equipment of the "Children's Houses" because the children themselves do everything. They sweep the rooms, dust and wash the furniture, polish the brasses, lay and clear away the table, wash up, sweep and roll up the rugs, wash a few little clothes, and cook eggs. As regards their personal toilet, the children know how to dress and undress themselves. They hang their clothes on little hooks, placed very low so as to be within reach of a little child, or else they fold up such articles of clothing, as their little serving-aprons, of which they take great care, and lay them inside a cupboard kept for the household linen.

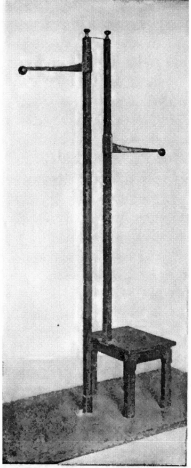

Fig. 2.—The Montessori Paedometer.

In short, where the manufacture of toys has been brought to such a point of complication and perfection that children have at their disposal entire dolls' houses, complete wardrobes for the dressing and undressing of dolls, kitchens where they can pretend to cook, toy animals as nearly lifelike as possible, this method seeks to give all this to the child in reality — making him an actor in a living scene.

My pedometer forms part of the equipment of a "Children's House." After various modifications I have now reduced this instrument to a very practical form. (Fig. 2.)

The purpose of the pedometer, as its name shows, is to measure the children. It consists of a wide rectangular board, forming the base, from the center of which rise two wooden posts held together at the top by a narrow flat piece of metal. To each post is connected a horizontal metal rod — the indicator — which runs up and down by means of a casing, also of metal. This metal casing is made in one piece with the indicator, to the end of which is fixed an india-rubber ball. On one side, that is to say, behind one of the two tall vertical wooden posts, there is a small seat, also of wood. The two tall wooden posts are graduated. The post to which the seat is fixed is graduated from the surface of the seat to the top, whilst the other is graduated from the wooden board at the base to the top, i.e. to a height of 1.5 meters. On the side containing the seat the height of the child seated is measured, on the other side the child's full stature. The practical value of this instrument lies in the possibility of measuring two children at the same time, and in the fact that the children themselves cooperate in taking the measurements. In fact, they learn to take off their shoes and to place themselves in the correct position on the pedometer. They find no difficulty in raising and lowering the metal indicators, which are held so firmly in place by means of the metal casing that they cannot deviate from their horizontal position even when used by inexpert hands. Moreover they run extremely easily, so that very little strength is required to move them. The little india-rubber balls prevent the children from hurting themselves should they inadvertently knock their heads against the metal indicator.

The children are very fond of the pedometer. "Shall we measure ourselves!" is one of the proposals which they make most willingly and with the greatest likelihood of finding many of their companions to join them. They also take great care of the pedometer, dusting it, and polishing its metal parts. All the surfaces of the pedometer are so smooth and well polished that they invite the care that is taken of them, and by their appearance when finished fully repay the trouble taken.

The pedometer represents the scientific part of the method, because it has reference to the anthropological and psychological study made of the children, each of whom has his own biographical record. This biographical record follows the history of the child's development according to the observations which it is possible to make by the application of my method. This subject is dealt with at length in my other books. A series of cinematograph pictures has been taken of the pedometer at a moment when the children are being measured. They are seen coming of their own accord, even the very smallest, to take their places at the instrument.

The Method

The technique of my method as it follows the guidance of the natural physiological and psychical development of the child, may be divided into three parts:

-Motor education.

-Sensory education.

-Language.

The care and management of the environment itself afford the principal means of motor education, while sensory education and the education of language are provided for by my didactic material.

The didactic material for the education of the senses consists of:

(a) Three sets of solid insets.

(b) Three sets of solids in graduated sizes, comprising:

(1) Pink cubes.

(2) Brown prisms.

(3) Rods: (a) colored green; (b)' colored alternately red and blue.

(c) Various geometric solids (prism, pyramid, sphere, cylinder, cone, etc.).

(d) Rectangular tablets with rough and smooth surfaces.

(e) A collection of various stuffs.

(f) Small wooden tablets of different weights.

(g) Two boxes, each containing sixty-four colored tablets.

(h) A chest of drawers containing plane insets.

(i) Three series of cards on which are pasted geometrical forms in paper.

(k) A collection of cylindrical closed boxes (sounds).

(l) A double series of musical bells, wooden boards on which are painted the lines used in music, small wooden discs for the notes.

Didactic Material for the Preparation for Writing and Arithmetic

(m) Two sloping desks and various iron insets.

(n) Cards on which are pasted sandpaper letters.

(o) Two alphabets of colored cardboard and of different sizes.

(p) A series of cards on which are pasted sandpaper figures (1, 2, 3, etc.).

(q) A series of large cards bearing the same figures in smooth paper for the enumeration of numbers above ten.

(r) Two boxes with small sticks for counting.

(s) The volume of drawings belonging specially to the method, and colored pencils.

(t) The frames for lacing, buttoning, etc., which are used for the education of the movements of the hand.

Motor Education

The education of the movements is very complex, as it must correspond to all the coordinated movements which the child has to establish in his physiological organism. The child, if left without guidance, is disorderly in his movements, and these disorderly movements are the special characteristic of the little child. In fact, he "never keeps still," and "touches everything." This is what forms the child's so-called "unruliness" and "naughtiness."

The adult would deal with him by checking these movements, with the monotonous and useless repetition "keep still." As a matter of fact, in these movements the little one is seeking the very exercise which will organize and coordinate the movements useful to man. We must, therefore, desist from the useless attempt to reduce the child to a state of immobility? We should rather give "order" to his movements, leading them to those actions towards which his efforts are actually tending. This is the aim of muscular education at this age. Once a direction is given to them, the child's movements are made towards a definite end, so that he himself grows quiet and contented, and becomes an active worker, a being calm and full of joy. This education of the movements is one of the principal factors in producing that outward appearance of "discipline" to be found in the "Children's Houses." I have already spoken at length on this subject in my other books.

Muscular education has reference to:

The primary movements of everyday life
(walking, rising, sitting, handling objects).

The care of the person.

Management of the household.

Gardening.

Manual work.

Gymnastic exercises.

Rhythmic movements.

In the care of the person the first step is that of dressing and undressing. For this end there is in my didactic material a collection of frames to which are attached pieces of stuff, leather, etc. These can be buttoned, hooked, tied together — in fact, joined in all the different ways which our civilization has invented for fastening our clothing, shoes, etc. (Fig. 3.) The teacher, sitting by the child's side, performs the necessary movements of the fingers very slowly and deliberately, separating the

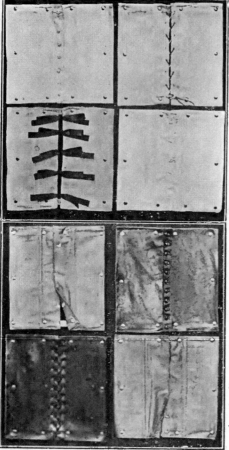

movements themselves into their different parts, and letting them be seen clearly and minutely.

For example, one of the first actions will be the adjustment of the two pieces of stuff in such a way that the edges to be fastened together touch one another from top to bottom. Then, if it is a buttoning-frame, the teacher will show the child the different stages of the action. She will take hold of the button, set it opposite the buttonhole, make it enter the buttonhole completely, and adjust it carefully in its place above. In the same way, to teach a child to tie a bow, she will separate the stage in which he ties the ribbons together from that in which he makes the bows.

FIG. 3.—FRAMES FOR LACING AND BUTTONING.

In the cinematograph film there is a picture which shows an

entire lesson in the tying of the bows with the ribbons. These lessons are not necessary for all the children, as they learn from one another, and of their own accord come with great patience to analyze the movements, performing them separately very slowly and carefully. The child can sit in a comfortable position and hold his frame on the table. (Fig. 4.) As he fastens and unfastens the same frame many times over with great interest, he acquires an unusual deftness of hand, and becomes possessed with the desire to fasten real clothes whenever he has the opportunity. We see the smallest children wanting to dress themselves and their companions. They go in search of amusement of this kind, and defend themselves with all their might against the adult who would try to help them.

In the same way for the teaching of the other and larger movements, such as washing, setting the table, etc., the directress must at the beginning intervene, teaching the child with few or no words at all, but

FIG. 4.—CHILD BUTTONING ON FRAME. (PHOTO TAKEN AT MR. HAWKER'S SCHOOL AT RUNTON.)

with very precise actions. She teaches all the movements: how to sit, to rise from one's seat, to take up and lay down objects, and to offer them gracefully to others. In the same way she teaches the children to set the plates one upon the other and lay them on the table without making any noise.

The children learn easily and show an interest and surprising care in the performance of these actions. In classes where there are many children it is necessary to arrange for the children to take turns in the various household duties, such as housework, serving at table, and washing dishes. The children readily respect such a system of turns. There is no need to ask them to do this work, for they come spontaneously — even little ones of two and a half years old — to offer to do their share, and it is frequently most touching to watch their efforts to imitate, to remember, and, finally, to conquer their difficulty. Professor Jacoby, of New York, was once much moved as he watched a child, who was little more than two years old and not at all intelligent in appearance, standing perplexed, because he could not remember whether the fork should be set at the right hand or the left. He remained a long while meditating and evidently using all the powers of his mind. The other children older than he watched him with admiration, marveling, like ourselves, at the life developing under our eyes.

The instructions of the teacher consist then merely in a hint, a touch — enough to give a start to the child. The rest develops of itself. The children learn from one another and throw themselves into the work with enthusiasm and delight. This atmosphere of quiet activity develops a fellow-feeling, an attitude of mutual aid, and, most wonderful of all, an intelligent interest on the part of the older children in the progress of their little companions. It is enough just to set a child in these peaceful surroundings for him to feel perfectly at home. In the cinematograph pictures the actual work in a "Children's House" may be seen. The children are moving about, each one fulfilling his own task, whilst the teacher is in a corner watching. Pictures were taken also of the children engaged in the care of the house, that is, in the care both of their persons and of their surroundings. They can be seen washing their faces, polishing their shoes, washing the furniture, polishing the metal indicators of the pedometer, brushing the carpets, etc. In the work of laying the table the children are seen quite by themselves, dividing the work among themselves, carrying the plates, spoons, knives and forks, etc., and, finally, sitting down at the tables where the little waitresses serve the hot soup.

Again, gardening and manual work are a great pleasure to our children. Gardening is already well known as a feature of infant education, and it is recognized by all that plants and animals attract the children's care and attention. The ideal of the "Children's Houses" in this respect is to imitate the best in the present usage of those schools which owe their inspiration more or less to Mrs. Latter.

For manual instruction we have chosen clay work, consisting of the construction of little tiles, vases and bricks. These may be made with the help of simple instruments, such as molds. The completion of the work should be the aim always kept in view, and, finally, all the little objects made by the children should be glazed and baked in the furnace. The children themselves learn to line a wall with shining white or colored tiles wrought in various designs, or, with the help of mortar and a trowel, to cover the floor with little bricks. They also dig out foundations and then use their bricks to build division walls, or entire little houses for the chickens.

Among the gymnastic exercises that which must be considered the most important is that of the "line." A line is described in chalk or paint upon a large space of floor. Instead of one line, there may also be two concentric lines, elliptical in form. The children are taught to walk upon these lines like tight-rope walkers, placing their feet one in front of the other. To keep their balance they make efforts exactly similar to those of real tight-rope walkers, except that they have no danger with which to reckon, as the lines are only drawn upon the floor. The teacher herself performs the exercise, showing clearly how she sets her feet, and the children imitate her without any necessity for her to speak. At first it is only certain children who follow her, and when she has shown them how to do it, she withdraws, leaving the phenomenon to develop of itself.

The children for the most part continue to walk, adapting their feet with great care to the movement they have seen, and making efforts to keep their balance so as not to fall. Gradually the other children draw near and watch and also make an attempt. Very little time elapses before the whole of the two ellipses or the one line is covered with children balancing themselves, and continuing to walk round, watching their feet with an expression of deep attention on their faces.

Music may then be nsed. It should be a very simple march, the rhythm of which is not obvious at first, but which accompanies and enlivens the spontaneous efforts of the children.

When they have learned in this way to master their balance the children have brought the act of walking to a remarkable standard of perfection, and have acquired, in addition to security and composure in their natural gait, an unusually graceful carriage of the body. The exercise on the line can afterwards be made more complicated in various ways. The first application is that of calling forth rhythmic exercise by the sound of a march upon the piano. When the same march is repeated during several days, the children end by feeling the rhythm and by following it with movements of their arms and feet. They also accompany the exercises on the line with songs.

Little by little the music is understood by the children. They finish, as in Miss George's school at Washington, by singing over their daily work with the didactic material. The "Children's House," then, resembles a hive of bees humming as they work.

As to the little gymnasium, of which I speak in my book on the "Method," one piece of apparatus is particularly practical. This is the "fence," from which the children hang by their arms, freeing their legs from the heavy weight of the body and strengthening the arms. This fence has also the advantage of being useful in a garden for the purpose of dividing one part from another, as, for example, the flower-beds from the garden walks, and it does not detract in any way from the appearance of the garden.

Sensory Education

My didactic material offers to the child the means for what may be called "sensory education."

In the box of material the first three objects which are likely to attract the attention of a little child from two and a half to three years old are three solid pieces of wood, in each of which is inserted a row of ten small cylinders, or sometimes discs, all furnished with a button for a handle. In the first case there is a row of cylinders of the same height, but with a diameter which decreases from thick to thin. (Fig. 5.) In the second there are cylinders which decrease in all dimensions, and so are either larger or smaller, but always of the same shape. (Fig. 6.)

Lastly, in the third case, the cylinders have the same diameter but vary in height, so that, as the size decreases, the cylinder gradually becomes a little disc in form. (Fig. 7.)

The first cylinders vary in two dimensions (the section); the second in all three dimensions; the third in one dimension (height). The order which I have given refers to the degree of ease with which the child performs the exercises.

The exercise consists in taking out the cylinders, mixing them and putting them back in the right place. It is performed by the child as he sits in a comfortable position at a little table. He exercises his hands in the delicate act of taking hold of the button with the tips of one or two fingers, and in the little movements of the hand and arm as he mixes the cylinders, without letting them fall and without making too much noise and puts them back again each in its own place.

In these exercises the teacher may, in the first instance, intervene, merely taking out the cylinders, mixing them carefully on the table and

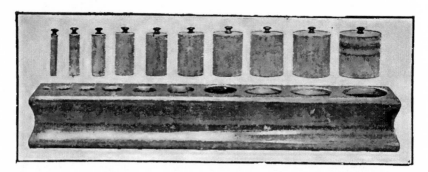

FIG. 5.—CYLINDERS DECREASING IN DIAMETER ONLY.

FIG. 6.—CYLINDERS DECREASING IN DIAMETER AND HEIGHT.

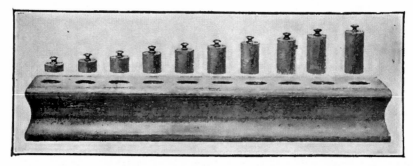

FIG. 7.—CYLINDERS DECREASING IN HEIGHT ONLY.

then showing the child that he is to put them back, but without

FIG. 8.—CHILD USING CASE OF CYLINDERS.

FIG. 9.—THE TOWER.

FIG. 10.—CHILD PLAYING WITH TOWER. (PHOTO TAKEN AT MR. HAWKER'S SCHOOL AT RUNTON.)

performing the action herself. Such intervention, however, is almost always found to be unnecessary, for the children see their companions at work, and thus are encouraged to imitate them.

They like to do it alone; in fact, sometimes almost in private for fear of inopportune help. (Fig. 8.)

But how is the child to find the right place for each of the little cylinders which lie mixed upon the table? He first makes trials; it often happens that he places a cylinder which is too large for the empty hole over which he puts it. Then, changing its place, he tries others until the cylinder goes in. Again, the contrary may happen; that is to say, the cylinder may slip too easily into a hole too big for it. In that case it has taken a place which does not belong to it at all, but to a larger cylinder. In this way one cylinder at the end will be left out without a place, and it will not be possible to find one that fits. Here the child cannot help seeing his mistake in concrete form. He is perplexed, his little mind is faced with a problem which interests him intensely. Before, all the cylinders fitted, now there is one that will not fit. The little one stops, frowning, deep in thought. He begins to feel the little buttons and finds that some cylinders have too much room. He thinks that perhaps they are out of their right place and tries to place them correctly. He repeats the process again and again, and finally he succeeds. Then it is that he breaks into a smile of triumph. The exercise arouses the intelligence of the child; he wants to repeat it right from the beginning and, having learned by experience, he makes another attempt. Little children from three to three and a half years old have repeated the exercise up to forty times without losing their interest in it.

If the second set of cylinders and then the third are presented, the change of shape strikes the child and reawakens his interest.

The material which I have described serves to educate the eye to distinguish difference in dimension, for the child ends by being able to recognize at a glance the larger or the smaller hole which exactly fits the cylinder which he holds in his hand. The educative process is based on this: that the control of the error lies in the material itself J and the child has concrete evidence of it.

The desire of the child to attain an end which he knows, leads him to correct himself. It is not a teacher who makes him notice his mistake and shows him how to correct it, but it is a complex work of the child's own intelligence which leads to such a result.

Hence at this point there begins the process of auto-education.

The aim is not an external one, that is to say, it is not the object that the child should learn how to place the cylinders, and that he should know how to perform an exercise.

The aim is an inner one, namely that the child train himself to observe; that he be led to make comparisons between objects, to form judgments, to reason and to decide; and it is in the indefinite repetition of this exercise of attention and of intelligence that a real development ensues.

The series of objects to follow after the cylinders consists of three sets of geometrical solid forms:

(1) Ten wooden cubes colored pink. The sides of the cubes diminish from ten centimeters to one centimeter. (Fig. 9.)

With these cubes the child builds a tower, first laying on the ground (upon a carpet) the largest cube, and then placing on the top of it all the others in their order of size to the very smallest. (Fig. 10.) As soon as he has built the tower, the child, with a blow of his hand, knocks it down, so that the cubes are scattered on the carpet, and then he builds it up again.

(2) Ten wooden prisms, colored brown. The length of the prisms is twenty centimeters, and the square section diminishes from ten centimeters a side to the smallest, one centimeter a side. (Fig. 11.)

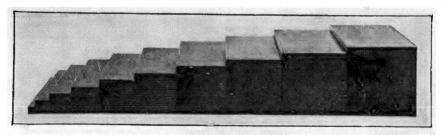

FIG. 11.—THE BROAD STAIR.

The child scatters the ten pieces over a lightcolored carpet, and then beginning sometimes with the thickest, sometimes with the thinnest, he places them in their right order of gradation upon a table.

(3) Ten rods, colored green, or alternately red and blue, all of which have the same square section of four centimeters a side, but vary by ten centimeters in length from ten centimeters to one meter. (Fig. 12.)

FIG. 12.—THE LONG STAIR.

The child scatters the ten rods on a large carpet and mixes them at random, and, by comparing rod with rod, he arranges them according to their order of length, so that they take the form of a set of organ pipes.

As usual, the teacher, by doing the exercises herself, first shows the child how the pieces of each set should be arranged, but it will often happen that the child learns, not directly from her, but by watching his companions. She will, however, always continue to watch the children, never losing sight of their efforts, and any correction of hers will be directed more towards preventing rough or disorderly use of the material than towards any error which the child may make in placing the rods in their order of gradation. The reason is that the mistakes which the child makes, by placing, for example, a small cube beneath one that is larger, are caused by his own lack of education, and it is the repetition of the exercise which, by refining his powers of observation, will lead him sooner or later to correct himself. Sometimes it happens that a child working with the long rods makes the most glaring mistakes. As the aim of the exercise, however, is not that the rods be arranged in the right order of gradation, but that the child should practice by himself if there is no need to intervene.

One day the child will arrange all the rods in their right order, and then, full of joy, he will call the teacher to come and admire them. The object of the exercise will thus be achieved.

These three sets, the cubes, the prisms, and the rods, cause the child to move about and to handle and carry objects which are difficult for him to grasp with his little hand. Again, by their use, he repeats the training of the eye to the recognition of differences of size between similar objects. The exercise would seem easier, from the sensory point of view, than the other with the cylinders described above.

As a matter of fact, it is more difficult, as there is no control of the error in the material itself. It is the child's eye alone which can furnish the control.

Hence the difference between the objects should strike the eye at once; for that reason larger objects are used, and the necessary visual power presupposes a previous preparation (provided for in the exercise with the solid insets).

During the same period the child can be doing other exercises. Among the material is to be found a small rectangular board, the surface of which is divided into two parts — rough and smooth. (Fig. 13.) The child knows already how to wash his hands with cold water and soap; he

FIG. 13.—BOARD WITH ROUGH AND SMOOTH SURFACES.

then dries them and dips the tips of his fingers for a few seconds in tepid water. Graduated exercises for the thermic sense may also have their place here, as has been explained in my book on the "Method."

After this, the child is taught to pass the soft cushioned tips of his fingers as lightly as possible over the two separate surfaces, that he may appreciate their difference. The delicate movement backwards and forwards of the suspended hand, as it is brought into light contact with the surface, is an excellent exercise in control. The little hand, which has just been cleansed and given its tepid bath, gains much in grace and beauty, and the whole exercise is the first step in the edu cation of the "tactile sense, "which holds such an important place in my method.

When initiating the child into the education of the sense of touch, the teacher must always take an active part the first time; not only must she show the child "how it is done," her interference is a little more definite still, for she takes hold of his hand and guides it to touch the surfaces with the finger-tips in the lightest possible way. She will make no explanations; her words will be rather to encourage the child with his hand to perceive the ditferent sensations.

When he has perceived them, it is then that he repeats the act by himself in the delicate way which he has been taught.

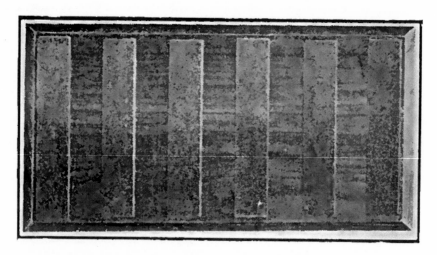

FIG. 14.—BOARD WITH GUMMED STRIPS OF PAPER.

After the board with the two contrasting surfaces, the child is offered another board on which are gummed strips of paper which are rough or smooth in different degrees. (Fig. 14.)

Graduated series of sandpaper cards are also given. The child perfects himself by exercises in touching these surfaces, not only refining his capacity for perceiving tactile differences which are always growing more similar, but also perfecting the movement of which lie is ever gaining greater mastery.

Following these is a series of stuffs of every kind: velvets, satins, silks, woolens, cottons, coarse and fine linens. There are two similar pieces of each kind of stuff, and they are of bright and vivid colors.

The child is now taught a new movement. Where before he had to touch, he must now feel the stuffs, which, according to the degree of fineness or coarseness from coarse cotton to fine silk, are felt with movements correspondingly decisive or delicate. The child whose hand is already practiced finds the greatest pleasure in feeling the stuffs, and, almost instinctively, in order to enhance his appreciation of the tactile sensation he closes his eyes. Then, to spare himself the exertion, he blindfolds himself with a clean handkerchief, and as he feels the stuffs, he arranges the similar pieces in pairs, one upon the other, then, taking off the handkerchief, he ascertains for himself whether he has made any mistake.

This exercise in touching and feeling is peculiarly attractive to the child, and induces him to seek similar experiences in his surroundings. A little one, attracted by the pretty stuff of a visitor's dress, will be seen to go and wash his hands, then to come and touch the stuff of the garment again and again with infinite delicacy, his face meanwhile expressing his pleasure and interest.

A little later we shall see the children interest themselves in a much more difficult exercise.

There are some little rectangular tablets which form part of the material. (Fig. 15.) The tablets, though of identical size, are made of wood of varying qualities, so that they differ in weight and, through the property of the wood, in color also.

FIG. 15.—WOOD TABLETS DIFFERING IN WEIGHT.

The child has to take a tablet and rest it delicately on the inner surfaces of his four fingers, spreading them well out. This will be another opportunity of teaching delicate movements.

The hand must move up and down as though to weigh the object, but the movement must be as imperceptible as possible. These little movements should diminish as the capacity and attention for perceiving the weight of the object becomes more acute and the exercise will be perfectly performed when the child comes to perceive the weight almost without any movement of the hands. It is only by the repetition of the attempts that such a result can be obtained.

Once the children are initiated into it by the teacher, they blindfold their eyes and repeat by themselves these exercises of the baric sense. For example, they lay the heavier wooden tablets on the right and the lighter on the left.

When the child takes off the handkerchief, he can see by the color of the pieces of wood if he has made a mistake.

A long time before this difficult exercise, and during the period when the child is working with the three sorts of geometrical solids and with the rough and smooth tablets, he can be exercising himself with a material which is very attractive to him.

This is the set of tablets covered with bright silk of shaded colors. The set consists of two seperate boxes each containing sixty-four colors; that is, eight different tints, each of which has eight shades carefully graded. The first exercise for the child is that of pairing the colors; that is, he selects from a mixed heap of colors the two tablets which are alike, and lays them out, one beside the other. The teacher naturally does not offer the child all the one hundred and twenty-eight tablets in a heap, but chooses only a few of the brighter colors, for example, red, blue and yellow, and prepares and mixes up three or four pairs. Then, taking one tablet — perhaps the red one — she indicates to the child that he is to choose its counterpart from the heap. This done, the teacher lays the pair together on the table. Then she takes perhaps the blue and the child selects the tablet to form another pair. The teacher then mixes the tablets again for the child to repeat the exercise by himself, i.e., to select the two red tablets, the two blue, the two yellow, etc., and to place the two members of each pair next to one another.

Then the couples will be increased to four or five, and little children of three years old end by pairing of their own accord ten or a dozen couples of mixed tablets.

When the child has given his eye sufficient practice in recognizing the identity of the pairs of colors, he is offered the shades of one color only, and he exercises himself in the perception of the slightest differences of shade in every color. Take, for example, the blue series. There are eight tablets in graduated shades. The teacher places them one beside another, beginning with the darkest, with the sole object of making the child understand "what is to be done."

She then leaves him alone to the interesting attempts which he spontaneously makes. It often happens that the child makes a mistake. If he has understood the idea and makes a mistake, it is a sign that he has not yet reached the stage of perceiving the differences between the graduations of one color. It is practice which perfects in the child that capacity for distinguishing the fine differences, and so we leave him alone to his attempts!

There are two suggestions that we can make to help him. The first is that he should always select the darkest color from the pile. This suggestion greatly facilitates his choice by giving it a constant direction.

Secondly, we can lead him to observe from time to time any two colors that stand next to each other in order to compare them directly and apart from the others. In this way the child does not place a tablet without a particular and careful comparison with its neighbor.

Finally, the child himself will love to mix the sixty-four colors and then to arrange them in eight rows of pretty shades of color with really surprising skill. In this exercise also the child's hand is educated to perform fine and delicate movements and his mind is afforded special training in attention. He must not take hold of the tablets anyhow, he must avoid touching the colored silk, and must handle the tablets instead by the pieces of wood at the top and bottom. To arrange the tablets next to one another in a straight line at exactly the same level, so that the series looks like a beautiful shaded ribbon, is an act which demands a manual skill only obtained after considerable practice.

These exercises of the chromatic sense lead, in the case of the older children, to the development of the "color memory." A child having looked carefully at a color, is then invited to look for its companion in a mixed group of colors, without, of course, keeping the color lie has observed under his eye to guide him. It is, therefore, by his memory that he recognizes the color, which he no longer compares with a reality but with an image impressed upon his mind.

The children are very fond of this exercise in "color memory"; it makes a lively digression for them, as they run with the image of a color in their minds and look for its corresponding reality in their surroundings. It is a real triumph for them to identify the idea with the corresponding reality and to hold in their hands the proof of the mental power they have acquired.

Another interesting piece of material is a little cabinet containing six drawers placed one above another. When they are opened they display six square wooden "frames" in each. (Fig. 16.)

FIG. 16.—CABINET WITH DRAWERS TO HOLD GEOMETRICAL INSETS.

Almost all the frames have a large geometrical figure inserted in the center, each colored blue and provided with a small button for a handle. Each drawer is lined with blue paper, and when the geometrical figure is removed, the bottom is seen to reproduce exactly the same form.

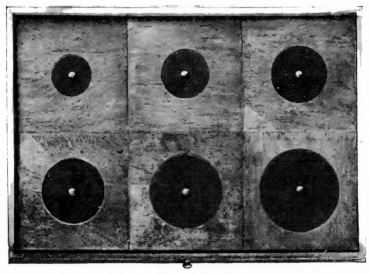

FIG. 17.—SET OF SIX CIRCLES.

The geometrical figures are arranged in the drawers according to analogy of form.

(1) In one drawer there are six circles decreasing in diameter. (Fig. 17.)

FIG. 19--Set of Six Triangles

(2) In another there is a square, together with five rectangles in which

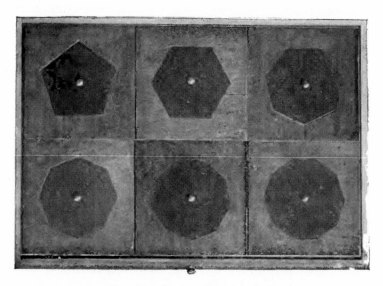

FIG. 20.—SET OF SIX POLYGONS.

the length is always equal to the side of the square while the breadth gradually decreases. (Fig. 18.)

(3) Another drawer contains six triangles, which vary either according to their sides or according to their anyles (the equilateral, isosceles, scalene, right angled, obtuse angled, and acute angled). (Fig. 19.)

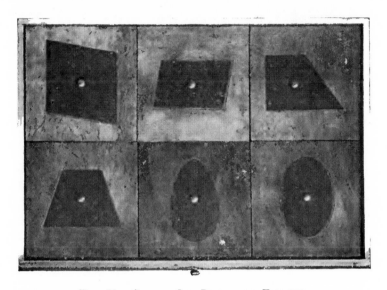

FIG. 21.—SET OF SIX IRREGULAR FIGURES.

(4) In another drawer there are six regular polygons containing from five to ten sides, i.e., the pentagon, hexagon, heptagon, octagon, nonagon, and decagon. (Fig. 20.)

(5) Another drawer contains various figures: an oval, an ellipse, a rhombus, and a trapezoid. (Fig. 21.)

(6) Finally, there are four plain wooden tablets, i.e., without any geometrical inset, which should have no button fixed to them; also two other irregular geometrical figures. (Fig. 22.)

Connected with this material there is a wooden frame furnished with a kind of rack which opens like a lid, and serves, when shut, to keep firmly in place six of the insets which may be arranged on the bottom of the frame itself, entirely covering it. (Fig. 23.)

This frame is used for the preparation of the first presentation to the child of the plane geometrical forms.

The teacher may select according to her own judgment certain forms from among the whole series at her disposal.

Fig. 22.—Set of Four Blanks and Two Irregular Figures.

At first it is advisable to show the child only a few figures which differ very widely from one another in form. The next step is to present a larger number of figures, and after this to present consecutively figures

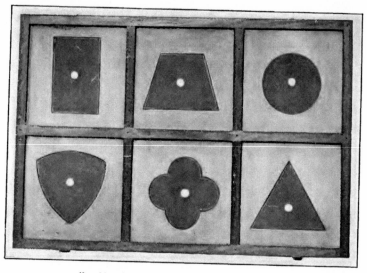

Fig. 23.—Frame to hold Geometrical Insets.

more and more similar in form.

The first figures to be arranged in the frame will be, for example, the circle and the equilateral triangle, or the circle, the triangle and the square. The spaces which are left should be covered with the tablets of plain wood. Gradually the frame is completely filled with figures; first, with very dissimilar figures, as, for example, a square, a very narrow rectangle, a triangle, a circle, an ellipse and a hexagon, or with other figures in combination.

Afterwards the teacher's object will be to arrange figures similar to one another in the frame, as, for example, the set of six rectangles, six triangles, six circles, varying in size, etc.

This exercise resembles that of the cylinders. The insets are held by the buttons and taken from their places. They are then mixed on the table and the child is invited to put them back in their places. Here also the control of the error is in the material, for the figure cannot be inserted perfectly except when it is put in its own place. Hence a series of "experiments," of "attempts" which end in victory. The child is led to compare the various forms; to realize in a concrete way the differences between them when an inset wrongly placed will not go into the

FIG. 24.—CHILD TOUCHING THE INSETS. (MONTESSORI SCHOOL, RUNTON.)

aperture. In this way he educates his eye to the recognition of forms.

The new movement of the hand which the child must coordinate is of particular importance. He is taught to touch the outline of the geometrical figures with the soft tips of the index and middle finger of the right hand, or of the left as well, if one believes in ambidexterity. (Fig. 24.) The child is made to touch the outline, not only of the inset, but also of the corresponding aperture, and, only after having touched them, is he to put back the inset into its place.

The recognition of the form is rendered much easier in this way. Children who evidently do not recognize the identities of form by the eye and who make absurd attempts to place the most diverse figures one within the other, do recognize the forms after having touched their outlines, and arrange them very quickly in their right places.

The child's hand during this exercise of touching the outlines of the geometrical figures has a concrete guide in the object. This is especially true when he touches the frames, for his two fingers have only to follow the edge of the frame, which acts as an obstacle and is a very clear guide. The teacher must always intervene at the start to teach accurately this movement, which will have such an importance in the future. She must, therefore, show the child how to touch, not only by performing the movement herself slowly and clearly, but also by guiding the child's hand itself during his first attempts, so that he is sure to touch all the details – angles and sides. When his hand has learned to perform these movements with precision and accuracy, he will be really capable of following the outline of a geometrical figure, and through many repetitions of the exercise he will come to coordinate the movement necessary for the exact delineation of its form.

This exercise could be called an indirect but very real preparation for drawing. It is certainly the preparation of the hand to trace an enclosed form. The little hand which touches, feels, and knows how to follow a determined outline is preparing itself, without knowing it, for writing.

The children make a special point of touching the outlines of the plane insets with accuracy. They themselves have invented the exercise of blindfolding their eyes so as to recognize the forms by touch only, taking out and putting back the insets without seeing them.

Corresponding to every form reproduced in the plane insets there are three white cards square in shape and of exactly the same size as the wooden frames of the insets. These cards are kept in three special cardboard boxes, almost cubic in form. (Fig. 25.)

FIG. 25.—SERIES OF CARDS WITH GEOMETRICAL FORMS.

On the cards are repeated, in three series, the same geometrical forms as those of the plane insets. The same measurements of the figures also are exactly reproduced.

In the first series the forms are filled in, i.e., they are cut out in blue paper and gummed on to the card; in the second series there is only an outline about half a centimeter in width, which is cut out in the same blue paper and gummed to the card; in the third series, however, the geometrical figures are instead outlined only in black ink.

By the use of this second piece of the material, the exercise of the eye is gradually brought to perfection in the recognition of "plane forms." In fact, there is no longer the concrete control of error in the material as there was in the wooden insets, but the child, by his eye alone, must judge of identities of form when, instead of fitting the wooden forms into their corresponding apertures, he simply rests them on the cardboard figure.

Again, the refinement of the eye's power of discrimination increases every time the child passes from one series of cards to the next, and by the time that he has reached the third series, he can see the relation between a wooden object, which he holds in his hand, and an outline drawing; that is, he can connect the concrete reality with an abstraction. The line now assumes in his eyes a very definite meaning; and he accustoms himself to recognize, to interpret and to judge of forms contained by a simple outline.

The exercises are various; the children themselves invent them. Some love to spread out a number of the figures of the geometric insets before their eyes, and then, taking a handful of the cards and mixing them like playing cards, deal them out as quickly as possible, choosing the. figures corresponding to the pieces. Then as a test of their choice, they place the wooden pieces upon the forms on the cards. At this exercise they often cover whole tables, putting the wooden figures above, and beneath each one in a vertical line, the three corresponding forms of the cardboard series.

Another game invented by the children consists in putting out and mixing all the cards of the three series on two or three adjoining tables. The child then takes a wooden geometrical form and places it, as quickly as possible, on the corresponding cards which he has recognized at a glance among all the rest.

Four or five children play this game together, and as soon as one of them has found, for example, the filled-in figure corresponding to the wooden piece, and has placed the piece carefully and precisely upon it, another child takes away the piece in order to place it on the same form in outline. The game is somewhat suggestive of chess.

Many children, without any suggestion from any one, touch with the finger the outline of the figures in the three series of cards, doing it with seriousness of purpose, interest and perseverance.

¡We teach the children to name all the forms of the plane insets.

At first I had intended to limit my teaching to the most important names, such as square, rectangle, circle. But the children wanted to know all the names, taking pleasure in learning even the most difficult, such as trapezium, and decagon. They also show great pleasure in listening to the exact pronunciation of new words and in their repetition. Early childhood is, in fact, the age in which language is foimed, and in which the sounds of a foreign language can be perfectly learned.

When the child has had long practice with the plane insets, he begins to make "discoveries" in his environment, recognizing forms, colors, and qualities already known to him — a result which, in general, follows after all the sensory exercises. Then it is that a great enthusiasm is aroused in him, and the world becomes for him a source of pleasure. A little boy, walking one day alone on the roof terrace, repeated to himself with a thoughtful expression on his face, "The sky is blue! the sky is blue!" Once a cardinal, an admirer of the children of the school in Via Guisti, wished himself to bring them some biscuits and to enjoy the sight of a little greediness among the children. When he had finished his distribution, instead of seeing the children put the food hastily into their mouths, to his great surprise he heard them call out, "A triangle! a circle I a rectangle!" In fact, these biscuits were made in geometrical shapes.

In one of the people's dwellings at Milan, a mother, preparing the dinner in the kitchen, took from a packet a slice of bread and butter. Her little four-year-old boy who was with her said, "Kectangle." The woman going on with her work cut off a large comer of the slice of bread, and the child cried out, "Triangle." She put this bit into the saucepan, and the child, looking at the piece that was left, called out more loudly than before, "And now it is a trapezium."

The father, a working man, who was present, was much impressed with the incident. He went straight to look for the teacher and asked for an explanation. Much moved, he said, "If I had been educated in that way I should not be now just an ordinary workman."

It was he who later on arranged for a demonstration to induce all the workmen of the dwellings to take an interest in the school. They ended by presenting the teacher with a parchment they had painted themselves, and on it, between the pictures of little children, they had introduced every kind of geometrical form.

As regards the touching of objects for the realization of their form, there is an infinite field of discovery open to the child in his environment. Children have been seen to stand opposite a beautiful pillar or a statue and, after having admired it, to close their eyes in a state of beatitude and pass their hands many times over the forms. One of our teachers met one day in a church two little brothers from the school in Via Guisti. They were standing looking at the small columns supporting the altar. Little by little the elder boy edged nearer the columns and began to touch them, then, as if he desired his little brother to share his pleasure, he drew him nearer and, taking his hand very gently, made him pass it round the smooth and beautiful shape of the column. But a sacristan came up at that moment and sent away "those tiresome children who were touching everything."

The great pleasure which the children derive from the recognition of objects by touching their form corresponds in itself to a sensory exercise.

Many psychologists have spoken of the stereognostic sense, that is, the capacity of recognizing forms by the movement of the muscles of the hand as it follows the outlines of solid objects. This sense does not consist only of the sense of touch, because the tactile sensation is only that by which we perceive the differences in quality of surfaces, rough or smooth. Perception of form comes from the combination of two sensations, tactile and muscular, muscular sensations being sensations of movement. What we call in the blind the tactile sense is in reality more often the stereognostic sense. That is, they perceive by means of their hands the form of bodies.

It is the special muscular sensibility of the child from three to six years of age who is forming his own muscular activity which stimulates him to use the stereognostic sense. When the child spontaneously blindfolds his eyes in order to recognize various objects, such as the plane and solid insets, he is exercising this sense.

There are many exercises which he can do to enable him to recognize with closed eyes objects of well defined shapes, as, for example, the little bricks and cubes of Froebel, marbles, coins, beans, peas, etc. From a selection of different objects mixed together he can pick out those that are alike, and arrange them in separate heaps.

FIG. 26.—SOUND BOXES.

In the didactic material there are also geometrical solids — pale blue in color — a sphere, a prism, a pyramid, a cone, a cylinder. The most attractive way of teaching a child to recognize these forms is for him to touch them with closed eyes and guess their names, the latter learned in a way which I will describe later. After an exercise of this kind the child when his eyes are open observes the forms with a much more lively interest. Another way of interesting him in the solid geometrical forms is to make them move. The sphere rolls in every direction; the cylinder rolls in one direction only; the cone rolls round itself; the prism and the pyramid, however, stand still, but the prism falls over more easily than the pyramid.

Little more remains of the didactic material for the education of the senses. There is, however, a series of six cardboard cylinders, either closed entirely or with wooden covers. (Fig. 26.)

When these cases are shaken they produce sounds varying in intensity from loud to almost imperceptible sounds, according to the nature of the objects inside the cylinder.

There is a double set of these, and the exercise consists, first, in the recognition of sounds of equal intensity, arranging the cylinders in pairs. The next exercise consists in the comparison of one sound with another; that is, the child arranges the six cylinders in a series according to the loudness of sound which they produce. The exercise is analogous to that with the color spools, which also are paired and then arranged in gradation. In this case also the child performs the exercise seated comfortably at a table. After a preliminary explanation from the teacher he repeats the exercise by himself, his eyes being blindfolded that he may better concentrate his attention.

We may conclude with a general rule for the direction of the education of the senses. The order of procedure should be:

(1) Recognition of identities (the pairing of similar objects and the insertion of solid forms into places which fit them).

(2) Recognition of contrasts (the presentation of the extremes of a series of objects).

(3) Discrimination between objects very similar to one another.

To concentrate the attention of the child upon the sensory stimulus which is acting upon him at a p:articular moment, it is well, as far as possible, to isolate the sense; for instance, to obtain silence in the room for all the exercises and to blindfold the eyes for those particular exercises which do not relate to the education of the sense of sight.

The cinematograph pictures give a general idea of all the sense exercises which the children can do with the material, and any one who has been initiated into the theory on which these are based will be able gradually to recognize them as they are seen practically carried out. . It is very advisable for those who wish to guide tne children in these sensory exercises to begin themselves by working with the didactic material. The experience will give them some idea of what the children must feel, of the difficulties which they must overcome, etc., and, up to a certain point, it will give them some conception of the interest which these exercises can arouse in them. Whoever makes such experiments himself will be most struck by the fact that, when blindfolded, he finds that all the sensations of touch and hearing really appear more acute and more easily recognized. On account of this alone no small interest will be aroused in the experimenter.

For the beginning of the education of the musical sense, we use in Rome a material which does not form part of the didactic apparatus as it is sold at present. It consists of a double series of bells forming an octave with tones and semitones. These metal bells, which stand upon a wooden rectangular base, are all alike in appearance, but, when struck with a little wooden hammer, give out sounds corresponding to the notes doh, re, mi, f ah, soh, lah, ti, doh, doh #, re#, fah#, soh #, lah#.

One series of bells is arranged in chromatic order upon a long board, upon which are painted rectangular spaces which are black and white and of the same size as the bases which support the bells. As on a pianoforte keyboard, the white spaces correspond to the tones, and the black to the semitones. (Fig. 27.)

At first the only bells to be arranged upon the board are those which correspond to the tones; these are set upon the white spaces in the order of the musical notes, doh, re, mi, fah, soh, lah, ti, doh.

To perform the first exercise the child strikes with a small hammer the first note of the series already arranged (doh). Then among a second series of corresponding bells which, arranged without the semitones, are

Fig. 27.—Musical Bells.

mixed together upon the table, he tries, by striking the bells one after the other, to find the sound which is the same as the first one he has struck (doh). When he has succeeded in finding the corresponding sound, he puts the bell thus chosen opposite the first one (doh) upon the board. Then he strikes the second bell, re, once or twice; then from among the mixed group of bells he makes experiments until he recognizes re, which he places opposite the second bell of the series already arranged. He continues in the same way right to the end, looking for the identity of the sounds and performing an exercise of pairing similar to that already done in the case of the sound-boxes, the colors, etc.

Later, he learns in order the sounds of the musical scale, striking in rapid succession the bells arranged in order, and also accompanying his action with his voice — doh, re, mi, fah, soh, lah, ti, doh. When he is able to recognize and remember the series of sounds, the child takes the eight bells and, after mixing them up, he tries by striking them with the hammer, to find doh, then re, etc. Every time that he takes a new note, he strikes from the beginning all the bells already recognized and arranged in order — doh, re, doh re, mi; doh, re mi, fah; doh, re mi, fah, soh, etc. In this way he succeeds in arranging all the bells in the order of the scale, guided only by his ear, and having succeeded, he strikes all the notes one after the other up and down the scale. This exercise fascinates children from five years old upwards.

If the objects which have been described constitute the didactic material for the beginnings of a methodical education of the auditory sense, I have no desire to limit to them an educational process which is so important and already so complex in its practise, whether in the long established methods of treatment for the deaf, or in modern physiological musical education. In fact, I also use resonant metal tubes, small bars of wood which emit musical notes, and strings (little harps), upon which the children seek to recognize the tones they have already learned with the exercise of the bells. The pianoforte may also be used for the same purpose. In this way the difference in timbre comes to be perceived together with the differences in tone. At the same time various exercises, already mentioned, such as the marches played on the piano for rhythmic exercises, and the simple songs sung by the children themselves, offer extensive means for the development of the musical sense.

To quicken the child's attention in special relation to sounds there is a most important exercise which, contrary to all attempts made up to this time in the practice of education, consists not in producing but in eliminating, as far as possible, all sounds from the environment. My "Wesson of silence" has been very widely applied, even in schools where the rest of my method has not found its way, for the sake of its practical effect upon the discipline of the children.

The children are taught "not to move"; to inhibit all those motor impulses which may arise from any cause whatsoever, and in order to induce in them real 'immobility' it is necessary to initiate them in the control of all their movements. The teacher, then, does not limit herself to saying, "Sit still," but she gives them the example herself, showing them how to sit absolutely still; that is, with feet still, body still, arms still, head still. The respiratory movements should also be performed in such a way as to produce no sound.

The children must be taught how to succeed in this exercise. The fundamental condition is that of finding a comfortable position, i.e., sl position of equilibrium. As they are seated for this exercise, they must therefore make themselves comfortable either in their little chairs or on the ground. When immobility is obtained, the room is half-darkened, or else the children close their eyes, or cover them with their hands.

It is quite plain to see that the children take a great interest in the "Silence"; they seem to give themselves up to a kind of spell: they might be said to be wrapped in meditation. Little by little, as each child, watching himself, becomes more and more still, the silence deepens till it becomes absolute and can be felt, Just as the twilight gradually deepens whilst the sun is setting.

Then it is that slight sounds, unnoticed before, are heard; the ticking of the clock, the chirp of a sparrow in the garden, the flight of a butterfly. The world becomes full of imperceptible sounds which invade that deep silence without disturbing it, just as the stars shine out in the dark sky without banishing the darkness of the night. It is almost the discovery of a new world where there is rest. It is, as it were, the twilight of the world of loud noises and of the uproar that oppresses the spirit. At such a time the spirit is set free and opens out like the corolla of the convolvulus.

And leaving metaphor for the reality of facts, can we not all recall feelings that have possessed us at sunset, when all the vivid impressions of the day, the brightness and clamor, are silenced? It is not that we miss the day, but that our spirit expands. It becomes more sensitive to the inner play of emotions, strong and persistent, or changeful and serene.

"It was that hour when mariners feel longing, And hearts grow tender." (Dante, trans. Longfellow.)

The lesson of silence ends with a general calling of the children's names. The teacher, or one of the children, takes her place behind the class or in an adjoining room, and "calls" the motionless children, one by one, by name; the call is made in a whisper, that is, without vocal sound. This demands a close attention on the part of the child, if he is to hear his name. When his name is called he must rise and find his way to the voice which called him; his movements must be light and vigilant, and so controlled as to make no noise.

When the children have become acquainted with silence, their hearing is in a manner refined for the perception of sounds. Those sounds which are too loud become gradually displeasing to the ear of one who has known the pleasure of silence, and has discovered the world of delicate sounds. From this point the children gradually go on to perfect themselves; they walk lightly, take care not to knock against the furniture, move their chairs without noise, and place things upon the table with great care. The result of this is seen in the grace of carriage and of movement, which is especially delightful on account of the way in which it has been brought about. It is not a grace taught externally for the sake of beauty or regard for the world, but one which is born of the pleasure felt by the spirit in immobility and silence. The soul of the child wishes to free itself from the irksomeness of sounds that are too loud, from obstacles to its peace during work. These children, with the grace of pages to a noble lord, are serving their spirits.

This exercise develops very definitely the social spirit. No other lesson, no other "situation," could do the same. A profound silence can be obtained even when more than fifty children are crowded together in a small space, provided that all the children know how to keep still and want to do it; but one disturber is enough to take away the charm.

Here is demonstration of the cooperation of all the members of a community to achieve a common end. The children gradually show increased power of inhibition; many of them, rather than disturb the silence, refrain from brushing a fly off the nose, or suppress a cough or sneeze. The same exhibition of collective action is seen in the care with which the children move to avoid making a noise during their work. The lightness with which they run on tiptoe, the grace with which they shut a cupboard, or lay an object on the table, these are qualities that must be acquired hy all, if the environment is to become tranquil and free from disturbance. One rebel is sufficient to mar this achievement; one noisy child, walking on his heels or banging the door, can disturb the peaceful atmosphere of the small community.

Language and Knowledge of the World

The special importance of the sense of hearing comes from the fact that it is the sense organ connected with speech. Therefore, to train the child's attention to follow sounds and noises which are produced in the environment, to recognize them and to discriminate between them, is to prepare his attention to follow more accurately the sounds of articulate language. The teacher must be careful to pronounce clearly and completely the sounds of the word when she speaks to a child, even though she may be speaking in a low voice, almost as if telling him a secret. The children's songs are also a good means for obtaining exact pronunciation. The teacher, when she teaches them, pronounces slowly, separating the component sounds of the word pronounced.

But a special opportunity for training in clear and exact speech occurs when the lessons are given in the nomenclature relating to the sensory exercises. In every exercise, when the child has recognized the differences between the qualities of the objects, the teacher fixes the idea of this quality with a word. Thus, when the child has many times built and rebuilt the tower of the pink cubes, at an opportune moment the teacher draws near him, and taking the two extreme cubes, the largest and the smallest, and showing them to him, says, "This is large"; "This is small." The two words only, large and small, are pronounced several times in succession with strong emphasis and with a very clear pronunciation, "This is large, large, large"; after which there is a moment's pause. Then the teacher, to see if the child has understood, verifies with the following tests: "Give me the large one. Give me the small one." Again, "The large one."

"Now the small one." "Give me the large one." Then there is another pause. Finally, the teacher, pointing to the objects in turn asks, "What is this?" The child, if he has learned, replies rightly, "Large," "Small." The teacher then urges the child to repeat the words always more clearly and as accurately as possible. "What is it?" "Large." "What!" "Large." "Tell me nicely, what is it?" "Large."

Large and small objects are those which differ only in size and not in form; that is, all three dimensions change more or less proportionally. We should say that a house is "large" and a hut is "small." When two pictures represent the same objects in different dimensions one can be said to be an enlargement of the other.

When, however, only the dimensions referring to the section of the object change, while the length remains the same, the objects are respectively "thick" and "thin." We should say of two posts of equal height, but different crosssection, that one is "thick" and the other is "thin." The teacher, therefore, gives a lesson on the brown prisms similar to that with the cubes in the three "periods" which I have described:

Period 1. Naming. "This is thick. This is thin."

Period 2. Recognition. "Give me the thick. Give me the thin."

Period 3. The Pronunciation of the Word, "What is this?"

There is a way of helping the child to recognize differences in dimension and to place the objects in correct gradation. After the lesson which I have described, the teacher scatters the brown prisms, for instance, on a carpet, says to the child, "Give me the thickest of all," and lays the object on a table. Then, again, she invites the child to look for the thickest piece among those scattered on the floor, and every time the piece chosen is laid in its order on the table next to the piece previously chosen. In this way the child accustoms himself always to look either for the thickest or the thinnest among the rest, and so has a guide to help him to lay the pieces in gradation.

When there is one dimension only which varies, as in the case of the rods, the objects are said to be "long" and "short," the varying dimension being length. When the varying dimension is height, the objects are said to be "tall" and "short"; when the breadth varies, they are "broad" and "narrow."

Of these three varieties we offer the child as a fundamental lesson only that in which the length varies, and we teach the differences by means of the usual three periods, and by asking him to select from the pile at one time always the "longest," at another always the "shortest."

The child in this way acquires great accuracy in the use of words. One day the teacher had ruled the blackboard with very fine lines. A child said, "What small lines !" "They are not small," corrected another; "they are thin"

When the names to be taught are those of colors or of forms, so that it is not necessary to emphasize contrast between extremes, the teacher can give more than two names at the same time, as, for instance, "This is red." "This is blue." "This is yellow." Or, again, "This is a square." "This is a triangle." "This is a circle." In the case of a gradation, however, the teacher will select (if she is teaching the colors) the two extremes "dark" and "light," then making choice always of the "darkest" and the "lightest."

Many of the lessons here described can be seen in the cinematograph pictures; lessons on touching the plane insets and the surfaces, in walking on the line, in color memory, in the nomenclature relating to the cubes and the long rods, in the composition of words, reading, writing, etc.

By means of these lessons the child comes to know many words very thoroughly — large, small; thick, thin; long, short; dark, light; rough, smooth; heavy, light; hot, cold; and the names of many colors and geometrical forms. Such words do not relate to any particular object, but to a psychic acquisition on the part of the child. In fact, the name is given after a long exercise, in which the child, concentrating his attention on different qualities of objects, has made comparisons, reasoned, and formed judgments, until he has acquired a power of discrimination which he did not possess before. In a word, he has refined his senses; his observation of things has been thorough and fundamental; he has changed himself.

He finds himself, therefore, facing the world with psychic qualities refined and quickened. His powers of observation and of recognition have greatly increased. Further, the mental images which he has succeeded in establishing are not a confused medley; they are all classified — forms are distinct from dimensions, and dimensions are classed according to the qualities which result from the combinations of varying dimensions.

All these are quite distinct from gradations. Colors are divided according to tint and to richness of tone, silence is distinct from non-silence, noises from sounds, and everything has its own exact and appropriate name. The child then has not only developed in himself special qualities of observation and of judgment, but the objects which he observes may be said to go into their place, according to the order established in his mind, and they are placed under their appropriate name in an exact classification.

Does not the student of the experimental sciences prepare himself in the same way to observe the outside world! He may find himself like the uneducated man in the midst of the most diverse natural objects, but he differs from the uneducated man in that he has special qualities for observation. If he is a worker with the microscope, his eyes are trained to see in the range of the microscope certain minute details which the ordinary man cannot distinguish. If he is an astronomer, he will look through the same telescope as the curious visitor or dilettante, but he will see much more clearly. The same plants surround the botanist and the ordinary wayfarer, but the botanist sees in every plant those qualities which are classified in his mind, and assigns to each plant its own place in the natural orders, giving it its exact name. It is this capacity for recognizing a plant in a complex order of classification which distinguishes the botanist from the ordinary gardener, and it is exact and scientific language which characterizes the trained observer.

Now, the scientist who has developed special qualities of observation and who "possesses" an order in which to classify external objects will be the man to make scientific discoveries. It will never be he who, without preparation and order, wanders dreaming among plants or beneath the starlit sky.

In fact, our little ones have the impression of continually "making discoveries" in the world about them; and in this they find the greatest joy. They take from the world a knowledge which is ordered and inspires them with enthusiasm. Into their minds there enters "the Creation" in stead of "the Chaos"; and it seems that their souls find therein a divine exultation.

Freedom

The success of these results is closely connected with the delicate intervention of the one who guides the children in their development. It is necessary for the teacher to guide the child without letting him feel her presence too much, so that she may be always ready to supply the desired help, but may never be the obstacle between the child and his experience.

A lesson in the ordinary use of the word cools the child's enthusiasm for the knowledge of things, just as it would cool the enthusiasm of adults. To keep alive that enthusiasm is the secret of real guidance, and it will not prove a difficult task, provided that the attitude towards the child's acts be that of respect, calm and waiting, and provided that he be left free in his movements and in his experiences.

Then we shall notice that the child has a personality which he is seeking to expand; he has initiative, he chooses his own work, persists in it, changes it according to his inner needs; he does not shirk effort, he rather goes in search of it, and with great joy overcomes obstacles within his capacity. He is sociable to the extent of wanting to share with every one his successes, his discoveries, and his little triumphs. There is therefore no need of intervention. "Wait while observing." That is the motto for the educator.

Let us wait, and be always ready to share in both the joys and the difficulties which the child experiences. He himself invites our sympathy, and we should respond fully and gladly. Let us have endless patience with his slow progress, and show enthusiasm and gladness at his successes. If we could say: "We are respectful and courteous in our dealings with children, we treat them as we should like to be treated ourselves," we should certainly have mastered a great educational principle and undoubtedly be setting an example of good education.

What we all desire for ourselves, namely, not to be disturbed in our work, not to find hindrances to our efforts, to have good friends ready to help us in times of need, to see them rejoice with us, to be on terms of equality with them, to be able to confide and trust in them – this is what we need for happy companionship. In the same way children are human beings to whom respect is due, superior to us by reason of their"innocence" and of the greater possibilities of their future. What we desire they desire also.

As a rule, however, we do not respect our children. We try to force them to follow us without regard to their special needs. We are overbearing with them, and above all, rude; and then we expect them to be submissive and well-behaved, knowing all the time how strong is their instinct of imitation and how touching their faith in and admiration of us. They will imitate us in any case. Let us treat them, therefore, with all the kindness which we would wish to help to develop in them. And by kindness is not meant caresses. Should we not call anyone who embraced us at the first time of meeting rude, vulgar and ill-bred? Kindness consists in interpreting the wishes of others, in conforming one's self to them, and sacrificing, if need be, one's own desire. This is the kindness which we must show towards children.

To find the interpretation of children's desires we must study them scientifically, for their desires are often unconscious. They are the inner cry of life, which wishes to unfold according to mysterious laws. We know very little of the way in which it unfolds. Certainly the child is growing into a man by force of a divine action similar to that by which from nothing he became a child.

Our intervention in this marvelous process is indirect; we are here to offer to this life, which came into the world by itself, the means necessary for its development, and having done that we must await this development with respect.

Let us leave the life free to develop within the limits of the good, and let us observe this inner life developing. This is the whole of our mission. Perhaps as we watch we shall be reminded of the words of Him who was absolutely good, "Suffer the little children to come unto Me." That is to say, "Do not hinder them from coming, since, if they are left free and unhampered, they will come."

Writing

The child who has completed all the exercises above described, and is thus prepared for an advance towards unexpected conquests, is about four years old.

He is not an unknown quantity, as are children who have been left to gain varied and casual experiences by themselves, and who therefore differ in type and intellectual standard, not only according to their "natures," but especially according to the chances and opportunities they have found for their spontaneous inner formation.

Education has determined an environment for the children. Individual differences to be found in them can, therefore, be put down almost exclusively to each one's individual "nature." Owing to their environment which offers means adapted and measured to meet the needs of their psychical development, our children have acquired a fundamental type which is common to all. They have coordinated their movements in various kinds of manual work about the house, and so have acquired a characteristic independence of action, and initiative in the adaptation of their actions to their environment. Out of all this emerges a personality, for the children have become little men, who are self-reliant.

The special attention necessary to handle small fragile objects without breaking them, and to move heavy articles without making a noise, has endowed the movements of the whole body with a lightness and grace which are characteristic of our children. It is a deep feeling of responsibility which has brought them to such a pitch of perfection. For instance, when they carry three or four tumblers at a time, or a tureen of hot soup, they know that they are responsible not only for the objects, but also for the success of the meal which at that moment they are directing. In the same way each child feels the responsibility of the "silence," of the prevention of harsh sounds, and he knows how to cooperate for the general good in keeping the environment, not only orderly, but quiet and calm. Indeed, our children have taken the road which leads them to mastery of themselves.

But their formation is due to a deeper psychological work still, arising from the education of the senses. In addition to ordering their environment and ordering themselves in their outward personalities, they have also ordered the inner world of their minds.

The didactic material, in fact, does not offer to the child the "content" of the mind, but the order for that "content." It causes Mm to distinguish identities from differences, extreme differences from fine gradations, and to classify, under conceptions of quality and of quantity, the most varying sensations appertaining to surfaces, colors, dimensions, forms and sounds. The mind has formed itself by a special exercise of attention, observing, comparing, and classifying.

The mental attitude acquired by such an exercise leads the child to make ordered observations in his environment, observations which prove as interesting to him as discoveries, and so stimulate him to multiply them indefinitely and to form in his mind a rich "content" of clear ideas.

Language now comes to fix by means of exact words the ideas which the mind has acquired. These words are few in number and have reference, not to separate objects, but rather to the order of the ideas which have been formed in the mind. In this way the children are able to "find themselves," alike in the world of natural things and in the world of objects and of words which surround them, for they have an inner guide which leads them to become active and intelligent explorers instead of wandering wayfarers in an unknown land.

These are the children who, in a short space of time, sometimes in a few days, learn to write and to perform the first operations of arithmetic. It is not a fact that children in general can do it, as many have believed. It is not a case of giving my material for writing to unprepared children and of awaiting the "miracle."

The fact is that the minds and hands of our children are already prepared for writing, and ideas of quantity, of identity, of differences, and of gradation, which form the bases of all calculation, have been maturing for a long time in them.

One might say that all their previous education is a preparation for the first stages of essential culture — writing, reading, and number, and that knowledge comes as an easy, spontaneous, and logical consequence of the preparation — that it is in fact its natural conclusion.

We have already seen that the purpose of the word is to fix ideas and to facilitate the elementary comprehension of things. In the same way writing and arithmetic now fix the complex inner acquisitions of the mind, which proceeds henceforward continually to enrich itself by fresh observations.

Our children have long been preparing the hand for writing. Throughout all the sensory exercises the hand, whilst cooperating with the mind in its attainments and in its work of formation, was preparing its own future. When the hand learned to hold itself lightly suspended over a horizontal surface in order to touch rough and smooth, when it took the cylinders of the solid insets and placed them in their apertures, when with two fingers it touched the outlines of the geometrical forms, it was coordinating movements, and the child is now ready — almost impatient to use them in the fascinating "synthesis" of writing.

The direct preparation for writing also consists in exercises of the movements of the hand. There are two series of exercises, very different from one another. I have analyzed the movements which are connected with writing, and I prepare them separately one from the other. When we write, we perform a movement for the management of the instrument of writing, a movement which generally acquires an individual character, so that a person's handwriting can be recognized, and, in certain medical cases, changes in the nervous system can be traced by the corresponding alterations in the handwriting. In fact, it is from the handwriting that specialists in that subject would interpret the moral character of individuals.

Writing has, besides this, a general character, which has reference to the form of the alphabetical signs.

When a man writes he combines these two parts, but they actually exist as the component parts of a single product and can be prepared apart.

Exercises for the Management of the Instrument of Writing
(The Individual Part)

In the didactic material there are two sloping wooden boards, on each of which stand five square metal frames, colored pink. In each of these is inserted a blue geometrical figure similar to the geometrical insets and provided with a small button for a handle. With this material we use a box of ten colored pencils and a little book of designs which I have prepared after five years' experience of observing the children. I have chosen and graduated the designs according to the use which the children made of them.

The two sloping boards are set side by side, and on them are placed ten complete "insets" that is to say, the frames with the geometrical figures. (Fig. 28.) The child is given a sheet of white paper and the box of ten colored pencils. He will then choose one of the ten metal insets, which are arranged in an attractive line at a certain distance from him. The child is taught the following process:

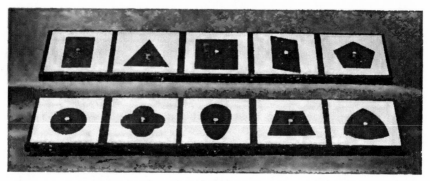

FIG. 28.—SLOPING BOARDS TO DISPLAY SET OF METAL INSETS.

He lays the frame of the iron inset on the sheet of paper, and, holding it down firmly with one hand, he follows with a colored pencil the interior outline which describes a geometrical figure. Then he lifts the square frame, and finds drawn upon the paper an enclosed geometrical form, a triangle, a circle, a hexagon, etc. The child has not actually performed a new exercise, because he had already performed all these movements when he touched the wooden plane insets. The only new feature of the exercise is that he follows the outlines no longer directly with his finger, but through the medium of a pencil. That is, he draws, he leaves a trace of his movement.

The child finds this exercise easy and most interesting, and, as soon as he has succeeded in making the first outline, he places above it the piece of blue metal corresponding to it. This is an exercise exactly similar to that which he performed when he placed the wooden geometrical figures upon the cards of the third series, where the figures are only contained by a simple line.

This time, however, when the action of placing the form upon the outline is performed, the child takes another colored pencil and draws the outline of the blue metal figure.

When he raises it, if the drawing is well done, he finds upon the paper a geometrical figure contained by two outlines in colors, and, if the colors have been well chosen, the result is very attractive, and the child, who has already had a considerable education of the chromatic sense is keenly interested in it.

These may seem unnecessary details, but, as a matter of fact, they are all-important. For instance, if, instead of arranging the ten metal insets in a row, the teacher distributes them among the children without thus exhibiting them, the child's exercises are much limited. When, on the other hand, the insets are exhibited before his eyes, he feels the desire to draw them all, one after the other, and the number of exercises is increased.

The two colored outlines rouse the desire of the child to see another combination of colors and then to repeat the experience. The variety of the objects and the colors are therefore an iriducement to work and hence to final success.

Here the actual preparatory movement for writing begins. "When the child has drawn the figure in double outline, he takes hold of a pencil "like a pen for writing," and draws marks up and down until he has completely filled the figure. In this way a definite filled-in figure remains on the paper, similar to the figures on the cards of the first series. This figure can be in any of the ten colors. At first the children fill in the figures very clumsily without regard for the outlines, making very heavy lines and not keeping them parallel. Little by little, however, the drawings improve, in that they keep within the outlines, and the lines increase in number, grow finer, and are parallel to one another.

When the child has begun these exercises, he is seized with a desire to continue them, and he never tires of drawing the outlines of the figures and then filling them in. Each child suddenly becomes the possessor of a considerable number of drawings, and he treasures them up in his own little drawer. In this way he organizes the movement of writing, which brings him to the management of the pen. This movement in ordinary methods is represented by the wearisome pothook connected with the first laborious and tedious attempts at writing.

The organization of this movement, which began from the guidance of a piece of metal, is as yet rough and imperfect, and the child now passes on to the filling in of the prepared designs in the little album. The leaves are taken from the book one by one in the order of progression in which they are arranged, and the child fills in the prepared designs with colored pencils in the same way as before. Here the choice of the colors is another intelligent occupation which encourages the child to multiply the tasks. He chooses the colors by himself and with much taste. The delicacy of the shades which he chooses and the harmony with which he arranges them in these designs show us that the common belief, that children love bright and glaring colors, has been the result of observation of children without education, who have been abandoned to the rough and harsh experiences of an environment unfitted for them.

The education of the chromatic sense becomes at this point of a child's development the lever which enables him to become possessed of a firm, bold and beautiful handwriting.

The drawings lend themselves to limiting, in very many ways, the length of the strokes with which they are filled in. The child will have to fill in geometrical figures, both large and small, of a pavement design, or flowers and leaves, or the various details of an animal or of a landscape. In this way the hand accustoms itself, not only to perform the general action, but also to confine the movement within all kinds of limits.

Hence the child is preparing himself to write in a handwriting either large or small. Indeed, later on lie will write as well between the wide lines on a blackboard as between the narrow, closely ruled lines of an exercise book, generally used by much older children.

The number of exercises which the child performs with the drawings is practically unlimited. He will often take another colored pencil and draw over again the outlines of the figure already filled in with color. A help to the continuation of the exercise is to be found in the further education of the chromatic sense, which the child acquires by painting the same designs in water-colors. Later he mixes colors for himself until

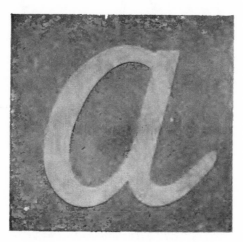

FIG. 29.—SINGLE SANDPAPER LETTER.

he can imitate the colors of nature, or create the delicate tints which his own imagination desires. It is not possible, however, to speak of all this in detail within the limits of this small work.

Exercises for the Writing of Alphabetical Signs

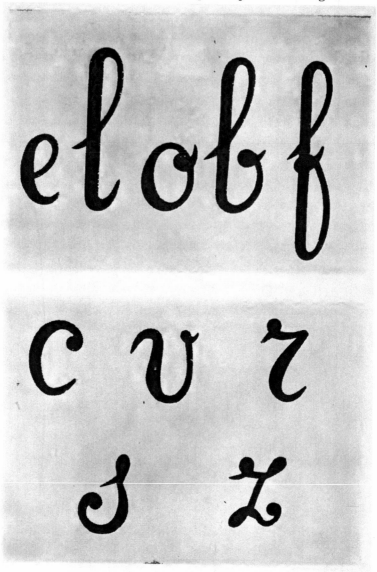

FIG. 30.—GROUPS OF SANDPAPER LETTERS.

In the didactic material there are series of boxes which contain the alphabetical signs. At this point we take those cards which are covered with very smooth paper, to which is gummed a letter of the alphabet cut out in sandpaper. (Fig. 29.) There are also large cards on which are gummed several letters, grouped together according to analogy of form. (Fig. 30.)

The children "have to touch over the alphabetical signs as though they were writing." They touch them with the tips of the index and middle fingers in the same way as when they touched the wooden insets, and with the hand raised as when they lightly touched the rough and smooth surfaces. The teacher herself touches the letters to show the child how the movement should be performed, and the child, if he has had much practice in touching the wooden insets, imitates her with ease and pleasure. Without the previous practice, however, the child's hand does not follow the letter with accuracy, and it is most interesting to make close observations of the children in order to understand the importance of a remote motor preparation for writing, and also to realize the immense strain which we impose upon the children when we set them to write directly without a previous motor education of the hand.

FIG. 31.—BOX OF MOVABLE LETTERS.

The child finds great pleasure in touching the sandpaper letters. It is an exercise by which he applies to a new attainment the power he has already acquired through exercising the sense of touch. Whilst the child touches a letter, the teacher pronounces its sound, and she uses for the lesson the usual three periods. Thus, for example, presenting the two vowels i, o, she will have the child touch them slowly and accurately, and repeat their relative sounds one after the other as the child touches them, "i, i, i! o, o, o!" Then she will say to the child: "Give me i!" "Give me o!" Finally, she will ask the question: "What is this. To which the child replies, "i, o." She proceeds in the same way through all the other letters, giving, in the case of the consonants, not the name, but only the sound. The child then touches the letters by himself over and over again, either on the separate cards or on the large cards on which several letters are gummed, and in this way he establishes the movements necessary for tracing the alphabetical signs. At the same time he retains the visual image of the letter. This process forms the first preparation, not only for writing, but also for reading, because it is evident that when the child touches the letters he performs the movement corresponding to the writing of them, and, at the same time, when he recognizes them by sight he is reading the alphabet.

The child has thus prepared, in effect, all the necessary movements for writing; therefore he can write. This important conquest is the result of a long period of inner formation of which the child is not clearly aware. But a day will come — very soon — when he will write, and that will be a day of great surprise for him — the wonderful harvest of an unknown sowing.

The alphabet of movable letters cut out in pink and blue cardboard, and kept in a special box with compartments, serves "for the composition of words." (Fig. 31.)

In a phonetic language, like Italian, it is enough to pronounce clearly the different component sounds of a word (as, for example, m-a-n-o), so that the child whose ear is already educated may recognize one by one the component sounds. Then he looks in the movable alphabet for the signs corresponding to each separate sound, and lays them one beside the other, thus composing the word (for instance, mano). Gradually he will become able to do the same thing with words of which he thinks himself; he succeeds in breaking them up into their component sounds, and in translating them into a row of signs.

When the child has composed the words in this way, he knows how to read them. In this method, therefore, all the processes leading to writing include reading as well.

If the language is not phonetic, the teacher can compose separate words with the movable alphabet, and then pronounce them, letting the child repeat by himself the exercise of arranging and rereading them.

In the material there are two movable alphabets. One of them consists of larger letters, and is divided into two boxes, each of which contains the vowels. This is used for the first exercises, in which the child needs very large objects in order to recognize the letters. When he is acquainted with one half of the consonants he can begin to compose words, even though he is dealing with one part only of the alphabet.

The other movable alphabet has smaller letters and is contained in a single box. It is given to children who have made their first attempts at composition with words, and already know the complete alphabet.

It is after these exercises with the movable alphabet that the child is able to write entire words. This phenomenon generally occurs unexpectedly, and then a child who has never yet traced a stroke or a letter on paper writes several words in succession. From that moment he continues to write, always gradually perfecting himself. This spontaneous writing takes on the characteristics of a natural phenomenon, and the child who has begun to write the "first word" will continue to write in the same way as he spoke after pronouncing the first word, and as he walked after having taken the first step. The same course of inner formation through which the phenomenon of writing appeared is the course of his future progress, of his growth to perfection. The child prepared in this way has entered upon a course of development through which he will pass as surely as the growth of the body and the development of the natural functions have passed through their course of development when life has once been established.

For the interesting and very complex phenomena relating to the development of writing and then of reading, see my larger works.

The Reading of Music

When the child knows how to read, he can make a first application of this knowledge to the reading of the names of musical notes.

In connection with the material for sensory education, consisting of the series of bells, we use a didactic material, which serves as an introduction to musical reading. For this purpose we have, in the first place, a wooden board, not very long, and painted pale green. On this board the staff is cut out in black, and in every line and space are cut round holes, inside each of which is written the name of the note in its reference to the treble clef.

There is also a series of little white discs which can be fitted into the holes. On one side of each disc is written the name of the note (doh, re, mi, fah, soh, lah, ti, doh).

The child, guided by the name written on the discs, puts them, with the name uppermost, in their right places on the board and then reads the names of the notes. This exercise he can do by himself, and he learns the position of each note on the staff. Another exercise which the child can do at the same time is to place the disc bearing the name of the note on the rectangular base of the corresponding bell, whose sound he has already learned to recognize by ear in the sensorial exercise described above.

Following this exercise there is another staff made on a board of green wood, which is longer than the other and has neither indentures nor signs. A considerable number of discs, on one side of which are written the names of the notes, is at the disposal of the child. He takes up a disc at random, reads its name and places it on the staff, with the name underneath, so that the white face of the disc shows on the top. By the repetition of this exercise the child is enabled to arrange many discs on the same line or in the same space. When he has finished, he turns them all over so that the names are outside, and so finds out if he has made mistakes. After learning the treble clef the child passes on to learn the bass with great ease.

FIG. 32.—THE MUSICAL STAFF.*

To the staff described above can be added another similar to it, arranged as is shown in the figure. (Fig. 32.) The child beginning with doh, lays the discs on the board in ascending order in their right position until the octave is reached: doh, re, mi, fah, soh, lah, ti, doh. Then he descends the scale in the same way, returning to doh, but continuing to place the discs always to the right: soh, fah, mi, re, doh. In this way he forms an angle. At this point he descends again to the lower staff, ti, lah, soh, fah, mi, re, doh, then he ascends again on the other side: re, mi, fah, soh, lah, ti, and by forming with his two lines of discs another angle in the bass, he has completed a rhombus, the rhombus of the notes."

After the discs have been arranged in this way, the upper staff is separated from the lower. In the lower the notes are arranged according to the bass clef. In this way the first elements of musical reading are presented to the child, reading which corresponds to sounds with which the child's ear is already acquainted.

DIDACTIC MATERIAL FOR MUSICAL READING.

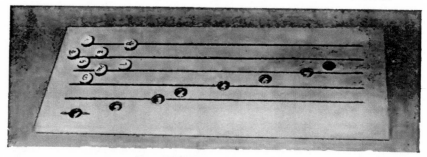

FIG. 33.

On the wooden board, round spaces are cut out corresponding to the notes. Inside each of the spaces there is a figure. On one side of each of the discs is written a number and on the other the name of the note. They are fitted by the child into the corresponding places.

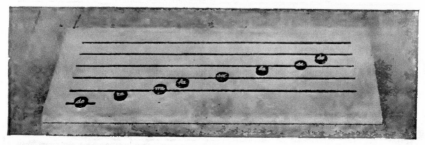

FIG. 34.

The child next arranged the discs in the notes cut out on the staff, but there are no longer numbers written to help him find the places. Instead, he must try to remember the place of the note on the staff. If he is not sure he consults the numbered board (Fig. 33).

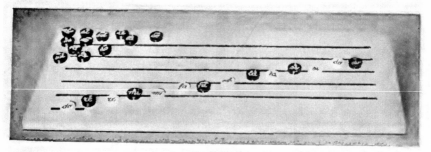

FIG. 35.

The child arranged on the staff the semitones in the spaces which remain where the discs are far apart: do-re, re-mi, fah-soh, soh-la, la-si. The discs for the semitones have the sharp on one side and the flat on the other, e.g., re♯-mi♭ are written on the opposite sides of the same disc.

DIDACTIC MATERIAL FOR MUSICAL READING.

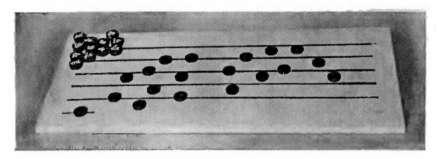

FIG. 36.

The children take a large number of discs and arrange them on the staff, leaving uppermost the side which is blank, i.e., the side on which the name of the note is not written. Then they verify their work by turning the discs over and reading the name.

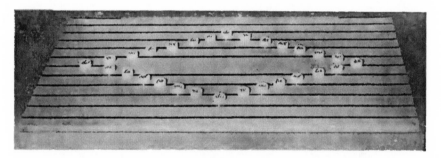

FIG. 37.

The double staff is formed by putting the two staves together. The children arrange the notes in the form of a rhombus.

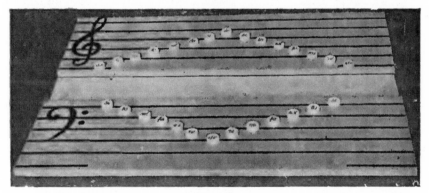

FIG. 38.

The two boards are then separated and the notes remain arranged according to the treble and bass clefs. The corresponding key signatures are then placed upon the two different staves.

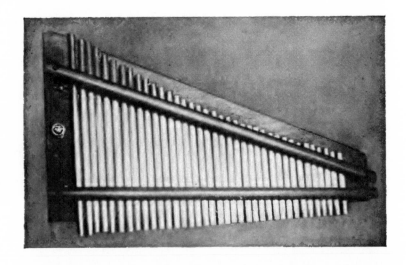

Fig. 39.—Dumb Keyboard.

For a first practical application of this knowledge we have used in our schools a miniature pianoforte keyboard, which reproduces the essentials of this instrument, although in a simplified form, and so that they are visible. Two octaves only are reproduced, and the keys, which are small, are proportioned to the hand of a little child of four or five years, as the keys of the common piano are proportioned to those of the adult. All the mechanism of the key is visible. (Fig. 39.) On striking a key one sees the hammer rise, on which is written the name of the note. The hammers are black and white, like the notes.

With this instrument it is very easy for the child to practice alone, finding the notes on the keyboard corresponding to some bar of written music, and following the movements of the fingers made in playing the piano.

The keyboard in itself is mute, but a series of resonant tubes, resembling a set of organ-pipes, can be applied to the upper surface, so that the hammers striking these produce musical notes corresponding to the keys struck. The child can then pursue his exercises with the control of the musical sounds.

Arithmetic

The children possess all the instinctive knowledge necessary as a preparation for clear ideas on numeration. The idea of quantity was inherent in all the material for the education of the senses: longer, shorter, darker, lighter. The conception of identity and of difference formed part of the actual technique of the education of the senses, which began with the recognition of identical objects, and continued with the arrangement in gradation of similar objects. I will make a special illustration of the first exercise with the solid insets, which can be done even by a child of two and a half. When he makes a mistake by putting a cylinder in a hole too large for it, and so leaves one cylinder without a place, he instinctively absorbs the idea of the absence of one from a continuous series. The child's mind is not prepared for number "by certain preliminary ideas," given in haste by the teacher, but has been prepared for it by a process of formation, by a slow building up of itself.

To enter directly upon the teaching of arithmetic, we must turn to the same didactic material used for the education of the senses.

Let us look at the three sets of material which are presented after the exercises with the solid insets, i.e., the material for teaching size (the pink cubes), thickness (the brown prisms), and length (the green rods). There is a definite relation between the ten pieces of each series. In the material for length the shortest piece is a unit of measurement for all the rest; the second piece is double the first, the third is three times the first, etc., and, whilst the scale of length increases by ten centimeters for each piece, the other dimensions remain constant (i.e., the rods all have the same section).

The pieces then stand in the same relation to one another as the natural series of the numbers 1, 2, 3, 4, 5, 6, 7, 8, 9, 10.

In the second series, namely, that which shows thickness, whilst the length remains constant, the square section of the prisms varies. The result is that the sides of the square sections vary according to the series of natural numbers, i.e., in the first prism, the square of the section has sides of one centimeter, in the second of two centimeters, in the third of three centimeters, etc., and so on until the tenth, in which the square of the section has sides of ten centimeters. The prisms therefore are in the same proportion to one another as the numbers of the series of squares (1, 4, 9, etc.), for it would take four prisms of the first size to make the second, nine to make the third, etc. The pieces which make up the series for teaching thickness are therefore in the following proportion: 1: 4: 9: 16: 25: 36: 49: 64: 81: 100.

In the case of the pink cubes the edge increases according to the numerical series, i.e., the first cube has an edge of one centimeter, the second of two centimeters, the third of three centimeters, and so on, to the tenth cube, which has an edge of ten centimeters. Hence the relation in volume between them is that of the cubes of the series of numbers from one to ten, i.e.,1: 8: 27: 64: 125: 216: 343: 512: 729: 1000. In fact, to make up the volume of the second pink cube, eight of the first little cubes would be required; to make up the volume of the third, twenty-seven would be required, and so on.

The children have an intuitive knowledge of this difference, for they realize that the exercise with the pink cubes is the easiest of all three and that with the rods the most difficult. When we begin the direct teaching of number, we choose the long rods, modifying them, however, by dividing them into ten spaces, each ten centimeters in length, colored alternately red and blue. For example, the rod which is four times as long as the first is clearly seen to be composed of four equal lengths, red and blue; and similarly with all the rest.

When the rods have been placed in order of gradation, we teach the child the numbers: one, two, three, etc., by touching the rods in succession, from the first up to ten. Then, to help him to gain a clear idea of number, we proceed to the recognition of separate rods by means of the customary lesson in three periods.

We lay the three first rods in front of the child, and pointing to them or taking them In the hand in turn, in order to show them to him we say: "This is one" "This is two" "This is three" We point out with the finger the divisions in each rod, counting them so as to make sure, "One, two: this is two" "One, two, three: this is three"

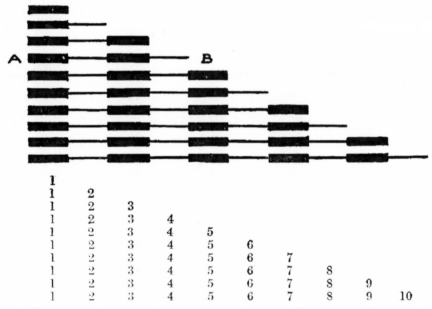

1									
1	2								
1	2	3							
1	2	3	4						
1	2	3	4	5					
1	2	3	4	5	6				
1	2	3	4	5	6	7			
1	2	3	4	5	6	7	8		
1	2	3	4	5	6	7	8	9	
1	2	3	4	5	6	7	8	9	10

Fig. 40.—Diagram Illustrating Use of Numerical Rods.

Then we say to the child: "Give me two" "Give me one" "Give me three" Finally, pointing to a rod, we say, "What is this!" The child answers, "Three," and we count together: "One, two, three."

In the same way we teach all the other rods in their order, adding always one or two more according to the responsiveness of the child.

The importance of this didactic material is that it gives a clear idea of number. For when a number is named it exists as an object, a unity in itself. When we say that a man possesses a million, we mean that he has a fortune which is worth so many units of measure of values, and these units all belong to one person.

So, if we add 7 to 8 (7 + 8), we add a number to a number, and these numbers for a definite reason represent in themselves groups of homogeneous units.

Again, when the child shows us the 9, he is y handling a rod which is inflexible — an object complete in itself, yet composed of nine equal parts which can be counted. And when he comes to add 8 to 2, he will place next to one another, two rods, two objects, one of which has eight equal lengths and the other two. When, on the other hand, in ordinary schools, to make the calculation easier, they present the child with different objects to count, such as beans, marbles, etc., and when, to take the case I have quoted (8 + 2), he takes a group of eight marbles and adds two more marbles to it, the natural impression in his mind is not that he has added 8 to 2, but that he has added 1 + 1 + 1 + 1 + 1 + 1 + 1 + 1 to 1 + 1. The result is not so clear, and the child is required to make the effort of holding in his mind the idea of a group of eight objects as one united whole, corresponding to a single number, 8.

This effort often puts the child back, and delays his understanding of number by months or even years.

The addition and subtraction of numbers under ten are made very much simpler by the use of the didactic material for teaching lengths. Let the child be presented with the attractive problem of arranging the pieces in such a way as to have a set of rods, all as long as the longest. He first arranges the rods in their right order (the long stair); he then takes the last rod (1) and lays it next to the 9. Similarly, he takes the last rod but one (2) and lays it next to the 8, and so on up to the 5.

This very simple game represents the addition of numbers within the ten: 9 + 1, 8 + 2, 7 + 3, 6 + 4. Then, when he puts the rods back in their places, he must first take away the 4 and put it back under the 5, and then take away in their turn the 3, the 2, the 1. By this action he has put the rods back again in their right gradation, but he has also performed a series of arithmetical subtractions, $10 - 4$, $10 - 3$, $10 - 2$, $10 - 1$.

The teaching of the actual figures marks an advance from the rods to the process of counting with separate units. When the figures are known, they will serve the very purpose in the abstract which the rods serve in the concrete; that is, they will stand for the uniting into one whole of a certain number of separate units.

The synthetic function of language and the wide field of work which it opens out for the intelligence is demonstrated, we might say, by the function of the figure, which now can be substituted for the concrete rods.

The use of the actual rods only would limit arithmetic to the small operations within the ten or numbers a little higher, and, in the construction of the mind, these operations would advance very little farther than the limits of the first simple and elementary education of the senses.

The figure, which is a word, a graphic sign, will permit of that unlimited progress which the mathematical mind of man has been able to make in the course of its evolution.

In the material there is a box containing smooth cards, on which are gummed the figures from one to nine, cut out in sandpaper. These are analogous to the cards on which are gummed the sandpaper letters of the alphabet. The method of teaching is always the same. The child is made to touch the figures in the direction in which they are written, and to name them at the same time.

In this case he does more than when he learned the letters; he is shown how to place each figure upon the corresponding rod. "When all the figures have been learned in this way, one of the first exercises will be to place the number cards upon the rods arranged in gradation. So arranged, they form a succession of steps on which it is a pleasure to place the cards, and the children remain for a long time repeating this intelligent game.

After this exercise comes what we may call the "emancipation" of the child. He carried his own figures with him, and now using them he will know how to group units together.

For this purpose we have in the didactic material a series of wooden pegs, but in addition to these we give the children all sorts of small objects — sticks, tiny cubes, counters, etc.

The exercise will consist in placing opposite a figure the number of objects that it indicates. The child for this purpose can use the box which is included in the material. (Fig. 41.) This box is divided into compartments, above each of which is printed a figure and the child places in the compartment the corresponding number of pegs.

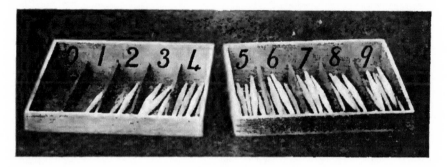

FIG. 41.—COUNTING BOXES.

Another exercise is to lay all the figures on the table and place below them the corresponding number of cubes, counters, etc.

This is only the first step, and it would be impossible here to speak of the succeeding lessons in zero, in tens and in other arithmetical processes — for the development of which my larger works must be consulted. The didactic material itself, however, can give some idea. In the box containing the pegs there is one compartment over which the is printed. Inside this compartment "nothing must be put," and then we begin with one.

Zero is nothing, but it is placed next to one to enable us to count when we pass beyond 9 — thus, 10.

If, instead of the piece 1, we were to take pieces as long as the rod 10, we could count 10, 20, 30, 40, 50, 60, 70, 80, 90. In the didactic material there are frames containing cards on which are printed such numbers from 10 to 90. These numbers are fixed into a frame in such a way that the figures 1 to 9 can be slipped in covering the zero. If the zero of 10 is covered by 1 the result is 11, if with 2 it becomes 12, and so on, until the last 9. Then we pass to the twenties (the second ten), and so on, from ten to ten. (Fig. 42.)

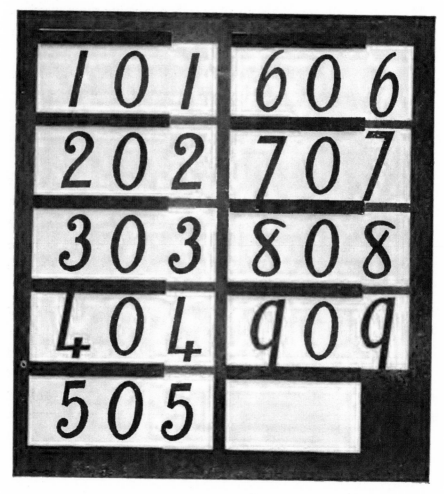

FIG. 42.—ARITHMETIC FRAME.

For the beginning of this exercise with the cards marking the tens we can use the rods. As we begin with the first ten (10) in the frame, we take the rod 10. We then place the small rod 1 next to rod 10, and at the same time slip in the number 1, covering the zero of the 10. Then we take rod 1 and figure 1 away from the frame, and put in their place rod 2 next to rod 10, and figure 2 over the zero in the frame, and so on, up to 9. To advance farther we should need to use two rods of 10 to make 20.

The children show much enthusiasm when learning these exercises, which demand from them two sets of activities, and give them in their work clearness of idea.

In writing and arithmetic we have gathered the fruits of a laborious education which consisted in coordinating the movements and gaining a first knowledge of the world. This culture comes as a natural consequence of man's first efforts to put himself into intelligent communication with the world.

All those early acquisitions which have brought order into the child's mind, would be wasted were they not firmly established by means of written language and of figTires. Thus established, however, these experiences open up an unlimited field for future education. "What we have done, therefore, is to introduce the child to a higher level — the level of culture — and he will now be able to pass on to a school, but not the school we know to-day, where, irrationally, we try to give culture to minds not yet prepared or educated to receive it.

To preserve the health of their minds, which have been exercised and not fatigued by the order of the work, our children must have a new kind of school for the acquisition of culture. My experiments in the continuation of this method for older children are already far advanced.

Moral Factors

A brief description such as this, of the means which are used in the "Children's House," may perhaps give the reader the impression of a logical and convincing system of education. But the importance of my method does not lie in the organization itself, but in the effects which it produces on the child. (Jt is the child who proves the value of this method by his spontaneous manifestations, which seem to reveal the laws of man's inner development [See the chapters on Discipline in my larger works.] Psychology will perhaps find in the "Children's Houses" a laboratory which will bring more truths to light than thus hitherto recognized; for the essential factor in psychological research, especially in the field of psychogenesis, the origin and development of the mind, must be the establishment of normal conditions for the free development of thought.

As is well known, we leave the children free in their work, and in all actions which are not of a disturbing kind. That is, we eliminate disorder, which is "bad," but allow to that which is orderly and "good" the most complete liberty of manifestation.

The results obtained are surprising, for the children have shown a love of work which no one suspected to be in them, and a calm and an orderliness in their movements which, surpassing the limits of correctness have entered into those of "grace." The spontaneous discipline, and the obedience which is seen in the whole class, constitute the most striking result of our method. (The ancient philosophical discussion as to whether man is born good or evil is often brought forward in connection with my method, and many who have supported it have done so on the ground that it provides a demonstration of man's natural goodness. Very many others, on the contrary, have opposed it, considering that to leave children free is a dangerous mistake, since they have in them innate tendencies to evil.

I should like to put the question upon a more positive plane.

In the words "good" and "evil" we include the most varying ideas, and we confuse them especially in our practical dealings with little children.

The tendencies which we stigmatize as evil in little children of three to six years of age are often merely those which cause annoyance to us adults when, not understanding their needs, we try to prevent their every movement, their every attempt to gain experience for themselves in the world (by touching everything, etc.). The child, however, through this natural tendency, is led to coordinate his movements and to collect impressions, especially sensations of touch, so that when prevented he rebels, and this rebellion forms almost the whole of his "naughtiness."

What wonder is it that the evil disappears when, if we give the right means for development and leave full liberty to use them, rebellion has no more reason for existence?

Further, by the substitution of a series of outbursts of joy for the old series of outbursts of rage, the moral physiognomy of the child comes to assume a calm and gentleness which make him appear a different being.

It is we who provoked the children to the violent manifestations of a real struggle for existence. In order to exist according to the needs of their psychic development they were often obliged to snatch from ns the things which seemed necessary to them for the purpose. They had to move contrary to our laws, or sometimes to struggle with other children to wrest from them the objects of their desire.

On the other hand, if we give children the means of existence the struggle for it disappears, and a vigorous expansion of life takes its place. This question involves a hygienic principle connected with the nervous system during the difficult period when the brain is still rapidly growing, and should be of great interest to specialists in children's diseases and nervous derangements. The inner life of man and the beginnings of his intellect are controlled by special laws and vital necessities which cannot be forgotten if we are aiming at health for mankind.

For this reason, an educational method, which cultivates and protects the inner activities of the child, is not a question which concerns merely the school or the teachers; it is a universal question which concerns the family, and is of vital interest to mothers.

To go more deeply into a question is often the only means of answering it rightly. If, for instance, we were to see men fighting over a piece of bread, we might say: "How bad men are!" If, on the other hand, we entered a well-warmed eating-house, and saw them quietly finding a place and choosing their meal without any envy of one another, we might say: "How good men are!" Evidently, the question of absolute good and evil, intuitive ideas of which guide us in our superficial judgment, goes beyond such limitations as these. We can, for instance, provide excellent eating-houses for an entire people without directly affecting the question of their morals. One might say, indeed, that to judge by appearances, a well-fed people are better, quieter, and commit less crime than a nation that is ill-nourished; but whoever draws from that the conclusion that to make men good it is enough to feed them, will be making an obvious mistake.

It cannot be denied, however, that nourishment will be an essential factor in obtaining goodness, in the sense that it will eliminate all the evil acts, and the bitterness caused by lack of bread.

Now, in our case, we are dealing with a far deeper need — the nourishment of man's inner life, and of his higher functions. The bread that we are dealing with is the bread of the spirit, and we are entering into the difficult subject of the satisfaction of man's psychic needs.

We have already obtained a most interesting result, in that we have found it possible to present new means of enabling children to reach a higher level of calm and goodness, and we have been able to establish these means by experience. The whole foundation of our results rests upon these° means which we have discovered, and which may be divided under two heads — the organization of work, and liberty.

It is the perfect organization of work, permitting the possibility of self -development and giving outlet for the energies, which procures for each child the beneficial and calming satisfaction. And it is under such conditions of work that liberty leads to a perfecting of the activities, and to the attainment of a fine discipline which is in itself the result of that new quality of calmness that has been developed in the child.

Freedom without organization of work would be useless. The child left free without means of work would go to waste, just as a new-born baby, if left free without nourishment, would die of starvation. The organization of the work, therefore, is the corner-stone of this new structure of goodness; but even that organization would be in vain without the liberty to make use of it, and without freedom for the expansion of all those energies which spring from the satisfaction of the child's highest activities.

Has not a similar phenomenon occurred also in the history of man! The history of civilization is a history of successful attempts to organize work and to obtain liberty. On the whole, man's goodness has also increased, as is shown by his progress from barbarism to civilization, and it may be said that crime, the various forms of wickedness, cruelty and violence have been gradually decreasing during this passage of time.

The criminality of our times, as a matter of fact, has been compared to a form of barbarism surviving in the midst of civilized peoples. It is, therefore, through the better organization of work that society will probably attain to a further purification, and in the meanwhile it seems unconsciously to be seeking the overthrow of the last barriers between itself and liberty.

If this is what we learn from society, how great should be the results among little children from three to six years of age if the organization of their work is complete, and their freedom absolute 1 It is for this reason that to us they seem so good, like heralds of hope and of redemption.

If men, walking as yet so painfully and imperfectly along the road of work and of freedom, have become better, why should we fear that the same road mil prove disastrous to the children?

Yet, on the other hand, I would not say that the goodness of our little ones in their freedom will solve the problem of the absolute goodness or wickedness of man. We can only say that we have made a contribution to the cause of goodness by removing obstacles which were the cause of violence and of rebellion.

Let us "render, therefore, unto Caesar the things that are Caesar's, and unto God the things that are God's."

The Absorbent Mind

Table of Contents

The Child and the World Reconstructed

In modern times the psychic life in the new-born child has called forth great interest. Many scientists and psychologists have made observations of children from 3 hours to the 5th day from birth. Others, after having studied children carefully, have come to the conclusion that the first two years are the most important of life. Education during this period must be intended as a help to the development of the psychic powers inherent in the human individual. This cannot be attained by teaching because the child could not understand what a teacher would say.

Unexploited Riches

Observation, very general and wide-spread, has shown that small children are endowed with a special psychic nature. This shows us a new way of imparting education! A different form which concerns humanity itself and which has never been taken into consideration. The real constructive energy, alive and dynamic, of children, remained unknown for thousands of years. Just as men trod upon the earth first and cultivated its surface in later times, without knowing of or caring for the immense riches that lay hidden in the depth, so is man now-a-days progressing in civilization without knowing of the riches that lie buried inside the psychic world of the child and indeed, for thousands of years, from the very beginning of humanity itself, man has continued repressing these energies and grinding them into the dust. It is only today that a few have begun to suspect their existence. Humanity has begun to realize the importance of these riches which have never been exploited something more precious than gold; the very soul of man.

These first two years of life furnish a new light that shows the laws of psychic construction. These laws were hitherto unknown. It is the outer expression of the child that has revealed their existence. It shows a type of psychology completely different from that of the adult. So here begins the new path. It is not the professor who applies psychology to children, it is the children themselves who teach psychology to the professor. This may seem obscure but it will become immediately clear if we go somewhat more into detail: the child has a type of mind that absorbs knowledge and instructs himself. A superficial observation will be sufficient to show this. The child of two speaks the language of his parents. The learning of a language is a great intellectual acquisition. Now who has taught the child of two this language? Is it the teacher? Everyone knows that that is not so, and yet the child knows to perfection the names of things, he knows the verbs, the adjectives etc. If anyone studies the phenomenon he will find it marvelous to follow the development of language. All who have done so agree that the child begins to use words and names at a certain period of life. It is as if he had a particular time-table. Indeed, he follows faithfully a severe syllabus which has been imposed by nature and with such exactitude that even the most pains-taking school would suffer in comparison. And following this time-table the child learns all the irregularities and different syntactical constructions of the language with exacting diligence.

The Vital Years

Within a child there is a very scrupulous teacher. It is he who achieves these results in every child, no matter in what region he is found. The only language that man learns perfectly is acquired at this period of childhood when no one can teach him. Not only that, but no matter what help and assistance he will get later in life if he tries to learn a new language, he will not be able to speak it with the same exactitude as he does the one acquired in childhood. There is a psychic power in the child that helps him. It is not merely a question of language. At two years he is able to recognize all the things and persons in his environment. The more one thinks about it the more it becomes evident that the construction the child achieves is immense: for all that we possess has been constructed by the child we once were, and the most important faculties are built in the first two years of life. It is not merely a question of recognizing what it is around us or understanding and dealing with our environment. It is the whole of our intelligence, our religious sentiment, our special feelings of patriotism and caste that are built during this period of life when no one can teach the child. It is as though nature had safeguarded each child from the influence of human intelligence in order to give the inner teacher that dictates within, the possibility of making a complete psychic construction before the human intelligence can come in contact with the spirit and influence it.

At three years of age the child has already laid the foundations of the human personality and needs the special help of education in the school. The acquisitions he has made are such that we can say the child who enters school at three is an old man. Psychologists say that if we compare our ability as adults to that of the child it would require us 60 years of hard work to achieve what a child has achieved in these first three years. And they express themselves by the strange words that I have mentioned above: at three a child is already an old man. Even then this strange ability of the child to absorb from the environment is not finished. In our first schools the children came at three years of age; no one could teach them because they were not receptive. But they gave striking revelations of the greatness of the human mind. Our school is not a real school; it is a house of children, i.e., an environment specially prepared for the children where the children absorb whatever culture is spread in the environment without any one teaching them. In our first school the children who attended came from the lowest class of people; the parents were quite illiterate. Yet these children at 4 years knew how to read and write. Nobody had taught them. Visitors were surprised to see children of so tender an age writing and reading. "Who has taught you how to write?" they asked and the children would look up in wonder and answer, "Taught? no one has taught me," This seemed at the time a miracle. That children so small could write was in itself wonderful, but that they should do so without having received any teaching seemed impossible. The press began to speak about spontaneous acquisition of culture, Psychologists thought that these children were special children and we shared this opinion for a long time. It was only after some years that we perceived that all children have this power of absorbing culture. If this is so, we reasoned, if culture can be taken in without fatigue then let us put different items of culture for them to absorb. So the children absorbed much more than reading and writing, subjects like botany, zoology, mathematics, geography and so on were taken with the same ease, spontaneously, without any fatigue.

So we found that education is not what the teacher gives: education is a natural process spontaneously carried out by the human individual. It is acquired not by listening to words, but by experiences upon the environment. The task of the teacher then becomes not one of talking, but one of preparing a series of motives of cultural activity spread in a specially prepared environment. My experiences have lasted for 40 years now and as the children developed, here and there, in different nations, parents asked me to continue the education for older children and so we found that individual activity is the only means of development: that this is true for the preschool child as well as for the young people in primary and other schools.

The New Man Arises

In front of our eyes arose a new figure. It was not a school or education. It was Man that rose; Man who revealed his true character as he developed freely; who showed his greatness when no mental oppression was there to restrict his soul. And so I say that any reform of education must be based upon the development of the human personality. Man himself should become the center of education. And it must be remembered that man does not develop only at the university: man starts his development from birth and before birth. The greatest development is achieved during the first years of life, and therefore it is then that the greatest care should be taken. If this is done, then the child does not become a burden; he will reveal himself as the greatest marvel of nature. We shall be confronted by a child not as he was considered before a powerless being an empty vessel that must be filled with our wisdom. His dignity will arise in its fullness in front of our eyes as he reveals himself as the constructor of our intelligence, as the being who, guided by the inner teacher, in joy and happiness works indefatigably, following a strict time-table, to the construction of that marvel of nature: Man. We, the human teachers, can only help the great work that is being done, as servants help the master. If we do so, we shall be witnesses to the unfolding of the human soul, to the rising of a New Man who will not be the victim of events, but who will have the clarity of vision to direct and shape the future of human society.

Education for Life

The School and Social Life

It is necessary from the very beginning to have an idea of what we intend by an education for life that starts from birth and even before birth. It is necessary to go into detail about this question, because recently, for the first time, a leader of the people has formulated the necessity not only of extending education to the whole course of life, but also of making 'defense of life' the center of education. I say for the first time when I refer to a political and spiritual leader, because science has not only expressed the necessity of it, but from the beginning of this century it has given positive contributions which show that the conception of extending education to the whole life can be done with certainty of success. Education, as a help and protection to life, is an idea which certainly has not entered the field of action of any ministry of education, neither in America North or South nor in Europe. Education as conceived up to today is rich in methods, in social aims and finalities, but it takes hardly into any consideration whatever life itself. There are many official methods of education adopted by different countries, but no official system of education considers life itself or sets out to protect development and help the individual from birth. If education is protection to life, you will realize that it is necessary that education accompany life during its whole course. Education as conceived today prescinds from both biological and social life. If we stop to think about the question we soon realize that all those who are undergoing education are isolated from society. Students must follow the rules established by each institution and adapt themselves to the syllabus recommended by the ministry of education. If we think about it we find also that in these schools no consideration is given to life itself. If the high school student for instance has not enough food, that is no concern of the school. In the recent past if there were children who were partly deaf, they were marked out by their receiving lower marks because they were unable to hear what the teacher said, but the defects of the child were not taken into consideration. If a child was defective in sight he also received bad marks because he could not write as beautifully as other children. Physical defects have not been taken into consideration until very lately and when this was done, it was from the point of view of hygiene. Even now, however, no one worries about the danger there is for the mind of the student, danger due to defects in the methods of education adopted. What school worries about the kind of civilization the children are forced to live in? The only thing officialdom is bothered about is whether or not the syllabus has been followed. There are social deficiencies apt to strike the spirit of young men attending the university and which do strike them, but what is the official admonition? "You students should not concern yourselves with politics. You must attend to your studies and after you have formed yourselves, then go into the world," Yes. That is quite so, but education today does not form an intelligence capable of visualizing the epoch and the problems of the times in which they live. Scholastic mechanisms are foreign to the social life of the times: its study does not enter the realm of education. Who has ever heard of any ministry of education that is called upon to solve any social problem acutely felt in the country? Never has such a case occurred because the world of education is a sort of retreat where the individuals, for the whole of their scholastic life, remain isolated from the problems of the world. They prepare themselves for life by remaining outside of life.

There may be, for instance, a university student who dies of tuberculosis. That is very sad indeed. But as a university, what can be done? At the most it can provide to be represented at the funeral. There are many individuals who are extremely nervous; when they go into the world, they will be useless not only to themselves, but will be a cause of trouble to their family and to their friends. That may be so, but I, as authority, am not concerned with peculiarities of psychology. I am only concerned with studies and examinations. Who passes them will receive a diploma or a degree. That is as far as the schools of our times go. Those who study sociology or problems of society have said that the people who come from school or university are not prepared for life, not only that, but most are diminished in their possibilities. Sociologists have compiled statistics and have found that there are many criminals, many mad and many more who are considered 'strange': they conclude by saying that the schools must do something to remedy this.

This is a fact. The school is a world apart and if there are social problems the school is expected to ignore them. It is the sociologists who say that schools must do something, but the school itself has not the possibility of doing so, because the school is a social institution of long standing and its rules cannot be modified unless there is some outside power which enforces this modification. These are some of the deficiencies that accompany education and therefore the life of all who go to school.

The Pre-School Age

What about the child from birth to the seventh year, or of the child before its birth? It is taken into no consideration whatever by the school. This age is called pre-scholastic and this means it falls outside the concern of the school. And as to people who are just born what could the school do about them? Wherever institutions have been created for children of pre-school age, these are hardly ever governed by the ministry of education. They are controlled by municipalities or private institutions who dictate their own rules and regulations. Who is concerned as a social problem with the protection of the life of the small child? No one! Society says that small children belong to the family and not to the state. Today great importance is given to the first years of life. But what is it that is being recommended? A modification of the family, a modification in the sense that mothers must be educated. Now, the family does not form a part of school, but of society. So we see how the human personality or the care of the human personality is broken into pieces. On one side there is a family which is one part of society, but is generally isolated from society, from social care. On the other the school, also kept apart from society, and then the university. There is no Unitarian conception of the social care of life. There is one piece here, one piece there and each one ignores the other. Even those new sciences that reveal the harm of this isolation such as social psychology and sociology are themselves isolated from the school. So nowhere is there a reliable system of help for the development of life. When a statesman says that education must be a help to life, we realize the importance of it. It is, as I mentioned before, nothing new to abstract science, but socially it is something that does not yet exist. It is the next step to be taken by civilization. Everything is prepared however: criticism has revealed the errors of the existing conditions, others have shown the remedy to be applied at different stages of life. Everything is ready for the construction. The contributions of science may be compared to the stones cut and ready for the building, but what is necessary is some one who takes the stones and puts them together to make the new building necessary for civilization. That is why the resolution of this Indian leader is of such great importance. It is a step that will permit civilization to rise higher and it is to the building of this step, that in the field of applied science, we strive and work.

The Task of Education and Society

What is the conception of education that takes life as the center of its own function? It is a conception that alters all previous ideas about education. Education must no longer be based upon a syllabus but upon the knowledge of human life. Now, if this is so and it has to be so the education of the new-born acquires a sudden great importance. It is true that the new-born cannot do anything, cannot be taught in the ordinary sense, it can only be observed, it can be studied so as to find out what are the needs of the new-born life. Observation has been carried out by us with a view of discovering what are the laws of life, because if we wish to help life the first thing we must do is to know the laws governing life. Not- only this, because if it were merely knowledge that we sought then we would remain in the field of psychology; but if we are concerned with education our action cannot be limited merely to knowledge. This knowledge must be spread, for all must know what is the psychic development of the child. Education then acquires a new dignity, a new authority, because education will then tell society: "These are the laws of life. You cannot disregard them and you must act in this way."

Indeed if society wishes to give compulsory education it means that education must be given, practically, otherwise one cannot call it compulsory; and if education is to be given from birth, then it is necessary for society to know what are the laws of the development of the child. Education can no longer remain isolated from society but must acquire authority over society. Social machinery must arrange itself around what is to be done so that life be protected. All must be called upon to collaborate: mothers and fathers must, of course, do their part well, but if the family has not sufficient means, then society must give not only knowledge, but enough means to educate the children. If education means care of the individual and if society recognizes that such and such a thing is necessary for the child for its development and the family is not capable of providing for it, then it must be society which provides for the child. The child must not be abandoned by the state. Thus education, instead of remaining apart from society, is bound to acquire authority over society. It is evident that society must have control over the human individual, but if education is considered as a help to life, this control will not be one of restraint and oppression, but a control of physical help and psychic aid. It will be realized by these few words that the next step for society is that of allotting a great deal of money to education.

Step by step the needs of the child during the years of growth have been studied scientifically and the results of this study are being given out to society. The education conceived as a help to life takes in every one not only the child. That means that social conscience must take over responsibility for education and that education will spread its knowledge to the whole of society in every step it takes, instead of remaining isolated from society as it does today. Education as protection to life affects not only the child, but the mothers and fathers as well as the state and international finance. It is something which moves every part of society, indeed it is the greatest of social movements. Education as it is today! Can we imagine anything more immobile, stagnant and indifferent? Today if economy is to be made in a state, education is the first victim. If we ask any great statesman about education he will tell us: "I do not know anything about education. Education is a specialization. I have even entrusted the education of my children to my wife and she has given them to the school." In future it will be absolutely impossible for any head of the state to answer in this fashion when one speaks about education.

The Child Builder of Man

Now, let us take another point. Let us take the statements made by different psychologists who have studied small children from their first year of life. What conception does one derive from them? Generally that from now on instead of growing haphazardly, the individual will grow scientifically, with better care. He will achieve better development and growth. This is the common idea: "The individual will grow stronger, the individual will grow more balanced in mind and have a stronger character," In other words the extreme conception is that besides being provided with physical hygiene, the growing child will be provided with mental hygiene. But this cannot be all. Let us suppose that science has made some discoveries about this first period of life, and this is not merely a supposition. .Indeed there are powers in the small child that are far greater than is generally realized, because it is in this period that the construction, the building-up of man takes place, for at birth, psychically speaking, there is nothing at all zero! Indeed not only psychically, for at birth the child is almost paralytic, he cannot do anything, he cannot speak, even though he sees all that happens around him. And behold him after a while; the child, talking, walking and passing on from conquest to conquest until he has built up man in all his greatness, in all his intelligence. If we consider this we begin to have a glimpse of reality. The child is not an empty being who owes whatever he knows to us who have filled him up with it. No, the child is the builder of man. There is no man existing who has not been formed by the child he once was. In order to form a man great powers are necessary and these powers are possessed only by the child. These great powers of the child which we have described for long, and which at last have attracted the attention of other scientists, were hitherto hidden under the cloak of motherhood, in the sense that people said that it is the mother who forms the child, the mother who teaches him to talk, walk etc., etc. But I say that it is not the mother at all. It is the child himself who does all these things. What the mother produces is the new-born babe, but it is this babe who produces the man. Suppose the mother dies, the child grows just the same. Even if the mother is not there, and even if the mother has not the milk necessary to feed him, we give other milk to the child and that is how he continues to grow. It is the child who carries out the construction and not the mother. Suppose we take an Indian child to America and entrust him to some Americans. This child will learn the English language and not an Indian language. By English, we mean American English. So it is not the mother that gives the knowledge. He takes it himself and if these Americans really treated the child as one of their own, this Indian child would acquire the habits and customs of the American people and not those of the Indian people. So none of these things is hereditary. The father and mother cannot claim the credit: it is the child who, making use of all that he finds around him, shapes himself for the future.

The child needs special aid in order to build man properly and society must give this its attention. Recognizing the merits of the child does not diminish the authority of the father and the mother for when they come to realize that they are not the constructors, but merely the helpers of this construction, then they will be able to do their duty better; they will help the child with a greater vision. Only if this help is well given will the child achieve a good construction, not otherwise. So the authority of parenthood is not based upon an independent loftiness but upon the help that is given to the child. Parents have no authority other than that. Let us consider another aspect. Everyone will have heard of Karl Marx who was the originator of a social reform when he made the workers realize that whatever society enjoys was due to their work and that everything we have in our environment has been made by some man or woman. Our daily life is based upon these workers and if they ceased to produce, our social and political life would cease. This is part of the theory of Karl Marx. The workers are those who really give us the possibility of carrying on our lives; they produce the environment and provide everything, food, clothing, every means of life. When people realized this, the working man no longer appeared as the poor laborer who depended for his bread on his employer; he assumed his real importance. Previous to that all importance was given only to princes, kings and capitalists, but later the merits of the workers came to light. And the real contribution of the capitalist was realized as the supplier of the means that the workers needed to carry out their work; also that the better were the conditions afforded to the worker, the better and more accurate was his product.

Let us carry this idea into our field. Let us realize that the child is the worker who produces man. The parents furnish the means of construction to the worker. The social problem confronting us then is of much greater importance, because from the children's work, humanity itself is produced, not an object. Childhood does not produce one race, one caste, one social group, but it produces the whole of humanity. This is the reality that humanity must envisage: it is the child that society must take into consideration, this worker who produces humanity itself. The two social questions really present a striking resemblance, e.g. before Karl Marx expounded this idea, the working men were not considered. They had to do whatever they were told just as the child has to; the workers' needs and his dignity as a man were not considered. In the work of the child, the needs of life physical and psychic are not considered, and his dignity of man is non-existent. What have socialists and communists done? They have started a movement in order to obtain better conditions of life for the working man. Also to the child, this constructor, we must give better means of life. Workers ask for more money; more money must also be given to those who produce humanity. The workers wish to free themselves from restraints and repressions. We must free childhood from repression that weighs upon it. The conditions of this constructor of man are more dramatic than those of the constructor of the environment. Bettering the conditions of life for the constructor of man will bring about a betterment in humanity. We must follow this great worker from the moment he starts, at birth, follow him until he reaches adulthood; and provide him with means necessary for a good construction. We must remember that he is going to form that humanity which with its intelligence is building civilization. The child is the builder of our intelligence, and it is our human intelligence which guides our hands and produces what we call civilization.

If life itself is taken into consideration and studied, we shall know the secret of humanity. We shall have in our hands the power of governing and helping humanity. The social vision of Karl Marx brought about a revolution. It is a revolution that we are preaching when we speak about education. It is a revolution inasmuch as everything that we know today will be changed. Indeed I consider it the last revolution. It will be a non-violent revolution because if the slightest violence is offered to the child, then his psychic construction will be faulty. This delicate construction of human normality, as it should be, needs protection; it must be carried out without the slightest violence being offered to it. Indeed all our effort has been to remove obstacles from the path of the growth of the child. We have taken away from him the dangers and misunderstandings that surrounded him.

This is what is intended by education as a help to life; an education from birth that brings about a revolution: a revolution that eliminates every violence, a revolution in which everyone will be attracted towards a common center. Mothers, fathers, statesmen all will be centered upon respecting and aiding this delicate construction which is carried on in psychic mystery following the guide of an inner teacher.

This is the new shining hope for humanity. It is not so much a reconstruction, as an aid to the construction carried out by the human soul as it is meant to be, developed in all the immense potentialities with which the new-born child is endowed.

The Periods of Growth

According to the modern psychologists who have followed children from birth to university age, there are in the course of development different and distinct periods. This conception is different from the one which was held previously and which considered that the human individual when young holds very little and then becomes more capable as it grows, the conception of something small that developed, i.e., something small which grows, but which holds always the same form. That was the old conception about the human mind. Today psychology recognizes that there are different types of psyche and different types of mind at different periods of life. These periods are clearly distinct from one another. It is curious to say that these periods correspond to different phases in the development of the physical body. The changes are so great, psychically speaking, that certain psychologists, trying to render them clear, have exaggerated and they have expressed themselves in this fashion: "Growth is a succession of births." At a certain period of life, a psychic individuality ceases and another is born. These successive births take place during the period of growth. The first of these periods goes from birth to six years. This period shows notable differences, but during its whole length the type of mind is the same. From zero to 6 the period shows two distinct sub-phases. The first from to 3 years shows a type of mentality which is unapproachable by the adult, i.e., upon which the adult cannot exert any direct influence and, indeed, there is no school for such children. Then there is another sub-phase from 3 to 6 in which the type of mind is the same, but the child begins to become approachable in a special manner. This period is characterized by the great transformations that take place in the individual. In order to realize this, it is sufficient to think about the difference there is between a new-born babe and a child of 6. How this transformation takes place does not concern us for the moment, but the fact is that at 6 years the individual becomes, according to the usual expression, intelligent enough to be admitted to school.

The next period is from 6 to 12 years. This period is one of growth, but without transformations. It is a period of calm and serenity. It is also psychically speaking a period of health and strength and security. Now if we look at the physical body, we see signs that seem to mark the limit between these two psychic periods. The transformation that takes place in the body is very visible. I will cite only one item: the child loses his first set of teeth and starts growing the second.

Then there is the third period which goes from 12 to 18 years, which is also a period of such transformation that it reminds us of the first period. This last period can also be sub-divided into two sub-phases, one that extends from 12 to 15 and one from 15 to 18. This period is also distinguished physically by transformations in the body which achieves maturity. After 18 man is considered completely developed and there is no longer any considerable transformation. Man merely becomes older.

The curious thing is that official education has recognized these different psychic types. It seems to have had a subconscious intuition of them. The first period from to 6 years of age has been clearly recognized because it has been excluded from compulsory education and it has been noticed that at 6, there is a transformation. People seem to have reasoned that the child of 6 years is sufficiently intelligent to be admitted to school. In doing so they have unconsciously admitted that the child knows a great many things; for if he were completely ignorant, he would not be able to attend school. If, for instance, children do not know how to orientate themselves, how to walk, how to understand when somebody talks and so forth, even at 6, they would be unable to attend school. So we might say that this has been a practical recognition. But they never thought, these educators, that if the child can come to school, find his way about and understand the ideas transmitted to him, he must have learned to do so, because at birth he was unable to do any of these things. Who has taught him then? Not the teachers, because, as we saw, during this period the child is excluded from school. It has never even entered their minds that there must be a very elaborate procedure to enable the new-born individual who had no intelligence, no co-ordinated movement, no will, and no memory, to understand what we say.

An unconscious recognition was also given to the second period, because in many countries at 12 years of age children generally leave the elementary school and enter high school. Why have they chosen the period from 6 to 12 and why do they consider it the proper period in which to give the basic and elementary items of culture? As this happens in every country of the world, it means that it was not done by chance. It means that there must be a psychic basis common to all children that made this possible. It had been recognized by reasoning based upon experience. It has been found that during this period, the child can submit to the mental work necessary in schools. He understands what a teacher says and he has enough patience to listen and to learn. During this whole period, he is constant in his work, as well as strong in health. It is because of these characteristics that this period is considered as the most profitable for imparting culture. After the 12th year of age, usually there is the beginning of a higher sort of school. By this official education has recognized that at that year a new type of psychology begins in the human individual. That this type has two divisions has also been felt. It is shown by the fact that they have divided high schools into two parts.

We have in our country an inferior and a superior high school. The inferior high school lasts three years and the superior sometimes two and sometimes three. Here we have a period which is not as smooth and calm as the preceding one. Psychologists say that it is a period of such psychic transformation that it may be compared to the first period from to 6. Usually during this period the character is not steady, there is indiscipline and some sort of rebellion. Physical health also is not as strong and secure as during the second period. But the school pays no heed to this. A certain syllabus has been elaborated and children are forced to follow it, whether they like it or not. In this period also the children have to sit and listen to the teachers, have to obey implicitly and spend their time memorizing things.

Then comes the university. The university also does not differ essentially from the types of school that precede it, except perhaps by the intensity of study. Here also the professors come, they talk and students listen. When I was young, men did not shave, they had beards. And it was curious to see in the lecture halls all these men fully bearded, some of them with pointed beards, some with square ones; some had long beards and some had them short, while the most different varieties of moustaches were displayed. Yet all these men mature and more than mature were as little children. They had to sit and listen; they had to submit to the jibes of the professors; they had to depend for their cigarettes, for their street-car fares on the liberality of their fathers who scolded them if they failed in the examinations. They were adult men! These men, whose intelligence, whose experience was going to direct the world, whose instrument of work was to be the intelligence and to whom were allotted the highest professions, were the future doctors, engineers, lawyers. And what good is a degree today? Is one's life assured on receiving one's degree? Who goes to a doctor who has only just received it? And if somebody wants to build a beautiful house, does he go and ask the services of a newly fledged engineer. Or if I have a law suit on my hands, am I going to employ a newly accredited lawyer? No. And why? For the simple reason that all these years of study, all these years of listening, do not form 'man'; only practical work and practice do that. Thus we find that young doctors have to serve in hospitals, and lawyers have to practice in the office of an established lawyer. The same plan has to be followed for the engineer. This apprenticeship lasts for years and years, before they can have a practice of their own. And in order to be able to find a place to practice, they must have an opportunity and protection. There have been very strange cases resulting from this in many countries. A typical one took place in New York. There was a procession exclusively of intellectuals; hundreds of them who had been unable to find any sort of employment. They bore a banner with this information: "We are without work; we are starving. What are we to do?" Such is the situation, even today. There is no planning. Education is without control, but some sort of acknowledgment is given to the fact that during growth there are different types at different periods of life. There are different mental types and to each mental type has been allotted a different phase of education, elementary, high school and university.

The Period of Creation

When I was young, the children from 2 to 6 years were not taken into consideration at all. Now there are pre-school institutions of different kinds. There is the creche for small children and the so-called Montessori school, nursery and kindergarten schools for children from 3 to 6. But today, as then, the most important part of education is considered to be university education, because from the university come the people who have best cultivated that part of man's mind which we call intelligence. Now that the psychologists have come to study life, there is a tendency to go to the other extreme, and there are other people besides me who say that the most important part of life is not the university, but the first period the period that extends from to 6 years, because it is during this first period that intelligence, the great instrument of man, is formed; and not only intelligence, but the whole of the psychic faculties are constructed during this period. This has made a great impression upon all who have had any sensibility towards psychic life. Today many meditate upon the small child; upon the new-born, and the one year old, who create the personality of man; and they feel the same emotion, the same deep impression as those who in olden times used to meditate upon death. What is it that takes place when death comes? This is what attracted meditation and sentimentality in the past. Today a similar meditation is being carried out upon man who has just entered the world. This is a Man, this is the being who has been created with the highest and loftiest intelligence. Why is he to have such a long and painful infancy? No animal has a period of infancy so painful and so long. This is what attracts the attention of the thinkers. "What is it that takes place during this period?" they ask themselves.

Certainly it is a period of creation because before nothing existed, and then, a year or so after birth, the child knows everything. It is not as if a child were born with a little bit of intelligence, with a little bit of memory, with a little bit of will which after a while grows. There is nothing! Individuality starts from zero! It is not as though there were a little voice that later developed, as is the case, for instance, for the kitten, who at birth is able to mew even if imperfectly, or for the bird or the calf. Man is absolutely mute. The only means of expression he has is that of crying. In the case of the human being, it is not a question of development. It is a question of creation that starts from zero. If you do not exist, you cannot hope to grow. That is the tremendous step the child takes, the step that goes from nothing to something. We are not capable of it. Our mind is not capable of it.

A type of mind different from ours, endowed with different powers is necessary to accomplish this. And it is not a small creation that the child achieves. It is the creation of all. He creates not only the language, but the organs that make it possible for us to speak. Every physical movement he creates, every side of our intelligence. He creates all that the human mind, the human individual is endowed with. It is a tremendous achievement!

This is not done with a conscious mind. We are conscious; we have a will and if we want to learn something, we go about it. There is no consciousness in the small child, no will. For both consciousness and will have to be created. The child's mind is not the type of mind we adults possess. If we call our type of mind the conscious type, that of the child is an unconscious mind. Now an unconscious mind does not mean an inferior mind. An unconscious mind can be full of intelligence. One will find this type of intelligence in every being and every insect has it. It is not a conscious intelligence even though sometimes it looks as if it were endowed with reason. It is of an unconscious type and while he is endowed with it the child performs his wonderful achievements. The child of one year has already seen all things that are in his environment and is capable of recognizing them.

How has he been able to take in this environment? This is due to one of the special characteristics that we have discovered in the child: a power of such intense sensitivity that the things which surround him in the environment awaken in him an intense interest and such a great enthusiasm that they seem to penetrate into his very life. The child takes all these impressions not with his mind, but with his life. The acquisition of language is the most evident example of this. How is it that the child acquires language? It is said that the child is endowed with the sense of hearing, that he hears the voice of the human being and thus he learns to speak. Let us admit this. It is a fact. Why, however, amongst all the millions of different sounds and noises that surround him, does he hear just the voice of man? If it is true that the child hears, and if it is true that he takes only the language of human beings, it means that the human language must have made a great impression on the child. These impressions must be so strong, they must cause such an intensity of feeling and such a great enthusiasm as to set in motion invisible fibers within the body that begin to vibrate in order to reproduce those sounds. We can compare it to something similar in ourselves. Sometimes one goes to a concert. After a while one begins to see rapt expressions on the faces of the public; heads and hands begin to move. What has brought them into movement if not the impressions caused by the music? Something similar must happen in the unconscious mind of the child. The voice causes such impressions that the impressions aroused in us by music seem almost non-existent in comparison. One can almost see these movements of the tongue that thrills, of the minute chords that tremble and of the cheeks, everything vibrating and becoming tense, preparing in silence to reproduce those sounds that have caused so much emotion in the unconscious mind. And how is it that the child acquires language in its exactness? It is so exactly and firmly acquired that this language forms part of his psychic personality, it is called his mother-tongue, and it is as clearly distinguished from all other languages that he may learn, as a set of false teeth may be distinguished from the natural set. How is it that these sounds which in the beginning have no meaning suddenly bring to his mind understanding, ideas? He has not merely taken in the words. He has taken 'the sentence, the construction of the sentence.' If we do not understand the construction of the sentence, we cannot understand language. If we say, for instance, "the glass is on the table" it is the order of the words that gives the sense. If one said to them, "glass the on is table" it would be difficult to get the idea. It is the sequence of words that we understand. The child has absorbed the constructions of the language.

The Absorbent Mind

How does it take place? It is said "he remembers these things," but in order to remember, he has to have memory and he had no memory; he has still to construct it. He would have to have the power of reasoning in order to realize that the construction of a sentence is necessary in order to understand it. But he has no reasoning power. He has to construct it.

Our mind, such as it is, could not do it; to accomplish it a different type of mind is needed, and that is what the child possesses, a type of intelligence different from ours. We might say that we acquire with our intelligence, the child absorbs with his psychic life. The child merely by going on with his life, learns to speak the language belonging to his race. It is like a mental chemistry that takes place in the child. We are vessels; impressions pour in, and we remember and hold them in our mind, but we remain distinct from our impressions, as water remains distinct from the glass. The child undergoes a transformation. The impressions not only penetrate the mind of the child, but form it. They become incarnate. The child makes its own 'mental flesh' by using the things that are in his environment. We have called his type of mind "Absorbent Mind" It is difficult for us to conceive the powers of the absorbent mind of the small child, but certainly it is a privileged form of mind. If only it could continue, if only it persisted! Just think. The child is born and for some months he lies in his house. After a while he walks, goes around, does things and he enjoys himself, he is happy; he lives from day to day and by doing this he learns movements; language comes into his mind with all its constructions; the possibility of directing his movements to suit his life and many other things. Whatever is in his environment comes to be part of his mind: habits, customs, religion. Think how wonderful it would be if, while merely enjoying ourselves, merely by existing, just because we had such a type of mind, we could become doctors or lawyers or engineers. Think of it. Children learn the language with all the perfection or imperfection they find in their environment without going to school. How wonderful would it be if one could learn German merely by walking with a German. Instead how hard have we to work. Arid how much have we to study when we have to learn the different subjects.

Little by little the child becomes conscious of all the things, these form his consciousness. And so we see the path followed by the child. He acquires all unconsciously, gradually passing from unconscious to conscious, following a path of pleasure and love, this consciousness seems to us a great acquisition. To become conscious; to acquire a human mind! But we pay for it. Because as soon as we become conscious, every new acquisition causes hard work and fatigue.

Movement is another of these wonderful acquisitions. At birth the child moves very little, then gradually his body becomes animated. He starts to move. The movements that the child acquires, just as is the case with language, are not formed by chance. They are determined in the sense that they are acquired during a special period. When the child begins to move, his absorbent mind has already taken in the environment. Before he starts to move, an unconscious psychic development has already taken place. As he starts to move, he begins to become conscious. If you watch a small child of three, he is always playing with something. That means he is elaborating with his hands, putting into his consciousness, what his unconscious mind had taken in before. It is by this experience in the environment in the guise of playing that he goes over the things and the impressions that he has taken into his unconscious mind. It is by means of work that he becomes conscious and constructs Man. He is directed by a marvelously grand mysterious power which little by little he incarnates and thus he becomes a Man. He becomes a man by means of his hands, by means of his experience, first through play, then through work. The hands are the instrument of the human intelligence. And by means of this experience he becomes a man, he takes a definite form and becomes limited because consciousness is always more limited than unconsciousness and sub-consciousness.

He comes to life and begins his mysterious work and little by little he becomes the wonderful personality adapted to his time and to his environment. He builds his mind, until little by little he has constructed memory; until little by little he has constructed understanding, reasoning power; until little by little, he has arrived at his 6th year. Then suddenly we educators discover that this individual understands, that he has the patience to listen to what we say, whereas before we had no power to reach him. He lived on another plane, different from ours. In this book we are concerned with this first period. And a study of the psychology of the child in the first years of his life is so marvelous, so full of miracles, that all who understand it cannot help but feel a great emotion. Our work is not to teach, but to help the absorbent mind in its work of development. How marvelous it would be if by our help, if by an intelligent treatment of the child, if by understanding the needs of his physical life and by feeding his intellect, we could prolong the period of functioning of the absorbent mind! What a service we should render if we could help the human individual to absorb knowledge without fatigue, if man could find himself full of knowledge without knowing how he had acquired it, doing it almost by magic. And why should it not be possible? Is not nature full of magic, full of miracles?

The discovery of the fact that the child is endowed with an absorbent mind has brought about a revolution in education. Now it is easy to understand why the first is the most important amongst the periods of development. The creation of human character takes place within its span; and once we have understood this, it also becomes clear that we must help the child in his creative work. For there is no age in which the child is more in need of intelligent help than in this period. It is evident that if the child meets with obstacles, his creative work becomes less perfect. We do not any longer help the child because he is a small and weak being. No! We have realized that the child is endowed with great creative powers, that these great powers are delicate in their nature and can be thwarted if obstacles are placed in their path. It is these powers we wish to help, not the small child, not his weakness. When we understand that these powers belong to an unconscious mind which must become conscious by work and experience carried out in the environment, when we realize that the child's mind is different from ours, that we cannot reach it and teach him things, that we cannot directly intervene in this process of passing from the unconscious to the conscious and of constructing the human faculties; then the whole conception of education will change and will become that of a help to the child's life. Education will take the guise of an aid to the psychic development of man and not of making him memorize ideas and facts.

This is the new path of education and how to help this mind in its different processes, how to second the different powers and how to give strength to the different qualities of this mind will be the object of our study in this book.

A New Orientation

In our days there is a definitely new orientation in biological studies. Previously all study was carried out on the adult being. For instance, when animals or plants were studied by scientists it was the adult specimen which came under consideration. This applied also to the studies upon humanity. It was always the adult that was taken into consideration, e.g. in the study of morality, in the study of sociology, it was always the adult. Another field which attracted the attention and meditation of the thinkers was death and this was logical because the adult being as he proceeds in life is headed towards death. The study of morality was, we might say, the study of the conditions and rules of social contact amongst adults. It is true that there are moral ideas such as love for one another, the sacrifice of one's self for the welfare of other beings and so forth, but all these are difficult virtues. They require a preparation and an effort of the will. Today scientists seem to have taken the opposite direction. It seems as though they were proceeding backwards. Both in the study of human beings and of other types of life, they consider not only the very young beings, but their very origin. So biology directs its attention to embryology, to the life of the cell and so forth. From this orientation towards the origin a new philosophy has sprung up but this philosophy is not of an idealistic nature. Rather, we might say, it is scientific because it springs from observation and not from abstract deductions of thinkers. The progress of this philosophy proceeds side by side with the progress in the discoveries made in the laboratories.

When one enters the field of origins, the field of embryology, one sees things which do not exist in the fields that concern adults, or if they do exist, they are of a very different nature. Scientific observations reveal a type of life which is quite different from the one that humanity was accustomed to consider previously. It is by this new field of research that the personality of the child has been thrown into the limelight. A very banal consideration will show that the child does not progress towards death like the adult, the child progresses towards life because the purpose of the child is the construction of man in the fullness of his strength and in the fullness of his life. When the adult arrives, the child is no longer. So the whole life of the child is a progress towards perfection, a progress of ever greater achievement. Even from this banal observation, one can deduct that the child can find joy in the fulfilment of a task of growth and perfection. The child's is a type of life in which work, the fulfilment of one's task, brings joy and happiness, whereas in the field of adult, work is something which is usually a rather painful process. This process of growth, this proceeding in life is for the child something that expands and enlarges, inasmuch as the older the child becomes, the more intelligent and stronger he becomes. His work, his activity help the child to acquire intelligence and strength, whereas in the case of adults, it is rather the contrary. Also in this field of the child, there is no competition, because no one can do the work that the child does in order to construct the man that he has to construct. In other words, nobody can grow for him.

The adults who are near the child usually are protectors of the child. So one can see that, in the case of human beings, it is in the field of the child that examples and inspiration for a better society can be found. It is not a question of an ideal. It is a reality. As this field is different and also as it represents a better kind of life, it deserves to be studied.

Now let us go still further back in the life of the child, i.e. to the period before birth. Already before birth the child has contact with the adult because as an embryo life is spent in the body of the mother. Before the embryo, there is the germinal cell which is the result of two cells which come from adults. So from either side when one goes towards the origin of the life of human beings, and when one goes on following the child towards the completion of his task of growth, one finds the adult. The child's life is the line that joins the two generations of adult life. The child's life which originates and is originated, starts from the adult and finishes in the adult. This is the way, the path of life, and it is from this life that touches the adult so intimately that a great light can be derived. That is why its study is so fascinating.

The Two Lives

Nature furnishes special protection to the young. They are born amidst love, the very origin of the child is love. Once he is born, he is surrounded by the love of his father and mother. So it is not in strife that he is generated and that is his protection. Nature gives to the parents love for their young and this love is not something artificial, or enforced by reason, such as the idea of brotherhood that all people aspiring to unity are trying to arouse. It is in the field of the child's life that can be found the type of love which shows what ought to be the ideal moral attitude of the adult community, because only here can be found love that naturally inspires self-sacrifice. It inspires the dedication of an ego to somebody else, the dedication of one's self to the service of other beings. In the depth of their sentiment all parents give up their own life in order to dedicate it to their children. This sacrifice that the father and mother make is something natural that gives joy. It does not appear as sacrifice. Nobody for instance says: "Oh, this poor man has two children etc." But one says: "How lucky this man is to have a wife and children. What a joy it must be for her to have such lovely children!" And yet there is a real self-sacrifice on the part of the parents for their children, but it is a sacrifice which gives joy. It is life itself, so that the child inspires that which in the adult world represents an ideal: renunciation, self-sacrifice which are almost impossible to attain. What businessman, if, on the market, there is something rare he needs, tells another rival firm: "Here you take it, I do not want it?" But if they are both hungry and if there is only a small piece of bread, what father or mother would not say to the child: "You eat it. I am not hungry?" This is a very lofty sort of love that can be found only in the world of children. It is nature that gives it. So there are two different lives. The adult has the privilege of taking part in both. In one life because of the child and in the other because he is a member of society. The better of the two is the part which concerns the child because in this life his loftiest sentiments are developed.

Now it is curious that, if the study is carried out among animals instead of among men, these two types of life are also to be found. There are, for instance, the wild and ferocious animals which seem to change their instincts when they have a family. Everybody knows how tender are tigers and lions for their young and how brave becomes the timid deer. It seems as if there were a reversal of instinct in all animals when they have young ones to protect. It is a sort of imposition of special instincts over the ordinary ones. Timid animals, even to a greater degree than we, possess an instinct of self-preservation, but when they have young ones, this instinct of self-preservation changes into an instinct of protection for the young. So with many birds. Their instinct for the protection of life is to fly away as soon as any danger approaches, but when they have young ones, they do not fly away, but some remain frozen upon the nest in order to cover the betraying whiteness of the eggs. Others feign being wounded, keep themselves just out of reach of the dog's jaws and attract them away from their young who remain in hiding. Ordinarily instead of taking the chance of being caught, they fly away. There are many instances of this kind and in every form of animal life there will be found two sets of instincts: one set for self-protection and another set of instincts for the protection of the lives of their young. One of the books which most beautifully describes this is a book of the French biologist J. H. Fabre in which he concludes by saying that it is to this great mother-instinct that the species owes its survival. This is true because if the survival of the species were due only to the so-called weapons for the struggle for existence, how could the young ones defend themselves? They have not as yet developed these weapons. Are not the small tigers toothless and the young birds without feathers?

Therefore, if life is to be saved and if the species is to survive, it is necessary first of all to provide protection for the young who though unarmed are building up their weapons.

If life owed its survival only to the struggle of the strong, the species would perish. So the real reason, the main factor of the survival of the species, is the love that the adults feel for their young. If we study nature, the fascinating part is to see the revelation of intelligence that there is even in the lowest of the low, as we consider them. Each one is endowed with different kinds of protective instincts; each one is endowed with a different kind of intelligence and all this intelligence is expended for the protection of the young, whereas if one studies their instincts for self-protection, these do not show so much intelligence and there is not the same variety of instinct in this field. There is not the finesse of detail that made Fabre fill 16 volumes, treating mainly of the protective instincts among insects. So studying among all different kinds of life, one sees that two sets of instincts are necessary and two types of life. When we carry this to the field of human life, were it for nothing but for social reasons, the study of the life of the child is necessary for the consequences it has in the adult. And this study of life must go to the very origin.

Embryology

There are today different sciences which take into consideration the life of the child and the life of the living being from its very beginning. One of the most interesting is the study of embryology which is also carried out in a new fashion. Thinkers and philosophers in all times have wondered about the marvel of a being who did not exist before and becomes a man or a woman who will have intelligence, thoughts, and who will be able to show the greatness of his soul. How does this come about? How are the organs made which are so complicated and so marvelous P How are the eyes formed and the tongue, that allows us to speak, and the brain and all the other infinite details of the human organism? How are they formed? In the beginning of the XVIIIth century scientists thought that there must be in the egg-cell a minute ready-made man or woman. It was so small that one could not see it but it was there and afterwards it merely grew. This was thought to be so also for the mammals. Two schools disputed as to whether it was the man who had this in his generating cell or the woman. And they fought carrying on learned discussions in the Universities. At that time there was a young man who made use of the microscope, which had just been invented, saying to himself: "I am going to see what really happens." He started to study the germinal cell. He came by observations to the conclusion that there is nothing pre-existing.

He said that the being builds itself and described how it is formed. The germinal cell divides itself into two, the two divide into four and by multiplication of cells, the being is formed. (See fig. 1.) The learned university men who were fighting with each other became angry. Who is this ignorant person who says that nothing exists? Why, this is against religion! And the situation became so bad for this poor man that he was chased out of his country. He remained an exile and died in a foreign country. For 50 years though the microscopes were multiplied, nobody dared to look into the secret again. But meanwhile what this first man had said had begun to penetrate and people thought that it might be true. Another scientist after 50 years made the same study and found that what the first man had said was true. He said it to every one arid this time

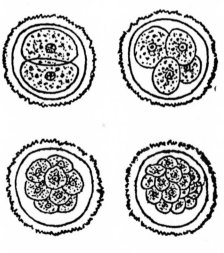

Fig. 1
The multiplication of the germinal cell.

every one believed it, and a new branch of science arose which today is very advanced: Embryology.

Today embryology has developed to the point that it begins to reason and says that it is true that there is nothing pre-existing, that there is no ready-made man or ready-made woman who grows and grows until he becomes a full-grown man or woman; but there is a pre-established plan of construction which is surprising, because it seems so well made, so well reasoned out, that it appears as if somebody had thought it out and fixed it. It is as though some one wanted to build a house and started by collecting bricks before beginning to build the walls of the house. And the same happens with this primitive cell: first it accumulates a number of cells, by sub-division and multiplication, and then builds three walls. When the three walls have been built, the second phase begins the phase of the construction of the organs.

Now the construction of the organs takes place in an extraordinary way. It begins by one cell at one point. I do not know what happens there. I do not know if it is something of a chemical nature or if it is a sort of sensitiveness. I believe no one does. The fact is that around that point an extraordinary activity begins. There the rate of multiplication of cells becomes feverish whereas elsewhere it continues in the same calm fashion. When this feverish activity ceases, an organ has been built. There are several of these points and each one of them builds up a definite organ. The discoverer has interpreted the phenomenon in this fashion: there are points of sensitivity around which a construction takes place. These organs develop independently one from the other. It is as though the purpose of each of these cellular points were to build something for themselves only, and the intensity, the activity, is such that in each of these organs the cells become so united, so imbued with what we might call their ideal that they actually transform themselves and they become different from the other cells. So the cells assume a special form according to the organs that they are constructing. Then when the different organs are formed independently one of the other, something else comes, which puts them into relation and communication. When they are all united, so united and so interconnected that one cannot live without the other, the child is born. It is the circulatory system that joins them together. And after the circulatory system, the nervous system is finished, to make more intimate the union. And then one sees the plan of construction. This plan of construction is based upon a point of enthusiasm from which a creation is achieved. And once the creation of the organs is a fact, they are destined to unite, to join together. This plan is the same for all superior animals and for man. It is followed by them all for the development of each.

The modern idea is therefore that there is but one plan of construction common to all lives. Embryos are in fact so similar that in the recent past there was a theory that evolution had proceeded along a path of different degrees of animality; so that man for instance came from the monkey, that mammals and birds came from reptiles, these from amphibians, the latter from fishes etc. The embryos of each were thought to pass through the stages of all the preceding ones before achieving birth; so that in the embryos there was a synthesis of the evolution of the species, Today this is an abandoned theory. Today science looks merely at the facts and says that nature has but one method of construction, that there is only one plan of construction in nature.

Now if we have this in mind, then many obscure facts are better understood, e.g. the psychic development of the child, because not only the human body, but also the human psyche is constructed following the same plan. It starts from nothing, or at least from what appears to be nothing, in the same way as the body starts from that primitive cell which appears in no way different from other cells. In the new-born child, also psychically speaking, there seems to be nothing which is already built up, just as there was not a ready-made man in the primitive cell. And in the psychic field also, organs are built around a point of sensitivity. There is at first the work of accumulation of material, just as we said there was an accumulation of cells by a multiplication in the case of the body. This is done by what I have called the 'absorbent mind' After that come points of sensitivity. These are so intense that we adults cannot even imagine anything approaching it. We gave an example of this when we illustrated the acquisition of language. From these points of sensitivity, it is not the psyche that is developed, but the organs of this psyche. Here also each organ develops independently of the other, e.g., language, being able to judge distances, or being able to orient oneself in the environment, or being able to stand on two legs and other co-ordinations. Each of these items develops around an interest, but independently one of the other. Now this point of sensitivity is so acute that it attracts the individual towards a certain set of actions. None of these sensitivities occupies the whole period of development. Each occupies only part of the time; long enough to ensure the construction of a psychic organ. After the organ has been formed, the sensitivity disappears, but during this period there are powers so great that we cannot imagine them, because we have lost them and therefore cannot even have an idea of what they are. When all the organs are ready, they unite, in order to form what we call the psychic unity.

Biological studies carried out upon different animals have revealed that all of them build their adult species by means of these sensitive periods. One cannot understand the construction of the psyche of the child, unless one has an idea of these sensitive periods. When one knows of them, then the whole attitude towards childhood is bound to change. As a consequence we are better able to help the psychic development of the child if we know when these sensitive periods occur.

People say: "What about the previous generations? How did they develop into healthy and strong beings if they did not know about them?" It is true that humanity did not scientifically know the sensitive periods, but in previous civilizations mothers applied an instinctive treatment of their children which enabled them if not to second the needs of a sensitive period at least not to disturb it too much. Nature which in its plan has devised the sensitive periods so as to achieve the construction of the psychic organs has also put an instinct in mothers that guides them to give protection. And when one studies the simply living mothers in the treatment of their children, then one understands how well mothers of past generations must have aided the development of their children and how well they seconded the special sensitivities. It is in the sentiments that nature has put in the hearts of parents that the reason is to be found for the spiritual strength of previous generations.

Today, on account of civilization, mothers have lost this instinct. Humanity is headed towards degeneration. That is why it is as important to study the maternal instinct as it is to study the phases of the natural development of children. In the past the mother not only gave physical life, not only the first nourishment, but she also gave protection to growth as other mothers belonging to animal species give it even today. And if today in humanity the maternal instincts tend to disappear as they do, then a very real danger looms ahead of humanity. Today, we are face to face with the great practical problem that mothers must co-operate and science must find some way of aiding and protecting the psychic development of the child as it has found a way of protecting the physical development. The artificial life of the West has deprived most children of their mother's milk and the children would have starved if science had not intervened and supplied the child with some other sort of physical nourishment. In the psychic field, maternal love is a force, it is one of the forces of nature. This must receive today the attention of science,

science must enlighten the mothers by means of the discoveries made in the field of the psyche of the children so that henceforth mothers can help consciously instead of unconsciously. Now that circumstances no longer give free play to instincts in the mother, a consciousness of the child's needs must be given to her. Education must come to the rescue and give mothers this knowledge. Education that starts from birth means to give a conscious protection to the psychic needs of the children. It is certain that in this effort to give protection to the psychic needs of the children, the mothers must be the first to be invited and interested. And if the life of today has become so artificial that the child cannot achieve its development, then society must create institutions which will fulfil the needs of the children. When should schools begin? We started from $3^{1/2}$, then we went to 3, then $2^{1/2}$, then 2. Now the children of one year are brought to school. But education meant to give protection to life, must reach further down until it includes the new-born child.

The Miracle of Creation

This passing from a cell to a complete organ is something which is incomprehensible, but it is a fact. It does exist, but it is so marvelous that no one can understand it and if one reads the modern scientific books upon this subject, one finds a word used which before was anathema to scientists. It is the word 'miracle,' Because though it is something that happens continuously, nevertheless it is miraculous and wonder at this miracle is felt just the same. No matter what animals are observed, a bird or a rabbit or any sort of vertebrate, one sees that it is composed of organs which in themselves are extremely complicated and what causes great wonder and surprise is to see how these very complicated organs are closely connected one with the other. If one considers the circulatory system, one sees in it a drainage system so fine, so complicated and so complete that no system of drainage invented by the most advanced type of civilization can be compared to it. Also the intelligence service of collecting impressions from the environment, which is carried out with sense organs, is so marvelous that no modern instrument can approach it. What can for instance approach the marvel of the eye or of the ear? And if one studies the chemical reactions that take place in the body, one sees that there are special chemical laboratories in which substances are evolved, placing and holding together other substances that we in our most modern and most powerful laboratories are unable to unite. If we consider communications in the human system, the most evolved and perfect communication systems which include telephone and wireless, telegraphy and telephones and all that we may imagine which have been evolved and put together they, when compared to the communications that there are in the body by means of the nervous system, are as nothing. And if one studies the best organized army, one will never find the obedience that the muscles have, which carry out the commands of one strategic director whom everyone obeys immediately. These obedient servants exercise themselves in a special work, in a special fashion, so as to be ready to obey whatever commands come to them. If we consider that all these complicated organs, organs of communication, muscles obedient as soldiers, nerves that penetrate each little cell in the body, come from one cell, the primitive cell which is spherical in its form, we realize the wonder of nature. Each living animal, each living mammal, and man, this marvelous being, all of them come from one primitive cell which, when examined, differs in no way from other cells and looks very very simple. If we, who are accustomed to big things, consider the size of these primitive cells, we shall probably receive a shock. It is the 1/30th part of an inch, or 1/10th of a millimeter. To realize what this means, consider the size of a point made by a sharp pencil and try to put 10 such dots one against the other, no matter how tiny they are a millimeter will not hold ten of them. So imagine how microscopic is the cell, this cell from which man comes. And when this cell develops, it develops isolated from the parent because it is protected, it is enclosed in a sort of envelope that keeps it separate from the adult that contains it. This is true for all animals. The cell is isolated from the parent so that the adult resulting from it is actually the product of the work of this cell originated by the adult. This has been the cause of meditation for a long time because the greatest men in different spheres, such as Napoleon or Alexander or Gandhi, Shakespeare or Dante, etc., as well as the humblest of the humble among the human beings, every one has been constructed by one of these tiny cells. This mystery not only provoked meditation but has also roused the attention of many scientists who have made these cells the object of their studies. By observation with a powerful microscope, it has been found that each cell contains a certain number of points which as they can be very easily colored by chemical means have been called 'Chromosomes' Their number differs in the different species. In the human species for instance, there are 48. In others there are 15, in some 13 so that the number of chromosomes distinguishes the species to which they belong. Scientists thought that these chromosomes had something to do with the formation of the organs. Recently much more powerful microscopes have been invented. These allow one to see things which it was absolutely impossible to see previously. They have been called ultra-microscopes, and by their means people have been able to see that each of the chromosomes was a sort of a little box which contained a sort of chain, composed of about 100 little grains. The chromosomes break up, the grains free themselves and the cell becomes the depositary of some four thousand little grains that have been termed 'genes' (fig. 2.) The word genes implies the idea of generation. They have been so called because the characteristics of the body are formed by their combinations.

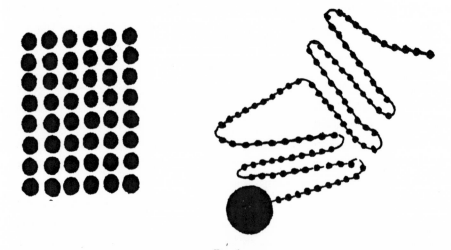

Fig. 2
A chain of 100 genes shown linearly and each contained in one of the 48 chromosomes disposed geometrically on the left.

This is really science. Yet if one stops to think what this implies, one realizes how mystic this dry scientific statement sounds, for this cell is so tiny as to be almost invisible, yet it contains within itself the heredity of all times. In this little speck, there is the whole experience, the whole history of the human kind. Before any apparent change is visible in the primitive cell, already a combination among these genes has taken place. They have already arranged themselves to determine exactly the form of the nose, the color of the eyes etc. of the being that will result from this primitive cell. Not all the genes are employed in the formation of a body. A sort of struggle takes place between these genes; only a few combine and these give the outer characters of the individual while others remain hidden and obscure. For instance, there is the famous example of Mendel who made an experiment. He crossed a plant with red flowers and one of the same kind with white flowers and then the seeds of the new plant were sown. These produce either three plants with white and one with red flowers or the contrary. So out of 40 seeds, 30 will come with red flowers and 1 with white flowers or 1 with red and 30 with white. If the circumstances are good, it is the superior qualities that prevail; but if the circumstances are not favorable, then it is the worse qualities that come forth. So according to the circumstances in which the cell finds itself, you can have a more beautiful individual or a less beautiful individual, a stronger individual or a weaker individual. And this is due to the combinations between the genes. The combinations are so many that every human being is different from every other and even if one observes families that have many children, though all the children are generated by the same parents, yet some are beautiful, others ugly; some are tall, others short and so forth.

Today much time is spent in studying what are the circumstances which will make the better characters come forth; a new science has arisen, Eugenics, which shows how man has by his intelligence succeeded in acquiring influence even over heredity. Human intelligence has understood that heredity can be influenced only at the stage when the primitive cell is formed and changes can be made. Thus man becomes a sort of god who takes in hand the powers of life and orients the path it will take. Nothing much has been done in this direction in the field of humanity, but in that of plants and animals, man has been able to influence heredity to a great extent. What does it mean when one has the power of life in one's hand? It means that we can dispose of heredity so as to transform the species. This is the fascinating part that in our days focuses on this science the interest of hundreds upon hundreds of people. Today this interest is not academic or philosophical. Today it has invaded the practical field. Great numbers of plants and animals have been transformed. Some years ago, for instance, two young men carried out certain biological experiments and a race of stingless bees was produced which made a great deal more honey. So man has been able to influence the life of these insects and to create a species that has become harmless and produces more of a nourishing substance that humanity appreciates. In the same way certain plants have been transformed so as to produce much more food than they did previously. Men have also transformed simple roses into the many beautiful varieties that today gladden our eyes and delight our sense of smell. In the case of flowers great achievements have been made. Man has captured a secret of life. He has become a sort of magician who has embellished life with the magic wand of his intelligence; because of it, the world is much richer and more pleasant. We begin to see one of the aims of the life of man, one of the reasons which makes him one of the great cosmic forces. He has not been placed in the world in order to enjoy beautiful things. He has been placed here to make the world better. Man has intelligence because he has to make a better world than that which he has found. It is as though man were the continuation of the creation, as though he had been sent to employ his intelligence in order to help and make creation more perfect. Intelligence is the great gift that has been given to him. Man has been able to enter a field that permits him to have control over life. Hitherto man had to follow life as it was, but now he can control it. So the study of embryology is no longer an abstract and fruitless study. It is a study which has allowed man to penetrate certain secrets of life and to be able to control by means of these secrets the beings that are to come. Now, if by a stretch of imagination we think that psychic development follows a similar procedure, then we can imagine that man, who has penetrated the secrets of physical development, can also control and help psychic development.

alike amongst themselves. Only they are smaller than the primitive cell. (Fig. 3.)

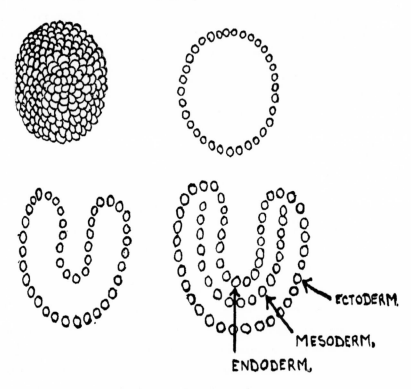

Fig. 3
Upper left the primitive ball of cells (morula) consisting of a single
wall (right). Below left the introflected double-walled gastrula
and to the right the third inner wall is formed.

This chapter about genes and heredity is separate from pure embryology. Embryology considers only the way in which the primitive cell produces the individual. To do this, the ultra -microscope or special reasoning are not required. It is merely a question of observation. From one cell, two are generated and these remain joined. Then the two become four, the four eight, eight become sixteen and so on. This continues until hundreds of cells are produced which are similar to the bricks that are used for the construction of a house. Eventually a sort of hollow sphere is produced. Curiously enough, in the oceans, there are certain animals which are just like that, a hollow ball, and they are called 'volvo' because they are always going round. Then these balls become inflected and form two walls and later a third wall is formed between the two. So the first construction consists of these three walls. Up to now all cells are Recently studies have permitted the discovery of the way in which these organs are formed. I mentioned this fact in the previous chapter. This discovery Was made very recently, between 1929 and 1930 i.e., after the first world war. Now this is 14 years ago. Before a discovery is made and this discovery is made public and every one knows about it, 14 years are, we might say, as yesterday. Now the figure reproduced here does not correspond to a reality. (Fig. 4.)

SENSITISATION. INCREASED ACTIVITY.   GRADIENTS,

PHYSIOLOGICAL GRADIENTS.

FIG. 4

It is something imaginary made in order to show points of sensitivity. There are these spots in which cells begin to multiply very fast and it is in these special points that organs are formed. While one person discovered this in America, in England independently somebody else was also doing research work and he made the same discovery. The American called these points 'gradients,' the Englishman, as he made his discovery upon the nervous system, called them 'points of sensitization' and 'sanglion.'

Each of the three walls of the gastrula produces a set of organs. The external one produces the skin, the sensory organs and nervous system. And this illustrates that the external layer is in relation with the environment, because the skin gives us protection and the nervous system places us in relation to the environment. The innermost one develops organs used for nourishment such as the intestines, stomach, the glands of digestion, liver, pancreas, and the lungs. The organs of the nervous systems are called organs of relation because they allow us to put ourselves in relation with the environment. The organs of the digestive and respiratory systems are called vegetative organs because they make vegetative life possible. The third or middle wall produces all the rest, the skeleton that sustains the whole body and the muscles. Now it is curious to see how each one of these walls has a special purpose and this purpose remains the same for each kind of animal. As long as they are in the stage of walls, the cells are more or less alike, simple. Is this not intelligent? First three walls are made, then the organs. And is it not curious that the plan of the whole is made while each of the three layers is still independent of the other? After this, each of the cells that are going to form organs begins to transform itself. They assume the form best suited to perform a function which, however, they do not carry out in the embryo. So that this fine specialization of the cells which transform themselves for a certain function takes place before the function begins.

Here I have reproduced some of these cells (Fig. 5.). There are the liver cells which are pentagonal in form; there are the cells of the muscles which are very long, and the triangular ones are those that make the bones. While these bone-cells are very soft, they take carbonate of calcium from the blood and form bones. There are others which are very interesting because they are a sort of little cup and these little cups exude a sort of sticky substance. They also have a sort of fringe of fibers called cilia which vibrate so as to catch any dust that may enter the throat with their gluey mucus and move it up to the mouth. And then there are the heroes, who sacrifice their life for the welfare of others. These are the cells of the skin. The skin which sacrifices itself for the protection of the other organs, covers the whole body. The outer layer of the skin dies; its cells sacrifice themselves and underneath there is another layer which is getting ready to sacrifice its life for the safety of all. Those with the long filaments are the cells of the nervous system. Then there are the red cells of the blood which go on continuously taking oxygen to the other cells. They take back and throw away the poisonous gases that have formed. The marvelous thing is that though the red corpuscles of the blood are in enormous numbers, yet their number is determined.

Before the work starts, these are some of the types of cells. Each of these cells prepares itself for the work it has to do. When they have formed

Here I have reproduced some of these cells (Fig. 5.).

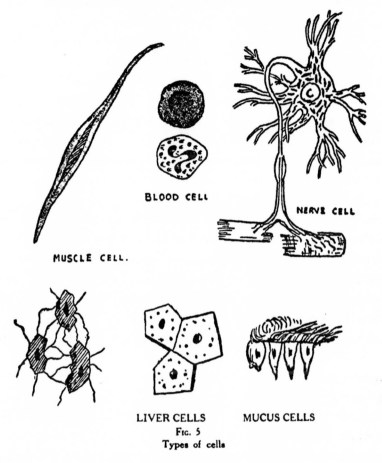

MUSCLE CELL.

BLOOD CELL

NERVE CELL

LIVER CELLS   MUCUS CELLS
Fig. 5
Types of cells

themselves for this special work, they can no longer transform themselves. A nervous cell can never be transformed into a liver cell. And so when they have transformed themselves as if imbued with a great ideal and dedicated themselves to the work that fulfils it, their task is fixed, because they have specialized themselves for it. Is it not the same in our human society? There are, we might say, special groups of men who form the organs of humanity. In the beginning each individual performs many tasks. In the primitive society, when people are few, one has to know a little of everything. One is a mason, a doctor, a carpenter and everything. But when society is evolved, then there is specialization of work. Each man chooses a type of work and his psyche becomes so involved in this work that he can do only that work and nothing else. For example, a doctor cannot be a shoemaker. The training for a profession is not only learning a technique, the individual undergoes a psychic transformation for the task that he is to perform so that one prepares himself not only technically, but, what is more important, one acquires a special psychic personality, which is suited for that special work. One finds one's ideal realized in it. One's life is that.

The same seems to happen in the case of the body. When each cell has specialized to form the different organs, something else comes that achieves a union among them all. It is composed of two complex organs which do not function for themselves but function in order to achieve the unity among all others. They are the circulatory and nervous systems. The first system is a sort of a river in which there are substances and these are carried to all. But it is not only a distributor, it is also a collector. The organs produce certain things which are needed by other organs that are far away from them. See what perfection has been achieved by this river! Each organ takes from it what it needs for its life and throws into the river whatever it has produced so that other organs can take of it according to their need.

Do we not find the same in our society to day? Has it not developed a circulatory system. All the substances that are produced are thrown into circulation and each one takes from it what is useful for his life and what is produced is thrown into the stream of commerce so that it becomes available to others. The merchants, the traveling salesmen who go about everywhere, are they not like red corpuscles? If we look at human society, we can better understand the functioning of the embryo because in society also the functioning is such that things produced in Germany are consumed in S. America, things which are produced in England are consumed in India and so forth. We can deduce from this that society has reached an embryonic stage in which the circulatory system begins to function, but with many defects still. The defects of circulation reveal that our society has not finished its development.

The one thing we do not find in human society is something corresponding to the specialized cell of the nervous system. We might almost conclude that this organ of direction has not yet been evolved by society as the the chaotic state of our world very clearly indicates. In the absence of this specialization, there is nothing that gives sensibility to all and can harmoniously direct the whole of society. What happens in democracy, for instance, which is the most evolved sort of social organization that civilization has produced? It permits all to choose their own leader by elections. If we transport this to the field of embryology, one could say: "I think the liver cell is most suited to govern"; and another: "I think that those cells which are inside the bones are more suited, because they have a strong structure." And another might say: "I want some one heroic who will defend us. The skin cell must be at the work of direction," If such a situation arose in the field of embryology, it would appear absurd, inconceivable, because if there must be specialized cells at all it is surely the cell which directs the functions of the whole. The work of direction is the most difficult task and requires greater specialization than any other. So it is not a question of election. It is a question of being fit and prepared for the work. He who has to direct others, must have transformed himself. Thus there can be no leader unless he has first transformed himself. But this principle that goes from specialization to function is fascinating. It becomes even much more fascinating when we discover that this is the plan adopted by nature for all branches of life, that it is the plan that nature follows when it creates. If we show an interest in embryology, it is not only because of this plan, and because of the fact that one can acquire control over development, but because it runs parallel step by step to what we have discovered in the psychic field.

One Plan, One Method

Neither the discoveries nor the theories that arise from modern discoveries explain fully the mystery of life and of its development. But certainly they do show and illustrate facts. These furnish us with sufficient data to enable us to see how growth takes place. Every new detail discovered shows an added realization, but does not explain it. These phenomena can be fully observed and they give an explanation of events of ordinary life. One of the things which is observed for instance is that the plan of construction is only one and all types of animal life follow it. Now when I say that it is a plan, I do not mean that we actually see a plan drawn up like a draftsman's. But what we see occurring in front of our eyes, shows us that all the details follow a certain

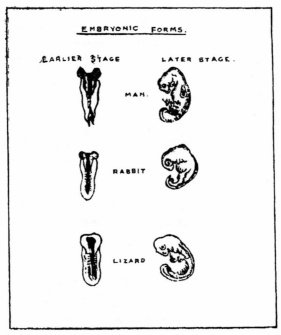

Fig. 6

invisible plan. The plan can be seen materially in the embryo, it can be followed in the psychology of children and it can also be recognized in society. If one observes the embryos of different animals, one easily sees that the plan of development followed is the same. This is no new discovery. Fig. 6. shows the embryos of three different animals at two different stages. The earlier stage is on the left and the more advanced on the right. The animals are: Man on top, rabbit below it, and lizard below that. And this is one of the revelations I mentioned. As the picture shows, in order to realize themselves, the vertebrates have to pass through the same stages of development and the same forms. For instance you can see a striking resemblance between man and lizard at this stage of embryonic development. Yet when the embryo has finished developing, the difference is immense. So there is a period when all beings are alike.

We can also say with the same certainty that, psychically speaking, there is a period in which all the human beings are alike. And when we say that the new born is a psychic embryo, we must understand that all new-born children are alike. There can therefore be but one means of treating or educating children of this age, i.e., if education is to start from birth, there can be but one method. There can be no question of special methods for Indian children or Chinese or Japanese or European children. Here there is an absolute method which is the same for all. There is a period of incarnation in which every human being acts in the same fashion, i.e., every human being incarnates itself in the same way; all have the same psychic needs and follow the same procedure in order to achieve the construction of man. No matter what type of man results from the work of the child, no matter if it is a genius, or a laborer, a saint or a murderer, each in order to become what he is in the end, must pass through these stages of growth, these phases of incarnation. What we must take into consideration is this process of incarnation, we must not pre-occupy ourselves with what the individual will become later on. We cannot interfere with that. First of all we do not know it, and then we should not have the power to achieve it if we knew. What must preoccupy us, what must take our energies is the assistance to those laws of growth that are common to all.

This brings us to the question of the methods of education. There must be there can be only one method of education. The method which helps the natural laws of growth and of development, alike for all. This is not an idea; it is a fact, an evident fact and it shows that it cannot be a philosopher or a thinker to dictate this or that method of education. The only one who can dictate the method is nature itself which has established certain laws, which has infused certain needs into the growing being. It is the aim of satisfying these needs, seconding these laws, which must dictate the method of education; not the more or less brilliant ideas of a philosopher.

This is specially so in the first years of life. It is true that afterwards differences arise in the individuals but it is not we who cause these differences; we cannot even provoke them. There is an inner individuality, an ego which develops spontaneously, independently of us and we cannot do anything about it. We cannot make, for instance, a genius, or a general or an artist. We can only help that individual who is to be a general or a leader to realize his potentialities. No matter what they are, if they are leaders or poets or artists or geniuses, or merely common men, they must pass through these stages: embryonic stages before birth, psycho-embryonic stages after birth, in order to realize their mysterious future self. What we can do is merely to remove the obstacles so that the mysterious being that each individual is to realize can be achieved, because by removing those obstacles, the work can be done better.

We call this fundamental effort of self-realization 'incarnation.' This is the first practical point: there is a process of incarnation, this process of incarnation is the same for all, and our aim in education must be to help this process of incarnation.

Further Outcome of Embryology

The three embryos of fig. 6 are very similar, one to the other. However, when they have finished their development, these beings are very different from one another. Now let us continue to illustrate this question of the development of embryos by following the reasoning of the most modern thinkers. What we have already seen is very striking: the existence of genes, the existence of points of sensitivity around which organs are formed and then the formation of two systems the circulatory system and the nervous system which connect and unite intimately all that has been created. After these organs have come into relation, there is something that is even more mysterious. This is the fact that it is not merely organs that are created and that come to be intimately connected one with the other, but that there come living beings free and independent. It is not merely the construction of those organs and putting them in connection with one another, the whole of these organs, the same in every being, form in each case a being different from the other: each has its own character. This is what is extraordinary. This problem has not yet been solved by science. There is the theory of evolution, but it is a theory and not a fact. Observation unfolds all the facts without explaining them. Whenever there is no explanation a void remains and this is important. The important fact is to recognize that there is a void. If we accept a theory, e.g., that of evolution which covers all the facts, then our intelligence is set at rest. But once the void has been noticed, the intelligence becomes restless and sets out to find an explanation. These voids lead people to think, to study facts until a new discovery is made and with each discovery, one more void is filled and one step forward in knowledge is made.

There was a discovery first made public in 1930 (this seems to be an important year for embryology). It was made in the laboratories of a biologist of Philadelphia. These modern laboratories of America are very well staffed and endowed so that each scientist can dedicate himself to the study of one special detail. One of these studied for seven or eight years but one type of animal, a very inferior sort of amphibian and he studied it for such a long time because the facts did not correspond to the scientific theories which were expounded at the time. Now to give a full explanation of what this man has discovered would be boring and not easy to understand. I just mention it in passing. This scientist discovered that the parts which were first formed were those parts which directed the functioning of the individual and that the formation of the executive organs comes afterwards. Every body knows that we have a nervous system and among other things we have a brain and in our brain are located certain parts each of which deals with an organ. There is a part of the brain which deals with sight and it is called the visual center. Now what this scientist discovered was that the part of the nervous system which was meant to direct sight was formed first, much before the nerve of sight and much before the eye. This was absolutely contrary to the scientific theory of the time. The conclusion he came to was this: that in animals the psychic part is formed before the being itself is formed i.e., the instincts of the animals are there before the animal has finished building itself physically. This means that generation concerns not only the body, and the different inner organs but also the psyche, also the instincts of each animal, and that the habits of these animals are fixed before the organ is formed.

Behaviorism

This is the new idea. The habits that the animal is going to have are fixed in the nerve centers much before the organ is built. Now if this psychic part is preexisting, what does it mean? It means that the organ finishes its own construction, molding itself to the requirements of the psyche, of the instincts. This method of reasoning brings us to the conclusion that animals have their habits pre-established before birth and the organs are built in such a fashion as best to fulfil these habits and these instincts. So according to this new theory, what is important in nature is the habits, the customs of animals. It is interesting to see that the organs, of whatever the animal, are the best suited to carry out the command of its instincts. The new theory has arisen from years and years of study and from observation of facts, not from pre-established ideas. This brings us to the conclusion that the habits of animals are now-a-days more important than the form of the body which was the center of interest in previous times. The term used in this generalization of facts is what is designated as 'behavior,' It includes in its meaning the habits and customs of the animals described. The new theory is known in modern books, especially in America, as 'Behaviorism.' It is a new light that has come into the field of science. The old ideas which held that animals assume their habits because they had to adapt themselves to their environment have gone. The old theory held that it was the will of the adult which provoked the transformations necessary so that the body became adapted to the environment, that the efforts which animals made to keep alive, this 'instinct of self-preservation,' caused a transformation in the successive generations and gradually the species became adapted. The species which could not do this perished. This was called the 'survival of the fittest,' This theory averred that by means of continuous efforts carried out during generations, a sort of perfection came about and this was then transmitted to the next generation.

The new theory does not do away with all this, but places the behavior of the animal at the center of all its habits. The facts observed are that the animal which strives for adaptation is successful only if its efforts are expended within its behavior-pattern. So the animal which successfully carries out its experiences of life upon the environment does so along the lines of its behavior. Let us illustrate this by an example. Let us take the cows. They are powerful animals, strong and well armed. In the geological history of the earth, the course of their evolution can be traced. They make their appearance when the earth is already well covered with vegetation. One might ask oneself why this animal has limited itself to feed only on grass which is the most indigestible food that can be found, so much so that in order to digest it the poor animal has had to develop four stomachs. If, as the old theory said, it was a question of self-preservation of survival, how much easier it would have been to eat something else of which there was an abundance in the surroundings. It would have been very simple and very easy. But today after millions and millions of years, we still see cows, when in natural surroundings, eating only grass. They stand with lowered heads, chewing and chewing. It is very seldom that you can make them raise their heads so that one can look into their beautiful eyes. Immediately after they have given you a look, down goes their head. If you observe the animal, you will see that it crops the grass near the roots, but it never uproots the plant. It seems to know that in order to keep the grass alive, it must be cut near the roots because if the latter are cut, the plant dies, whereas if they are cut like this, they develop under ground. The roots expand and occupy more ground and so the grass travels and spreads instead of dying. Now if one studies the history of evolution, one finds that only very late in the history of the earth grass appears and one also finds the tremendous importance that grass has for other vegetation; because grass ties together the loose grains of sand which otherwise would be carried away by the wind. Not only does it render the ground firm, but it fertilizes it also. No other vegetation could have grown if the grass had not prepared the way first. That is the importance of grass. Two things are necessary for its upkeep, besides cutting: one is manure, the other is rolling i.e., putting a heavy weight upon it. Now, tell me what artificial agricultural machine can be more marvelously fit for these three tasks than the cow herself. So efficient is this machine that besides helping the growth of grass it also produces milk. What a wonderful agriculturist of nature is the cow. Her behavior gives us one more reason to be grateful to her. We thought that she gave us milk and manure and nothing else. At the most we may have thought that the cow is an example of patience. But much more does humanity owe to the cow. It is something which has been ignored by humanity at large, but which has been felt by the subconscious mind in India, where the cow is worshiped. It is the upkeep of the earth, the life of other plants that we owe to the cow. The patience she has is more than the superficial patience that we admire. It is the patience of generations and generations.

A Task in Life

Now if the cow were conscious, she would be conscious merely of the fact that she is hungry, that she likes grass, just as in India the people like chapatis, rice and curry and other people like something else. But certainly the cow will never realize, will never think, will never be conscious of the fact that she is an agriculturist. Yet the behavior of the cow is just such as to help nature in its work of agriculture.

Now, let us take the example of crows and vultures who eat the refuse of nature. Why, with the abundance of food there is in the world, should the vultures eat rotten carcases and the crows excrements and whatever dirt they find in the environment? They have wings. They can and do fly long distances in search of their food. So it would not be difficult for them to find something more appetizing, such as other animals less endowed with strength and the possibility of movement do find. But can you imagine the amount of mortality there would be if this refuse were not removed from the earth? What an amount of illness, of plague and other diseases of all kinds would there be, if there were not some instrument whose only task in life is to keep the environment clean? They have by nature been allotted the task of cleaning the environment. Tell me what is the difference between the mass of workers that in Ahmedabad go back after their work, streaming from the mills towards their homes, and the hundreds of crows we see flying back at dusk towards their roost, after having done their work of cleaning and sweeping? This is their behavior.

These two examples have been given taking them from the choice of food. We might take hundreds and we should find that each species has chosen a particular kind of food. We might conclude that animals have no free choice of food. They do not eat merely to satisfy themselves. They eat to fulfil a mission upon the earth, the mission which is prescribed for them by their behavior. Certain it is that all these animals are benefactors of nature and the benefactors of all other living beings. They work to preserve the harmony of creation. They work out creation, because creation is achieved by the collaboration of all the living and non-living beings. And these two do their part in it by their behavior. Other animals there are which eat in such tremendous quantity that it cannot be explained merely on the ground of the upkeep of life. They do not eat in order to keep themselves alive. They keep alive in order to eat, for instance, the earth-worms. They eat only earth, although there is so much choice of foods. These earthworms eat daily a quantity of food which is 200 times the volume of their body. This is measured by their droppings. This is a species of being that does not eat in order to keep alive, especially when one considers the amount of other better food there is at its disposal. The worm is a worker of the earth. It was Darwin himself who first said that without the worms the earth would be less productive. The worms render the earth fertile. So there are forms of body or details of the body which go beyond the direct advantage of the individual.

Take the bees. They come out in hot weather. They are covered with a sort of fur or a sort of yellow and black velvet. This fur is not necessary in a hot country, but it collects the pollen from flowers which the bee itself does not use. This pollen, however, is useful to other flowers to which it is brought by them and which are thus fertilized. So the work of the bee is not useful to itself alone, it is useful for the propagation of plants so that one might say that this fur has been developed by the bees for the propagation of plants, not for themselves. Don't you begin to see in this behavior that animals sacrifice themselves for the welfare of other types of life, instead of trying to eat as much as possible merely for their own existence or upkeep? The more one studies the behavior of animals and of plants, the more clearly one sees that they have a task to perform for the welfare of the whole.

There are certain unicellular animals which live in the ocean and drink such an enormous quantity of water that if they were calculated to the proportion of man, they would need to drink a gallon of water per second during their whole life. Certainly one could call this intemperance, for these animals cannot do it to satisfy their thirst. It is not a vice, however, it is rather like a virtue. They must work at high speed because their task is to filter all the water of the ocean, to eliminate from it certain salts which would be a terrible poison for all the other inhabitants of the ocean.

The same is true of corals. Corals are inferior animals and if the theory of evolution were true, it would be incomprehensible that having been among the first animals to appear, they have remained for millions of years always the same. Why have they not changed? Because they have a function to fulfil and they fulfil it in a perfect manner. This is the same function as that of the animals mentioned above: to eliminate from the ocean the poisonous matter which is brought into it by the flow of rivers. Their work is that of coating themselves with those salts. This has been going on for millions and millions of years and so we can imagine the enormous quantity of rock they have accumulated. They accumulate enormous quantities and these animals have been entrusted with the formation of new continents. Look at the innumerable little islands of the Pacific Ocean that today have come into the lime-light on account of the war which has been fought between the Japanese on one side and the Allies on the other. Those islands are constructions made by these animals, the corals. They are the tops of mountains that today are rising out of the water, forming islands. If we study the rocks on dry land, we find that many of them are formed by animals. Even in the Himalayas much of the massif is of coralline origin. We may well say that these corals are the constructors of our continents.

So the more one studies the functions of these animals, the more one finds, that these functions are not for the upkeep of the animal's body only, but that all give their contribution to the harmony of the whole. Let us say then that these animals are not merely inhabitants of the earth: they are the constructors and workers of this earth, they keep it going. This is the vision given by these new discoveries. Once given this light, by studying the geological epochs of the past, we find testimony of similar work carried out by animals which are now extinct. There has always been this relation between the animals and the earth, of the animals between themselves and between the animals and the vegetation. A new science has arisen from this which is called Ecology, a science which is widely applied today and forms an important part of the study in universities. Ecology is a study of the different behaviors of animals, and it reveals that they are not here to compete with each other, but to carry out an enormous work serving the harmonious upkeep of the earth. When we say they are workers, we mean that each one of them has a purpose, a special aim to fulfil and the result of these tasks is our beautiful world.

A fundamental study today is to consider the task of each upon this earth. Behavior does not merely fulfil the desire to continue to live. It serves a task which evidently remains unknown and unconscious to the being, because it does not form part of what one might wish. If animals were to become self-conscious, they would be conscious of their habits, of the beauty of the places in which they live, but certainly the corals would never realize or understand that they are the builders of the world, nor would the worms which fertilize the earth consider themselves agriculturists, nor would others consider themselves the purifiers of the environment and so forth. The purpose which places the animals in relation to the earth and its upkeep would never enter their consciousness. Yet life and its relation with the surface of the earth, the purity of the air, the purity of water are dependent upon these tasks. So there is another force which is not the force of the desire for survival, but a force which harmonizes all the tasks. Let us say that each one is important, not because it is beautiful, or because it has succeeded in the struggle for existence, but because it carries out tasks which are useful to the whole and the effort of each is to try and reach the place allotted to it and the task which it is to fulfil. That is why we said that there was a pre-established plan, and that the organs were formed to fulfil this plan. This pre-established plan puts the animals in relation with the task that they have to accomplish upon the earth. Nor is the purpose of life to perfect oneself, nor only to evolve. The purpose of life is to obey the hidden command which ensures harmony among all and creates an ever better world. We are not created only to enjoy the world, we are created in order to evolve the cosmos. Today the influence of the existence of a cosmic plan is gradually changing the theory of the linear evolution of past times.

Man's Universality

The vision given by the theory of Behaviorism shows how each animal species has a task to perform upon the environment and the individuals belonging to that species faithfully carry out the task which has been allotted to them, although they live and function independently from those who have generated them. We may have the impression that animals are free, that they have a free choice and that they struggle with others to have the upper hand. If we look more closely, we see that their freedom is merely to carry out what is in the behavior of each and each one moves according to the dictates of this behavior. We see certain animals that proceed by running, other animals by skipping, others by walking slowly and sedately, others by crawling and so forth. If we observe more closely still we find that each species has a task assigned at a different level in the environment, so that certain animals live upon the plains, others live upon the hills, others live upon the mountains, some live in frozen lands and others in torrid zones.

Now, when we study the human kind and compare it with the animal kind, we find some differences and an important one is that the human kind has not had allotted to it a special kind of movement or a special kind of residence. Certainly, it is a facilitation of life to have one's task assigned by nature. The study of nature shows, however, that there is no animal which is as capable as man to adapt itself to any climate or to any place upon this earth. We find man in frozen lands where certain animals such as tigers or elephants cannot live. Yet if you look in the jungle where elephants and tigers are to be found there man can also be found. Man can be found even in deserts. So we can see that man has been allotted no fixed place. He can adapt himself and can live in any part of the world, for he is destined to invade every part of the world. Let us say then that because of this adaptability, man is the only being who is free to go wherever he likes upon this earth.

If we look at the behavior of animals, we find that this behavior is expressed in their movements, which stand in relation to the work that they carry out, whereas man has no special movements. Man is capable of the most varied movements which he can acquire very rapidly and very perfectly. Also man can do certain things which no animal has ever been able to do or will ever be able to do. Man has done them from his first appearance upon the earth: he works with his hands. There is no limit to man's behavior. Each animal, for instance, has one language. If we take for example an English dog, it will bark in the same fashion as a dog in America. But if we take a Tamilian and bring him to Italy, he will not understand the language there and the Italians will not understand him. Mankind has the most varied languages. The same can be said for movements: man can walk, run, jump and crawl also. Like the fish man can swim. Birds can fly. Man can fly better than birds. Not only this, man is capable of artificial movements such as dancing.

Each animal has but one sort of movement. Man has a great variety of movements. So his behavior is not fixed like that of the animals. Another thing is also certain. In the child none of these abilities we have mentioned are present. So we can conclude that though it is true that the abilities of man are infinite, each has to be acquired by the human individual during childhood. It is by an active conquest, by work, that he acquires language. He who is born without movement, who is born almost paralyzed, by means of exercise can learn to walk, to run and to climb like any animal. But all these capabilities he must acquire by his own effort. Everything must be conquered by him. Whatever abilities man possesses, there must have been a child who conquered them. So we might say that the values of man have their beginning in the work of the child.

We saw that men are to be found everywhere on the earth, in every possible condition and, strange to say, each one is contented and glad to live where he lives. If we consider the Eskimoes, we find that to them happiness of life consists in the great wide plains covered with snow, in those lights that break the long darkness with vivid colors, in the noise of the winds that howl and penetrate not only the body, but are music to the soul. The cold climate and everything that goes with those conditions of life give them happiness. Nowhere else can they be happy except there. The same can be said for others. The men who live in the tropics find that climate, that special food and those customs essential for their life and happiness. No matter where we look, we will always find the same. Man is in love with his own country. There are certain people who live in places which seem to be absolutely unsuited even to the possibility of life. In Finland, the country is rocky, cold and for long months covered with snow and ice. Yet the recent war between Finland and Russia shows what attachment, what fascination this barren land seems to exercise upon the Finns. If we take Holland, we find that its inhabitants are extremely proud of and attached to their land though we can hardly call it land because it is only by a tremendous amount of work that they wrest the land from the water of the sea and once they have wrested it away, they have to surround it with dykes and they have to pump out the water continuously. And if they have to build a house, they build first the ground upon which the house is to stand, because otherwise the house would sink. They have to sink trees vertically side by side and create an artificial wooden platform upon which can be put the foundations of the house. A country with most undesirable conditions, yet see with what ferocity they fought for that piece of land! And how beautiful it seems to them! It has produced some of the greatest painters. It is this attachment, this affection to the place, to the country, which makes it possible that the whole earth is peopled by men. Because if each people sought for the best conditions of life, for the most fertile of the lands, much of the world would be uninhabited. It is this attachment, this love for whatever country one lives in, that makes the whole world inhabited by human beings.

Now, the curious part is that when we consider man in his adult stage, we see that he is one of the least adaptable beings. An Indian certainly does not like to live anywhere except in India. If the Indian adult goes outside for study or for work, he is always hankering to come back. And we who are accustomed to the Mediterranean environment and a temperate climate, we cannot adapt ourselves to the icy North. Yes, it is very nice to go to the desert to see strings of camels traveling along. It is fascinating and romantic, but not pleasant to live there.

We are attached to our environment, but also to the times we live in. If we consider Europe of some years ago, it had a much simpler life than it has now-a-days. There were no railways or other fast means of communication. Traveling was done by horse carriages, horses had to be changed, people spent days and days to go from one country to another. In order to get news of their family, they would have to wait for months. Suppose a modern man from America came into such conditions. He would find it impossible to live. Or let us take somebody who lived a few centuries back. Everything was calm and peaceful. No trains, no electric light, no trams, no underground rumblings of sub-ways, no noise. If a person of those days were taken to New York today with its tremendous traffic, all the bustle and noise that goes on there day and night, where people always hurry, where darkness becomes a fantastic display of electric light advertisements, where no peace, no silence is to be found, he would say: "I cannot live in this place,"

So here we see a contrast. Previously we have described man who is capable of loving and adapting himself to the worst conditions that the earth can present and who can live happily no matter in what country. Now we find that men of different centuries could not live and adapt themselves to the more evolved stage of civilization of more modern times just like we could not adapt ourselves to the slow fashion of living of the previous age. We are happy to live in our age as our forefathers were happy to live in their ages.

We see that as society and civilization evolve, conditions change and if men were fixed in their behavior like animals, they would not be able to adapt themselves to the new conditions. Let us consider language. No language is born as it is now. Language evolves like everything else. First it is simple. Then it becomes more complicated. How is it that those who live in a time when language is so complicated, take it without pain and without paying any attention to it learn it so easily?

Where does the explanation lie? We face a contradiction. There is a sort of mystery. Man must adapt himself to the changing conditions of civilization. The older humanity becomes, culture progresses the more. So there must be a continuous adaptation on the part of man, not only to geographical changes as we saw, but also to the continuous changes of civilization. And yet as we saw, adult man is not very adaptable. Here is a real enigma!

The Child Instrument of Adaptation

The solution is found in the child, whom we can call the instrument of the adaptability of humanity. The child whom we saw born without any special movement, not only acquires all the human faculties, but also adapts the being that it constructs to the conditions in his environment. And this takes place because of the special psychic form of the child, for the child's psychic form is different from that of the adult. Psychologists today show great interest in the study of this different form of psychology. The child stands in a different relationship to the environment. We may admire an environment. We may remember an environment, but the child absorbs it into himself. He does not remember the things that he sees, but he forms with these things part of his psyche. He incarnates in himself the things which he sees and hears i.e., in us there is no change, in the child transformations take place. We merely remember an environment while the child adapts himself to it. This special kind of vital memory, that does not remember consciously, but absorbs images into the very life of the individual has received from the psychologists a special name: they have called it Mneme.

We have an example of this in language. The child does not remember the sounds of language. The child incarnates these sounds and he can pronounce them better than anybody else. He speaks the language according to all its complicated rules and all its exceptions, not because he studies and remembers it by means of ordinary memory, perhaps his memory never takes it consciously. Yet this language forms a part of his psyche, forms a part of him. This is a phenomenon different from mere mnemonic activity. It is a psychic feature that characterizes an aspect of the child's psychic personality.

There is in the child an absorbent sensitivity towards whatever is in his surroundings. And it is by beholding and absorbing the environment that one becomes adapted to it. This faculty reveals a subconscious power that is only found in the child.

The first period of life is the period of adaptability. We must be very clear as to what we mean by adaptability in this case. We must distinguish it from the adaptability in the adult. The biological adaptability of the child is that which makes the only place one really loves to stay in, the place where one is born. Just as the only language that one speaks well is one's mother tongue. Now an adult person who goes to a country other than his own, never adapts himself to it in the same fashion or to the same degree.

Let us take the example of those men who go voluntarily to another country in order to spend their life there, e.g. the missionaries. Missionaries are people who by their own will choose to go and live in another country. And yet if you speak to them, they usually say: "We sacrifice our lives by living in this country," This denotes the limitations of the adaptability of the adult.

Let us now take the child. The child is an individual who loves whatever locality he is born in to the point that he could not be happy anywhere else, no matter how hard is the life there. So the man who loves the frozen plains of Finland and another who loves the dunes of Holland has each received his adaptation, his love for his country, from the child he once was.

It is the child who practically and actually realizes this adaptation. The adult finds himself prepared, adapted, suited to his country, so that he feels the love and special fascination for the place where he lives, so that happiness and peace for him are only found there.

In former times, in Italy, the people who were born in a village lived and died there and never moved away from it. Later people who got married sometimes moved elsewhere and gradually the original population were scattered from their native places. By and by a strange malady came about. People became pale, sad, weak, anaemic looking. Many cures were tried but in vain. So at last when it could not be cured in any other way, the doctor said to the relatives: "I think you had better send this person to get a breath of his native air," And the person was sent to his home town, or the farm, or wherever he was born and after a little while he came back fully cured. People said that a breath of the native air, was better than any amount of medicine, but the air itself was often much worse than that of the place where one was suffering. What this person really needed was the quiet given to his subconscious by the conditions of the place where he had lived as a child.

Now there is nothing more important than this absorbent sort of psyche which forms man and adapts him to no matter what social conditions, to no matter what climate, to no matter what country. It is upon this that we must concentrate and work. When one says: "I love my country," one does not say something superficial, something artificial. It is something which forms a part of one's own self, of one's own life.

From what we have said above we can also understand how the child absorbs by this type of psyche, the customs that he finds in the land, the habits, etc., and thus forms the individual who is typical of his race. This 'local' behavior of man, i.e., of man suited to the special country in which he lives, is a mysterious construction which takes place during childhood. It is evident that men acquire customs, habits, mentality, etc. peculiar to their own surroundings because none of them is natural to humanity. So we have now a fuller picture of the work of the child. He constructs a behavior suited not only to the time and to the place, but also to the mentality of the place. Here in India there is a great respect for life, a respect which leads to veneration also of animals. This cannot be acquired by an adult person. It is not by saying: "Oh, life must be respected" that this feeling is acquired. I may reason that those people are right and feel that I also must respect animal life, but with me it is not a sentiment, it is reasoning. What I cannot feel is the sort of veneration that some Indians feel for the cow, for instance, whereas people who possess it can never get rid of it. Other people have their religion and even if their mind eventually rejects it, still at heart they feel uneasy, restless. These things form part of us as we say in Europe: "they are in our blood," The things that together form the personality, sentiments of caste and all sorts of other feelings that make a typical Italian, a typical Englishman, a typical Indian, are constructed during childhood by this mysterious sort of psychic power that psychologists call Mneme. This is true for everything, even for certain types of characteristic movement that distinguish different races. There are certain people in Africa who develop and fix qualities which are provoked by the need of defense against wild animals. They do certain exercises in order to render their hearing sharper. Sharpness of hearing is one of the special characteristics of the individual of that special tribe. In the same way all characteristics are absorbed by the child and fixed in the individual. There are certain religious sentiments which remain in spite of the fact that the mind may later on reason otherwise and reject the teachings of this religion. Something continues in the sub-conscious, because what has been formed by the child can never be totally destroyed. This Mneme, which may be considered as a superior natural memory, not only creates characteristics, but holds them alive in the individual. The individual changes, it is true, but those things which are formed by the child remain in the personality just as the legs remain, so that each man has this special character.

One would like to change individual adults. Often we say: "This person does not know how to behave?" Often we call such and such a person bad-mannered. He or she knows it, they feel humiliated, because they recognize that they have 'a bad character,' but the fact is that it cannot be changed. In the same way in which this type of psychology leads the child to the wonderful acquisitions of civilization, to the complications and elaborations of modern language, it also leads him to fix in his psyche certain things which reason would like to eliminate from the personality, but which cannot be changed. The same phenomenon explains the adaptation to, we might say, different phases of history, because, while an adult of olden times could not adapt himself to modern times, the child adapts himself to the level of civilization which he finds, no matter what the level of that civilization may be and succeeds in constructing a man suited to those times and those customs.

So today the child begins to be visualized as it should be, as the connection, the joining link between different phases of history and different levels of civilization. Childhood is now considered by psychologists as a very important period because they realize that if we wish to give new ideas to the people, if we wish to alter the habits and customs of the country, or if we wish to accentuate more vigorously the characteristics belonging to a people, we must take as our instrument the child, as very little can be done by acting upon adults. If one has really a vision of better conditions, of greater enlightenment for people, it is only the child that one can look upon in order to bring about the desired results. If there are people who think that their customs are degenerate, or others who want to revive old ones, the only individual with whom they can work is the child. They will never have success with the adults. If anybody wants to have an influence upon society, he must orientate himself towards childhood. In past times people tried to influence adults. Now they have understood better and they start schools for children because in the children the construction of humanity takes place. They construct with what we give them. Let us suppose that a statesman wanted to try and change the customs of his people. Strange as it may sound, this person must take into great consideration the children of his country. This has actually happened recently among different nations. A person set out to make warrior-like people out of those who were very peaceful, of a loving nature. He tried with the grown-ups, but in the end he had to take the young children. Mussolini did so in Italy, Hitler followed suit in Germany. The Fascist hymn begins with the words 'Youth, Youth,' This was the main trend of their policy, to make use of the creative spirit of youth, but soon they had to go towards even younger people and soon the hymn should have sounded. 'Infancy, Infancy,' By taking children of three years and younger and by creating around them an atmosphere of enthusiasm, of dignity, of activity, in one generation the character of the whole people was changed.

The mentality we fight today was neither the original character of the Italian people nor perhaps that of the Germans, but by creating an atmosphere, an enthusiasm based upon 'our glory' around the children, these rooted so firmly this warrior-spirit in their psyche that no matter what disaster may fall upon the nation, this spirit will not die. With older people one can reason, but not with the young ones. They will fight till they are dead. If they are defeated they will continue to fight underground. And you see the different methods and how even ordinary democracy is not the answer to our needs, for children cannot choose a leader because they do not understand. We cannot hold a meeting of children of three years in order to make them understand political idealism or to make them warriors. In order to influence them, you must do so by means of the environment, because the child absorbs the environment, he takes everything from the environment and incarnates it in himself. He can do everything. He is really omnipotent, whereas the adult who is already formed cannot change. So we have in front of us a clear vision. If we wish to change a generation, if we wish to influence it either towards good, or evil, if we want to reawaken religion or add culture, whatever it is that we may wish to do, we must take the child.

The power of the psyche is something parallel to what has been discovered in the embryo. By action upon the embryo, you can either make a monster or a more perfect being. Indeed, experiments have been made by transferring the sanglion and arms have been made to develop on the back. But in an adult, one could not do it. It is the same here for the psyche. You cannot create man, but you can make him more perfect by acting upon the psychic embryo. This gives great power to the adults and to education because it confers control over psychic growth and psychic development. This power is immense if we compare it to the power society has had when it acted merely upon the adult. The child gives us a new hope and a new vision. Perhaps a great many modifications which would bring more understanding, greater welfare, greater spirituality can be brought about in the future humanity.

The Psycho-Embryonic Life

Let us repeat again that the child at birth is endowed with psychic life. If this be so, this psychic life may not have begun then. If it exist, it may already have been built, otherwise how could it be there? Also in the embryo there may be psychic life. When one conceives this idea, one wonders at what period of embryonic life the psychic life begins. Let us consider certain cases. We know there are occasions when a child is born at 7 instead of at 9 months and at 7 months the child is already so complete that it can live. Therefore its psychic life is capable of functioning like that of the child who is born at 9 months. I do not want to insist upon this question, but this example will suffice to illustrate what I mean when I postulate that all life is psychic life, and that even as an embryo the child is endowed with a psyche. As a matter of fact, each type of life has a specific quantity of psychic energy, a specific kind of individual psyche, no matter how primitive the form of life is. Even if we consider unicellular beings, we find that there is a kind of psyche, they move away from danger, towards food, etc. To give an example, there is a unicellular being which is called the little vampire of the spirogyra. This little being, out of all the plants in the water, feeds upon a special weed. In order to do this it must have a specific psychic individuality which makes it choose this plant. It must, in other words, be endowed with a specific behavior.

Each type and especially every animal form of life has a special irresistible way of conducting its life which shows that their actions are directed by a special form of psyche. If we were to leave the strictly scientific field we might say that there is a psychic director who distributes all the activities upon the earth using different types of life to do so. In other words today life is considered as a great energy, one of the energies of cosmic creation. Therefore, why should it surprise us when people state that the new-born child is endowed with psychic life? Indeed if it were not so, how could it be alive?

This conclusion made a great impression because previously the child had been considered void of psychic life. Many began to study and meditate upon the fact that the child is endowed with a psychic life even before birth.

If one is endowed with psychic life, one receives impressions and at birth a great shock must be felt by the child. This is a new point which makes thinkers dwell upon the drama of birth, the fact of a psychic life, of a living being thrown all of a sudden from one environment into another vastly different. This sudden change of environment is even more impressive when one considers the condition of the child at birth. The newborn child is not fully developed and indeed the more people study it, the more they realize how incomplete it is even physically. Everything is unfinished. The legs with which he will walk upon the earth and invade the whole world are still cartilaginous. The same is true of the cranium that encloses the brain which is in need of a strong defense, but in the new-born child the head is not yet ossified. Only a few of its bones are developed. More important still is the fact that the nerves themselves are not completed so that there is a lack of central direction and therefore a lack of unification between the organs, so that this being, whose bones are not yet developed, is at the same time unable to obey the urge to move because every urge is transmitted by nerves and they are not yet fully developed. So in the human new-born, there is no movement whilst among animals the new-born walk almost at once. The conclusion is this: the child at birth is still in an embryonic stage. Thus we must consider the child as possessing an embryonic life that extends before and after birth. This life is interrupted, we might say, by a great event, the great adventure of birth, by which he plunges into a new environment. The change in itself is terrific; it is as though one went from the earth to the moon. But this is not all; in order to make this great step the child must make a tremendous physical effort. Generally the fact that the child goes through so difficult an experience is not considered. When a child is born, people think only about the mother, and how difficult it has been for her. The child, however, passes through a greater trial than the mother, especially if one considers that the child is not even complete, but is nevertheless endowed with a psychic life. Let us therefore remember that the new-born child does not possess developed psychic faculties because he has yet to create them, this psychic embryo, which even physically is not complete, must create its own faculties.

Let us then continue to reason along this line. This being which is born, powerless, motionless, must be endowed with a behavior that leads it towards movement. The formation of those human faculties which do not exist and which must be created, represents a further period of embryonic life: the psycho-embryonic life.

This physically incomplete new-born child must complete the complicated being who is man: he must create man's psychic faculties.

After birth psychic development takes place following the line dictated by behavior. In other words, it is the psychic development which creates movement. The instincts which in other animals seem to awaken at birth, as soon as the animal comes into contact with the outer environment, must in man be built by the psyche. It is the psyche which must construct the human faculties and along with that the movements to correspond to those faculties. And while this goes on the physical part of the embryo finishes its development. The nerves become myelinized and the cranium ossified. It seems as though the human embryo were born incomplete because its final form and its functions must wait until the psyche has built itself.

Little chickens, when they come out of the egg but wait for the hen to show them how to pick up food and immediately start to behave like all other chickens. This is so now, this was so in previous generations and it is to be expected that it will always be so. For man this is not the case, because man, before he starts to move, must develop his psyche. Therefore he is born incapable of movement. The psyche must be constructed according to the evolution of man, according to the environment in which man finds himself, according to the conditions he finds around him, because he must build man suited to his time and conditions.

The movements are built up together with the psyche i.e., the psyche while it develops its faculties, also develops the movements that express them and thus such behavior is built that man is adapted to his time and to his conditions. The first active experiences upon the environment must wait until the formations of the psychic faculties have been laid.

Several consequences follow this fact. One is that from birth itself the most important side of life in man is the psychic life, not movement, because movements must be created following the guide and dictates of the psychic life. Intelligence is what distinguishes man from all animals. The first act of man in this life must therefore be the construction of intelligence. While both the skeleton and the nervous system await the construction of this intelligence, the body remains inert. It has to wait, because this is not the body of a being whose behavior is prefixed. Nature has taken its precautions, it has deprived man of the power of movement and made his body soft-boned, because before starting on his experience upon the environment, he must wait until he has made a great psychic acquisition. It is logical that if psychic life is to construct itself by incarnating the environment, the intelligence must observe and study first, it must gather a great quantity of impressions from it, just like the physical embryo begins with a great accumulation of cells before starting to build its special organs.

The first period of life has been reserved in order that impressions may be collected from the environment. This is logical because how could man orient himself in the environment if he started to walk immediately after birth, unless he were endowed with fixed instincts like those of the animals?

This is the marvelous part. In the life of man the first period is one of the greatest psychic activity. It is then that the accumulation of impressions is made upon which intelligence builds itself afterwards.

Also, as it is towards his environment that the movements of man are directed and as man is born in different environments and in different historical epochs, as he must adapt himself to them, it is imperative that at first the psyche receive and accumulate a great deal of nourishing matter which lays the foundation of this special adaptation to the specific environment and historical epoch in which the individual is born. The first year of life then appears to us as a period of the greatest activity leading to the absorption of everything that there is in the environment. In the second year the physical being nears completion, its movement begins to become determined. This shows how clearly nature has planned that the movements of man be determined by psychic life.

This is all the more impressive because people in olden times said that children who cannot move and cannot speak were psychically speaking non-existent. What a change! Then people thought that the small child had no psychic life whereas now it is known that the main activity during this first year is of the brain.

Now if with this vision, we consider again the newborn child, we seem better to understand why the size of the head of the one year old child is double the size of that of the new-born child. And at the third year its size is already half of that of an adult. And when the child is four years of age, the size of its head is 8/10 of that of the adult. (Fig. 7.)

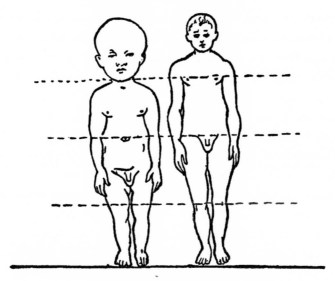

Fig. 7
A new-born child and an adult brought to the same scale
show the difference in the proportions of their bodies.

How clearly one sees then that the human being grows especially in intelligence, in psychic life, and that all the rest of growth is but that of an instrument of this psychic life as it develops its faculties.

This, if it shows anything, shows the importance of the first year for the rest of life and that the child of man is characterized by his intelligence. This also shows the greatest difference there is between man and the animals. Animals merely have to obey the instincts of their behavior. Their psychic life is limited to that. In man there is another fact: the creation of human intelligence. What man will do in the future we do not know and we cannot know from the new-born child. The intelligence of the child will have to take in the present of a life which is in evolution, which goes back hundreds of thousands of years in its civilization and which has stretching in front of it a future of hundreds, of thousands, of millions of years perhaps: a present that has no limit either in the past or in the future, and that is never for a moment the same: its aspects are infinite whereas for the others there is but one aspect which is always fixed.

For man there is no limit. Human intelligence is the center which must be taken into consideration when man is studied. Certainly this psychic life which has the possibility of going towards the infinite, which is destined to go towards the infinite, must begin in some mysterious fashion. It begins before birth because in the mind of the new-born we find powers so strong that they have the possibility of creating any faculties, of adapting man to any condition.

The various impulses of man have as their basis this psychic life. This point must be clearly visualized before we go on and before we can understand the psychic development of the child. There is something else which must be considered and that is the essence of the mind of the child and its way of functioning, because this mind is so very hungry in the first year of life that it wants to gather impressions of everything that exists in its environment. It does not absorb anything consciously. It is life with its powers that guides the development of the child. What is the nature of this psychic life? We must understand this if we are to understand some of the future actions of the child. How does the child re-act to external things?

Birth Terror and its Reactions

Psychologists are today struck by what they call the 'difficult adventure of birth,' and conclude that the child at birth must undergo a great shock of fright. Today one of the scientific terms of psychology is 'birth terror' Certainly, it is not a conscious terror, but if his conscious psychic faculties were developed, he would express himself by bitter words: "Why have you thrown me into this terrible world? What can I do? How shall I be able to adapt myself to a life which is so different from my own? How am I going to adapt myself to the terrific amount of sounds, I who had never heard even the slightest whisper before? How shall I take upon myself these very difficult functions which you, my mother, took upon yourself for me? How can I digest and breathe? How shall I be able to withstand these terrific changes of climate in the world, I who have been in a temperature that was always of the same agreeable warmth of your body?"

Now, the child is not conscious of all this. He could not say that he is suffering from birth terror. There must be a psychic feeling different from the conscious, because if he were conscious the child would say "Why have you abandoned me? You have left me who am wounded. You have abandoned me, who have no strength. How had you the courage to do so?"

This would be his reasoning if he were conscious, but he is not conscious. Yet in his sub-conscious he is very sensitive, and he must feel very nearly something corresponding to what we have expressed above.

This must be taken into consideration by those who study life. The child must be helped in his first adaptation to our environment as his psyche must, through birth, receive a terrific shock. There is no doubt that the child can feel fright.

Very often we have seen children who, if quickly lowered into the bath in the first hours of life, made a grasping movement, as one does when one is falling. That shows that they felt frightened.

What help is there in nature? Nature does give help to the young in this difficult adaptation. Nature gives mothers the instinct of keeping their child close to their own body and to protect him from light. And the mother herself has been made powerless by nature during this period. Not too much energy is left to her. By keeping quiet for her own sake she gives the needed quiet to the child. It is as though sub-consciously the mother were reasoning: "This child has received a terrific shock. I must keep it close to me."

She warms it with her warmth and she protects it from too many impressions.

Human mothers do not do this with the enthusiasm we see in mothers of other types of life. We see the mother-cats who hide their young in some dark hole and they are very jealous if somebody comes near them, whereas human mothers seem to have lost this animal instinct. As soon as the child is born somebody comes, washes it, dresses it, puts it into the light to see the color of the eyes, etc. That is why the human kind is in danger. It is no longer nature that guides, but human reasoning and the reasoning is faulty because it is not enlightened by understanding. It is a reasoning which considers that the child is not a being endowed with a psyche. This birth-terror, it has been observed today, leads to something much more terrible than vocal protests, it leads to wrong characters assumed by the child as it develops. The consequence is a psychic transformation, or rather, instead of taking the path which we might say is normal, the child takes a wrong path. The faulty characters are to be found not only in the child, but remain in the adult. They have been included in the general term of 'psychic regressions.' Instead of progressing, instead of going forward along the path of life, individuals suffering from a negative reaction to birth-terror seem to remain attached to something which existed before birth. These characters of regression are several, but they all give the same impression. It is as though the child were reasoning in this fashion: "My goodness, how terrible is this world, I am going back to where I came from." The long hours of sleep in the new-born are considered normal, but too long sleep is not normal even in the new-born and it is considered as a sort of refuge due to a psychic repulsion from the world and a means to seek oblivion from the earth.

And is it not so? Is not sleep the kingdom of the sub-conscious? If something unpleasant troubles our mind, let us sleep. For in sleep there are dreams, not realities, in sleep there is a life in which there is no necessity for struggle. Sleep is a refuge, a getting-away from the world. Another fact is the position of the body in sleep. In the new-born child the natural position is to double up with the hands near the face, and the legs next to the body. This however continues also in some older people, and is, we might say, a refuge into the pre-natal position. Then there is another fact. This is clearly a character of regression. When children wake up, they start crying as if they were frightened, as if they were living again through that terrible moment of birth which brings one into a difficult world. Often they suffer from nightmares. These form a part of the terror of life.

Another expression of this tendency is to attach oneself to somebody as though one was afraid of being left alone. This attachment is not affection. It is something which has fear in it. The child is timid and always wants to remain near someone, the mother preferably. He is not happy to go out, but would always like to remain at home isolated from the world. Everything in the world that should make him happy frightens him, he feels repugnance from new experiences. The environment instead of proving attractive, as it should to a being in course of development, is repellent. And if a child, from the very first infancy feels repulsion towards this environment, which ought to be its means of development, certainly this child will not develop normally. He will not be the child who conquers, who is destined to take the whole of his environment and incarnate it in himself. He will do so, but with difficulty and incompletely. He is the very picture of the saying 'To live is to suffer,' To do something is, to him, to go against his own nature. Even respiration seems to be hard. People of this sort require much more sleep and rest; even digestion seems to be difficult. So you see what sort of life this type of child prepares for himself in the future, for these characters are things not only of the present, but also of the future. He is of the type who cries easily. He will always require somebody to help him. He will be indolent, sad and depressed. And these are not passing features. They remain as characteristics for life. Even when an adult, he will feel repulsion for the world, will fear to meet people and be always timid. It is evident that such beings are inferior to others in the struggle for existence in social life. It will not be the lot of these people to have joy, courage and happiness.

This is the terrible answer of the subconscious psyche. We forget with our conscious memory, but though the subconscious appears not to feel and though it does not seem to remember, it does something worse. The impressions made there, are made upon the Mneme; they remain engraved as characteristics of the individual. Therein lies the great danger to humanity. The child, not properly cared for, will take revenge on society through the individual that it forms. The treatment does not foment rebels as it would amongst adults, it forms individuals who are weaker, inferior to what they ought to be; it forms characters that will be an obstacle to the life of the individual, and individuals who will be an obstacle to the progress of civilization.

The Conquest of Independence

The characteristics of regression are developed when the child has been unable to achieve the first adaptation i.e., soon after birth. Certain tendencies which can be traced back to this remain also in the adult.

Modern psychologists describing these characters of regression say that when they are not there, then the child presents tendencies which are very clearly and very strongly set towards independence. Then development is a conquest of ever greater independence. It is as though an arrow had been sent flying from the bow and it goes straight, sure and strong. So does the child proceed along the path of independence. This is normal development: an ever growing and more powerful activity shown along the path that leads to independence. The conquest of independence begins from the first commencement of life. As the being develops, it perfects itself and overcomes every obstacle that it finds on its way. A vital force is active in the individual and leads it towards its own evolution. This force has been called Home.

If one had to find something to compare to this Horme in the conscious psychic field, one would have to compare it to the force of will, although there is very little analogy between the two. The force of will is something too small and too much attached to the consciousness of the individual, whereas the Horme is something which belongs to life in general, to what we might call a divine force which is the promoter of all evolution. This vital force of evolution is expressed in the child by a will to perform certain actions. This will cannot be broken by anything short of death. I call it 'will' because we possess no better word to describe it. It is not will, however, because will implies consciousness and reasoning. It is a subconscious vital force which urges the child to do certain things and in the normally growing child its unhindered activity is manifested in what we call 'joy of life,' The child is enthusiastic, always happy.

These conquests of independence are in the beginning the different steps of what is generally known as natural development. In other words, if we examine natural development closely, we can describe it as the conquest of successive degrees of independence. This is true not only of the psychic, but also of the physical field. The body also has a tendency to grow, a tendency so strong that nothing can stop it short of death.

Let us then examine this development. The child at birth frees himself from a prison, the prison of the body of the mother. At birth he becomes independent of the functions of the mother. The new-born child is endowed with an urge, an impulse to face the environment and to absorb it. We might say that he is born with the 'psychology of conquest of the world' He absorbs it in himself and in absorbing it, he forms his psychic body.

This is the characteristic of the first period of life. It is evident that if the child feels this urge, if the first impulse he feels is the desire to conquer the environment, this environment must exert an attraction on the child. Therefore we say, using words which are really not appropriate to describe the fact, that the child feels 'love' for the environment.

The first organs which begin to function in the child are the sensory organs. Now what are sensory organs but organs of prehension, instruments by means of which we grasp the impressions which, in the case of the child, must be incarnated?

When we gaze, what do we see? We see everything there is in the environment. As soon as we start hearing, we also hear every sound there is in the environment. We might say that the field of prehension is very wide, that it is almost universal. This is the way of nature. One does not take in sound by sound, noise by noise, object by object, we begin by taking in everything, a totality. The distinctions of object from object, sound from noise, sounds from sounds, come later as an evolution of this first global gathering in.

This is the picture of the normal child's psyche. At first it takes in the world and then it analyses it.

Now let us suppose another type who does not feel this irresistible attraction for the environment, a type in whom this great fondness has suffered damage by fright, by terror. It is evident that the development of the first type must be different from that of the second.

Let us continue to examine the development of the child by considering the child at six months of age. Certain phenomena present themselves which are looked upon as sign-posts of normal growth. At the age of 6 months the child undergoes certain physical transformations. Some of these are invisible and have been discovered only through experiments, e.g., the stomach begins to secrete chloric acid which is necessary for digestion. It is also at six months that the first tooth makes its appearance. This is a further perfection of the body which at birth is not finished and develops along a certain path of growth. It also means that at six months the child is capable of living without the milk of his mother, or at least of supplementing milk with other substances. This is a further conquest of independence. If we consider that the child up to that age had been absolutely dependent upon his mother's milk because if he were to take anything else he would not be able to digest it, we realize what a great degree of independence he acquires at this period. The 6 months' child seems to reason: "I do not want to live upon my mother. I am a human being and I can eat everything now." An analogous phenomenon takes place in adolescents who begin to feel the humiliation of being dependent on their family. They do not want to live on them. They would like to live by their own resources.

It is also at about this epoch (which seems to be a critical moment in the life of the child) that he begins to utter the first syllables. This is the first stone in the great building which will develop later into language which is another great step, another great conquest of independence. When the child acquires language, he can express himself and does not have to depend upon other people to guess his needs. Instead of somebody having to guess what he, the child, wants, he can express himself. He can tell everybody: "Do this. Do that" Thus he comes into communication with humanity, because without language how can one communicate? This conquest of language and this possibility of intelligent communication with others is a tremendous step towards independence. Before acquiring it the child may be compared to a deaf and dumb person, because he cannot express himself and he cannot understand what other people say. After the conquest of language it is as if he suddenly acquired ears and the possibility of uttering the speech of the people around him.

A long time after that, at one year of age, the child starts to walk. This is to become free of a second prison, because now he can run on his own two legs and if you come near him, he can get away. He can say: "I can run on my two legs, I can express with language my thoughts to men like you."

Thus man develops gradually and by means of these successive steps of independence, he becomes free. It is not a question of will, it is, a phenomenon of independence. Really, it is nature that is giving to the child the opportunity of growing, gives him independence and at the same time leads him to freedom.

The 'conquest of walking' is very important, especially if one considers that, in spite of being very complex, it is achieved in the first year of life and is made together with all the other conquests of language, of orientation, etc. To walk is for the child a physiological conquest of great importance. Animals do not need to make it. It is only man who has this prolonged and refined type of development. In his growth he has to make three different achievements, three conquests, before being physically able to walk, or even to stand erect on his two legs. Look at those majestically looking animals, the oxen. Imagine if at one year of age calves just began to stand on their legs. Indeed they do not. They begin to walk as soon as they are born. Yet these animals are inferior to us, even if they are gigantic in construction. We are so apparently powerless because the construction of man is much more refined and takes therefore much more time.

The power of walking and being able to stand on one's two legs entails a thorough development composed of different items. One of them concerns the brain. There is a part of the brain called the 'cerebellum' which is situated under its larger portion. (See fig. 8).

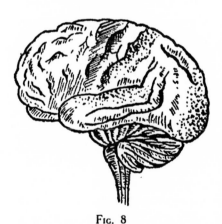

Fic. 8

The cerebellum at the base of the brain

It is just at six months that the cerebellum develops rapidly and this rapid development of the cerebellum continues until the child is 14 or 15 months. Then the growth of the cerebellum is slower but continues nevertheless until the child is 41/2 years, the possibility of standing on two legs and of being able to walk erect depends on the development of the cerebellum. In the child this development can easily be followed. We see the two developments following each other step by step: the child begins to its up at six months of age, starts to crawl at 9 months, stands at 1 and walks between 12 and 13 months, while at 15 months the child walks with security.

The second item of this complex development is the completion of certain nerves. If the spinal nerve, through which the direct command to the muscles must pass, were not completed, it could not pass and it is only during this period that the nerves become completed. How complex is development and how many things have to come into harmony before the conquest of walking can be made. This however is not all. There is a third achievement to be made: the development of the skeleton. The legs of the child are not completely ossified, as we have seen. They are cartilaginous and that is why they are so soft. If this is the case, how can they support the weight of the body? Therefore the skeleton has to be complete before the child can start to walk. Still another thing is that the bones of the cranium were not united at birth and only now they become complete, so that, if the child falls down, he is not in danger of injuring his head.

If by means of education we wished to teach the child how to walk before this time, we could not do it, because the fact of being able to walk is dependent on a series of physical developments, which take place simultaneously. If one tried one could not achieve anything without seriously damaging the child. Here it is nature which directs. Everything depends on her and has to obey her exact commands. At the same time, if you tried to keep the child who has started to walk and run from doing so, you would not be able to do it, because in nature whenever an organ is developed, this must be put in use. Creation in nature is not to make something, but also to allow it to function. As soon as the organ is complete, it must immediately be used in the environment. In modern language these functions have been called "experiences upon the environment." If these experiences do not take place, then the organ does not develop normally because the organ, incomplete at first, must be used in order to accomplish its completion.

The child can only develop by means of experiences upon the environment, we call them 'work.' As soon as language appears the child begins to chatter and no one can silence him. Indeed one of the most difficult things is to make a child stop talking. Now if the child were not to talk or to walk, then he would not be able to develop normally. There would be an arrest in his development. Whereas the child walks, runs, jumps and by doing this he develops his legs. Nature first makes the instruments, and then develops them by means of functions, through experiences upon the environment. When, therefore, the child has increased his independence by the acquisition of new powers, he can only develop normally if left free to function. When the child has acquired independence, it is by exercising this independence that he will develop. Development does not come of itself, but, as modern psychologists express it, 'the behavior is affirmed in each individual by the experiences this individual carries out upon the environment,' If therefore we think of education as a help to the development of the child's life, we cannot but rejoice when a child shows signs of having attained a certain degree of development. We cannot help saying: "My child has today said his first word" and rejoice about it. Especially inasmuch as we know we cannot do anything to bring about this event. If, however, we realize that, although the development of the child cannot be destroyed (because nature is too strong for us, thanks be to God), it can however be kept incomplete or retarded if the child is not given an opportunity of carrying out experiences upon the environment, then a problem does arise: The problem of education.

The first problem of education is to furnish the child with an environment which will permit him to develop the functions that nature has given to him. This is not an indifferent question. It is not a question of merely pleasing the child, of allowing him to do as he likes. It is a question of co-operation with a command of nature, with one of her laws which decrees that development should take place by means of experiences upon the environment. With his first step the child enters a higher level of experiences.

If we observe the child who has reached this level, we see that he has a tendency to acquire still further independence. He wants to act in his own way, i.e., he wants to carry things, to dress and to undress alone, to feed himself, etc. And it is not by following our suggestions that the child begins to do things. On the contrary he has such a strong urge, such a vital impulse that our efforts are usually spent in restraining him from doing things. It is not the child that we fight when we do this, it is nature. It is not the child's will that we fight, he merely collaborates with nature and obeys her laws and step by step, first in one thing, then in others, he acquires ever increasing independence from those who surround him, until a moment comes when he will want to acquire mental independence too. Then he will show the tendency to develop his mind through his own experiences and not through the experiences of other people. He begins to seek out the reason of things. And thus it is that the human individuality is constructed during this period of childhood. This is not a theory. This is not an opinion. These are clear natural facts, they are observed facts. When we say that we must render the freedom of the child complete, when we say that his independence and his normal functioning must be assured by society, we do not speak about a vague ideal. We speak because we have observed life, we have observed nature and nature has revealed this fact. It is only through freedom and by experiences upon the environment that man can develop.

Now, when we speak of independence and freedom for the child, do not transfer to this field the ideas of independence and freedom that we hold as ideal in the world of adults. If the adults were to examine themselves and give a definition of independence and freedom, they could not do so with exactness. In reality they have a very miserable idea of what freedom is. They have not the largeness that nature has. The child offers the majestic vision of nature that gives life by giving freedom and independence. She gives it with determined laws regarding the time, and the needs: she makes freedom a law of life: either be free or die. I believe that nature offers us help and aid for the interpretation of our social life. It is as though the child offered us the picture of the whole and we in our social life took only small details. The child is right in this sense that what he shows leads to reality, to truth. When there is a natural truth, there can be no doubt about it. It is interesting therefore to consider the freedom of the child which is achieved through growth.

What is the aim of this ever increasing conquest of independence? From where does it arise? It arises in the individuality that forms itself, that is able to function by itself. But in nature all living beings have the tendency towards this. Every living being functions by itself. So in this also the child obeys the plan of nature. He achieves that freedom which is the first rule of life in every being.

How does the child acquire this independence? He acquires it by means of continuous activity. How does the child realize his freedom? By means of continuous effort; what life cannot do is to arrest itself, to stop. Independence is not static. It is a continuous conquest. And by means of continuous work, one acquires not only freedom but strength and self-perfection.

Let us consider the first instinct of the child: he seeks to act alone, i.e., without help from others. His first conscious act of independence t is to defend himself from those who try to help him. And in order to act by himself, he tries to make an ever greater effort. If, as many of us think, the best idea of well-being is to sit down, do nothing and let other people work for us r then the ideal state would be that of the child before birth. The child might as well go back to the body of the mother, because the mother would do everything for the child. If we think so, why should one learn a language in order to communicate with others? No, nature has other intentions. She forces the child to make this difficult conquest of language so that he can enter into communication with other beings. Or again, if we adopted rest as the ideal of life, then the child might say: "I have nice sweet milk from my mother. It is easily digestible. Why should I want any other food? I shall stick to it. Why should I have to take the trouble of chewing coarser food that I have to secure for myself? No! No! I am going to stick to mother's milk." Or again: "Why walk? Somebody carries me in her arms. I have something like an automobile of my own. See the tremendous effort I must make in order to walk, I have to develop my bones, my brain and even finish the insulation of the nerves in the spinal chord. Why should I go to all this trouble? Why should I be so uncouth and bad-mannered as to insist upon knowing things for myself? Why, when there are so many wise people around me, people who have instruction and culture and who can tell me things?" But the reality shown by the child is not so. The child reveals that nature's teachings are quite different from the ideals that society has forged for itself. The child seeks independence through work: independence of body and of mind. The child seems to say: "I do not mind how much you know, I want to know things for myself. I want to have experience in the world and to perceive it with my own effort; you keep your own knowledge and let me acquire mine." We must understand clearly that when we give freedom and independence to the child, we give freedom to a worker who is impelled to act and who cannot live except by his work and his activity. This is the form of existence for living beings, and as the human being is also living, he also has this tendency. And if we try to stop it then, we produce a degeneration in the individual.

Everything in creation is activity and in life this is all the more so. Life is activity and it is only through activity that perfection of life can be sought and found. The social aspirations that have come to us through the experience of past generations: an ideal life of less hours of work, of people working for us, of idling as long as we can, is what nature shows as the characteristic of a degenerate child. These aspirations are the characteristics of regression of the child who was not helped in the first days of its life to adapt itself and who has acquired a disgust for the environment and for activity. He it is who wants to be helped by other people, who wants to have servants, wants to be carried or driven in a perambulator, who sleeps too long, who shuns the company of other people. These are the characteristics that nature has shown as belonging to degeneration. These are the characteristics which have been recognized, analyzed and described as the tendency to go back to embryonic life. He who is born and grows normally goes towards independence. The one who shuns it is degenerate.

Quite another problem of education faces us in these degenerate children. How to cure regression? Regressions retard or deviate normal development. The deviated child has no love for the environment, because the environment presents too many difficulties, too much resistance. Today the deviated child holds the center in the scientific field of psychology which we could better call 'psycho-pathology' Pedagogy teaches that the environment must offer the least resistance. It is sought, therefore, to diminish the avoidable obstacles and resistance that the environment presents to the child, and, if possible, to eliminate them altogether. Nowadays we try to give attraction to the environment. The environment must be rendered pleasing, beautiful, because it is necessary, especially in the case of one who feels repulsion for the environment to arouse sympathy and benevolence towards it. The environment must be made as attractive as possible so as to overcome diffidence and disgust. We must give pleasant activity to the child, because we know that it is through activity that development takes place. The environment must contain plenty of motives for interesting activity which are an invitation for the child to carry out his experiences upon the environment. These are clear principles for the deviated child, principles which are dictated by life, by nature, and which bring those who have acquired regressive characteristics from the tendency to idle to the desire of working, from lethargy and sluggishness to activity, from that state of fright which sometimes translates itself into attachment to somebody whom they never want to leave, into a freedom of joy, freedom to go towards the conquest of life.

From inertia to work! That is the path of the cure just as from inertia to work is the path of development for the normal child. If a new education is to be envisaged, this must be its basis, for it has been formulated by nature herself.

Care to Be Taken at Life's Beginning

The absorbent mind of the child orients itself in the environment; so it is necessary to prepare the environment with much care.

We must remember that there are different periods of development in the life of the child. One period is soon after birth, and this is so important a period that it is impossible to deal with it in a book as short as this. I feel that in the future there will be people who will specialize in this type of study, at present there are only very few.

If we study the animals we shall see that nature has provided special protection to the mammals, giving special care at this period. Nature has arranged that mothers isolate themselves from the rest of their species just before the time when they give birth to their little ones and they remain isolated for some time before coming back. This is very evident in animals who live in herds or packs. Horses do this, cows do, elephants, wolves, deer, dogs, all do this. During this time the little new-born animal has time to adapt itself to the new environment, alone, except for its mother's love watchful guidance and care. In this period the baby animal gradually expresses the behavior of its kind. During this short period of isolation there is a continued psychological reaction on the part of the little one to all the stimuli of the environment, and that reaction is according to the special features of the behavior of its kind. So that, when the mother returns to the herd with her baby, the little one enters the community with its own special preparation for living there already established. It is either a little horse, psychically speaking, or a little wolf, or a little cow, psychically not merely physically.

The child has no fixed behavior, but he has to take in the environment, therefore it is necessary to take special care of the environment which surrounds this newborn child. This care is of utmost importance in order to aid the absorption of the environment, so that the child may feel attracted towards it instead of repelled, and does not develop phenomena of regression. The progress, growth and development of the child depend on his love for the environment; we must therefore take care that he can absorb it with interest. Science nowadays takes this into great consideration. Without entering into too many details we can enunciate certain principles. The child should remain as much as possible in contact with his mother and the environment must not present obstacles, such as great differences of temperature from that to which the child has been accustomed before birth. Not too much light, not too much noise, for the child has come from a place of perfect silence and darkness. Today, in the modern Nursing Homes, the mother and child are placed in a glass-walled room where the temperature is easily controllable, so that it may be gradually assimilated to that of the normal temperature outside. The glass is blue so that the light entering the room is very subdued, and the air also is regulated. Care should also be taken in the way how the child is handled and moved. It has been customary to handle the child as if it were an object without feelings, and it was plunged into a low bath and rapidly and roughly dressed (roughly in the sense that any handling of a new-born child is rough, because it is so delicate a thing, psychically as well as physically), Today science has come to the conclusion that the newborn child should be touched as little as possible, and should not be dressed, but rather kept in a room the temperature of which is sufficient to keep the baby warm and free from droughts of cold air. The way of transporting the baby is also changed: he is carried by means of a soft mattress, something like a hammock, so that he remains in a level and horizontal position, similar to his pre-natal position. He is not lifted up or down but treated as we treat wounded people who need great care. Sick people today are not lifted up and then taken to a cart and drawn along; there is a stretcher which is at the same level as the bed, and the invalid is carried very, very carefully, so that there are no bumps and jumps. This is done for adult people. The tendency today is to give the baby the same care and consideration, only even more refined and perfect. This is more than merely hygienic care, because hygiene is something else again. Today the nurses of the child have a cloth in front of their mouth and nose, so that microbes from them may not enter the environment of the new-born child. He is protected from them. Nowadays mother and child are considered as two organs of one body which are in communication. The adaptation to the environment then takes place successfully and naturally for the child, since mother and child have a special connection with each other. It is considered as a kind of magnetism. There are certain forces within the mother to which the child is accustomed and these forces are a necessary aid for the child during the first difficult days of adaptation. We can say that the child has changed his position in relation to the mother. He is now outside the mother's body whereas before he was inside, but the rest is the same. They are still in close communication and this magnetism that goes from the mother to the child remains intact. This is how these things are considered in our modern times, but only a few years ago the first thing that was done at birth, even in the best Nursing Homes, was to separate the mother from the child. The child was taken away and bathed and then brought back to his mother. The treatment I have described above is the 'last word' in the scientific treatment of the child. Nature shows us that this special care is not necessary to the child during the whole period of childhood. Just as, after a time, the mother cat brings her kittens out and does not hide them any more, so after a little time the human baby and mother can come out of their isolation into to the social world.

Usually, as soon as a baby is born, all the relatives go and see this baby. They pat him and say: "How beautiful he is, he looks just like the father, (or mother, or both!)" They kiss it and caress it. This should be stopped. The richer the children the more unhappy they often are, the unhappiest of all are perhaps the king's children. In olden times, when the queen gave birth to an heir to the throne, the king himself took the baby out on to a balcony. The little one was wrapped in a bundle of clothes, and shown to the people who were assembled in the square outside the palace. Imagine this and how it would give rise to regressions!

It is interesting to note that the social questions of the child are not the same as those of the adult. We might say also that the economic position has a bearing upon the child which is the reverse of that which it has upon the adult, for we find that while among the adults it is the poor who suffer, amongst the children it is often the rich who suffer most. It is among the rich that the mother gives the child to a nurse for care, while the poor mother follows the proper method of keeping her child with her. The children of working mothers also usually receive more substantial food from their mothers, because the mothers are healthy and produce more milk which is of a more substantial quality than that of rich mothers, who do not need to work and are often inert and so their milk is scarce and poor in quality. This is one of the main reasons why a child is given to a nurse. The mother does not feed the child owing to unsuitable milk, and in olden times the baby was given to a 'wet nurse,' who was a healthy peasant woman with plenty of good milk.

There is therefore not a general question of rich and poor; in the world of children things and values change altogether.

Once this first period is passed the child adapts himself happily to the environment without feeling any repugnance. Then he begins traveling on the path of independence that we have described, on which the child, we might say, opens its arms to the environment, receives the environment and absorbs it to the extent of making his own, the customs of the environment in which he lives.

The first activity in this development, which we might call a conquest, is the activity of the senses. Owing to the lack of completeness in its bony tissues, the child is inert, without movement of limbs, so his activity cannot be that of movement. His activity is purely that of the psyche taking in the impressions of the senses. The child's eyes are very active, but we must have very clear in our minds that (as science has described in modern times) the child is not merely struck by the light on its eyes. The child is not passive. He certainly receives impressions, but he is also an active research worker in the environment. This is the new idea; it is he, the child, who seeks these impressions; he is not a victim of impressions that are all around him and that strike him, but he seeks them.

Now, if we look at the animal species, we see that they have a type of apparatus in the eyes similar to that which we have, a sort of photographic machine. But these animals are specialized in their use of it: they are attracted towards certain things more than others so that they are not struck by the whole of the environment. They have a guide in them that makes them follow certain lines and through their eyes they follow that guide of their behavior. So they direct themselves towards those things for which their behavior is made. From the very beginning there is a guide; the senses perfect themselves and are then used always following this guide. The eye of the cat will perfect itself in the dim light of the night (as does that of other nocturnal prowlers), but the cat, although interested in the darkness, is attracted by moving things and not by still things. As soon as something moves in the darkness, the cat pounces upon it; to the rest of the environment it pays no attention. There is not a general awareness of the environment, therefore, but an instinctive move towards specialized things. In the same way, there are insects which are attracted by flowers of special colors, because in the flowers of those colors they find their food. Now, an insect just emerged from a chrysalis could not have any experience along that line; it has a guide which directs it and the eye serves to follow that guide. Through this guide the behavior of the species is realized. The individual, therefore, is not the victim of his senses, neither is it dragged by them; the senses are there and work in the service of their owner, following a guide.

The child has a special faculty. His senses are not limited like those of animals, but his senses also are in the service of a guide. The cat is limited to things that move in the environment, it is attracted only by them. The child has no such limitation. The child observes his surroundings and experience has shown us that his tendency is to take in everything. He does not merely take them in by means of his camera-like eye, but a kind of psycho-chemical reaction takes place so that these impressions form an integral part of his psyche. We might make this observation which is an impression and not a scientific statement that the person who is merely dragged by his senses, who is the victim of his senses, has something wrong within him. His guide may be there, but instead of acting it has become enfeebled in some way and so the person becomes the victim of his senses. Therefore it is of the utmost importance that the guide which is within each child should be taken care of and kept alive.

To make clearer what happens in this absorption of the environment, I would like to make a comparison. There are certain insects who resemble leaves and others resembling sticks. These insects can be quoted as analogies to what takes place in the psyche of the child. They live on sticks and leaves and resemble them so closely that they have become as one with their environment. Something like that happens in the child. He takes the environment in and transforms himself accordingly like leaf-insects or stick-insects. This is very interesting indeed! The impressions that the environment gives to them are so great that some biological or psycho -chemical transformation makes them resemble their environment. They become like the thing they love. This power of taking in the environment and transforming accordingly, is now discovered to exist in all types of life, in some physically as in the insects mentioned and in some other animals, but psychically in the child. It is to be considered as one of the greatest activities of life. The child does not look at things as we do. We may look at a house and say: "How beautiful!" and then we see something else and we have but a vague memory of those things afterwards. But the child constructs himself by means of the profound way in which he gathers them especially in the first period of life. It is in infancy, by virtue of the unique powers of infancy, that the child acquires the human characteristics that distinguish him, such as language, religion, racial character, etc. Thus he constructs the adaptation to the environment. In that environment he is happy and develops taking in its customs, language, etc. He does not refuse food if the word for food differs from that in his own country. He constructs an adaptation to each new environment. What does it mean to build up adaptation? It means to transform oneself so that one becomes suited to one's environment, so that this environment forms a part of oneself. We must therefore observe these facts as the child absorbs his environment.

The child is in need of an environment in order to develop himself. Having accepted that, the next point is, what are we to do? What sort of environment must be prepared for the child so that it may be of assistance to him? It is a very embarrassing question. If we were dealing with a child of three years, he might be able to tell us. We should have to put flowers and beauty in the environment; we should have to provide those motives of activity which belong to his path of development. We could easily find out that certain motives of activity would have to be in the environment in order to offer an opportunity for functional exercise to this child. But when the baby has to take in the environment in order to build up adaptation, what sort of environment can we prepare for him? There can be but one answer to this: the environment for the baby-child must be the world, the world that is around him, all of it! It is evident that if the child is to acquire language, he must be among people who speak, otherwise he will not be able to do so; if he is to acquire any powers or faculties he must be among people who habitually use those powers and faculties. If the child is to take in customs and habits he must be constantly among people who themselves follow them. That is why we find that the child who is among cultured people who use many words and many small refinements of behavior, acquires many more words and many more little refinements than the less fortunate child.

This really is a strikingly revolutionary statement. It is a contradiction of what has happened in the last few years, since, as a consequence of hygienic reasoning, people have come to the conclusion or misconclusion that the child should be isolated! What has happened is that the child has been placed in a nursery. When it was discovered that the nursery, hygienically speaking, was not good enough, the hospital was taken as a model and the child was left undisturbed and made to sleep as much as possible like a sick person. Let us realize that if this is progress this exclusively hygienic care it is a social danger.

If the child is kept in nurseries, in a sort of prison,, with as his sole companion a nurse who obstructs more or less the development of the child, because no expressions of truly maternal sentiment or feeling are shown to the child, there are serious obstacles to normal growth and development; serious retardation and dissatisfaction, one might say psychic hunger on the part of the child, is bound to result with harmful effect. Instead of staying with his mother, who loves him and with whom there is a special current of communication, the child has a nurse who does not speak much to the child because of the hygienic habit of covering her mouth. How then can he learn the language? He must be protected from the sun or cold so a hood is put up over his perambulator and he sees only the face of the nurse or the hood and is shut away from all other parts of the environment. The richer the children the worse their lot, because this is life in a prison for them. Instead of nice beautiful mothers they have nurses, sometimes very experienced, but then old and ugly and the more aristocratic the family, the more formal it is and the parents see still less of the child. Many families see their child for a moment once a week because 'the nurse knows how to deal with the child. Mother says: "I do not deal with him," After that period, they put the child in a boarding school!

The treatment of the child is really a social question and today more and more we begin to realize that it must be changed. Once this has been understood people begin to worry very much as in America which is awake now to the need for this new sort of aid to the child. They study how the child should be treated, and there is a growing conviction that as soon as the child can come out of doors, one should bring him along in the midst of one's work and allow him to see as much as possible. Then the perambulator is built very high, because the higher the child the better he can see. The nursery also has undergone a transformation. It conforms as rigorously to the requirements of hygiene as a hospital room, but the walls are full of pictures and the child lies on a stand which is slightly sloping and fitted high up, so that he can command a view of the whole of the environment and not of the ceiling only. This is the first throne for the child. The idea has been understood that the child must be placed in a position to see everything.

The absorption of language presents a more difficult problem especially to nurses who themselves belong to a social environment different from that of the child. Here also there is another side to the question. The child must be brought with us when we converse with our friends. Usually when we go to call on a friend or when a friend comes to see us, the child is taken away and put back in the nursery. If we want to aid the child we must put him in our midst so that he can see how we do things and can hear the conversation. He does not register it consciously, but if he sees the people round him talking, eating, etc., he receives a sub-conscious impression that he takes in and this will help his growth. Also when we take him for an outing what will he like? We cannot say so definitely, but we can observe him. Here again mothers and rightly prepared nurses, when they see the child interested in something, will stop and let the child examine and inspect it as long as he likes. The nurse, instead of dragging along a cart with something in it as she used to do in the old days, considers the child and the little face lights up with interest as he is allowed to examine what attracts him. How, indeed, can we know what is going to be of interest to the child on any particular day? We must be at his service. Our whole conception is therefore revolutionized, and this revolution must be brought about among adults. The adult world must realize that the child constructs a vital adaptation to the environment and must therefore have full, complete contact with the environment, for if the child is unable .to construct this adaptation, we face a social problem of the first order. All the social problems we have today are due to a lack of adaptation on the part of somebody, either in the moral field or in others. This is a fundamental problem, a question of fundamental importance. This conclusion, of course, points to the fact that the education of the small child will in the future become the most basic and important consideration of society.

Then how is it possible that we knew nothing of it before? Our grandparents and great-grandparents knew nothing of these things and yet children grew up and humanity existed. This is the sort of statement that usually comes into the mind of a person who hears something new! They say: "Humanity is very old and people must have lived. I have grown up myself; my children have grown up and yet we had no such theory before. In spite of the lack of such preparation, people have acquired their language and in many countries certain customs have become so strong that they have become prejudices. How has that taken place? How is it that without any such preparation I have become one of my race?"

Let us consider this question for a little while. One of the most interesting studies is the study of the behavior of human groups at different levels of civilization. Every one seems more intelligent than we in the West with our ultra-modern ideas! In most other countries we see that children are not treated as disastrously as by the rich ultra-modern Westerner. We see that in most countries the child accompanies his mother everywhere. The mother and child are as one body. Wherever the mother goes the child goes with her. In the street she talks and the child listens. The mother has an altercation with some tradesman about prices, the child is present. Whatever the mother does the child sees and hears, and for how long does that last? During the whole period of breast-feeding. The mother has to feed her child and so sis she goes to work or goes out she cannot leave the child. To her it is not merely a question of feeding the child, it is really a question of attraction between the mother and child. "I do not like to leave the child, because I love him." she would say. Nature has arranged that milk and love solve the problem of adaptation to the environment on the part of the child. So here is the picture: the mother and child are but one person divided into two. Where civilization has not destroyed the possibility, the mother loves the child and takes him about with her, everywhere. She says, and rightly: "I do not trust anyone with my child." Is this mother a jailer then? No! She goes everywhere and so does the child. The child hears the mother speaking in a normal way to many people. She speaks whatever she has to say and the child takes part. People say that mothers are loquacious; yes, because they have to aid the development of the child and his adaptation to his environment. If the child were to hear only the words that the mother addresses to himself, he would not learn much. Instead, the child learns language in its construction. It is not language consisting only of disconnected words, it is language taken from the people who speak. It is really marvelous that the child is able to absorb the language of the environment in which he lives, but this can only happen if he lives among people. Therefore I stress the necessity of the child being brought out into the world.

Again, if we study the different human groups, races or nations, there are other characteristics to observe: the fashion of transporting the child is one of these characteristics. Ethnological studies are made and people go about observing these and other customs and there are many interesting things to be seen. One of the greatest interest is to see how women carry their children. They usually lay the child on a bed or in a bag and do not carry him in their arms. In some countries the child is fastened to a piece of wood and put on the shoulders of the mother, when the mother goes to work. Certain people tie the child on the neck, others on the back, others use a basket. But each race has found some means of carrying the child along. There is always the question of breathing to consider. The child is usually carried with his face against the back of the mother, there is the danger of suffocation to be considered, and so precautions are taken. The Japanese put their children in such a way that the neck of the child comes above the shoulder of the person who is carrying it, and the first traveler who went to Japan, called the Japanese two-headed people, on account of this habit. In India the child is carried on the hip, and the Red Indian straps it on the back; the child is in a sort of cradle and is fastened to the mother back to back, so that the child sees whatever is behind her. Each country has different habits and customs, but the child never leaves the mother. It never enters the head of the mother to leave the child behind any more than she would leave her hair behind. In Africa among a certain tribe there was to be a coronation ceremony for a queen. To the surprise of the missionaries who witnessed the ceremony, the queen had her child along with her. It never entered her head to leave the child at home. Another curious fact with these people is that the period of breast-feeding lasts for a long period. In some countries it lasts one year, in others one and a half or up to two years. It is not necessary, because the child has the necessary means now to eat anything. In fact he does eat a great many things besides drinking his mother's milk, but since the mother continues to feed him, it means that she takes the child along with her and so involuntarily ensures the proper aid of a full social environment during this important period. The mother says nothing to the child but he has his eyes and he goes about. The mother carries him and the child comes to know people in the street and the market, carts and buses. He sees all these things without anybody telling him anything. And when mothers go to market and fix the price for fruits, if you look at the face of the child she carries, it is curious to see the intensity of interest there is in his eyes. The mother is un ˜ expressive in her face but the child is intensely expressive. Another interesting factor is that the small child who is being carried about never cries, unless he is ill or wounded. Sometimes the child falls asleep, but he never cries. Among the enormous quantity of photographs taken in these countries, you never see a child crying. The photographs have been taken of the mother, of course, to show her customs, but incidentally we notice that one feature of them is that the child does not cry, whereas what people complain about in Western countries is: "My child is always crying," and "what do you do when a child cries?" What can one do? Crying is the problem in Western countries. Today the answer of psychologists is this: the child cries and is agitated, he has fits of crying and 'tempers,' because he suffers from mental starvation. He is mentally undernourished. He is kept in prison with a restricting guardian over him. The only remedy is this: to take the child out of prison and allow him to go into society. What nature shows us is this treatment of the child which is unconsciously followed in many races. This treatment has to be understood and applied consciously by us as we use our observation and intelligence.

On Language

Let us consider the development of language in the child. In order to understand language, we must reflect on what language is. It is so fundamental that we might well call it the basis of normal human life, because through it men join together to form a group. It brings about the transformation of the environment that we call civilization.

There is a central point that distinguishes humanity: it is not guided to do this or that fixed task as animals are. We never know what man will do, hence men must come into harmony with each other or they will never do anything. In order to come into accord and to take intelligent decisions together, it is not sufficient to think, not even if all of us were geniuses. What is necessary is that we must understand one another. This understanding one another is possible only by means of language. Language is the instrument of thinking together. Language did not exist on the earth until man made his appearance. Yet after all, what is it? A mere breath, a series of sounds put together not even logically, just put together.

Sounds have no logic, the collection of sounds that occur when we say 'plate' have in themselves no logic. What gives sense to these sounds is the fact that men have agreed that those special sounds shall represent this special idea. Language is the expression of agreement among a group of men, and it is only the group who has agreed on those sounds who can understand them. Other groups have other sounds to represent the same idea. Language is a sort of wall that encloses a group of men and separates it from other groups. That is why language has become almost mystical, it is something that unites groups of men even more than the ideas of nationality. Men are united by language, and language has become more complicated as man's thought has become more complicated; it has grown with man's thought.

The curious thing is that the sounds used to compose words are few, yet they can unite in so many ways to make so many words. How complicated are the combinations of these sounds! Sometimes one is placed before another, sometimes after another, sometimes softly, sometimes with force, with closed lips, with open lips, etc., etc. It needs a great memory to remember them all and the ideas represented by these words. Then there is the thought itself, as a whole, which must be expressed and this is done by a group of words which we call a sentence. The words must be placed in a special order in that sentence so as to conform to the thought of man and not just to string together a number of things in the environment. There is therefore a set of rules in order to guide the hearer as to the intentional thought of the speaker. If man wishes to express a thought, he must put the name of the object here and an adjective near it and another noun there. The number of words used is not sufficient, their position must be considered. If we want to test this, let us take a sentence with a clear meaning, write it out, cut the written sentence into its separate words and mix them; the sentence will not make sense, yet there are exactly the same words. So here also there must be agreement among men. Language therefore might be called the expression of a supra-intelligence. On first consideration we feel that language is a faculty with which we are endowed by nature, but after further thought we realize that it is above nature. It is a supra-natural creation produced by conscious collective intelligence. Around it there grows a sort of network that extends and increases and there is no limit to the extension and increase, so that there have been languages so complicated, so difficult to remember for ever, that they have died. They extended so far and gradually became so complicated that it was impossible to retain them, and they disintegrated. And if one wished to study Sanskrit or Latin one would study for eight years, ten years, and even then one would not succeed in speaking this language completely and in its perfection.

There is nothing more mysterious than the underlying reality that to do anything, men must come together in agreement and to that they must use language, this most abstract instrument.

This problem is always worrying humanity, but it mast be solved, because language has to be given to the new-born child. Attention to this problem has led people to consider and realize that it is the child who takes in language. The reality of this absorption is something very great and mysterious which men have not sufficiently considered. It is said: "Children are among people who speak, so they speak." This is a very profound statement indeed! especially when one considers the complications. Yet people have gone on for thousands of years to think of it so superficially.

Another thought has entered men's minds through their study of this problem of language; a language might be difficult and complicated for us to learn and yet it has been spoken once by the uncultured people of the country to which it belonged. Latin is a difficult language, even for those who speak the modern languages that have developed from Latin, but the language that the slaves of imperial Rome spoke was this same complicated and difficult Latin! And what did the uncultured peasants speak as they labored in the fields? This complicated Latin! And what did the children of three years speak in imperial Rome? They expressed themselves in this complicated Latin and understood it as it was spoken to them. It is probably the same in India. Long ago, the people who worked in the fields and roamed in the jungle spoke Sanskrit. To-day this mystery has aroused curiosity and the result is that the development of language in children is receiving attention and, let us remember, it is development, not teaching. The mother does not teach language to her little one. Language develops naturally as a spontaneous creation. And what strikes one is that language develops following certain laws and in certain epochs that development reaches a certain height. This is true for all children whether the language of their race be simple or complicated. Even today there are some very simple languages spoken among certain primitive people; the children who live among them attain the same development in their language as the children with a more difficult language do. There is a period for all children when only syllables are spoken; then words are spoken and finally the whole syntax and grammar is used in its perfection. The differences of masculine and feminine, of singular and plural, of tenses, of prefixes and suffixes, all are used by children. The language may be complicated and with many exceptions to the rules, yet the child who absorbs it learns it all and can use it in the same time as the African child learns the few words of his primitive language.

If we look at the production of the different sounds we also find it follows laws. All the sounds which compose words are made by putting into use certain mechanisms. Sometimes the nose is employed together with the throat, and sometimes it is necessary to control the muscles of the tongue and cheek, etc. Different parts of the body come together to construct this mechanism. Its construction is perfect in the mother tongue, the language taken by the child. Of a foreign tongue, we adults cannot even hear all the sounds, let alone reproduce them. We can only use the mechanism of our own language. Only the child can construct the mechanism of language, and he can speak any number of languages perfectly if they are in his environment.

This construction is not the result of conscious work, but takes place in the deepest layer of the sub-conscious of the child. He begins this work in the darkness of the sub-conscious and it is there that it develops and fixes itself as a permanent acquisition. It is this that lends interest to the study of language. We, adults, can conceive only a conscious wish to learn a language and set about to learn it consciously. We must however have another conception of a natural, or rather supra-natural mechanism that takes place outside of consciousness, and this mechanism, or series of mechanisms, is fascinating. They take place in a depth not directly accessible to adult observers. Only the external manifestations can be seen, but these are very clear in themselves if we observe them properly, since they take place in all humanity. Especially striking is the fact that the sounds of any language keep their purity age after age; another curiosity is that complications are taken in as easily as simplicities. No child becomes 'tired' of learning his mother tongue, his mechanism elaborates his language in its totality.

There comes to my mind a sort of comparison to this absorption of language by the child. My idea has nothing to do with the various factors of the phenomenon, nor with reality, but it gives a picture of something similar that we can experience. If, for instance, we wish to draw something, we take a pencil or colors and draw it, but we can also take a photographic picture of the thing and then the mechanism is different. The photograph of a person is taken on a film. This film does not have to do much work, and if there were instead of one a group of ten people to be photographed, the film would have no more work than before; the mechanism works instantaneously. It would be just as easy to take a thousand people if the camera were large enough. If we photograph the title of a book, or if we photograph a page of that book filled with minute or foreign characters, the effort is the same for the film. So the mechanism of the film can take in anything, simple or complicated, in the fraction of a second. Whereas, if we have to draw a man it will take some time, and if we have to draw ten men it will take more time. If we copy the title of a book it will also take some time, if we have to copy a page of minute and foreign characters it will take much more time.

Then, too, the photograph is taken in darkness and still in darkness it undergoes the process of development, then it is fixed, still in darkness, and finally it can come to the light and is unalterable. So it is with the psychic mechanism for language in the child. It begins deep down in the darkness of the sub-conscious, is developed and fixed there, and then it is seen openly. Certain it is that some mechanism does exist, (whether I have made a good comparison or not) so that this understanding of language may be realized. Once one has envisaged this mysterious activity, one wants to find out how it happens; so there is today a deep interest in the investigation of this mysterious feature of the deep subconscious.

This however is only part of the activity of observation that adults can perform; the other part is to watch the external manifestations, because it is only of these external manifestations that we can have proof; but this observation must be exact. Nowadays several people are engaged in this. Observations have been carried out day by day from the date of birth to two years of age and beyond: what happened on each day, how long the development remained at the same level, etc. From these observations certain things stand out like milestones. They have revealed the fact that there is a mysterious inner development that is very great, while the corresponding external manifestation is very small, so there is evidently a great disproportion between the activity of the inner life and the external expression. Another thing that stands out in all these observations of outer manifestations is that there is not a regular linear development, but development manifests itself in jerks. There is the conquest of syllables, for instance, at a certain time and then for months the child emits nothing but syllables there is no progress externally. Then suddenly he says a word; then he remains with one or two words for a long time. Again there seems no progress and one feels almost disheartened to see this slow external progress. It seems so sluggish, but the acts reveal to us that in the inner life there is a continuous and great progress.

After all is this not illustrated also in the actions of society? If we look at history, we see that man for centuries lived at the same level, primitive, stupid, conservative, incapable of progress; but this is only the outer manifestation seen in history. There is an inner growth going on and on, until an explosion suddenly comes! And then another period of placidity and little progress externally and then another revelation!

So it is with the child and this language of man. There is not merely small steady progress of word by word, but there are also explosive phenomena, as psychologists call them, happening without reason or teaching. At the same period of life in each child comes suddenly this cataract of words, and all pronounced perfectly. In three months the children use with ease all the complications of nouns, suffixes and prefixes, and verbs. All this happens at the end of the second year for every child. So we must be heartened by this action of the child and wait. (And at the sluggish epochs in history we may hope for the same; perhaps humanity is not so stupid as it appears, perhaps wonderful things will happen which will be explosions of internal life.) These explosive phenomena and eruptions of expression continue after the age of two years; the use of simple and compound sentences, the use of the verb in all its tenses and modes, even in the subjunctive, the use of subordinate and co-ordinate clauses appear in the same sudden explosive way. So is completed the expression of the language of the group (race, social level, etc.,) to which the child belongs. This treasure which has been prepared by the sub-conscious is handed over to the consciousness, and the child, in full possession of this new power, talks, and talks, and talks, till the adults say: "For goodness' sake can't you stop talking!"

After this great landmark at two and a half years, which seems to indicate a border-line of intelligence when man is formed, language still continues to develop, without explosions, yet with great vivacity and spontaneity. This second period lasts from two and a half to four and a half or five years. This is the period when the child takes in a great number of words, and perfects the rendering of sentences. Certainly if the child is in an environment of a few words or of 'slang,' he will use those words only, but if he lives in an environment of cultured speech and rich vocabulary, the child will fix it all. The environment is very important, yet in any case an enrichment of vocabulary will come about. Great interest is being taken in this fact. In Belgium scientific observers discovered that the child of only two and a half years knew two hundred words, but by the time of five years he knew and used thousands of words, and all this happens without a teacher; it is a spontaneous acquisition. After he has learnt all this, we allow the child to come to school and say: "I will teach you the alphabet!"

We must keep clearly in mind this double path that has been followed: that of the sub-conscious activity which prepares the language, and then that of the consciousness gradually coming to life and taking from the sub-conscious what it has to give. And what have we at the end? MAN the child of five who can speak his language well, knows and uses all the rules. He does not realize all the sub-conscious work, but in reality he is MAN who has created language. The child has created it for himself. If the child did not have these powers and did not spontaneously acquire language, there would have been no work possible in the world of men and no civilization. We see, therefore, how important is MAN in this period of his life: he constructs all. If it were not for him, civilization would not exist, for he alone constructs its foundation. So we should give him the help he needs and not leave him to wander alone.

The Call of Language

What I want to illustrate is a fact that will arouse little sympathy, I am afraid, because we human adults think we are above mechanisms and live in the abstract. How interesting however are these wonderful mechanisms. Mechanisms are basic things, they are material facts. Material things are not only flesh and blood, but also mechanisms. All know that in the mechanism of the nervous system there are the sense-organs, the nerves and nerve-centers, and the motor organs. The fact that there is a mechanism concerning language goes somewhat beyond such material facts. It was towards the end of the last century that the brain-centers which deal with language were discovered. There are in the cortex of the brain two special centers dealing with language: one is the center for heard language, auditory receptive speech, and one the center for the production of language, that is of spoken, motor speech. If we consider the question from the physiological point of view, there are also two organic centers: one for hearing the language (the ear) and one for speaking the language (the mouth, throat and nose, etc.), and these two centers develop separately, both psychically and physiologically. The receptive or hearing center is in relation with that mysterious side of the psyche in which language is developed in the deepest part of the sub-conscious, and the activity of the motor center is manifested when we speak.

It is evident that this second part, which deals with the movements necessary for the emission of language, is slower to develop, and is manifested after the other. Why? Because it is the sounds heard by the child that provoke those delicate movements which produce sound. This is very logical, because if humanity does not have a pre-established language (which it does not, considering that it creates its own), then it is necessary that the child first hears the sounds of his group's created language before he can reproduce them. Therefore the movement for reproducing sounds must be based on a sub-stratum of impressions on the psyche, on those sounds, because it is on the sounds which have been felt (impressed on the psyche) that movement depends.

This is easy and logical to understand, but it has not come because of logic, but because of a mechanism in nature. And what logic is there in nature? In nature one first notices facts and after seeing them, one says: "How logical they are!" and then, "There must be a directing intelligence behind the facts," The mysterious intelligence which acts in the creation of things is much more visible here in the psychic phenomena than it is in flowers even t with all their beautiful colors and shapes.

It is clear that at birth, these two activities of the heard and the spoken language do not exist. What does exist then? Nothing exists, yet at the same time everything is there. What exists are these two centers, centers free of all sound and of all heredity yet capable of taking in language, and of elaborating the movements necessary for its emission. These two points are part of the mechanism for developing language in its totality. Going more deeply into the matter we see that both a sensibility and an ability exist which are centralized. It is easy to see also that the elaboration of language begins after birth, since it depends on the hearing of language and before birth the child cannot hear anything. Activity must come afterwards. It is marvelous that all is prepared so that, when the child is born, it can start on its work.

Now let us study the organs as well as the mechanism. Certainly the creation of this mechanism is marvelous, but all creation is marvelous. Is it not marvelous to think of the creation of the ear (the organ of heard language) before the child is born? There, in that mysterious environment, this very delicate and complicated instrument has developed spontaneously. How marvelously is it constructed, as if some musical genius had built it up. A musician, yes, because the central part of the ear is a sort of harp, with the possibility of vibrating with different sounds according to the length of the 4 strings. The harp in our ear has sixty-four strings all placed in gradation and as the size of the ear is so small they have been arranged in the form of a snail's shell. What intelligence! Respecting the limits of space, yet building up all that is necessary for musical sounds. And who is going to play on these strings? For if no one plays on it, the harp may remain silent against the wall for years. We see a drum in front of the harp, and when something touches that drum, one or more of the harp strings vibrate; so the drum plays the harp and we hear the music of speech. Not all the sounds of the universe are taken in by the ear, because there are only sixty-four strings, but quite a complex music can be played on it. By means of it a language, with all its delicate and fine complications, can be transmitted. And if this complicated instrument has created itself in the mysterious pre-natal life, why should it be that after birth something else is created, i.e., the language that the child finds in his environment and must create for himself? We shall see.

For the moment let us look at nature; how marvelous she is, and how quick! Even if the child is born at seven months, all is complete and ready. Nature is never late! How does this instrument transmit the sounds it receives through the nervous fibers to the brain, where the special centers are located to collect these special sounds? That is also mysterious, but these are facts of nature. The curious thing is that psychologists, who have studied new-born children, say that the sense most sluggish to develop is that of hearing. They say it even seems that the child is deaf. All sorts of noises are made round the child and there is no reaction. This is because these centers are centers for language, for words, and it seems as though this powerful mechanism responds and acts only in relation to these special sounds the spoken word so that thus, in time, will be produced the mechanism of movement, which will reproduce those same sounds.

If this special isolation of the centers were not provided for, imagine what would happen to man? If the centers were free to take anything, then the child who was born on a farm would be impressed only by the sounds of the farm, and would say: "Moo, Moo" and grunt and cackle. The child born near a station would only make the sounds of the whistling and puffing trains. It is because nature has built and has isolated these centers specially for language that man can speak. There have been cases of wolf-children, children who, for one reason or another, have been abandoned in the jungle, and by some wonderful means have managed to live. These children, although they have lived in the midst of all kinds of bird- and animal-sounds, those of water and of falling leaves, have nevertheless remained entirely dumb. They produced no sound whatever, because they did not hear the sounds of human speech, which alone provoke the mechanism of spoken language. All this I relate to show that there is a special mechanism for language. This distinguishes humanity, it possesses this mechanism; not to possess language, but to possess this mechanism for creating its own language characterizes humanity. Words are the result of a sort of elaboration performed by the child, but the child himself is not a mechanism, far from it.

Let us imagine the ego in this mysterious period, just after birth, as a sleeping self. This sleeping ego suddenly wakes up and hears a delightful music. If this mysterious ego could talk, it would say: "I have entered the world, and they have welcomed me with music, a music, so divine, so soul-penetrating, that my whole being, my very fibers have begun to vibrate to it. No other sound reached me, because this reached my soul and I heard no other sound but this divine call!" And if we remember the great propulsive powers which create and conserve life, we can see how this music produces a thing that remains everlasting. What takes place in the mneme of the newborn child now, remains for ever. Every group of humanity loves music, creates its own music and its own language. Each group responds to its music with movements of the body and this music attaches itself to words, but those words have no sense in themselves, it is we who give the sense. In India there are many languages, but music unites all. The impressions on the new-born child have remained. There are no animals that make music and dance, but all humanity does it wherever it is.

These sounds of language then are fixed in the sub-conscious. What goes on inside we cannot see, but the outer manifestations give us a guide. Sounds are fixed and this is an integral part of the mother tongue. We might call it an alphabet. Then syllables come, then words, just spoken as a child will read sometimes from a primer, without knowing what it all means. But how intelligently the child works! Inside the child himself is a little teacher, like one of the old-fashioned teachers who make the child recite the alphabet, then syllables and finally words. Only the human teacher does it at the wrong time when the child already possesses his language. The teacher inside the child does things at the right time, so the baby fixes sounds, then syllables. It is a gradual construction as logical as the language. Afterwards words come and then we enter the field of grammar. Names of things (nouns) come first. That is why it is so illuminating to follow the teachings of nature, because nature is a teacher, and it teaches the child the most arid part of language. It is a real school with methods. It teaches nouns and adjectives, conjunctions and adverbs, verbs in the infinitive, then the conjugation of verbs, the declensions of nouns, then prefixes and suffixes and all the exceptions. Then there is the examination; he shows he can use them. We then see what a good teacher there has been and what a diligent pupil, because he uses them all quite correctly in the examination. Isn't he clever? One should applaud him, but no one takes any notice of him. Much later when he is at the school we adults have chosen for him, he is given a medal and we say "What a clever teacher he has."

But it is the small child who is really a living miracle! This is what the teacher should see in the child: a pupil who has learnt in such a fashion that the teacher herself could not learn better. In two years he has learnt everything! This is a deep mysterious fact. Let us then follow the manifestations the child gives in these two years, because thus it will be easier to follow what the child has done. On examining these manifestations, we see a gradual and ever-awakening consciousness and then, suddenly, this consciousness becomes predominant and wishes to master all. At four months (some say earlier, and I am inclined to agree with them) the child perceives that this mysterious music that surrounds him and touches him so deeply, comes from the human mouth. It is the mouth (the lips that move) which produces it. This is seldom noticed, but if we watch a baby we see with what intensity he watches the lips. Consciousness is already seen taking a hand in the matter, for consciousness takes a propulsive part in the work. Certainly, movement has been unconsciously prepared, all the exact co-ordinations of minute fibers have not been achieved consciously, but consciousness gives interest, enlivens and makes a series of keen, alert researches.

After two months of this observation of the mouth, the child produces his own sounds (at six months of age). All of a sudden, this baby, who has been unable to say anything except an occasional interjectional noise, one morning wakes up (before you) and you hear him saying: "Ba-ba-ba," "Ma-ma-ma," etc. It is he who invented 'Papa' and 'Mama,' He now goes on for so long a time with these syllables only that we say he cannot do any more. After a great effort he has reached this. Let us remember, it is the effort of the ego who has made a discovery and is conscious of his powers; a little man who is no longer a mechanism, but an individual using mechanisms. We arrive at the end of the first year of life, but before that, at ten months, the child has made another discovery: that this language from the mouth of people has a purpose. It is not merely music. When we say: "Dear little Baby, how sweet you are!," he realizes: "this is meant for me" and so he begins to realize there is some purpose in these sounds addressed to him. Two things therefore have happened by the end of the first year: in the depths of the unconscious he has understood: on the heights of consciousness he has created language, though at the moment it is only babbling, just repeating sounds and combinations of sounds.

At one year of age the child says his first intentional words. He babbles just the same, but it is intentional, and intention means conscious intelligence. What has happened within? Having studied him we know that he has much more within him than is shown by these unobtrusive manifestations. More and more the child has realized that language refers to the environment round him and he goes on to the conscious mastery of it. Here a great struggle arises within the child, a struggle of consciousness against mechanism. It is the first struggle of man, it is the first war between the parts! To illustrate this I can use my own experience. I know many things, I want to express them to an English-speaking audience, but I do not have the language. I only know a little English and my words would be a useless babbling. I know that my audience is intelligent and we could exchange ideas, but, alas, I only babble. This epoch when the intelligence has many ideas and knows people could understand them, but cannot express these ideas through lack of language is a dramatic epoch in the life of the child. It gives the first disappointments of life. If I had no translator, what could I do? What can the child do? He goes to school in his subconscious, and his desire spurs him to learn. It is the conscious impulse to be able to express himself that makes this hurried acquisition of language possible. Imagine his attention to language at this time!

A being who is so desirous of expressing himself, needs to go to a teacher to give him the words clearly. Are we any use as such teachers? No; we don't help him at all; we merely repeat to him his own babbling. If he did not have this inner teacher, he would learn nothing at all. It is this inner teacher who makes him go to adult people who are talking to each other, not to him. The impulse forces him to take the language with exactness, but we do not give it. Yet after one year of age he could indeed go to school; to one of our schools where intelligent people talk to him intelligently. Some people have understood this difficulty of the child between one and two years, and the importance of giving to the child the opportunity of learning exactly. Just a few days before I wrote this, I received a communication from Ceylon in which someone wrote: "How glad we are that there are now schools in our country for our small child!" They have understood the need there. So besides those who say: "What a pity we have no University!" There are also those who say: "How glad we are to have these schools for small children!" We must realize that since the child has grammatical knowledge we can talk to him grammatically and help him with the analysis of sentences. The new teachers of children between the ages of one and two years should know the development of language. Mothers must know it, as it is important, and teachers should know it in a scientific fashion. Then the child need not go about to find people talking to others, not to himself, in order to receive the aid he needs. We become the servants of nature that creates, and of nature that teaches, and a whole syllabus and method is ready for us.

What can I do with my babbling if I want to tell something that is very important? I may not have much self-control, I may become agitated, enraged, and begin to cry. That is what happens to the child of one or two years. He wants to show by one word what he wants us to know, but he cannot and hence tantrums. Then people say: "See man's innate perversity coming out!" (What! in a man of one year!) The origin of war is there in this child of one year, who gets angry and violent for no reason at all, as we think. We say: "We care for him, we dress him, we do things for him, yet he makes all these naughty scenes," Poor little man who is working towards independence! To be so misunderstood! And yet this poor being who has no language and whose only expression is one of rage, has yet the power of making his own language. The rage is merely an expression that comes after the obstructed effort to try to make words, and he does make some sort of words.

There is another period at about one and a half years when the child has recognized another fact; namely, that each object has a name. This is marvelous because it means that among all the words he has heard, he has been able to pick out nouns, especially concrete ones. There was a world of objects, now there are words for these objects. Unfortunately, with nouns alone one cannot express everything, so he has to use one word to express a whole idea. Psychologists therefore give special attention to these words that are meant to express sentences, and they call them fusive words or 'one-word sentences.' Let us suppose porridge is eaten with milk, the child then may call out: "Ma pa" meaning: "Mother I am hungry, I want some porridge," He is expressing one whole sentence in a word. Another feature of this fusive speech, this forced language of the child, is that there are alterations in the words themselves; there are often abbreviations. A Spanish baby will use 'to' instead of 'paletot' which means 'overcoat'; and 'palda' for 'espalda' which means 'shoulder' This is a modification, an abbreviation of the words We use, and sometimes they are so different that we might say that the child uses a foreign language. There is a 'child-language,' but very few take the trouble to study it. Teachers of children of this age, should study this in order to help the child and bring calm to his tormented soul.

These two child-words 'to' and 'palda' were the manifestation of a mental conflict in a child, and the child was so enraged and agitated that many people did not know what to do with it. The mother of the child was carrying her coat over her arm and the child was screaming, screaming. At last, at my suggestion, the mother put on her coat and immediately the screaming ceased, the child was calm and crowed happily: "To palda," meaning to say: "That is right; a coat is meant to be worn over the shoulders." So you see another fact, that this mysterious language of the child can reveal the psychology of the child at this age, his urge and need for order and his distress at disorder. A coat was not meant to be carried carelessly over the arm; it was the wrong place for it, and the disorder was more than the child could bear.

I have another instance, an incident that reveals that a child of one and a half years can understand a whole conversation and the sense of it. Some five people were discussing the merits and demerits of a child's story-book. They had been discussing for some time, and the conversation ended with the remark: "It all ends happily." Immediately the little one, who was in the room, began to shout: "Lola, lola!" The people thought it wanted its nurse and was calling her by her name. But no! It became more agitated and cried in distress and rage, not yet self-controlled, and then at last it managed to get hold of the book and turning to the back cover pointed to the picture of the child about whom the story was written, and said again: "Lola, lola!" The adults had taken the end of the printed story as the end of the book, but for the child the last picture, which was on the back cover, was the end, and in that picture the child was crying: "how could they say it ended happily?" It had followed the whole conversation, knew it was about that book, and had understood what was said and that a mistake had been made by these adults. Its understanding was complete and detailed, but its speech was not sufficient. It could not even pronounce the correct word for 'cries' which is 'llora' in Spanish, so it said 'lola.' The one word 'lola,' was used to tell these adults: "You are wrong; it does not end happily: he cries."

This illustrates why I say that it is necessary to have a special 'school' for children of the age of one and one and a half years. Mothers, and society in general, must take special care that the children have frequent experiences of the best language. Let the child come with us when we visit our friends and also when we go to meetings, especially where people speak with emphasis and clear enunciation.

Obstacles and Their Consequences

I now wish to deal with certain inner sensitivities, so that we may understand the hidden tendencies of the child. We might compare this to a sort of psychoanalysis of the invisible mind of the child. In Fig. 9. I represent by symbols the language of the child, and that may clarify the idea.

For the symbolic representation of the nouns (names of things) that children use, I have used a black triangle; for the verbs, a red circle; and different symbols for other parts of speech. These symbols are shown in Fig. 10. So if we say that the child uses two to three hundred words at a certain age, I represent this by symbols in order to give a visual impression of it. It is then sufficient to have eyes to see the development of language and it does not matter whether we speak English, Gujarati, Tamil, Italian or Spanish, because the symbols for the parts of speech are the same.

All the nebulous patches at the left hand side of the diagram represent the efforts of the child to speak, his first exclamations, interjections, etc. Then we see two sounds come together and syllables are formed, and then three sounds together and the first words are spoken. A little further to the right of the diagram, we see a grouping of words, some nouns that children use, then two word phrases (a sentence with diffused meaning), just a few words to mean quite a lot. Then there is a great explosion into words. This is an exact representation of the actual number of words that psychologists have found children to use. At one side of this picture of the explosion we see a patch of words which are nearly all nouns, then next to that, different parts of speech in a confused combination, but soon after two years the next stage is represented, i.e., words in order. There is an explosion of sentences. So the first explosion is of words and the second explosion is of thoughts.

There must be a preparation for this. It is hidden, a secret, but though it is secret it is not a hypothesis, because the results indicate efforts. One can realize the great efforts the child has had to make in order to express his thoughts. As adults do not always understand what the child means, at this stage there is the rage and agitation I mentioned before. This agitation forms an integral part of the life of children. All the efforts which the child will carry out, if not crowned with success, will produce agitation. It is a known fact that the deaf and dumb are often quarrelsome. The explanation lies in their inability to express their thoughts. There is an inner wealth and richness which tries to find expression; it does so in the ordinary child, but amidst great difficulties.

There is a period of difficulties which we must take into consideration; difficulties caused by the environment and by the child's own limitations. This is the second difficult period of adaptation, the first was that of birth when the child was suddenly called upon to function for himself, whilst his mother had hitherto done it for him. We saw then, that unless great care and understanding were shown, birth terror affected the child and caused regressions. Certain children are stronger than others, certain others have a more favorable environment, and these go straight to independence, the path of normal development, without regressions. A parallel situation is seen at this period. The conquest of language is a laborious conquest towards a greater independence, and it ends in the freedom of language, but there are parallel dangers of regression too.

We must also remember another characteristic of this creative period, viz., every impression and the result of it has a tendency to remain permanently registered. This is true for the sounds and for grammar. Children taking in knowledge now retain it for the rest of their life; so also if there are obstacles at this period their effect will remain permanently. This is the characteristic of every epoch of creation. A struggle, fright or other obstacles, may produce effects that remain for the rest of life, since the reactions to those obstacles are absorbed like everything else in development. (In the same way if there is a spot of light on the photographic film we mentioned above, all the prints of that film will show that spot.) In this epoch therefore we have not only a development of the character, but also a development of certain deviated psychic characteristics which children will manifest as they grow older. Knowledge of the mother-tongue and the faculty of walking are acquired at this epoch of the child's life, during the creative period which goes beyond the age of two and a half years, but is then less strong. The acquisition of these two faculties takes place now, but their growth and development continue afterwards. So also it is with any defects and obstacles acquired now; they remain, and grow; and so many defects that adult people present are attributed to this distant epoch of their life.

The difficulties that mar normal development are included in the term repression, (this term is particularly used in psycho-analysis, but also in psychology generally). These repressions, now known to the general public, refer to this age in childhood. Examples of these repressions may be given in connection with language itself, though there are many more having a relationship with other human activities. The mass of words that explodes must have freedom of emission. Also when the explosion of sentences occurs and a child gives regular form to his thoughts there must be freedom of expression. Great emphasis is laid on freedom of expression, because it is not only connected with the immediate present of the developing mechanism, but also with the future life of the individual. There have been certain cases where, at the age when the explosion should take place, nothing occurred; at more than three or three and a half years the child still used only the few words of a much earlier age and appeared as a dumb child, although his organs of speech were perfectly normal. This is called 'psychic mutism' and it has a purely psychological cause, it is a psychic illness. This is the epoch of the origin of psychic illnesses and psycho-analysis (which is really a branch of medicine) studies them. Sometimes psychic mutism disappears suddenly like a miracle; a child speaks suddenly, well and completely, with a full grasp of grammar, as he is already prepared inwardly, only the expression had been hindered by some obstacle. We have had children in our schools of three and four years of age who had never spoken and then suddenly spoke. They had never even spoken the words of the two-year old, they were absolutely dumb and then suddenly they spoke. By allowing them free activity and a stimulating environment, they suddenly manifested this power. Why does this happen? Because either a great shock or persistent opposition has impeded the child hitherto from giving forth the wealth of his language.

There are adult people also who find difficulty in speaking; they have to make a great effort and they look as if they were not sure what to say, there is a hesitation. There are different reasons for this hesitation:

(a) they do not have the courage to speak,

(b) they do not have the courage to pronounce
the words,

(c) they have a difficulty in using sentences,

(d) they speak more slowly than a normal person
and say "er, um, ah" etc.

They find a difficulty in themselves which is fatal and remains throughout life; it represents a state of permanent inferiority in the person.

There are also psychic impediments which prevent an adult speaker from articulating words clearly; cases of stuttering and stammering. This is a defect that has had birth during the period when the mechanisms themselves were being organized. So there are different epochs of acquisition and corresponding regressions may occur at those epochs:

First period: Mechanism of words is acquired, Corresponding regression stammering Second period: Mechanism of sentence (expression of thought) is acquired, Corresponding regression hesitation in the formulation of thoughts.

These regressions are related to the sensitivity of the child; as he is sensitive to receive, in order to produce, so also he is sensitive to obstacles that are too strong for him. The results of this thwarted sensitivity then remain as a defect for the rest of life. It is because this sensitivity of the child is greater than anything we can imagine that these things take place.

Let us then study these obstacles. It is an adult who is responsible for these anomalies, an adult who acts too violently in his dealings with the child. Nonviolence must be exaggerated, because what may not be violence for the adult is often violence for the child. We do not realize when we are violent to children, so we must study ourselves. The preparation for education is a study of oneself; and the preparation of a teacher who is to help life is more than a mere intellectual preparation, it is a preparation of character, a spiritual preparation.

The sensitivity of the child presents various aspects, but some things are common to all. One is a sensitivity to shocks at this period. Another common feature is sensitivity to the calm but cold, determined effort of the adult to prevent outer manifestations of children: "You mustn't do this!" "It is not done," Those who have the good fortune (!) to have what is called a well-trained nurse for their children should especially beware of this tendency in her; she very often has it. That is why this type of impediment is so frequent among aristocrats, they do not lack physical courage, but when they speak they stutter and stammer. I wish to stress this question of violence. It must be understood from the child's point of view, and we must be very delicate in our behavior. It has happened to me to be violent to children and I have given an example in one of my books. [Cf. The Secret of Childhood] A child put his pair of outdoor shoes on the nice silk coverlet of his bed. I removed them very determinedly, put them on the floor and brushed the coverlet vigorously with my hand, to demonstrate that it was not the place for shoes. For two or three months after that, whenever the child saw a pair of shoes, he changed their position and then looked round for some silk coverlet or cushion to clean. The answer of the child to my too vigorous (violent) lesson, was not a crude, rebellious spirit. He did not say: "Do not talk, I will put my shoes where I like!," but an abnormal development. The child is so often non-violent in his reactions. I wish he were not, rebellion would be better than taking the faulty path to anomalies. The child with tantrums has found out how to defend himself and may arrive at normal development, but when a child responds by changing his character, this affects his whole life. Yet people take no notice of this, they only worry about tantrums!

There is another fact: certain senseless fears and 'nervous' habits which we find in adults can be traced to violence to the child's sensitivity. Some of; the senseless fears concern animals, cats and hens; some concern remaining in a room with the doors closed, etc. No reasoning, no persuasion can help the victims of these fears. I once had a colleague, a Professor of Pedagogy in a University of Italy. She was forty-five years old and she came to me one day and said: "You are a doctor and will understand. Every time I see a hen I am terribly frightened, I have to make an effort not to shriek. I tell nobody; they would laugh at me." Perhaps, as a tiny girl of two and a half years, she went to fondle a fluffy baby-chick and met the sudden agitated frenzy of the watchful mother-hen. The feathered fury of that hen gave her a shock which remained. These kinds of unreasonable fears are included under the name phobias; some are so common that they have special names such as claustrophobia (the fear of closed doors, of a confined space). Many more examples could be given if we entered the field of medicine. I mention them to illustrate the mental form of children of this age.

Our action is not reflected merely in a sweet or naughty child, but in the adult who will result from this child. Therefore, I repeat, this epoch of the child's life is very important for the rest of his life and for humanity; it must be studied. This study is very important, but it hardly exists as yet. It is necessary to embark on this path, which is a path of discovery. It is necessary to try and penetrate into the mind of the child, as the psychoanalyst penetrates into the sub-conscious of the adult. It is difficult because we often do not understand their language, or if we do, we don't understand the meaning they give to the words they use. Sometimes it is necessary also to know the rest of the life of the child; it is a sort of research work or detective work, but a research work of great utility because through it we bring peace to this difficult period. We need a translator, an interpreter of the child and his language, and this interpretation will allow us to understand the child's state of mind. I myself have worked in this sense and tried to become the interpreter of the child and it has been curious to see how the children run to this interpreter, because they realize there is someone who can help them. This eagerness of the child is something entirely different from the affection of the child who is petted or caressed. The interpreter is to the child a great hope, someone who will open to him the path of discovery when the world had already closed its doors. This helper is taken into the closest relationship, a relationship that is more than affection because help is given, not merely consolation.

In a house where I was living and working I used to rise early in the morning, before the rest of the family, and work. One day a little child of the family, not more than one and a half years old, came in at this early hour. I thought he had got up because he was hungry and wanted food, so I said: "What would you like?" He said: "I want worms," I was startled and said: "Worms? Worms?" The child realized I did not understand, but was trying to do so, so he gave me some more help and added: "Egg." I thought: "This can't be a breakfast that he wants; what does he want?" Then he added another word: "Nena, egg, worms," Light came to my mind. I remembered a fact (and that is why I say you must know something of the circumstances of the child's life). The previous day his little sister, Nena, was filling up the oval inset, drawing with colored pencils. This little one had wanted the pencils and the sister had defended herself and told him to go away. Now, (see the mind of the child), he did not oppose his sister, but waited for his chance, and with what patience and determination. I gave him the pencil and the inset. There was a great light on the face of the child, but he could not make the 'egg' so I had to make it for him. Then after I had made the oval, he filled it up with wavy lines. His sister had used the usual straight lines, but he thought he knew something better, so he made wavy lines, 'worms,' He had waited till he knew everyone was asleep but his interpreter, then he came to her for he felt she would help him. It is not tantrums, violent reactions, but patience that is the real characteristic of this age in all children; patience to wait for their opportunity. Violent reactions or tantrums express a state of exasperation, when he cannot attain his expression.

This interpreter of words can give light in order to penetrate into the mind of the child. From the example given one can see that the little child tries to carry out the activities followed by older children. If one introduces the child of three years to an activity, the child of one and a half also wants to do it. Probably he will be impeded and stopped from doing it, but he will try, A small child in our house wanted to copy his sister of three, who was learning her first steps in dancing. The teacher had wanted to know how to teach so young a child to dance ballet, etc. We said: "Never mind, you try it; what does it matter whether she learns or not; you will receive your salary." Knowing that we were working to help the child, she agreed to try. Immediately the one and a half year old, said: "Me, too!" The teacher said: "Absolutely impossible," and when we said: "Try it," she said it was derogatory to her dignity as a teacher of ballet to teach a baby of one and a half years. We suggested she put her dignity in her pocket, so at last she came to the house, somewhat disgruntled, threw her hat on the sofa and began to play a march. The little one was immediately furious, and shrieked and would not move. The teacher said: "You see, you can't teach one so small," But the child was not distressed about the dancing; he was having a discussion with the hat, addressing it with fury. He did not use the name of the hat itself, nor that of the teacher; he just used two words which he repeated with concentrated fury: "Hat-rack! Hall!" meaning: "This hat must not be here on the sofa, but on the hat-rack in the hall!" He had forgotten the dance and the pleasures of life, he had his duty to perform of changing disorder into order before anything else. When the hat was on the hat-rack, his fury went and he was ready to dance. Till then the fundamental need for order erased everything else. So this study allows us to penetrate into the mind of the child to a depth where psychologists generally do not go. The patience of the child in my first example and the passion for order in the second make a picture which it is difficult for us to realize and understand. If we take these pictures, together with that which I mentioned above of the child who understood a whole conversation and disagreed with the final opinion of the happy ending to the story, we see that there is a whole mental life, a whole psychic picture usually hidden from us by our own blindness.

Every discovery of the mind of the child at this age must be made known, and not as knowledge to be gained for ourselves, as the knowledge of Sanskrit for instance, but in order to help the child to adapt himself to the environment around him. We must be a help to life all the time, even if it means we have to spend great energy as an interpreter. The task of the teacher of small children is very noble. It belongs to a science that will develop in the future, and will help mental development and the growth of character. Above all we must carry it out so that children may avoid those defects that make certain individuals inferior to others. We must remember, if nothing else, that we must realize:

1. That education in the first two years of life is important to the whole life.

2. That the child is endowed with great intelligence which we cannot see.

3. That he has an extreme sensitivity which may (under any violence) bring forth, not re-action only, but defects incorporated in his personality.

Movement and Total Development

It is necessary to consider movement from a new point of view. Because of some misunderstanding, movement is considered less noble than it is, especially the movement of the child. In education as a whole movement is sadly neglected and all importance is given to the brain. Only physical education which up till recently held a very inferior place considers movement, although disconnected from the intelligence.

Let us consider the organization of the nervous system in all its complexity. First of all we have the brain itself; then the senses which take the images which are to be passed to the brain and thirdly we have the nerves. But what is the aim of the nerves and where do they go? Their purpose is to give energy, movement to the muscles (the flesh). This complex organism, therefore, consists of three parts: (1) the brain (the center); (2) the senses and (3) the muscles. Movement is the conclusion and the purpose of the nervous system. Without movement we cannot speak of an individual at all. If we think of a great philosopher he speaks of his meditations or writes of them, and so must use his muscles. If he does nothing with his meditations, of what use are they? Without the muscles, the expression of his thoughts would not exist.

If we turn to animals, their behavior is only expressed through movement. Therefore, also if we wish to consider the behavior of man, we must take man's movements into consideration. The muscles are part of the nervous system.

The nervous system in all its parts puts man into relationship with his environment; that is why it is also called the System of Relation. It puts man into relationship with the inanimate and animate world and therefore with other individuals; without it there would be no relationship between an individual and his environment.

The other organized systems of the body are comparatively selfish in their aims, because they are exclusively at the service of the body of the individual and of nothing else. They merely allow one to live, or to vegetate as we say;

hence they are called the systems and organs of the vegetative life. So there is this difference:

The vegetative systems serve only to help the individual in growing and vegetating.

The nervous system serves to put the individual in relation with other individuals, it is a sort of Minister of Foreign Affairs.

The vegetative systems help man to enjoy the maximum comfort and purity of body and health; hence we go to places with cool air, good hotels, etc. If we consider the nervous system from a similar point of view, we shall make a mistake; even if we think it is only to give us the most beautiful impressions and purity of thought and continuous uplift to loftier levels. It is nice to be pure in this field also, but it is a mistake to lower the nervous system to the level of merely vegetative life. If this criterion of mere purity and uplift of the individual is upheld, the individual is led to spiritual selfishness. It is the greatest mistake one can make. The behavior of animals does not tend merely to be beautiful and graceful in movement; it has a purpose deeper than that. So has man a purpose which is not just to be purer and finer than others. Of course, man can and should be beautiful and take only the finest things on the loftiest levels, but if that is his only aim, his life would be useless. What would be the use of this mass of brain then, or of these muscles?

There is nothing in this world which does not form part of a universal economy; and if we have spiritual richness, aesthetic greatness, it is not for ourselves, it is part of the spiritual, universal economy and must be used for the universe. The spiritual powers are wealth, but not personal wealth; they must be put into circulation for the rest to enjoy; they must be expressed, made use of, and in this way complete the cycle of relationship. If I content myself to become pure so that I may go to heaven, I might as well die. I should have left aside the greatest part of my life and the greatest part of the aim of my life. If one should believe in reincarnation and say: "I shall have a better life next time if I live well now," this is selfish. We have reduced the spiritual to the vegetative level. We are always thinking of ourselves, of ourselves in eternity. We are egotists for eternity. The other point of view must be taken into consideration, not only in the practice of life, but also in education. There must be completeness of function. Nature has endowed us with functions; therefore it is necessary that they be exercised.

Let us make a comparison. If we have lungs, a stomach, a heart, it is necessary that these function in order to have health. Why not apply the same rule to the nervous system? If we have a brain, senses and organs of movement, they must function, and if we do not exercise every part we cannot even understand them with certainty. Even if we wish to uplift ourselves, make our brains finer for instance, we cannot do so unless we use all the parts. Perhaps movement is the last part that will complete the cycle. In other words, we can obtain spiritual uplift through action. This is the point of view from which to consider movement; it is part of the nervous system and cannot be discarded. The nervous system is one, a unity, though it has three parts. Being a unity, it must be exercised in its totality to become better.

One of the mistakes of modern times is to consider movement separately from the higher functions. People think that the muscles are merely there and have to be used in order to keep better bodily health. In order to keep fit or as recreation we play tennis. If we do that we can breathe more deeply. What an idea! Or we go for a walk to ensure better digestion and sleep, forsooth! This mistake is penetrating education. This is, physiologically speaking, as though a great prince had been made use of to serve a shepherd. This great prince the muscular system has become a handle to turn in order to stimulate the vegetative system. This is the great mistake. It leads to separation: physical life is put on one side and mental life on the other. The result is that, since the child must develop physically as well as mentally, we must include physical exercise, games, etc. What has mental life to do with physical pastimes? Nothing. Yet we cannot separate two things that nature has put together. If we consider physical life on one side and mental life on the other, we break the cycle of relation, and the actions of man remain separated from the brain. The motor actions of man are used to aid better eating and breathing, whereas the real purpose is that movement be the servant of the whole life and of the spiritual, universal economy of the world.

The motor actions of man must be co-ordinated to the center the brain and put in their right place; this is fundamental. Mind and activity are two parts of the same cycle and, moreover, movement is the expression of the superior part. Otherwise we make man a mass of muscles, but without a brain. Something is out of place as with a broken bone and the limb does not serve any more. Man then develops his vegetative life and the relation between the motor part and the brain is left out. There is a self-determination of the brain apart from movement and muscles. This is not independence; it is to break something that nature in her wisdom has put together. If mental development is spoken of, people say: "Movement? There is no need for movement; we are talking about mental growth!" When they think of mental improvement they imagine all are sitting down, moving nothing. But mental development must be connected with movement and is dependent on it. This is the new idea that must enter educational theory and practice.

Up to the present most educationists have considered movement and muscles as a help to breathing, improving the circulation, etc., or, if movement is indulged in, it is to acquire greater muscular strength. It remains a part of physical education only. What is the individual supposed to do with it?

Our new conception stresses the importance of movement as a help to the development of the brain, once it is placed in relation to the center. Mental development and even spiritual development can and must be helped by movement. Without movement there is no progress and no health (mentally speaking). This is a fundamental fact which must be taken into consideration. I might be asked to demonstrate these facts, but they are not ideas, nor even personal experiences. They are demonstrated whenever we observe nature, her facts, and the precision given to this observation conies from watching the development of the child. Watching him, one sees that he develops his mind by using his movements. The development of language, for instance, shows an improvement of understanding accompanied by an ever extending use of the muscles of production. Besides this and other examples the child, scientifically observed, shows that he develops his intelligence generally through movement. Observations made all over the world have shown that the child demonstrates that movement helps psychic development, that development expresses itself in its turn by further movement and action. So it is a cycle, because both psyche and movement belong to the same unity. The senses also help. Without opportunity for sensorial activity the child is less intelligent. That is why the examination of the development of the small child is of such great aid to the whole of education.

Now muscles (flesh), the activity of which is directed by the brain, are called voluntary muscles; that means that they are moved by the will of the individual. The will is one of the greatest expressions of the psyche. Without that energy psychic life does not exist. Therefore, since the voluntary muscles are the muscles depending on the will, they are a psychic organ. The muscles are the main part of the body. Take a mammal and take off its flesh, what is left? Skeleton, bones. What is their purpose? To support the muscles, so they also belong to this section. Take them away then. What is left? Very little. The main part which has been developed by nature has been taken away. And if we look at someone and say how beautiful he is, or the opposite, the form which we contemplate is given by muscles attached to the bones. All animals endowed with an inner skeleton owe their form to voluntary muscles and when we see a camel in proud disdain or a lady walking gracefully or a child playing, we see merely form given to each by its own flesh (muscles). These muscles are interesting to study in form and number. They are in great quantity. People who study medicine say that students must forget them seven times before they remember them and even then they forget! Some are delicate, some bulky, some short, some long, they have different functions. A curious fact is that if one muscle functions in one direction, there is always another functioning in the opposite direction, and the more vigorous and refined this play of opposite forces, the more refined the movement resulting therefrom. The exercise one takes to attain more harmonious movement is an exercise to put more harmony in the opposition. So what is important is not agreement, but opposition in agreement.

The child or person is not conscious of this opposition, but nevertheless it is the way movement takes place. In animals the perfection of movement is given by nature. The gracefulness of the tiger's pounce or the running up and down of the squirrel is due to a wealth of opposition put into play to attain that harmony, like a complicated piece of machinery working well, like a watch with wheels going in opposite directions; when the whole mechanism runs smoothly, we have the correct time. So the mechanism of movement is very complicated and more refined then one could imagine. In man this mechanism is not pre-established before birth and so it must be created, achieved through practical experiences on the environment. The number of muscles in man is so great that he can achieve any movement, so we do not speak of exercise of movement, but of co-ordination of movement. This co-ordination is not given, it has to be created and achieved by the psyche. In other words the child creates his own movements and, having done so, perfects them. The child has a creative part in this work and then achieves a development of what he has created through a series of exercises.

It is really marvelous that man's movements are not limited and fixed, but that he can control them. Some animals have a characteristic ability to climb or to run; these are not man's characteristic movements, but he can do both very well. Certain animals have a characteristic ability to burrow in the earth; it is not a characteristic of man, yet he can go deeper than any of them. So his characteristic is that he can do all movements and extend them further than any animal; he can make some of them his own. So we might say that his characteristic is universal versatility, but there is one condition: he must construct them himself. He must work and create by will, and repeat the exercises for coordination sub-consciously as to their purpose, but voluntarily as to his initiative. So he can conquer all. As a matter of fact, however, no individual conquers all his muscles, but all are there. Man is like very wealthy people, he is so wealthy that he can only use part of his wealth; he chooses which part. If a man is a professional gymnast, it is not that special muscular ability was given to him; nor is a dancer born with certain refined muscles for dancing; he or she develops them by will. Anyone, no matter what he wants to do, is endowed by nature with such a wealth of muscles that he can find among them what he needs, and his psyche can direct and create any development. Nothing is established, but everything is possible, provided proper direction is given by the individual psyche.

It is not in man to do the same standardized thing as in animals of the same species. Even if the same thing is done by some, it is done in a different manner. We all write, but each has his own handwriting. Each has his own path always.

We see in movement as it is developed the work of the individual, and the work of the individual is expressing his psychic life; it is the psychic life itself. It has at its disposal a great treasure of movements, so movement is developed in service of the central part, i.e. of the psychic life. If man does not develop all his muscles, even of those he does develop some are only for rough work. So man's psychic life is limited in as much as his muscles only develop for rough action, not for refined action. It is limited also by the type of work that is accessible or chosen. The psychic life of those who do no work is in great danger. We might say that though all muscles cannot be put in motion, it is dangerous for the psychic life to go below a certain number. If the number of muscles in use is not sufficient, then there is a weakness of the whole life. That is why gymnastics, games, etc., were introduced in education; too many muscles were being left aside.

The psychic life must use more muscles or else we also shall have to follow the double path of ordinary education alternating physical and mental activities. The purpose in using these muscles is not to learn certain things. Some forms of 'modern' education develop movement just because there is a desire to serve a certain direct purpose in social life; e.g. one child must write well because he is going to be a teacher and another is going to be coal heaver so he must shovel well. This narrow and direct training does not serve the purpose or aim of movement. Our purpose must be that man develop the co-ordination of movements necessary for his psychic life; to enrich the practical and executive side of psychic life. Otherwise the brain develops apart from realization through movement and cannot fulfil its directive function regarding movement and that brings only revolution and disaster in the world. Movement then works by itself, undirected by the psyche, and so brings destruction. As movement is so necessary to the human life of relations with the environment and other men, it is on this level that movement must be developed, in service of the whole. It is not work to be first in one's art or profession.

The principle and idea today are too much directed towards self-perfection, self-realization. If we understand the real aim of movement this self-centralization cannot exist; it must expand into the immensity of space. We must, in short, keep in mind what might be called the 'philosophy of movement,' Movement is what distinguishes life from inanimate things. Life, however, does not move in a haphazard fashion, it moves with a purpose and according to laws. In order to realize this fact let us just imagine what the world would be like if it were quiet, without movement. Imagine what it would be like if all the plants stopped living, if the movement within the plant ceased. There would be no more fruits, nor flowers. The percentage of poisonous gas in the air would increase and cause disaster. If all movement stopped, if the birds remained motionless on the trees, or if insects fluttered to the ground and remained still, if the wild beasts of prey did no longer move through the jungles, or the fish stopped swimming in the oceans, what a terrible world it would be!

Immobilization is impossible, the world would become a chaos if movement ceased or if living beings moved without purpose. Nature gives a useful purpose to each living being. Each individual has its own characteristic movements with its own fixed purpose. The creation of the world is a harmonious co-ordination of all these activities with a set purpose.

And imagine what a society of men would be like if it were without movement! The movement of humanity shows the intelligence of a personality. Think what would happen if all men stopped moving for even one week only. Everyone would die. Work and movement are one, the question of movement is a social question. It is not a question concerning individual gymnastics. If the whole society of men all over the world did nothing but performing some physical jerks, humanity would die in a short time. All its energies would be consumed for nothing.

Society is formed by a complexity of individuals, each of whom moves differently from the other, following his own individual purpose. The individual moves in order to carry out this purpose. The basis of society is formed by movement with a useful aim. When we speak about 'behavior,' the behavior of men and animals, we refer to their purposeful movements. This behavior is the center of their practical life. It is not confined to the practical life in a house, cleaning the rooms, washing clothes, etc. This is important of course, but everyone in the world must move with a larger purpose, everyone must work not for himself alone, but also for others. It is strange that man's work must also be work in the service of others. If this were not so, his work would have no more meaning than gymnastic exercise. All work is done for others as well. Dancing is perhaps one of the most individual movements, but even dancing would be pointless without an audience, without a social or transcendental aim. The dancers who perfect their movements with so much trouble and fatigue, dance for others. Tailors who spend their lives sewing, could not possibly wear all the clothes they make. Yet tailoring, like gymnastics, requires many trained movements.

If we have a vision of the cosmic plan in which every form of life in the world is based on purposeful movements, having their purpose not in themselves alone, we shall be able to understand and to direct the children's work better.

Intelligence and the Hand

The study of the mechanical development of movement is considered to be very important, because it is a complicated machine, each part of which is of great value. That is why the movement of small children has been studied with great attention and as nothing is hidden, but all is manifested outwardly, it can be very clearly followed.

In all animals the four limbs develop in movement together, but in man the one pair of limbs develops differently from the other pair. This clearly shows that their function is different. The function of the legs is quite different from the function of the arms. Another thing which stands out is that the development of walking and equilibrium is so fixed in all men that one might call it a biological fact. We might say that after birth man will walk and all men will do exactly the same thing with their feet, but we do not know what the individual man will do with his hands. We do not know what particular activity of the hands is possible or has been possible in the past; their function is not fixed. So the types of movement have a different meaning when considering hands or feet.

It is certain that the function of the feet is biological, yet it is connected with an inner development in the brain. At the same time only man walks on two limbs, all mammals walk on four. Once a man achieves the art of walking on two legs he continues to walk on two legs only and to keep the difficult state of erect equilibrium constantly. This equilibrium is difficult to attain, it is a real conquest. It demands that man put his whole foot on the ground, whereas most animals walk on tiptoe, as a small resting place is sufficient when using four legs. The foot used for walking can be studied from a physiological, biological and anatomical point of view; it has connections with all of them.

If the hand does not have this biological guide, because actions are not fixed, then with what is it connected? If not connected with biology and physiology, it must have a psychological connection. The hand then depends on the psyche for development, and not only on the psyche of an individual ego, but also on the psychic life of different epochs. We see that the development of the hand is connected with the development of the intelligence in man and r if we look at history, it is connected with the development of civilization. We might say that, when man thinks, he thinks and acts with his hands and almost as soon as man appeared on the earth, he left traces of work done by his hands. In great civilizations of past ages there are always samples of his handiwork. In India we can find work so fine that it is almost impossible to imitate it; and in Ancient Egypt there are also traces of very fine delicate work. If the civilization was of a less refined type, then the handiwork remaining is also of a rougher type.

The development of the hand therefore goes side by side with the development of the intelligence. Certainly the refined type of handiwork needed the attention and guidance of the intelligence to carry it out. In the Middle Ages in Europe there was an epoch of great intellectual awakening and at the same time they covered with beautiful illuminations the writing that conveyed the new thoughts. Even the life of the spirit, which seems so far from the earth and the things of the earth, was nevertheless affected, for we see the result in the temples where the people worshiped, and this is to be found wherever there is spiritual life.

St. Francis of Assisi whose spirit was perhaps the simplest and purest once said: "You see these mountains; these are our temples and from these we must seek inspiration." Yet when once asked to build a church he and his spiritual brethren being poor used the rough stones that were available. They all carried the stones to build the chapel and why? Because if there is a free spirit it needs to be materialized in some kind of work and the hands must come into use. Everywhere are the traces of the hand of man, and in these traces we can read the spirit of man and the thought of his time.

If we talk of Christianity, it may be difficult to make its influence demonstrable, but when we see countries covered with churches, with works of art and beautiful cloth of all kinds, with hospitals and educational institutions, we can realize its spiritual and cultural effect.

And if we look into the dim past, of which not even bones are left, what gives us knowledge of the peoples and their times? Their works of art. When we look into these prehistoric times, we see there the rougher sort of civilization based on strength: the statues and works of art are formed from huge masses of stones and we wonder how they got there. Elsewhere we see finer works of art and we say: "Here was a more refined race." How do we know? No man of them is left, but the works of man tell us. So that we can see that the hand has followed the intelligence, spirit and emotions, and touching all these, has left us the traces of man. Even if we do not take the psychological point of view, we still see that all changes in man's environment have been made by the hand of man. Really, it would se$m that the purpose of having intelligence was almost to have hands, because if the intelligence of man had merely built up his spoken language in order to communicate with others, nothing would have been left behind when that race of men died out. They would have stated their wisdom by mere breath. It is because the hands have accompanied the intelligence that civilization has been built up, therefore we can well say that the h and is the organ of that immense treasure given to man.

The hands therefore are connected with psychic life. In fact those who study the hand show that there is an intuition that the history of man is printed in the hand, that it is a psychic organ. Therefore the study of the psychic development of the child must be closely linked up with the study of the development of the hand. The child has clearly shown that his development is connected with the hand which reveals this psychic urge. We can express it this way: the intelligence of the child will reach a certain level without the use of the hand; with the hands it reaches a still higher level, and the child who has used his hands has a stronger character. So we see that even the development of character, which seems so completely within the psychic field, remains rudimentary, if it has no opportunity of practicing on the environment (which means through the hand). The child has shown us most clearly that if (through circumstances in the environment) he cannot use his hands, his character remains on a very low level, incapable of obedience, of initiative, lazy and sad, whereas the child who has been able to work with his hands shows also a development and firmness of character. This reminds us of an interesting point in the Egyptian civilization when work with the hand was present everywhere, in the fields of art, of construction, of religion; if we read the inscriptions on the burial places of that time the highest praise accorded to any man was that he was a person of character. The development of character was important to them and they were people of great works carried out by the hand. This is one more instance of the fact that the movement of the hand follows through history the development of character and civilization. It shows how the hand is connected with the individuality. And if we examine how all these people walked, we always find of course that they walked on two legs, erect and with equilibrium. Probably they danced and ran a little differently, but they always used two legs for ordinary locomotion.

It is therefore clear that the development of movement is twofold; one part is biological and the other, though using the muscles, is nevertheless connected with the inner life. If we study the child we consequently study two developments: the development of the hand apart from that of equilibrium and walking. It is when the child wants to transport heavy things that his legs must help him, otherwise there is no connection. These feet that are able to walk and transport him to various parts of the earth, take him there so that he can work with his hands, A man walks and walks and gradually covers the face of the earth 9 and through this invasion by walking he lives and dies, but he leaves behind him the trace of his passage in the work of his hands.

When we studied language we saw that speech is connected especially with hearing, whereas in the development of movement we see this is connected with sight; first of all because we must have eyes to see where to put our feet, and when we work with our hands we must see what we do. These are the two senses specially connected with development: hearing and sight. In the development of children first of all there is observation of the environment, because he must know the environment in which he has to move. This observation is carried out before he can move and then he orients himself in it; so the orientation in the environment and movement are both connected with psychic development. That is why the new-born babe is immobile at first, when he moves he follows the guide of his psyche.

The first development in movement is that of grasping or prehension; as soon as the hand grasps something the consciousness is called to this hand which has been able to do so. Prehension is unconscious at first and then conscious. The hand calls for the attention of consciousness whereas the feet do nothing of the sort. When the consciousness is called to this fact, prehension is developed, so that what was instinctive prehension becomes intentional prehension, and it is at six months that the child shows this development. At ten months observation of the environment has awakened the interest of the child and he wants to catch hold of it; intentional prehension is accompanied by desire and mere prehension ceases. After this begins the exercise of the hand, it begins to change the places of objects' There is a vision of the environment, there is a desire and the hand begins to do something in the environment. Before one year of age the child carries out many actions with his hand that are ever so many types of work. He opens and closes doors, drawers, puts stoppers in bottles, puts objects on one side and then puts them back, etc. it is through these exercises that the child acquires ability.

What has happened to the other pair of limbs? Neither intelligence nor consciousness has been called forth. There is something anatomical happening however: the rapid development of the cerebellum, the director of equilibrium. It is as though a bell rang and called an inert body to get up and attain equilibrium. The environment has nothing to do with it; the cerebellum orders it and the child, with effort and help, sits up and then gets up by itself. Psychologists say, man gets up in four periods. Then the baby turns on his tummy and walks on four limbs, and if, during this time when he begins crawling, you give him two fingers, he will make the feet go one in front of the other, but on his toes. Before this, even with the help of two fingers, he would not walk, the cerebellum and not the environment is responsible.

When at last he stands by himself, he rests his whole foot on the ground; he has attained the normal erect position of man and can walk if he holds on to something (mother's skirt). After a little while he can walk alone. The tendency now is to say: "Goodbye; I have my two legs, and off I go!" Another stage of independence is attained, for the acquisition of independence is the beginning of doing things by oneself. The philosophy of these steps of development tells us that independence and development of man is attained by effort. To be able to do without other people's help is independence, it is not comfort. If independence is there the child progresses very rapidly; if it is not there the progress is very slow. So if we keep this picture in mind we know the way of dealing with the child, and it is a useful guide. We are taught not to help him, whereas we always fall on him to help him. The child who is capable of walking alone must walk by himself, because all development is strengthened by exercise and all acquisition confirmed by exercise. When a child of even three years is carried, as I have often seen, his development is not helped, but hindered. Immediately the child has acquired independence the adult who should continue to help him becomes an obstacle to the child. It is therefore clear that we must not carry the child, but permit him to walk, and if his hand wants to work, we must give him motives of intelligent activity. The child by his actions goes to greater conquests of independence.

It has been noticed that there is a very important and visible factor at one and a half years of age in both the development of the hands and of the feet, this fact is strength. This child who has acquired agility and ability is now a strong man. His first urge in doing anything is to use the maximum effort; not merely to exercise, but to make the maximum effort (so different from the adult). This is brought about by nature which seems to admonish: "You have the possibility and agility to go about, now become strong or it is of no use." It is now that the contact of hands and equilibrium takes place. Then what do we see? The child instead of merely walking, likes to walk far and carry heavy loads. Man is destined not only to walk, but to shoulder his load. The hand that has learnt to grasp must exercise itself also by sustaining and carrying weight. So we see the one and a half year old with a large jug of water, adjusting his equilibrium and walking slowly. There is the tendency also to break the laws of gravity and overcome them. Having learnt to walk, why not be satisfied to walk? No! He must climb and to do so must grasp something with his hand and pull himself up. This is no longer a grasping to possess, but grasping with a desire to go up. It is an exercise of strength, and there is a whole period of this exercise of strength. Again there is the logic of nature here, since man must exercise his strength. Then what follows next? The child, capable of walking, sure of his strength, seeing the actions of men around him, has a tendency to imitate them. Nature's first task for him is to take in, to absorb the actions of the humanity of his period. So there is an imitative period in which the child imitates the actions of his surroundings not because someone tells him to imitate them, but because of an inner urge. This imitation is only seen if the child is free to act. We then see the logic of nature:

1 . To make man stand erect.

2. To make him go around and acquire strength.

3. To make him take in the actions of the people around him.

There is a preparation in time that precedes the action. First he must prepare himself and his instruments, then he must get strong, then look at others and start doing something. While he does that, nature also tells him to prepare by gymnastics, to climb chairs and steps. Then only comes the stage when he wants to do things by himself. "I have prepared myself and now I want to be free, thank you!" No psychologist has taken into sufficient account that the child becomes a great walker who is in need of long walks. Usually we carry him or put him in a perambulator and so the poor child can only walk in imagination.

He can't walk, we carry him; he can't work; we do it for him: on the threshold of life we give him an inferiority complex.

Development and Imitation

In the last chapter we left the child at the age of one and a half years; this age has become a center of interest and is considered of the greatest importance in education. It may seem strange that this period should seem so important, but we must remember that it is the point where the preparation of the upper and the lower limbs coincides. Also it will appear natural if we consider that the child at that epoch is on the eve of the disclosure of his fullness of manhood for at two years he reaches a point of completion with the explosion of language. On the eve of that event, at 1 2/2 years, he is already making efforts to express what is within him. It is an epoch of effort and an epoch of construction.

Once the importance of something has been discovered, everybody at once sets to work. Humanity is generous, but ignorant, so when they learn of something they precipitate themselves, usually with too much enthusiasm, and so also in this instance. Philosophers, psychologists, sociologists and others have centered their interest on the child of 1 ½ to 2 years of age. This is an epoch of development in which special care must be taken not to destroy the tendencies of life. If nature has given us such clear indications that this is the period of maximum effort we must support this effort. This is a general statement, but those who observe become more exact in the details they give. They state that at this epoch the child begins to show an instinct of imitation. This, in itself, is not a new discovery, because at all times people have said that children imitate, but hitherto this was a superficial statement. Now it is realized that the human child must understand before it imitates; this is logical, but it had not occurred to anyone before. The old idea was that we only had to act and the children would follow, there was hardly any further responsibility for the adult. Of course it was also said that we had to set a good example. This sets forth the importance of all adults, especially teachers. They must set a good example if there is to be a good humanity. Mothers also were specially included. The feeling was that children who have bad examples will grow up badly. The adult therefore stressed that he had set a good example for his children to imitate and the real responsibility was thrown on the heads of the children surrounding him, it was their fault if they did not profit by the good example the adults so generously gave to them. The result was unhappiness everywhere, for although children ought to become models of perfection, they were far from it. We wanted a perfect humanity and thought humanity was to be perfect by imitating us, but we were imperfect; what a confusion! Nature has not reasoned like we, she has reasoned another way; she does not bother about perfection in adults. What is important is that in order to imitate, the child has to be prepared to do so. It is this preparation that matters and it depends on the efforts of the individual child. The example offers a motive to imitation, it is not the aim. It is the effort of imitation which develops, not the attainment of the examples given. In fact the child once launched on the part of this effort often surpasses in perfection and exactitude the example, which served as an incentive.

Some people think: "If I want my child to be a pianist, let me (or a teacher) be a pianist and the child will imitate," But it is not as simple as that and many of us know that a child has to prepare his hands in order to gain the necessary agility enabling him to do anything on the pianoforte. Yet we follow this simple reasoning in matters which are on lofty levels. We read or tell the child stories of heroes and saints and think the child will imitate. It is not so easy. His spirit must be prepared. One does not become great by imitation. An example may furnish inspiration and interest, the instinct of imitation spur the effort, but even then one must have a preparation to carry this out and, in education, nature has shown that without preparation no imitation is possible. The effort does not aim at imitation, it aims at creating in oneself the possibility of imitation, of transforming oneself into the thing desired. Hence the value of indirect preparation in all things. Nature does not merely give the power of imitation, but that of transforming oneself to become what the example demonstrates. And if we, as educationists, believe in helping life, we must see which are the things we must help.

If one observes a child of this age, one sees that there are certain activities that the child sets out to do. To us they may seem absurd, but that does not matter. He must carry them out completely. There is a vital urge to carry out certain things, and if the cycle of this urge is broken, the result is deviation and lack of purpose. The possibility of carrying out this cycle of activity is considered important now, just as the indirect preparation is considered important; it is an indirect preparation. Even all through life we prepare for the future indirectly. In the lives of those who have done something in the world, there has always been a previous period of something worked for; it may not have been on the same lines as the final work, but there is intense effort on some line which gives a preparation of the spirit, and this effort must be fully expanded, the cycle must be completed. So if we see any intelligent activity in the child, even if it seems to us absurd or not according to our wishes (as long as it is not dangerous to life and limb of course!), we must not interfere, because the child must complete his cycle of activity. Children of this age show many interesting forms of carrying out this cycle of activity; one sees children below two years of age carrying big heavy weights far beyond their strength, and for no apparent reason. In a house of a friend of mine were very heavy footstools, and a child of one and a half years carried all of them with much effort from one end of the room to the other. Children will help to lay the table and carry large loaves of bread in front of them so that they cannot even see their own feet. They will continue doing these activities, carrying things back and forth, until they are tired. The adult's usual reaction is to have sympathy for the child's effort, they go to help him and take the weight from him, but psychologists have recognized that such 'help,' which is an interruption of the child's own chosen cycle of activity, is one of the greatest repressions of this age. The deviations of many 'difficult' children are traced back to this interrupted cycle of activity. Another effort is to climb staircases; for us to climb up a difficult staircase is an aim, but not for the child. Having accomplished the climbing he is not satisfied, he must come back to the starting point to complete the cycle and this too they repeat many times. The wooden or concrete slides we see in children's playgrounds offer opportunities for these activities; it is not the coming down that is important, it is the joy of going up, the joy of effort.

It is so difficult to find people who do not interrupt that all the psychologists ask for places where children can work uninterruptedly, and hence the schools for very little children are very important and the most important of all are those for little ones from 1 1/2 years. All sorts of things are created in those schools: small houses in trees with ladders to climb up and go down. The house is not to live in or rest in, but a point to reach so that you can go up there and come down again: effort is the purpose, but the house gives a center of interest. We notice it with our own material: if the child wants to carry something, it always chooses either the brown stairs or the cylinder blocks because they are so heavy. So too the climbing instinct which is so apparent in children is merely an effort to pull himself up, he looks for difficult things in the environment to climb on, like a chair. But a staircase is a very great joy, for there is a tendency in the child to go up. I have seen a child who was climbing a very steep staircase from one floor of a house to the other; the steps were so steep that they reached to the child's middle and he had to use both hands to pull himself up and then put his legs round in a most difficult position, but he had the constancy to reach the top, 45 steps. Then he looked back to see what he had achieved, overbalanced and went head over heels backwards down the stairs. They were thickly carpeted and when he had reached the last bump and was at the bottom again, he was facing right round into the room. We thought he would cry, but he laughed as if to say: "How hard to go up and how easy to come down"; Sometimes these efforts are efforts of attention and fine co-ordination of movement, not merely efforts of strength. One child of 1 ½ years I knew, who was free to go round the house, came to a store-room where there were twelve large napkins, starched and ironed, ready to be put away. The baby took the top one with both hands, happy to see that it came away from the pile, went along the corridor and laid it on the floor in the farthest corner. Having done that he came back for another and put that in the same place; he did this for all the twelve napkins and each time he took one, he said; "One." Having put them all in the corner, from our standpoint the work was finished, but no! As soon as the last one was in the corner, he started from there and brought them all back in exactly the same way, saying: "one," each time, and left them where he found them. The attention and the tension of the child during the whole time was marvelous to see and his face had a delighted expression as he went away at last on further business of his own.

These examples of cycles of activity have no outer purpose in themselves, but the child is carrying out exercises giving fine co-ordination of his own movements^ And what has he done thereby? He has prepared himself to imitate certain things. There must be an object in these exercises, but the object is not the real aim; they obey an inner urge. When he has prepared himself, he can imitate, and the environment affords inspiration, The dusting of the floor or the making of bread he sees being done, serve him as an inspiration to do likewise.

Walking and Exploring

Let us consider the child of two years and this need for walking which most psychologists do not consider. It is natural that the child should show the tendency to walk, he is preparing man and all essential human faculties are being built. A child of two years can walk for a mile or two miles and, if he likes to climb, so much the better. The difficult points in a walk are the interesting ones. We must realize what walking means to the child; it is different from our idea. The idea that he could not walk for any distance came because we expect him to walk at our rate. That is as sensible as if we were to tie ourselves to a horse and if, when we became tired trying to keep up with him, he would say: "Never mind, you get on my back and we will both get there," The child does not want to 'get there,' he wants to walk, but his legs are disproportionate in size to ours and disproportionate to the size of his own body (cf. Fig. 7), so we must not make the child follow us, we must follow the child. The need to 'follow the child' is clearly demonstrated here, but we must remember that it is the rule for all education of children in all fields. The child has his own laws of growth and, if we want to help him grow, we must follow him, not impose ourselves on him. The child walks with his eyes as well as his legs, and it is the interesting things in the environment that carry him along. He walks and sees a lamb eating, he is interested and sits down by it, watching; then he gets up and goes further, he sees a flower sits down by it and sniffs at it; then he sees a tree, walks up to it and round and round it four or five times and then sits down and looks at it. In this way he covers miles; they are walks full of resting periods and at the same time full of interesting information, and if there is something difficult like a boulder in the way, that is the height of his happiness. Water is another great attraction. Sometimes he will sit down and say: "Water," happily and all you can see is a tiny stream falling drop by drop. So he has an idea of walking different from that of his nurse, who wants to arrive at a spot in the quickest possible time. She takes him to a park for a walk or a so-called 'airing' in a perambulator, the hood up, so that he cannot see too many things.

The habits of the child are like those of the primitive tribes of the earth. They did not say: "Let us go to Paris," Paris was not there. Nor did they say: "Let us catch a train to go to . . . ," there were no trains. So their habit was to walk till they found something interesting that attracted them, a forest that might supply wood, a place to sow crops, and so on. So does the child proceed, it is a natural fashion. This instinct of moving about in the environment, passing from attraction to attraction forms part of nature itself, and of education. Education must consider the walking man who walks as an explorer. This is the principle of scouting which is now a relaxation from education, but should form part of education and come earlier in life also. All children should walk in this fashion, guided by attraction; and it is here that education can give help to the child by giving him a preparation in school, e.g. by introducing him to the colors, the shapes and forms of leaves, the habits of insects and other animals, etc. All these give points of interest to him when he goes out. The more he learns, the more he walks. He should explore and that means to be guided by an intellectual interest which we must give. Intelligent interest leads man to walk and to move about.

Walking is a complete exercise; there is no need of other gymnastic efforts. He breathes and digests better and has all the advantages we ask of sports. Beauty of body is formed by walking, and if you find something interesting to pick up and classify, or a trench to dig, or wood to fetch for a fire, then with these actions accompanying walking, the stretching of arms and bending of the body, the exercise is complete. As man studies more he has many interests calling him, and his intellectual interest augments his activity of body. If the child is capable of following these interests, he finds other things he did not know, and so his intellectual interest grows . The path of education has to follow the path of evolution; walking about made man see more things, so should the life of the child expand and expand.

This must form part of education, especially today r when people do not walk, but go in vehicles, and there is a tendency towards paralysis and sloth. It is no good to cut life in two and to move limbs by sport and then move the head by reading a book. Life must be one whole, especially at an early age when the child must construct himself according to the plan and laws of development.

From Unconscious Creator to Conscious Worker

We have been dealing with a part of the development of the child which we have compared to that of the embryo. This type of development continues till 3 years of age. It is full of events because it is a creative period. Yet although it is a period in which the greatest number of events take place, it may nevertheless be called the forgotten period of life. It is as if nature had traced a dividing line; on one side there are events which it is impossible to remember; on the other side remembrance begins. The forgotten period is the psycho-embryonic period of life, and may be compared to the physioembryonic period before birth which nobody can remember.

In this psycho-embryonic period, there are developments which come separately and independently, such as language, the movement of the arms, the movement of the legs, etc., and there are certain sensorial developments like that of the eye in which the muscles are not needed. Like the physical embryo in the prenatal period, which had organs unfolding one by one, each separate from the other, so in this period the psychic embryo develops faculties separately and we remember nothing of either. This is because there is no unity of the personality. Everything is developing, one after the other, so there cannot be unity as yet; that can come only with completed parts.

When the age of three years has been reached, it is as though life began again, for then the life of consciousness begins fully and clearly. These two periods the unconscious psycho-embryonic period and the later period of conscious development seem to be separated by a very definitely marked line. The faculty of conscious memory was not developed in the first period; only when consciousness comes is there unity of the personality and therefore memory.

Psychically speaking, before three years there is construction and creation (as in the physical embryo in the pre-natal period), and after three years there is development of the faculties created. The border line is compared with the river Lethe of Greek mythology, the river of Forgetfulness, Certainly it is very difficult to remember what happened before three years of age, still more before two years. Psycho-analysis has tried by all sorts of means to bring the consciousness of the individual back to its own history, to the beginning, but no individual could ordinarily and reliably remember further back than three years of age. This is a very dramatic situation, because it is during this first period that everything is created, starting from nothing and yet the memory of the individual who accomplished all this cannot recall anything, not even the memory of the adult man who is the result of this creation.

This sub-conscious and unconscious creation this forgotten child seems to be erased from the memory of man and the child coming to us at three years of age seems to be an incomprehensible being. The communication between him and us has been taken away by nature, so either we have to know the period or to know nature herself.

If we do not take into consideration the natural laws of development and if children take a form of life that departs from its earlier part, the adult must know this former life or there is a danger that the adult destroys what nature would have made. If therefore, because of social development or the way of civilization, man abandons the natural path of life, there is a great danger since the natural provisions are taken away. As humanity in the development of civilization has given protection only to the physical and not to the psychic part of man, the child finds himself in a prison. If civilization is not given the necessary light regarding the natural laws of psychic development the child very likely lives in an environment full of obstacles to normal expression. It must be remembered that during this period the child is entirely in the care of the adult, because it cannot yet provide for himself, and we adults, if not enlightened by the wisdom of nature or science, will present the greatest obstacles to the life of the child.

After this period the child has acquired certain special faculties which allow him to defend himself, because he can speak for himself. If he feels the oppression of the adult, he can run away or have tantrums. Nevertheless, the aim of the child is not to defend himself, but to conquer the environment and in it the means for his development. In this later period he must develop by means of exercises in the environment, but what exactly must he develop? That which he has created in the previous period. So the period from three to six years of age is a period of conscious construction when a child takes consciously from the environment. He has forgotten the things and events of the epoch before three years of age, but, using the faculties he created then, he can now remember. The powers he created are brought to the surface by the experiences consciously carried out in the environment by the child. These experiences are not mere play nor are they haphazard, they are consciously brought about by work. The hand, guided by the intelligence, does a sort of work. If then in the first period, the child was a sort of contemplative psychic being, observing the environment in apparent passivity and then taking from it what he needed for his construction, i.e., constructing the elements of his being, in the second period he is following the will. At first it was as if a force outside his will led him; now it is the child's own ego which guides him, and now he shows the activity of his hands. It is as though this child who before received the world through his unconscious intelligence, now takes it by his hands, using his hands. There is therefore another sort of development: that of perfecting former acquisitions. The development of language for example continues spontaneously to four and a half years, but we have seen that at two and a half years it is already complete in all its details. Now he acquires enrichment and perfection.

Yet though this is a period of perfectionment, the child still retains the embryonic power of absorbing without fatigue. The absorbent mind continues, but now his hand and its experiences help him to develop and enrich further his acquisitions. The hand becomes the direct organ of prehension to the intelligence; so while the child previously absorbed the world and developed his intelligence merely by walking about, now he must develop by working with his hands; further psychic development takes place this way. He lives not merely because he has life; he must have an environment in which to express his work. If we watch the child of this age we see that he is continuously at work, happy, lighthearted, but always busy with his hands. It is called the 'blessed age of play!' Adults have always noticed this, though only lately has it been scientifically studied. In Europe and America, where the trend of civilization has taken humanity farther from nature, society offers any number of toys to correspond to the activity of the child. Instead of the means to create the intelligence, he is given only mostly useless toys. At this age he has the tendency to touch everything, the adults let him touch some things and forbid others. The only real thing they let him touch at will is sand, play with sand is stimulated all over the world. Where there is no sand, compassionate men bring it to rich children. If there is no sand or only a little, water may be allowed, but not too much of it, because the child gets wet, and water and sand make dirt which adults have to wash.

Toys and Reality

When the child tires of sand, he is given small copies of things used by adults: toy-kitchens and houses, toy-pianos, etc., but these in a form which render them useless to the child. The adults say: "Children want them; they see us working so they want to do the same," But the things they give them to work with are useless; the copies of fruits are stone fruits, they cannot prepare them nor eat them. It is a mockery. The child is lonely, so he is given a mockery of the human figure, the doll. These dollies are more real than father and mother, all sorts of presents are given to it in clothes, jewels, etc. We know that up to four and a half years the child perfects his language, yet the only being he can freely talk to is his dolly, and dolly cannot answer him

The toy has become so important in the West, that people think it is a help to the intelligence. It is certainly better than nothing, but if we watch the child, we see he always wants new ones, he breaks them, he develops nervous and moral complaints. People who study the child superficially say that as he breaks the toy, he seems to find delight in taking everything apart and in destroying everything. This is an artificially developed characteristic due to the circumstances which deprive the child of the right things. He is not even quiet with his toys or not for more than a few minutes. It is Nurse who loads the perambulator with toys, and takes them out for the child. When they arrive at the park, the child is often not interested. Very often the child deliberately takes a look at it and then smashes it on the ground. Those psychologists who study phenomena and not their cause, say that the child has an instinct of destruction and another observation that has been made by these superficial observers is that the child does not fix his attention on any of these toys. Both these criticisms of the child are true, but superficial, the cause of this behavior is not investigated. The real trouble is that children have no real interest in these things, because there is no reality in them. It is the misunderstanding by the adult that has led to this life of lack of attention on the part of the children; this useless life, a mockery of life instead of real life. The child cannot exercise the energies that nature has given him to perfect his individuality, they are wasted and worse than wasted. So the result is that the child cannot develop normally and the longer he lives in this environment full of toys, the less capable he becomes of adapting himself to the real environment, and gradually his personality is completely deformed. It is here and now that he seriously and consciously tries to perfect himself through imitation of his elders. His consciousness develops through the experiences of life and these are denied to him, so of course he is deformed.

In countries which have not developed such a toy-civilization for children, you find children greatly different from those of the West. They are much more calm, healthy and cheerful They take their inspiration from the activities they see around them. They are normal human beings. They take the objects of the adults and use them. When mother washes, or makes bread or chapaties the child does it too, if he has suitable things. It is like imitation, but it is intelligent, selective imitation, it finds real inspiration in those around him; he is preparing for the environment in which he lives.

There are clearly two periods in this early phase of development:

The first period: to 3 years; the child absorbs the environment.

The second period: 3 to 6 years; the child realizes the environment by the work of his hands.

This fact cannot be doubted; the child must handle things for purposes of his own. When, as lately in the West, toys are made which are in proportion to the child so that he can be active with them as the adults are active, then the child changes his character and becomes calm, serene and attentive. This shows that children do not merely play, but are intelligently active. These activities, however, are performed in order to fill a psychic need of the child, not for the need of the environment. This activity has superficially been attributed to an Instinct of Imitativeness; but it is more than this. One sees that the child does not use objects that are not in his usual environment. Why not? Because the child's work is to produce an individual who is suited to his environment.

Once this has been understood, one can no longer speak of play with sand and imitation as the essential characteristics of the child, as if the child were a monkey. This imitation is but a means of learning what is in the environment, and nature wishes to give joy in the fulfilment of special things. The new trend nowadays is not to give children toys, but to furnish them with an environment full of things with which they can perform the same actions as the adults of their race and community. We provide motives of activity with objects built in proportion to their strength and body; and as we usually work at home or on the land, it is necessary that the children have their own home and their own land. Not only toys for children, but houses for them; not toys for children, but land for them with tools to carry out work on the land; not dolls for children, but other children and a social life in which the child is not just seated on a chair and has to be still while the teacher acts, but where he acts himself; an environment where he can act, talk and find all the instruments necessary for intelligent, constructive activities. All these today substitute the toys of the past.

When this idea, which is just now taking hold of the public imagination, was first expressed, it caused surprise. Prof. Dewey of America, a famous educationist, was persuaded of this idea and set out to hunt for objects proportionate to children. He himself, though a University professor, went to all the New-York stores to look for small brooms, chairs, tables, plates, etc. He found NOTHING not even the idea of manufacturing them existed. There were innumerable toys of all kinds; whole furnished houses of minute size, little horses and carriages, nothing for the child. However, the multiplication of toys did one thing. Dolls which started very small increased until they were almost the size of a child; and as the dolls grew, the objects for the dolls grew; they became larger and larger, but never large enough for a child to use really. The child was now almost on the threshold of fulfilment, but the door was yet closed. The adults had spent millions and millions in order to make him happy, and had succeeded in giving him an expensive mockery. We said: "Make all these things a little bigger and the child can use them as he needs to use them." So the step was taken and the dawn of a new world was realized; there were real houses and real objects for children to use in order to perfect the preparation that had been made in the previous period from to 3 years. Once the result was seen, these objects were made everywhere, and a new industry and a new source of wealth came into being.

Prof. Dewey was so certain that in New-York he would find the things he was searching for that when he failed to find them anywhere, he said: "The child has been forgotten," and I say, "What a discovery!" But, alas, he is forgotten in other ways too, he is the forgotten citizen, living in a world where there is everything for all, except for him; for him only mockery, a desert. He wanders ambling aimlessly, crying in tantrums, destroying the mockeries provided, only seeking for the satisfaction of his soul. And standing in front of him the adult could not see the real being of the child.

Once this barrier was broken and the veil of unreality torn asunder, once the child was given real things, we expected happiness, readiness to act with the objects, but this was not the only thing which took place. The child showed a completely different personality. The first result was an act of independence, as if he said: "I want to be self-sufficient; keep your aid." This has been one of the revelations that the freed child has given. The child has not become a wealthier being with bigger objects than when he played with toys; he has become a man seeking independence. He was a surprise to all around him, nurses, mothers, teachers. He refused help, he wanted to be alone. No one had ever imagined that his first act would have been that of refusing assistance, and that, as he worked, nurses and mothers would have to be observers only.

This environment was not merely proportionately constructed, it was one of which he became master. Social life and development of character came spontaneously. It is not the happiness of the child that is the aim, but that he become the constructor of man, independent in function, the worker and master of his environment. This is the light that the beginning of the conscious life of the individual reveals.

The New Teacher

The problems facing village education, especially in countries like India, the primitive circumstances under which such work is started, might be something similar to what happened in the beginning of my work which was very surprising to all. I believe that the facts which we were fortunate enough to witness would not have happened but for certain circumstances. No one else in the world has recognized them, because if Prof. Dewey, for instance, had found the objects he was seeking in the stores of New-York and had been able to organize a house for children with all these activities, nothing would have happened, as nothing happens in so many schools which are richly endowed. Nothing would have happened as objects are not enough. It is not lack of objects alone that matters, but certain other things as well that obscure the real characteristics of children. What will happen cannot be foreseen, because what is needed is freedom for the child and not wealth, and that freedom we cannot understand unless we experience it. No one could have seen it in my experiment but for a chance which gave the necessary conditions. They were:

1. Extreme poverty and a social condition of extreme hardship. It was not a class of working people among whom we worked, those were rich compared with the parents of the children I had. This extreme poverty was a favorable condition. The child who is extremely poor may suffer from lack of food, but he finds himself in natural conditions. Now that we see that the development of the child is directed by natural laws, we see that the child who has a greater number of natural conditions has much greater opportunities to reveal his inner wealth than one living in rich, artificial conditions.

2. The parents of the children Were illiterate, therefore unable to give help to their children in learning.

3. The teachers were not teachers. If they had been real teachers, I do not think these results would have been achieved. In America they never succeeded so well, because they looked for the best teachers. Who is believed to be a good teacher? It means usually one who has studied all the things

which do not help the child; such teachers are full of prejudices and ideas about the child which are not conducive to giving freedom to the child. As is the case with a 'good' nurse who thinks she must help the child to do everything, so these teachers think they must help the child's mind. It is this teaching, this imposition of the teacher on the child, which hinders him.

Who would have thought of imposing the three conditions mentioned above in order to have a successful experiment? One would naturally have thought to give just the contrary.

The great success which we obtained augurs well for similar attempts and experiments in India, because one of the complaints is the lack of good teachers. One must take simple persons and make use of them. In Indian villages also the parents are probably illiterate, so much the better for the children. And as to poverty, it is universally recognized as the first condition for the development of spiritual qualities. It is difficult to tell all to give up their riches, and it might not work, but religious leaders in all countries have renounced the world and sought poverty. We need not impose poverty, but it must not frighten us, as it is the most favorable condition for spiritual development we can find, if accepted with assent. If we want to experiment in giving freedom to the child, the field of poverty is the best. If one wants an easy experiment and sure success, go and work among the poor children. We offer them objects and an environment they do not possess. An object scientifically constructed, offered to a child who has nothing, is taken with passionate interest and awakens mental concentration and meditation. Forty-two years ago this fact caused great surprise. Concentration had never been recognized in children of three years, yet it is a basic factor because it means to take intense hold of the environment, item by item, exploring each one of them and dwelling on each of them. Under the usual unsatisfactory conditions, the child flits from one thing to another and concentrates on nothing, but that is not his characteristic, it is forced on him by an unsatisfactory environment.

Also, in a small child of three years that mysterious teacher which urges the child to work is still active within him; and when we speak of a free child (i.e., with inner freedom) we speak of a child free to follow the powerful guides of nature within him. These guides are extremely wise, and lead the child to seek exactness, precision and the full achievement of what he undertakes. The child is led by nature to go into all the details (e.g. to dust the top, sides, bottom and all the groves of a table). This is what we want for success in education. What any teacher requires of his pupils is attention and concentration on what the teacher does, so that they can carry out exactly any instruction and all is done completely. This is the maximum any teacher can expect in order to have success. The surprising revelation that the children have given us is that this is the natural behavior when a child is free. Given freedom and no interruptions by the teacher, he performs full, complete, concentrated work. At this age of three years, he does not receive with facility from others, because he is constructing himself. Too many teachers are inclined to put so many things before the child, to interrupt him continuously and teach continuously, instead of letting the children have their own experience. The child of this age, therefore, who develops by spontaneous work, following the guides of nature, cannot develop in this fashion with a teacher who teaches. Also the teacher aiming at success (i.e., that the child do what the teacher thinks important, such as obeying her or him) and convinced that she must go from the easy to the difficult, from the simple to the complex, by gradual steps, when instead a child goes from the difficult to the easy and with great strides; such a teacher is not a help in our work, and most teachers are like that, because they have been trained so. Inevitable conflict would arise between the child and such a teacher. Another prejudice such teachers have is that of fatigue. If a child is interested in what he is doing, he goes on and on. The child is not fatigued. When however the teacher makes him change every few minutes and 'rest,' he gets fatigued. As the completed cycle of physical activity gives added strength to the very little ones, so do mental activities with the older ones.

These prejudices are so impregnated in teachers educated in the usual type of Training Colleges, that to get rid of them, you would have to kill the teacher. No new vision of the mind would get rid of them. It is the same with some of the prejudices of society, nothing short of a bloody revolution can help. Some of the most modern Colleges have this prejudice of the need for rest so badly that they have interruptions and rest every three quarters of an hour or half an hour on a carefully graduated plan. The result is extreme indifference in the minds of the people educated. Interest and enthusiasm only can produce anything of value and these are automatically killed. Modern pedagogy sees things from a superficial and erroneous point of view, because it takes no notice of the inner life. The guide of the psychic activities is completely ignored. Also the pedagogical world (or it leaders) is ruled by human logic, but human logic is one thing and the logic of nature another. Human logic says we must distinguish between mental and physical activities, for mental work we must be immobile in a class room and for physical work the mental faculties are not required. It cuts the child in two. When he thinks he may not use his hands, and when he uses his hands his head is not considered. Thus we get men with a head and no body at one time and with a body and no head at another. Consequently there are problems and trouble of all sorts for the teacher. Yet nature shows that the child cannot think without his hands and that the hands are the instruments of intelligence. Objects must occupy the hands and interest the mind. Our experience has shown us that, when the child thinks, he is continually moving. So indeed great men often give us the thoughts they gained as they walked about, meditating (cf. the peri-pathetic school of philosophy). What do people who philosophize do? They go into convents and walk hours alone under trees, meditating. In this period between three and six years, it has been clearly revealed that movement and mind go together; yet many think it is impossible to have schools where children study and continuously walk about.

From this we can realize that a well-prepared teacher (in the usual sense) is the worst teacher for the child. The greatest effort in our method is that of trying to free the teacher from the prejudices he or she may possess and the greatest success is the teacher who can best free herself or himself from them. The measure of how well they succeed is seen in how far they are still cloaked by prejudice. So if education of a great number is envisaged and there is a scarcity of teachers, what can we say but: "Thank God!" It is one of the best conditions.

The new teachers found among simple folk must understand certain fundamental things which, however, are not difficult. In my first experiment I instructed the 'teacher' (who was the daughter of the door-keeper of the tenements) to take certain objects and to present them in a certain fashion to the child and then to leave the child alone with them and not to interfere. Uneducated as she was, she was able to do this exactly. A full fledged teacher would probably have been unable to do that. In the first place he might have thought it below his intelligence and, even if he had done it, he would not have done it so simply. He would have launched a verbose attack of explanations on the class, whereas anything beyond the necessary and sufficient causes distraction and confusion. My uneducated 'teacher' did exactly what she was told and, to her surprise and mine, the children worked and worked with these objects with wonderful results. She was so surprised that she thought there were angels or some spiritual agencies at work. Then the children exploded into writing when she had taught them nothing of writing and when visitors came and asked the children: "Who taught you to write?" they would say: "No one taught us to write," She would add in an awed manner: "No, I haven't taught him to write," She would come to me, half frightened, to say: "Madame, at 2 o'clock yesterday the child started to write!" She could not understand how he could write at 2 o'clock, and perfect sentences in beautiful handwriting too, when he had not written anything in his life before, even up to 1 o'clock. We had given them the cursive letters, then we thought they might find reading easier if we gave them letters of the print-type, but before we had them prepared, the children were already reading books and did not need them. Now, after forty-two years, we know that these explosions occur and can understand why they occur. These incidents, however, happened before we knew the reason of them. Now we know that the child is endowed with an absorbent mind which takes from the environment without fatigue, so that culture, if properly prepared and presented, can be taken as the mother tongue is taken, with the greatest ease. The only thing necessary is to construct a material, scientifically exact, which can be handled by the children. Then a great many items of culture can be brought down to the period of three to six years of age.

Experience has shown that the teacher must withdraw more and more, therefore the task of those who have to train these teachers is easy. Tell them: "Do not do anything, but prepare for the children; they will work." It brings into actual fact a great truth: "Self-renunciation can bring great truths." Our task is to teach the teacher where he or she intervened needlessly. We call this part of our work 'the method of non-intervention.' The teacher must measure what is needed and limit her work to that, like a good servant carefully prepares a drink for his master and then leaves it for his master to complete the work, i.e., drinking it. He does not force his master to drink, that is not his business. His business is only to prepare. So must the teacher act towards the children. It might be good to send teachers to study with a good servant so that they might learn to be humble; not to impose themselves on the child, but to be vigilant and prepare all for the child and then put it at his disposal and leave him.

People who are in charge of children of this age have to serve the psychic needs of the children. It is not indispensable to know them scientifically. If we say to a mother: "Carry the child of one year always with you, so that he may see the world, and take him where people talk so that he may hear his mother tongue" the mother can understand and the teacher can explain it very easily. Also the teacher can tell the mother not to carry a child when he is old enough to walk, not to be afraid of letting him carry heavy things if he wants to do so. All these things are easy to understand if the mind is not encumbered with prejudices.

It is difficult perhaps to understand the psychological reasons for all this, but the practical things themselves are not difficult to tell or to understand, just as putting a seed in the ground or looking after a plant does not require the effort of studying vegetable biology in the University. We must distinguish between the practice of nature, and the science that man has built round that practice. Practice is easy. All the marvelous results always come from the expenditure of the spontaneous energy of the child which is usually impeded in ordinary schools.

Let us consider the illiteracy of the parents. Illiteracy brings about other conditions of ignorance, so that when the child comes home and shows how he can wash his hands, the mother thinks: "How clever he is!" and the child is uplifted. Also when the child whose mother and father cannot write, writes his first word, their adoring admiration again brings uplift to the child, whereas the richer parents will probably say: "Oh! ah! yes!, but do they teach you art at school?" and the child is chilled and loses interest. Or if a child dusts something the better-class mother kills the joy of the little one, because she says it is sweeper's work and she did not send her child to school to learn that. Or if it is mathematics he learns, she is afraid he will get brain-fever and wants to stop the work. So either the child gets an inferiority-complex or a superiority-complex and thinks it is not necessary for him to do certain things. The real problems are with the literate, cultured parents and if they are pedagogues themselves, so much the worse, because then they think they know all about education.

A Social Problem Solved

The conditions, therefore, which we think bad for an experiment, are really good. Success will not limit itself to the children, it will influence the parents. In my first experimental "House of Children" when they had started doing exercises of practical life and were interested in the details of them, they would tell their mothers that they must not have spots on their dress and must not spill water. "You do it like this," so the mothers began to care for their dress and appearance. This shows the power the child has of transforming the environment. It is the child probably who is the only force who will lead illiterate persons to educate themselves. The parents in my first 'House of Children' came to me to learn how to read and write, because their children could do it. In dealing with children of this age one handles almost a magic wand in social life. First there is the marvel of the transformation of the child himself, secondly there is the touching marvel (it causes emotion) that the child is able to do much more than one had expected, and this rouses in the spirit of the adult a sort of reverence for the spirit of childhood, hence it achieves a transformation and an education of the adults.

If one envisages a social reform on a large scale and plans according to the old method, one has to make a plan covering many years (the Sargent Scheme covers 40 years). If one has to prepare teachers with all the prejudices of psychology all over the world, we can calculate how long it will take to train them. These teachers begin with children of seven who have passed the sensitive stage and being faced with this dead-weight (the children do not possess the enthusiasm natural to the little ones for the same things) they force and force and the children become more and more bored. The child who, before, had at least a relative freedom, now finds himself under a teacher who fusses and tells him to do this, that and the other. It will take forty, eighty, a hundred years, two centuries perhaps before the work is completed. If, on the contrary, we consider these psychological facts which are easy to practice, then things are not so difficult, because we tap and make use of natural energies which always exist. It is necessary to understand the child at different ages, certainly, but then practically all is done. Such facts as the smaller child's better memory than the older one's, for instance, when remembered, make things quite simple.

We see that the child learns better than with the old methods and that the whole of education is shifted downwards, towards birth, from eight to four years. Thus so many years are saved and as the absorbent mind and the sensitive periods are functioning at this age, which means that all things are taken with interest and enthusiasm, the wish to continue is present and education does not have to be imposed.

What about the teacher? She will work long hours with the children since the children do so, but in a very different way. Once a teacher has become a good teacher in this sense, she is happy. A newspaper-man in America once visited his cousin, a Montessori teacher, and found her lying on a deck-chair and thought she had vacation. She told him to be quiet and not to disturb the children. He could not see. or hear any children, but looking through a window he found them all working quite happily without any noise on the lawn. Children educated in this way will always work, also without the teacher if she is late or away. The possibility of a reform on a large scale is much more rapid and easy to attain in this way.

In my first experiment I used to give instructions ta the teachers once a week and after ten months there was the explosion into writing. Today our observations have made it plain to us how these miracles happened, but when they happened we did not know the reasons, so it is not indispensable to know them. If we put a plant in the earth, we must know how much soil and water it wants, and then water it regularly. Then, one day, we shall see the flower coming. We do not need to know the anatomy of the flower or the acidity of the soil, etc. We only have to wait in patience and look for the flowers. So with the education of children, all that is necessary are adults, simple and of good will.

In all countries where children live in a simple r natural way, in so-called backward countries, where education seems to present the greatest problems, the great miracles of our early experiments will easily be repeated and a great and urgent problem solved. Simple teachers are perhaps better than others and all these little children will lead the rest of the world. Those who feel the appeal of this work must not be afraid of the task: what must be kept in mind are not the difficulties of the theories we have given, but the vision of the first experiment before any of these theories were developed.

Further Elaboration Through Culture and Imagination

The period between three and six years is most interesting; it follows the period of the spiritual embryo (0 to 3 years). The passage between these two periods is not very marked. Usually only one period is considered, the period from 0–6, but it is really divided into two parts. The first part concerns the creation of the psychic life, and the second part is a sort of period of perfectionment or fixation. Certain faculties developed in the first period are rendered secure. Also in the first period there is a prevalence of the unconscious part, whereas in the second period consciousness guides development. It is, therefore, not only a period of fixation, but of greater perfection. We no longer have the embryo, but man who is completing himself. The second period shows a special form of activity, because consciousness falling upon the world grasps the world and handles it, and in this handling the conquests that were not clear before, become clear and perfect. The child not only takes in the environment, but realizes himself. This is the period in which the conscious individuality is established and this is done spontaneously. It is still a period forming part of creation and is still closed to outside influences such as an adult mentality trying to impose or transmit something directly. The child, therefore, cannot be educated in the ordinary sense of the word by a teacher, but education must come through the natural bases. The natural laws of development compel the child of this age to experiment on the environment by the use of his hands, both in cultural and other matters. It is the passage from nothing to life. Only recently this has become known, before then the whole psychic life of the child was buried under the indifference of humanity to him. Now it has made itself suddenly known to those who did not know of it.

It was the explosion into writing that first caught the attention of the public to the child's psychic life. It is not an explosion of writing only, the writing was like the smoke out of a pipe, the real explosion was of the human self in the child. He might be compared to a mountain which seems to be solid and eternally the same r but contains a hidden fire. One day there is an explosion and out comes the fire through the outer heaviness. It is an explosion of fire, smoke and unknown substances, from which those who can see, will be able to tell us what the earth contained. Our explosion was similar and it happened because of circumstances which, as I explained in the previous chapter, were the least favorable (apparently) for such a revelation. These revelations came also on bases which were 'non-existent' The poverty and ignorance, the lack of proper teachers, syllabus and rules were basic 'nothings,' We found nothingness, and because there was nothingness, the soul was able to expand itself. The obstacles had been removed, but no one knew (at that time) what the obstacles were. It is well to understand this, because in the child lies a great energy a latent cosmic energy. It is important for us to know this, because if we know it is there and wait for its flashing revelations, we are on the road to success. It was not a method of education which caused these explosions, because the method did not exist when the explosions occurred. The following up of psychology and the building up of the method came as a result of these volcanic revelations of the children. The explosion came as the result of a discovery not of a method. The Press spoke of it from the first as of a 'discovery of the human soul.' From it sprang the new science which followed step by step the revelation of the children.

I will explain these phenomena a little. They are facts, they should not be attributed to intuition, but to perception. I have described what I saw. The facts seen are the foundation of the new science; these facts can be found in my previous books.

Two groups of facts are important in these revelations, one is that the mind of the child is capable of acquiring culture at a period of life when nobody would have thought it possible, but can only take it by his own activity. Culture cannot be received from another, but only through the work and increased realization of oneself. Nowadays, when we are aware of the powers of the absorbent mind during the period from three to six years, we know this possibility to take in culture at a very early age. The other important group of facts deals with the development of the character. Development of the character has pre-occupied education at all times, but all educators have agreed that the age from three to six years is not the age to influence character in a systematic fashion. No one thinks of real discipline for children so young; only later can discipline be imposed. Also it was thought that it was the adult who had to influence the character of young people and the problem of changing evil into good is an eternal problem. We were wrong: this is the time for developing character, but the child must develop his own character according to the laws of growth. We have already seen a great deal of how the mind is formed, but it is interesting to dwell in some detail on the contents and working of the mind at this period and we shall deal with the formation of character in another chapter.

The child is especially interested in and concentrates on those things he has already in his mind, those that were absorbed during the previous period, for whatever has been conquered has a tendency to remain and the mind dwells on it. So, for instance, the explosion into writing was due to the special sensitivity for, and conquest of language. As the sensitivity ceases at five and a half to six years, it was clear that writing could be achieved with such joy and enthusiasm only before this age, while older children of six or seven were not capable of doing this and did not feel the same enthusiasm. So our method came from the observation of the children, from the observation of facts. It was seen that children had prepared the organs necessary for writing previously, so indirect preparation was adopted as an integral part of the method. Thus certain bases of the method could be fixed. We had seen that nature prepares indirectly in the embryo; she does not give orders until she knows that the individual has the organs which enable him to obey. That is why the child cannot do anything by mere imitation and obedience; it must be provided with the means to be obedient. Both mind and character were helped by the observation of these facts. Earlier it was thought that all that was needed was good example by the adult and good will from the child, but the adults lacked a wisdom that nature possesses, i.e., that the means must be prepared for the command to be obeyed, and this is not done directly. To receive frequent and successive commands does not create obedience; obedience is attained indirectly by inner preparation. Obedience to arbitrary commands of the adult cannot achieve development. The child has in himself such a fountain of wisdom to guide him, that it is evident that frequent and ill-founded interference by the adult is not a help, but an obstacle to his development. The necessity of a prepared and well organized environment for the child and freedom for the child to expand its soul within it stands out very clearly now.

If, as we found, the child again takes up the conquests of the first period in order to elaborate them in the second period, the first period can furnish us with a guide for the second period which follows the same method of development. Let us take language: in the first period we have seen that the child follows a method which is almost grammatical: he successively absorbs and uses sounds, syllables, nouns, adjectives, adverbs, conjunctions, verbs, prepositions, etc. We then know that we should help the child in the second period by following the same grammatical method. The first teaching is that of grammar. It seems absurd to our usual way of thinking, that teaching should begin with grammar at three years of age, and that before he knows how to read or write, he should learn grammar. If we stop to think of it, however, what is the basis of construction of a language if not grammar? When we (and the child) speak, we speak grammatically. If, therefore, we give him grammatical help at four years of age when he perfects his language in construction and enlarges his vocabulary, we give a real help. By giving him grammar, we allow him to absorb more perfectly the language spoken around him. Experience has shown us that these children were keenly interested in grammar and that this was the right time to give it. In the first period (0 to 3 years) the acquisition was almost unconscious; now it has to be perfected consciously by conscious exercise. Another thing we noticed was that the child of this age acquires a large number of words; there was a special sensitivity and interest in words and he spontaneously took in any number of new words. Many experiments were carried out and it was seen that all children considerably enriched their vocabulary at this age. The words acquired were those used in the environment of course, so a cultured environment gave a child the opportunity to learn many words; but in any environment the instinct was to absorb the greatest possible number of words; the child had a hunger for words. In a cultured environment he can take thousands and thousands of words. To give many to him is a help at this age. If unaided he takes them with effort and without order; the help will consist in reducing the effort and giving order.

Another detail in the method was established as a result of this observation, to give many words. The uncultured 'teachers' we had in our first experiment noted this fact and they wrote words for the children. They wrote as many as they knew, but presently they came to a halt and they came to me and said that they had given all the words relating to dress, house, street, names of trees, etc., but the children wanted more words! So we thought, why not give to the children at this age the words necessary for culture, e.g. all the names of the geometrical figures they had been handling in the sensorial apparatus, polygons, trapezium, trapezoid, etc. The children took them all in one day! So we went to scientific instruments, thermometer, barometer, etc. Then we gave them botanical names, sepals, petals, stamens, pistil, etc. They were all taken in with enthusiasm. "Do you not have any more?" they asked, and the

teachers complained that when they took them for a walk, they knew the names of all the motor cars which we, of course, do not know. The thirst for words is insatiable and the power for taking them inexhaustible, while in the period that follows this is not the case. Other things develop then, but there is difficulty in later periods to remember strange words. We found that our children who had the opportunity of learning these words early, recalled and remembered them easily when they found them later in the ordinary schools, at 8 or 9 or even 12 or 14 years, while those children who then met them for the first time found it difficult to remember them. So the logical conclusion is to give scientific names at this age, of 3 to 6 years. They are not given mechanically of course, but in connection with specially prepared apparatus, so that they are based on real understanding and experience. To us foreign names are long, complicated and difficult to remember, yet the foreign child says his name with the utmost ease. In Italian there are many strange names for foreigners, but there is no difference for the Italian child between these and other words like triangle. To help this remarkable thirst for words in the children we give them the words of the various classifications in all subjects, botany, zoology, geography, etc., like the different parts of a leaf, of a flower, of geographical features, etc. They are all easily represented and apparent in the environment and therefore most suitable. They offer no difficulty. The difficulty was with the teachers who did not know these words and found it difficult to remember which was which.

In Kodaikanal I once saw older children of 14 years of age, who were studying in the ordinary school, puzzled over the name of a part of the flower, a tiny child of three years said: "pistil," and ran off to play. The child of this early age does not take words indifferently as any ordinary easy thing; it is as if a light is lit in the child and he is profoundly interested. We showed to older children of 7 or 8 years the classification of roots according to the botany books and a small child came in and asked of an older child what were the new charts on the wall. He was told and later we found plants pulled out of the garden, because the tiny ones were so interested that they wanted to see which roots those plants had. When we saw their interest, we gave this knowledge to them and then the parents complained that the children pulled up the plants in their gardens, washed them and said they wanted to see roots.

What is the limit of the words the children will learn? I do not know! Does the mind of the child limit itself in taking in objects and the facts about the things they can see? No; the child has a type of mind that goes beyond concrete limits. It has the power of imagining things. This power of visualizing things that are not present to the eye, reveals a higher type of mind. An object I can see is an easy thing to know, but when I have to make an image for myself (to imagine) it is more difficult. If the mind of man were restricted only to the things he could see, it would be very limited indeed. Man sees without seeing; culture is not made up of the knowledge of things seen. Geography gives an example. If we have never seen a lake or snow, we have to imagine them, imagination has to be put into activity. Up to what point can children imagine things? We did not know, so we began with some experiments starting with children of 6 years. We saw that they did the opposite of what we imagined. We had thought they would be interested in big things, but they were interested in the details. We took the globe; they knew the world, they had heard of it so much. 'The world' is a phrase to which no sensorial image corresponds, yet the child forms an idea of what it is, which shows that he has a power of imaginative understanding, of abstraction. We prepared special small globes. We covered the earth with "star dust" and the oceans with deep and bright blue. The children began to say: "This is land," "This is water," "This is America," "This is India," They loved the globe so much that it became a favorite object in our classes. The mind of the child between 3 and 6 years fixes not only the functions of the intelligence in relation with objects, but also those of imagination and intuition. This means that the intelligence must have a great and vivid power at this age beyond that of merely absorbing through the senses. It has a higher power, that of imagination, which enables the individual to 'see' things he cannot see. This may seem an exaggeration in relation to children of this age, but if we think about it, we realize it is not such an exaggeration, since psychology has always said that this is a period of imagination. Even the most ignorant people tell their children fairy tales, and they love them immensely, as if they were anxious to use this great power of imagination. They call a table a house, a chair a horse, etc. Everyone realizes that the child likes to imagine, but he is given tales and toys as the only help. If the child can realize a fairy and visualize fairyland, it is not difficult for him to visualize America, etc. Instead of only hearing vaguely about America, a globe with the general shape of America is a concrete help to his imagination. Imagination is endeavoring to find the truth of things, a fact which is often forgotten. If in the child's environment the word 'America' or 'World' had never been mentioned by anyone, then it might be difficult for him to show interest in it, but since he hears the word so often, it enters his mind and he clothes it with imagination. The mind is not the passive entity one imagines, the mind of man is a flame, an all-devouring flame, it is never still, but always active.

When those children of six years had the globe and were talking about it, a child of three and a half came in and said: "Let me see! Is this the world?" "Yes," said the older ones, a little surprised, and the child of three and a half said: "Now I understand, because I have an uncle who has gone three times round the world. How was it round? How did he go? Now I understand" At the same time he realized this was only a model for he knew the world was immense; he had taken it from the conversation round him.

We had a child of four and a half, who also asked to see the older ones' globes and he looked steadily at one. The bigger children were talking of America, taking no notice of him. Presently the tiny one interrupted them: "Where is New York?" The older ones, surprised, showed it to him. Then he said "Where is Holland?" Still more surprised, they showed it to him. Then, touching the blue part, he said: "Then this is the sea" The older ones were interested, so the little one said "My father goes to America twice a year; he stays in New York." After he has started, Mother says, "Papa is on the sea," For many days she says it; then she says: "Papa is in New York," Then after a while she says: "He is on the sea again" and then one day she says: "He is in Holland, and we go to meet him at Amsterdam," He had heard so much about America, that when the older children were talking about it, he was very eager to know about it and felt: "I have discovered America," And what a rest it must have been for him, for he had been trying to find an orientation in the mental environment as he used to do in the physical environment. In order to take the mental world of his time, he has to take words from the adults and cloak them with images. This is the fact.

Playing with toys and imagination through fairy tales represent two needs of that special period of life: the first, to place oneself in direct relation with the environment, to master the environment, and by this a great mental development is acquired by the child. The other reveals the strength of the imagination, so much so that he turns it on his toys. If we then give him real things to imagine about, this is a help to him and places him in more accurate relation with his environment too.

At this age children often want information. They ask questions to know more of the truth of things. It is well known that the child is curious, always asking questions. If all these questions come together, it means that the child is in need of knowledge. The questions of children are also interesting if one consider them not as a nuisance, but as the expression of a mind seeking information. Children of this age are not able to follow long explanations, so we do not give him a long explanation of the world, but a globe. Usually people give too exhaustive explanations. A child asked his father once why the leaves were green. The father thought how intelligent his child was, so he gave a long explanation of chloroplasm and chlorophyll and of the blue rays of the sun, etc. Presently he heard the child mumbling and listened; the child said: "Oh, why did I ask Papa? I want to know why the leaves are green, not all this about chlorophyll and the sun!"

Play, imagination and questions are the three characteristics of this age; this is known by all and misunderstood by all. Sometimes questions are difficult like: "Mamma, where did I come from?" but the child has reasoned to come to this question. An intellectual lady who guessed beforehand that her child would ask this question one day, determined to tell him the truth and when the child asked her the question at four years of age, she said: "My child, I made you." The answer was quick and short and the child was immediately quiet. After a year or so she told him: "I am making another child now," and when she went into the Nursing Home, she said she would come back with the child she had made. When she arrived back, she said: "Here is your little brother; I made him as I made you," By this time the child was six years old, so he said: "Why don't you tell me really how we come into the world? I'm big now; why don't you tell me truth? When you told me last time you were making a child, I watched you, and you did nothing" Even telling the truth is not as easy as it seems, so it needs a special wisdom on the part of teachers and parents to know how to help this imagination.

The teacher requires a special preparation, because it is not our logic that solves problems. In no point on which we have touched, does our logic help, we have to know the child's development and to shed our preconceived ideas.

Great tact and delicacy is necessary for the care of the mind of a child from three to six years, and an adult can have very little of it. Fortunately the child takes more from the environment than from the teacher. We must know the psychology of the child and serve him where we can.

Character and its Defects in Young Children

The education of character was one of the most important items in old pedagogy; it was one of its main aims. At the same time no clear definition of what is character was given, nor of the way to educate it. Old pedagogy only said that mental education is not sufficient, practical education is not sufficient; character is needed, but it is an unknown quantity X . These old educationists have some intuition of it, for what they really mean is the realization of the value of man, but when you go to these values, there also they are not clear. Like many other things in education, it is vague. Value is given to certain things, such as the virtues: courage, constancy, certainty of what one ought to do, moral relations with one's neighbors. In the question of character moral education plays a part.

All over the world we find the same vague ideas. It seems to me that this question must be looked at from a different point of view, and instead of speaking about the education of the character we ought to speak of the construction of the character, the development of the character in and through the effort of the individual. A demonstration of this active creation of the character, not its education from outside, was shown by the children in my first school. Let me illustrate some points of this construction, which give a new idea to education.

From the point of view of life, we could consider everything about character as behavior in man. As I have mentioned before, the life of the individual from 18 years can be divided into three periods: 6 years (with which we deal in this book), 6–12 years and the last period form 12–18 years; each again divided into two sub-phases. In considering each of these groups, the type of mentality which each represents is so different that they might appear to belong to different people.

As we have seen, the first period is a period of creation; it is here that the roots of character are to be found, although when the child is born he has no character. The period from 6 years is therefore the most important part of life regarding character too, since here it is formed. Everyone has recognized that at this age the child cannot be influenced by outside example and pressure, so it must be nature herself that lays the foundation of the character. The child at this age has no understanding of or interest in what is good or bad; he lives outside our moral vision of life. This is recognized, because we do not call the child of this age evil or bad, but naughty, indicating that this behavior is infantile. We shall, therefore, not speak of evil and good or of morality in this book because those terms have a different meaning at this age. I mention this, because people ask all kinds of questions as to the use of the good example of forefathers, of patriotism, etc. They are important, but they do not concern this age; in the second period (6–12 years) lies the beginning in the child's consciousness of the problem of good and evil, not only in his own actions, but in, and among, other people too. The question of good and evil comes into the light of consciousness as a special characteristic of this age: the moral conscience begins to form itself; later it leads to social conscience. In the third period (12–18 years) comes the feeling of patriotism, of belonging to a group and of the honor of the group. I mention this now to make clear that it does not belong to the age of 6 years.

I mentioned above that, although the character of each period is so different that it seems to belong to different people, yet each period lays the foundation for the next period. In order to develop normally in the second period, one must have lived well in the first period. It is like the caterpillar and the butterfly which are so different to look at and so different in their habits; yet the fineness of the butterfly is attained by the true life of the caterpillar it was before, and not by imitating the example of another butterfly. In order to construct the future one must attend to the present. The more fully one period is lived as regards its needs, the more successful the next period will be.

Life begins at the conception of the individual If conception is brought about by two pure beings, not by alcoholics or drug-addicts, etc., then the resulting individual will be free from certain hereditary taxations on life. The right development of the embryo depends on the conception. For the rest the child can be influenced, but only by the environment, i.e. during gestation, by the mother. If the environment is favorable, the result is a strong healthy being. A fact worth considering is that this conception and gestation have an influence on the nervous system of the child (that is the reason why, if a shock or accident happens, he may become an idiot), so what happens after birth is due largely to the period of gestation. The first important thing in life is therefore conception, then gestation, then birth. We have mentioned the shock at birth and that this might give rise to regressions; these characteristics of regression are serious, but not so serious as alcoholism or hereditary illness (as epilepsy, etc.). This shows us that, as we go on, the danger of the obstacles grows less and less, but the characteristics are always of a psychic kind. They influence the individual either in the direction of regression or in that of independence.

After birth come the three important years which we have already studied. During these two or three years, there are influences that can alter the child and alter his character in after-life, e.g. if the child has had some shock or met too great obstacles during this time, phobias may develop or we may have a timid or melancholic child. The character, therefore, develops in relation to obstacles or freedom from obstacles during this period. If during conception, gestation, birth and this period the child has been treated scientifically, then at the age of three years the child should be a model individual. This ideal of perfection is never fully attained as, amongst other reasons, during these developments the child has met with many accidents. At three years we meet with one or fifty or a million children with different characteristics. We have so many different results of different experiences and these different characteristics are of different importance according to the seriousness of the experience. If the characteristics are due to difficulties after birth, they are less serious than those of the period of gestation, and these in their turn are less serious than those of conception. If they are due to the post-natal age, they can be cured between 3 and 6 years, because then perfectionment is attained and defects are adjusted. If, however, the defects are due to shock at birth or earlier, then they are very difficult to correct. So there are certain imperfections that may appear, but there is an active period of perfectionment and the erasure of certain defects of post-natal life is possible, but idiocy, epilepsy, paralysis, etc., which may even be hereditary cannot be cured by any help we can give. It is interesting to know that all but these organic difficulties can be cured, but if these defects, developed from 3 years, are not corrected now by treatment at the age of 3–6 years, they will not only remain, but will be increased by the wrong treatment during the period from 3–6 years. Then, by the age of 6 years, there may be a child with the defects of the period from

3 years strengthened, and with the newly acquired difficulties of the sub-phase from 3–6 as well. These in their turn will have an influence over the second period and the development of the conscience of good and evil.

All these defects have a reflection on the mental life and on intelligence. Children are less able to learn if they have not met with good conditions of development in the previous period. A child of six years of age, therefore, is an accumulation of characteristics that may not be really his, but are acquired under the influence of circumstances. If a child has been neglected from 3 to 6 years, he may not have the moral conscience that develops from 7 to 12 years or he may not have the normal intelligence. We then have a child with no moral character and no ability to learn, more troubles are added, and he is a man with scars due to the difficulties he has gone through.

In our schools (and in many other modern schools) we keep a record of the biological details of each child in order to see how to treat the child. If we know the troubles of the different periods, we can orient ourselves as to how serious they are and how to treat them. We therefore ask the parents if there is hereditary illness, we enquire after the age of the parents at the birth of the child, make tactful enquiries as to the mother's life during the period of gestation, whether she had falls, etc. Then, if the birth has been a normal one, whether the baby was well or suffered from asphyxia. There are the questions regarding the home life of the child, if parents have been severe or if the child has had shocks. If we have problem-children or naughty children, we try to find a reason for it in the life the child has led previously to that time. When they come to us at three years, almost all of them show strange characteristics, but they are curable. We can briefly consider the familiar types of these deviations.

All these manifestations which are faulty and not normal, enter the field of what is usually called character. All children are different and the general idea is that each child must have a different treatment to cure his defects, but we distinguish two main groups of faulty characteristics, one belongs to the strong children who fight and overcome obstacles and the other group to the weaker ones who succumb to adverse conditions.

Defects of the Strong Children

Violent tantrums, anger, acts of rebellion and aggression. One of the most common features is disobedience and another is destructiveness. Then there is the desire for possessions; so we have selfishness and envy (the latter not manifesting itself passively, but by trying to have what other children have). Inconstancy (very common in children); incapability of attention; inability to co-ordinate the movements of the hands so that they drop and break things; a disorderly mind and strong imagination. Also they frequently shout, shriek and make loud noises; they interrupt and they tease and torment and often are cruel to the weak and to animals. Frequently too they are gluttons. These are a few of their troubles.

Defects of the Weak Children

These are of a passive type and have negative defects such as sloth, inertia, crying for things and wanting people to do things for them; they want to be amused, are easily bored. They have a fear of everything and cling to adults. Then too they have the fault of lying (a passive form of defense) and of stealing (a passive form of grabbing other's possessions,) and many more.

There are certain physical characteristics which are concomitant with these difficulties; i.e., these physical defects have a psychic origin, but are confused with real physical illnesses. One of these is the refusal of food and loss of appetite; the contrary defect is indigestion due to gluttony; both are of a psychic origin. Then there are nightmares, fear of the dark, agitated sleep which in their turn affect the physical health and then anaemia results. Certain forms of anaemia and liver trouble are due to psychic facts. There are neuroses too. All these have a psychic origin, as is shown because no medicine can cure them.

All these characteristics enter into what is called moral problems and behavior. Many of these children (especially the strong type) are not felt as a blessing in the family, the parents try to get rid of them and hand them over to nurses or schools and they become orphans with their parents living. They are ill with a healthy body. This leads to the depression of life called naughtiness. They are problems and their parents want to know what to do with them. Some ask questions, some try to solve their own problems. Some adopt severity convinced that if you stop them at once, they will be cured, these defects checked as soon as they appear will not develop, they think. All means are used: slapping, scolding, sending them to bed without food, but it is found that they become more ferocious and bad, or develop the passive equivalent of the same defect. Then the persuasive line is tried, we will reason with them and their affection is exploited: "Why do you hurt Mummie," or one washes one's hands of the whole thing, and leaves them alone. Discussions start: "My sister's children do what they like and see what they are!" "What about your children?" "Oh, I tell their father, who beats them," "And are they good?" "Oh, no, they are just like their father!" Then there are the people who leave their children alone. These children usually belong to the passive type, they do nothing, and the mother thinks her boy good and obedient, and when he clings to her, she says how much he loves her; he loves her so much that he will not go to sleep without her. But somehow she finds he is slow and retarded in speech and he is too weak to walk. "He is healthy, but he is so sensitive, he is afraid of everything! He doesn't want to eat either; he is a spiritual child because I have to tell him stories to make him eat, he must be a saint or a poet!" Finally she thinks he is ill and the doctor is called to give medicine. These psychic illnesses make a fortune for the child's doctor.

All these problems can be understood and solved if we know of the cycles of activity necessary for the construction of the personality; if we realize the children's need to hear men and see the actions of men and carry out their own experiences. We know that all these troubles are due to faulty treatment in the earlier period; they have been startled mentally, their mind is empty because they had no means of constructing it. This starved mind (of which psychology takes much notice now) is the main cause of these defects and another cause is the lack of spontaneous activity guided by the constructive impulses of the child which we have studied. Hardly any children have been able to find the conditions necessary for full development. They have been isolated from people, made to sleep all the time; the adults have done everything for them; they have not been able to complete cycles of activity without interruption. They have not been able to observe objects, because when they handled them, they were taken away; seeing them only and unable to handle them, made them want to possess them, so when they did get hold of a flower or an insect they pulled them apart, not knowing what to do with them. And the passive child has developed inertia instead.

Fear also is traceable to the early period. If, when the little child fell down all the stairs, the adults had all rushed to help him and made a fuss (as they usually do) he would have felt fear instead of laughing. Our actions are often the cause of fear in children.

One of the facts that made our schools remarkable was the disappearance of these defects. It was due to one thing: the children could carry out their experiences on the environment, and these exercises were nourishment to the mind; that is why all these common defects disappeared. Round the interest in their activity they repeated exercises and passed from one period of concentration to another. When the child has reached this stage and is able to concentrate and work round an interest, defects disappear; the disorderly become orderly, the passive active and the disturber becomes a helper. This is a marvelous fact and the disappearance of these defects made us understand that they were acquired, not real characteristics. Children were not different in that one told lies and another was disobedient. All the troubles came from the same cause: the children had lacked the necessary means for psychic life.

So what advice can one give to mothers? To tell them to give their children work and interesting occupations; not to help them unnecessarily, and not to interrupt them if they have started any intelligent action. Sweetness, severity, medicine do not help at all. Children are suffering from mental starvation. If anyone is suffering from physical starvation, we do not call him stupid or hit him or sentimentalize over him; that would do no good; what he needs is to eat. So it is with this question too; neither harshness nor sweetness will solve the problem. Man is by nature an intellectual creature and he needs mental food almost more than physical food. Unlike animals, he must construct his own behavior and life is life for this need. So if he is on the road where he can construct the behavior for which life has been given to him, all will be well. Physical illness disappears, nightmares disappear, digestion is normal without gluttony. He becomes normal, because the psyche is normal.

This is not a question of moral education, but regards the development of character. Lack of character, faulty character disappear without the need of preaching or of an example by the adult. Neither threats nor promises are necessary, but just conditions of life.

A Social Contribution of the Child: Normalization

All the characteristics we described in the last chapter when tracing the behavior of the strong and weak children, are not considered evil by general opinion; some are considered good traits. Those children who showed a passive character and were attached to their mother are considered good. Other traits still are considered as signs of superiority; children who are always bustling about, are extremely healthy and have vivid imaginations are all considered superior. They usually pass from one thing to another, but the parents think they are bright children.

So we might say the world considers three types of children:

1 . Those whose traits need to be corrected;

2. Those who are good (passive) and serve as models;

3. Those who are considered superior.

The two latter types are considered desirable and the parents are proud of such children; even when (as with the last type) they feel a certain discomfort when they are near, they still speak proudly of them.

I have insisted on this point and drawn attention to this classification, as these features have been noticed during the centuries, and no other characteristics have been noticed but these. Yet what I have seen in my first school, and in others, is that all these characteristics disappeared at once, as soon as a child became interested in work that attracted his attention. So-called bad traits, the so-called good and the so-called superior, all disappeared and only one type of child appeared with none of the traits I have described. This means that the world hitherto has not been able to measure good or bad or superior; what we considered so, was not really so. It reminds me of a mystical saying: "Nothing is right except you, O Lord; all the rest is erroneous." The children of our schools revealed that the real aim of all children was constancy at work, and this had never been seen before. Neither had spontaneity in the choice of work, without the guide of a teacher, ever been seen before. The children, following some inner guide, occupied themselves in work (different for each) that gave them calm serenity and joy, and then something else appeared that had never yet appeared in a group of children: a spontaneous discipline. This struck people even more than the explosion into writing. This discipline in freedom seemed to solve a problem which had been insoluble. The solution was: to obtain discipline, give freedom. These children going about seeking for work in freedom, each concentrated in a different type of work, yet as a whole group presented the appearance of perfect discipline. We shall return to this question of the real nature of the children that finally obtained, but meanwhile we will describe the change which took place in the children.

All children, if placed in an environment allowing ordered activity, show this new appearance, so there is one psychic type common to all humanity, which hitherto had remained hidden under the cloak of other apparent characteristics. This change that came over our children and made them appear as of one uniform type, did not come gradually, but suddenly. It always came when the child was concentrated in one activity; so that if there was a lazy child, we did not urge him to work. We merely facilitated contact with the means of development in the prepared environment. As soon as he found work all his trouble disappeared at once. It is not reasoning with the children that will do good; it is something within themselves that sets to work.

The human individual (especially in the period of construction) is a unity and constructs a unity, when the hand is working and the mind is guiding it. I recognized that when the mind and hand are not united, there is no unity in the individuality and it is then that these superficial traits of badness,' 'goodness' and 'superiority' appear. This conclusion is the result of my observations of children, it certainly is no a priori idea of mine. This is the new point which came to light and which is perhaps most difficult to understand, probably because we live in a world of virtues and defects (which are rewarded or punished) and among children who have always shown the traits outlined above, because they had no opportunity to express anything else. It is not necessary to have an adult as a guide and mentor to conduct, but it is essential to give the child opportunities of work which have been denied to him heretofore.

The passage from the superficial to the normal traits is always through a function, through intelligent activity of hand and mind together. In figure 9 on one side we see all the different characteristics of children as we usually know them, represented by lines raying out. They are innumerable. The middle thick perpendicular line symbolizes concentration on one point; it is the line of normality. When the children are able to concentrate, then all the lines on the right of this middle line disappear and only one type is seen revealing characteristics represented by the lines on the left. The loss of all the superficial characteristics is not achieved by an adult, but by the child passing along the main line of functioning with his whole personality; then normality is achieved.

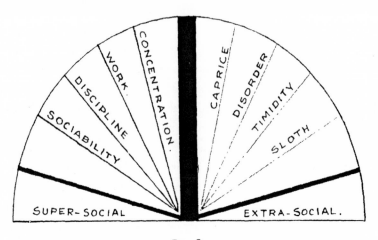

FIG. 9
Normal and deviated features of the child's character

I shall now give some examples of what appeared in some schools after the first school which had such unusual conditions. People came from all parts of the world to take my Courses and then went back to their own countries and started schools there. Most of these schools were for rich children, who have more defects,, because they have much less chance of normal functioning, having so many servants. The first letters I received from these students were letters of dismay; records of tremendous disorder, and they described in detail all the usual defects, e.g.

1 . One child used material as if it were a train or an aeroplane, etc. he joked and talked loudly and molested other children (the old superior type).

2. Another child was snobbish and superior to wards the apparatus and was lazy.

3. A little one was attached to his brother, took exactly what his brother took, and when his brother got up, he got up too, etc.

4. Other children were almost pathological cases, e.g. afraid to touch water, etc., and one about 3 did not speak at all.

A collection of children like these, all together, made a confusion for the teacher too. One said that they threw the material on the ground and danced on it. The teachers who expected little angels to drop down from heaven were therefore bitterly disappointed.

After some months the tone of the letters began to change. The transformation which we call 'normalization' had occurred. Teachers who had no connection with each other (some were in New Zealand, others in Rome, in France, in America, or in England) all wrote the same thing: "such and such a child has found some work and he has changed himself." The child who followed his brother everywhere, one day took the pink tower by himself and his attention became fixed on it. When his elder brother went into another room, the little one did not follow him, so that the big brother had such a shock that he said in an almost offended tone: "What is this? You are doing the pink tower when I am drawing in the other room?" The little one had found his own value and no longer needed the moral support of his brother. Another child would not come to school or stay in school without his mother; she would put herself in a corner and say she would stay and if she tried to slip away, the child would immediately cry. One day the child became interested in washing a table; the mother thought this was a good opportunity to slip away, but she hesitated to do so without some intimation to the child lest he should scream later when he found her not there. She, therefore, said to him, "I am going," The little one said, "All right, goodbye Mummie," and never needed her any more either to stay in school or to accompany him to school The children who had been attached to their mother and brother, had not had freedom for independence, so they were unable to do anything alone. Someone always had to function for them. As soon as both became interested in work and the mind guided the hand, they found their own independence and functioned for themselves.

The romping child who used the material as trains and aeroplanes became interested in the geometrical insets; he went round the shapes and the frames and fitted them in with his eyes shut. At once his wild fancies disappeared. Instead of saying: "This is an engine." "This is an aeroplane" etc., he said: "This is a trapezium," "This is an octagon," etc. He was attached to reality now, not to fantasy; and his hands which had previously dropped everything, now became very definite, precise and careful in their work. He became calm and serious with all the material. If one examines these things, one might say that this little fellow, living in a world of fantasy, had had nothing of real value to occupy his attention, so he occupied himself with what he found around him; neither had his hands had any opportunity to hold anything for any real purpose. When the mind, which had been running about in fantasy apart from the hands which had nothing to do, became a guide for the hands which were doing something real, there suddenly came a united individuality and the real work in its turn was now nourishing the mind.

The child who had a fear of water, especially of pouring water (and had probably been scolded with some violence for playing with water) became interested in the baric sense tablets at last. She was very happy; and when she had finished that, she did some other work. Then she suddenly realized that she was no longer afraid of pouring water; and she was so happy that seeing some children using water colors, she immediately went to fill all their little jars with fresh water and took that task as a special one for herself.

One child had a trait of not sitting down, even though tired. We tried to find out what had happened earlier in her life to account for this peculiarity. The mother said she had never scolded her for sitting down at any time, and then the father remembered an incident which happened when the child was about one and a half years of age. She had a new dress and she went to sit on a newly painted stool, and the mother said suddenly: "Be careful! don't sit on that! there now you have made a mess!" This was the cause of the fear of sitting, and the question was how to cure her. I said: "Take no notice of her; let her find her own interest," After a time she became interested in some work and repeated the activity full of interest. Wanting to continue she "unconsciously" drew a chair to herself and sat down. From that moment she lost her fear of sitting down. The child of 3 years who did not talk, was examined by a doctor; there was nothing organically wrong which would prevent her from talking. She was given electric treatment, but that did not help. She spent some time in school wandering about, doing nothing and saying nothing of course. At last she became interested in some work and we could see her face light up. When she had finished, she ran to the teacher and said: "Come and see what I have done!" her first words.

Also digestive trouble, nightmares and other things disappeared and at home too the children became calmer. One child always afraid of the dark, became interested in work at school, and one evening at home, when her mother needed something from a dark outhouse, she said: "I'll go and fetch it Mummie," She was no longer afraid of the dark.

So too the over-obedient, passive children changed, the passivity and the over-obedience disappeared through concentrated spontaneous activity.

We must repeat that this was not a sporadic phenomenon. It happened in our schools all over the world, so we realized that this type of calm, serene, unafraid child was the real, normal child and showed the real behavior and character of childhood. It was only afterwards that I fully understood what this actually meant, viz., that the child must construct himself, as we have been expounding in this and our other books. If the conditions do not allow this, normality disappears, but once the conditions for building the psyche are there, the normal type appears. We therefore called the type that developed in our schools 'normalized' children and the others deviated children. One of the greatest and most interesting factors was the extraordinary discipline of normalized children, each occupied in the work of his choice. The newspapers said: "It is marvelous if it is true, but it is incredible," Everyone who visited these schools tried to find out what trick I used, they were sure it must be a trick. Some said it was my personal hypnotism that produced the result, but I said: "This happened in New York; and I was in Rome." Others thought that the children had been prepared before by the teacher or that she used her eyes in some way to express approval or disapproval, but who would have gone through all this trouble to prove something that had not been seen before?

A public occasion which also demonstrated the genuineness of these phenomena was at the World Fair in San Francisco, at the time of the opening of the Panama Canal. Among the educational exhibits had been built a small Montessori classroom with glass walls so that the public could watch from outside without disturbing the children at work. Helen Parkhurst, the later ordinator of the 'Dalton Plan,' was then the teacher. The door was locked at night and the key left with a caretaker. One day the caretaker had an accident and did not turn up, so the people were outside waiting and also the children with their teacher. The teacher said: "We can't get in today to work," but one child saw an open window and said: "Lift us up and we can get through the window and work," The window was of a size proportionate to the children, so the teacher said: "That is all right for you, but I cannot get in," The children answered, "Never mind; you don't work anyhow; you can sit outside and watch us with the other people," It is not a theoretical principle that I am advocating, they are facts which were witnessed by the whole world.

At one time there was an earthquake in Italy which destroyed the city of Messina; after the earthquake many children were found who had lost their parents, and were suffering from terrible shock and obviously had to be helped by the State. They were collected together in an orphanage and sixty of them, who were the most depressed and of a suitable age, were chosen to try and give them some special consolation by using this new method. They were of course most difficult to treat and so a special environment was made for them to help their independence. It was very beautiful and bright with many exercises of practical life. In a few months they were so happy that they skipped about as they laid tables in the garden for lunch. People outside wondered what had happened. What had really happened was this: into the exercises of practical life many complications had been incorporated which were given with great exactness of detail. Among the people helping them were aristocrats who taught them many refined details of social manners that were not known outside aristocratic circles, and these details and the precision they demanded caught the children's interest and they began to have a new life. People outside said that these children were both perfect gentlemen and ladies, and perfect servants. It is the number and exactness of details that call forth the attention; on a gross action the mind does not dwell, on exactness of detail the mind must dwell. One American authoress, Dorothy Canfield-Fisher, came to see these children and as a result she wrote The Montessori Mother, a book which is still in print. In the case of these children it was a depression of life that was cured; life had gone to its lowest extremity through the shock the children had received, and now it came bubbling up again.

From all this we must conclude that the first psychic need of the child is to live according to his own psychic laws. Activity brings him to the normal behavior of man, because it is not merely ordinary activity as with an adult, it is a need of life. The child must develop, functioning individually, going towards independence, the mind linked with the hand. If the natural laws are not obeyed, innumerable difficulties arise; if natural laws are obeyed the difficulties disappear. If therefore working with the hands according to free choice in a prepared environment expands the activities of the first period and perfects them, it is possible between the ages of three and six years to overcome all difficulties. The facts are simple, but they are the facts of life, witnessed all over the world in the last forty years. On the basis of these facts new characteristics have been revealed, and a new organization of schools has commenced; schools where the children are active and the teacher is mostly passive, acting indirectly through the environment.

This transformation of character does not take place in all children. Certain organic forms of defects and illnesses which originated in the pre-natal state, we cannot help or cure. The small angle represented at the left of our diagram represents these. They are the congenital, mental and moral defective who will grow up to be the idiots and criminals of our society. They are relatively a very small proportion of humanity, but this proportion of the criminals, the idiots and the mad is increased by the numbers of those who could have been helped before they were six years old, but were not helped. So we begin to understand a little of the problems of society. In the United States of America, for instance, statistics give us the figure of 100,000 as the number of new admissions to the mental asylums every year; and since every one of these has been crazy for ten years at least, one can realize how many crazy and mad people there must be in the United States, and how many are still at large. This is not natural, most of these could have been helped, but only before the age of six years. Jails also are full and special jails are built for youths, another tragedy.

The small angle to the right of the diagram also represents those whom we do not help; they are the saints and geniuses of society who do not need us. Normalization is for the great mass of men, not for the very few exceptions on either side, those who do not need it because they are great personalities as saints and geniuses, and those who cannot be helped because their defects are pre-natal in origin, the criminals and the mad. We have hopes that through understanding many can be helped and that the number of the insane and criminal can be much reduced, but the schools and social life must alter for they are responsible for much of the trouble. Hence, this first institution of mine is important, and we owe a great debt of gratitude to these first children for, without their example, we could not have known all this. The child is the great citizen who has shown the way of bettering society, the simplicity and uniqueness of the way are all the contributions of the child. It is only through work that re-organization can be achieved, but work that gives joy, not work imposed against the laws of life.

Character-Building a Conquest, Not a Defense

In the previous chapter we mentioned that the defects that arose after birth were lost by children if they had the proper environment before the age of 6 years. The disappearance of these defects was not due to the general practice of attacking them one by one; they all disappeared suddenly in the same fashion when the children's interest was centered on one activity. Then began a series of phenomena which was constant. All normalized children acted in a uniform manner, i.e. they continued to work concentrated on something, serene and tranquil. This, at the time, was surprising, because it had never before been seen in small children. They also showed a special characteristic not seen in adults and not before seen in children: they worked with the maximum effort, and continued their activity till the task was completely finished and with exactitude. This accomplishment of a task with exactitude is uncommon even in adults; the children do this to the extreme limit, for, having perfectly completed their work once, they repeat it many times often carrying these repetitions to what seems to us absurdity. They will polish a brass vessel ten times over or repeat forty times and even two hundred times the exercise with the cylinders. Obviously children do not work with an outer aim; it is evident that they have another aim which is not external, but dictated by nature. These repeated and concentrated activities always share one feature; the mind and the hand are engaged in it together. We must envisage this and try to understand it. These children are building the character of man, they are elaborating the inner qualities which we admire in a man of character: the ability to decide rapidly, constancy in work. These qualities have not been developed in response to preaching or to our examples. We must study character from a positive point of view: character is only acquired through long and gradual exercise which lasts for years. This is achieved in the period from 3 to 6 years and this creation and elaboration of qualities of character are carried out along the lines that nature established for the formation of the human personality. As between and 3 years of age certain acquisitions are elaborated (e.g. language) so here the creation and elaboration of character is achieved following natural guides. All the acquisitions from to 3 years were made through the absorbent mind so that the child, merely by living among others, absorbed the language, etc., but from three to six years, he must construct and he constructs his character in an active fashion. The construction of character is accompanied by work so that at six years of age the construction of mental qualities and character has been fundamentally accomplished. If we take this into consideration it becomes clear, not only that we cannot teach the virtues of character, but that we must not disturb the normalized child of three to six years when he is building his character. If we intervene unnecessarily we interrupt this construction. The work of education for children of this age is therefore not to preach to them; there is only one way of helping this spontaneous development of character and that is to prepare the environment for their development and then to respect their intelligent activities and leave them alone. It is useless to put examples in front of these children. For one thing, they may do better than the example already; and in any case it is useless to preach to them, it is like talking to the wind. Even ordinary parents understand something of this, that is why they smack them because they know that it is useless to talk to them.

The revelations of our children pointed the way to us to place this part of education on a scientific basis. At a later age it is possible to approach the mind of the child directly and we can intervene with preaching and exhortations. After six years only one can become a missionary of morality to the child; between the ages of six and twelve years the conscience is awakened and the child sees the problems of what is right and what is wrong. Still more success is attainable between twelve and eighteen years when the child begins to feel ideals like patriotism and the social aspect of religion, etc. Then we can become missionaries to them and also to adults. The moralizing activity of preaching is always carried out among adults, so there is plenty of time for our missionary efforts. The only trouble then is that after six years of age they cannot spontaneously develop qualities of character, and the missionaries, imperfect themselves, have difficulties, because they are trying to act on smoke not on fire. Educationists lament that they can teach science, literature, etc., but that these young people have no character, and when character is lacking, the propelling force of life is lacking. It is only in those who, through storms and mistakes of the environment, have nevertheless been able to rescue some or all of these characteristics, that there is character. The fault lies in the fact that we did not give them the opportunity of constructing their own character through the normal activities natural to them and undisturbed by us, before they were six years old. Now we cannot make these young people concentrated if they lack the power of concentration. If we tell them to be constant in their work and attend to it exactly, how can they do it if they lack the power? It is as though someone said "Walk straight" and we had no legs to do it. These abilities can only he acquired by exercise and not by command. I cannot play on the piano or the veena even if commanded and willing to do so, because I do not have the ability; the chance has been lost. Many things lost to the child during the creative period cannot be created again. What can we do then? Society generally says: "Be patient with youth; we can only persist in our good intentions and examples"; and we think with patience and time we shall achieve something. We achieve nothing; with the passage of time we become older, but we create nothing. Nothing can be achieved only with time and patience; if you do not use the opportunities of the creative period when they are there, you can wait for eternity with the patience of Job.

Another point becomes clear if we look at humanity, which is really an undeveloped mass of confused minds. Everybody repeats: "All are different from each other," but these different individuals can be grouped in different categories. If we could become mental eagles and look at them from above we should see these categories. It seems that, as with children, these adults differ in defects, but have something deep and profound, common to all of them, but remaining hidden. In all men there is a tendency, though sometimes vague and subconscious, to better themselves, a trend towards spirituality. Indeed these actions on the defects of character, have later on the quality of stimulating improvement. Both individuals and society have this in common: continued progress. This is a fact both externally and internally speaking and means that there is a little lamp in the subconscious of humanity which leads it to betterment. In other words the behavior of man is not fixed as in other animals, but can progress, so it is natural that man has this urge to progress.

In figure 10 we see in the center a red circle, the center of perfection, around it is an aura of blue which represents the category of humanity of the stronger normal type. The white space round that represents the great mass of people not-well-developed in various degrees. On the periphery is a small brown circle between two black lines which represents those outside the circle of normal humanity, the very few extra-social or anti-social people (the extra-social being the imbecile and insane and the anti-social, the criminals). The criminals and the insane have not been able to adapt themselves to society; all the others have been able to adapt themselves to a greater or smaller degree. The problems of education, therefore, are all with people who have been able to adapt themselves to some extent.

That adaptation to the environment is the work of the child under six years, so here is the origin of human character. What a tremendous problem it is, finding or not finding easy adaptation! There are the people who have more or less perfectly adapted themselves, they more or less answer the needs of society, they are those represented in the white circle. Those in the blue circle are nearer to perfection, stronger because they have a greater amount of vital energy or found a better environment, while the others have less vital force or met with many obstacles. In society, those in the blue circle are recognized as having the stronger character and the others are said to have a weaker character. People in the blue circle have a natural attraction to the perfection represented by the center, whereas the people in the white circle feel an attraction to the extremity, the outer circumference. So there is a category of people who feel an attraction to, and are sliding down towards, the anti- and extra-social belt, as if they were climbing with difficulty and slipped down. They meet many temptations and if they do not continually make an effort, they slide down; they feel themselves becoming inferior. We have to sustain these morally so that they do not slip in temptation. It is not an attraction of pleasure, because no one enjoys slipping towards criminality or insanity; it is like an irresistible attraction of gravity and involves continuous fighting against it. It is this effort to resist the tendency to slip downwards that is considered a virtue. Virtue, in fact, prevents us from falling down into a moral chasm. Such people are told to take care not to Jail and they will do penance; they will put a rule on their life to keep them from falling; they will attach themselves to someone better than they are; they will pray to the Omnipotent to help them against temptation. More and more they clothe themselves in virtues, but it is a very difficult life. Penance is not a joy of life; it is an effort of one climbing a cliff and clinging to some projection so as not to be dashed on the rocks. Youth feels this pull of gravity and it is the educationists who try to help them by examples and exhortation. They serve as a model, though they feel the pull sometimes as much as the youths do. How many times they say: "I must be a model, or what will my pupils do?" And they feel the restraint of model-hood. Both pupil and educationists are in the category of the virtuous people the white circle; this is the environment of the education of character and morals today and so it has been accepted as the only education. Hence the majority of people are always in the white circle and humanity generally considers that this is the true man, who is continually on the defense.

In the blue circle are the stronger people with an attraction to perfection. There is no pull of gravity, but a real attraction to get nearer to perfection. This may often be an aspiration without the possibility of actual perfection, but in any case they go towards it naturally and almost without effort. They are not people that are not thieves because of fear of the police or that make an effort against the sense of possession; they are not people led towards violence, but refraining from it by virtue; they are not attracted by the possessions of those around them nor are they violent. They feel only one attraction, that of the center of perfection and they feel that because it has become a quality of their life. They do not need virtue in the same way, because they are less subject to the pull of gravity towards imperfection. They hate imperfection. When they go towards the center of perfection they do not feel it as a sacrifice, but as their dearest wish; they want to go.

Let us make a physical comparison, and consider the question of vegetarians and non-vegetarians. Many who eat meat, abstain from eating meat on certain days of the week, and in Lent they fast for forty days, which means they go without meat and some other things. It often is one long, dreary period of penance to them and they feel very virtuous. After this period there comes a reaction and they gorge on all sorts of meat perhaps. During Lent they are tempted and say: "O, Lord, help me!" These are virtuous people who observe the rules of other people and religious leaders. They are pure, but in the blue field are the celestial ones, the vegetarians, who have no temptation to eat meat; they avoid it. It is of no use sending a missionary against meat-eating to the vegetarians; they observe non -meat-eating better than he does.

Let us take another example: the physically strong: and the weak (e.g. a sufferer from chronic bronchitis). The latter needs protection for his lungs with many warm wraps and woollen garments; perhaps too he needs baths and massage for bad circulation. These seem quite normal people, they are not in hospital, but take care of themselves. Or perhaps their digestion is not good and they have to eat special food in special ways at special times in order to keep well. All these people keep afloat among the normal people, but with a lot of care and attention to details, and with the fear of the hospital and death always in the environment. They are always attached to doctors and nurses and people of the family and they have a constant cry of "Help me" But look at those who enjoy good health, they eat what they like and do not care about rules. They go out in the cold because they enjoy it, and they jump into an icy stream for a swim when others hardly dare to put their nose out of doors. Polar explorers feel the adventure as a joy; they don't worry about the physical discomforts. In the whitish field of virtues, too, Sadhus and Babus are needed and spiritual mentors of all kinds or there is a fall into the abyss or chasm of temptation. But the people in the blue field do not need these in the same way and they have joys the others could not dream about.

Let us then go to the circle of perfection in our effort to put character on a basis of facts. What is perfection? Is it perhaps to possess all the virtues to the highest degree, and to attain what? Here also we must put something possible and factual. By character we mean the behavior of humanity, which is urged (even if subconsciously in many) towards progress. This is the general trend: humanity and society must progress in evolution. Some people feel the attraction towards God, but let us consider for the present a merely human center of perfection, which is the progress of humanity. Some individual makes a discovery and society progresses on that line. It is the same in the spiritual field, an individual reaches a level and gives a push forward to society. All that we know, spiritually speaking, and all that we see, physically speaking, has been the result of some man's attainment. If we study geography or history we see continuous progress, because from time to time some man puts a point in the red circle, of perfection and this is an attraction, but only to the people in the blue field, who are sure of themselves and who do not need rules or penance. They do not have to spend energy fighting temptation, thus they can use the same energy to achieve things impossible to those who have to struggle in order to keep safe from temptation. So Admiral Byrd submitted himself to the humiliation of one who seeks to collect money in order to do what? to explore the South Pole and expose himself to all the sufferings of a polar expedition. He felt nothing of the suffering, he felt the attraction of the red circle of perfection, of reaching something not yet reached.

To conclude we might say that humanity is too wealthy in those who are in the white circle and too poor in those who are in the blue circle from the point of view of character. There are too many people in need of crutches to enable them to avoid temptation; and if the world continues to center education on this level, it is keeping the people down on this level. Imagine a missionary from the white field coming to children in the blue field and telling them to renounce meat or they will fall; such children would say: "I cannot fall, I feel no attraction for meat," Or another missionary says: "You must cover yourself or you will catch a cold," the child would say: "I do not need to cover myself, I have no fear of cold," Let us realize that this tendency in education to provide mentors from the whitish field, tends to push all the children down to this level (even if it is only to resist) and not up and towards the center of perfection. If we look at all the syllabuses of education, we see the scarcity of information they give and the aridity of them. It is humiliating this education of today and brings about an inferiority complex and an artificial reduction of human strength. It does this by its very organization. It puts limits to knowledge, and limits below the level of man. It gives men crutches, when they could have strong legs to run with it is a wrong education based on the inferior qualities of man not on the superior qualities. It is by the effort of man himself, that men are today a mass of inferior beings. They have not built their character before six years of age. We must try and reconstruct the real level, try to allow the child to use his creative powers; and probably the blue space which is not one of perfection, but of attraction towards perfection, not of defense, but of conquest, will invade the whole of the whitish space . If there is only one epoch in man's life when he can construct himself psychically, and the construction is not then made or is badly made on account of a wrong environment, then we naturally obtain a mass of undeveloped individuals. Supposing, however, that we allow the character to develop according to nature and give an opportunity for constructive activity, not exhortations only, then the world will need another type of education.

Take away artificial limitations and set in front of humanity great things to be accomplished. I can read all the histories and philosophies and remain a dunce, but give the means which lead to great efforts and the result will be different. We must cling to something which finds a response in man in order to do this. The qualities which we can encourage are the creative qualities which are built up in the creative period, and if we do not allow them to establish themselves then they are not there later, and it is useless to preach and give examples.

This is the difference between the old and the new education: we wish to help the construction of man by himself at the right period; to help all possibilities to ascend to something great in order that something may really be done now. Society has built walls and barriers, we must destroy them and show the horizon. The new education is a revolution, but non- violent, the non-violent revolution. After that, and if it succeeds, it will be impossible to have a violent revolution.

The Sublimation of Possessiveness

Having given a glimpse of the general phenomena, let us observe in detail the facts which took place and the interpretation we gave to them. These facts that presented themselves, both because of the age of the children and of the intensity the children showed, were very surprising and arresting, but even more so because of the relation between the character shown by the children and the loftier characteristics of humanity.

If one studies all the phenomena which took place, one can see in them all a process of construction. This process of construction may be compared to the action of caterpillars at a certain stage. Instead of moving about on many twigs as they had been doing, they stay in one spot and become very active there, and after a little time one sees a cloud of threads hardly visible, so diaphanous they are, but this is the beginning of a strong cocoon. As with the caterpillar, the first phenomenon we notice is a phenomenon of concentration on one thing. In a child of three and a half, who was in our first school, this concentration was striking for its intensity; there were many other stimuli in the environment, but it was impossible to break her concentration. A similar degree of concentration can be observed in some adults, but only in exceptional characters as for instance in Archimedes, who was so intensely concentrated in his geometrical problems, that although enemy soldiers had entered the city and were penetrating his house, he said merely: "Don't disturb my circles!" He had not realized that the city had fallen to the enemy. Poets also have been known to continue their work without noticing a noisy carnival procession outside. But it is only with geniuses that such concentration is noticed in adults. The phenomenon in the three and a half year old child was not of the same type of concentration. In the child such concentration is given by nature, and when we see it repeated by different children in different countries, we decide that it must be a part of the pattern of construction. As with the compass the fixing of one point is necessary before anything can be done, but once it is fixed any design can be drawn, so with the construction in the child the fixing of the attention is the first stage. It need not always be fixed on the same thing, but unless it is fixed, construction cannot begin. It is as if the individuality found a center and once that has been done, it can possess what it achieves. So with us, if we want to organize, we must have a concentration diffused over everything connected with the work in hand. Without this concentration the object with which the child is concerned possesses the child, he is led by all the stimuli, but once this fixity of concentration obtains, then the child possesses and controls the environment.

When in the adult world, we find a person changing his interest frequently, we speak of him as inconsistent in character and we know that such people are unable to undertake anything responsible in life, whereas when we see a person with a deep aim, who can distribute his attention and organization on things given to him, we feel that such a person will do something in the world. We tend to ponder on these things and say we should like to have our young students concentrated on their work, but we cannot manage to bring it about. This means then that it is not among the items that one can give by ordinary educational means. As it is difficult to get from older children (college and high school students) who would have thought of getting it from three and a half year óld children? It would be impossible to think that any teacher could provoke such concentration when the rest of the class were dancing and jumping about; all the more impossible to obtain it in a whole class, yet, it happened in that class of the Messina orphans whom I mentioned in a previous chapter. There were sixty of them working in one large room or hall, and a hundred students came in and ranged themselves round the walls, and the children did not notice their entrance or look up.

This phenomenon shows that nature is constructing some great item of the human psyche, and from this already one can understand that the elements of the human will are being built. It is not by an already existent strength of will that the children achieve this concentration, it is by nature; nature builds the will in this way. After this all the gyrations and deviations disappear and character is formed. What takes place after this fact? We see constancy (repetition of exercise) with no outer aim and therefore with an inner aim; and this constancy is characteristic of children, we adults do not possess it. We may have constancy in pursuing a long work, but not in repeating the same work. This repetition of the children is a sort of training for character which the adult will be able to use, but which the child constructs. There are certain adult people who do not have the patience to see the child repeating all these exercises of exactness; it is done so often. The child does not yet have the will for this constancy, he does it by nature, but through it he builds the will of the adult which will later persist in carrying out any task that must be carried out. And if we see how nature practice each single exercise separately and so often, we see how impossible it is to obtain any constancy or will from youth who have not had these possibilities of practice and of developing the elements of the will. People who do not have these are not to be blamed, they had no opportunity to construct them.

There is another thing that takes place after this first fixation of concentration and that is the determination by the child of the action he will carry out. Children in our classes, who are choosing their work freely, are exercising this determination of action. This also is constructed by repetition, every day, for years. We often find ourselves with adults who can never decide what they want, we say they have no will. Quite a majority of people are like this and when we find a person who can express clearly what he wants and what we want, we say he has a strong will and can determine his actions. Children determine their action by nature's law, the adult by mental reflection. It is evident that in order to exercise this power of determination of actions, it is necessary to have independence from an adult who tells the child what to do every moment of his life, because it is evident that this determination comes from inner development and inner forces. If someone, stronger for the time being, usurps the office of the inner guide, then the child cannot develop either determination or concentration. So if we wish these qualities to develop, then the first thing is that the child must become independent of the adult. If we look at child life anywhere, we find that the strongest instinct is to be free from the adult and this is true for all species. And how logical it is when one looks at the conclusion! But the child does not do it by logic, he does it by nature; so nature gives a special design that the child must follow. This indicates a parallel in the development of the character in man and the behavior of animals, because the animal has to follow a certain pattern and does so by freeing itself from the adult of its species. There are natural laws that guide growth and construction and the individual must follow these laws if he has to construct his character his psyche.

We can witness the construction of the psyche in every item and element. The character of man is not the result of education, it is a cosmic fact; it is willed by nature. It is not the result of our imposition, it is a fact of creation not of education.

Let us consider some of the defects that disappear. One of the most common defects of children who have not been able to develop properly is an urge for possession. It is expressed by the saying "wishing for the moon," What is this if not an instinctive impulse? Now in normalized children the active possibility of interesting themselves in any object, leads them to the stage where it is no longer the object, but the knowledge of it which fixes the attention, and then a change takes place in this possessiveness. It is a curious fact that children who want objects for physical possession, after a little time lose or break those objects. The defect of possession is accompanied by the defect of destructiveness, but if it is an object that has no lasting interest for us, this is understandable. It has only caught the interest for a moment and then is thrown on one side. Take a watch for instance; it is meant to tell the time and that is its real value. A tiny child cannot tell the time so the real interest in the watch is not there and quickly he breaks it. An older child may want to know how it is built and opens up the case and sees all the wheels which in their working give the time. This complicated machinery then interests the child for its function not for any outer aim. It has happened that people have felt this feeling for its function so strongly that it gives a passionate interest. History gives us examples, Louis XVI of France had this passion for the functioning of watches and he spent much of his time in a laboratory of watches. The Emperor Charles V, who ruled a large part of Europe, also had this interest; he had twelve watches, which he tried to keep constantly at the exact time, but he couldn't succeed in keeping them together, so he said: "If I can't keep twelve watches together, how can I hope to keep all Europe together? I had better retire," and he became a monk. This is a second type of possession interest in how it works. We can notice this in other fields. Children pluck flowers merely to possess and the result is that they destroy them. Always material possession and destruction go hand in hand. Do we not see it in the world at the present time? If instead the child knows the parts of the flower, the kinds of leaves, the direction the stem takes, etc., then there is no possessiveness and destruction. He is interested, an intellectual interest centered on the plant or an intellectual possession. The child will destroy also butterflies, if he merely seeks to possess the insect, but if his interest is aroused in its life and function, it is still centered on the butterfly, but to observe not to possess and destroy. And this intellectual possession showed itself in such a great attraction that we might call it a love, and it brought the child to care for these things in a delicate and refined manner.

So we can say that this possessiveness because of an intellectual interest is raised to a superior level and that intellectual interest urges the child to progress through this life they study. Instead of the instinct of possession, on this higher level we see three things: to know, to love and to serve. Possession transformed into love and when it has arisen, there is not only conservation of the object, but service of it. Then it is said that an instinctive impulse is sublimated. In the same way curiosity becomes sublimated into scientific research. Curiosity becomes an impulse to learn and from this the strength and attraction for study comes. It is interesting to observe that when the child has become the lover and admirer of one object, he becomes zealous in the upkeep of all the objects. It was the transformation of children in our first class which showed how children go from possession to a higher level of love and service. Their copy books when completely filled showed no 'dog's ears' nor smudges nor blots, but were neat and even decorated.

If we look at humanity, at the greatness of humanity, as revealed by history and evolution, we see that it is an instinct of man to attain this sublimation. He tries to enter every field and protect and better it, so he helps life by intellectual penetration into the laws of life. The farmer serves his plants and animals all his life; the scientist loves his microscope and lenses and shows his love in the extreme care and delicacy of his handling them. Humanity starts by grabbing with its hands and by destroying, and ends by loving things intellectually and serving them. Once in a while we have reversals as in the recent war when loads of lead fell on cities and destroyed them, but these are incidents only. Generally the rule is to serve and to love. It is in man to be brought out because it is in nature. The children who tore plants out of the garden, now watch for the plant's growth, count its leaves, measure its sides. It is no longer my plant, but the plant. This sublimation and love is given by knowledge, by penetration of the mind. Destructiveness cannot be overcome by preaching; the child still wants the thing for himself so that no other shall have it. If we try to correct him by smacking, or moralizing or exploiting his emotions sentimentally, he may alter for five minutes, but he comes back to the same starting point. Only work and concentration which give knowledge first and then love will achieve the transformation. It is a revelation of the spiritual man to know, to love and to serve. It comes only by one's own experience and development, not through preaching. As soon as the attention of the intellect on details is there, love comes, the desire to know all details, so that we may not unwittingly hurt.

To know, to love and to serve is preached in all religions, but it is the child who is the constructor of our spirituality; he has revealed that nature has a plan for our behavior or character, a careful plan determined in age and functioning and needing freedom and intense activity following life's own laws. Repetition of the exercise is followed in intellectual as well as physical exercises; and it is not physics or botany or cleaning one's shoes that is achieved merely, but the will and the elements of the spirit are built. The adult can make use of that will which the child builds up, so the child is the spiritual builder of us all. Discoveries we make, when adults, often fall on our own heads (as actually in the recent war) because we have forgotten the soul the child has built or, more often, prevented him from building it normally.

Social Development

The first work the child has to do is to find the way and the means to concentration which lays the foundations of the character and prepares social behavior. This immediately shows the importance of the environment, because no one will be able to give concentration or to organize the child from without. He has to organize himself. The importance of our schools is that there the child has a chance of finding the kind of work that will give him concentration. A closed environment (our school or class-room) favors concentration; we know this because when people want to find concentration they build a temple or a shrine. Through an activity that promotes concentration in a closed environment character is formed and the creation of the individual achieved. In ordinary schools children are mostly admitted after the age of five years only when they have already finished the first and most important period of formation, or, if they have not had the opportunity to do so, at least the age for it is passed, whereas our school is a protective environment where the first elements of character may be formed and acquire their particular importance. That is why the question of the prepared environment in education, when first proclaimed to the world, gave rise to such a great interest. Artists, architects and psychologists got together to prepare carefully the size and the height of the rooms and the artistic elements of the school. This interest arose, because for the first time we had the conception of a school which was not merely a shelter, but aimed at helping the concentration of little children. It was more than a protective environment, it was a psychic environment. In this environment it is not so much the form, size, etc., but the objects it contains that matter, because concentration can only take place if a child has an object. These objects are not casually chosen, they are special objects determined by our experience with the children themselves.

The first idea was to enrich the environment with many objects and the children were given freedom to choose what they desired among these objects.

We found that the children chose only certain objects, others remained unused, so we eliminated them from the environment. The objects we now have decided on, were chosen by the children themselves, and we did not work on these experimental lines in one country only, we tried it out all over the world. There were certain objects that all children chose, those we put in as essential; there were certain objects that children in all countries rarely used, (even though adults thought they would use them), those we eliminated. Wherever there were our normalized children and freedom of choice this happened, and it reminded me of insects that go only and always to certain flowers which they need. Here with the children there is the need of certain stimuli. The children chose those objects which aided their construction of themselves. In the beginning there were many toys, but the children did not use them. There were many types of objects for teaching color, the children chose only one type: the color tablets which we now use. This happened in all countries alike. Also with the size of the objects and the intensity of color the choice of the children was taken as the determining factor. This brought about the system of determination and limitation of objects in our method. This principle has a bearing on social life as well. If there are too many objects or more than one set of material for a group of about 30 to 40 children, there is confusion. The objects therefore are few though the children are many.

In a class of many children there will only be one copy of each object. If a child wants to use an object which is already being used, he cannot do it and when the children are normalized they will wait till the other has finished using that material. Thus certain social qualities develop which are of great importance, e.g., the child knows that he must respect objects being used by another, not because someone has told him, he simply must, it is a fact he has found by social experience. There are so many of them, there is only one object, the only thing to do is to wait. As this happens every hour of the day for years, this experience of respecting and waiting enters into the life of each individual as an experience which matures with the passing of time.

Thus a transformation and adaptation take place and what is this but building social life? Basically society is not founded upon liking, but on a combination of activities which must harmonize together. By these children's experience another social virtue is developed: patience. This patience is a sort of abnegation of impulses. Thus the features of the character we call virtues come by themselves. One cannot teach this type of morality to children of three years, but experience can. As normalization was not achieved by the children in other environments, this was thrown into greater relief. In the outside world children were snatching at this age, but our children waited. People said: "How could you obtain this sort of discipline in such small children?" It was a question of a prepared environment and freedom within it, and thus certain qualities came out which usually do not appear in children from three to six years, neither much between adults of 25 to 30 years!

The interference of the adult in this adjustment of social behavior is almost always wrong. E.g., two children may walk on the line, one mistakes the direction and it looks like an unavoidable head-on collision. The adult would have the impulse to turn one of the children round, but the children solve their own problem and they solve it every time, not always in the same way, but always satisfactorily. There are many problems of a similar kind in other fields of activity. They arise continuously and the children find great pleasure in solving these problems. If the adults step in to adjust, the children get nervous, but if they are left alone they solve them peacefully. This is also an exercise of social experience and if these problems are solved peacefully, there is continuous experience of social situations which could not be given by the teacher. Generally if a teacher interferes, she has an idea quite different from that of the children and disturbs the social harmony of the class. If there is such a problem, we should, but for exceptional cases, leave the children alone and mind our own business, because in so doing we are able to see how the children solve these problems and observe a manifestation of the behavior of childhood, of the real behavior which the adult does not know at all. Through all these daily experiences a social construction takes place. Generally the teacher has no patience and interferes. In fact, this is so instinctive that in the first days of my work, as the teachers could not resist this impulse, I said: "Tie yourself to a post" and several people did it materially. Other teachers instead of doing that had a rosary, and every time they had an impulse to interfere and someone (or they themselves) checked it, they moved a bead. They always found it wiser not to .interfere and they could count how many times they refrained from doing so.

Ordinary educators do not understand our work for social life; they think that Montessori schools cater for subjects of the curriculum, but not for social life. They say: "If the children work by themselves where is social life?" But what is social life but to solve problems, behave and make plans to suit all? They think of social life as sitting together and listening to a teacher or someone else but this is not social life at all. In fact in ordinary life social experiences are limited to the 'interval' or to the occasional excursions, whilst our children live and work in a community all the time.

Differences of character are revealed and different experiences are possible when there is a great number of children in a class. They do not take place when the children are few. Indeed the greatest perfectionment of children takes place through these social experiences.

Let us now give some consideration to the constitution of this society of children. It was brought about by chance, but by a wise chance. Those children who found themselves together in a closed environment were of different ages (from 3 to 6 years). Usually this is not found in schools, unless the older children are mentally dull. Children are usually classified by age, only in a few schools we find this vertical grouping in one class. The children themselves, however, made us see the difficulty of trying to give culture to children of the same age and capacity. A mother may have six children, but her household runs smoothly. If some of those children are twins, triplets or quadruplets, then difficulties begin, because it is fatiguing for the mother to deal with four children all needing the same thing. The mother with six children of different ages is better off too than the mother with only one child. One child is always difficult. The real difficulty is not that he is petted, but that he has no society and he suffers more than other children. Families often find difficulty with the first child, but not with later children; they think it is due to their greater experience, but it is really because the child has society.

Society is interesting because of the different types that compose it. An Old Men's or Old Women's Home is the most deadly thing. It is a most unnatural and cruel thing to put people of the same age together. It is one of the most cruel things we do to children; it breaks the thread of social life, there is no nourishment for social life. In most schools there is first the separation of the sexes and then that of the ages, separated into classes. This is a fundamental error leading to all sorts of mistakes; it is an artificial isolation which cannot develop the social sense. We generally have co-education for small children. Really co-education is not so important, boys and girls could have different schools, but there should be children of different ages in the classes. Our schools have shown that children of different ages help each other, the small one sees what the elder one does and asks about it, and the older one gives an explanation. This is really teaching, but the explanation and teaching of a child of five years is so near to the understanding of the child of three years that the little one understands easily, whereas we should not reach his intelligence.

There is a sort of harmony and interchange of ideas between them which is not possible between an adult and a child so small. We can see this if we compare it with adult society. A university professor gives a talk to illiterates and the latter cannot understand anything, so it is not wise to ask them to help in the work with illiterates. They do not easily find the means, the level should not be so far distant. That is why adult education is so difficult. When the first Popular University in Rome was founded, all the big University professors wanted to help. One of them tried to teach hygiene to these poor ill-educated people. The subject was plague and he showed pictures of the bacilli. The audience asked: "What are bacilli?" He answered: "You see them on this slide." Then he was asked: "What is a slide?" and he answered: "It is a slip of glass which you put under a microscope," The next question was: "What is a microscope?" etc., etc. So the professor gave up the chair in the Popular University. In the problem of educating the masses one should not go to the great professors, but to people of goodwill and basic knowledge who can transmit it in simple language.

We teachers are incapable of making a child of three years understand many things, but a child of five years can make him understand; there is a natural mental osmosis between them. Also the child of 3 years can become interested in what the child of 5 years does because it is not so very different from the possibilities of the child of 3 years. All the older children become heroes and teachers and all the smaller ones are great admirers. The small ones go to the older ones for inspiration and then work by themselves. In ordinary schools where there are children of the same age it is true that those with more ability could teach the others, but the teacher does not usually allow it. They merely ask to give the correct answers when others cannot and so envy arises. With younger children there is no envy, they are not humiliated by being taught by an older one, because they know they are smaller and feel that when they are big they can do the same. There is love and admiration, real brotherhood. In the old schools the only way to reach a higher level is by competition, which means envy, hate, humiliation and all things depressive to life and anti-social. The intelligent child becomes vain and gathers power over others, whereas the child of five with the child of three feels himself a protector. It is difficult to imagine how much this atmosphere of protection and admiration increases and deepens in its action: the class becomes a group cemented by affection. The children come to know each others character and appreciate each other. In ordinary schools they merely know: "That fellow got the first prize, that other fellow got zero." Brotherhood cannot develop in these conditions and yet this is the age of construction for social and anti-social qualities, according to the environment; it starts at this age.

People become worried whether the five years old will acquire sufficient knowledge if he is always teaching younger ones. In the first place, he is not always teaching, he has his freedom and it is respected. Apart from that, in teaching he fixes his own knowledge, because he has to analyze and re-handle it in order to to teach, so he sees it with greater clarity. The older child also is benefitted by this exchange.

The class of children from three to six years of age is not rigidly separated from that of the seven to nine year old ones either, so the six year old gets his inspiration from the next class. All our walls are only half walls and there is always easy access from one class to another as all the children are free to move from class to class. If the three years old goes to the class of the seven to nine years old ones he does not stay long, because he sees he cannot get anything that is useful to him. There are limitations therefore, but no separation and all the groups are in communication. The groups have their own environment, but they are not isolated. There is the possibility of an intellectual walk, A three years old can see a nine years old extracting the square root, he asks him what he is doing. If the answer gives him no inspiration he goes back to his own class where there are objects of inspiration, but the six year old would be interested and would find inspiration there. With this freedom one can see the limits of the intelligence of each age. That is how we found that the children of eight and nine years understood the extraction of the square root being done (at that time) by children of twelve and fourteen years. Thus he also understood that the child was interested in and capable of algebra at eight years. It is therefore not only the age which leads to progress, but also the freedom to move about.

It is intellectual height which is important. In society you find people of all ages, in all history we do not find any instance of a society divided into age groups. In the ordinary schools divided in age groups there is nothing which is social despite all its claims. This intercourse between children of different ages brings harmony and happiness, because the older children find they are real teachers even though they have not been to Teachers' Training Colleges and are not B.T.s. These children do teach, whereas, judging by examination results, apparently qualified teachers do not teach!

There is animation everywhere and there is no inferiority-complex. The smaller child is animated, because he does understand what the older one does, and the older one is animated, because he can teach what he knows; so there is an enhancement of forces, of psychic forces.

These and other facts show that all these phenomena which seemed so extraordinary were not really so extraordinary. They were merely the result of natural laws being obeyed.

All these energies are thrown away in ordinary education. If henceforth they are no longer wasted, there will be new psychic wealth for the new generations. It comes without much expenditure: few teachers and by tying those few to poles!

It is by studying the behavior of these children and their re-actions to each other in this atmosphere of freedom that the real secret of society is revealed. They are fine and delicate facts that have to be examined with a spiritual microscope, but they are of the utmost interest since they reveal facts inherent in the very nature of man. These schools, therefore, are thought of as laboratories for psychological research, although it is not really research, but observation that is carried out. It is this observation which is important.

There are facts the importance of which is very great, e.g., that the children solve their own problems. If we observe the children without intervening, we notice one great fact, vis., that children do not help each other in the same way as we do. We see children carrying heavy objects and no other child goes to help them, or they put all the apparatus away after a complicated exercise and nobody helps. They respect each other and only help when help is a real necessity. This enlightens us greatly, because they evidently have an intuition of, and show respect for, the essential need of the child not to be helped uselessly. There was once a child who had spread all the geometrical cards on the floor with all the geometrical insets. Suddenly there was music, a procession passing, all the children ran to look except the little fellow with all the material. He did not go, because he would not dream of leaving all the material about like that. It should be put away and normally nobody would help him, but there were tears in his eyes, because he too wanted to see the procession. The others realized the emergency and all came back and helped him. Adults do not possess this fine discrimination in determining when to help. They help each other frequently when it is not necessary. A gentleman will often (as a matter of good manners) adjust a chair at a table to help a young lady to sit down when she is quite capable of sitting down unaided, or take her arm in going downstairs although she is quite capable of walking without his support, but when someone loses his fortune then nobody helps. When help is needed, nobody helps, when help is not needed all help! So here is a point where the adult cannot teach the children, because he himself does not know the right way as well as the children do. I think that probably the subconscious of the child still retains the memory of his desire and need to make the maximum effort and that is why instinctively he does not help others where help would be a hindrance.

Another interesting feature is the way children deal with a disturber, perhaps a child newly admitted to the school and not accustomed to the behavior there. He disturbs and is a real problem for the teacher and the children. The teacher generally says: "That is very naughty. This is not nice," sometimes: "You are a bad boy," but the reaction of the children is interesting. One child approached such a newcomer and said: "You are naughty, but don't worry about it, when we came we were as naughty as you," The naughtiness was recognized as a misfortune and the child was trying to console the naughty one and bring out the real boy. He had compassion for him. What a change there would be in society if the evil doer evoked compassion and we made an effort to console him. It would mean compassion for him as we have when he has a physical illness. Wrong doing is often a psychic illness due to an unfavorable environment or the condition of birth or some such misfortune. It ought to evoke compassion and help, not merely punishment. This would change our social structure for the better. With our children if an accident happens, e.g., a vase that falls down, the child who has dropped it is often desperate, because they do not like destruction and also it suggests inferiority, they are incapable of carrying it. The instinctive reaction of the adult is to say: "See it is broken; why do you touch these things when I have told you not to do so?" Or at least they would tell him to pick up the pieces, because they think the child will take the lesson more seriously if he has to clear up the results of the accident. But what do the children do? They all run around to help; with the sound of help in their little voices, they say: "Never mind! We can get another glass." And some of them will pick up the pieces and another will wipe up the water that has run over the floor. So there is an instinct that attracts them to help one who is weak with encouragement and consolation and this is an instinct of social evolution. Indeed a great part of our social evolution has come about when society went out to help the weak. All our medical sciences developed on this principle, so that from this instinct has come help not only for those who were the object of compassion, but for the whole of humanity. It is not an error to encourage those who are weak and those who are inferior, it is the correct thing and it carries forward the whole of society. Children show these sentiments as soon as they become normalized, not only for each other, but for animals too.

Everyone thinks that respect to animals has to be taught, as they think that children tend to cruelty towards them. This is not so, they have an instinct to protect them. We had in our school at Kodaikanal a baby-goat. I used to feed it daily and held the food high so that the little one used to rise up to it on its hind legs. I was interested in watching the baby-animal do this and it seemed to enjoy it. But one day a little child with a look of anxiety on his face came and held the goat with his two hands under its body, because he thought the baby-animal should not have to depend on only his two hind legs. This was a very delicate sentiment.

Another manifestation in our schools is the admiration for those who do better than oneself. The children are not only not envious at all, but the achievements of other children evoke an enthusiastic admiration and joy. This was what happened in the famous incident of the explosion into writing. It was the first written word and it caused a great joy and laughter and they looked at the writer with admiration and then it suddenly inspired them to write: "I can do this too! "The good work of one brought the uplift of the whole group. It was the same with the enthusiasm for the alphabet, so that it happened once that the whole class formed a procession with the letters as flags, and there was so much joy and shouting in glee that people came up from downstairs (we were on the roof) to see what all the joy was about. "They are enthusiastic over the alphabet," said the teacher.

There is an evident communication among the children based on a high sentiment and so there is unity in the group. From these instances one realizes that there is a sort of attraction in an atmosphere of high sentiment when the children are normalized. As the older ones are attracted to the little ones and the little ones attracted to the older ones, so the normalized are attracted to the non-normalized (new) children and vice versa.

Society by Cohesion

I would like to relate another episode out of my memorable experience. One day I thought I would give a lesson on a subject which in itself was hardly attractive. I taught the children how to blow their noses and they evidently were greatly interested in my lively demonstrations. I showed them how different people blow their noses, some ostentatiously unfolding their handkerchief and making a lot of noise, and on the other hand the well-educated person who does so almost hiding the necessary movements and even with the least perceptible noise. What struck me was the serious way in which the children followed me. Not one began to laugh. When I had finished, to my immense surprise, the audience of infants burst out into loud applause. Never had I witnessed such manifestation. Never, as far as I know, in world history had a gathering of small children applauded a speech.

Yet, not two or three children only, but all of them at the same time clapped with great enthusiasm their small hands which until then had only "worked," I went out as usual and after having walked along the footpath for a little while I turned round and saw to my amazement that all the children had been following me. They really looked like a swarm of bees, only they moved so silently that I had not been aware of them. What a curious situation! What would the passers-by have said if they had seen a lady walking in the street, followed at some distance by this solid group of forty-five tiny children? I turned to them and said calmly: "Now run back to school, all of you, but on tiptoe and take care not to knock against the door-post," I gave this instruction, because I knew that exactitude in actions has great interest for such young children. As by magic they all turned their back on me and ran off on tiptoe. When they reached the door they made a wide curve and avoided the corner, Centering through the center of the door-opening. Thus they disappeared.

"Why such enthusiasm?" I thought. Perhaps I had happened to touch a social question to which they were very sensitive. In fact all children are generally humiliated on account of their dirty noses. In Italy vulgar people call the child "a snotty one" instead of calling him a child. Small children have always dirty noses and the mothers of the people sometimes attach a handkerchief to the child's dress with a safety-pin, right in front of their body. This evidently they feel as a humiliating sign of inferiority. Perhaps that was the reason of the success of my lesson. I had given them a lesson instead of showing contempt. Now they had acquired knowledge which redeemed them and raised their personal dignity. My action had somehow been similar to that of a popular leader, of a revolutionary who tries to raise the masses and defends their human dignity.

This miniature episode was really surprising, but the main fact was that these children felt and acted as a group. They really formed a society of children, united by a mysterious bond, and acted as one body. This bond was formed by a common sentiment felt by each individual. Although they were "independent individuals," although they did not depend on one another, they were all moved by the same impulse.

Such a society seems to be more closely connected to the absorbent mind than to consciousness.

The lines of construction which we have observed seem to be analogous to those which we can follow through the microscope when we observe the work of the cells building up an organism. Evidently also society has an embryological phase which can be observed in its initial formation among children in course of development.

It is very interesting to see how, slowly, they seem to become conscious of forming a community which acts as such. They seem to become aware of belonging to a group and of contributing to the activity of that group. They not only begin to be interested in it, but I would almost say that they delve into it with their spirit. When they reach this stage they do not act mechanically any longer, they aim at success, they give special consideration to the honor of the group. This first step towards full social consciousness I call "clan spirit" comparing it to those primitive human societies wherein the individuals already love, defend and appreciate the value of their group as an aim of each individual's activity.

The first manifestations of this phenomenon amazed us also, because they appeared independently of any influence of ours. They came forth as facts successively expressing development, just as at a certain age the teeth are seen to pierce the gums. This association brought about by natural urges, directed by a power within itself, animated by a social spirit, I call 'Cohesive Society,'

I came to this conception by some spontaneous manifestations of children which amazed us very much. Let me give an example of them: I knew that some important visitors from the United States were to come and see the school the next day. I, however, could not possibly be there to receive them. Before going away I told the children as a matter of confidence: To-morrow some people are coming to see the school. How happy I would be if they said: "This is the school with the nicest children in the world." I uttered this sentence without any afterthought, almost involuntarily, and did not think it would have the slightest consequence.

When I came back to the school another day I found the teacher quite excited, she was in tears when she spoke to me. "You should have seen these children! Every one of them worked and they were full of enthusiasm. They greeted the visitors very politely. I was really moved to see how each of them did his best. Whoever directed them? It must have been the holy Angels themselves!" They evidently felt the honor of their clan and acted in a way even more impressive than when they only obeyed their vital urges. They had been capable of feeling something beyond their individual needs.

Similar experiences were often repeated. When the Ambassador of the Argentine wished to see this famous school where children of only four and five years old worked on their own, read and wrote spontaneously and behaved with discipline not imposed by the authority of the teacher, he was really very incredulous. Instead of announcing his visit he wished to pay a surprise-call. Unfortunately he came just on a holiday and the school was closed. This school was the 'Casa dei Bambini' established in the block of flats where the children lived with their families. A small child happened to be in the court-yard when the Ambassador came along and heard his expressions of disappointment. The child understood that he was a visitor and told him: "It does not matter that the school is closed, the janitor has the keys and we are all at home." The door was opened and all the children came to their class and began to work. They felt a kind of responsibility to do well for the honor of their clan. Nobody received any personal benefit from it, nobody wished to distinguish himself, all co-operated for their community. The teacher heard about it only the day after.

This social feeling that had not been instilled by any teaching and was completely different from a competitive sentiment or a personal interest, was like a gift of nature. Yet, it was definitely an achievement which these children had reached through their own efforts. As Coghill says: "Nature determines behavior, but it is developed only by means of experiences in the environment." Nature evidently gives a design for the construction of the personality and of society, but this design is realized only through the obedient activity of the child when he is in a position of bringing it to actuality. In doing so he illustrates the successive phases of development. This clan -spirit which pervades the cohesive society corresponds closely to what the modern American psychologist and educationist, Washburne, calls 'social integration,' He maintains that this is the key to social reform and should constitute the basis of the whole of education. Social integration is realized when the individual identifies himself with a group to which he belongs. A person possessing it thinks of the success of the group rather than of personal credit. Washburne tries to explain his conception by means of a comparison to the Oxford and Cambridge boat-races. "Each individual there makes the greatest possible effort for the honor of his team, fully aware of the fact that he personally will not derive any benefit nor any credit from it. If this were the case in every social enterprise, from nation-wide enterprises to those in industry, etc., and if all let themselves be spurred by the desire of success for the whole of which each forms part, the entire human society would be regenerated. In the schools the development of this feeling of integration of the individual with society should be fostered, because," he adds, "this is what is lacking everywhere and leads society to failure and ruin."

The example of a society where social integration exists can be given: it is the cohesive society of young children, achieved by the magic powers of nature.

We must consider it and treasure it where it is actually being created, because neither character nor sentiments can be given through teaching: they are the product of life.

Cohesive society, however, is not the same as the organized society that rules the destiny of man. It is merely the last phase in the evolution of the child, it is the almost divine and mysterious creation of a kind of social embryo.

Organized Society

At once after six years of age when the child enters another phase of development which marks the transition of the social embryo to the social new -born, another spontaneous form of social life appears very clearly. It shows an organized association, fully conscious of itself. The children then look for principles and laws established by man himself. They seek a leader who directs the community. Evidently obedience to the rules and the leader forms the connective tissue of this society. This obedience has, as we know, been prepared in the embryonic stage which precedes this period of development. MacDougall describes this type of society which children of six and seven years of age already begin to form. They submit to other, older children as if urged by an instinct which he calls the gregarious instinct. Often neglected and abandoned children now organize gangs groups associated especially in revolt against the principles and the authority of adults. These natural urges, however, which often lead to a rebellious attitude have been sublimated in the Boy Scouts movement. The latter answers a real social need of development, instilled in the very nature of children and youths.

This 'gregarious instinct' is different from the force of cohesion which was the basis of the society of infants. These successive societies which continue to develop until they reach the society of adults are all consciously organized societies, they all require man-made rules and a leader to direct them.

Life in society therefore is an innate fact, belonging to human nature as such. It develops as an organism, having different characteristics during its natural evolution. We would compare it to the manufacture of cloth, to weaving and spinning in the manufacture of home-spun cloth which is such an important part of Indian cottage industry. Without doubt we then have to begin at the beginning and consider first that small white fluffy tuft which the cotton plant produces around its seed. So when we wish to consider the construction of human society we must begin with the child and look at him in the surroundings of the family which has given birth to him. The first thing that is done with cotton, which is also the first work in Gandhi's village schools, is to purify the cotton harvested from the plants. The black bits left behind in the cotton by the shell of the cotton seeds have to be cut out. The first activity corresponds to what we do when we gather the children from amongst their homes and purify them of their deviations and help them to concentrate and normalize themselves. Then comes the spinning. Gandhi who has indicated spinning as a means to achieve the liberation and re-birth of India has placed a great symbol in front of the Indian people. Spinning corresponds, in our simile, to the formation of the child's personality accomplished through work and social experiences. This is the basis of all: the development of the personality. If the thread is well spun and strong, the cloth woven from it will equally be so. The quality of the cloth depends upon it. In this symbolic sense the Mahatma's emphatic assertion: "I have consideration only for those who spin," is very right. It is indeed the principal thing to be considered, because cloth woven from threads without resistance has no value.

Then comes the stage when the threads are put on a loom, on a limited frame. The threads are taken up and all stretched in the same direction and then fixed to the staffs at both ends of the loom. The threads are all parallel, of equal length, separate and they do not touch each other. They form the woof of a piece of cloth, but are not cloth. However, without this woof cloth could not be woven. If the threads break or go astray without being fixed in the same direction, the spool cannot shoot through them. This woof corresponds to the cohesive society. In the embryonic preparation of human society it depends on the activity of the children who act upon the urges of nature in a limited environment, corresponding to the loom. In the end they associate themselves, everyone tending to the same aim.

The actual weaving then takes place by passing the spool through these threads and thus uniting them all, keeping each one firmly in place by means of the transversal threads closely pressed together on the woof. This stage corresponds to the real organized society of men which is fixed by rules under the direction of an acknowledged leader whom all obey. Then only we have a real piece of cloth which remains intact even when taken off the loom. It has an existence independent of the loom and once taken off it can be utilized. An unlimited amount can be produced. Men do not form a society because each individual has turned towards some aim in the environment and has concentrated himself upon it on his own account, as happens in the cohesive society of small children, but the final form of human society rests on organization.

The two things, however, are interlinked. Society does not depend only on organization, but also on cohesion. The latter in fact is the more fundamental of the two and serves as a basis for the construction of the former. Good laws and a good leader cannot keep the masses together and make them act, unless the individuals themselves be already oriented towards something that fixes them, and makes a group out of them. The masses in their turn are more or less strong and active according to the degree of development of the personality of the individuals who make them up. The organization of society depends therefore not only on circumstances and events, but first of all on the formation of the individuals and their inner orientation.

The Greeks, e.g., had as the basis of their social constitution the formation of the personality. Their leader, in later times, Alexander the Great, conquered with but few men the whole of present day Persia. Let us also look at the Muslims: they represent a formidable union, not so much on account of their laws and leaders, but because they are united in cohesion by a common ideal. Periodically they take to the road in masses and go as pilgrims to Mecca. These pilgrims do not know each other, they have no private interests nor ambition: they are all individually directed towards the same goal. Nobody pushes them on, nobody commands them, and yet they are capable of immense sacrifices to achieve their aims. These pilgrimages are accomplished only by cohesion.

In the history of Europe during the Middle Ages we see something that the leaders of our war-torn times try in vain to achieve: then there were really the United Nations of Europe. And how did it happen? The secret of this success lay in the fact that all the individuals of the nations and European empires had been conquered by one and the same religious faith which formed a formidable force of cohesion. Then we really saw kings and emperors each ruling his own people according to his own laws, but all subject to and dependent on the force of Christianity. Cohesion, however, does not suffice to construct a society which acts practically upon the world creating civilizations by means of intelligence and labor. In our own times, we observe the Jews who are united by a millenarian force of cohesion: but they are not organized and do not exist as a national power. They are only the woof of a people.

It is noteworthy that in the most recent times we had a new example of this in history. Mussolini and Hitler were the first to realize that in order to achieve success in conquest the individuals should be prepared from their very infancy. The "Figli della Lupa" (sons of the wolf the name of the organization of Fascist children) and the "Balilla italiani" (name of the organization of older children) just as the "Hitler Jugend" (Hitler Youth, as the Nazi youth organization was called) were set up years before these two leaders began to step up the armament of their countries in view of war. They prepared the children and the youths during the years of schooling and imposed upon them from the outside an ideal that would unite them. This was a new, logical and scientific procedure whatever its moral value may have been. These leaders understood the need to have a "cohesive society" as the basis of their plans and prepared it from infancy.

The cohesive society, however, is a natural fact and must be constructed spontaneously on the creative urges of nature. Nobody can substitute himself for God and whoever tries to do so in society becomes a devil like the adult who in his pride crushes by repression the creative energies of the child-personality. Also the force of cohesion in adults is something which is attached to cosmic directives, to ideals superior to the mechanism of organization. There ought to be two societies, interwoven among themselves, one of them, we might say, has its roots in the subconscious and creative unconscious mind, the other depends upon men who act consciously. We could also express it as follows: one begins in childhood and the other is superimposed upon it by the adult, because, as we have seen in the beginning of this volume, it is the absorbent mind of the child which incarnates the characteristics of the race. Which are the characteristics it incarnates almost as if it realized another form of heredity found only in man; a heredity which does not depend upon the hidden genes of the germinative cell, but comes from the other creative center, the child? The characteristics which the child incarnates when he lives as a spiritual embryo are not the discoveries of the intellect, nor of human labor, but those characters which are found in the cohesive part of society. He, the child, gathers them and incarnates them. By means of these characteristics he builds his personality: thus he becomes a man with a particular language, a particular religion, a particular set of customs. What is fixed, and fundamental, what is 'basic,' to use a fashionable term, in an ever-changing society is its cohesive part.

When we leave the child to develop, when we leave him to build up the adult man from the invisible roots of creation, then we can learn the secrets upon which depends our individual and social strength.

Instead of this and we have only to look about to see it nowadays men only judge and act and regulate themselves by the conscious and organizatory part of society. They wish to strengthen and assure the organization as if they alone were its creators. They have no consideration for the bases indispensable to that organization. They only allow for human direction and their aspiration goes towards the discovery of a leader.

How many hope for a new Messiah, for a genius of conquering and organizing power! After the first world-war it was proposed to found schools for the preparation of leaders, because it was seen that those there were had insufficient training and were unfit to direct world events. There were really attempts to try and find out by means of mental tests which were the supernormal persons, youths who in their school years were the most intelligent, in order to train them for leadership. But who could train them if precisely there are no good leaders, teacher-leaders?

It is not the leaders who are lacking, or rather the question is not limited to this detail. The question is much vaster and it is the masses themselves who are completely unprepared for the social life of our actual civilization. The problem, therefore, is to train the masses, to re-constitute the character of all the individuals, to harvest the treasures hidden in everyone of them and to develop their values. No leader can achieve this, however great his genius may be.

Just as a great literary genius would not be sufficient to make literates out of millions of illiterates, even if he had unlimited powers, because it would be necessary for those millions to learn how to read and to write, each one individually, (and this can be done by children only), so also in this far greater question.

This is the most practical and urgent task of our critical times. The fact is that the human masses are inferior to what they could be. We saw it in the diagram of the two forces of attraction, one coming from the center and the other from the periphery. The great task of education must consist directly in trying to save normality which on its own strength tends towards a center of perfection. Now, instead, all that is done is to prepare artificially weak and abnormal men, predisposed to mental diseases, in need of unceasing care and small exercises in virtue so that they may not fall towards the periphery where, once fallen, they become extra-social beings. This which actually happens now is really a crime of lese-humanity which has a repercussion on everyone of us and which may yet destroy us. The mass of illiterates which covers half of the surface of the earth does not really weigh upon society; what does weigh upon it is the fact that we are ignorant regarding the creation of man, that we trample upon the treasures deposited by God himself in every child without even being aware of it, because here is the source of the intellectual and moral values which can raise the whole world upon a higher plane. We weep in front of the dead and we aspire towards saving humanity from destruction, but it is not the salvation from dangers, it is the elevation that is the destiny of everyone of us which should stand before our mind's eye. It is not death, but the lost paradise that should afflict us.

The greatest danger lies in our ignorance, in the ignorance of us who look for pearls in oyster shells, for gold in rocks, for coal in the very entrails of the earth, but ignore the spiritual germs, the nebulae of creation, which the child hides within himself when he comes into our world to renew mankind.

If this spontaneous organization and the possibility to move easily and at will from one class to another were allowed for in ordinary schools, it would bring a great betterment, because in the ordinary schools people start from the opposite point of view. They believe children are not active in learning and so they urge or encourage, punish or give prizes to foster activity. Competition also they use as an encouragement to give animation to effort. People generally seem to be animated by a search for the evil in whatever there is in order to fight against it. The attitude of the adult is to seek evil to suppress it, then to criticize and judge malevolently is a necessity. But the correction of an error is a humiliation and discouragement and as this is the basis of education generally, the whole of it is based on a lowering of the level of life. No copying allowed, so no union, it is a sin in the school to help an inferior pupil; the pupil who helps one who does not know his work is considered as guilty as the one who accepts the help, so a morality is imposed which lowers the level. Again we hear all the time "Don't fidget!" "Don't prompt!," "Don't help!" "Don't answer when not asked!" All DON'Ts, all negations. What must we do with this situation? Even if the average teacher did try to uplift his class, he would do it in a way opposite to that of the children. The maximum he would say is probably: "Don't be envious if one is better than you " or "Don't seek revenge if someone has upset you," Ordinary education apparently cannot be understood without negation. The general idea is that everyone is wrong and we must help them to become less wrong than they are. But children do things that do not occur to the teacher; they would admire the one who was better than they, not merely be just 'not envious.' One cannot however command admiration of a rival, so the teacher is limited. What can she do? Certain attitudes of the spirit cannot be commanded if they do not exist. If the existence however is there and is instinctive (as it is) then how important it is to hold and encourage it. It is the same with the law: "Don't seek revenge." The child frequently makes one who hurts him or takes his place in the lime-light his friend, but one cannot command that. One must have sympathy and love for those who do evil, but it is not possible to command that. One must give help to the incapable, but one cannot command that. So there are sentiments in the soul of the child which cannot be commanded, but are there naturally and should be upheld. Unfortunately they are generally stifled and all the work in schools is in the inferior white zone of figure 10, with its pull towards the periphery of the anti-social and the extra-social. The teacher first thinks that the child is incapable and must be made capable, then he proceeds to do so by saying: "Don't do this or that"; "Don't slide to the periphery" in other words. An effort is made to keep the sliders from sliding and that is all. But all the time normalized children are showing us an exaggeration of good instead of this emphasis on avoiding evil. The interruption of work by the hours fixed by a time-table and the periods of rest is also negative. "Don't work too hard at one thing or you will be tired," whereas the child shows clearly the desire for the maximum effort. The ordinary schools could never help the creative instincts of children, because there is an exaggeration of activity on the part of the child. The exaggerated activity, to work a great deal, to find all work beautiful, to console the afflicted and help the weak are all instincts of these young children. A comparison between the ordinary school and normalized children reminds me of the Old Testament of the Bible and the New Testament. The Ten Commandments of the Old Testament the book of the old religion are mostly negative: "Don't kill," "Don't steal," all don'ts; these are for inferior people and are necessary for those who are confused, but the New Testament shows Christ as similar to the children; it says positive things an exaggeration of what one would usually do; e.g.,: "Love your enemy" an exaggeration of positiveness. So also when there came people who seemed superior to many, who followed the laws and wanted approbation for that, Christ said: "I have come for the sinners" (the inferior). To this the children's nature corresponds. It is an exposition of the exaggeration of good. What, however, are the consequences? It is not sufficient to teach these principles to man nor is it sufficient for man to have them; it is useless to repeat: "Love your enemy"; even if it is said, it is said in church, but not on the battlefield, there just the opposite is done. The people who say: "Don't kill" are merely drawing attention to the evil in order to protect themselves, because the good to them is unpractical. Loving your enemy seems unpractical so it mostly remains an empty ideal.

Why does this happen? Because the root of good does not exist in the heart of man; it may have been there once, but it is dead, it has disappeared. If during the whole period of education hate, rivalry, competition have been encouraged, how can we expect people grown in this atmosphere to be good at twenty or thirty, because somebody preaches goodness? I say, it is impossible. No sensorial organ in the spirit has been prepared to collect this preaching or if it began to be prepared, it was destroyed, so the preaching flies away on the wings of the wind.

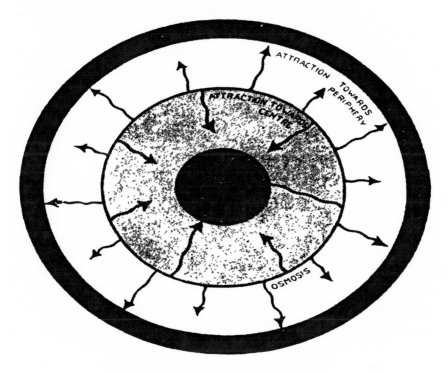

Fig 10 Circles of attraction towards superior and inferior types

Creative instincts, not preaching are the important things, because they reveal a reality, young children act as nature urges them to act and not because the teacher tells them to do so. Good should come about by reciprocal aid, by union brought about by spiritual cohesion. This society by cohesion which has been revealed by the children is the basis of all organization; that is why I maintain that it is not we who can teach children between the ages of three and six years. We can observe in a refined manner and see how development is achieved by every daily and hourly exercise. That which nature gives is developed by constant exercise. Nature provides a guide but it is also revealed that to develop anything in any field, continuous experience and effort is necessary. If I have not had the opportunity for this, preaching is useless.

Growth comes from activity, not from intellectual understanding, hence the education of small children is important, and especially between the ages of three and six years, because this is the embryonic period for the formation of character and for the formation of society (just as the period from birth to three years is the embryonic period for the formation of the psyche; and the prenatal period, the embryonic period for the formation of physical life.) The things that the children carry out between the ages of three and six do not depend on doctrine, but on a divine directive given by God to the spirit undergoing construction. They are germs of behavior and can develop only with the right environment of freedom and order.

Error and its Control

When we say that the children are free in our schools, organization is necessary, an organization more detailed than in other schools, so that the children may be free to Work. The child, by carrying out experiments in a prepared environment, perfects himself, but a certain amount of apparatus is then necessary and space is necessary. Once the child has achieved concentration, he continues to be concentrated through many activities, and as he becomes more and more active, the teacher becomes less and less so, till she is almost put aside.

We have mentioned that through exercises repeated in freedom the children join together in a special society and this society is so much more refined than ours that it inspires the wish and conviction that the children should be left free and not interfered with. It is a phenomenon of life, a phenomenon as delicate as the phenomena of embryonic life and it should not be touched. If these conditions are present it can happen with any of our materials.

In this environment there is a definite relation between the teacher and the child. The teacher's task, which is determined in detail, shall be outlined in another chapter, but one of the things she must not do is to interfere, to praise, to punish or to correct errors. This seems a wrong principle to most educationists and when we find them opposed to our method, it is always on this point. They say: "How can we improve the children's work if we do not correct the errors?" In ordinary education the fundamental task is to correct both in the moral and intellectual field, else the teacher does not feel she has done her job. Education walks on the two feet of the giving of prizes and of giving punishments; but if a child is given prizes and punishments it means that he does not have the energy to guide himself and that the teacher is hovering over the child and directing him. In our schools they automatically disappeared because there was no need for them. Prizes and punishments come from outside, so when they are given the spontaneity of spirit disappears; and as this is a method of spontaneity, it makes no sense to give prizes or punishments. This is so difficult to understand that even in so-called Montessori schools they are given; how often have I been invited to a prize-giving in such Montessori, schools! Whereas if the children are given freedom, they are absolutely indifferent to prizes.

In my first experiment, the teacher who was, as I have mentioned, the caretaker's daughter, also had this idea of prizes and punishments. After all it is so common in the home as well as in the school, that it is almost incarnated in the soul of man. I was against it then, but had no method as yet, and I tolerated it because the poor teacher had to have something to do. She made big 'military' crosses in gold or silver paper as rewards and pinned them to the breasts of the children rewarded, with a silk ribbon. I did not think much of the idea, but I left it alone. One day I went to the school and found a child seated all by himself on a chair in the middle of the room and wearing a large cross. I asked: "Have you given a prize to this one?" The teacher said: "No, he was being punished; that is why he is sitting alone." The cross had actually been given to another child, but it was in his way as he worked, so he gave it to the child in the middle who had nothing to do and with whom it would not interfere! And the child in the middle was indifferent both to the cross and to the punishment! We found also that sweets and such rewards were not appreciated.

The abolition of prizes might not have aroused much trouble, because after all it would mean an economy. Only a few get them in any case, and those at the end of the year. But punishments! That was a different matter, they happen every day throughout the year and 'corrections' are still more frequent. What does this correction, in copy-books for example, mean? It means putting a mark A, B, or C or 10 or 0. How can the marking of a zero be a correction? Then the teacher says: "You always make the same errors; you don't listen when I speak; you will fail in the examination," All these corrections in books and these accusations of the teacher result in a lowering of energy and interest. To say: "You are bad" or "You are a dunce" is humiliating; it is an insult, an offence, but it is not a correction, because in order to correct oneself one must become better, and how can a child become better if he is below level already and then we humiliate him further? In olden times teachers used to put donkey's ears to children when they were stupid, and beat the tips of the fingers of those who could not write. If they had used all the paper in the world making donkey's ears and beaten the fingers to pulp, they would have corrected nothing. Experience and exercise alone correct errors, and the acquisition of faculties demands long exercise. If a child lacks discipline he becomes disciplined through work and association with others in a society of cohesion, not by telling him that he is undisciplined. If you tell a child he cannot do something, he could quite easily tell you: "You are telling me that? I know I can't." That is not correction, but a presentation of facts. Correction and perfection come only when the child can exercise himself in freedom for a sufficiently long time.

Errors can be made and the children may not always see them, but teachers also can make errors and not know they are errors. Unfortunately the teacher usually starts as if she were a perfect being and an example, so if she makes a mistake she certainly does not tell the child about it. Her dignity is based on always being right. In the ordinary school she must be infallible, so the whole of education there is on a false basis.

Let us consider error itself. It is necessary to admit that we all make errors; it is a reality of life so that admission in itself is a great step in our progress. If we are to walk on the path of truth and reality we must admit that we all make mistakes or else we should be perfect. So the best thing is to become friendly with the error and then it will not frighten us any more, but will be a friendly person living among us and will perform its task, because it has one. Many errors are corrected spontaneously through life. A child of one year walking on the line, walks unsteadily, rolls, falls, but finally it walks correctly. He corrects his errors through growth and experiences. We have an illusion that we are walking along the path of life towards perfection, we are all the time making errors and do not correct them. We do not recognize them, so we are out of reality altogether and in illusion. The teacher who poses as perfect and does not recognize that she makes errors, is not a good teacher. No matter where we look, we always find Gentleman Error! If we set out on the path towards perfection, we must look carefully at error, because perfection will come by correcting it. We should use a light to show the error. We must know there is error as there is life; it is as real as that.

The exact sciences (mathematics, physics, chemistry, etc.) have called attention to errors, because these sciences purposely make them stand out. The scientific study of error has begun with the positive sciences, those which are considered to be without error, because they measure exactly and can appreciate error. There are therefore two things in life: (I) to reach a certain exactness: (ii) to appreciate error in exactness. Whatever science gives, she gives as an approximation, not as an absolute, and this approximation is considered with the result. For example, an anti-microbe injection is certain in 95% of the cases, but it is important to know that there is 5% uncertainty. Also in taking a measurement it is stated correct to so many thousandths of an inch. In science no data are given or accepted unless with the indication of probable error and what gives importance to the data is the calculation of the error. No data are considered seriously, unless the amount of probable error is given and attached to the result, it is as important as the result itself. So if it is so important for the exact sciences, how much more important it is for our work. Then error becomes something interesting and important, and the knowledge of it is necessary for correcting or controlling.

We then reach a scientific principle, which is also a principle of truth, i.e., the 'control of error.' In whatever is done in school by teacher or children or by others, there must be error and this must so enter into the school-life that there is no outside correction, but an individual, independent control of error, that tells us whether we are right or not. I must know whether I have worked rightly or not, therefore error becomes interesting to me whereas before it was superficial. In the usual school one makes errors without knowing it, unconscious and indifferent to it, for it is not I, but the teacher who makes me conscious of errors. How far off from the field of freedom! If I do not have the ability of controlling my error, I have to go to someone else who may know no better than I. Instead, how important one becomes, when one knows one is making mistakes and can control them! One of the greatest realizations of psychic freedom is to realize that we may make a mistake and can control it; to recognize and control error without help. One thing that makes for indecision of character is that we are unable to control anything without the help of someone else. There is a sense of inferiority, of discouragement and a lack of confidence, when one has to rely on others to tell one where one is wrong. So the control of error becomes the guide which tells us whether we are proceeding on the right path or not. We have an instinct to go towards perfection; we want to be able to know for ourselves whether we are on the right path.

Supposing I want to go somewhere and I can drive a car, but I do not know the road; this often happens in life. In order to be sure that I go right, I take a map; also I see several signs which tell me where I am. I may have been seeing signs which said "2 miles to Ahmedabad," but if then I suddenly see a sign that says "50 miles to Bombay," I know I have gone wrong somewhere. The map and the signs have helped me; if I had had no map I should have had to ask and be told many things probably contradictory in their advice. If there is no guide or control it is impossible to go on.

What is necessary therefore in positive science and in practical life must also be included in education from the very beginning: the possibility of a control of error. So with the teaching and the material must go the control of error. The way to go forward is to have freedom and a sure way, with the means of telling ourselves when we make a mistake. When this principle is realized in the school and in practical life, it does not matter whether the teacher or the mother is perfect or not. Errors in older people become interesting and the children have sympathy with them. It becomes something interesting, but completely detached. It becomes an inherent fact in nature, and how much affection it provokes in the hearts of children that we can all make mistakes. Another factor enters the relationship between mother and child. The fact that we can all make mistakes makes us more friendly. Brotherhood comes along the path of errors, not along the path of perfection. If one is perfect one cannot change any more, two 'perfect' people together usually fight, because there is no possibility of change and of understanding each other. If one has grown up without error, there is no progress and no help possible, because one cannot help the perfect. If, therefore, we think we are perfect, we are not in the field of truth; one is misled by the illusion of perfection one puts before one's eyes, but never achieves. Let us make a geometrical comparison: we can superimpose squares one on the other, as is done in one of our children's exercises with inscribed squares. As we continue inscribing squares to a further and further degree, we gradually reduce the difference between the last one and that immediately before it. If we think of this as gradually reducing the 'error' between the squares, we find that, however small it eventually becomes, yet we never reach the complete elimination of error. Let us look at one of the earliest practical exercises the children do. We have cylinders all of the same height, but differing in diameter which fit into corresponding sockets. Recognizing that they differ is first perfectionment, holding them with three fingers is another perfectionment. The child begins to place them in their sockets, but when he has finished he sees that he has made a mistake for a thick one is left whilst there is only a thin hole for it to fill, and some of the others are loose and rattle, so he looks at them again and observes them more carefully than before. The child knows he can make a mistake and that if he does so, one cylinder cannot be fitted. If there were not this possibility of mistake there would not be the same interest. It is this that makes him repeat the exercise again and again. So the material has two requirements to meet: (I) to refine the senses of the child, (ii) to provide a possibility of control of error.

The above mentioned material has a control of error which is very material and visible, so a little child of two years can use it and with it acquire the knowledge of control of error on the path to perfection. With daily practice in such exercises the child gains power to control error and becomes sure of himself. To be sure of oneself does not mean perfection, but it means to know one's possibilities and, therefore, to be able to do something. He may say: "I am not perfect; I am not omnipotent but I know this thing and my strength and I also know that I can make mistakes and control them, so I am sure of my path." There is prudence, certainty and experience. These lead towards perfection, not that some one says, one is this, that or the other. In other words to arrive at this sureness is not so simple as one supposes; to be on the path towards perfection is not so simple either. To tell anyone he is silly, stupid, brave, good or bad is a betrayal of humanity; one must be sure for oneself and it is necessary to give the means of development and the control of error for this.

Let us look a little later at a child thus trained. There are mathematical exercises, e.g., multiplication sums. With the sum there is a table of multiplication, which serves as a control of error. Without it there is no possibility of being sure whether one is right; so instead of the teacher correcting, we let the child get into the habit of controlling his own errors. This control of error is more attractive than the exercise itself. So with reading. The child has an exercise of written cards to put with the specimens of those names, and then there are cards with the names written underneath to control his work. The attraction is in finding out whether he was right or not.

If in the practice of school-life there comes this opportunity for constant control of error, this leads to perfection. The interest in the progress to perfection and the control of error is so important to the child that progress is ensured. By nature the child leans to exactness and so this control interests him very much. In one of our schools a child had a reading command which said: "Go out, close the door and come back," The child studied it and started to carry it out; then she came to the teacher and said: "Why did you write it like this? It cannot be done. How can I come back if the door is closed?" So the teacher said: "Yes, my mistake" and rewrote it, and the child said with a smile, "Yes, now I can do it."

Fraternity arises from this interest in the control of error. Error divides men, but control of error is a means of fraternity. It becomes a universal interest to overcome error no matter where it is found. The error itself becomes interesting. It becomes a link and certainly it becomes a means of cohesion among all beings, but especially between the child and the adult. Finding a small error in the adult does not lead to lack of respect or a lowering of dignity. Error is detached from the person and made a thing apart which can be controlled. Thus simple steps lead to great things.

The Three Degrees of Obedience

The main preoccupations in ordinary character education concern the will and obedience, and generally the two ideas are opposed in the minds of those preoccupied with them. One of the main aims is to curb the will of the child, to substitute for it the will of the adult and to demand obedience from him.

I would like to clarify these ideas, basing myself not on any opinion of my own, but on my experience. First of all we must admit that there is a great confusion in these topics. Some biological studies tell us that the will of man is part of a universal power (horme), and that this universal force is not physical, but a force of life along the path of evolution. All life is urged irresistibly towards evolution, and this urge is called horme. Evolution is governed by laws and is not haphazard or casual. These laws of life show us that the will of man is an expression of that force and shapes his behavior. In childhood this force becomes partly conscious as soon as the child carries out a certain self-determined action and then this force is developed in children, but only through experience. So let us begin by saying that the will is something which must develop and, being natural, it obeys natural laws.

Confusion in this subject is also shown by the thought that the voluntary actions of children are naturally disorderly and sometimes violent. This is so generally admitted because people see these sorts of actions in the child and think they express his will. It is not so, these actions do not belong to the field of the universal force or horme. Let us consider the behavior of adults; suppose we mistook convulsions in a man for voluntary manifestations, or actions performed in a frenzy of anger to be directed by his will, that would clearly be absurd. We do not think so; we think of a person of will primarily as someone who carries out something purposive and difficult. If we consider voluntary actions to be mainly disorderly movement in adult or child, then of course we feel we must curb the will, or 'break it' as the older generation used to say; and if we find it necessary to break this ' will,' then, of course, we must substitute our will for the child's by means of his 'obedience' to us.

The real fact is that the will of man (child) does not lead to disorder or violence; these are a mark of deviation and suffering. The will in its natural field is a force which compels us to carry out actions considered to benefit our life. The task given by nature to the child is growth, so the child's will is a force urging to growth and development.

A will that wills what the individual does enters upon a road of conscious development. Our children choose their own work spontaneously and, repeating this exercise of choice, develop a consciousness of their actions. What at first was a hormic impulse urging the child to act now becomes an effort of the will. At first he acted instinctively, now he acts consciously and voluntarily: this is an awakening of the spirit.

The child himself has understood this difference and expressed it in a way that will ever be a precious remembrance of our experience. A society lady once visited the school and, having the old frame of mind, said to a child: "So, this is a place where you do what you like, is it not?" The child answered: "No, Madam, we do not do what we want, we want what we do." The child felt the difference between doing what one likes and liking what one does.

One thing ought to be clear: the conscious will is a power which is developed by means of exercise, of work. Our aim is definitely to cultivate the will, not to break it. The will can be broken almost instantaneously, the development of the will is a slow process unfolding itself by means of continuous activity carried out in relation to the environment. It is easy enough to destroy; the devastation of a building can be accomplished in a few seconds by a bomb or an earthquake. How difficult instead is the construction of a building! It requires accurate knowledge of the laws of equilibrium, of tension,, even art is necessary in order to achieve a harmonious construction.

If all this is needed to achieve a lifeless construction, how much more for the construction of the human soul I It takes place from within. The constructor, therefore, can be neither the mother nor the teacher. They are not the architects, they are not almighty to say, like God in the Bible: "Let there be light, and the light was made." They can only help the creative work that comes from the child himself. That should be their function and their aim, but it is equally in their power to destroy it, to break it by repression. This point, darkened by so many prejudices, deserves to be made clear.

The prejudice prevailing in ordinary education suggests that everything can be achieved by mere teaching (that is by directly addressing the child's hearing) or by upholding oneself as an example to be imitated (which is a kind of visual education). The personality instead can only develop by means of individual exercise, through activity. The child is commonly considered as a receptive being instead of as an active individual. This happens in every field. Even the development of the imagination is considered in this fashion. Children are told fairy tales, enchanting scenes of princes and lovely fairies and thus one tries to develop the imagination. The child, however, then only receives impressions and does not really develop his imaginative powers which are the highest of human intelligence. In the case of the will this error is still more serious, because ordinary education does not only deny the will a chance to develop, it actually obstructs this development and directly inhibits the expression of the will. Every attempt at resistance on the part of the child is repressed as a form of rebellion against this pretension. The educator really tries to destroy the child's will. The educative principle of teaching by example does not lead the teacher to picture a fantastic world of princes and fairies, here the teacher goes as far as to uphold himself as a model. And so both imagination and will remain inert, their activity is confined to follow the teacher who tells stories and who acts.

We must deliver ourselves of these illusions and courageously face reality.

In traditional education the teacher reasons in a way which in itself may seem logical enough. It runs like this: "In order to educate I must be good and perfect (this means that I must disguise myself as a kind of Father Christmas who offers gifts to the children). I know what should be done and what should not be done. It is, therefore, sufficient that the children imitate me and obey me." Obedience is the secret basis of teaching.

I do not remember which renowned educationist pronounced the maxim: "All the virtues of the child can be resumed in one: obedience." but there it is.

The task of the teacher then becomes easy and exalting! He says: "In front of me there is an empty being or a being full of naughtiness I shall now transform him creating him almost to my image and likeness." He repeats to himself the words of the Bible: "and God created man to His own image and likeness."

The adult, of course, is unconscious of thus putting himself in God's place. He forgets above all the other part of the biblical story where it is told how the devil became such precisely on account of his pride urging him to take the place of God.

The poor child! this being who bears within himself the work of a Creator much greater than the teacher, the father or the mother whose likeness he is forced to acquire. In other times teachers used the stick to achieve this aim and even recently in an otherwise highly civilized nation teachers declared: "If we must renounce the stick, we must also renounce education." Besides, in the Bible we find among the proverbs of Solomon the famous one declaring that if we do not use the stick we are bad parents because we condemn our children to hell. Discipline is enforced by threats and fear. This leads to the conclusion that the child who does not obey is bad, the child who obeys is good.

In this era of the theories of democracy and liberty, when we ponder over this attitude, we are inclined to judge the old type of teacher as that of a tyrant. This, however, would not be true, that kind of teacher is not a tyrant. A tyrant is much more intelligent. Tyrants have a certain will-power, some originality and a certain dose of imagination. Teachers of the old type instead have only illusions and prejudices and uphold unreasonable rules. The difference between a tyrant and an old fashioned teacher lies in this: the tyrant uses violent means to achieve the success of his aims, the teacher uses violent means to reach the failure of his aims. It is a fundamental error to think that the will of the individual must be destroyed in order that he may obey, i.e., that he may accept and execute the decision of somebody else's will. If we applied this reasoning to intellectual education we ought to say that it is necessary to destroy the child's intelligence in order that he may receive our culture in his own mind.

To obtain the obedience of individuals who have well developed their own will, but decide to follow ours by their own free choice, is very different indeed. This latter type of obedience is an act of homage, an acknowledgment of a superiority in the teacher, which could make him feel proud and satisfied of himself.

Will and obedience are connected in as much as the will is the foundation and obedience marks a second phase in a process of development. Obedience has thus a higher meaning than is generally realized in education. It may be considered as a sublimation of the individual will.

Also obedience must be interpreted in a way which places it among the phenomena of life and can then be considered as one of the characteristics of nature.

In our children, in fact, we witness the development of obedience as a kind of evolution. It appears spontaneously, as a surprise. It represents the destination of a long process of perfectionment.

If there were not this quality in the human soul, if men could not reach the point of being able to obey by an evolutional process, society could not exist. If we throw but a superficial glance at the affairs of the world we easily discover up to what extent people obey. This kind of obedience is exactly the reason that causes whole groups of humanity to fall into a chasm of destruction. An obedience without control, an obedience leading whole nations to disaster. There is no lack of obedience in the world, far from it! Obedience as a natural consequence of the development of the human soul is very evident indeed, but the control of obedience is sadly lacking.

Our observation of children in a environment prepared to help their natural development has clearly shown us the growth of obedience as one of its most characteristic coefficients and this observation throws a great deal of light upon the subject.

We have clearly seen in the course of our experience that obedience in children is developed in the same way as the other qualities of the character; it follows hormic urges at first, then passes on to a conscious level where it is further developed along several degrees.

Let us first specify what we really and practically mean by obedience. It is after all what has always been meant by it: a teacher commanding the children what to do and the children obeying the command by realizing it.

The natural development of obedience in the child can be divided according to three degrees.

In the first degree the child obeys only occasionally, not always. This fact which could be attributed to whimsical behavior, should be analyzed.

Obedience is not connected only with what is usually called "willingness," it depends on facts of formation. A certain ability and a certain measure of maturity are necessary in order to be able to perform the commanded action. Obedience, therefore, should be judged in relation to development and vital conditions. It is impossible to command "walk on your nose," because this is physiologically impossible. Neither is it possible to command "write a letter" to a person who cannot write. It is necessary, therefore, to establish first the material possibility to obey in relation to the development reached. That is why a child of to 3 years of age is not an obedient child, he has not yet constructed himself. He is taken up by the unconscious elaboration of the mechanisms of his personality and has yet to reach the point where he can establish them so that they may serve his own purpose in order to then dominate them consciously. This represents a progress in development. In fact, the customs and the ways in which adult and child live together have led the adult not to expect obedience from a child of 2 years of age. At this stage the adult can only inhibit more or less violently the actions of such an undeveloped child, should he reprove them.

Obedience, however, does not consist of inhibition only. It consists of the performance of actions corresponding to the will of another person, not to that of the child himself. Although the life of an older child is not taken up by the same primitive preparation which we mentioned for the child between and 3 years of age, where it takes place in the secrecy of his life, even at this later stage we find analogous facts. Also the older child must have developed certain abilities in order that he may obey, i.e., that he may act according to the will of another, and abilities are not developed over night. They are the result of an interior formation passing through several stages. As long as this period of formation lasts it may happen that now and then the child succeeds in performing an action which corresponds to an acquisition just made, but only when the acquisition has become a permanent asset can the will dispose of it. This is also seen when the child labors to make those primitive mechanical acquisitions of the motor functions, when he acts under the compulsion of the hormic urges of life. A child of about 1 year of age can make his first steps, but then he falls down and perhaps he will not be able to repeat them for a long time. It is only when the mechanism of walking is completely established that the child can walk whenever he likes. This is a very important point. The obedience of the child at this later stage depends above all on the stage of development of his capacities. It may therefore happen that he can obey the teacher once, but not after that. This inability to repeat the act of obedience is then attributed to "unwillingness," If so, the teacher with her insistence and criticism may become an obstacle to the inner development that is taking place. In the history of Pestalozzi, the famous Swiss educationist, who had such a great influence on education in schools all over the world, we find a very noteworthy point. Pestalozzi was the first to introduce a so-called paternal gentleness in the treatment of pupils. He was always ready to show sympathy and to forgive. One thing, however, was not included in his forgiveness; whimsical behavior, a child now obeying then disobeying. Who had once executed a command was capable of it and if at another time he did not obey the same command, Pestalozzi would not admit any excuse. That was the only time when he showed himself severe instead of indulgent. If this happened in the case of Pestalozzi, how often will not ordinary teachers commit the same mistake!

On the other hand nothing is more harmful than discouragement at the very time when a facet of development is being constructed. When the child is not yet really master of his own actions, when they do not yet obey his own will, he is even less able to correspond to the will of another person. That is why it may happen that he obeys once, being unable to repeat this act of obedience. This does not even happen in childhood alone. How often will a beginner who plays a musical instrument play a piece quite nicely whilst he is unable to do it a second time? The day after he will be asked to do it again, but he cannot do it as well as he did the day before. The willingness to do so is not at fault, but we face an imperfectly established ability.

What we call the first degree of obedience, therefore, is the period when a child can obey, but is not always able to do so. It is a period when obedience and disobedience exist together.

The second degree is reached when the child can always obey, i.e. there are no obstacles concerning development. His abilities firmly acquired can be called upon and directed not only by his own will, but also by the will of another person. This possibility is a great gift. We could compare it to the ability to translate from one language into another. The child can absorb the will of another person and act accordingly. This is the highest level which generally education tries to reach. The ordinary teacher does not aspire after a stage beyond that when the child obeys all the time. The young child, however, goes far beyond our expectations, as always when he is given the opportunity to follow the laws of nature. The child does not stop here, but goes on towards the: third degree of obedience. Here obedience surpasses the relation to an acquired ability which brings it within reach of the child. Here obedience is directed towards a superior personality, towards the teacher who has served and helped the child. It is as if the child became conscious of the fact that the teacher is capable of things higher than those which he could do by himself. It is as if he said to himself: "This person who is greater than I am can penetrate into my intelligence by her power, she can make me as great as she is herself. She acts in me!" This thought seems to give the child a great and deep joy. To be able to receive directions from this superior life causes a new form of enthusiasm and joy. It is quite a sudden discovery. The child then becomes anxious and impatient to obey. To what could we compare this marvelous natural phenomenon? Perhaps to the spirit of the Saint who said: "I am leaping to obey." Or we might compare it, on quite another plane, to the instinct of the dog who loves his master and through his obedience executes the will of a man. When his master shows him a ball, the dog looks at it intensely and when the master throws it away, he jumps and triumphantly returns it waiting for the next command. The dog is craving for commands, he is excited and waves his tail full of joy. He runs to obey. The third degree of obedience of the young child is somewhat similar, but the child shows his desire to obey in a different manner. In any case, he obeys with a surprising promptitude, and seems impatient to do so.

The findings of a teacher with ten years' teaching experience gives an interesting illustration. She had a class of children which she directed very well, but she could not abstain from advising them. One day she said: "Put everything away, before going home tonight." The children did not wait for her to end her sentence, but as soon as they had heard "Put everything away," they started immediately to put everything carefully, but quickly in its place. Then they heard, to their surprise, "when you go home to-night." Their obedience had become so instantaneous that the teacher felt that she had to be very careful in the wording of her requests. This time she ought to have expressed herself like this: "Before you go home to-night, put everything in its place." She said similar things happened whenever she expressed herself without due care and she felt very responsible whenever she spoke on account of the children's immediate reaction. It was a strange experience for her, because orders seem the natural attribute of authority. Instead of feeling the weight she carried, she keenly felt the tremendous responsibility of her position of authority. She could obtain silence so easily that it was only necessary to write the word silence on the blackboard, and even then, the moment she started to form the letters and long before she had finished the word, all the children were silent.

The Silence Lesson

My own experience, too, which led me to introduce the 'silence -lesson,' proves this attitude of obedience which in this case was a phenomenon of collective obedience. It proved a marvelous and unexpected correspondence by a whole group of children who almost identified themselves with me.

Once I came into a class that was already seriously at work; the children had already developed their will I entered this class of forty-five children with a baby of four months in my arms. It was an old Italian custom to place a baby's legs together and wrap them tightly round and round with cloth so that the legs and feet were perforce quite still and fixed. Showing the baby to the children I said: "I have brought you a visitor; see how still he is; I am sure you could not keep so still," I meant it as a joke and thought they would laugh, but all became serious and put their legs and feet together and were still without movement. I thought they had not understood my joke so I said: "If only you could feel how gently he breathes; you could not breathe as gently as that because your chests are bigger." Now, I thought, they will laugh, but no, they remained with their feet together and also controlling their breath so that it should make no noise and they looked seriously at me, I then said: "I will walk out very quietly, but the baby will be quieter than I; he will not move or make any noise," I took the child back to its mother and came back; they were still there motionless and with a look on their faces as if to say: "See you made a little noise but we are as quiet as that baby," So all the children had the same will, all were urged to do the same thing, and the result was a class of forty-five children perfectly immobile and silent. People would have thought, "what a wonderful discipline" and would have wondered how it was obtained. How? by an attempt to make the children laugh! The result was a silence which was very striking, so much so that I said "What a silence!" and the children seemed to understand and feel the silence and remained quite still, controlling their breath, and I began to hear sounds that I had not heard before, the ticking of the clock, the drip from a leaking tap outside, the buzzing of flies. Adults generally do not know this silence; even in church they get up and kneel down and move about, put coins in the collection-box, etc. etc.; so their idea of silence is very superficial. This silence was a cause of great joy to the children, and the silence lesson which is a feature of our schools now, developed from this experience.

From this exercise of silence could be measured the strength of will of these children, and with the exercise the strength of this will became greater and greater and the period of silence lengthened. So we added to this the whispering of the name of each child, and as each heard his name he came quietly while the others remained immobile, and, since each child came carefully and slowly so as not to make a noise, how long the last child to be called had to wait! They therefore had developed to a great degree their strength of will. When we say we must teach children to inhibit this or that, we must remember that children are capable of much greater inhibition than we are capable of, and after all will and inhibition give obedience. Inhibition of impulses is one of the great results of this exercise as well as the control of one's actions. Hence it came to be a part of our method: on one side, the will to choose and be freely active, and on the other side inhibition. The children thus developed into people of great will; in that environment they could do what they willed ̄act or refrain from action, and they formed a group wonderful to see.

To have absolute silence we must all agree; if one person does not agree, the silence is broken; therefore a consciousness comes that we must act together and produce a result. Thus a conscious social relationship comes about.

I had unintentionally stimulated this first silence by bringing the baby into the room, but I could not always depend on that, so how was I to arouse this interest again? I found the best way was by saying simply: "Would you like to make silence?" Immediately there was great enthusiasm and I found to my surprise that I could command silence and the children obeyed me. The adult gave a command which all obeyed. Obedience had developed in the children, because all the elements were there. I merely said something and they obeyed; so in developing the will, unseen and unexpected obedience had come.

Obedience is the last phase of the development of the will, so the development of the will makes obedience possible. With our children it leads to a phase when the teacher, whatever he commands, is promptly obeyed. What he then feels is that he should be careful not to take advantage of this type of obedience of the children. He becomes aware of the real nature of the character which a leader should have. A leader should feel a great responsibility for the orders he issues. A leader, therefore, is not somebody with a sense of great authority, but somebody with a sense of great responsibility.

The Montessori Teacher

From all that we have mentioned it may be understood that a Montessori teacher has to be quite different from a teacher in an ordinary school, and one must be careful not to consider this too superficially, because there are certain Montessori teachers who take things too literally. They say: "The children must be active and the teacher must not interfere," so they abandon the children and they do nothing.

In the presentation of the means of development the teacher has a very active task; also the fashion in which they must be presented and their details indicate a very active teacher; therefore, the part the teacher plays is a complex one. It is not that the Montessori teacher is inactive and the teacher of the ordinary school active, but all the activities our teacher has to perform are a preparation, a guidance, and the subsequent "inactivity" of the teacher is a sign of success. Complete outer inactivity of the teacher represents a task successfully accomplished, we might say it is an ideal aim, and blessed are the teachers who have brought their class to the stage where they can say: "Whether I am present or not, the class functions" Each child through his activity has achieved independence and now the group has achieved independence. That is the mark of success, but to arrive at this there is a path to follow; the teacher too must develop.

One thing we must have clearly before our eyes, i.e., that the Montessori teacher and the ordinary teacher are on different levels. One cannot transform an ordinary teacher into a Montessori teacher; one must create anew. To begin with, we might say that the first step for the teacher is self -preparation. She has to prepare her imagination, because in the ordinary school the teacher knows what her children are like as far as their immediate behavior shows and she knows she has to care for them and bring them up, whereas the Montessori teacher sees a child who is not there yet, materially speaking. This is the main difference. Our teachers are on a superior level, not on the material level. Teachers who come to our schools must have a sort of faith in the child who will reveal himself through work. The teacher becomes detached from any idea regarding the level on which the children may be. The different types of children r who are all deviated, do not affect her, she sees a different type of child who lives in a spiritual field. The teacher has faith that the children she has actually before her will show their real self when they find any work which attracts them. What does she look for? What is her expectation? To wait till one or two of the children become concentrated.

On the path of the teacher's own spiritual evolution in this work there are three stages:

First Stage. The teacher becomes the guardian and custodian of the environment; she therefore concentrates on the environment instead of being caught up by all these deviated children. She concentrates on the environment because from there the cure will come. The environment holds the attraction that will polarize the will of the children. As in our countries where each bride has her own home and makes it as attractive as possible for herself and her husband, instead of paying over-much attention to her husband she pays attention first to the house in order to make it into an environment in which a normal and constructive relationship can be formed. She tries to make it a peaceful, comfortable house, full of interesting stimuli. In such a house, the essential part is cleanliness and order: everything in its place, clean, shining and bright. This is the first care of the wife. In the school also the first care of the teacher should be this: order and care of the material so that it be always beautiful, shining and in repair and nothing missing, so that everything looks new to the children and is complete and ready for use at any time. This also means that the person of the teacher must be attractive. She should be young, beautiful, with flowers in her hair, scented with cleanliness, happy and full of dignity. This is the ideal. Everyone can translate it as they like, but we must remember that when we present ourselves in front of children, we must realize they are great people. The appearance of the teacher is the first step to real understanding and real respect for the children. She should study her movements and make them as gentle and graceful as possible. The child of this age has a great ideal of his mother; we don't know of what type the mother is, but very often we hear a child say when he sees a beautiful lady: "How beautiful she is, just like my mother!" Actually the mother may not be so beautiful at all, but to the child she is and everyone whom he admires is "as beautiful as my mother," So this care for one's appearance ought also to form part of the order in the environment of the child; the most living part of the environment is the teacher.

This care of the environment then, is the first work of the teacher and must precede everything else; it is an indirect work. Unless it is completely attended to, there will never be any worthwhile and continuous results in any other field physical, mental or spiritual.

Second Stage. Now we come to the children, having first ordered the environment. What to do with these children still disorderly with these aimlessly wandering minds which we wish to attract in order to fix them on work? I sometimes use a term which is not always appreciated: the teacher must be seductive, she must seduce the children at this stage. Imagine a child entering a black dirty environment with a dirty teacher and being given an object to which he is supposed to be attracted! Surely the teacher must be attractive first, in appearance and in manner. In this respect our teachers and the teachers in ordinary schools may be alike, but this is all before the period of concentration.

Before concentration sets in the teacher can do what she likes more or less, because she upsets nothing important. She can intervene in the children's activities if necessary. I have read of a Saint who tried to attract the abandoned boys of the streets of a town who were learning bad habits. What did he do? He tried every means to amuse them. That is what the teacher must do at this stage. The use of poetry, rhymes, singing, stories, drama, clowning; anything is good enough except the stick. The teacher who fascinates the children attracts them and this leads to some exercise, which is not very important but it does attract them. A vivacious teacher can attract more easily, then why not make use of it? To say brightly: "Now what about changing the furniture today" and then work with them, the teacher herself carrying things carefully and suggesting how to carry, doing all this brightly. Or: "How about polishing this beautiful brass bowl?" or: "Shall we go into the garden and collect some flowers?" If the teacher is attractive the action will be attractive.

This is the second period in the development of the teacher. If there is some child who persists in molesting others at this stage, the practical thing is to interrupt his actions. Whilst we have said so often that when a child is concentrated in work one must not, under any circumstances, intervene and interrupt his cycle of activity, and so prevent his full expression, obviously here the contrary is the right technique: to interrupt and so to break his thread of disturbing activities. The interruption can be an exclamation merely, or it can be getting interested in him; multiplying your attention to him is like a lot of electric shocks to him and will bring a reaction in time. If a child is bothering others, one might say: "How are you, Johnnie? Come here, I want to give you something to do!" Probably he will not want to do that, so you say: "So you don't want to do that) All right, let's go into the garden then," and go with him or let your helper take him and then his naughtiness comes under your care and the children are not troubled.

Third Stage. Now comes the third stage when the children are interested in something, usually some exercise of practical life, because one cannot give any other material until one has been able to present it properly and that we cannot do while they are not concentrated on anything. When the child becomes interested in an object, the teacher must not interrupt, because this activity obeys natural laws and has a cycle; and if it is touched, it disappears like a soap-bubble and all its beauty with it. The teacher must be very careful now, non-interference means non-interference, in any form. Often mistakes are made by teachers here. A child who has been a nuisance, at last does a piece of concentrated work; the teacher passes and sees him and says: "Good!" that is enough, the damage is done. The child will probably not look at work for another two or three weeks. Also if a child has a difficulty and the teacher interferes to show how to deal with it, the child will leave the teacher with the work and go away. The interest of the child was not in the mere task, but in conquering that difficulty. If the teacher is going to conquer it instead, well let her, my interest is gone. Also if the child is lifting heavy things, the teacher will go to help and frequently the child will then just dump the things and walk off. Praise, help or even noticing a child are often sufficient interruption to destroy activity. Indeed, even the child's seeing one looking at him will do it. After all if we are concentrated in something and someone comes and looks over our shoulder or looks at us from somewhere nearby, our concentration disappears. The great principle which leads to the success of the teacher is this: as soon as concentration appears, pay no attention, as if the child did not exist. We can note what he does in a single glance, without paying any attention that makes him aware of us. Now the child will begin to choose his own actions. This may cause problems in a class where more than one may want the same material. In the solution of these problems also, we must not interfere unl/ we are asked; the children will solve them. Our duty is only to present objects when the child exhausts the activities possible with the old on/

This ability of the teacher to refrain from interfering comes with practice, just as all the other abilities. She must act as if she were there to serve the children; if she wants a good example, she can study a good servant. He prepares everything that pleases his master, but he does not tell him what to do. He keeps the master's hair -brushes in order, but he does not tell him when he must tidy his hair; he prepares his food carefully, but he does not order him to eat. He presents it well and with exactness and unobtrusiveness and then disappears. So must we act to this master of ours the growing spirit of the child. This is the master we serve, the child-spirit. When he shows a wish, we are ready to satisfy it. The servant does not intrude on the master if he is alone, but when the master calls, the servant is immediately there to do what he wants and he answers: "Yes, sir," He admires if asked to do so and says: "How beautiful" if that is expected of him, even if he does not see any beauty himself. So with the child who has done some concentrated work. We must not intrude, but if he shows us what he has accomplished and wants our approbation, we give it generously.

This is the plan and the technique: to serve, and serve well; to serve the spirit. This is something new, especially in the realm of education. It is true we would all like to serve children, but does the ordinary teacher know how to serve or what to do? She will see he is dirty and she will wash him; that his clothes are in disorder and she will dress him. This is the idea of the ordinary teacher, viz., that if one is to serve children, one must do everything for them, wash, dress and feed them. But we are not this type of teacher; we are not servants of the body. We know that if a child is to develop, he must do these things himself. The basis of our teaching is that the child shall not be served in this sense. The child must acquire physical independence by being sufficient unto himself. Independence of will by choosing alone and freely, independence of thought by working alone and uninterrupted. The consciousness we have that development is a straight path to independence must give us the clue. We must help the child to act by himself, will for himself, think for himself. This is the art of the servant of the spirit, an art which can be expressed perfectly in the field of childhood. It is only then that we can see the development of those marvelous characteristics in children, that we have talked about.

These qualities of a social being are wonderful to behold, and the joy of the teacher is to be able to see the manifestations of the spirit of the child. It is a great privilege since usually they are hidden, and as they appear, the teacher who knew of them by the inspiration of her faith, welcomes them. Here is the child as he should be: the worker who never tires, the calm child, the child who seeks the maximum effort and who tries to help the weak, who knows how to respect others and shows us characteristics which make us know him as the true child.

So the teacher gradually begins to say: "I know my children" and by saying that she says: "I have seen the reality of these facts. I have seen the child as he should be, a child even superior to what I had supposed." This is to have knowledge of childhood. The ordinary teacher may say: "I know my children; this is Johnnie, his father is a carpenter, his mother is a very clever manager in the home." "I have been to this little girl's home; I have eaten with her family," etc. "I have given much time and thought to them; I know them." But with our teachers it is not these superficial facts that they know, but the secret of childhood. They have penetrated into this secret and have a knowledge far superior to ordinary knowledge, just as their love and care was far superior to that of the ordinary teacher. The Montessori teacher has a deep love because she loves the deep knowledge of the secret of the children. Perhaps for the first time one understands what love really is on these occasions when the child manifests his spirit. "They are very touching, they touch me so deeply that they change me as does any love worthy of the name. I have been so touched that I cannot help talking about it And what have I loved? These manifestations of the human spirit. It is these revelations, this spirit which has transformed me. It is possibly the highest form of love, for I may not remember the child's name, but the manifestation of the human spirit has deeply moved me, I am in love with it."

Ordinary teachers say that they love their pupils: "When they pass me, I rub their hair or I kiss them. I enquire after them when they are ill," But this is personal love, only. So there are two different levels. One is material, and on this the whole conception of the old education is founded. Children are material beings; if you think of spiritual things in connection with children, you think of the prayers or rituals you can teach them. But our level is spiritual, our love not material. The children have brought us to it; so when the teacher says she knows her children she refers to something superior which the children have revealed. And when she says: "I serve my children," she means: "I serve the spirit of man which must liberate itself. I know them, i.e. I know the spirit of man."

This difference of level has really been brought about not by the teacher, but by the children. It is the teacher who finds herself brought up to this level which she did not know existed. The child has made the teacher grow up to his level; now she is there and she is happy. Her happiness before was perhaps to have as little to do as possible and to draw as high a salary as possible and what other satisfaction? Perhaps her authority over the children and her feeling that she is the ideal which the children follow and whom they obey. She may be satisfied by a sense of power and vanity. Perhaps also she thinks of going a step higher in her material career, to become a headmistress or inspector. But there is no real happiness in this. The spiritual happiness that one may derive from the spiritual manifestations of the children, these teachers have never felt; yet to have this one would be ready to leave the lesser happiness. How many headmasters and teachers in high schools have resigned their posts and salaries and gone to little children^ to find this joy? I do know of two doctors of medicine in Paris who left their profession to do this work in order to see for themselves these phenomena, and they found that what they actually did was to pass from a lower level to a higher one.

What is the greatest height of a Montessori teacher's success? To be able to say: "Now the children work as if I did not exist," She has become nothing and the children have become all. The ordinary teacher may say: "I have brought my children up to this level; I have taught this; I have developed their intellectual powers; I have .... I have . . . ," But what have they done? Nothing. They have not developed; they have imposed themselves and crushed and impeded. This is the crime of the schools, especially at the period of development before six years. All we should be able to say is: "I have helped this life to achieve its creation" and that is real satisfaction. The Montessori teacher of children up to six years knows she has helped humanity in an essential period of development. She may not know anything of the material facts of the children, though actually some she will be bound to know because the children will talk to her freely. She need not mind what happens afterwards to these children, whether they go to secondary schools and colleges or cease their schooling earlier; she is satisfied to know that in this formative period they have achieved what they had to achieve. She says: "I have served the spirit of these children so that they have achieved development and I have accompanied them in all their experiences," She does not care what the ordinary inspector says, it is of no importance, it is a ridiculous remnant of old times. The teacher who has to wait on inspectors' reports is a person in a miserable position and out of the reality of spiritual life, even if she prays five times a day. Spiritual life is perpetual life from one morning to the next morning. It is to live on a spiritual level, not merely to say prayers.

The ordinary teacher says: "How humble these teachers seem, they are not interested even in their own authority" and some say: "How can your method succeed, when you pretend that these teachers renounce all the usual things?" But they have not renounced; they have simply entered another life where the values are different; where there are the real values of life unknown to the former life. All the principles are different, take the principle of justice. In the old schools justice was important. "The teacher has power, dignity and justice" it used to be said. What was this justice? Treating all alike: "I don't mind if the children are rich or poor; if punishment is necessary, all are punished," If any child made mistakes he got a zero for his work, in some cases even if he was deaf; all had to be treated alike. Human society is based on this 'justice.' Even in democratic countries justice frequently only means that there is one law for all the rich and powerful and the starving man. Justice is usually connected with trials, prisons, sentences. The Law Courts are called the Palace of Justice, and to say: "I am an honest man" means I have had nothing to do with justice (i.e., the police and the law courts.) In schools also the teacher is careful not to caress a child because if so she must caress all she must be just. This is a justice which levels all down to the lowest level; as if, spiritually, we cut off the heads of the taller ones to bring them to the same level as the others. On the higher level of educational work, justice is really spiritual, it seeks that every child achieve the maximum of its individual abilities. Justice is to give to any human being all help that will enable him to reach his full spiritual stature, and those who serve the spirit in all ages, must give help to these energies. This will perhaps be the organization of the future society. So called justice at present is ridiculous, it is the freedom where one man has no chance and others have all the chances and take no advantage of them. Nothing need be lost of these spiritual treasures and compared to them economic treasures lose their value. Whether I am rich or poor does not matter if I can reach full expression, the economic problem will then adjust itself. When humanity can achieve its spiritual self to the full, it will be more productive; and economic things will lose their exclusive value. Men do not produce with their feet or their bodies, but with their spirit and intelligence. All insoluble problems will be solved.

The children develop an ordered society unaided. We adults need police, lathis, soldiers, machine-guns. The children solve their own problems in peace. They have shown us that freedom and discipline are the two sides of the same coin, because scientific freedom leads to discipline. Usually coins have two sides, one beautifully engraved with a face or figure, the other flatter and with lettering. The flat side is freedom and the beautifully engraved side discipline. This is so true that when we find a class of undisciplined children this serves as a control of error for the teacher, for she says on seeing it: "I have made a mistake against this class somewhere" and so she corrects it. The ordinary teacher thinks this is a humiliation; it is not. It is a technique of the new education. In serving the children, we serve life. By helping nature we go to the next level of super-nature, since a law of nature is to go higher continuously. And it is the children who have built this beautiful structure to another level. The laws of nature are order, so when order comes spontaneously we know we have reached the cosmic order. One of the missions of children is to draw adult humanity to a higher level. I cannot develop this point here, important as it is, but it is a fact. The children draw us to a spiritual level and solve the problems of the material level. Let me quote some phrases which have helped us to keep in mind all these things we have mentioned. It is not a prayer, but a memorandum and so for Montessori teachers an invocation, a kind of syllabus, our only syllabus:

"HELP US, O LORD, TO PENETRATE INTO THE SECRET
OF THE CHILD SO THAT WE MAY KNOW HIM, LOVE
HIM AND SERVE HIM, ACCORDING TO YOUR LAWS OF
JUSTICE AND FOLLOWING YOUR DIVINE WILL."

The Fountain Source of Love the Child

In our Courses we always see a gathering of workers that are typically Montessorian. There are babies, young people, older people, professional people, non-professional people, cultured and illiterate people and there is no leader among us. Our Courses are apparently heterogeneous unlike most other courses of culture. Students following our courses have to have some degree of culture, but that is the only limit, within it we can have matriculates and professors side by side, lawyers and doctors, and those who would be their patients. In Europe we used to have people from all countries and in America we once had an anarchist among us! With all these differences of people there have never been any conflicts between the students. How is this? It is because we have all been linked by a common ideal. In Belgium, such a small country that it might be fitted in one of the tips of India, there are nevertheless two languages: French and Flemish. The people are divided politically as a result. Seldom has it been possible to draw all these people together in a conference, but in a Montessori Course it happened. It was so unusual, that in newspapers it was commented: "For many years we have been trying unsuccessfully to get these parties together, now we have it in this course to study the child." This is the power of the child: all are familiar with children, whatever their religious or political feeling, and all love children, hence the uniting influence of the child. Adults have formed some strong and ferocious convictions and these convictions divide them into groups. When they begin to speak of these convictions, their religious and political ideals, they begin to fight.

But on one point the child they all feel alike; that is why socially the child is so important. It is evident that this is a point from which one can start in order to put the world into harmony. It is one point on which all have a delicate sensitivity. When we speak of the child, all are touched, all feel love, all are sensitive. The whole of humanity is held by this deepest emotion which kindles friendly sentiments. It is a form of love. When one touches the child, one touches love. One does not know how to define this love; all feel it, but cannot describe it. We may say: "I feel this love; it exists, but its root and its vastness I do not know," Just as we are aware of things through our senses, so we have this feeling of love; we are impressed by it. We feel it is there, even though, when we consider much in the life of the adult, it is as if we had forgotten it. When an adult thinks of another adult, usually forces of defense arise, but when we think of the child the strong and hard accretions soften and disappear, we become sweet and gentle because now we are dealing with the basis of life. This is so not only for humans, but for all living beings. It comes when the young appear. There are then these two aspects of adult life: that of defense and that of love, but the fundamental one is that of love as one feels it for the child, because without the child the adult would not exist.

Let us try to understand this love more consciously. Let us consider what prophets and poets have said about it, for they have been able to give form and expression to this great energy which we call love. Certainly there is nothing more beautiful or uplifting than the words of poets who have given this form to love so that man can visualize it to some extent; this love which is the energy at the base of all existence. Even the most ferocious of men when they read these statements of poets and religious men may say: "How beautiful!" That means that this love has remained in them and keeps vibrating in them, despite the manner of their life. Were it not so, they would call such things, nonsense, stupidity, vapidity and so on. Although it does not seem to have entered their lives, yet they are influenced by it. It means that they are thirsty for love even without their knowing it.

It is curious that even in times such as these when war is most destructive and has reached all the corners of the world, when one would think that to talk of love would be most ironic, people do talk of it. They are planning for unity, which is love. This means that it is a basic force. So now, at this time, when it would seem that everything might lead men to say: "Away with this thing called love; let us have reality which has been proved to be destruction, for are not cities, forests, women, children, animals all destroyed?," still there is talk of reconstruction and love; even while they destroy, people talk of it. If we look and listen to all around us, the wireless, newspapers, common talk, we hear the Pope, Truman, Churchill, the directors of the churches, those against the churches, the cultured and the illiterate, the rich and the poor and all the followers of all the "isms" and theologies, all saying "love," And if this is so, (and there could be no stronger proof than there is to day of the force and impressiveness of this love) then why should not humanity study this great fact of love? Why should it be only spoken of when hate is raging? Why should it not be studied and analyzed always, so that its energy can be made use of? And why not see why this energy has not been studied before so that it could be used to combine the other forces of which we know? Man has put so much of his mental energies into the study of other natural facts. In those fields he has worked laboriously and long and discovered many things. Why not put a little of this energy into the study of this force which should unite humanity? I feel that all contributions that give an illustration of love should be taken in with energy and avidity and great prominence should be given to them. I mentioned that poets and prophets have spoken of it, often as if it were an ideal; but it is real, it has always been there and is eternal.

We must realize too that if we feel this reality of love at the present time, it is not because we were taught it in school. Even if we were taught the beautiful descriptions of love, the words were few and they would have disappeared, the memory of them would have vanished in the multitudinous events that have followed since then. When people appeal with so much energy for love, it is not because they heard of it in their youth or read of it in poetry or in religion; it is the expression of something not learnt by heart, but of something given to us as part of the great heritage of our life. It is Life which speaks, not poets and prophets. Love can be considered from another side, besides that of religion and poetry. It is from the point of view of Life itself that we must consider it; then love is not merely the fruit of imagination or aspiration, but a reality which is an eternal energy and cannot be extinguished.

I would like to say a few words about this reality and about those things which the poets and prophets have said also. This energy we call love is the greatest cosmic energy. Even when we use such terms we still speak of it disparagingly, because it is more than an energy it is creation itself and is better expressed in the phrase "God is Love."

Now to come to more concrete things. I would like to be able to quote from all poets and prophets, but I do not know them nor do I know their language. But I know all have wonderful verses. Let me quote from one I know who showed great vehemence in his expression when speaking of love. It is the best-known of all religious or poetic descriptions in Christendom, and says:

"If I speak with the tongues of men, and of angels, and have not charity, I am become a sounding brass or a tinkling cymbal. And if I should have prophecy, and should know all mysteries, and all knowledge, and if I should have all faith, so that I could remove mountains, and have not charity, I am nothing. And if I should distribute all my goods to feed the poor, and if I should deliver my body to be burned, and have not charity, it profiteth me nothing." (St. Paul in I. Cor. XIII)

We could say to such a person: "You must know what love is since you feel it so strongly, it must be something formidable, tell us about it in detail." But when the description of this mighty sentiment is given, it is so simple. The illustrations he has used might be found in our present civilization which can move mountains and work even greater miracles than that, for we can speak in a whisper from one corner of a continent to a corner in another continent where we are heard. But all this is nothing, if there is not love. We also have organized great institutions to feed the poor and clothe them, but if we have not love it is like playing a drum which gives sound because it is empty. What then is this love? St. Paul who gave us a description of its lofty grandeur, as quoted above, continues, but he does not furnish a philosophical theory, he writes:

"Charity is patient, is kind: charity envieth not, dealeth not perversely: is not puffed up. Is not ambitious, seeketh not her own, is not provoked to anger, thinketh no evil. Rejoiceth not in iniquity, but rejoiceth with the truth: beareth all things, believeth all things, hopeth all things, endureth all things."

It is a long enumeration of facts, a long description of features, but all these features remind us strangely of the qualities of children. They seem to describe the powers of the absorbent mind. The absorbent mind receives all, it does not judge, it never repels, it does not react. It absorbs all and incarnates it in man. The child achieves incarnation in order to adapt himself to life with other men and become equal to them. The child suffers all: if he comes into the world in a cold and frozen environment there he forms himself to live in it and the adult he will be one day will only be happy in that environment. If he enters the world in a torrid region, there he will construct himself so that he could not live and be happy in another climate. Be it the desert which receives him, be it the plains fringing the ocean, be it the slopes in the high mountain ranges, he enjoys it all and there alone he reaches the highest well-being.

The absorbent mind believes all, hopes all. It receives poverty as it receives wealth, it receives all faiths as it receives the prejudices and customs of his environment: it incarnates it all within itself.

This is the child!

And if it were not like this, mankind would not reach stability in any of the most different parts of the world, it would not achieve its continuous progress in civilization without ever having to start afresh.

The absorbent mind forms the basis of the miraculous society created by man and appears to us in the guise of the small and delicate child who solves the mysterious difficulties of human destiny by the virtues of love.

If therefore we study the child a little better than we have done hitherto, we find love in all its aspects and analyzed. It is not analyzed by the poet or the prophet but by what the child shows by reality. If we consider the description given by St. Paul and then look at the child, we say, "Here it is that all these are found; so here is the great treasure itself."

The treasure then is to be found not merely near those who study poetry and religion, but within every human being. This miracle is sent to all; the representative of this tremendous force is to be found everywhere. Man makes a desert of strife and God continues to send this rain. So it is easy to understand that all the creations of adults, great achievements as they are, without love lead nowhere, to nothing. But if this love present in the child is taken among us, if its values and potentialities are realized and developed, our achievements, already great, will be tremendous. The adult and the child must come together; the adult must be humble and learn from the child to be great. It is curious that among all the miracles which humanity has performed, there is only one miracle that he has not taken into consideration: the miracle that God has sent from the beginning: the Child.

Supposing we put a little levity into this weighty subject and tell a little story. A certain young man wished to marry and recounted all the praises of the lady of his choice. An elder guide responded in writing and this is what happened: The young man praises her beauty; the guide writes a zero. The young man finding beauty is not enough, states that she is rich; the guide writes zero.

The young man says, she is learned, but the guide again writes zero. The young man says: "All this means nothing, well, she is athletic, she rides, swims, plays tennis." Again the guide writes zero. The young man goes on describing all sorts of qualities which his lady-love possesses and the guide continues to write zero against them. Then the young man says: "She is of good character," and the guide says: "That is something," and writes a figure one in front of all the zeros. All the other merits acquire their value from this one quality and with that one in front of all the zeros her total value increases a thousandfold. So it is with civilization, all the achievements are naught and lead to destruction, but if love is there they all acquire a great value. This teaching of the child as a power of love is not as the teaching of St. Paul, it is not an understanding of love with the mind. It is not that man has taught this love to children. Since he is not even capable of describing it, how can he teach it? It is a force of nature and is in the child. It means that there is this force that nature has placed in the very constitution of man, it is therefore more important than anything else and must be put before all the creations of man. This brings us to another field, to that of love not as a phantasy of man, but as a force in Natura Creatrix. Let us analyze the forms and aspects that this love can assume.

That which we call love we have in our consciousness. It is the part of the universal energy that we feel consciously. But one may say that universal energy has nothing to do with humanity. Let us analyze it: it is an attraction, and what is attraction but a universal force. Let us consider the universe. What keeps the stars where they are and makes them move along the fixed path they follow? Attraction. Why do bodies fall to the ground? By attraction. What is it that works among the atoms of matter so that they construct wholes? Attraction. If this attraction did not exist there would be chaos, nothing would be in existence. There would be no heaven and no stars without attraction. And if there were no attraction to the earth, when we jump we would remain up in the air and so would everything else! Chemical affinity which brings certain elements together could not manifest itself without attraction. And attraction is love. So we could say with St. Paul, "If I made the stars and everything on earth, but I had no love or attraction, nothing would exist." Love is not merely sympathy, but the very essence of existence.

If we consider conscious love, we can analyze further. All animals have at certain moments the instinct of reproduction, which is a form of love. This form of love is a command of nature because without this attraction nothing would continue. So a little atom of this universal energy is lent to them for a little moment in order that the species may be continued. They feel it for a moment and then it disappears. This shows how measured and economical nature is in lending love; just sufficiently and no more, given in small doses and based on command. When the young come, the parents feel a special love for them which leads them to protect the species, and all the young ones are kept near the mother. But as soon as the young are sufficiently grown, love disappears suddenly from one moment to another. It is not a sentiment as we think, but an energy given very carefully and economically, just a small ray to penetrate the darkness of consciousness, but as soon as the work is done, it disappears. So, love can take this aspect and then what does it convey to us? That this supposed sentiment is not merely a sentiment. It is true that it lasts longer in man than in animals, but it is not a sentiment really (apart from its encouragement or discouragement). Cosmically it is an energy lent to every living being and withdrawn as soon as the immediate purpose is fulfilled.

So this force is given within measured limits to man also, but even so it is greater than any other force, because it carries him to social organization. It must be treasured and developed and expanded to the maximum. Man can sublimate this force lent to him and make it vaster and vaster to reach abstraction. To bring it into the field of abstraction and to treasure it, this is the work of man. Let us take it and bring it into the field of imagination and make it general. Let us treasure it because this is the force that holds the universe together. This part, that we possess consciously, is given to us, and if this force is renewed in man every time a child is born, it must be treasured. By this force man can hold together all things that he can do with his hand and his intelligence.

Love is a gift of the Universal Consciousness for a special aim and purpose, as is everything lent to man by the Cosmic Consciousness. If the aim is not fulfilled, then nothing can sustain itself and all crumbles away. We can understand the words of the saint that all is nothing unless love is there. More than electricity which gives light in the darkness, more than the etheric waves which allow our voices to travel over wide distances, more than any energy that man has discovered and exploited is this love; above all things it is the most important. All that man can do with the forces of electricity or of etheric waves depends on the consciousness of him who uses them. This energy of love is given to us so that each one of us contains it when a child comes and it opens out as a fan. Even if later circumstances destroy it, we feel a yearning for it. So we must study it and use it more than any other force in the environment, because it is not lent to the environment as other forces are, but it is lent to us. The study of love and its utilization will lead us to the fountain whence it springs and that is the Child. This is the new path that man must follow.

Printed in the United Kingdom by
Lightning Source UK Ltd., Milton Keynes
140845UK00001B/18/P